MOTOROLA
Semiconductor Products Inc.

MICROPROCESSOR
APPLICATIONS MANUAL

CONTRIBUTORS

Alvin W. Moore   Karl E. Fronheiser

Vinay Khanna   John M. DeLaune

Gary G. Sawyer   Mark E. Eidson

Thomas C. Daly   James F. Vittera

McGRAW-HILL BOOK COMPANY

*New York   St. Louis   San Francisco   Auckland   Düsseldorf
Johannesburg   Kuala Lumpur   London   Mexico   Montreal
New Delhi   Panama   Paris   São Paulo   Singapore
Sydney   Tokyo   Toronto*

MOTOROLA SERIES IN SOLID-STATE ELECTRONICS

THE ENGINEERING STAFF, MOTOROLA INC., SEMICONDUCTOR PRODUCTS DIVISION:
Analysis and Design of Integrated Circuits
THE ENGINEERING STAFF, MOTOROLA INC., SEMICONDUCTOR PRODUCTS DIVISION:
Integrated Circuits: Design Principles and Fabrication
HAMILTON AND HOWARD: Basic Integrated Circuit Engineering
COMPUTER APLICATIONS GROUP, MOTOROLA INC., SEMICONDUCTOR PRODUCTS DIVISION: Microprocessor Applications Manual

34567890   HDHD   784321098765

Circuit diagrams external to Motorola products are included as a means of illustrating typical Microprocessor applications; consequently, complete information sufficient for construction purposes is not necessarily given. The information in this manual has been carefully checked and is believed to be entirely reliable. However, no responsibility is assumed for inaccuracies. Furthermore, such information does not convey to the purchaser of the semiconductor devices described any license under the patent rights of Motorola Inc. or others.

Motorola reserves the right to change specifications without notice.

EXORciser MIKBUG *and* EXbug *are trademarks of Motorola Inc.*

Library of Congress Cataloging in Publication Data

Motorola Semiconductor Products Inc.
  Microprocessor applications manual.

  (Motorola series in solid-state electronics)
  Includes index.
  1. Microprocessors.   I. Title.
  QA76.5.M66   001.6′4   75-28444
  ISBN 0-07-043527-8

PREFACE

General purpose Microprocessing Units (MPUs), architecturally descended from the minicomputer and implemented as integrated circuit semiconductor products, are an exciting reality for today's electronics business. The current availability of several general purpose MPUs in production quantities (and the accompanying competitive prices) have generated widespread interest among potential users. The electronics industry trade press (magazines, newspapers, etc.) has responded with enthusiasm and there has been a flurry of editorials and articles covering the subject. The media has given extensive coverage to market potential, comparative descriptions of the various devices available, and, to a lesser extent, "how to use them" articles. In the applications area, they are hampered by two considerations: (1) their format requires that they concisely present only the salient features without burying their readers in a mountain of detail; (2) much of the interesting work is proprietary in nature and, thus, cannot be publicized.

The semiconductor manufacturers have also added to the information gap by taking a "business as usual" attitude toward their new products; in many cases, they have been slow to realize that they are now providing a significant subsystem and must provide more information than their classical data sheets and application notes.

This book was written in the attempt to partially close this information gap by providing detailed applications information for a representative general purpose microprocessing unit. If it is assumed, as it was here, that the reader is not necessarily familiar with MPUs, the description of even a simple system is burdened by a considerable body of information concerning the MPU itself. In addition to the system considerations, such topics as architecture, instruction set, addressing modes, interrupt structure, etc., must be covered. For this reason, only the Motorola MC6800 and its family of associated parts are dealt with here. However, the system design considerations and hardware/software discussions are generally applicable to designs based on other MPUs.

The book's primary audience was intended to be practicing system/circuit designers with some previous experience in developing electronic equipment using bipolar digital integrated circuits. While no particular computer/MPU experience is assumed, a basic understanding of classical computer architecture and some experience with assembly language programming will be of value. An attempt was made to treat each topic in sufficient detail to be useful to a general technical audience.

Chapter 1 describes the architecture of the M6800 system and provides a brief description of the elements required for a rational microcomputer system. In addition, the addressing modes and instruction set of the MC6800 MPU are introduced and discussed.

Chapter 2 is a collection of various programming techniques with emphasis on arithmetic operations and peripheral control routines. This chapter introduces a practice that is followed throughout the remainder of the book: Programming examples that are reproduced as assembly listings (computer print-outs from the host computer's terminal) have been "debugged" and can be used as is if they fit the reader's requirements.

Detailed descriptions of the M6800 interrupt structure and Input/Output (I/O) devices used with the system are provided in Chapter 3. The concepts of interrupt control/prioritizing and direct memory access are introduced in context with the I/O control material.

Chapter 4 provides additional details on auxiliary circuitry used in typical microcomputer systems. Included are: clock circuitry, use of supervisory controls (i.e., Reset, Interrupt Request, Three-state Control, etc.), and interface/enabling considerations. This chapter also provides specific examples for such system problems as interrupt prioritizing, direct memory access, and the use of non-family memory devices.

A typical Point-of-Sale terminal design based on an MPU is described in Chapters 5 and 6. The system described is representative of equipment that has traditionally been implemented with small and medium scale integrated circuits. The executive control program, special processing routines, and the overall hardware configuration is presented in Chapter 6. Individual control routines for a variety of peripheral devices are discussed in Chapter 5. As mentioned earlier, each of these subroutines was prepared with the intention that it could be used "as is" for specific applications. However, sufficient information (flow-charts, program comments, etc.) is included to indicate the modification procedure for similar but different problems. In both chapters, particular emphasis is given to the tradeoffs between "software" and "hardware" that should be made when designing with microprocessors.

Chapter 7 was included to provide familiarization with a typical assembler and simulator in order to enable readers to use the remainder of the book without excessive reference to other material. This chapter also describes typical support products that can be used to reduce the time and effort required during the development of MPU systems.

I would like to acknowledge the support given by our secretary, Beverly Leap, and our Technical Art Director, Stan Bennett; without their efforts this book could not have been produced.

Al Moore

TABLE OF CONTENTS

TABLE OF CONTENTS (Continued)

TABLE OF CONTENTS (Continued)

TABLE OF CONTENTS (Continued)

TABLE OF CONTENTS (Continued)

TABLE OF CONTENTS (Continued)

LIST OF FIGURES

LIST OF FIGURES (Continued)

LIST OF FIGURES (Continued)

CHAPTER 4

LIST OF FIGURES (Continued)

LIST OF FIGURES (Continued)

LIST OF FIGURES (Continued)

LIST OF FIGURES (Continued)

LIST OF FIGURES (Continued)

LIST OF TABLES

LIST OF TABLES (Continued)

CHAPTER 1

1.   INTRODUCTION TO THE MC6800 MICROPROCESSOR

Motorola has elected to provide a microprocessor family of parts headed by the MC6800 Microprocessing Unit (MPU). The MC6800 MPU is an eight-bit parallel microprocessor with addressing capability of up to 65,536 words. It is TTL compatible requiring only a single five-volt supply and no external TTL devices for bus interface in small systems.

In support of the MPU are several memory and I/O interface devices. To date, the family consists of a 128 X 8 RAM (MCM6810), a 1024 X 8 ROM (MCM6830), a parallel I/O interface (MC6820 PIA), and an asynchronous serial I/O interface (MC6850 ACIA). In keeping with the family concept, each operates on a single five-volt power supply and is compatible with the system bus signals. The family of parts is not a chip set in the sense that the MPU operation is dependent upon other family elements; the MC6800 is a self-contained microprocessor capable of operating with virtually any MOS or standard TTL device. The significant point is that the other family members merely add additional capability and/or flexibility. They provide excellent tools in configuring a full microprocessor operating system.

1-1   SYSTEM ORGANIZATION

Before describing the individual parts in any detail, an explanation of the MPU bus and control structure will serve to demonstrate how a system is brought together. Figure 1-1-1 is organized to show the processor's inputs and outputs in four functional categories; data, address, control, and supervisory.

The width and drive capability of the Data Bus has become a standard means of measuring microprocessors. The MC6800 has an 8-bit bidirectional bus to facilitate data flow throughout the system. The MPU Data Bus will drive up to 130 pf and one standard TTL load. As a result of the load characteristics of the RAM, ROM, ACIA, and PIA, the MPU can drive from 7 to 10 family devices without buffering.

Using the family I/O interface devices allows the 16-bit Address Bus to assume additional responsibility in the M6800 system. Not only does the Address Bus specify memory, but it becomes a tool to specify I/O devices. By means of its connections to the Data Bus, Control Bus, and selected address lines, the I/O interface is allocated an area of memory. As a result, the user may converse with I/O using any of the memory reference instructions, selecting the desired peripheral with a memory address.

In addition to the Data and Address Bus, a Control Bus is provided for the memory and interface devices. The Control Bus consists of a heterogeneous mix of signals to regulate system operation. Following is a brief review of the designated Control Bus signals shown in Figure 1-1-1. $\phi2$ is one phase of the system clock applied to the MPU. It is applied to the enable or chip select inputs of the family parts to insure that the devices are enabled only when the address bus and VMA are stable. $\overline{\text{Reset}}$ is used to reset and start the MPU from a power down condition. It is also routed to the $\overline{\text{Reset}}$ inputs of the PIAs for use during power on initialization. $\overline{\text{Interrupt Request}}$ is generated by the PIA, ACIA, or user defined hardware to notify the MPU of a request for service.

Read/Write (R/W) and Valid Memory Address (VMA) are MPU outputs characterizing the Data Bus and Address Bus, respectively. R/W designates whether the MPU is in a Read or Write mode for each cycle. VMA indicates to memory and I/O that the MPU is performing a read or write operation in a given cycle. This signal is applied to the enable or chip select inputs of each family device in order to disable data transfer when VMA is low.

The last set of signals in Figure 1-1-1, the MPU Supervisory, is used for timing and control of the MC6800 itself. Note that three of the Supervisory signals are shared with the control bus and affect the memory and I/O devices as well.

$\phi1$ is one of the two clock phases to the MPU. Non-Maskable Interrupt ($\overline{\text{NMI}}$) is similar to the interrupt request input mentioned earlier, except that $\overline{\text{NMI}}$ will always be serviced regardless of the state of a programmable interrupt mask contained within the processor. Data Bus Enable (DBE) is the three-state control signal for the MPU data bus. Normally, this signal will be $\phi2$, derived from the clock. Three-State Control (TSC) affects the address bus and the R/W line in the same manner that DBE controls the data bus. This signal can be used, for example, to accomplish a direct memory access by putting the Address Bus and the R/W line in the high impedance state. The last supervisory input is the $\overline{\text{Halt}}$ signal. When $\overline{\text{Halt}}$ is low, the MPU will stop processing. In the $\overline{\text{Halt}}$ mode, all three-state signals will be in a high impedance state (address, data and R/W), VMA will be low, and Bus Available will be high.

The Bus Available supervisory output from the MPU is normally in an inactive low state. It is brought high by the occurrence of the $\overline{\text{Halt}}$ input low or by execution of a WAIT instruction. In either case, the MPU stops program execution and sets Bus Available high, indicating that all the three-state buffers are in the high impedance state. If the MPU has stopped as a result of the $\overline{\text{Halt}}$ signal, Bus Available will remain high until the $\overline{\text{Halt}}$ input is again taken high. If the MPU has stopped as a result of the WAIT instruction, it is waiting for an interrupt and Bus Available will remain active until a non-maskable interrupt or interrupt request occurs. Bus Available may be used to signal external hardware that the MPU is off the bus for multiprocessor or direct memory access applications.

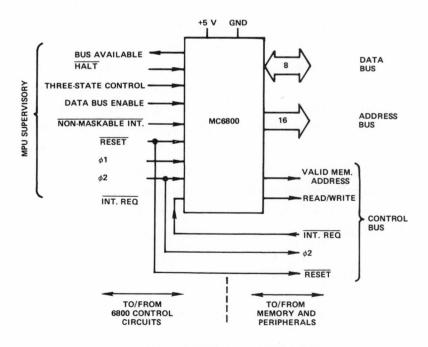

FIGURE 1-1-1. MC6800 Bus and Control Signals

1-1.1 M6800 FAMILY ELEMENTS

With the MC6800 as the focal point, a variety of memory and I/O devices may be tied onto the bus network. The busses will provide TTL compatible voltage levels ($V_{OH} = 2.4$ volts, $V_{OL} = 0.4$ volts) while driving capacitive loads up to 130 picofarads with current loads of up to 1.6 ma sink current and 100 μa source current.

1-1.1.1 Memory On The Bus

Memory is connected in a straightforward fashion by tieing directly to the MC6800 busses. Motorola currently provides two byte oriented memory devices as part of the microprocessor family: The 128 X 8 RAM (MCM6810) and the 1024 X 8 ROM (MCM6830). Block diagrams of the RAM and ROM are shown in Figures 1-1.1.1-1 and 1-1.1.1-2, respectively. Notice that the data lines have three-state buffers permitting the memory data signals to wire-OR directly onto the system data bus. Address decoding is minimized by providing multiple enable (E) inputs. The enable inputs, when active, select the specified device as defined by the address inputs. For a small to medium size system, no additional address decoding is necessary. The memories operate from a single 5 V power supply and are TTL compatible. Static operation eliminates the need for clocks or refresh.

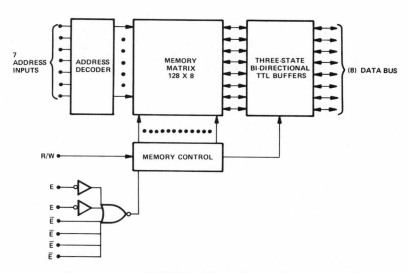

FIGURE 1-1.1.1-1. MCM6810 RAM Functional Block Diagram

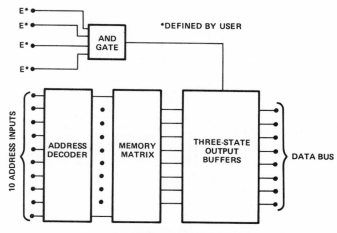

FIGURE 1-1.1.1-2. MCM6830 ROM Functional Block Diagram

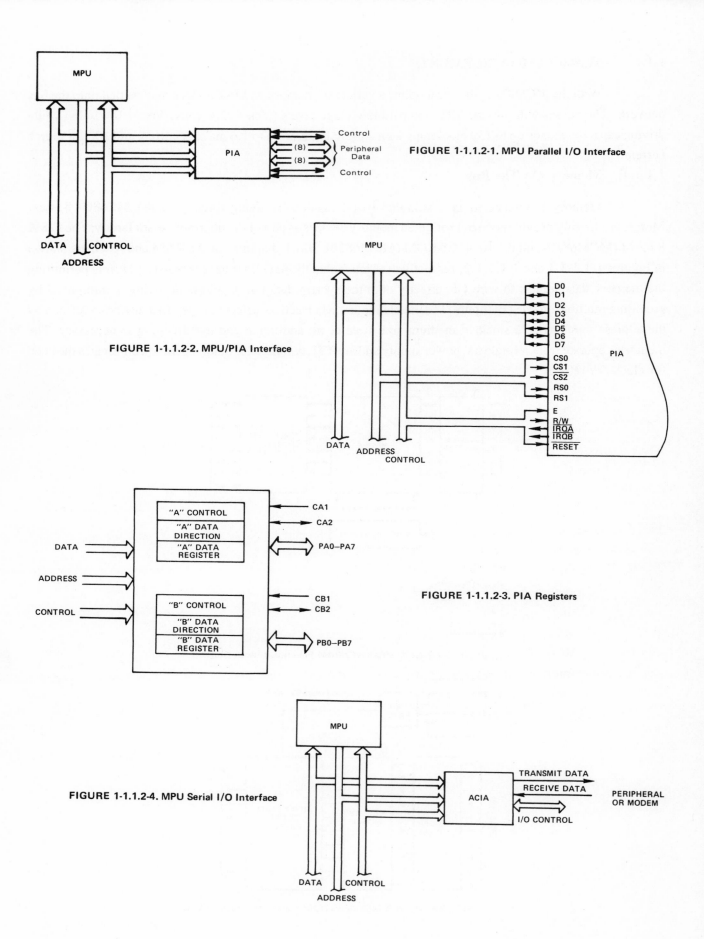

FIGURE 1-1.1.2-1. MPU Parallel I/O Interface

FIGURE 1-1.1.2-2. MPU/PIA Interface

FIGURE 1-1.1.2-3. PIA Registers

FIGURE 1-1.1.2-4. MPU Serial I/O Interface

1-1.1.2 I/O On The Bus

The family I/O devices are also tied directly to the bus network. In the M6800 architecture, I/O is configured to respond to MPU instructions in the same fashion as memory. This is accomplished by tapping off the MPU busses such that I/O has a "memory" address that the MPU references. Two devices available for interfacing the microprocessor with the outside world are the MC6820, Peripheral Interface Adapter (PIA), for parallel interface, and the MC6850, Asynchronous Communication Interface Adapter (ACIA), for serial interface. Both are designed to tie directly to the MPU busses and transfer signals between peripherals and the MPU under program control.

Interfacing the MPU to a variety of I/O devices is straightforward with the Peripheral Interface Adapter (PIA). It is a programmable general purpose parallel interface device designed to interface the MPU to peripherals through two 8-bit bidirectional peripheral data busses and four control lines as shown in Figure 1-1.1.2-1.

The MPU/PIA interface consists of three elements: 8 data lines, 5 address lines, and 5 control lines (see Figure 1-1.1.2-2). The data lines are bidirectional common to the MPU data bus. The PIA taps off 5 bits from the 16-bit MPU address bus. These 5 inputs are utilized to select the PIA (CS0, CS1, $\overline{CS2}$) as well as registers within the PIA (RS0 and RS1).

The PIA uses all of the signals on the MPU Control Bus. The R/W input ties directly to the MPU R/W output to control direction of data flow. The PIA has two independent Interrupt Request outputs that may be wire-ORed together and tied to the $\overline{IRQ}$ line of the Control Bus or applied separately to prioritizing circuitry. The $\overline{Reset}$ input may be tied directly to the MPU control bus to initialize the PIA to an all zero condition when required. Finally, the Enable input is the timing signal to be supplied to the PIA. This input is typically the $\phi2$ clock.

The PIA is programmable in the sense that the MPU can Read and/or Write into its internal registers. There are a total of six 8-bit registers in the PIA. They are separated into an A and B side, each side containing a Control Register, Data Direction Register, and an Output Data Register (Figure 1-1.1.2-3). To define operation of the PIA control lines, an 8-bit word is loaded into the Control Register. Likewise, to define the PIA/peripheral data lines to be inputs or outputs, an 8-bit word is loaded into the Data Direction Register. Finally, data being transferred to peripherals may be saved in the PIA Output Data Register.

Motorola has also made available a serial interface device to accommodate asynchronous data transfer. The MC6850 Asynchronous Communications Interface Adapter (ACIA) is a general purpose programmable interface for use between the MPU and asynchronous I/O as shown in Figure 1-1.1.2-4. The ACIA ties into the MPU Address, Data, and Control Busses enabling the MPU to handle the serial I/O using memory reference instructions.

The MPU/ACIA interface consists of three elements (see Figure 1-1.1.2-5): 8 data lines, 4 address lines, and 3 control lines. The data lines are bidirectional common to the MPU data bus. Four of the sixteen MPU address signals are used to select a particular ACIA (CS0, CS1, $\overline{CS2}$), and to select registers within the ACIA (RS).

The control signals from the bus are Read/Write (R/W) and Enable (E). The R/W input is common to the MPU control bus R/W signal and the E input in a typical application is the $\phi2$ clock.

The internal structure of the ACIA is centered around four registers (Figure 1-1.1.2-6): Control, Status, Transmit Data, and Receive Data. The ACIA is programmed by storing an 8-bit word into the write only Control Register. This register controls the function of the receiver, transmitter, interrupt enables, and the

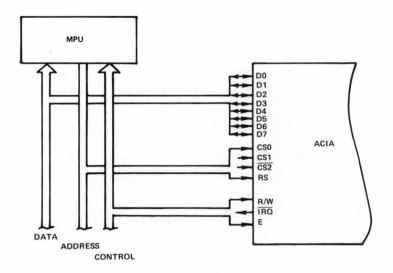

FIGURE 1-1.1.2-5. MPU/ACIA Interface

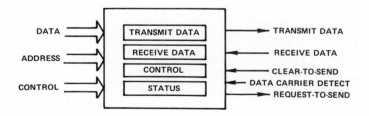

FIGURE 1-1.1.2-6. ACIA Registers

modem control signals. ACIA status and error conditions are monitored by reading the 8-bit Satus Register. The ACIA also has independent transmit and receive data buffers to save data and perform serial/parallel transformation.

1-1.2   TYPICAL SYSTEM CONFIGURATION

With the preceding material as background, the family devices and bus structure can be combined in a system configuration. Figure 1-1.2-1 shows a system controlled by the MC6800 containing one each RAM, ROM, PIA, and ACIA. With the exception of suitable peripherals, this block diagram represents all of the hardware required for a fully operational MPU system. The family of parts represents 5 devices, clock circuitry can be designed with 2 devices, and start-up can be accomplished with one device[1]. Therefore, a functional system can be configured with as few as eight devices and have both parallel and serial I/O capability.

The configuration of Figure 1-1.2-1 represents typical interconnections regardless of the size of the system. The data bus is shared fully between all devices in the system. The control bus is shared by all devices, with each tapping off signals as required. The I/O devices wire-OR all interrupt request signals to the MPU $\overline{IRQ}$ input. The PIA has two interrupts and the ACIA, one. VMA and $\phi2$ are both required inputs to the family devices and are, therefore, applied to the inputs as shown in Figure 1-1.2-1. $\phi2$ guarantees that all busses are stable and VMA designates a valid memory cycle whenever a memory or I/O device is enabled.

1-1.2.1   Memory Allocation

The Address Bus lends itself to very flexible memory allocation. Different combinations of signals may be tapped off the Address Bus to define where in "memory" each device is located. The chip select signals (CS0, CS1, $\overline{CS2}$) of the PIA/ACIA and the enable inputs of the RAM/ROM are used to select specific devices. In Figure 1-1.2-1, for example, A2, A14, and A15, are used to enable the PIA for MPU data transfer. The least significant address bits (A0, A1) are then utilized to select a memory word or I/O register within the selected device. Therefore, a given address will specify the device, and a location within the device.

Table 1-1.2.1-1 shows the "memory map" of the example system. This map represents the area in memory where each device is located, including I/O. For example, address bits A14 and A15 are both tied to the $\overline{E}$ inputs of the RAM. Therefore, whenever both of these address signals are low, the RAM will be conversing with the MPU on the data bus. It should be noted that without address decoding, the devices will be allocated a block of memory because the "don't care" address bits may be either logical "0" or "1", thereby widening the devices apparent address band. Having defined the memory map, the user may then determine the address of registers in a specific I/O device. Table 1-1.2.1-2 shows the corresponding register addresses for each ACIA and PIA register. Notice that bit 2 of the control registers (CRAb2 and CRBb2) and R/W are used to assist the address signals to select PIA and ACIA registers, respectively.

1-1.2.2   Hardware Requirements

The final point to consider is that the example configuration represents a minimum system. To expand the system, the user need only make further use of the bus network. If, for example, an additional PIA is required, A4, A14, and A15 may be tied to CS0, CS1, and $\overline{CS2}$, respectively. This procedure could be continued to add multiple memory and I/O devices without address decoding.

---

[1]See Chapter 4 for typical clock and start-up circuits.

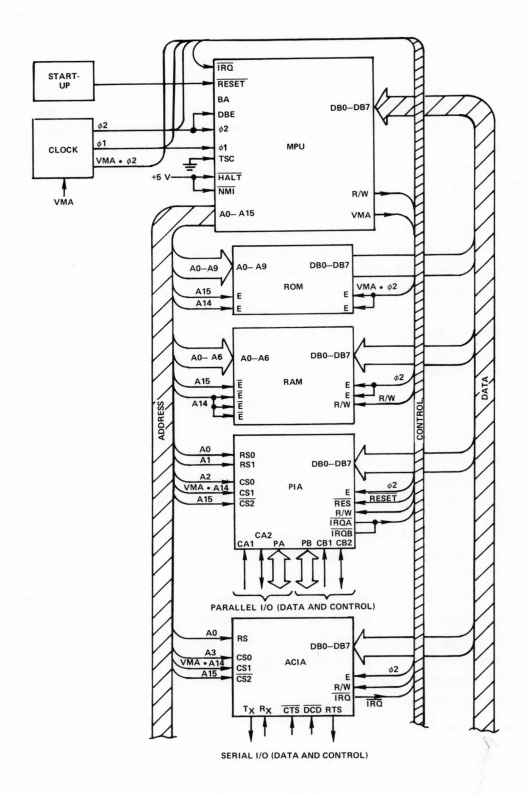

FIGURE 1-1.2-1. MPU Minimum System

The MC6800 microprocessor complemented by its family of parts was designed with ease of use in mind. Interfacing peripherals to the microprocessor with PIAs and ACIAs eases the burden of hardware design and minimizes software requirements by distributing intelligence to these interfaces. Power supply requirements are uncomplicated: one five-volt supply throughout the family. Neither decode nor buffering circuitry is required in systems containing less than 7 to 10 family devices. As the system grows, the design may require buffers to prevent overloading or address decoders to more precisely define memory blocks. Be that as it may, the rules don't change and bussing continues to be straightforward.

						ADDRESS										DEVICE	MEMORY MAP
15	14	13	12	11	10	9	8	7	6	5	4	3	2	1	0		
0	0	·	·	·	·	·	·	·	X	X	X	X	X	X	X	RAM	0000-007F HEX
1	1	·	·	·	·	X	X	X	X	X	X	X	X	X	X	ROM	C000-C3FF HEX
0	1	·	·	·	·	·	·	·	·	·	·	·	1	X	X	PIA	4004-4007 HEX
0	1	·	·	·	·	·	·	·	·	·	·	1	·	·	X	ACIA	4008-4009 HEX

X = Variable address   0 = Logical zero
· = Don't care   1 = Logical one

TABLE 1-1.2.1-1

ADDRESS(HEX)			I/O REGISTER
(4004-4007)	RS1	RS0	(PIA)
4004	0	0	Data direction register A (CRAb2 = 0)
4004	0	0	Peripheral interface register A (CRAb2 = 1)
4005	0	1	Control register A
4006	1	0	Data direction register B (CRBb2 = 0)
4006	1	0	Peripheral interface register B (CRBb2 = 1)
4007	1	1	Control register B
(4008-4009)	RS		(ACIA)
4008	0		Control register (write only)
4008	0		Status register (read only)
4009	1		Transmit data register (write only)
4009	1		Receiver data register (read only)

TABLE 1-1.2.1-2

A hardware configuration similar to that described in the preceding Section provides the nucleus for a system based on the M6800 Microprocessor Family. Three additional elements are required to complete a typical system design: (1) the actual peripheral equipment that is dictated by the system specification; (2) any auxiliary electronics required to control the peripherals; (3) the ''intelligence'' that enables the MPU to perform the required control and data processing functions.

In an MPU based design, ''intelligence'' refers to the control program, a sequence of instructions that will guide the MPU through the various operations it must perform. During development, the designer uses the MC6800's predefined instruction set to prepare a control program that will satisfy the system requirements. The program, usually called ''software'' at this point, is then stored in ROM memory that can be accessed by the MPU during operation, thus becoming the system's intelligence. Once in ROM, the program is often called ''firmware'', however, it is common to find the terms software and firmware used interchangeably in this context.

Definition of suitable peripheral interfaces is discussed in detail in Chapter 5. The remainder of this Chapter provides the background information necessary for generation of the control program. Source statement format and the MPU's addressing modes are introduced in this section. The instruction set is described in Section 1-3.

The MPU operates on 8-bit binary numbers presented to it via the Data Bus. A given number (byte) may represent either data or an instruction to be executed, depending on where it is encountered in the control program. The M6800 has 72 unique instructions, however, it recognizes and takes action on 197 of the 256 possibilities that can occur using an 8-bit word length. This larger number of instructions results from the fact that many of the executive instructions have more than one addressing mode.

These addressing modes refer to the manner in which the program causes the MPU to obtain its instructions and data. The programmer must have a method for addressing the MPU's internal registers and all of the external memory locations. The complete executive instruction set and the applicable addressing modes are summarized in Figure 1-3-1, however, the addressing modes will be described in greater detail prior to introducing the instruction set later in this chapter. A programming model of the MC6800 is shown in Figure 1-2-1. The programmable registers consist of: two 8-bit Accumulators; a 6-bit Condition Code Register; a Program Counter, a Stack Pointer, and an Index Register, each 16 bits long.

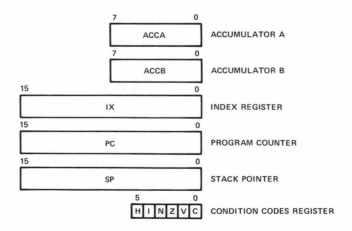

FIGURE 1-2-1. Programming Model of MC6800

1-2.1 SOURCE STATEMENTS

While programs can be written in the MPU's language, that is, binary numbers, there is no easy way for the programmer to remember the particular word that corresponds to a given operation. For this reason, instructions are assigned a three letter mnemonic symbol that suggests the definition of the instruction. The program is written as a series of source statements using this symbolic language and then translated into machine language. The translation can be done manually using an alphabetic listing of the symbolic instruction set such as that shown in Table 7-1.1. More often, the translation is accomplished by means of a special computer program referred to as a cross-assembler. The cross-assembler and other "software" design aids available to the user are described in Chapter 7.

During assembly, each source statement or executive instruction is converted to from one to three bytes of operating code (opcode), depending on the addressing mode used. The term "executive instruction" is used here to distinguish between statements that generate machine code and "assembly directives" that are useful in controlling and documenting the source program but generate no code. The Assembly Directives are described in Section 7-1.1.

Each statement in the source program prepared by the user may have from one to four fields: a label, a mnemonic operator (instruction), an operand, and a comment. The four fields are illustrated in the following typical source statement:

Label	Operator	Operand	Comment
BEGIN1	TST	DATA1B	TEST CONTENTS OF DATA1B

(This instruction causes the MPU to test the contents of the memory location labeled DATA1B and set the Condition Code Register bits accordingly.)

Each source statement must have at least the mnemonic operator field. An operand may or may not be required, depending on the nature of the instruction. The comment field is optional, at the programmer's convenience, for describing and documenting the program.

1-2.2 LABELS

Labels and their use are described in greater detail in Chapter 7. In general, they may correspond to either a numerical value or a memory location. This use of symbolic references to memory permits programming without using specific numerical memory addresses. For instance, the operand label "DAA1B" in the example may be anywhere in memory. Labels are required for source statements that are the destination of jump and branch instructions. In the example, "BEGIN1" identifies the statement as the destination of a branch or jump instruction located elsewhere in the control program. That instruction will, in turn, have "BEGIN1" as its operand.

Labels may be up to six characters long and use any alphanumeric combination of the character set shown in Table 7-1.1-2 with the restriction that the first character be alphabetic. Three single character labels, A, B, and X, are reserved for referring to accumulator A, accumulator B, and the Index Register, respectively.

1-2.3 ADDRESSING MODES

1-2.3.1 Inherent (Includes "Accumulator Addressing" Mode)

The successive fields in a statement are normally separated by one or more spaces. An exception to this rule occurs for instructions that use dual addressing in the operand field and for instructions that must distinguish between the two accumulators. In these cases, A and B are "operands" but the space between them and the operator may be omitted. This is commonly done, resulting in apparent four character mnemonics for those instructions.

The addition instruction, ADD, provides an example of dual addressing in the operand field:

	Operator	Operand	Comment
	ADDA	MEM12	ADD CONTENTS OF MEM12 TO ACCA
or	ADDB	MEM12	ADD CONTENTS OF MEM12 TO ACCB

The example used earlier for the test instruction, TST, also applies to the accumulators and uses the "accumulator addressing mode" to designate which of the two accumulators is being tested:

	Operator	Comment
	TSTB	TEST CONTENTS OF ACCB
or	TSTA	TEST CONTENTS OF ACCA

A number of the instructions either alone or together with an accumulator operand contain all of the address information that is required, that is, the address is "inherent" in the instruction itself. For instance, the instruction ABA causes the MPU to add the contents of accumulators A and B together and place the result in accumulator A. The instruction INCB, another example of "accumulator addressing", causes the contents of accumulator B to be increased by one. Similarly, INX, increment the Index Register, causes the contents of the Index Register to be increased by one.

Program flow for instructions of this type is illustrated in Figures 1-2.3.1-1 and 1-2.3.1-2. In these figures, the general case is shown on the left and a specific example is shown on the right. Numerical examples are in decimal notation. Instructions of this type require only one byte of opcode.

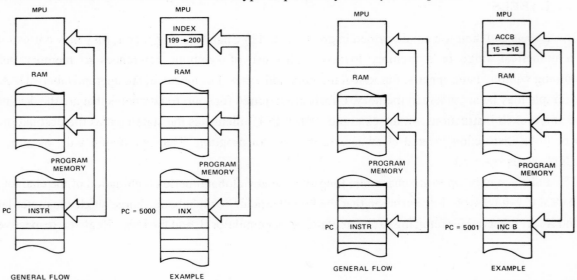

FIGURE 1-2.3.1-1. Inherent Addressing   FIGURE 1-2.3.1-2. Accumulator Addressing

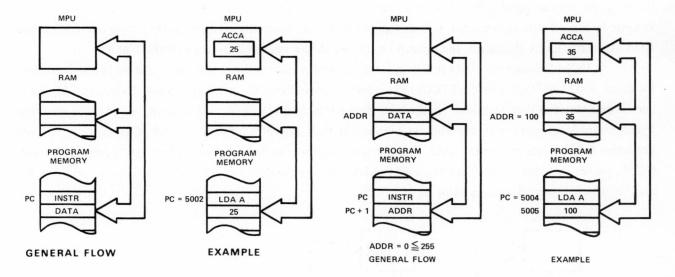

FIGURE 1-2.3.2-1. Immediate Addressing Mode   FIGURE 1-2.3.3-1. Direct Addressing Mode

1-2.3.2 Immediate Addressing Mode

In the Immediate addressing mode, the operand is the value that is to be operated on. For instance, the instruction

Operator	Operand	Comment
LDAA	#25	LOAD 25 INTO ACCA

causes the MPU to "immediately load accumulator A with the value 25; no further address reference is required. The Immediate mode is selected by preceding the operand value with the "#" symbol. Program flow for this addressing mode is illustrated in Figure 1-2.3.2-1.

The operand format allows either properly defined symbols or numerical values. Except for the instructions CPX, LDX, and LDS, the operand may be any value in the range 0 to 255. Since Compare Index Register (CPX), Load Index Register (LDX), and Load Stack Pointer (LDS), require 16-bit values, the immediate mode for these three instructions require two-byte operands. In the Immediate addressing mode, the "address" of the operand is effectively the memory location immediately following the instruction itself.

1-2.3.3 Direct and Extended Addressing Modes

In the Direct and Extended modes of addressing, the operand field of the source statement is the *address* of the value that is to be operated on. The Direct and Extended modes differ only in the range of memory locations to which they can direct the MPU. Direct addressing generates a single 8-bit operand and, hence, can address only memory locations 0 through 255; a two byte operand is generated for Extended addressing, enabling the MPU to reach the remaining memory locations, 256 through 65535. An example of Direct addressing and its effect on program flow is illustrated in Figure 1-2.3.3-1.

The MPU, after encountering the opcode for the instruction LDAA (Direct) at memory location 5004 (Program Counter = 5004), looks in the next location, 5005, for the address of the operand. It then sets the program counter equal to the value found there (100 in the example) and fetches the operand, in this case a value to be loaded into accumulator A, from that location. For instructions requiring a two-byte operand such as LDX (load the Index Register), the operand bytes would be retrieved from locations 100 and 101.

Extended addressing, Figure 1-2.3.3-2, is similar except that a two-byte address is obtained from locations 5007 and 5008 after the LDAB (Extended) opcode shows up in location 5006. Extended addressing can be thought of as the "standard" addressing mode, that is, it is a method of reaching anyplace in memory. Direct addressing, since only one address byte is required, provides a faster method of processing data and generates fewer bytes of control code. In most applications, the direct addressing range, memory locations 0-255, are reserved for RAM. They are used for data buffering and temporary storage of system variables, the area in which faster addressing is of most value.

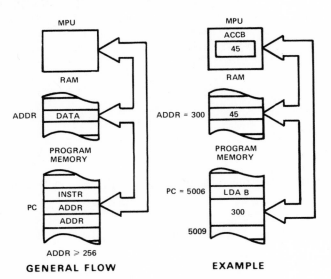

FIGURE 1-2.3-3-2. Extended Addressing Mode

1-2.3.4 Relative Addressing Mode

In both the Direct and Extended modes, the address obtained by the MPU is an absolute numerical address. The Relative addressing mode, implemented for the MPU's branch instructions, specifies a memory location relative to the Program Counter's current location. Branch instructions generate two bytes of machine code, one for the instruction opcode and one for the "relative" address (see Figure 1-2.3.4-1). Since it is desirable to be able to branch in either direction, the 8-bit address byte is interpreted as a signed 7-bit value; the 8th bit of the operand is treated as a sign bit, "0" = plus and "1" = minus. The remaining seven bits represent the numerical value. This results in a relative addressing range of ±127 with respect to the location of the branch instruction itself. However, the branch range is computed with respect to the next instruction that would be executed if the branch conditions are not satisfied. Since two bytes are generated, the next instruction is located at PC + 2. If D is defined as the address of the branch destination, the range is then:

$$(PC + 2) - 127 \leq D \leq (PC + 2) + 127$$

or $$PC - 125 \leq D \leq PC + 129$$

that is, the destination of the branch instruction must be within −125 to +129 memory locations of the branch instruction itself. For transferring control beyond this range, the unconditional jump (JMP), jump to subroutine (JSR), and return from subroutine (RTS) are used.

In Figure 1-2.3.4-1, when the MPU encounters the opcode for BEQ (Branch if result of last instruction was zero), it tests the Zero bit in the Condition Code Register. If that bit is "0", indicating a non-zero result, the MPU continues execution with the next instruction (in location 5010 in Figure 1-2.3.4-1). If the previous result was zero, the branch condition is satisfied and the MPU adds the offset, 15 in this case, to PC + 2 and branches to location 5025 for the next instruction.

The branch instructions allow the programmer to efficiently direct the MPU to one point or another in the control program depending on the outcome of test results. Since the control program is normally in read-only memory and cannot be changed, the relative address used in execution of branch instructions is a constant numerical value.

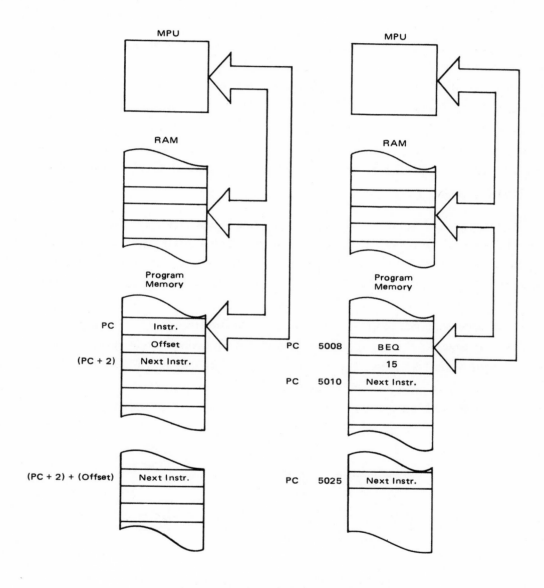

FIGURE 1-2.3.4-1. Relative Addressing Mode

1-2.3.5 Indexed Addressing Mode

With Indexed addressing, the numerical address is variable and depends on the current contents of the Index Register. A source statement such as

Operator	Operand	Comment
STAA	X	PUT A IN INDEXED LOCATION

causes the MPU to store the contents of accumulator A in the memory location specified by the contents of the Index Register (recall that the label ''X'' is reserved to designate the Index Register). Since there are instructions for manipulating X during program execution (LDX, INX, DEX, etc.), the Indexed addressing mode provides a dynamic ''on the fly'' way to modify program activity.

The operand field can also contain a numerical value that will be automatically added to X during execution. This format is illustrated in Figure 1-2.3.5-1.

When the MPU encounters the LDAB (Indexed) opcode in location 5006, it looks in the next memory location for the value to be added to X (5 in the example) and calculates the required address by adding 5 to the present Index Register value of 400. In the operand format, the offset may be represented by a label or a numerical value in the range 0-255 as in the example. In the earlier example, STAA X, the operand is equivalent to 0,X, that is, the 0 may be omitted when the desired address is equal to X.

1-2.3.6 Mode Selection

Selection of the desired addressing mode is made by the user as the source statements are written. Translation into appropriate opcode then depends on the method used. If manual translation is used, the addressing mode is inherent in the opcode. For example, the Immediate, Direct, Indexed, and Extended modes may all be used with the ADD instruction. The proper mode is determined by selecting (hexidecimal notation) 8B, 9B, AB, or BB, respectively (see Figure 1-3-1).

The source statement format includes adequate information for the selection if an assembler program is used to generate the opcode. For instance, the Immediate mode is selected by the Assembler whenever it encounters the ''#'' symbol in the operand field. Similarly, an ''X'' in the operand field causes the Indexed mode to be selected. Only the Relative mode applies to the branch instructions, therefore, the mnemonic instruction itself is enough for the Assembler to determine addressing mode.

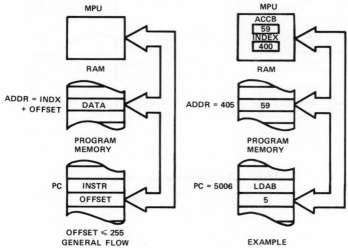

FIGURE 1-2.3.5-1. Indexed Addressing Mode

For the instructions that use both Direct and Extended modes, the Assembler selects the Direct mode if the operand value is in the range 0-255 and Extended otherwise. There are a number of instructions for which the Extended mode is valid but the Direct is not. For these instructions, the Assembler automatically selects the Extended mode even if the operand is in the 0-255 range. The addressing modes are summarized in Figure 1-2.3.6-1.

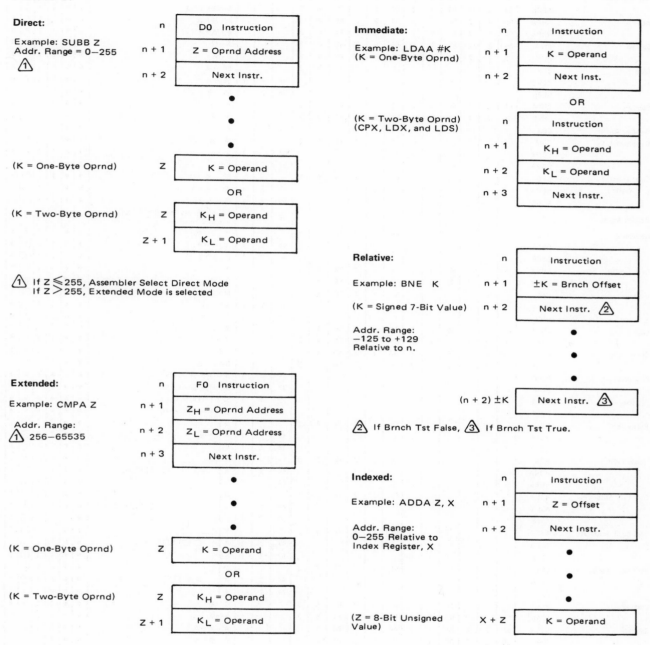

FIGURE 1-2.3.6-1. Addressing Mode Summary

ACCUMULATOR AND MEMORY OPERATIONS	MNEMONIC	IMMED OP	~	#	DIRECT OP	~	#	INDEX OP	~	#	EXTND OP	~	#	INHER OP	~	#	BOOLEAN/ARITHMETIC OPERATION (All register labels refer to contents)	5 H	4 I	3 N	2 Z	1 V	0 C
Add	ADDA	8B	2	2	9B	3	2	AB	5	2	BB	4	3				A + M → A	‡	•	‡	‡	‡	‡
	ADDB	CB	2	2	DB	3	2	EB	5	2	FB	4	3				B + M → B	‡	•	‡	‡	‡	‡
Add Acmltrs	ABA													1B	2	1	A + B → A	‡	•	‡	‡	‡	‡
Add with Carry	ADCA	89	2	2	99	3	2	A9	5	2	B9	4	3				A + M + C → A	‡	•	‡	‡	‡	‡
	ADCB	C9	2	2	D9	3	2	E9	5	2	F9	4	3				B + M + C → B	‡	•	‡	‡	‡	‡
And	ANDA	84	2	2	94	3	2	A4	5	2	B4	4	3				A • M → A	•	•	‡	‡	R	•
	ANDB	C4	2	2	D4	3	2	E4	5	2	F4	4	3				B • M → B	•	•	‡	‡	R	•
Bit Test	BITA	85	2	2	95	3	2	A5	5	2	B5	4	3				A • M	•	•	‡	‡	R	•
	BITB	C5	2	2	D5	3	2	E5	5	2	F5	4	3				B • M	•	•	‡	‡	R	•
Clear	CLR							6F	7	2	7F	6	3				00 → M	•	•	R	S	R	R
	CLRA													4F	2	1	00 → A	•	•	R	S	R	R
	CLRB													5F	2	1	00 → B	•	•	R	S	R	R
Compare	CMPA	81	2	2	91	3	2	A1	5	2	B1	4	3				A − M	•	•	‡	‡	‡	‡
	CMPB	C1	2	2	D1	3	2	E1	5	2	F1	4	3				B − M	•	•	‡	‡	‡	‡
Compare Acmltrs	CBA													11	2	1	A − B	•	•	‡	‡	‡	‡
Complement, 1's	COM							63	7	2	73	6	3				$\overline{M}$ → M	•	•	‡	‡	R	S
	COMA													43	2	1	$\overline{A}$ → A	•	•	‡	‡	R	S
	COMB													53	2	1	$\overline{B}$ → B	•	•	‡	‡	R	S
Complement, 2's (Negate)	NEG							60	7	2	70	6	3				00 − M → M	•	•	‡	‡	①	②
	NEGA													40	2	1	00 − A → A	•	•	‡	‡	①	②
	NEGB													50	2	1	00 − B → B	•	•	‡	‡	①	②
Decimal Adjust, A	DAA													19	2	1	Converts Binary Add. of BCD Characters into BCD Format	•	•	‡	‡	‡	③
Decrement	DEC							6A	7	2	7A	6	3				M − 1 → M	•	•	‡	‡	④	•
	DECA													4A	2	1	A − 1 → A	•	•	‡	‡	④	•
	DECB													5A	2	1	B − 1 → B	•	•	‡	‡	④	•
Exclusive OR	EORA	88	2	2	98	3	2	A8	5	2	B8	4	3				A ⊕ M → A	•	•	‡	‡	R	•
	EORB	C8	2	2	D8	3	2	E8	5	2	F8	4	3				B ⊕ M → B	•	•	‡	‡	R	•
Increment	INC							6C	7	2	7C	6	3				M + 1 → M	•	•	‡	‡	⑤	•
	INCA													4C	2	1	A + 1 → A	•	•	‡	‡	⑤	•
	INCB													5C	2	1	B + 1 → B	•	•	‡	‡	⑤	•
Load Acmltr	LDAA	86	2	2	96	3	2	A6	5	2	B6	4	3				M → A	•	•	‡	‡	R	•
	LDAB	C6	2	2	D6	3	2	E6	5	2	F6	4	3				M → B	•	•	‡	‡	R	•
Or, Inclusive	ORAA	8A	2	2	9A	3	2	AA	5	2	BA	4	3				A + M → A	•	•	‡	‡	R	•
	ORAB	CA	2	2	DA	3	2	EA	5	2	FA	4	3				B + M → B	•	•	‡	‡	R	•
Push Data	PSHA													36	4	1	A → M$_{SP}$, SP − 1 → SP	•	•	•	•	•	•
	PSHB													37	4	1	B → M$_{SP}$, SP − 1 → SP	•	•	•	•	•	•
Pull Data	PULA													32	4	1	SP + 1 → SP, M$_{SP}$ → A	•	•	•	•	•	•
	PULB													33	4	1	SP + 1 → SP, M$_{SP}$ → B	•	•	•	•	•	•
Rotate Left	ROL							69	7	2	79	6	3				M	•	•	‡	‡	⑥	‡
	ROLA													49	2	1	A	•	•	‡	‡	⑥	‡
	ROLB													59	2	1	B	•	•	‡	‡	⑥	‡
Rotate Right	ROR							66	7	2	76	6	3				M	•	•	‡	‡	⑥	‡
	RORA													46	2	1	A	•	•	‡	‡	⑥	‡
	RORB													56	2	1	B	•	•	‡	‡	⑥	‡
Shift Left, Arithmetic	ASL							68	7	2	78	6	3				M	•	•	‡	‡	⑥	‡
	ASLA													48	2	1	A	•	•	‡	‡	⑥	‡
	ASLB													58	2	1	B	•	•	‡	‡	⑥	‡
Shift Right, Arithmetic	ASR							67	7	2	77	6	3				M	•	•	‡	‡	⑥	‡
	ASRA													47	2	1	A	•	•	‡	‡	⑥	‡
	ASRB													57	2	1	B	•	•	‡	‡	⑥	‡
Shift Right, Logic.	LSR							64	7	2	74	6	3				M	•	•	R	‡	⑥	‡
	LSRA													44	2	1	A	•	•	R	‡	⑥	‡
	LSRB													54	2	1	B	•	•	R	‡	⑥	‡
Store Acmltr.	STAA				97	4	2	A7	6	2	B7	5	3				A → M	•	•	‡	‡	R	•
	STAB				D7	4	2	E7	6	2	F7	5	3				B → M	•	•	‡	‡	R	•
Subtract	SUBA	80	2	2	90	3	2	A0	5	2	B0	4	3				A − M → A	•	•	‡	‡	‡	‡
	SUBB	C0	2	2	D0	3	2	E0	5	2	F0	4	3				B − M → B	•	•	‡	‡	‡	‡
Subract Acmltrs.	SBA													10	2	1	A − B → A	•	•	‡	‡	‡	‡
Subtr. with Carry	SBCA	82	2	2	92	3	2	A2	5	2	B2	4	3				A − M − C → A	•	•	‡	‡	‡	‡
	SBCB	C2	2	2	D2	3	2	E2	5	2	F2	4	3				B − M − C → B	•	•	‡	‡	‡	‡
Transfer Acmltrs	TAB													16	2	1	A → B	•	•	‡	‡	R	•
	TBA													17	2	1	B → A	•	•	‡	‡	R	•
Test, Zero or Minus	TST							6D	7	2	7D	6	3				M − 00	•	•	‡	‡	R	R
	TSTA													4D	2	1	A − 00	•	•	‡	‡	R	R
	TSTB													5D	2	1	B − 00	•	•	‡	‡	R	R

FIGURE 1-3-1 MC6800 Instruction Set

INDEX REGISTER AND STACK POINTER OPERATIONS

POINTER OPERATIONS	MNEMONIC	IMMED OP	~	#	DIRECT OP	~	#	INDEX OP	~	#	EXTND OP	~	#	INHER OP	~	#	BOOLEAN/ARITHMETIC OPERATION	5 H	4 I	3 N	2 Z	1 V	0 C
Compare Index Reg	CPX	8C	3	3	9C	4	2	AC	6	2	BC	5	3				$(X_H/X_L) - (M/M+1)$	•	•	⑦	‡	⑧	•
Decrement Index Reg	DEX													09	4	1	$X - 1 \rightarrow X$	•	•	•	‡	•	•
Decrement Stack Pntr	DES													34	4	1	$SP - 1 \rightarrow SP$	•	•	•	•	•	•
Increment Index Reg	INX													08	4	1	$X + 1 \rightarrow X$	•	•	•	‡	•	•
Increment Stack Pntr	INS													31	4	1	$SP + 1 \rightarrow SP$	•	•	•	•	•	•
Load Index Reg	LDX	CE	3	3	DE	4	2	EE	6	2	FE	5	3				$M \rightarrow X_H, (M+1) \rightarrow X_L$	•	•	⑨	‡	R	•
Load Stack Pntr	LDS	8E	3	3	9E	4	2	AE	6	2	BE	5	3				$M \rightarrow SP_H, (M+1) \rightarrow SP_L$	•	•	⑨	‡	R	•
Store Index Reg	STX				DF	5	2	EF	7	2	FF	6	3				$X_H \rightarrow M, X_L \rightarrow (M+1)$	•	•	⑨	‡	R	•
Store Stack Pntr	STS				9F	5	2	AF	7	2	BF	6	3				$SP_H \rightarrow M, SP_L \rightarrow (M+1)$	•	•	⑨	‡	R	•
Indx Reg → Stack Pntr	TXS													35	4	1	$X - 1 \rightarrow SP$	•	•	•	•	•	•
Stack Pntr → Indx Reg	TSX													30	4	1	$SP + 1 \rightarrow X$	•	•	•	•	•	•

JUMP AND BRANCH OPERATIONS

OPERATIONS	MNEMONIC	RELATIVE OP	~	#	INDEX OP	~	#	EXTND OP	~	#	INHER OP	~	#	BRANCH TEST	5 H	4 I	3 N	2 Z	1 V	0 C
Branch Always	BRA	20	4	2										None	•	•	•	•	•	•
Branch If Carry Clear	BCC	24	4	2										C = 0	•	•	•	•	•	•
Branch If Carry Set	BCS	25	4	2										C = 1	•	•	•	•	•	•
Branch If = Zero	BEQ	27	4	2										Z = 1	•	•	•	•	•	•
Branch If ≥ Zero	BGE	2C	4	2										N ⊕ V = 0	•	•	•	•	•	•
Branch If > Zero	BGT	2E	4	2										Z + (N ⊕ V) = 0	•	•	•	•	•	•
Branch If Higher	BHI	22	4	2										C + Z = 0	•	•	•	•	•	•
Branch If ≤ Zero	BLE	2F	4	2										Z + (N ⊕ V) = 1	•	•	•	•	•	•
Branch If Lower Or Same	BLS	23	4	2										C + Z = 1	•	•	•	•	•	•
Branch If < Zero	BLT	2D	4	2										N ⊕ V = 1	•	•	•	•	•	•
Branch If Minus	BMI	2B	4	2										N = 1	•	•	•	•	•	•
Branch If Not Equal Zero	BNE	26	4	2										Z = 0	•	•	•	•	•	•
Branch If Overflow Clear	BVC	28	4	2										V = 0	•	•	•	•	•	•
Branch If Overflow Set	BVS	29	4	2										V = 1	•	•	•	•	•	•
Branch If Plus	BPL	2A	4	2										N = 0	•	•	•	•	•	•
Branch To Subroutine	BSR	8D	8	2											•	•	•	•	•	•
Jump	JMP				6E	4	2	7E	3	3				} See Special Operations	•	•	•	•	•	•
Jump To Subroutine	JSR				AD	8	2	BD	9	3					•	•	•	•	•	•
No Operation	NOP										01	2	1	Advances Prog. Cntr. Only	•	•	•	•	•	•
Return From Interrupt	RTI										3B	10	1		⑩					
Return From Subroutine	RTS										39	5	1	} See special Operations	•	•	•	•	•	•
Software Interrupt	SWI										3F	12	1		•	S	•	•	•	•
Wait for Interrupt	WAI										3E	9	1		•	⑪	•	•	•	•

CONDITIONS CODE REGISTER OPERATIONS

OPERATIONS	MNEMONIC	INHER OP	~	#	BOOLEAN OPERATION	5 H	4 I	3 N	2 Z	1 V	0 C
Clear Carry	CLC	0C	2	1	0 → C	•	•	•	•	•	R
Clear Interrupt Mask	CLI	0E	2	1	0 → I	•	R	•	•	•	•
Clear Overflow	CLV	0A	2	1	0 → V	•	•	•	•	R	•
Set Carry	SEC	0D	2	1	1 → C	•	•	•	•	•	S
Set Interrupt Mask	SEI	0F	2	1	1 → I	•	S	•	•	•	•
Set Overflow	SEV	0B	2	1	1 → V	•	•	•	•	S	•
Acmltr A → CCR	TAP	06	2	1	A → CCR	⑫					
CCR → Acmltr A	TPA	07	2	1	CCR → A	•	•	•	•	•	•

CONDITION CODE REGISTER NOTES:
(Bit set if test is true and cleared otherwise)

① (Bit V) Test: Result = 10000000?
② (Bit C) Test: Result = 00000000?
③ (Bit C) Test: Decimal value of most significant BCD Character greater than nine? (Not cleared if previously set.)
④ (Bit V) Test: Operand = 10000000 prior to execution?
⑤ (Bit V) Test: Operand = 01111111 prior to execution?
⑥ (Bit V) Test: Set equal to result of N ⊕ C after shift has occurred.
⑦ (Bit N) Test: Sign bit of most significant (MS) byte of result = 1?
⑧ (Bit V) Test: 2's complement overflow from subtraction of LS bytes?
⑨ (Bit N) Test: Result less than zero? (Bit 15 = 1)
⑩ (All) Load Condition Code Register from Stack. (See Special Operations)
⑪ (Bit I) Set when interrupt occurs. If previously set, a Non-Maskable Interrupt is required to exit the wait state.
⑫ (ALL) Set according to the contents of Accumulator A.

LEGEND:
OP   Operation Code (Hexadecimal);
~   Number of MPU Cycles;
#   Number of Program Bytes;
+   Arithmetic Plus;
−   Arithmetic Minus;
•   Boolean AND;
M_{SP} Contents of memory location pointed to be Stack Pointer;
+   Boolean Inclusive OR;
⊕   Boolean Exclusive OR;
$\overline{M}$ Complement of M;
→   Transfer Into;
0   Bit = Zero;

00   Byte = Zero;
H   Half-carry from bit 3;
I   Interrupt mask
N   Negative (sign bit)
Z   Zero (byte)
V   Overflow, 2's complement
C   Carry from bit 7
R   Reset Always
S   Set Always
‡   Test and set if true, cleared otherwise
•   Not Affected
CCR   Condition Code Register
LS   Least Significant
MS   Most Significant

FIGURE 1-3-1 (continued)

INSTRUCTION SET

The MC6800 instructions are described in detail in the M6800 Programming Manual. This Section will provide a brief introduction and discuss their use in developing MC6800 control programs.

The instruction set is shown in summary form in Figure 1-3-1. Microprocessor instructions are often divided into three general classifications: (1) memory reference, so called because they operate on specific memory locations; (2) operating instructions that function without needing a memory reference; (3) I/O instructions for transferring data between the microprocessor and peripheral devices.

In many instances, the MC6800 performs the same operation on both its internal accumulators and the external memory locations. In addition, the M6800 interfaces adapters (PIA and ACIA) allow the MPU to treat peripheral devices exactly like other memory locations, hence, no I/O instructions as such are required. Because of these features, other classifications are more suitable for introducing the MC6800's instruction set: (1) Accumulator and memory operations; (2) Program control operations; (3) Condition Code Register operations.

1-3.1   CONDITION CODE REGISTER OPERATIONS

The Condition Code Register (CCR), also called the Program Status Byte, will be described first since it is affected by many of the other instructions as well as the specific operations shown in Figure 1-3.1-2. The CCR is a 6-bit register within the MPU that is useful in controlling program flow during system operation. The bits are defined in Figure 1-3.1-1.

The instructions shown in Figure 1-3.1-2 are available to the user for direct manipulation of the CCR. In addition, the MPU automatically sets or clears the appropriate status bits as many of the other instructions are executed. The effect of those instructions on the condition code register will be indicated as they are introduced and is also included in the Instruction Set Summary of Figure 1-3-1.

b_5	b_4	b_3	b_2	b_1	b_0
H	I	N	Z	V	C

H = Half-carry; set whenever a carry from b_3 to b_4 of the result is generated by ADD, ABA, ADC; cleared if no b_3 to b_4 carry; not affected by other instructions.

I = Interrupt Mask; set by hardware or software interrupt or SEI instruction; cleared by CLI instruction. (Normally not used in arithmetic operations.) Restored to a zero as a result of an RT1 instruction if I_m stored on the stacked is low.

N = Negative; set if high order bit (b_7) of result is set; cleared otherwise.

Z = Zero; set if result = 0; cleared otherwise.

V = Overlow; set if there was arithmetic overflow as a result of the operation; cleared otherwise.

C = Carry; set if there was a carry from the most significant bit (b_7) of the result; cleared otherwise.

FIGURE 1-3.1-1. Condition Code Register Bit Definition

CONDITIONS CODE REGISTER OPERATIONS	MNEMONIC	BOOLEAN OPERATION	5 H	4 I	3 N	2 Z	1 V	0 C
Clear Carry	CLC	$0 \rightarrow C$	●	●	●	●	●	R
Clear Interrupt Mask	CLI	$0 \rightarrow I$	●	R	●	●	●	●
Clear Overflow	CLV	$0 \rightarrow V$	●	●	●	●	R	●
Set Carry	SEC	$1 \rightarrow C$	●	●	●	●	●	S
Set Interrupt Mask	SEI	$1 \rightarrow I$	●	S	●	●	●	●
Set Overflow	SEV	$1 \rightarrow V$	●	●	●	●	S	●
Acmltr A $\rightarrow$ CCR	TAP	$A \rightarrow CCR$			①			
CCR $\rightarrow$ Acmltr A	TPA	$CCR \rightarrow A$	●	●	●	●	●	●

R = Reset
S = Set
● = Not affected

① (ALL) Set according to the contents of Accumulator A.

FIGURE 1-3.1-2. Condition Code Register Instructions

1-3.2 NUMBER SYSTEMS

Effective use of many of the instructions depends on the interpretation given to numerical data, that is, what number system is being used? For example, the ALU always performs standard binary addition of two eight bit numbers using the 2's complement number system to represent both positive and negative numbers. However, the MPU instruction set and hardware flags permit arithmetic operation using any of four different representations for the numbers:

(1) Each byte can be interpreted as a signed 2's complement number in the range -128 to $+127$:

	2^6	2^5	2^4	2^3	2^2	2^1	2^0	
b_7	b_6	b_5	b_4	b_3	b_2	b_1	b_0	
1	0	0	0	0	0	0	0	(-128 in 2's complement)
1	1	1	1	1	1	1	1	(-1 in 2's complement)
0	0	0	0	0	0	0	0	(0 in 2's complement)
0	0	0	0	0	0	0	1	($+1$ in 2's complement)
0	1	1	1	1	1	1	1	($+127$ in 2's complement)

(2) Each byte can be interpreted as a signed binary number in the range -127 to $+127$:

2^6	2^5	2^4	2^3	2^2	2^1	2^0	
b_7	b_6	b_5	b_4	b_3	b_2	b_1	b_0
1	1	1	1	1	1	1	1	(-127 in signed binary)
1	0	0	0	0	0	0	1	(-1 in signed binary)
0	0	0	0	0	0	0	0	(0 in signed binary)
0	0	0	0	0	0	0	1	($+1$ in signed binary)
0	1	1	1	1	1	1	1	($+127$ in signed binary)

(3) Each byte can be interpreted as an unsigned binary number in the range 0 to 255:

2^7	2^6	2^5	2^4	2^3	2^2	2^1	2^0	
b_7	b_6	b_5	b_4	b_3	b_2	b_1	b_0	
0	0	0	0	0	0	0	0	(0 in unsigned binary)
1	1	1	1	1	1	1	1	(255 in unsigned binary)

(4) Each byte can be thought of as containing two 4-bit binary coded decimal (BCD) numbers. With this interpretation, each byte can represent numbers in the range 0 to 99:

2^3	2^2	2^1	2^0	2^3	2^2	2^1	2^0	
b_7	b_6	b_5	b_4	b_3	b_2	b_1	b_0	
0	0	0	0	0	0	0	0	(BCD 0)
0	0	1	0	0	1	1	1	(BCD 27)
1	0	0	1	1	0	0	1	(BCD 99)

The two's complement representation for positive numbers is obtained simply by adding a zero (sign bit) as the next higher significant bit position:

2^7	2^6	2^5	2^4	2^3	2^2	2^1	2^0	
a_7	a_6	a_5	a_4	a_3	a_2	a_1	a_0	
	1	1	1	1	1	1	1	(binary 127)
0	1	1	1	1	1	1	1	($+127$ in 2's complement representation)
	0	0	0	0	0	0	1	(binary 1)
0	0	0	0	0	0	0	1	($+1$ in 2's complement representation)

When the negative of a number is required for an arithmetic operation, it is formed by first complementing each bit position of the positive representation and then adding one.

	64	32	16	8	4	2	1	
a_7	a_6	a_5	a_4	a_3	a_2	a_1	a_0	
0	1	1	1	1	1	1	1	(+127 in 2's complement representation)
1	0	0	0	0	0	0	0	(1's complement)
							1	(add one)
1	0	0	0	0	0	0	1	(−127 in 2's complement representation)
0	0	0	0	0	0	0	0	(0 in 2's complement representation)
1	1	1	1	1	1	1	1	(1's complement)
							1	(add one)
0	0	0	0	0	0	0	0	("0" is same in either notation)
0	0	0	0	0	0	0	1	(+1 in 2's complement representation)
1	1	1	1	1	1	1	0	(1's complement)
							1	(add one)
1	1	1	1	1	1	1	1	(−1 in 2's complement representation)

Note that while +127 is the largest positive two's complement number that can be formed with 8 digits, the largest negative two's complement number is 10000000 or −128. Hence, with this number system, an eight bit byte can represent integers on the real number line between −128 and +127 and a_7 can be regarded as a sign bit; if a_7 is zero the number is positive, if a_7 is one the number is negative:

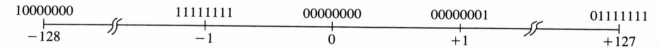

Since much of the literature on arithmetic operations presents the information in terms of signed binary numbers, the difference between 2's complement and signed binary notation is of interest. Signed binary number notation also uses the most significant digit as a sign bit (0 for positive, 1 for negative). The remaining bits represent the magnitude as a binary number.

±	64	32	16	8	4	2	1	
a_7	a_6	a_5	a_4	a_3	a_2	a_1	a_0	
1	1	1	1	1	1	1	1	(−127 in signed binary)
1	0	0	0	0	0	0	1	(−1 in signed binary)
0	0	0	0	0	0	0	0	(0 in signed binary)
0	0	0	0	0	0	0	1	(+1 in signed binary)
0	1	1	1	1	1	1	1	(+127 in signed binary)

An 8-bit byte in this notation represents integers on the real number line between −127 and +127:

```
11111111              10000001         00000000         00000001              01111111
  |——————— ƒƒ ——————————+———————————————+———————————————+————————— ƒƒ ——————————|
 −127                  −1              0               +1                    +127
```

Comparing this to the 2's complement representation, the positive numbers are identical and the negative numbers are reversed, i.e., -127 in 2's complement is -1 in signed binary and vice versa. In normal programming of the MPU, the difference causes no particular problem since numerical data is automatically converted to the correct format during assembly of the program source statements. However, if during system operation, incoming data is in signed binary format, the program should provide for conversion. This is easily done by first complementing each bit of the signed binary number except the sign bit and then adding one:

$\pm$	64	32	16	8	4	2	1	
a_7	a_6	a_5	a_4	a_3	a_2	a_1	a_0	
1	1	1	1	1	1	1	1	(-127 in signed binary)
1	0	0	0	0	0	0	0	(1's complement except for sign bit)
0	0	0	0	0	0	0	1	(add 1)
1	0	0	0	0	0	0	1	(-127 in 2's complement)

The MPU instruction set provides for a simple conversion routine. For example, the following program steps can be used:

10	CONVRT	TSTA	Test sign bit, a_7, and set N if $a_7 = 1$
20		BPL NEXT	Go to NEXT if N $= 0$
30		NEGA	Form 2's complement of A
40		ORAA %10000000	Restore sign bit
50	NEXT	STAA DATA1	Store data in DATA1

This routine assumes that the signed binary data is stored in accumulator A (ACCA). The program tests the sign bit and if the number is negative (N$=1$) performs the required conversion. The contents of ACCA and the N bit of the Condition Code Register would be as follows after each step of a typical conversion:

Instr	N	a_7	a_6	a_5	a_4	a_3	a_2	a_1	a_0	
TSTA	1	1	1	1	1	0	0	0	1	(-113 in signed binary)
BPL NEXT	1	1	1	1	1	0	0	0	1	
NEGA	0	0	0	0	0	1	1	1	1	(2's complement of ACCA)
ORAA #%10000000	1	0	0	0	0	1	1	1	1	(-113 in 2's complement)

Note that the sign bit status, N, is updated as the NEG and ORA instructions are executed. This is typical for many of the instructions; the Condition Code Register is automatically updated as the instruction is executed.

1-3.3 ACCUMULATOR AND MEMORY OPERATIONS

For familiarization purposes, the Accumulator and Memory operations can be further subdivided into four categories: (1) Arithmetic Operations; (2) Logic Operations; (3) Data Testing; and (4) Data Handling.

1-3.3.1 Arithmetic Operations

The Arithmetic Instructions and their effect on the CCR are shown in Figure 1-3.3.1-1. The use of these instructions in performing arithmetic operations is discussed in Section 2-1.

ACCUMULATOR AND MEMORY OPERATIONS	MNEMONIC	BOOLEAN/ARITHMETIC OPERATION (All register labels refer to contents)	COND. CODE REG.					
			5	4	3	2	1	0
			H	I	N	Z	V	C
Add	ADDA	A + M → A	↕	●	↕	↕	↕	↕
	ADDB	B + M → B	↕	●	↕	↕	↕	↕
Add Acmltrs	ABA	A + B → A	↕	●	↕	↕	↕	↕
Add with Carry	ADCA	A + M + C → A	↕	●	↕	↕	↕	↕
	ADCB	B + M + C → B	↕	●	↕	↕	↕	↕
Complement, 2's (Negate)	NEG	00 − M → M	●	●	↕	↕	①	②
	NEGA	00 − A → A	●	●	↕	↕	①	②
	NEGB	00 − B → B	●	●	↕	↕	①	②
Decimal Adjust, A	DAA	Converts Binary Add. of BCD Characters into BCD Format*	●	●	↕	↕	↕	③
Subtract	SUBA	A − M → A	●	●	↕	↕	↕	↕
	SUBB	B − M → B	●	●	↕	↕	↕	↕
Subract Acmltrs.	SBA	A − B → A	●	●	↕	↕	↕	↕
Subtr. with Carry	SBCA	A − M − C → A	●	●	↕	↕	↕	↕
	SBCB	B − M − C → B	●	●	↕	↕	↕	↕

*Used after ABA, ADC, and ADD in BCD arithmetic operation; each 8-bit byte regarded as containing two 4-bit BCD numbers. DAA adds 0110 to lower half-byte if least significant number >1001 or if preceding instruction caused a Half-carry. Adds 0110 to upper half-byte if most significant number >1001 or if preceding instruction caused a Carry. Also adds 0110 to upper half-byte if least significant number >1001 and most significant number = 9.

(Bit set if test is true and cleared otherwise)

① (Bit V) Test: Result = 10000000?

② (Bit C) Test: Result = 00000000?

③ (Bit C) Test: Decimal value of most significant BCD Character greater than nine? (Not cleared if previously set.)

FIGURE 1-3.3.1-1. Arithmetic Instructions

1-3.3.2 Logic Operations

The Logic Instructions and their effect on the CCR are shown in Figure 1-3.3.2-1. Note that the Complement (COM) instruction applies to memory locations as well as both accumulators.

1-3.3.3 Data Test Operations

The Data Test instructions are shown in Figure 1-3.3.3-1. Bit Test (BIT) is useful for updating the CCR as if the AND function was executed but does not change the contents of the accumulator. The Test (TST) instruction also operates directly on memory and updates the CCR as if a comparison (CMP) to zero had been executed.

1-3.3.4 Data Handling Operations

The Data Handling instructions are summarized in Figure 1-3.3.4-1. Note that the Clear (CLR), Decrement (DEC), Increment (INC), and Shift/Rotate instructions all operate directly on memory and update the CCR accordingly.

1-3.4 PROGRAM CONTROL OPERATIONS

Program Control operation can be subdivided into two categories: (1) Index Register/Stack Pointer instructions; (2) Jump and Branch operations.

1-3.4.1 Index Register/Stack Pointer Operations

The instructions for direct operation on the MPU's Index Register and Stack Pointer are summarized in Figure 1-3.4.1-1 Decrement (DEX, DES), increment (INX, INS), load (LDX, LDS), and store (STX, STS) instructions are provided for both. The Compare instruction, CPX, can be used to compare the Index Register to a 16-bit value and update the Condition Code Register accordingly.

The TSX instruction causes the Index Register to be loaded with the address of the last data byte put onto the "stack". The TXS instruction loads the Stack Pointer with a value equal to one less than the current contents of the Index Register. This causes the next byte to be pulled from the "stack" to come from the location indicated by the Index Register. The utility of these two instructions can be clarified by describing the "stack" concept relative to the M6800 system.

The "stack" can be thought of as a sequential list of data stored in the MPU's read/write memory. The Stack Pointer contains a 16-bit memory address that is used to access the list from one end on a last-in-first-out (LIFO) basis in contrast to the random access mode used by the MPU's other addressing modes.

The M6800 instruction set and interrupt structure allow extensive use of the stack concept for efficient handling of data movement, subroutines and interrupts. The instructions can be used to establish one or more "stacks" anywhere in read/write memory. Stack length is limited only by the amount of memory that is made available.

ACCUMULATOR AND MEMORY		BOOLEAN/ARITHMETIC OPERATION (All register labels refer to contents)	COND. CODE REG.					
			5	4	3	2	1	0
OPERATIONS	MNEMONIC		H	I	N	Z	V	C
And	ANDA	$A \bullet M \to A$	●	●	↕	↕	R	●
	ANDB	$B \bullet M \to B$	●	●	↕	↕	R	●
Complement, 1's	COM	$\overline{M} \to M$	●	●	↕	↕	R	S
	COMA	$\overline{A} \to A$	●	●	↕	↕	R	S
	COMB	$\overline{B} \to B$	●	●	↕	↕	R	S
Exclusive OR	EORA	$A \oplus M \to A$	●	●	↕	↕	R	●
	EORB	$B \oplus M \to B$	●	●	↕	↕	R	●
Or, Inclusive	ORA	$A + M \to A$	●	●	↕	↕	R	●
	ORB	$B + M \to B$	●	●	↕	↕	R	●

FIGURE 1-3.3.2-1. Logic Instructions

ACCUMULATOR AND MEMORY		BOOLEAN/ARITHMETIC OPERATION (All register labels refer to contents)	COND. CODE REG.					
			5	4	3	2	1	0
OPERATIONS	MNEMONIC		H	I	N	Z	V	C
Bit Test	BITA	$A \bullet M$	●	●	↕	↕	R	●
	BITB	$B \bullet M$	●	●	↕	↕	R	●
Compare	CMPA	$A - M$	●	●	↕	↕	↕	↕
	CMPB	$B - M$	●	●	↕	↕	↕	↕
Compare Acmltrs	CBA	$A - B$	●	●	↕	↕	↕	↕
Test, Zero or Minus	TST	$M - 00$	●	●	↕	↕	R	R
	TSTA	$A - 00$	●	●	↕	↕	R	R
	TSTB	$B - 00$	●	●	↕	↕	R	R

FIGURE 1-3.3.3-1. Data Test Instructions

ACCUMULATOR AND MEMORY

OPERATIONS	MNEMONIC	BOOLEAN/ARITHMETIC OPERATION (All register labels refer to contents)	COND. CODE REG. 5 H	4 I	3 N	2 Z	1 V	0 C
Clear	CLR	$00 \rightarrow M$	●	●	R	S	R	R
	CLRA	$00 \rightarrow A$	●	●	R	S	R	R
	CLRB	$00 \rightarrow B$	●	●	R	S	R	R
Decrement	DEC	$M - 1 \rightarrow M$	●	●	↕	↕	④	●
	DECA	$A - 1 \rightarrow A$	●	●	↕	↕	④	●
	DECB	$B - 1 \rightarrow B$	●	●	↕	↕	④	●
Increment	INC	$M + 1 \rightarrow M$	●	●	↕	↕	⑤	●
	INCA	$A + 1 \rightarrow A$	●	●	↕	↕	⑤	●
	INCB	$B + 1 \rightarrow B$	●	●	↕	↕	⑤	●
Load Acmltr	LDAA	$M \rightarrow A$	●	●	↕	↕	R	●
	LDAB	$M \rightarrow B$	●	●	↕	↕	R	●
Push Data	PSHA	$A \rightarrow M_{SP}, SP - 1 \rightarrow SP$	●	●	●	●	●	●
	PSHB	$B \rightarrow M_{SP}, SP - 1 \rightarrow SP$	●	●	●	●	●	●
Pull Data	PULA	$SP + 1 \rightarrow SP, M_{SP} \rightarrow A$	●	●	●	●	●	●
	PULB	$SP + 1 \rightarrow SP, M_{SP} \rightarrow B$	●	●	●	●	●	●
Rotate Left	ROL	M 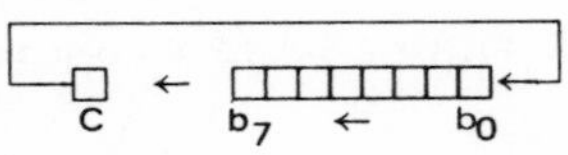	●	●	↕	↕	⑥	↕
	ROLA	A	●	●	↕	↕	⑥	↕
	ROLB	B	●	●	↕	↕	⑥	↕
Rotate Right	ROR	M 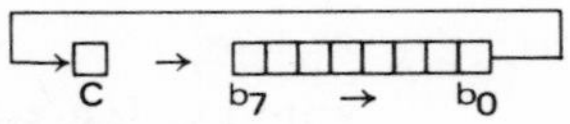	●	●	↕	↕	⑥	↕
	RORA	A	●	●	↕	↕	⑥	↕
	RORB	B	●	●	↕	↕	⑥	↕
Shift Left, Arithmetic	ASL	M 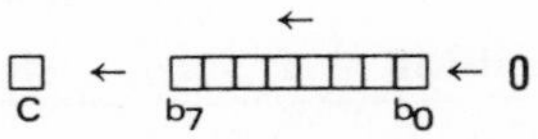	●	●	↕	↕	⑥	↕
	ASLA	A	●	●	↕	↕	⑥	↕
	ASLB	B	●	●	↕	↕	⑥	↕
Shift Right, Arithmetic	ASR	M 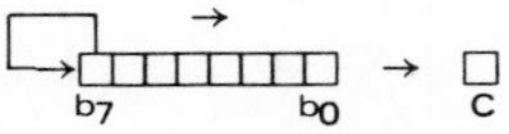	●	●	↕	↕	⑥	↕
	ASRA	A	●	●	↕	↕	⑥	↕
	ASRB	B	●	●	↕	↕	⑥	↕
Shift Right, Logic.	LSR	M 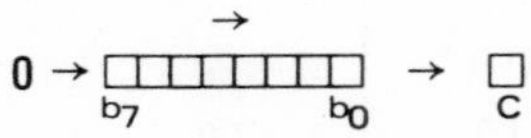	●	●	R	↕	⑥	↕
	LSRA	A	●	●	R	↕	⑥	↕
	LSRB	B	●	●	R	↕	⑥	↕
Store Acmltr.	STAA	$A \rightarrow M$	●	●	↕	↕	R	●
	STAB	$B \rightarrow M$	●	●	↕	↕	R	●
Transfer Acmltrs	TAB	$A \rightarrow B$	●	●	↕	↕	R	●
	TBA	$B \rightarrow A$	●	●	↕	↕	R	●

④ (Bit V) Test: Operand = 10000000 prior to execution?

⑤ (Bit V) Test: Operand = 01111111 prior to execution?

⑥ (Bit V) Test: Set equal to result of $N \oplus C$ after shift has occurred.

FIGURE 1-3.3.4-1. Data Handling Instructions

INDEX REGISTER AND STACK				5	4	3	2	1	0
POINTER OPERATIONS	MNEMONIC	BOOLEAN/ARITHMETIC OPERATION		H	I	N	Z	V	C
Compare Index Reg	CPX	$(X_H/X_L) - (M/M + 1)$		●	●	①	↕	②	●
Decrement Index Reg	DEX	$X - 1 \rightarrow X$		●	●	●	↕	●	●
Decrement Stack Pntr	DES	$SP - 1 \rightarrow SP$		●	●	●	●	●	●
Increment Index Reg	INX	$X + 1 \rightarrow X$		●	●	●	↕	●	●
Increment Stack Pntr	INS	$SP + 1 \rightarrow SP$		●	●	●	●	●	●
Load Index Reg	LDX	$M \rightarrow X_H, (M + 1) \rightarrow X_L$		●	●	③	↕	R	●
Load Stack Pntr	LDS	$M \rightarrow SP_H, (M + 1) \rightarrow SP_L$		●	●	③	↕	R	●
Store Index Reg	STX	$X_H \rightarrow M, X_L \rightarrow (M + 1)$		●	●	③	↕	R	●
Store Stack Pntr	STS	$SP_H \rightarrow M, SP_L \rightarrow (M + 1)$		●	●	③	↕	R	●
Indx Reg → Stack Pntr	TXS	$X - 1 \rightarrow SP$		●	●	●	●	●	●
Stack Pntr → Indx Reg	TSX	$SP + 1 \rightarrow X$		●	●	●	●	●	●

① (Bit N) Test: Sign bit of most significant (MS) byte of result = 1?

② (Bit V) Test: 2's complement overflow from subtraction of LS bytes?

③ (Bit N) Test: Result less than zero? (Bit 15 = 1)

FIGURE 1-3.4.1-1. Index Register and Stack Pointer Instructions

Operation of the Stack Pointer with the Push and Pull instructions is illustrated in Figures 1-3.4.1-2 & 1-3.4.1-3. The Push instruction (PSHA) causes the contents of the indicated accumulator (A in this example) to be stored in memory at the location indicated by the Stack Pointer. The Stack Pointer is automatically decremented by one following the storage operation and is ''pointing'' to the next empty stack location. The

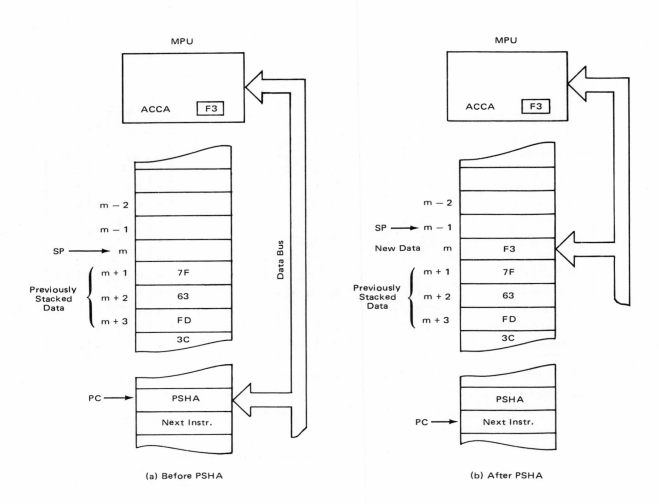

(a) Before PSHA　　　　　　　　　　　　　　　(b) After PSHA

FIGURE 1-3.4.1-2. Stack Operation, Push Instruction

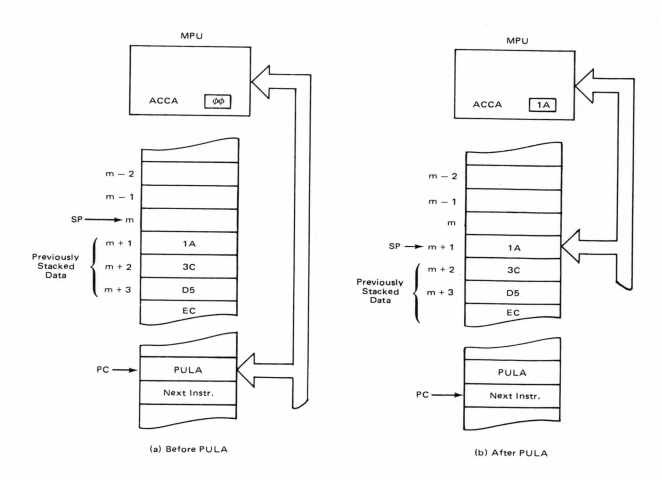

(a) Before PULA

(b) After PULA

FIGURE 1-3.4.1-3. Stack Operation, Pull Instruction

JUMP AND BRANCH OPERATIONS	MNEMONIC	BRANCH TEST	5 H	4 I	3 N	2 Z	1 V	0 C
Branch Always	BRA	None	●	●	●	●	●	●
Branch If Carry Clear	BCC	C = 0	●	●	●	●	●	●
Branch If Carry Set	BCS	C = 1	●	●	●	●	●	●
Branch If = Zero	BEQ	Z = 1	●	●	●	●	●	●
Branch If ≥ Zero	BGE	$N \oplus V = 0$	●	●	●	●	●	●
Branch If > Zero	BGT	$Z + (N \oplus V) = 0$	●	●	●	●	●	●
Branch If Higher	BHI	$C + Z = 0$	●	●	●	●	●	●
Branch If ≤ Zero	BLE	$Z + (N \oplus V) = 1$	●	●	●	●	●	●
Branch If Lower Or Same	BLS	$C + Z = 1$	●	●	●	●	●	●
Branch If < Zero	BLT	$N \oplus V = 1$	●	●	●	●	●	●
Branch If Minus	BMI	N = 1	●	●	●	●	●	●
Branch If Not Equal Zero	BNE	Z = 0	●	●	●	●	●	●
Branch If Overflow Clear	BVC	V = 0	●	●	●	●	●	●
Branch If Overflow Set	BVS	V = 1	●	●	●	●	●	●
Branch If Plus	BPL	N = 0	●	●	●	●	●	●
Branch To Subroutine	BSR	} See Special Operations	●	●	●	●	●	●
Jump	JMP		●	●	●	●	●	●
Jump To Subroutine	JSR		●	●	●	●	●	●
No Operation	NOP	Advances Prog. Cntr. Only	●	●	●	●	●	●
Return From Interrupt	RTI		①					
Return From Subroutine	RTS	} See special Operations	●	●	●	●	●	●
Software Interrupt	SWI		●	S	●	●	●	●
Wait for Interrupt	WAI		●	②	●	●	●	●

① (All) Load Condition Code Register from Stack. (See Special Operations)

② (Bit I) Set when interrupt occurs. If previously set, a Non-Maskable Interrupt is required to exit the wait state.

FIGURE 1-3.4.2-1. Jump and Branch Instructions

Pull instruction (PULA or PULB) causes the last byte stacked to be loaded into the appropriate accumulator. The Stack Pointer is automatically incremented by one just prior to the data transfer so that it will point to the last byte stacked rather than the next empty location. Note that the PULL instruction does not "remove" the data from memory; in the example, 1A is still in location (m + 1) following execution of PULA. A subsequent PUSH instruction would overwrite that location with the new "pushed" data.

Execution of the Branch to Subroutine (BSR) and Jump to Subroutine (JSR) instructions cause a return address to be saved on the stack as shown in Figures 1-3.4.2-3 through 1-3.4.2-5. The stack is decremented after each byte of the return address is pushed onto the stack. For both of these instructions, the return address is the memory location following the bytes of code that correspond to the BSR and JSR instruction. The code required for BSR or JSR may be either two or three bytes, depending on whether the JSR is in the indexed (two bytes) or the extended (three bytes) addressing mode. Before it is stacked, the Program Counter is automatically incremented the correct number of times to be pointing at the location of the next instruction. The Return from Subroutine instruction, RTS, causes the return address to be retrieved and loaded into the Program Counter as shown in Figure 1-3.4.2-6.

There are several operations that cause the status of the MPU to be saved on the stack. The Software Interrupt (SWI) and Wait for Interrupt (WAI) instructions as well as the maskable (IRQ) and non-maskable (NMI) hardware interrupts all cause the MPU's internal registers (except for the Stack Pointer itself) to be stacked as shown in Figure 1-3.4.2-7. MPU status is restored by the Return from Interrupt, RTI, as shown in Figure 1-3.4.2-8.

1-3.4.2 Jump and Branch Operations

The Jump and Branch instructions are summarized in Figure 1-3.4.2-1. These instructions are used to control the transfer of operation from one point to another in the control program.

The No Operation instruction, NOP, while included here, is a jump operation in a very limited sense. Its only effect is to increment the Program Counter by one. It is useful during program development as a "stand-in" for some other instruction that is to be determined during debug. It is also used for equalizing the execution time through alternate paths in a control program.

Execution of the Jump Instruction, JMP, and Branch Always, BRA, effects program flow as shown in Figure 1-3.4.2-2. When the MPU encounters the Jump (Indexed) instruction, it adds the offset to the value in the Index Register and uses the result as the address of the next instruction to be executed. In the extended addressing mode, the address of the next instruction to be executed is fetched from the two locations immediately following the JMP instruction. The Branch Always (BRA) instruction is similar to the JMP (extended) instruction except that the relative addressing mode applies and the branch is limited to the range within −125 or +127 bytes of the branch instruction itself (see Section 1-2.3.4 for a description of the addressing modes). The opcode for the BRA instruction requires one less byte than JMP (extended) but takes one more cycle to execute.

The effect on program flow for the Jump to Subroutine (JSR) and Branch to Subroutine (BSR) is shown in Figures 1-3.4.2-3 through 1-3.4.2-5. Note that the Program Counter is properly incremented to be pointing at the correct return address before it is stacked. Operation of the Branch to Subroutine and Jump to Subroutine (extended) instruction is similar except for the range. The BSR instruction requires less opcode than JSR (2 bytes versus 3 bytes) and also executes one cycle faster than JSR. The Return from Subroutine, RTS, is used at the end of a subroutine to return to the main program as indicated in Figure 1-3.4.2-6.

The effect of executing the Software Interrupt, SWI, and the Wait for Interrupt, WAI, and their

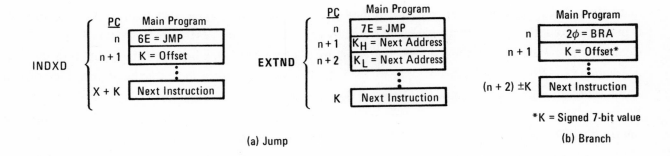

(a) Jump

*K = Signed 7-bit value

(b) Branch

FIGURE 1-3.4.2-2. Program Flow for Jump and Branch Instructions

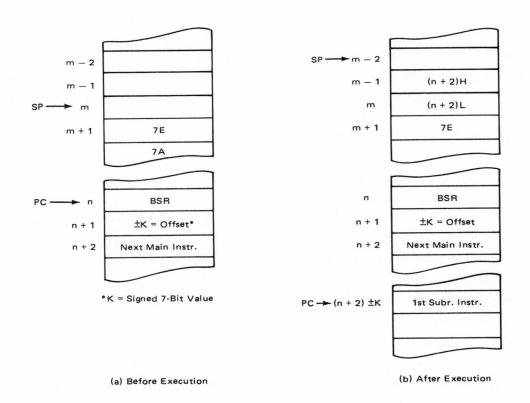

*K = Signed 7-Bit Value

(a) Before Execution

(b) After Execution

FIGURE 1-3.4.2-3. Program Flow for BSR

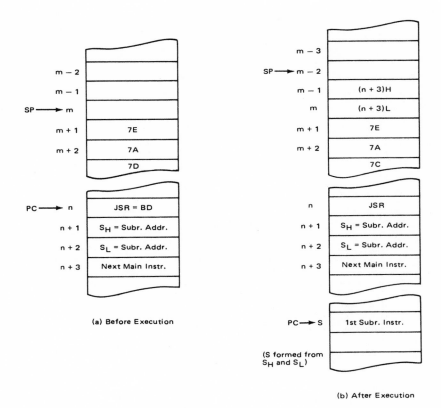

FIGURE 1-3.4.2-4. Program Flow for JSR (Extended)

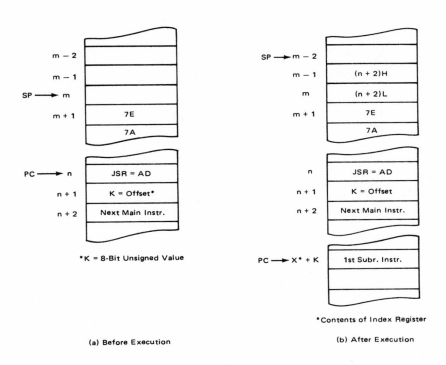

FIGURE 1-3.4.2-5. Program Flow for JSR (Indexed)

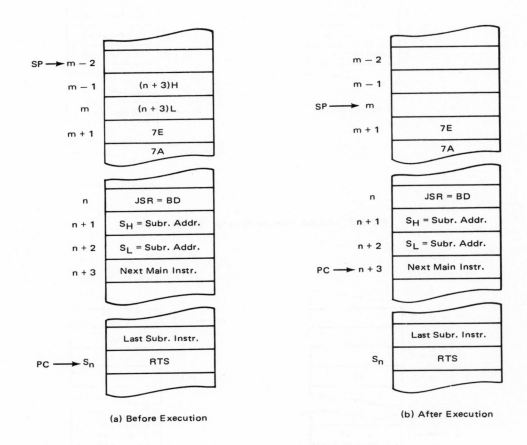

(a) Before Execution

(b) After Execution

FIGURE 1-3.4.2-6. Program Flow for RTS

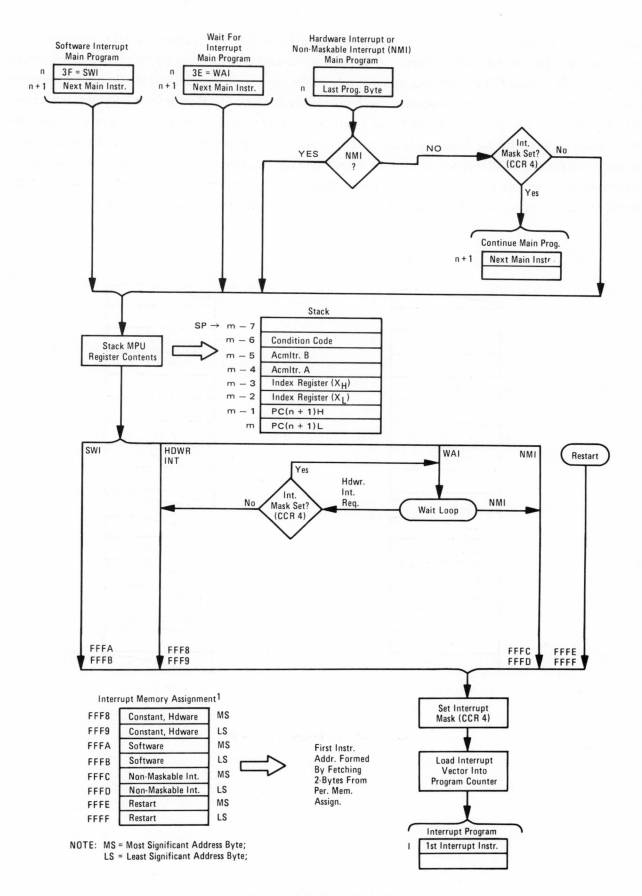

FIGURE 1-3.4.2-7. Program Flow for Interrupts

relationship to the hardware interrupts is shown in Figure 1-3.4.2-7. SWI causes the MPU contents to be stacked and then fetches the starting address of the interrupt routine from the memory locations that respond to the addresses FFFA and FFFB. Note that as in the case of the subroutine instructions, the Program Counter is incremented to point at the correct return address before being stacked. The Return from Interrupt instruction, RTI, (Figure 1-3.4.2-8) is used at the end of an interrupt routine to restore control to the main program. The SWI instruction is useful for inserting break points in the control program, that is, it can be used to stop operation and put the MPU registers in memory where they can be examined. The WAI instruction is used to decrease the time required to service a hardware interrupt; it stacks the MPU contents and then waits for the interrupt to occur, effectively removing the stacking time from a hardware interrupt sequence.

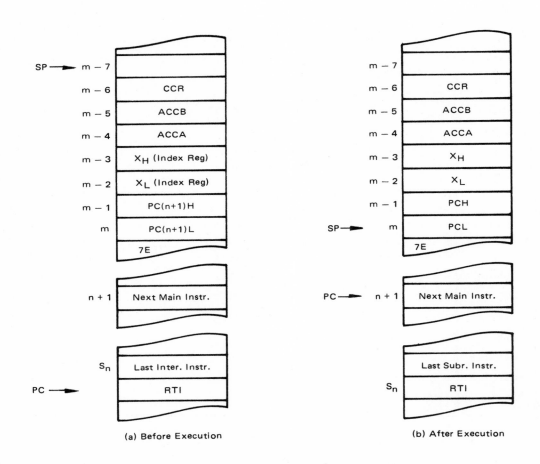

FIGURE 1-3.4.2-8. Program Flow for RTI

BMI :	N = 1 ;		BEQ :	Z = 1 ;
BPL :	N = ϕ ;		BNE :	Z = ϕ ;
BVC :	V = ϕ ;		BCC :	C = ϕ ;
BVS :	V = 1 ;		BCS :	C = 1 ;
BHI :	C + Z = ϕ ;		BLT :	N $\oplus$ V = 1 ;
BLS :	C + Z = 1 ;		BGE :	N $\oplus$ V = ϕ ;
		BLE :	Z + (N $\oplus$ V) = 1 ;	
		BGT :	Z + (N $\oplus$ V) = ϕ ;	

FIGURE 1-3.4.2-9. Conditional Branch Instructions

The conditional branch instructions, Figure 1-3.4.2-9, consist of seven pairs of complementary instructions. They are used to test the results of the preceding operation and either continue with the next instruction in sequence (test fails) or cause a branch to another point in the program (test succeeds).

Four of the pairs are used for simple tests of status bits N, Z, V, and C:

(1) Branch On Minus (BMI) and Branch On Plus (BPL) tests the sign bit, N, to determine if the previous result was negative or positive, respectively.

(2) Branch On Equal (BEQ) and Branch On Not Equal (BNE) are used to test the zero status bit, Z, to determine whether or not the result of the previous operation was equal to zero. These two instructions are useful following a Compare (CMP) instruction to test for equality between an accumulator and the operand. They are also used following the Bit Test (BIT) to determine whether or not the same bit positions are set in an accumulator and the operand.

(3) Branch On Overflow Clear (BVC) and Branch On Overflow Set (BVS) tests the state of the V bit to determine if the previous operation caused an arithmetic overflow.

(4) Branch On Carry Clear (BCC) and Branch On Carry Set (BCS) tests the state of the C bit to determine if the previous operation caused a carry to occur. BCC and BCS are useful for testing relative magnitude when the values being tested are regarded as unsigned binary numbers, that is, the values are in the range 00 (lowest) to FF (highest). BCC following a comparison (CMP) will cause a branch if the (unsigned) value in the accumulator is higher than or the same as the value of the operand. Conversely, BCS will cause a branch if the accumulator value is lower than the operand.

The fifth complementary pair, Branch On Higher (BHI) and Branch On Lower or Same (BLS) are in a sense complements to BCC and BCS. BHI tests for both C and Z = 0; if used following a CMP, it will cause a branch if the value in the accumulator is higher than the operand. Conversely, BLS will cause a branch if the unsigned binary value in the accumulator is lower than or the same as the operand.

The remaining two pairs are useful in testing results of operations in which the values are regarded as signed two's complement numbers. This differs from the unsigned binary case in the following sense: In unsigned, the orientation is higher or lower; in signed two's complement, the comparison is between larger or smaller where the range of values is between −128 and +127 (see Section 1-3.2 for a review of number systems).

Branch On Less Than Zero (BLT) and Branch On Greater Than Or Equal Zero (BGE) test the status bits for N $\oplus$ V = 1 and N $\oplus$ V = 0, respectively. BLT will always cause a branch following an operation in which two negative numbers were added. In addition, it will cause a branch following a CMP in which the value in the accumulator was negative and the operand was positive. BLT will never cause a branch following a CMP in which the accumulator value was positive and the operand negative. BGE, the complement to BLT, will cause a branch following operations in which two positive values were added or in which the result was zero.

The last pair, Branch On Less Than Or Equal Zero (BLE) and Branch On Greater Than Zero (BGT) test the status bits for $Z + (N \oplus V) = 1$ and $Z + (N \oplus V) = 0$, respectively. The action of BLE is identical to that for BLT except that a branch will also occur if the result of the previous result was zero. Conversely, BGT is similar to BGE except that no branch will occur following a zero result.

CHAPTER 2

2. PROGRAMMING TECHNIQUES

The objective of this Chapter is to present examples of programs and techniques that have been found useful in developing control programs for the MC6800 MPU. Much of the material in subsequent Chapters also covers programming methods. I/O techniques are discussed in Chapter 3. Chapter 5 is devoted to peripheral programming; Chapter 6 discusses system integration programming techniques. In this Chapter, the emphasis is on three programming areas: (1) arithmetic processing; (2) counter and delay operations; (3) use of the indexed addressing mode. In addition, Section 2-3 presents techniques for determining if a given program is usable and/or efficient for a particular application.

2-1 ARITHMETIC OPERATION

2-1.1 NUMBER SYSTEMS

The ALU always performs standard binary addition of two eight bit numbers with the numbers represented in 2's complement format. However, the MPU instruction set and hardware flags permit arithmetic operation using any of four different representations for the numbers:

(1) Each byte can be interpreted as a signed 2's complement number in the range -127 to $+127$:

$\pm$	2^6	2^5	2^4	2^3	2^2	2^1	2^0	
b_7	b_6	b_5	b_4	b_3	b_2	b_1	b_0	
1	0	0	0	0	0	0	1	(-127 in 2's complement representation)
1	1	1	1	1	1	1	1	(-1 in 2's complement representation)
0	0	0	0	0	0	0	0	(0 in 2's complement representation)
0	0	0	0	0	0	0	1	($+1$ in 2's complement representation)
0	1	1	1	1	1	1	1	($+127$ in 2's complement representation)

(2) Each byte can be interpreted as an unsigned binary number in the range 0 to 255:

2^7	2^6	2^5	2^4	2^3	2^2	2^1	2^0	
b_7	b_6	b_5	b_4	b_3	b_2	b_1	b_0	
0	0	0	0	0	0	0	0	(0 in unsigned binary)
1	1	1	1	1	1	1	1	(255 in unsigned binary)

(3) Each byte contains one 4-bit BCD number in the 4 LSBITS, the 4 MS bits are zeros. This is referred to as unpacked BCD and can represent numbers in the range of 0-9:

2^7	2^6	2^5	2^4	2^3	2^2	2^1	2^0	
b_7	b_6	b_5	b_4	b_3	b_2	b_1	b_0	
0	0	0	0	0	0	0	0	(BCD 0)
0	0	0	0	0	1	0	1	(BCD 5)
0	0	0	0	1	0	0	1	(BCD 9)

Always must be 0

(4) Each byte can be thought of as containing two 4-bit binary coded decimal (BCD) numbers. With this interpretation, each byte can represent numbers in the range 0 to 99:

2^3	2^2	2^1	2^0	2^3	2^2	2^1	2^0	
b_7	b_6	b_5	b_4	b_3	b_2	b_1	b_0	
0	0	0	0	0	0	0	0	(BCD 00)
0	0	1	0	0	1	1	1	(BCD 27)
1	0	0	1	1	0	0	1	(BCD 99)

Each of these number systems will be illustrated with programming examples after the condition code flags and instruction set have been introduced in more detail.

2-1.2   THE CONDITION CODE REGISTER

During operation, the MPU sets (or clears) flags in a Condition Code Register as indicated in Table 2-1.2-1:

b_5	b_4	b_3	b_2	b_1	b_0	
H	I	N	Z	V	C	Condition Code Register

H = Half-carry; set whenever a carry from b_3 to b_4 of the result is generated; cleared otherwise.

I = Interrupt Mask; set by hardware interrupt or SEI instruction; cleared by CLI instruction. (Normally not used in arithmetic operations).

N = Negative; set if high order bit (b_7) of result is set; cleared otherwise.

Z = Zero; set if result = 0; cleared otherwise.

V = oVerflow; set if there was arithmetic overflow as a result of the operation; cleared otherwise.

C = Carry; set if there was a carry from the most significant bit (b_7) of the result; cleared otherwise.

TABLE 2-1.2-1: Condition Code Register

2-1.3   OVERFLOW

The description of most of the condition code bits is straight forward. However, overflow requires clarification. Arithmetic overflow is an indication that the last operation resulted in a number beyond the ± 127 range of an 8-bit byte. Overflow can be determined by examining the sign bits of the operands and the result as indicated in Table 2-1.2-1 where the results for addition of A + B is shown.

Row	a_7	b_7	r_7	V	
1	0	0	0	0	
2	0	0	1	1	
3	0	1	0	0	
4	0	1	1	0	
5	1	0	0	0	(A + B) = R
6	1	0	1	0	
7	1	1	0	1	
8	1	1	1	0	

TABLE 2-1.3-1: Overflow for Addition

If the sign bits of the operands, a_7 and b_7, are different (rows 3 through 6 of the Table) no overflow can occur and the V flag is clear after the operation. If the operand sign bits are alike and the result exceeds the byte capacity, the sign bit of the result (r_7) will change and the overflow bit will be set. This is illustrated in the following example. The example follows actual ALU operation in that the starting number A is initially in the accumulator but is replaced by the result of the current operation.

V	7	6	5	4	3	2	1	0	
0	0	0	1	1	0	1	1	0	A = +54;
	1	0	0	0	0	1	1	1	B = −121; (negative numbers are in 2's complement notation)
0	1	0	1	1	1	1	0	1	R_0= A+B = −67; (signs of A & B different; no overflow)
0	1	0	1	1	1	1	0	1	R_0= −67;
	1	1	0	1	1	1	1	1	B = −33;
0	1	0	0	1	1	1	0	0	R_1= R_0 + B = −100; (Signs alike but byte capacity not exceeded; no overflow)

V	7	6	5	4	3	2	1	0	
	1	0	0	1	1	1	0	0	R_1= −100;
	1	1	1	0	0	0	0	0	B = −32;
1	0	1	1	1	1	1	0	0	R_2= +124 (Signs of R_1 & B alike and sign of result occurred)

Here the capacity of the register has been exceeded and the result is +124 rather than −132. Overflow is said to have occurred.

In subtraction operations, the possibility of overflow exists whenever the operands differ in sign. Overflow conditions For A − B are illustrated in Table 2-1.3-2.

Row	a_7	$\overline{b_7}$	r_7	V	
1	0	0	0	0	
2	0	0	1	1	
3	0	1	0	0	
4	0	1	1	0	(A − B) = R
5	1	0	0	0	
6	1	0	1	0	
7	1	1	0	1	
8	1	1	1	0	

TABLE 2-1.3-2: Overflow for Subtraction

Note that Table 2-1.3-2 is identical to the addition table except that b_7 has been replaced by $\overline{b_7}$. This is explained by the fact that the ALU performs subtraction by adding the negative of the subtrahend B to the minuend A. Hence, the ALU first forms the 2's complement of B and then adds. The subtraction table with b_7 negated then reflects the sign bits of two numbers that are to be added. If a_7 and $\overline{b_7}$ are alike, overflow will occur if the byte capacity is exceeded.

2-1.4 THE ARITHMETIC INSTRUCTIONS

Table 2-1.4-1 summarizes the instructions used primarily for arithmetic operations. The effect of each operation on memory and the MPU's Accumulators is shown along with how the result of each operation effects the Condition Code Register.

The carry bit is used as a carry for addition and as a borrow for subtraction and is added to the Accumulators with the Add With Carry Instructions and subtracted from the Accumulators in the Subtract With Carry instructions.

The Decimal Adjust instruction, DAA, is used in BCD addition to adjust the binary results of the ALU. Used following the operations, ABA, ADD, and ADC on BCD operands, DAA will adjust the contents of the accumulator and the C bit to represent the correct BCD Sum.

Table 2-1.4-2 shows the details of the DAA instruction and how it affects and is effected by the Condition Code Register bits.

2-1.4.1 Use of Arithmetic Instructions

Typical use of the arithmetic instructions is illustrated in the following examples:

The ABA instruction adds the contents of ACCB to the contents of ACCA:

ACCA	10101010	($AA)
ACCB	11001100	($CC)
ACCA	01110110	($76) with a carry.
CARRY	1	

The ADCA instruction adds the operand data and the carry bit to ACCA:

	b_7	b_6	b_5	b_4	b_3	b_2	b_1	b_0	
ACCA	1	0	1	0	1	0	1	0	$AA
OPERAND DATA	1	1	0	0	1	1	0	0	CC
CARRY								1	
ACCA	0	1	1	1	0	1	1	1	$77 with carry
CARRY								1	

In both of these examples, the 2's complement overflow bit, V, will be set as shown in Table 2-1.4.1-1.

ACCUMULATOR AND MEMORY OPERATIONS	MNEMONIC	IMMED OP	~	#	DIRECT OP	~	#	INDEX OP	~	#	EXTND OP	~	#	INHER OP	~	#	BOOLEAN/ARITHMETIC OPERATION (All register labels refer to contents)	H (5)	I (4)	N (3)	Z (2)	V (1)	C (0)
Add	ADDA	8B	2	2	9B	3	2	AB	5	2	BB	4	3				A + M → A	↕	•	↕	↕	↕	↕
	ADDB	CB	2	2	DB	3	2	EB	5	2	FB	4	3				B + M → B	↕	•	↕	↕	↕	↕
Add Acmltrs	ABA													1B	2	1	A + B → A	↕	•	↕	↕	↕	↕
Add with Carry	ADCA	89	2	2	99	3	2	A9	5	2	B9	4	3				A + M + C → A	↕	•	↕	↕	↕	↕
	ADCB	C9	2	2	D9	3	2	E9	5	2	F9	4	3				B + M + C → B	↕	•	↕	↕	↕	↕
Complement, 1's	COM							63	7	2	73	6	3				M̄ → M	•	•	↕	↕	R	S
	COMA													43	2	1	Ā → A	•	•	↕	↕	R	S
	COMB													53	2	1	B̄ → B	•	•	↕	↕	R	S
Complement, 2's (Negate)	NEG							60	7	2	70	6	3				00 − M → M	•	•	↕	↕	①	②
	NEGA													40	2	1	00 − A → A	•	•	↕	↕	①	②
	NEGB													50	2	1	00 − B → B	•	•	↕	↕	①	②
Decimal Adjust, A	DAA													19	2	1	Converts Binary Add. of BCD Characters into BCD Format	•	•	↕	↕	↕	③
Rotate Left	ROL							69	7	2	79	6	3				M	•	•	↕	↕	⑥	↕
	ROLA													49	2	1	A	•	•	↕	↕	⑥	↕
	ROLB													59	2	1	B	•	•	↕	↕	⑥	↕
Rotate Right	ROR							66	7	2	76	6	3				M	•	•	↕	↕	⑥	↕
	RORA													46	2	1	A	•	•	↕	↕	⑥	↕
	RORB													56	2	1	B	•	•	↕	↕	⑥	↕
Shift Left, Arithmetic	ASL							68	7	2	78	6	3				M	•	•	↕	↕	⑥	↕
	ASLA													48	2	1	A	•	•	↕	↕	⑥	↕
	ASLB													58	2	1	B	•	•	↕	↕	⑥	↕
Shift Right, Arithmetic	ASR							67	7	2	77	6	3				M	•	•	↕	↕	⑥	↕
	ASRA													47	2	1	A	•	•	↕	↕	⑥	↕
	ASRB													57	2	1	B	•	•	↕	↕	⑥	↕
Shift Right, Logic.	LSR							64	7	2	74	6	3				M	•	•	R	↕	⑥	↕
	LSRA													44	2	1	A	•	•	R	↕	⑥	↕
	LSRB													54	2	1	B	•	•	R	↕	⑥	↕
Subtract	SUBA	80	2	2	90	3	2	A0	5	2	B0	4	3				A − M → A	•	•	↕	↕	↕	↕
	SUBB	C0	2	2	D0	3	2	E0	5	2	F0	4	3				B − M → B	•	•	↕	↕	↕	↕
Subract Acmltrs.	SBA													10	2	1	A − B → A	•	•	↕	↕	↕	↕
Subtr. with Carry	SBCA	82	2	2	92	3	2	A2	5	2	B2	4	3				A − M − C → A	•	•	↕	↕	↕	↕
	SBCB	C2	2	2	D2	3	2	E2	5	2	F2	4	3				B − M − C → B	•	•	↕	↕	↕	↕

Rotate Left diagram: $C \leftarrow b_7 \leftarrow b_0$

Rotate Right diagram: $C \rightarrow b_7 \rightarrow b_0$

Shift Left Arithmetic diagram: $C \leftarrow b_7 \leftarrow b_0 \leftarrow 0$

Shift Right Arithmetic diagram: $b_7 \rightarrow b_0 \rightarrow C$

Shift Right Logic diagram: $0 \rightarrow b_7 \rightarrow b_0 \rightarrow C$

LEGEND:

OP	Operation Code (Hexadecimal);
~	Number of MPU Cycles;
#	Number of Program Bytes;
+	Arithmetic Plus;
−	Arithmetic Minus;
•	Boolean AND;
M_{SP}	Contents of memory location pointed to be Stack Pointer;
+	Boolean Inclusive OR;
⊕	Boolean Exclusive OR;
M̄	Complement of M;
→	Transfer Into;
0	Bit = Zero;

00	Byte = Zero;
H	Half-carry from bit 3;
I	Interrupt mask
N	Negative (sign bit)
Z	Zero (byte)
V	Overflow, 2's complement
C	Carry from bit 7
R	Reset Always
S	Set Always
↕	Test and set if true, cleared otherwise
•	Not Affected
CCR	Condition Code Register
LS	Least Significant
MS	Most Significant

CONDITION CODE REGISTER NOTES:

(Bit set if test is true and cleared otherwise)

① (Bit V) Test: Result = 10000000?

② (Bit C) Test: Result = 00000000?

③ (Bit C) Test: Decimal value of most significant BCD Character greater than nine? (Not cleared if previously set.)

⑥ (Bit V) Test: Set equal to result of N ⊕ C after shift has occurred.

TABLE 2-1.4-1. Arithmetic Instructions

Operation: Adds hexadecimal numbers 00, 06, 60, or 66 to ACCA, and may also set the carry bit, as indicated in the following table:

State of C-Bit Before DAA (Col. 1)	Upper Half-Byte (Bits 4—7) (Col. 2)	Initial Half-Carry H-Bit (Col. 3)	Lower Half-Byte (Bits 0—3) (Col. 4)	Number Added to ACCA by DAA (Col. 5)	State of C-Bit After DAA (Col. 6)
0	0—9	0	0—9	00	0
0	0—8	0	A—F	06	0
0	0—9	1	0—3	06	0
0	A—F	0	0—9	60	1
0	9—F	0	A—F	66	1
0	A—F	1	0—3	66	1
1	0—2	0	0—9	60	1
1	0—2	0	A—F	66	1
1	0—3	1	0—3	66	1

NOTE: Columns (1) to (4) of the above table represent all possible cases which can result from any of the operations ABA, ADD, or ADC, with initial carry either set or clear, applied to two binary-coded-decimal operands. The table shows hexadecimal values.

Effect on Condition Code Register:

H Not affected.

I Not affected.

N Set if most significant bit of the result is set; cleared otherwise.

Z Set if all bits of the result are cleared; cleared otherwise.

V Not defined.

C Set or reset according to the same rule as if the DAA and an immediately preceding ABA, ADD, or ADC were replaced by a hypothetical binary-coded-decimal addition.

TABLE 2-1.4-2. Effect of DAA Instruction

2's complement overflow after	carry after	b7 ACC after	b7 ACC before	b7 OPERAND (OR ACCB) before
0	0	0	0	0
1	0	1	0	0
0	0	1	0	1
0	1	0	0	1
0	0	1	1	0
0	1	0	1	0
1	1	0	1	1
0	1	1	1	1

TABLE 2-1.4.1-1 Truth Table for "Add with Carry"

The SUBA instruction subtracts the operand data from ACCA:

	b_7	b_6	b_5	b_4	b_4	b_2	b_1	b_0	
ACCA	0	1	1	0	0	1	0	1	$65
OPERAND DATA	1	0	0	0	0	1	1	1	$87
ACCA	1	1	0	1	1	1	1	0	$DE with a borrow
BORROW								1	

The SBCA instruction subtracts the operand and the borrow (carry) it from ACCA.

	b_7	b_6	b_5	b_4	b_3	b_2	b_1	b_0	
ACCA	1	0	1	1	1	1	0	0	$BC
OPERAND DATA	0	1	1	1	1	0	1	1	$7B
BORROW (carry)								1	C=1
	0	1	0	0	0	0	0	0	$40 no borrow
BORROW								0	

The 2's complement overflow and carry bits are set in accordance with Table 2-1.4.1-2 as a result of a subtraction operation.

2's complement overflow	carry after	b7 ACCA after	b7 ACCA before	b7 OPERAND before
0	0	0	0	0
0	1	1	0	0
0	1	0	0	1
1	1	1	0	1
1	0	0	1	0
0	0	1	1	0
0	0	0	1	1
0	1	1	1	1

TABLE 2-1.4.1-2: Truth Table for "Subtract with Borrow"

2-1.5 ADDITION AND SUBTRACTION ROUTINES

Most MPU based systems will require that the arithmetic instruction set be combined into more complex routines that operate on numbers larger than one byte. If more than one number system is used, routines must be written for each, or conversion routines to some common base must be used. In many cases, however, it is more efficient to write a specialized routine for each system requirement, i.e., hexadecimal (HEX) versus unpacked BCD multiplication, etc. In this section, several algorithms will be discussed with specific examples showing their implementation with the MC6800 instruction set.

The basic arithmetic operations are binary addition and subtraction:

ALPHA + BETA = GAMMA		ALPHA − BETA = GAMMA	
LDAA	ALPHA	LDAA	ALPHA
ADDA	BETA	SUBA	BETA
STAA	GAMMA	STAA	GAMMA

These operations are so short that they are usually programmed in line with the main flow. Addition of single packed BCD bytes requires only one more instruction. The DAA instruction is used immediately after the ADD, ADC, or ABA instructions to adjust the binary generated in accumulator A (ACCA) to the correct BCD value:

```
LDAA        ALPHA
ADDA        BETA
DAA
STAA        GAMMA
```

Carry	ACCA			
X	67	0110 0111	= ACCA	
X	+79	carry 0111 1001	= MEMORY	
O	146	0 1110 0000	= ACCA	binary result
	46	1 0100 0110	= ACCA	after DAA; the carry bit will also be set because of the BCD carry.

Since no similar instruction is available for BCD subtraction, 10's complement arithmetic may be used to generate the difference. The follow routine performs a BCD subtraction of two digit BCD numbers:

```
LDAA    #$99
SUBA    BETA        (99-BETA) = ACCA
SEC                 carry = 1
ADCA    ALPHA       ACCA + ALPHA + C = ACCA
DAA                 DECIMAL ADJUST (−100)
STAA    GAMMA       ALPHA-BETA = GAMMA
```

The routine implements the algorithm defined by the following equations.

ALPHA − BETA = GAMMA

ALPHA + (99-BETA) −99 = GAMMA   9's COMPLEMENT OF BETA

ALPHA + (99-BETA+1) −100 = GAMMA   10's COMPLEMENT OF BETA

One is added to the 9's complement of the subtrahend by setting the carry bit to find the 10's complement of BETA which is then added to the minuend ALPHA and saved in ACCA. The DAA instruction adjusts the result in ACCA to the proper BCD values before storing the difference in GAMMA. Since 100 has been added (99 + 1) to the subtrahend by finding the 10's complement, 100 must also be subtracted. This is accomplished by the DAA instruction since the resulting carry is discarded.

Multiple precision operations mean that the data and results require more than one byte of memory. The simplest multiple precision routines are addition and subtraction of 16 bit binary or 2's complement numbers. This is often called *double* precision since 2 consecutive bytes are required to store 16 binary bits of information. The following routines illustrate these functions:

```
LDAA        ALPHA +1
LDAB        ALPHA
ADDA        BETA +1     ADD LS BYTES
ADCB        BETA        ADD MS BYTES WITH CARRY FROM LS BYTES
STAA        GAMMA +1
STAB        GAMMA
```

```
LDAA        ALPHA +1
LDAB        ALPHA
SUBA        BETA +1     SUBTRACT LS BYTES
SBCB        BETA        SUBTRACT MS BYTES WITH BORROW FROM LS BYTES
STAA        GAMMA +1
STAB        GAMMA
```

Four digit BCD addition can be accomplished in a similar fashion with the use of the DAA instruction. The following routine has been expanded to a 2N digit addition where N is the max number of packed BCD bytes used:

```
START       CLC
            LDX         #N
LOOP        LDAA        ALPHA,X
            ADCA        BETA,X
            DAA
            STAA        GAMMA,X
            DEX
            BNE         LOOP
```

NOTE: ALPHA, BETA, and GAMMA must be in the direct addressing range and adjusted for offset for this example (See indexed addressing for further details).

This routine uses indexed address to select the bytes to be added, starting with the least significant. The carry is cleared at the start and is affected only by the DAA and ADCA instructions. This allows the carry to be included in the next byte addition.

Expanding subtraction to multiple precision is accomplished in a manner similar to the single byte case; 10's complement arithmetic is used. A suitable routine is shown in the Assembly Listing of Figure 2-1.5-1.

This routine first finds the 9's complement of the subtrahend and stores it in the result buffer. The carry is then set to add 1 to 9's complement, making it the 10's complement which is then added to the minuend and stored in the result buffer. Note that this routine has 2 loops, the first to calculate the 9's complement, the second to add and decimal adjust the result. The decimal add and subtract routines operate on 10's complement numbers as well as packed BCD numbers. A number is known to be negative in 10's complement form when the most significant digit in the most significant byte is a 9. When in the 10's complement form, this digit is reserved for the sign and the actual number of magnitude digits is one less than 2 times the number of bytes. A routine similar to the above subtract program will convert the 10's complement number to decimal magnitude with sign for display or output purposes:

```
DCONV       CLR         SINFLG      CLEAR SIGN FLAG
            LDAA        RESULT+1    GET MSBYTE
            BPL         END         POSITIVE:END
            LDX         #8          NEGATIVE:
DCONV1      LDAA        #$99
            SUBA        RSLT,X      SUBTRACT RESULT FROM
            STAA        RSLT,X      ALL 9's INCLUDING
            DEX                     SIGN DIGIT
            BNE         DCONV1
            LDX         #8
            CLRA
            SEC
DCONV2      ADCA        RSLT,X      ADD 1 TO RESULT
            DAA
            STAA        RSLT,X
            DEX
            BNE         DCONV2
            DEC         SINFLG      SET SIGN FLAG
END         RTS                     RETURN
```

The sign flag would be used to indicate plus when clear and minus when not clear.

```
00010                                    NAM     DSUB16
00030                                    OPT     SYMB,MEM=MEMSUB
00060           0000      SUBTRH EQU     0
00070           0008      MINUEN EQU     8
00080           0010      RSLT   EQU     16
00090  0100                        ORG     256
00092                           ◆ DECIMAL SUBTRACT SUBROUTINE FOR 16 DECIMAL DIGIT

00094                           ◆ THIS ROUTINE SUBTRACTS THE SUBTRAHEND ("SUBTRH")
00095                           ◆ FROM THE MINUEND ("MINUEN") AND PLACES THE
00096                           ◆ DIFFERENCE IN "RSLT."

00097                           ◆ THE MEMORY ALLOCATION IS AS FOLLOWS:
00097                           ◆                       ADDRESS RANGE      LSB
00097                           ◆     SUBTRAHEND            1-8            8
00097                           ◆     MINUEND              9-16           16
00097                           ◆     DIFFERENCE           17-24          24
00097                           ◆         ADDRESS VALUES ARE DECIMAL

00100  0100 CE 0008  DSUB    LDX     #8            SET BYTE COUNTER
00110  0103 86 99    DSUB1   LDA A   #$99
 )120  0105 A0 00            SUB A   SUBTRH,X      FIND 9'S COMPLEMENT
00130  0107 A7 10            STA A   RSLT,X        USE "RSLT" AS TEMP STORE
00140  0109 09               DEX                   DECREMENT BYTE COUNTER
00150  010A 26 F7            BNE     DSUB1         LOOP UNTIL LAST BYTE
00160  010C CE 0008          LDX     #8            RESTORE BYTE COUNTER
00170  010F 0D               SEC                   SET CARRY TO ADD 1 TO COMPL
00180  0110 A6 08    DSUB2   LDA A   MINUEN,X      LOAD MINUEND
00190  0112 A9 10            ADC A   RSLT,X        ADD COMPLEMENT SUBTRAHEND
00200  0114 19               DAA                   DECIMAL ADJUST
00210  0115 A7 10            STA A   RSLT,X        STORE DIFFERENCE
00220  0117 09               DEX                   DECREMENT BYTE COUNTER
00230  0118 26 F6            BNE     DSUB2         LOOP UNTIL LAST BYTE
00240  011A 39               RTS                   RETURN TO HOST PROGRAM

00251                           ◆ THE EXECUTION TIME OF THIS SUBROUTINE IS
00252                           ◆ 384 MPU CYCLES EXCLUDING THE RTS.

00254                                    END

SYMBOL TABLE

─SUB   0100 DSUB1   0103 DSUB2   0110 MINUEN 0008 RSLT    0010
─UBTRH 0000
```

FIGURE 2-1.5-1. Decimal Subtract Assembly Listing

2-1.6 MULTIPLICATION

Multiplication increases programming complexity. In addition to the addition and subtraction instructions, the use of the shift and rotate instructions is required. The general algorithm for binary multiplication can be illustrated by a short example:

(1) Test the least significant multiplier bit for 1 or 0.

    (a) If it is 1, add the multiplicand to the result, then 2.

    (b) If it is 0, then 2.

(2) Shift the multiplicand left one bit.

(3) Test the next more significant multiplier bit; then 1a or 1b.

DECIMAL	BINARY		
13	1101		MULTIPLICAND
11	1011		MULTIPLIER LSB=1; ADD MULTIPLICAND TO RESULT (A)
	1101	(A)	
13	1101	(B)	SHIFT MULTIPLICAND LEFT ONE BIT (B)
	100111	(C)	LSB+1 = 1; ADD MULTIPLICAND TO RESULT (C)
13	1101	(D)	SHIFT MULTIPLICAND LEFT ONE BIT (D)
	1101	(E)	LSB+2 = 0; SHIFT MULTIPLICAND LEFT 1 (E)
143	10001111	(F)	LSB+3 = 1; ADD MULTIPLICAND TO RESULT (F)
	128 + 15	= 143	

Signed binary numbers in 2's complement form cannot be multiplied without correcting for the cross product terms which are introduced by the 2's complement representation of negative numbers. There is an algorithm which generates the correct 2's complement product. Since positive binary numbers are correct 2's complement notations, they also may be multiplied using this procedure. It is called Booth's Algorithm. Simply stated the algorithm says:

(1) Test the transition of the multiplier bits from right to left assuming an imaginary 0 bit to the immediate right of the multiplier.

(2) If the bits in question are equal, then 5.

(3) If there is a 0 to 1 transition, the multiplicand is subtracted from the product, then 5.

(4) If there is a 1 to 0 transition, the multiplicand is added to the product, then 5.

(5) Shift the product right one bit with the MSBit remaining the same. (This has the same effect as shifting the multiplicand left in the previous example).

(6) Go to 1 to test the next transition of the multiplier.

The following example (Figure 2-1.6-1) shows the typical steps involved in an actual calculation.

A Flowchart and Assembly Listing for a program using the MC6800 instruction set is shown in Figures 2-1.6-2 and 2-1.6-3, respectively. The results of simulating this program, Figure 2-1.6-4, shows worst case processing time to be approximately 1.662 msec. The worst case condition results when alternate additions and subtraction are required in each of the 16 loops required to have the result in the proper location.

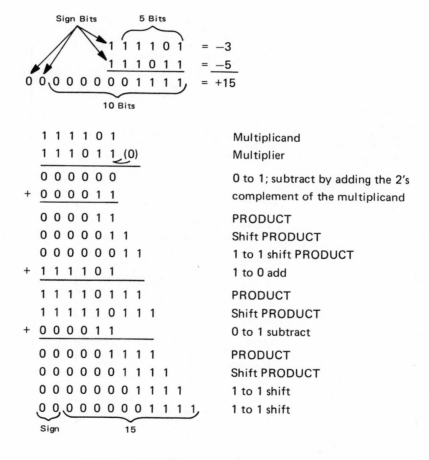

FIGURE 2-1.6-1. Multiplication Using Booth's Algorithm

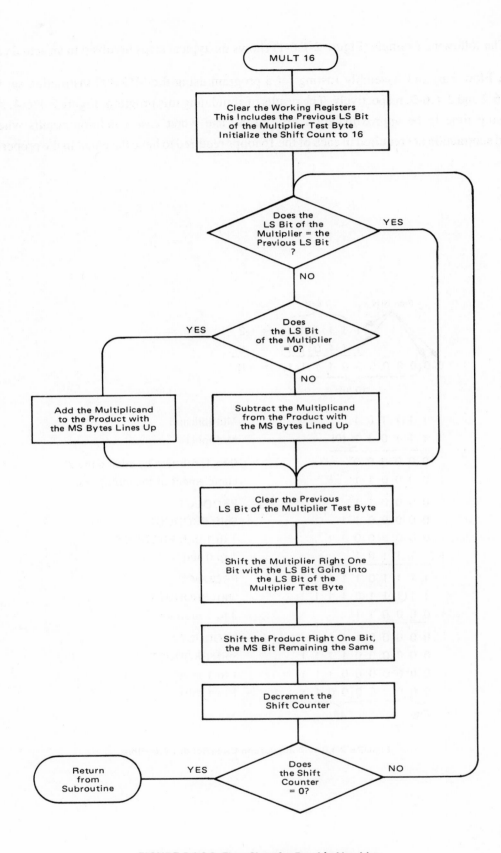

FIGURE 2-1.6-2. Flow Chart for Booth's Algorithm

```
00010                            NAM      MULT16
00020                            OPT      MEM
00030                    ◆
00040                    ◆   THIS ROUTINE MULTIPLIES TWO 16 BIT 2'S
00050                    ◆   COMPLIMENT NUMBERS USING BOOTH'S ALGORITHM
00060                    ◆
00070                    ◆   THE MULTIPLIER = Y = Y(MSB),Y(LSB) = Y,Y+1
00080                    ◆   THE MULTIPLICAND =XX=XX(MSB),XX(LSB) = XX,XX+1
00090                    ◆   THE PRODUCT = U = U(MSB),U+1,U+2,U+3
00100                    ◆   THE TEST BYTE FOR Y(LSB-1) = FF
00110                    ◆
00120 0080                       ORG      $80
00130 0080 0002     Y            RMB      2
00140 0082 0002     XX           RMB      2
00150 0084 0004     U            RMB      4
00160 0088 0001     FF           RMB      1
00170                    ◆
00180                    ◆   THE MULTIPLIER AND THE MULTIPLICAND MUST BE
00190                    ◆   STORED IN Y AND XX RESPECTIVELY, THEN A JSR TO
00200                    ◆   MULT16 WILL GENERATE THE 2'S COMPLIMENT PRODUCT
00210                    ◆   OF Y AND XX IN U.
00220                    ◆
00230                    ◆   THE MULTIPLICAND WILL BE UNCHANGED. THE
00240                    ◆   MULTIPLIER WILL BE DESTROYED.
00250                    ◆
00260 0400                       ORG      $400
```

FIGURE 2-1.6-3: Assembly Listing for Booth's Algorithm (Sheet 1 of 2)

```
00270  0400  CE 0005  MULT16  LDX     #5        CLEAR THE WORKING REGISTERS
00280  0403  4F               CLR   A
00290  0404  A7 83    LP1     STA   A  U-1,X
00300  0406  09               DEX
00310  0407  26 FB            BNE      LP1
00320  0409  CE 0010          LDX     #16        INIT'L SHIFT COUNTER TO 16
00330  040C  96 81    LP2     LDA   A  Y+1        GET Y(LSBIT)
00340  040E  84 01            AND   A  #1
00350  0410  16               TAB              SAVE Y(LSBIT) IN ACCB
00360  0411  98 98            EOR   A  FF        DOES Y(LSBIT) = Y(LSB-1) ?
00370  0413  27 1D            BEQ      SHIFT     YES: GO TO SHIFT ROUTINE
00380  0415  5D               TST   B            NO: DOES Y(LSBIT) = 0 ?
00390  0416  27 0E            BEQ      ADD        YES: GO TO ADD ROUTINE
00400  0418  96 85            LDA   A  U+1        NO:  SUBTRACT MULTIPLICAND
00410  041A  D6 84            LDA   B  U          PRODUCT WITH THE MSBYTES
00420  041C  90 83            SUB   A  XX+1       LINED UP
00430  041E  D2 82            SBC   B  XX
00440  0420  97 85            STA   A  U+1
00450  0422  D7 84            STA   B  U
00460  0424  20 0C            BRA      SHIFT     THEN GO TO SHIFT ROUTINE
00470  0426  96 85    ADD     LDA   A  U+1        ADD THE MULTIPLICAND TO THE
00480  0428  D6 84            LDA   B  U          PRODUCT WITH THE MSBYTES
00490  042A  9B 83            ADD   A  XX+1       LINED UP
00500  042C  D9 82            ADC   B  XX
00510  042E  97 85            STA   A  U+1
00520  0430  D7 84            STA   B  U
00530  0432  7F 0088  SHIFT   CLR      FF        CLEAR THE TEST BYTE
00540  0435  76 0080          ROR      Y         SHIFT THE MULTIPLIER RIGHT
00550  0438  76 0081          ROR      Y+1       ONE BIT WITH THE LSBIT
00560  043B  79 0088          ROL      FF        INTO THE LSBIT OF FF
00570  043E  77 0084          ASR      U         SHIFT THE PRODUCT RIGHT ONE
00580  0441  76 0085          ROR      U+1       BIT, THE MSB REMAINING THE
00590  0444  76 0086          ROR      U+2       SAME
00600  0447  76 0087          ROR      U+3
00610  044A  09               DEX              DECREMENT THE SHIFT COUNT
00620  044B  26 BF            BNE      LP2       IF NOT 0 CONTINUE
00630  044D  39               RTS
00640                         END
```

FIGURE 2-1.6-3: Assembly Listing for Booth's Algorithm (Sheet 2 of 2)

```
STRT: IB 16.
STRT: DB 16.
STRT: SD P,X,A,B,T.
STRT: HR 0A.
STRT: SP P400,T0.
? SM 80,55,55,AA,AB


? SM 80, 55,55,0AA,0AB

SM 80,55,55,0AA,0AA.
? R200

R 200
INST FAULT
HH  P    X    A  B    T
 0001 0000*  1C C7   0001662
```

```
? SM 80,0AA,0AB,55,55

SM 80,0AA,0AB,55,55.
? STRT

STRT: IB 16.
STRT: DB 16.
STRT::SD P,X,A,B,T.
STRT: SR P400,T0.
? R200

R 200.
INST FAULT
HH  P    X    A  B    T
 0001  0000 1C C7   0001635
? DM 80,8

DM 80.
 0080 00 00 55 55 E3 8E 71 C7 .
? STRT
```

```
STRT: IB 16.
STRT: DB 16.
STRT: SD P,X,A,B,T.
STRT: HR 0A.
STRT: SR P400,T0.
? SM 80,7F,0FF,7F,0FF

SM 80,7F,0FF,7F,0FF.
? R200
INST FAULT
HH  P    X    A  B    T
 0001 0000  *FE 7F 0001256
? DM 80,8

DM 80,8.
 0020 00 00 7F FF 3F FF 00 01
? EX
```

FIGURE 2-1.6-4: Simulation of Booth's Algorithm

In the transaction terminal design described in Chapter 6, it is necessary to multiply price by quantity, price by weight, and total price by tax. All these operations, as defined, require a 5 by 3 digit unpacked BCD multiply, where unpacked means one BCD digit per byte. Decimal point poisition is determined by the executive program's use of the subroutine buffers. The main multiply loop XKMPLY (refer to the flow chart of Figure 2-1.6-5 and the Assembly Listing of Figure 2-1.6-6) is similar to the basic multiply algorithm shown in the first example of this Section except that it has been modified to test the shifted multiplier byte for zero. This minimizes the number of shifts required to generate the correct result. This result or partial product is generated in ACCA and then decimal adjusted to determine the number of tens and the number of ones it contains. The number of ones results is in ACCA and the number of tens is in ACCB. ACCA is then added to the result buffer for the present partial product, ACCB is added to the result buffer for the next more significant partial product. The maximum number stored in any result buffer before it is added to the new partial product is 18 (9 max from its previous decimal adjustment plus 9 max from number of tens from the adjustment of the next least significant partial product.) This value, when added to the maximum partial product of 81, is less than 255, the maximum value in one byte so no carry or overflow will occur. This combined with the fact that the multiplication progresses from the least to the most significant byte says that the last partial product to be adjusted will be for the most significant result and that it and all previous result bytes will be in the proper decimal format.

The simulation for XKMULT gave the following results:

$$
\begin{array}{r}
99999 \\
\times\ 999 \\
\hline
99899001
\end{array}
$$
in 4.651 ms

$$
\begin{array}{r}
00009 \\
\times\ 007 \\
\hline
63
\end{array}
$$
in 1.108ms

$$
\begin{array}{r}
00079 \\
\times\ 700 \\
\hline
55300
\end{array}
$$
in 1.426 ms

$$
\begin{array}{r}
00005 \\
\times\ 100 \\
\hline
500
\end{array}
$$
in 974 ms

From this, the worst case multiplication is approximately 4.7 milliseconds, most of which is used up in determining the number of 10's and 1's in each partial product. The program is general in nature, i.e., it can easily be expanded (or shortened) to any number of unpacked BCD digits by increasing or decreasing the maximum value of the various address pointers and their corresponding memory buffers.

2-1.7   **DIVISION**

Another arithmetic routine developed for the transaction terminal demonstrator divides a timing

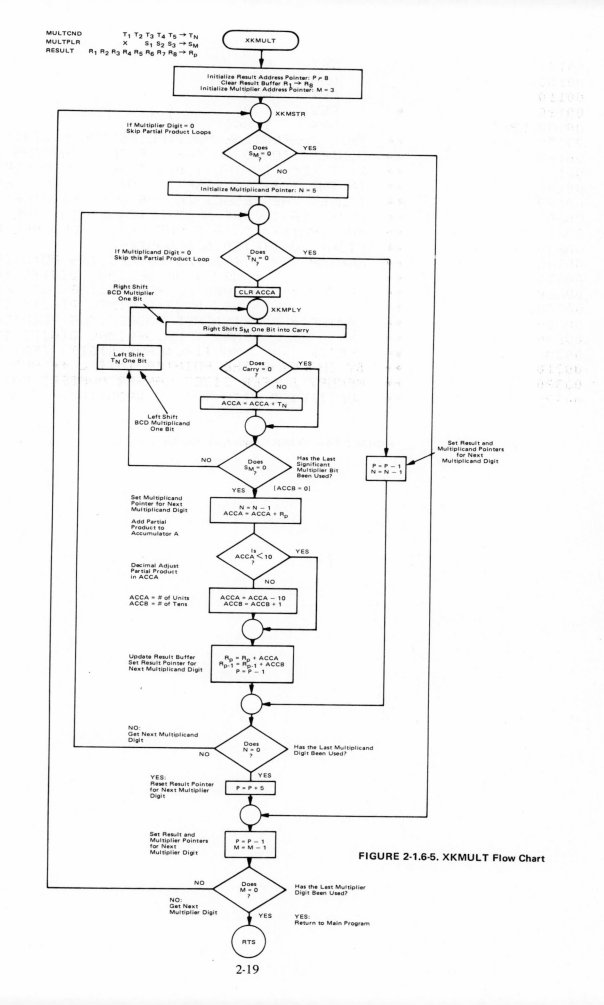

MULTCND T_1 T_2 T_3 T_4 T_5 → T_N
MULTPLR $\times$ S_1 S_2 S_3 → S_M
RESULT R_1 R_2 R_3 R_4 R_5 R_6 R_7 R_8 → R_p

FIGURE 2-1.6-5. XKMULT Flow Chart

2-19

```
00100                          OPT    L
00100                          NAM    XKMULT
00110                          OPT    MEM
00120                  ◆       REV    1.0
00130 5860                     ORG    $5860
00150                  ◆◆ THIS SUBROUTINE MULTIPLIES THE 5 DIGIT DECIMAL
00160                  ◆◆ NUMBER STORED IN THE 5 BYTES STARTING AT
00170                  ◆◆ XKMT (E5) BY THE 3 DIGIT DECIMAL NUMBER STORED
00180                  ◆◆ IN THE 3 BYTES STARTING AT XKMS (E2) AND
00190                  ◆◆ STORES THE RESULT IN THE 8 BYTES STARTING AT
00200                  ◆◆ XKMR (EA).  THE MULTIPLICAND [T], THE
00210                  ◆◆ MULTIPLIER [S] AND THE RESULT [R] ARE UNPACKED
00220                  ◆◆ RIGHT JUSTIFIED BCD NUMBERS
00240                  ◆◆ XKMTMM = M = INDEXED ADDRESSING POINTER FOR S
00250                  ◆◆            = MAX # OF DECIMAL DIGITS IN S
00260                  ◆◆ XKMTMN = N = INDEXED ADDRESSING POINTER FOR T
00270                  ◆◆            = MAX # OF DECIMAL DIGITS IN T
00280                  ◆◆ XKMTMP = P = INDEXED ADDRESSING POINTER FOR R
00290                  ◆◆            = MAX # OF DECIMAL DIGITS IN R
00300                  ◆◆ XKMSCR   =    MULTIPLICAND DIGIT SCRATCH PAD
00310                  ◆◆ BY CHANGING THE POINTER INIT'L ◆◆ AND THE
00320                  ◆◆ MEMORY BUFFER SIZES LARGER NUMBERS MAY BE
00330                  ◆◆ MULTIPLIED WITH THIS SUBROUTINE.
```

FIGURE 2-1.6-6: XKMULT Assembly Listing (Sheet 1 of 2)

```
00350  5860  CE 0008  XKMULT  LDX      #8        ** INIT'L P=8=N+M **
00360  5863  DF F6            STX      XKMTMP    INIT'L P POINTER
00370  5865  4F              CLR A
00380  5866  A7 E9    XKMLP1  STA A    XKMR-1,X   CLEAR RESULT BUFFER
00390  5868  09              DEX
00400  5869  26 FB           BNE      XKMLP1
00410  586B  CE 0003         LDX      #3        ** INIT'L M=3 **
00420  586E  E6 E1    XKMSTR  LDA B    XKMS-1,X   B=S
00430  5870  DF F2           STX      XKMTMM    SAVE M POINTER
00440  5872  27 3E           BEQ      XKMDCP    IF B=0 THEN GO TO NEXT "S"
00450  5874  CE 0005         LDX      #5        ** INIT'L N=5 **
00460  5877  A6 E4    XKMXTT  LDA A    XKMT-1,X
00470  5879  97 F8           STA A    XKMSCR    SAVE T IN XKMSCR
00480  587B  27 3E           BEQ      XKMTZO    GO TO NEXT "T"
00490  587D  37              PSH B             SAVE "S" ON STACK
00500  587E  4F              CLR A
00510  587F  54       XKMPLY  LSR B             RIGHT SHIFT ACCB INTO CARRY
00520  5880  24 02           BCC      XKMSHF    IF C=0 GO TO SHIFT T
00530  5882  9B F8           ADD A    XKMSCR    NO, A=A+T
00540  5884  5D       XKMSHF  TST B             SHIFT T:  DOES ACCB=0
00550  5885  27 05           BEQ      XKMC4     YES, FINISHED WITH THIS T.
00560  5887  78 00F8         ASL      XKMSCR    NO, LEFT SHIFT T ONE BIT
00570  588A  20 F3           BRA      XKMPLY
00580  588C  09       XKMC4   DEX               N=N-1
00590  588D  DF F4           STX      XKMTMN
00600  588F  DE F6           LDX      XKMTMP
00610  5891  AB E9           ADD A    XKMR-1,X   ADD R TO ACCA
00620  5893  81 0A    XKMLP3  CMP A    #10       DECIMAL ADJUST A
00630  5895  2D 05           BLT      XKMC2     A = #OF 1'S
00640  5897  80 0A    XKMC1   SUB A    #10
00650  5899  5C              INC B             B = #OF 10'S
00660  589A  20 F7           BRA      XKMLP3
00670  589C  EB E8    XKMC2   ADD B    XKMR-2,X   ADD R-1 TO ACCB
00680  589E  A7 E9           STA A    XKMR-1,X   R = R + A
00690  58A0  E7 E8           STA B    XKMR-2,X   R-1 = R-1 + B
00700  58A2  33              PUL B             RESTORE "S" FROM STACK
00710  58A3  09              DEX               P=P-1
00720  58A4  DF F6           STX      XKMTMP
00730  58A6  DE F4           LDX      XKMTMN
00740  58A8  26 CD    XKMC3   BNE      XKMXTT
00750  58AA  36              PSH A
00760  58AB  96 F7           LDA A    XKMTMP+1
00770  58AD  8B 05           ADD A    #5        ** INIT'L S=N **
00780  58AF  97 F7           STA A    XKMTMP+1   P=P+N(INIT'L)
00790  58B1  32              PUL A
00800  58B2  7A 00F7  XKMDCP  DEC      XKMTMP+1   P=P-1
00810  58B5  DE F2    XKMXTS  LDX      XKMTMM
00820  58B7  09              DEX               M=M-1
00830  58B8  26 B4           BNE      XKMSTR    IF M NOT 0 GO TO NEXT "S"
00840  58BA  39              RTS
00850  58BB  7A 00F7  XKMTZO  DEC      XKMTMP+1   P = P - 1
00860  58BE  09              DEX               N = N - 1
00870  58BF  20 E7           BRA      XKMC3
00880                        END
```

FIGURE 2-1.6-6: XKMULT Assembly Listing (Sheet 2 of 2)

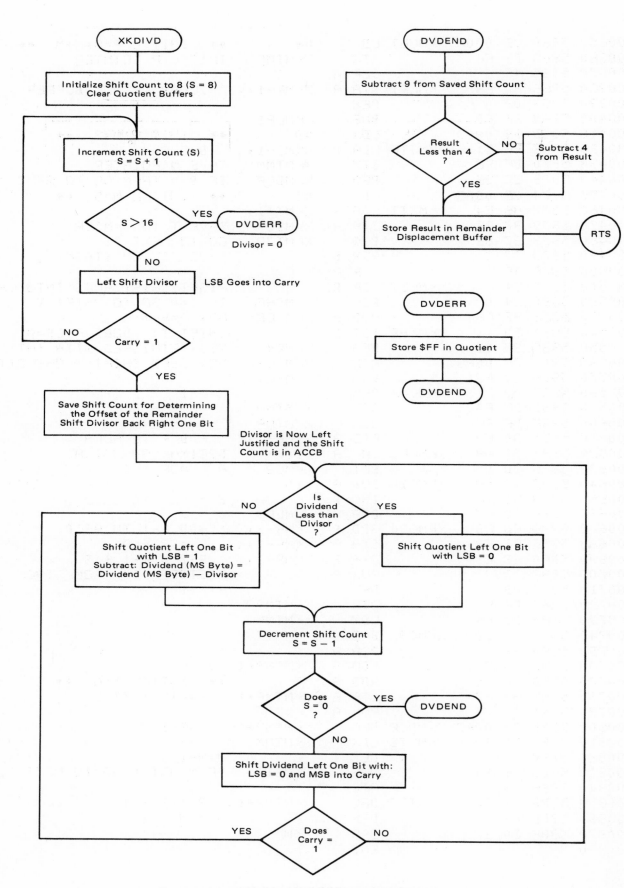

FIGURE 2-1.7-1. XKDIVD Flow Chart

count accumulated in the index register (up to 4 HEX digits) by the constant 7. This routine is used to determine an average module width during a portion of the UPC label scan routine. (See the description of the UPC label scanner in Chapter 5 for further details.) The routine permits division by a 2-digit Hex number as shown in Figures 2-1.7-1 and 2-1.7-2; it calculates the displacement of the remainder left in the dividend and sets the quotient to FFFF if division by zero is attempted.

The algorithm used for this straight forward binary division is as follows:

(1) Left justify the divisor byte.

(2) If the MS byte of the dividend is less than the divisor byte, shift quotient left one bit with the LS bit = 0; then 4.

(3) If the MS byte of the dividend is greater than or equal to the divisor, (2) shift the quotient left one bit with the LS Bit = 1; (b) subtract the divisor from the MS byte of the dividend, the result being stored in the MS byte of the dividend; then 4.

(4) Shift the dividend left one bit with the LS Bit = 0, and the MS Bit going into the carry.

(5) If the carry is set, go to 3a.

(6) If the carry is not set, go to 2a.

The process continues until the number of quotient shifts equals 8 + the number of shifts required to left justify the divisor. A simulation (Figure 2-1.7-3) shows a typical divide takes approximately 1 millisecond.

This section is, by no means, comprehensive. It is intended to provide some examples that can be used as is or that will suggest the direction for modifying them for other specialized applications.

```
00100                              OPT     L
00000                              NAM     XKDIVD
00010                              OPT     MEM
00020  5900                        ORG     $5900
00030                     *   SUBROUTINE TO DIVIDE AN UNSIGNED 4 DIGIT
00040                     *   HEX NUMBER [16 BIT BINARY] BY AN UNSIGNED
00050                     *   2 DIGIT HEX NUMBER [8 BIT BINARY].
00060                     *
00070                     *   THE DIVISOR = X = XKDVSR = [F9]
00080                     *   THE DIVIDEND = Y(M),Y(L)
00090                     *                = XKDVND,XKDVND+1
00100                     *                = [FA,FB]
00110                     *   THE QUOTIENT = Q(M),Q(L)
00120                     *                = XKQUOT,XKQUOT+1
00130                     *                = [FC,FD]
00140                     *   THE SHIFT COUNTER = S = ACCB
00150                     *   THE LEFT DISPLACEMENT OF THE REMAINDER = XKDSPL
00160                     *                                         = [FE]
00170                     *
00180                     *   THE DIVISOR AND THE DIVIDEND MUST BE LOADED
00190                     *   INTO XKDVSR AND XKDVND,XKDVND+1 RESPECTIVELY
00200                     *   THEN A JSR TO XKDIVD.
00210                     *
00220                     *   THE REMAINDER WILL BE IN Y(M) [XKDVND],
00230                     *   SHIFTED LEFT THE # OF BITS INDICATED IN XKDSPL
00240                     *   THE DIVISOR WILL BE BINARILY LEFT JUSTIFIED
00250                     *
```

FIGURE 2-1.7-2: XKDIVD Assembly Listing (Sheet 1 of 2)

```
00260  5900  C6 08    XKDIVD  LDA B   #8          INIT'L S=8
00270  5902  7F 00FC           CLR     XKQUOT      ZERO QUOTIENT BUFFER
00280  5905  7F 00FD           CLR     XKQUOT+1
00290  5908  5C       DVDLP0  INC B               S=S+1
00300  5909  C1 10            CMP B   #16
00310  590B  2E 24            BGT     DVDERR      IF S>16 DIVIDE ERROR
00320  590D  78 00F9           ASL     XKDVSR      IF S<16 LEFT SHIFT DIVISOR
00330  5910  24 F6            BCC     DVDLP0      IF C=0 CON'T LOOP
00340  5912  D7 FE            STA B   XKDSPL      IF C=1 XKDSPL = SHIFT COUNT
00350  5914  76 00F9           ROR     XKDVSR      SHIFT THE DIVISOR BACK 1
00360              ◆                               SHIFT COUNT NOW IN ACCB
00370              ◆                               DIVISOR LEFT JUST. IN X
00380  5917  96 FA            LDA A   XKDVND
00390  5919  91 F9    DVDLP1  CMP A   XKDVSR      IF THE DIVIDEND < DIVISOR
00400  591B  25 0D            BCS     DVNSUB      DON'T SUBTRACT
00410  591D  0D       DVDLP2  SEC                 IF THE DIVIDEND >OR= DIVISO
00420  591E  79 00FD           ROL     XKQUOT+1     SHIFT Q LEFT 1 BIT
00430  5921  79 00FC           ROL     XKQUOT      WITH LSB = 1
00440  5924  90 F9            SUB A   XKDVSR      Y(M) = Y(M)-X
00450  5926  97 FA            STA A   XKDVND
00460  5928  20 07            BRA     DVSHFT
00470  592A  0C       DVNSUB  CLC                 SHIFT Q LEFT WITH
00480  592B  79 00FD           ROL     XKQUOT+1     LSB =0
00490  592E  79 00FC           ROL     XKQUOT
00500  5931  5A       DVSHFT  DEC B               S = S-1
00510  5932  27 12            BEQ     DVDEND      IF S = 0   STOP
00520  5934  0C               CLC                 IF S > 0   SHIFT DIVIDEND
00530  5935  79 00FB           ROL     XKDVND+1     LEFT ONE BIT; LSB=0
00540  5938  79 00FA           ROL     XKDVND      MSB INTO CARRY
00550  593B  96 FA            LDA A   XKDVND
00560  593D  25 DE            BCS     DVDLP2      IF C = 1 GO TO LOOP2
00570  593F  20 D8            BRA     DVDLP1      GO TO LOOP 1
00580  5941  CE FFFF  DVDERR  LDX     #$FFFF
00590  5944  DF FC            STX     XKQUOT
00600  5946  D6 FE    DVDEND  LDA B   XKDSPL      GET SHIFT COUNT INTO ACCB
00610  5948  C0 09            SUB B   #9          XKDSPL = XKDSPL-9
00620  594A  C1 04            CMP B   #4          XKDSPL < 4
00630  594C  25 02            BCS     DVDLP3      YES: GO TO RETURN
00640  594E  C0 04            SUB B   #4          NO: XKDSPL=XKDSPL-4
00650  5950  D7 FE    DVDLP3  STA B   XKDSPL      DISPLACEMENT OF REMAINDER
00660              ◆                               STORED IN XKDSPL
00670  5952  39               RTS
00680                          END
```

FIGURE 2-1.7-2: XKDIVD Assembly Listing (Sheet 2 of 2)

```
STRT; SS.
STRT; IB.
STRT; DB 16.
STRT; SR P5860,S7FF,T0.
STRT; SD PABXCT.
STRT; HR 5.
? SR P5900
```

$$\frac{FFFF}{03} = 5555$$

```
SM 0F9,03,0FF,0FF.
```

```
R 100
```

```
MEM FAULT
 ◆1DC1   0000◆00◆02   000000 0001020 ≅ 1 ms
? DM 0FC,2
```

```
DM 0FC,2
 00FC 55 55 00
?
```

FIGURE 2-1.7-3: Simulation Results, Division

When microprocessor systems are initially considered as replacements for conventional logic designs there is a natural tendency to formulate such questions as: What is the program that replaces a flip-flop? A counter? A shift register? A one-shot? Etc.? Such questions are better posed as: What is the function that must be performed? The answer to the question then often falls in one of two categories: (1) The number of times something occurs must be determined (counted); (2) A particular time interval must be measured or generated prior to taking some action.

These functions are also commonly used for controlling internal program flow; the MC6800 provides a variety of ways for performing them. Short (up to 8-bits or decimal 255) counter requirement can be implemented using either of the two accumulators or any RAM location. The increment (INC) and decrement (DEC) instructions apply to random access memory locations outside the MPU as well as the accumulators. (The instruction set for the MC6800 is discussed in Section 1-3) The data test instructions BITA, BITB, CMPA, CMPS, CBA, TST (memory), TSTA, and TSTB that are available for updating the Condition Code Register combined with the branch instructions permit complete control of counter operations.

For applications requiring long counters (up to 16-bits or decimal 65,535) the Index Register and its full complement of instructions are available. When more than one long counter is required simultaneously, a short program can be written that permits two adjacent RAM locations to be used as a 16-bit counter:

```
                .
                .
                .
        INC     N+1         Increment mem. loc. (N+1)
        BNE     CNTNUE      if result not = 0 continue
        INC     N
CNTNUE  xxx     xxxxxx      Next program instruction
                .
                .
                .
```

This sequence effectively increments a 16-bit word located in memory locations N and N+1. A similar procedure is available for decrementing a 16-bit word:

```
                .
                .
                .
        TST     N+1         Mem. loc. N+1 = 0?
        BNE     NEXT        No, go decr. N+1
        DEC     N           Yes, first decr. N
NEXT    DEC     N+1         Decr. N=1
                .
                .
                .
```

In addition to their use for long counters, these instruction sequences can be used for modifying return addresses. During execution of subroutines and interrupt service routines the program counter containing the return address is stored on the stack, a designated area in RAM. The increment or decrement sequences can be used to change the program counter value on the stack and thus cause the return from subroutine or interrupt to be to a different location in the main program.

It is possible in some cases to use the index Register and Accumulators for two functions simultaneously when one is a counting function. As an example, assume that data from a peripheral device is to be entered into the MPU's memory via an MC6820 PIA[1]. The peripheral is to indicate the presence of data by setting a flag, bit 7 of the PIA's Control Register. Each time the flag is set the MPU is to retrieve the data from the PIA Data Register and store it in an internal memory location until a total of 8 bytes have been accumulated. Since the PIA's Data Register and Control Register look like memory to the MPU, a program is required that will cause the MPU to monitor one memory location for a change in a flag bit and then fetch the data from another location. This operation is to be repeated the specified number (8) of times.

The following sequence of instructions uses a single register, Accumulator B, for both the monitoring and counting functions:

```
              .
              .
              .
          LDAB    #08       Put 2's Compl. of byte count in ACCB.
LOOP1     BITB    PIACRA    Byte Available flag set?
          BPL     LOOP1     Not yet; loop back, chk. again.
          LDAA    PIADRA    Yes; Fetch byte.
          PSHA              Put byte on stack.
          INCB              Eight bytes yet?
          BNE     LOOP1     No, go wait for next byte.
          xxx     xxxxxx    Yes, continue with program.
              .
              .
              .
```

This program takes advantage of the fact that incrementing an accumulator containing FF cause it to "roll over" to 00. The two's complement of the required count is entered as the byte count. Since this will cause the sign bit (bit 7) of ACCB to be positive and since the BIT test does not affect ACCB but does update the Condition Code Register, the Bit test followed by the Branch on Plus instruction can be used to monitor the flag bit. As soon as bit 7 of the Control Register is set to one, the BPL test fails and the MPU fetches the current data byte by reading the Data Register (PIADRA) and then pushes the byte onto a stack location in RAM. The design of the PIA is such that the flag is automatically cleared by the LDAA PIADRA operation. The byte count is then "reduced" by incrementing ACCB and tested by the Branch on Not Equal Zero instruction. Unless the eighth byte has just been transferred the program loops back to wait on the next data byte. If the current byte was the eighth, the INC B instruction cause the count to roll over to zero, the branch test fails, and program flow falls through to the next instruction. The other test instructions (TST, CMP, and CBA) can also be used in a similar

---

[1]Operation of the PIA is described in detail in Section 3-4.

fashion since they too update the condition Code bits but do not affect register contents. Note also that it was not necessary to bring the contents of the Control Register into the MPU in order to examine the flag.

Delays can be generated in a variety of ways. A typical procedure is shown in the following sequence:

```
          .
          .
          .
          LDAA   #32        Takes 4 cycles to execute.
LOOP1     DECA              (2 cycles)
          BNE    LOOP1      (4 cycles)
          .
          .
          .
```

In this example, the MPU will go through LOOP1 32 times so that the total delay introduced by these instructions is, for a 1.0 μsec cycle time:

$$4 + 32\ (2+4) = 196\ \mu sec$$

The number of times through the loop is calculated as the program is developed. If, for instance, the required delay is 200 μsec, the value to be loaded into ACCA is determined from:

$$(200 - 4)/6 = 32.6 \approx 32$$

Note that since the nearest smaller integer is selected, the actual delay generated in only 196 μsec. If greater accuracy is required, the sequence above could be followed by two NOP instructions, since each NOP advances the program counter and takes up two cycles. Delays beyond the capacity of an 8-bit Register and a single loop can be generated by using the Index Register and/or multiple loops. It is also sometimes desirable to write the delay sequence as a callable subroutine that can be used to generate variable delays. This is illustrated by the following routine. This sequence assumes that the amount of delay, in milliseconds, is loaded into a RAM location identified as "DLYBFR" prior to calling the routine.

```
          .
          .
          .
DELGEN    LDAA   DLYBFR    (a) 4 cycles
LOOP1     LDAB   #165      (b) 4 cycles
LOOP2     DECB             (c) 2 cycles
          BNE    LOOP2     (d) 4 cycles
          DECA             (e) 42cycles
          BNE    LOOP1     (f) 4 cycles
          RTS              (g) 5 cycles
          .
          .
          .
```

The MPU will go through LOOP2 165 times each time it is entered: 165 (c+d) = (165)(6) + 990 cycles. For every time through LOOP1 there will be a total LOOP2 time plus the b, e, and f cycle times, or the total time, including the RTS cycle time, is:

$$\text{Total delay} = \text{DLYBFR} (990+4+2+4) + 5$$
$$= \text{DLYBER}(1000) + 5$$

If, for example, DLYBFR had been loaded with 17, indicating that a 17 msec delay was required, then for a 1.0 μsec cycle time. The total delay is 17,005 μsec = 17 msec with small error. The value 165 that is loaded into ACCB was of course selected to provide the desired scale factor, i.e., so that the delay could be entered as an integral number of milliseconds. Variation on these procedures can be used to generate virtually any amount of delay. Note that if for some reason it is undesirable to disturb the contents of the Accumulators or Index Register while generating a delay, RAM memory registers may be used. The INC and DEC instructions also operate directly on memory.

Data handling often involves the transfer of data between a microprocessor's memory and a time dependent peripheral. It is necessary to synchronize the data transfer program to the peripheral because the peripheral data clock is asynchronous with respect to the program clock. The I/O controller which handles the data transfer consists of both hardware and software. An implicit assumption is that the best trade-off occurs by minimizing the hardware in the controller.

In a microprocessor based I/O controller, it is necessary to determine:

(1) How fast can the microcomputer transfer program move data (as contrasted with a direct memory access scheme)?

(2) Will a given data transfer program work successfully in the system?

(3) Is there any processing time remaining after handling the data movement?

(4) Can any additional time dependent functions be performed?

(5) What is the maximum length routine that can be performed in addition to the data transfer?

An analysis is required that will provide a technique for testing the operation of a proposed program. In addition, if there is unused processing time in the system, it may be possible to eliminate additional hardware (e.g., buffer registers). If a given program does not work in the system, the analysis should enable the user to modify the program or add additional hardware to allow the system to work.

Specific examples of the word transfer problem for a floppy disk and the bit transfer problem for a cassette system will be used to illustrate the typical problems. The cassette data transfer example also illustrates the technique for increasing the amount of usable spare time by borrowing it from adjacent data cells. In this case, the spare time is used to refresh a display.

When a peripheral signals the MPU requesting processing time, it will be referred to as a Service Request, (SR). When the service request is periodic, as in the above mentioned examples, it is called a time dependent service request. Read or Write Data Transfers are both examples of such service requests and where the examples show programs or terms referring to a Read Data Transfer, they are meant to be illustrative of both Read and Write Data Transfers.

2-3.1   NOTATION USED SERVICE REQUESTS AND PROGRAMS AS WAVEFORMS ON A TIMING DIAGRAM

The process of synchronizing a data transfer program to a peripheral can be visualized more easily when the SR's and the program are both represented as waveforms on a timing diagram. The peripheral SR waveform is developed from the specifications of the peripheral which identify the maximum time, T_{1m} it takes to load the data buffer (the period during which data is invalid), and the minimum period, T_{0m} between service requests. The subscript m refers to the parameters of the mth peripheral.

The data transfer waveform is developed by writing the actual data transfer program and then calculating the time it takes to:

(1) Capture the data (T_{4m})

(2) Process the data (T_{2m} — includes period T_{4m})

(3) Loop in a synchronization delay loop until a SR is active. (nT_3 — where T_3 is the single loop time and n is the number of times the program loops).

These values are calculated by counting the number of processor clock cycles required to execute each function, and multiplying the numbers by the MPU clock rate. The waveforms and notation for a typical situation are illustrated in Figure 2-3.1-1. Figure 2-3.1-2 shows a flow chart for a data transfer program for a single peripheral. Figure 2-3.1-3 details the technique for calculating the program parameters and Figure 2-3.1-4 illustrates the relation between the peripheral word ready service request and the program timing. The values of the SR parameters are for a floppy disk data transfer.

The period T_{01} is the worst case (fastest) peripheral data word rate, and it is calculated taking into consideration floppy disk motor speed variations. The SR update time T_{11}, is the time during which a new word is being loaded into the data buffer, and at the end of which there exists an active SR.

The timing diagram of Figure 2-3.1-4 shows a processor clock running at a 1 μsec cycle time and shows how the word capture time is developed from a knowledge of the point in the instruction cycle when the word capture begins and ends. In this case, the program begins the word transfer at the positive edge of the fourth processor clock cycle during the LDAA RDCTL instruction and completes it at the negative edge of the fourth clock cycle during the LDAA RDDATA instruction which moves the data. Therefore, T_{41} is equal to the number of clock periods between initiation and the end of transfer, 8.5 cycles = 8.5μs. The first two instructions form the sync loop (T_3) and the total program represents the program processing time (T_{21}).

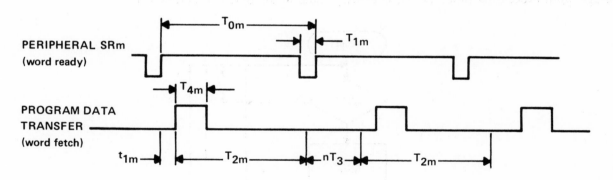

T_{0m} = Period of service request of mth peripheral (word ready period).

T_{1m} = Service request update time (Data Invalid) for m^{th} peripheral.

T_{2m} = Program Processing Time of the mth SR. Includes time to capture data.

T_3 = Synchronization Loop time when the program has checked and found no active service requests.

T_{4m} = Data Capture Time of the mth SR.

t_{1m} = Initial offset between the SR and Program Data Transfer Waveforms.

n = number of times the program goes through the synchronization delay loop.

FIGURE 2-3.1-1. Peripheral Service Request (SR) and Data Transfer Program Waveforms and Notation

2-3.2 DEVELOPMENT OF EQUATIONS AND INEQUALITIES USED TO TEST SUCCESSFUL SYSTEM OPERATION

A successful data transfer means that each time the peripheral indicates, via an SR, that a data word is available, the program is able to capture the data before it is replaced by the next data word. It is implied that the program is able to proces the data between data word transfers. (In the floppy disk data transfer program, processing involves storing the data in Random Access Memory (RAM) and checking whether it was the last word that needed to be transferred.) Similarly for data transfers to the peripheral, the program must make the data word requested available before the succeeding request arrives. In other words, a successful data transfer consists of avoiding an overrun (during READ) and underflow (during WRITE).

If the SR is not ative at the time that the program checks for a SR, (i.e., the data word is not ready), then the program goes into a synchronization (sync) loop, which causes a delay (T_3). At the end of a sync loop, the program again checks for an active SR.

In the following analysis, it is assumed that the values of the parameters detailed in Figure 2-3.1-1 are at their worst case limits and are constant for simplicity, the single SR model (where m = 1) will be used initially.

For the system to transfer data successfully the *average* word processing time T_{AVG} must be approximately equal to the peripheral data word SR period T_{01}.

$$T_{AVG} \approx T_{01} \tag{1}$$

More precisely stated, in the limit as the number of words transferred, p, approaches infinity, the average word processing time, T_{AVG}, is exactly equal to the byte cell period T_{01}.

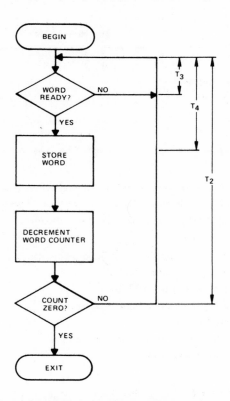

FIGURE 2-3.1-2. Flow Chart for a Typical Data Transfer Program for a Single Service Request

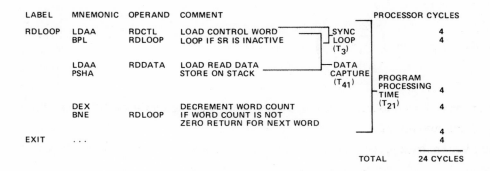

LABEL	MNEMONIC	OPERAND	COMMENT		PROCESSOR CYCLES
RDLOOP	LDAA	RDCTL	LOAD CONTROL WORD	SYNC LOOP (T_3)	4
	BPL	RDLOOP	LOOP IF SR IS INACTIVE		4
	LDAA	RDDATA	LOAD READ DATA	DATA CAPTURE (T_{41})	4
	PSHA		STORE ON STACK		4
	DEX		DECREMENT WORD COUNT		4
	BNE	RDLOOP	IF WORD COUNT IS NOT ZERO RETURN FOR NEXT WORD		4
EXIT	. . .				4

PROGRAM PROCESSING TIME (T_{21})

TOTAL   24 CYCLES

IF THE MPU CLOCK PERIOD IS $1\mu s$ THEN SYNC LOOP TIME $T_3 = 8\mu s$

PROGRAM PROCESSING TIME $T_{21} = 24\mu s$

DATA CAPTURE TIME $T_{41} = 8.5\mu s$ (See Text)

FIGURE 2-3.1-3. Data Transfer Program Indicating Method Used to Calculate Program Parameters

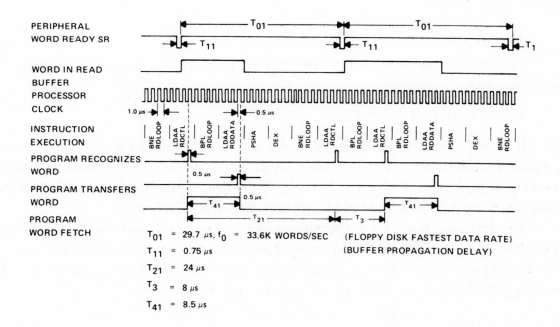

$T_{01} = 29.7\ \mu s$, $f_0 = 33.6K$ WORDS/SEC   (FLOPPY DISK FASTEST DATA RATE)

$T_{11} = 0.75\ \mu s$ (BUFFER PROPAGATION DELAY)

$T_{21} = 24\ \mu s$

$T_3 = 8\ \mu s$

$T_{41} = 8.5\ \mu s$

FIGURE 2-3.1-4. Relationship of Peripheral Data Stream to Program Timing

$$\lim_{p \to \infty} \text{T}_{\text{AVG}} = \text{T}_{01} \tag{2}$$

The time T_{AVG} consists of the program word processing time T_{21} and a time $n\text{T}_3$ while the program loops until the next word is ready. Stated mathematically,

$$\text{T}_{\text{AVG}} = \text{T}_{21} + \frac{1}{P} \left(\sum_{p=1}^{\infty} n_p \text{T}_3 \right) \tag{3}$$

Where n_p is the number of sync loops taken while waiting for the pth SR, and whose value may vary from 0 to n (n = n_p maximum).

The program byte processing time, T_{21}, must be equal to or less than the SR period T_{01}, or else the program could not keep up with the word rate of the peripheral. Therefore,

$$\text{T}_{21} \leq \text{T}_{01} \tag{4}$$

If the program loops n times in the sync delay loop before the next data word is ready, then equation (4) can be modified to read:

$$\text{T}_{21} + (n-1)\,\text{T}_3 \leq \text{T}_{01} \tag{5}$$

Also, the time $\text{T}_{21} + n\text{T}_3$ must be greater than T_{01} so that the program may begin the transfer of the next word even if the offset T_{11} is equal to zero. This is true simply because the program loops until the next word SR is active. Hence,

$$\text{T}_{01} < \text{T}_{21} + n\text{T}_3 \tag{6}$$

Therefore, the peripheral word ready period is bounded by $\text{T}_{21} + (n-1)\,\text{T}_3$ and $\text{T}_{21} + n\text{T}_3$ for successful operation:

$$\text{T}_{21} + (n-1)\,\text{T}_3 \leq \text{T}_{01} < \text{T}_{01} \leq \text{T}_3 \tag{7}$$

If $\text{T}_{01} = \text{T}_{21}$ then the program and peripheral are said to be synchronous. If $\text{T}_{01} > \text{T}_{21}$ (equation 4), then the offset T_{11} gets smaller and smaller until it is negative or zero, which means that after the program has processed one word, the next word will not be ready. At this time, the program goes into the synchronization loop, and samles the peripheral Word Ready line until the SR is again active.

The maximum value of the synchronization loop for which the system will work may be determined from the following argument. Since the peripheral SR and the program are independent, it is entirely possible that the SR occurs immediately after the program has initiated a sync loop. Since the data capture time is T_{41} and the data is invalid for a period T_{11} out of every T_{01}, it is necessary that:

$$\text{T}_3 \leq \text{T}_{01} - \text{T}_{11} - \text{T}_{41} \tag{8}$$

This is the inequality used to calculate the maximum permissible value of T_3.

2-3.3 Floppy Disk Data Transfer Routine

The parameters of the Floppy Disk Data transfer routine are listed in Figure 2-3.1-4. The parameters can now be tested with equations (7) and (8):

From Equation (7)

$$T_{21} \leqslant T_0 < T_{21} + T_3 \qquad n=1 \tag{9}$$

$$24 \leqslant 29.7 < 32\mu s$$

and from Equation (8)

$$T_3 \leqslant T_{01} - T_{11} - T_{41} \tag{8}$$

$$8 \leqslant 29.7 - 0.75 - 8.5$$

Both requirements are met and the program will transfer data successfully, (at a maximum rate when $T_{01} = T_{21}$).

$$\text{Max Data Rate} = \frac{1}{T_{21}} = \frac{1}{24\mu s} = 41.6K \text{ Bytes/sec.}$$

Note that in this example, the time left over in each data byte after processing is:

$$T_{01} - T_{21} = 29.7 - 24 = 5.7\mu s \tag{10}$$

This time is too small to be usable for other tasks by the M6800.

2-3.4   CASSETTE DATA TRANSFER ROUTINE

The data transfer routine of Figure 2-3.1-3 is equally valid for the case of word data transfer between the cassette and an MPU. The significant difference is the slower data rate, i.e., the SR period for word transfer is much longer. For the cassette with a worst case data transfer rate of 1.85 KBytes/sec (15KBits/sec):

$$T_{01} = \frac{1}{1850} = 540.5\mu s$$

All other parameters remain essentially the same.

$$T_{11} = 1\mu s$$

$$T_{21} = 24\mu s$$

$$T_3 = 8\mu s$$

$$T_{41} = 8.5\mu s$$

It may be verified that both Equation 7 and 8 are satisfied by the above parameters for n=65. The time available after processing the word is:

$$T_{01} - T_{21} = 540.5 - 24 = 516.5\mu s$$

This time is normally used up in synchronization delay loops. Since so much additional time is available, it may be possible to transfer cassette data in serial form (bit transfer), and eliminate the hardware associated with the serial to parallel conversion. The Serial Data Transfer Flow Chart and Program are shown in Figures 2-3.4-1 and 2-3.4-2 respectively. Equation 7 and 8 are both satisfied for n=4. The unused processing time per bit cell is:

$$T_{01} - T_{21} = 66.6 - 40 = 26.6\mu s \tag{11}$$

2-3.5 UTILIZATION OF MPU PROCESSING TIME

Assume that it is required that a program must service a cassette for serial data transfers, as described earlier, and simultaneously refresh a dynamic display (display without memory). Let the subscripts 1 and 2 be used to refer to parameters of the cassette and displays respectively. Assume that the program processing time T_{22}, to refresh the display, is longer than the available processing time in a single bit cell, i.e.

$$T_{22} > 26.6 \text{ s (From Equation 11)}$$

However, if the period of the display SR is longer than that of the Cassette ($T_{02} > T_{01}$) an interesting question arises. Is it possible to borrow time from adjacent data cells and process SR2 without losing SR1 data? The following analysis shows that it is, if the parameters meet certain requirements.

To maximize the utilization of an MPU's processing time the extra time spent in synchronization delay loops can be used for doing other routines. This is similar to adding a time equal to the additional delay loops to the program processing time T_{11}. The condition that must now be satisfied by the program and the peripheral SR period may be stated as:

$$T'_{21} \leqslant T_{01} < T'_{21} + T_3 \tag{11}$$

where

$$T'_{21} = T_{21} + (n-1) T_3 \tag{12}$$

and $(n-)$ T_3 is the additional time now used for processing. The length of the program processing time has been extended; however, there is still only one independent service request being serviced as illustrated in the flow chart in Figure 2A.

It is often required that the unused processing time be used to process SR's from another time dependent peripheral. Assume that it is required that the unused processing time be used to process SR's from a display, i.e., to refresh the display. Will the system be able to successfully handle the two SR's? This question leads to considering the program model for handling multiple SR's, and the conditions that must be satisfied for successful operation.

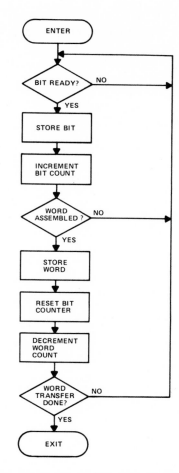

FIGURE 2-3.4-1. Flow Chart for Serial Data Transfer

LABEL	MNEMONIC	OPERAND	COMMENT	PROCESSOR CYCLES
LOOPC	LDAA	CLKDAT	LOAD CLOCK & DATA WORD (CLOCK IN BIT 7, DATA IN BIT 1)	4
	BPL	LOOPC	LOOP IF SR IS INACTIVE	4
	RORA		TRANSFER DATA BIT TO CARRY	6
	ROLB		ASSEMBLE WORD IN ACCUMULATOR B	6
	BCC	LOOPC	IF WORD IS NOT ASSEMBLED RETURN FOR NEXT BIT	4
	PSH B		STORE ASSEMBLED WORD ON STACK	4
	LDA B	#01	RESET BIT COUNTER	2
	DEC	COUNT	DECREMENT WORD COUNT	6
	BNE	LOOPC	IF WORD COUNT NOT ZERO RETURN FOR NEXT WORD	4
EXIT	. . .			
			TOTAL	**40 CYCLES**

At MPU clock rate of 1 MHZ

$$T_3 = 8\mu s$$

$$T_{21} = 40\mu s$$

$$T_{41} = 0.5\mu s$$

and $$T_{01} = \frac{1}{15000} = 66.6\ \mu s$$

FIGURE 2-3.4-2. Casette Bit Serial Data Transfer Program

2-37

2-3.6 PROGRAM MODEL FOR TWO PRIORITIZED SERVICE REQUESTS

When two independent periodic SR's are allowed, the program model for servicing them may be prioritized. The prioritizing is done such that the SR with the shorter period (hgher frequency) has the higher priority. Figure 2-3.6-1 indicates the programming model for two SR's where SR #1 (SR1) has higher priority. Notice that SR1 is tested first, regardless of which SR was last processed.

The parameters of the SR1, SR2 waveforms are derived as before, from specifications of the two peripherals. The parameters for the program are derived in conjunction with the prioritized model. For example, the synchronization loop time T_3, is now the time it takes the program to test for an active SR1, and

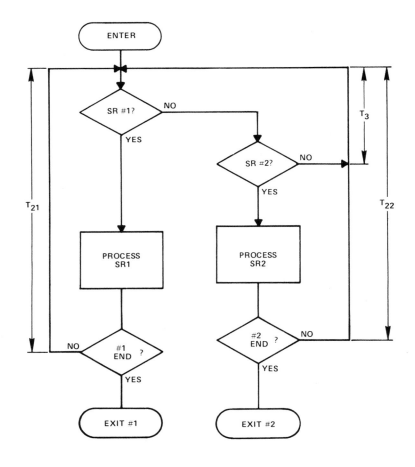

FIGURE 2-3.6-1. Program Model for Two Prioritized Time Dependent
Service Requests

then test for an active SR2, and find them both inactive. Similarly, T_{22}, the program processing time for SR2, includes the time to test for SR1, (which is inactive) and then test for SR2 (active), process SR2, and test if it is the end of SR2 processing.

2-3.7 REQUIREMENTS THAT MUST BE SATISFIED WHEN AN MPU SERVICES MULTIPLE SR's

The following requirements were developed by studying the failure mechanisms using the program model for two prioritized time-dependent service requests. A failure was defined as an overflow or underflow, and the program was run to process a very large number of consecutive SR's (up to 100,000 service requests). Each time there was a failure, the timing relationships between the two SR waveforms and the program processing waveform was studied to give a clue to the failure mechanism. The results are listed in Figure 2-3.7-1. Of the requirements listed in Figure 2-3.7-1, Equations 7 and 8 have already been discussed. Equation 12 is really implied by the program flowchart model for a single SR where the data capture time is included in the SR processing time.

Equation 13 states that the sum of the processing times expressed as a fraction of the SR frequency is no greater than unity. This is true because of the periodic nature of each SR and the fact that each SR uses T_{2m}/T_{om} of the MPU's processing time. As an example, if the cassette serial data transfer routine uses $40\mu s$ every $66.6\mu s$ then it uses $40/66.6 = 60\%$ (approx.) of the MPU's capability. Hence, 40% of the remaining MPU capability may be used by another SR. This result is used shortly to test the cassette-display service program.

For each SR it is required that:

A. $\quad T_{2m} \leqslant T_{om} < T_{2m} + nT_3$ (7)

B. $\quad T_3 \leqslant T_{om} - T_{1m} - T_{4m}$ (8)

C. $\quad T_{4m} \leqslant T_{2m}$ (12)

For the system it is required that:

D. $\quad 1 - \sum_m \left(\dfrac{T_{2m}}{T_{0m}}\right) \geqslant 0$ (13)

The equality is the synchronous case where no synchronization loops are taken.

E. For each peripheral when compared to the fastest peripheral k,

$\quad T_{0k} - T_{1k} - T_{4k} \geqslant T_{2n}$ for all $n \neq k$ (14)

Where k is the peripheral with the highest frequency of operation, and the SR's are prioritized by frequency with the highest frequency SR being first.

F. $\quad T_{0m} - T_{1m} - T_{4m} \geqslant T_{2k} + T_3$ (15)

FIGURE 2-3.7-1. Timing Constraints for Successful System Operation for Prioritized Multiple Service Requests

Equation 14 is best illustrated by the timing diagram in Figure 2-3.7-2 where SR2 and SR1 occur almost simultaneously, but SR2 is active first. This implies that just prior to this occurrence, the last SR from both SR1 and SR2 has already been processed and SR1 has been tested first, according to the prioritized model, and found to be inactive. SR2 must be processed in a time T_{22}; then data from SR1 must be captured in time T_{41}, before it becomes invalid. The data becomes invalid a time T_{11} prior to the next SR1. Therefore, the condition that must be satisfied is:

$$T_{01} - T_{11} - T_{41} \geq T_{22} \ (m=2) \tag{14}$$

Equation 15 implies that the program should be able to synchronize, then process SR1, and capture data from SR2 before it becomes invalid. This situation occurs after the last SR1 has just been processed, and then neither SR1 nor SR2 are active (see Figure 2-3.7-3). After the sync loop, SR1 is processed, and SR2 data must be captured:

$$T_{02} - T_{12} - T_{42} \geq T_{21} + T_3 \ (m=2) \tag{15}$$

Equations 14 and 15 are stated in a general form for m SR's in Figure 2-3.7-1 but they have been verified only for the case of two SR's. Equations 7, 8 and 13 of that Figure, however, must be satisfied by any set of m SR's.

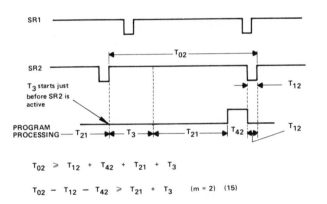

$$T_{02} \geq T_{12} + T_{42} + T_{21} + T_3$$

$$T_{02} - T_{12} - T_{42} \geq T_{21} + T_3 \quad (m = 2) \ (15)$$

FIGURE 2-3.7-2. Timing Diagram Showing Requirements of Equation 15 for Two SR's

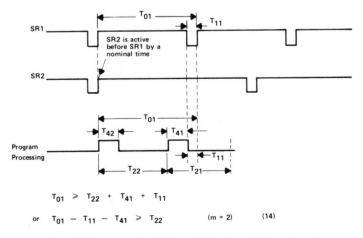

$$T_{01} \geq T_{22} + T_{41} + T_{11}$$

or $\quad T_{01} - T_{11} - T_{41} \geq T_{22} \quad (m = 2) \qquad (14)$

FIGURE 2-3.7-3. Timing Diagram Showing Requirements of Equation 15 for Two SR's

2-3.8 SERIAL DATA TRANSFER AND DYNAMIC DISPLAY REFRESH PROCESSING

The cassette serial data transfer program is now modified and extended to service both the cassette data SR and the Display Refresh SR. The combined program, listed in Figure 2-3.8-1 follows the model of two prioritized SR's of Figure 2-3.6-1. SR2 is generated by a 16 character dynamic display, and the characters are refreshed cyclically. Figure 2-3.8-2 lists the parameters of the two SR's and verifies that all requirements are met for the two SR's to be successfully serviced. Note that use of Equation 13 provides a measure of the efficiency of usage of the MPU processing time. In this case:

$$1 - \left(\frac{40}{66.6} + \frac{50}{130}\right) = 1 - 0.985 = 0.015$$

which implies that 98.5% of the total processing time is being used.

The amount of spare time remaining is calculated by multiplying the left-hand side of Equation 13 by the period of the highest frequency SR. Thus,

Unused processing time = $0.015 \times 66.6 = 1.00\mu$s every SR1 period.

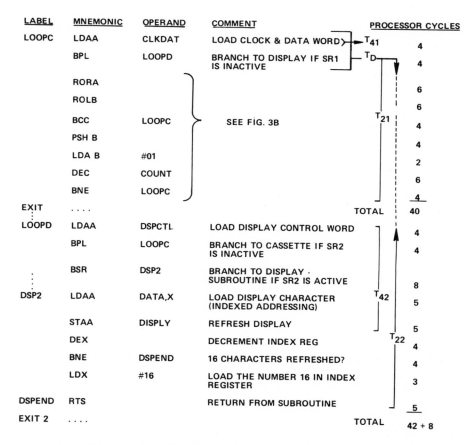

FIGURE 2-3.8-1. Serial Data Transfer and Dynamic Display Refresh Routine

PARAMETERS OF SR1 (SERIAL DATA)

T_{01} = 66.6μs

T_{11} = 1μs

T_{21} = 40μs

T_{41} = 0.5μs

$T_{21} \leq T_{01} < T_{21} + nT_3$

40 $\leq$ 66.6 $<$ 40 + 2 x 16

AND $T_3 \leq T_{01} - T_{11} - T_{41}$

16 $\leq$ 66.6 $-$ 1 $-$ 0.5

$T_{01} \leq T_{02}$

PARAMETERS OF SR2 (DISPLAY REFRESH)

T_{02} = 130μs

T_{12} = 1μs

T_{22} = 42 + 8 = 50μs

T_{42} = 26μs

T_3 = 16μs

$T_{22} \leq T_{02} < T_{22} + nT_3$

50 $\leq$ 130 $<$ 50 + 5 x 16

AND

$T_3 \leq T_{02} - T_{12} - T_{42}$

16 $\leq$ 130 $-$ 1 $-$ 26

FROM EQU. 13

$$1 - \sum_m \frac{T_{2m}}{T_{0m}} \geq 0$$

$$1 - \left(\frac{40}{66.6} + \frac{50}{130}\right) = 0.015 > 0$$

FROM EQU. 14

$T_{01} - T_{11} - T_{41} \geq T_{22}$

66.6 $-$ 1 $-$ 0.5 $>$ 50

FROM EQU. 15

$T_{02} - T_{12} - T_{42} \geq T_{21} + T_3$

130 $-$ 1 $-$ 26 $>$ 40 + 16

FIGURE 2-3.8-2. Serial Data Display SR Parameters and
System Requirement Test

2-3.9   INCREASING MPU PROCESSING EFFICIENCY WITH THE FLIP-FLOP MODEL FOR TWO "EQUAL" PERIOD SR'S

When the SR's have approximately equal SR periods, as in Read/Write, or bi-directional data flow, the processing time for SR2 may be reduced if a flip-flop model is used in place of the prioritized model. Figure 2-3.9-1 shows the Flip-Flop model in which, after completion of SR1 processing, the program checks SR2 first and vice versa.

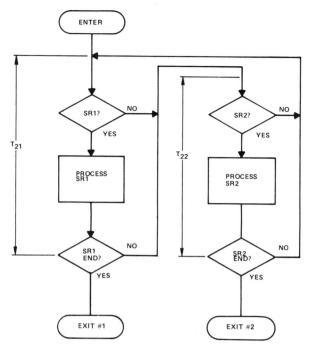

FIGURE 2-3.9-1. Flip-Flop Model for Two "Equal" Period SR's

The advantage gained in processing efficiency is reflected in the fastest data rate that the program can successfully transfer for both SR's. This can be illustrated using the example of cassette serial data transfer. Let SR1 and SR2 programs be identical in form such that:

$$T_{41} = T_{42} = 0.5\mu s$$

$$T_{11} = T_{12} = 1\mu s$$

$$T_3 = 16\mu s$$

$$MAX\ T_{01} = T_{02} = ?$$

If the prioritized model is used, then:

$$T_{21} = 40\mu s\ \text{and}\ \underline{T_{22} = 50\mu s}$$

because it takes $8\mu s$ to test if SR1 is active and this is always tested first.

In this case, the maximum data transfer rate for the two SR's may be calculated by using the equality in Equation 13.

$$\frac{40}{T_{01}} + \frac{50}{(T_{02} = T_{01})} = 1$$

$$T_{01} = \frac{1}{90\mu s} = 11.1\text{Kbits/sec.}$$

If the flip-flop model is used then.

$$T_{21} = T_{22} = 40\mu s$$

and the maximum data transfer rate for the two SR's may be calculated from Equation 13 as:

$$\frac{40}{T_{01}} + \frac{40}{(T_{02} = T_{01})} = 1$$

$$T_{01} = \frac{1}{80\mu s} = 12.5 \text{ Kbits/sec.}$$

This provides approximately a ten percent increase in maximum data rate.

Note, however, that when the flip-flop model is used there is an additional condition that now must be satisfied. This is required because both SR1 and SR2 may occur simultaneously. Therefore,

$$T_{01} \geqslant T_{02} \geqslant T_{21} + T_{22} \tag{16}$$

The techniques described in this section enable the user to determine if a given data transfer program will work in the microprocessor system. If it is found that the program does not work, the user may modify the program/hardware to allow the system to work. The techniques also provide a measure of the utilization of the microprocessor's capability. This provides the opportunity to add functions to or delete hardware from the system until the microprocessor is being used to its full capability. The techniques may be extended to cover operation of systems where interrupts are the periodic service requests.

2-4   USE OF INDEX REGISTER

Effective programming of the MPU makes extensive use of the Indexed Addressing mode. For this mode, the address is variable and depends on the current contents of the Index Register. A source statement such as

Operator	Operand	Comment
LDAA	X	Load ACCA from M=X

will cause the contents of the memory location specified by the contents of the Index Register to be loaded into accumulator A, that is, the effective address is determined by X. Since there are instructions for manipulating the contents of the Index Register during program execution (LDX, INX, DEX, etc.), the Indexed Addressing mode provides a dynamic "on the fly" way to modify program activity.

The Index Register can be loaded either with "constants" such as the starting address of a file in ROM or with a variable located in RAM that changes as the program runs. The Indexed Addressing mode also allows the address to be modified by an offset. The operand field can include a value that will be automatically added to X during execution. The format for this technique is:

Operator	Operand	Comment
STAA	K,X	Store ACCA in M=(X+K)

When the MPU encounters the opcode for LDAA (Indexed), it looks in the next memory location for the value to be added to X and calculates the required address, X + K in this example. (See Section 1-2.3.5 for additional information on the Indexed Addressing Mode.) The control program is normally in ROM, hence, the offset is a constant that was established during program development and cannot be changed during program execution.

There are numerous examples of indexed addressing techniques in the sample programs throughout this Manual, however, it is of interest to summarize some of the methods in this Section. A common usage is shown in the following sequence of instructions for setting a series of RAM locations to zero (perhaps part of an initialization routine):

Label	Operator	Operand	Comment
	.		
	.		
	.		
	LDX	#FIRST	Get starting Address
LOOP1	CLR	X	Clear current location.
	INX		Move to next location.
	CPX	LAST+1	Finished yet?
	BNE	LOOP1	No, continue clearing.
NEXT	xxx	xxxxxx	Yes, continue with program.
	.		
	.		
	.		

This sequence causes the consecutive memory locations FIRST through LAST to be cleared. The labels FIRST, LAST, NEXT, etc., will have been assigned specific values during assembly of the program. Note that only every other memory location would be operated on if a second INX had been included in the program:

	.		
	.		
	.		
	LDX		
LOOP1	CLR	X	
	INX		
	INX		
	CPX	LAST +2	
	BNE	LOOP1	
NEXT	xxx	xxxxxx	
	.		
	.		
	.		

This technique is commonly used to establish the "size" of the increment that will be stepped through. If the size of the step is large (many INXs) or if it is desirable to have a variable step size, another procedure can be used to advantage. The following sequence of instructions can be used to effectively add a variable offset to X:

Label	Operator	Operand	Comment
	.		
	.		
	.		
	LDAB	VALUE	Get variable into ACCB.
	LDX	#FIRST	Get Starting Address.
LOOP1	INX		Advance address pointer.
	DECB		Is ACCB zero yet?
	BNE	LOOP1	No, continue advancing pointer.
NEXT	xxx	xxxxxx	Yes, proceed with program.
	.		
	.		
	.		

This sequence has the effect of adding the contents of accumulator B to the Index Register, that is, a variable offset is generated. If, for example, the value in ACCB is one, the INX instruction increases X by one and the DECB instruction reduces ACCB to zero. The program flow falls through to NEXT since the BNE test fails but the Index Register is now loaded with X + 1 rather than X. A different value for B would cause the program to pass through the loop until B is reduced to zero. Since X is increased by one during each pass, the net effect is to add the variable "VALUE" to X.

This technique is illustrated in the following example: A program is required that will check for a zero result in every 8th location in a block of memory extending from FIRST to LAST. The first zero result encountered is to cause the program to branch to location ZROTST. If no zero results are encountered, processing is to continue:

Label	Operator	Operand	Comment
	.		
	.		
	.		
BEGIN	LDX	#FIRST	Get starting address.
START	LDAB	#$08	Load step size.
LOOP1	INX		Advance address pointer.
	DECB		Next location yet?
	BNE	LOOP1	No, continue advancing pointer.
	TST	X	Yes, test for zero result.
	BEQ	ZROTST	Branch to zero test if zero.
	CPX	LAST+1	Finished?
	BNE	START	No, move to next location.
NEXT	xxx	xxxxxx	Yes, continue with program.

In this case, the program will pass through LOOP1 eight times prior to each test, effectively adding eight to the value in the Index Register. Note also that the INX instruction could be replaced by the decrement X instruction, DEX, thus providing a means of "negative" or backward indexing if desired.

There is another "variable indexing technique" that combines the Indexed Addressing mode with suitable memory allocation to obtain dynamic indexed addressing. Assume that a program is required that will select a mask pattern that is determined by the current contents of a counter. The counter content is variable and depends on the results of previous program operation. Such sequences are useful for establishing particular bit patterns required by the program.

As an example, assume that one of the bit patterns shown below is required, depending on the current value of BITCNT, a value that has been previously computed and stored in RAM:

Bit Count	Bit Pattern							
	b_7	b_6	b_5	b_4	b_3	b_2	b_1	b_0
0	1	0	0	0	0	0	0	0
1	0	1	0	0	0	0	0	0
2	0	0	1	0	0	0	0	0
3	0	0	0	1	0	0	0	0
4	0	0	0	0	1	0	0	0
5	0	0	0	0	0	1	0	0
6	0	0	0	0	0	0	1	0
7	0	0	0	0	0	0	0	1

The following memory allocation can be used to permit indexed addressing of the desired pattern:

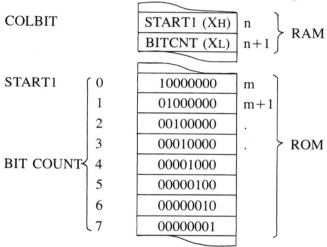

By putting the upper byte of the starting address of the table (upper byte of m = START1) in the RAM location immediately preceding BITCNT, the LDX instruction can be used to load the Index Register with the address of the desired bit pattern. This method has the limitation that the lookup table must begin (START1 above) at an address whose least two significant Hex digits are zero, that is, of the form XX00. Such tables can be at the beginning of any multiple of 256 ROM locations.

This technique is illustrated in the following sample program for updating a bit pattern stored in two PIA Output Registers, PIAORA and PIAORB. The registers contain a pattern for driving an external display array that must be updated to include the results of each new calculation of a word count, WRDCNT, and a bit count, BITCNT. The current update goes to PIAORA if the word count is odd and to PIAORB if even. The steps involved in the update are:

(1) Test WRDCNT for odd or even and set a flag.

(2) Get PIAORA (odd WRDCNT) or PIAORB (even WRDCNT) into accumulator A.

(3) Determine the bit pattern that corresponds to the current BITCNT.

(4) Combine with the contents of accumulator A, preserving any previously set bits.

(5) Write updated pattern back into appropriate PIA register.

The following program can be used if the memory allocation recommended above is used:

```
                .
                .
                .
        ROR     WRDCNT      Sets Carry if odd.
        ROR     COLFLG      Set sign bit on odd WRDCNT.
        BMI     TAG1        Get appropriate register.
        LDAA    PIAORB      * into
        BRA     TAG2        * ACCA
TAG1    LDAA    PIAORA      * for update
TAG2    LDX     COLBIT      Point to bit pattern.
        ORAA    X           Combine with previous pattern.
        TST     COLFLG      Put updated pattern.
        BMI     TAG3        * back.
        STAA    PIAORB      * out
        BRA     TAG4        * to
TAG3    STAA    PIAORA      * display
TAG4    xxx     xxxxxx
                .
                .
                .
```

Note that the single instruction LDX COLBIT is all that is required to locate a ROM location that depends on a dynamic program result.

CHAPTER 3

3. **INPUT/OUTPUT TECHNIQUES**

3-1 **INTRODUCTION**

Due to the type of applications in which they are used, the capability to efficiently handle Input/Output (I/O) information is perhaps the most important characteristic of microprocessor systems. The M6800 architecture incorporates supervisory controls and interface devices that permit a wide variety of I/O techniques to be used. This Chapter describes the I/O characteristics of the M6800 system and their use in typical applications.

Most I/O information can be placed in one of two general categories: (1) control and status signals; (2) data that is to be processed by the MPU. Much of the MC6800's flexibility in handling control and status information depends on three system features:

(1) Many of the routine peripheral control tasks can be delegated to the interface adapters.

(2) Because the design of the interface adapters allows the MPU to treat peripherals exactly like other memory locations, the memory reference instructions that operate directly on memory are also used to control peripherals.

(3) While all MPU's must be able to continuously control simple peripherals under program control, in many typical applications, the peripheral information to the MPU is often asynchronous in nature and is best handled on an interrupt basis. The interrupt structure of the MC6800 allows such applications to be processed in an orderly manner, that is, interrupts are handled without disrupting other system tasks in progress.

The currently available interface devices are described in detail in Section 3-4. The various interrupt control techniques are discussed in Sections 3-2 and 3-3.

In the M6800 system, all data movement between family elements (memory and/or peripheral interface adapters) is normally done through the MPU via the Data Bus. This means that the transfers are program controlled, that is, the movement is accomplished by execution of instructions such as Load, Store, Push, Pull, etc. Numerous examples of programmed controlled data transfers are shown throughout this manual. For example, a program for moving 8-bit bytes from a peripheral to memory (at the rate of 43,000 bytes per second) is described in conjunction with the floppy disk application discussed in Section 5-4.

In most system designs, it is possible to "speed up" data movement by surrendering program control and transferring data directly between the other system elements. This bypassing of the MPU, usually called Direct Memory Access (DMA), requires that the MPU be provided with supervisory signals. In addition, external hardware for generating addresses and controlling the transfer must be provided. The MC6800's supervisory control features allow DMA to be accomplished in a variety of ways. The details of implementation depend on the particular system configuration and timing requirements. Several methods and their relative merits are discussed in Section 3-5 of this Chapter.

In a typical application, the peripheral devices may be continuously generating asynchronous signals (interrupts) that must be acted on by the MPU. The interrupts may be either requests for service or acknowledgements of services performed earlier by the MPU. The MC6800 MPU provides several methods for automatically responding to such interrupts in an orderly manner.

In the control of interrupts, three general problems must be considered: (1) It is characteristic of most applications that interrupts must be handled without permanently disrupting the task in process when the interrupt occurs. The MC6800 handles this by saving the results of its current activity so that processing can be resumed after the interrupt has been serviced. (2) There must be a method of handling multiple interrupts since several peripherals may be requesting service simultaneously. (3) If some signals are more important to system operation or if certain peripherals require faster servicing than others, there must be a method of prioritizing the interrupts. Techniques for handling each of these problems with the MC6800 will be described in the following paragraphs.

The MPU has three hardware interrupt inputs, Reset ($\overline{\text{RES}}$)[1], Non-Maskable Interrupt ($\overline{\text{NMI}}$), and Interrupt Request ($\overline{\text{IRQ}}$). An interrupt sequence can be initiated by applying a suitable control signal to any of these three inputs or by using the software SWI instruction. The resulting sequence is different for each case.

3-2.1   INTERRUPT REQUEST ($\overline{\text{IRQ}}$)

The IRQ input is the mainstay of system interrupt control. Inputs to $\overline{\text{IRQ}}$ are normally generated in PIAs and ACIAs but may also come from other user-defined hardware. In either case, the various interrupts may be wire-ORed and applied to the MPU's $\overline{\text{IRQ}}$ input. This input is level sensitive; a logic zero causes the MPU to initiate the interrupt sequence[2]. A flow chart of the $\overline{\text{IRQ}}$ sequence is shown in Figure 3-2.1-1.

After finishing its current instruction and testing the Interrupt Mask in the Condition Code Register, the MPU stores the contents of its programmable registers in memory locations specified by the Stack Pointer. (Operation of the Stack Pointer is discussed in Section 1-3.4.1.) This stacking process takes seven memory cycles: two each for the Index Register and Program Counter, and one each for Accumulator A, Accumulator B, and the Condition Code Register. The Stack Pointer will have been decremented seven locations and is pointing to the next empty memory location.

The MPU's next step of setting the Interrupt Mask to a logic one is an important aspect of system interrupt control. Setting the mask allows the control program to determine the order in which multiple interrupts will be handled. If it is desirable to recognize another interrupt (of higher priority, for example) before service of the first is complete, the Interrupt Mask can be cleared by a CLI instruction at the beginning of the current service routine. If each interrupt is to be completely serviced before another is recognized, the CLI instruction is omitted and a Return from Interrupt instruction, RTI, placed at the end of the service routine restores the Interrupt Mask status from the stack, thus enabling recognition of subsequent interrupts.

Note that if the former method is selected (immediate enable of further interrupts), the original interrupt service will still eventually be completed. This is due to the fact that the later interrupt also causes the current status to be put on the stack for later completion. This process is general and means that interrupts can be

---

[1]The bar convention over the symbols is used to indicate an active low signal condition.

[2]$\overline{\text{IRQ}}$ is a maskable input. If the Interrupt Mask Bit within the MPU is set, low levels on the $\overline{\text{IRQ}}$ line will not be recognized; the MPU will continue current program execution until the mask bit is cleared by encountering the Clear Interrupt (CLI) instruction in the control program, or an RTI is encountered.

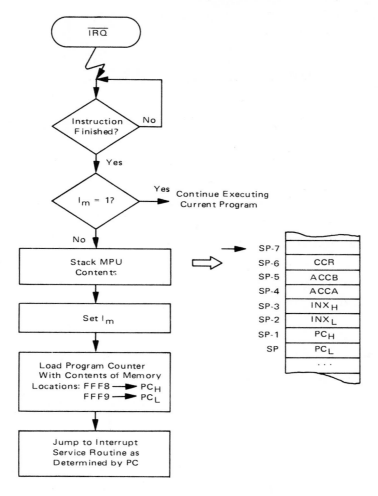

FIGURE 3-2.1-1: Hardware Interrupt Request Sequence

CONTENTS	ADDRESS
$\overline{RES}$ (Low Byte)	FFFF
$\overline{RES}$ (High Byte)	FFFE
$\overline{NMI}$ (Low Byte)	FFFD
$\overline{NMI}$ (High Byte)	FFFC
SWI (Low Byte)	FFFB
SWI (High Byte)	FFFA
$\overline{IRQ}$ (Low Byte)	FFF9
$\overline{IRQ}$ (High Byte)	FFF8

FIGURE 3-2. 1-2: Interrupt Vector, Permanent Memory Assignments

"nested" to any depth required by the system limited only by memory size. The status of the interrupted routines is returned on a Last-In-First-Out (LIFO) basis. That is, the last result to be stacked is the first to be returned to the MPU.

After setting the Interrupt Mask, the MPU next obtains the address of the first interrupt service routine instruction from memory locations permanently assigned to the $\overline{\text{IRQ}}$ interrupt input. This is accomplished by loading the Program Counter's high and low bytes from memory locations responding to addresses, FFF8 and FFF9, respectively. The MPU then fetches the first instruction from the location now designated by the Program Counter.

This technique of indirect addressing (also called vectoring) is also used by the other interrupt sequences. The "vectors" are placed in the memory locations corresponding to addresses FFF8 through FFFF as shown in Figure 3-2.1-2 during program development.

The MPU places two of the address bytes in the range FFF8 — FFFF on the Address Bus during interrupt sequences. It should be noted that the vector data is fetched from the memory locations that respond to these addresses even though they may not actually be FFF8 — FFFF. For example, in the memory allocation that was illustrated in Section 1-1.2.1 of Chapter 1, the ROM was assigned the 1024 memory locations between C000 and C3FF (decimal 49152 to 50175) by tying Address Lines A_{15} and A_{14} to the ROM's chip enables:

Address Lines	A_{15}	A_{14}	A_{13}	A_{12}	A_{11}	A_{10}	A_9	A_8	A_7	A_6	A_5	A_4	A_3	A_2	A_1	A_0
ROM Connections	E	E	X	X	X	X	A_9	A_8	A_7	A_6	A_5	A_4	A_3	A_2	A_1	A_0

Not Connected

Notice that if the MPU outputs the address FFFF (all ones) while fetching the vector data for a Reset, it is actually addressing memory location C3FF in the system memory.

The significant point is that the eight locations that *respond* to FFF8 — FFFF must be reserved for the interrupt vectors.

3-2.2 NON-MASKABLE INTERRUPT ($\overline{\text{NMI}}$)

As implied by its name, the Non-Maskable Interrupt ($\overline{\text{NMI}}$) must be recognized by the MPU as soon as the $\overline{\text{NMI}}$ line goes to logic zero. This interrupt is often used as a power-failure sensor or to provide interrupt service to a "hot" peripheral that must be allowed to interrupt.

Except for the fact that it cannot be masked, the $\overline{\text{NMI}}$ interrupt sequence is similar to $\overline{\text{IRQ}}$ (See Figure 3-2.2-1). After completing its current instruction, the MPU stacks its registers, sets the Interrupt mask and fetches the starting address of the $\overline{\text{NMI}}$ interrupt service routine by vectoring to FFFC and FFFD. (See Figure 3-2.1-2).

3-2.3 RESET ($\overline{\text{RES}}$)

The Reset interrupt sequence differs from $\overline{\text{NMI}}$ and $\overline{\text{IRQ}}$ in two respects. When $\overline{\text{RES}}$ is low, the MPU places FFFE (the high order byte of the $\overline{\text{RES}}$ vector location) on the Address Bus in preparation for executing the $\overline{\text{RES}}$ interrupt sequence. It is normally used following power on to reach an initializing program that sets up system starting conditions such as initial value of the Program Counter, Stack Pointer, PIA Modes, etc. It is also available as a restart method in the event of system lockup or runaway. Because of its use for starting the MPU from a power down state, the $\overline{\text{RES}}$ sequence is initiated by a positive going edge. Also, since it is normally used only in a start-up mode, there is no reason to save the MPU contents on the stack. The flow is shown in Figure 3-2.3-1. After setting the Interrupt mask, the MPU loads the Program Counter from the memory locations responding to FFFE and FFFF and then proceeds with the initialization program.

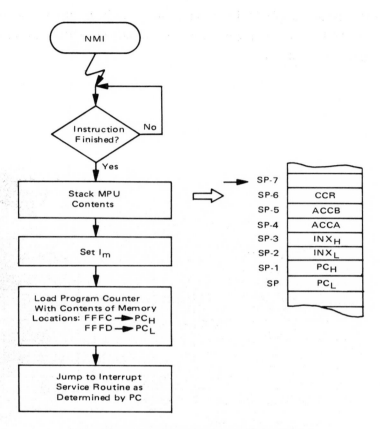

FIGURE 3-2.2.1: Non-Maskable Interrupt Sequence

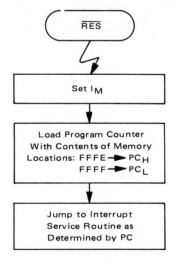

FIGURE 3-2.3-1: Reset Interrupt Sequence

3-2.4   SOFTWARE INTERRUPT (SWI)

The MPU also has a program initiated interrupt mode. Execution of the Software Interrupt (SWI) instruction by the MPU initiates the sequence shown in Figure 3-2.4-1. The sequence is similar to the hardware interrupts except that it is initiated by "software" and the vector is obtained from memory locations responding to FFFA and FFFB.

The Software Interrupt is useful for inserting break-points in the program as an aid in debugging and troubleshooting. In effect, SWI stops the process in place and puts the MPU register contents into memory where they can be examined or displayed.

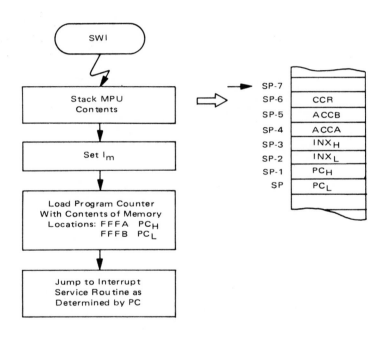

FIGURE 3-2.4-1: Software Interrupt Sequence

In the previous section, the various methods available for finding the "beginning" of an interrupt control program were described. If there is only one peripheral capable of requesting service, the source of the interrupt is known and the control program can immediately begin the service routine. More often, several devices are allowed to originate interrupt requests and the first task of the interrupt routine is to identify the source of the interrupt.

There is also the possibility that several peripherals are simultaneously requesting service. In this case, the control program must also decide which interrupt to service first. The $\overline{IRQ}$ interrupt service routine in particular may be complex since most of the I/O interrupts are wire-ORed on this line.

The most common method of handling the multiple and/or simultaneous $\overline{IRQ}$ interrupts is to begin the service routine by "polling" the peripherals to see which one generated the request. If the interrupts are generated by peripheral signals coming in through a PIA or an ACIA, the polling procedure is very simple. In addition to causing $\overline{IRQ}$ to go low, the interrupting signal also sets a flag bit in the PIA's or ACIA's internal registers. Since these registers represent memory locations to the MPU, the polling consists of nothing more than stepping through the locations and testing the flag bits[3].

Establishing the priority of simultaneous interrupts can be handled in either of two ways. The simplest is to establish priority by the order in which the PIAs and ACIAs are polled. That is, the first I/O flag encountered gets the service, so higher priority devices are polled first. The second method first finds all the interrupt flags and then uses a special program to select the one having highest priority. This method permits a more sophisticated approach in that the priority can be modified by the control program. For example, it might be desirable to select the lower priority of two simultaneous requests if the lower priority has not been serviced for some specified period of time.

Software techniques can, in theory, handle any number of devices to any sophistication level of prioritizing. In practice, if there are many sources of interrupt requests, the time required to find the appropriate interrupt can exceed the time available to do so. In this situation, external prioritizing hardware can be used to speed up the operation.

One method for implementing hardware prioritized interrupts is shown in block diagram form in Figure 3-3-1. With this technique, each interrupting device is assigned its own address vector which is stored in ROM memory similarly to the $\overline{RES}$, SWI, $\overline{IRQ}$, and $\overline{NMI}$ vectors. An external hardware priority encoder selects the interrupt to be recognized and directs the MPU to the proper locations in memory for obtaining the vectors.

Operation of the MPU itself is unchanged; after recognizing an $\overline{IRQ}$, the MPU still outputs addresses FFF8 and FFF9 as before. However, some of the address lines are no longer tied directly to memory but go instead to a 1-of-2 Data Selector. The other set of inputs to the Data Selector are generated by a Priority Encoder that outputs a binary number corresponding to the highest priority interrupt signal present at the time the interrupt was recognized by the MPU.

Detection of the FFF8 and FFF9 addresses by the Address Bus monitoring circuitry then causes the outputs of the priority encoder to be substituted for part of the normal address. Hence, even though the MPU outputs FFF8 and FFF9, other locations in ROM are read by the MPU. Suitable vectors for sending the MPU directly to the appropriate service routine are stored in these locations. Specific circuits for implementing this prioritizing method are described in Section 4-2.1.

---

[3] See Section 5-4 for a specific example of software polling.

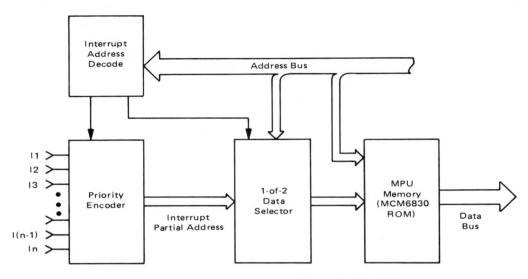

FIGURE 3-3-1: Hardware Interrupt Prioritizing Block Diagram

3-4   PROGRAM CONTROLLED DATA TRANSFERS

3-4.1   MC6820 PERIPHERAL INTERFACE ADAPTER

3-4.1.1   Input/Output Configuration:

The MC6820 Peripheral Interface Adapter (PIA) provides a flexible method of connecting byte-oriented peripherals to the MPU. The PIA, while relatively complex itself, permits the MPU to handle a wide variety of equipment types with minimum additional logic and simple programming. An Input/Output Diagram of the MC6820 is shown in Figure 3-4.1.1-1.

Data flows between the MPU and the PIA on the System Data Bus via eight bi-directional data lines, D0 through D7. The direction of data flow is controlled by the MPU via the Read/Write input to the PIA.

The "MPU side" of the PIA also includes three chip select lines, CS0, CS1, and $\overline{CS2}$, for selecting a particular PIA. Two addressing inputs, RS0, and RS1, are used in conjunction with a control bit within the PIA for selecting specific registers in the PIA. The MPU can read or write into the PIA's internal registers by addressing the PIA via the system Address Bus using these five input lines and the R/W signal. From the MPU's point of view, each PIA is simply four memory locations that are treated in the same manner as any other read/write memory.

The MPU also provides a timing signal to the PIA via the Enable input. The Enable (E) pulse is used to condition the PIA's internal interrupt control circuitry and for the timing of peripheral control signals. Since all data transfers take place during the $\phi2$ portion of the clock cycle, the Enable pulse is normally $\phi2$[4].

The "Peripheral side" of the PIA includes two 8-bit bi-directional data buses (PA0-PA7 and PB0-PB7), and four interrupt/control lines, CA1, CA2, CB1, and CB2. All of the lines on the "Peripheral Side" of the PIA are compatible with standard TTL logic. In addition, all lines serving as outputs on the "B" side of each PIA (PB0-PB7, CB1, CB2) will supply up to one milliamp of drive current at 1.5 volts.

---

[4]See Section 4-1.3 for exceptions required in some applications.

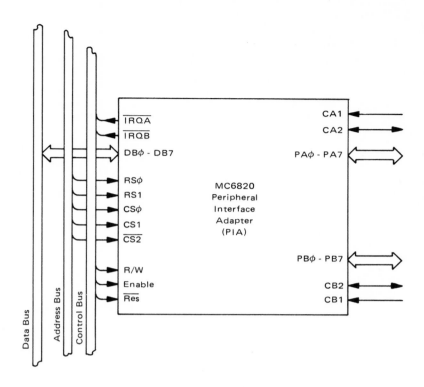

FIGURE 3-4.1.1-1: MC6820 PIA I/O Diagram

3-4.1.2 Internal Organization:

An expanded Block Diagram of the PIA is shown in Figure 3-4.1.2-1. Internally, the PIA is divided into two symmetrical independent register configurations. Each half has three main features: an Output Register, a Control Register, and a Data Direction Register. It is these registers that the MPU treats as memory locations, i.e., they can be either read from or written into. The Output and Data Direction Registers on each side represent a single memory location to the MPU. Selection between them is internal to the PIA and is determined by a bit in their Control Register.

The Data Direction Registers (DDR) are used to establish each individual peripheral bus line as either an input or an output. This is accomplished by having the MPU write "ones" or "zeros" into the eight bit positions of the DDR. Zeros or ones cause the corresponding peripheral data lines to function as inputs or outputs, respectively.

The Output Registers, ORA and ORB, when addressed, store the data present on the MPU Data Bus during an MPU write operation[5]. This data will also appear on those peripheral lines that have been

---

[5] As used here, an "MPU Write" operation refers to the execution of the "Store" instruction, i.e., writing into Output Register A is equivalent to execution of STAA PIAORA by the MPU. Similarly, an "MPU Read" operation is equivalent to execution of the "Load" instruction: LDAA PIAORA.

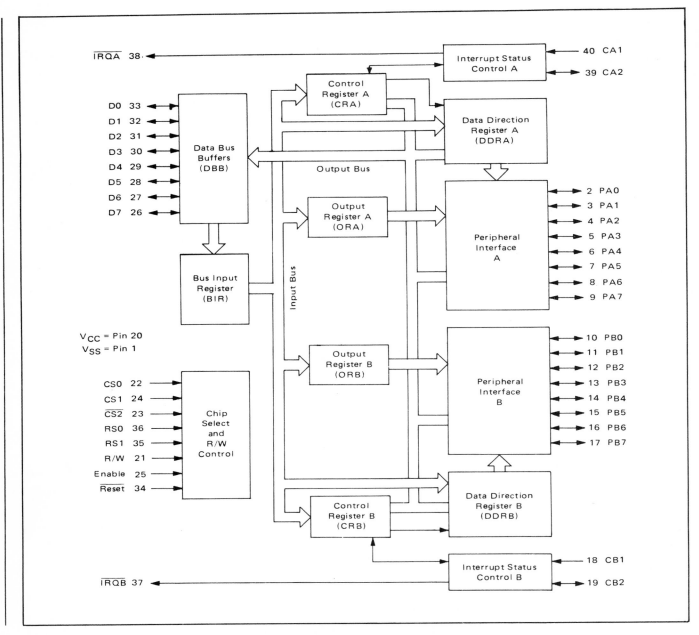

FIGURE 3-4.1.2-1: MC6820 PIA — Block Diagram

programmed as outputs. If a peripheral line has been programmed as an input, the corresponding bit position of the Output Register can still be written into by the MPU, however, the data will be influenced by the external signal applied on that peripheral data line.

During an MPU Read operation, the data present on peripheral lines programmed as inputs is transferred directly to the system Data Bus. Due to differing circuitry, the results of reading positions programmed as outputs differ slightly between sides A and B of the PIA. On the B side, there is three-state buffering between Output Register B and the peripheral lines such that the MPU will read the current contents of ORB for those bit positions programmed as outputs. (See Figure 3-4.1.2-2.) During an MPU Read of the A side, the data present on the Peripheral lines will effect the MPU Data Bus regardless of whether the lines are programmed as outputs or inputs. The bit positions in ORA designated as outputs will be read correctly only if the external loading on the Peripheral lines is within the specification for one TTL load. That is, a logic one level could be read as a logic zero if excessive loading reduced the voltage below 2.0 volts.

The two Control Registers, CRA and CRB, allow the MPU to establish and control the operating modes of the peripheral control lines, CA1, CA2, CB1, and CB2. It is by means of these four lines that control information is passed back and forth between the MPU and peripheral devices. The control word format and a summary of its features is shown in Figure 3-4.1.2-3.

The Data Direction Register access bit (b_2 = DDR Access) is used in conjunction with the register select lines to select between internal registers. For a given register select combination, the status of the DDR bit determines whether the Data Direction Register (b_2 of DDR = 0) or the Output Register (b_2 of DDR = 1) is addressed by the MPU.

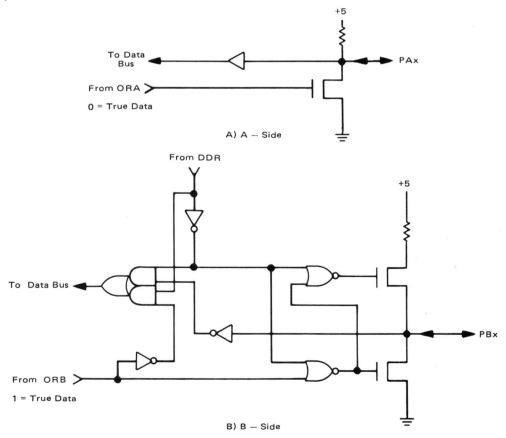

FIGURE 3-4.1.2-2: PIA Output Circuit Configurations

Determine Active CA1 (CB1) Transition for Setting Interrupt Flag IRQA(B)1 — (bit b7)

b1 = 0 : IRQA(B)1 set by high-to-low transition on CA1 (CB1).

b1 = 1 : IRQA(B)1 set by low-to-high transition on CA1 (CB1).

CA1 (CB1) Interrupt Request Enable/Disable

b0 = 0 : Disables IRQA(B) MPU Interrupt by CA1 (CB1) active transition.[1]

b0 = 1 : Enable IRQA(B) MPU Interrupt by CA1 (CB1) active transition.

1. IRQA(B) will occur on next (MPU generated) positive transition of b0 if CA1 (CB1) active transition occurred while interrupt was disabled.

IRQA(B) 1 Interrupt Flag (bit b7)

Goes high on active transition of CA1 (CB1); Automatically cleared by MPU Read of Output Register A(B). May also be cleared by hardware Reset.

---

b7	b6	b5	b4	b3	b2	b1	bφ
IRQA(B)1 Flag	IRQA(B)2 Flag	CA2(CB2) Control			DDR Access	CA1(CB1) Control	

IRQA(B)2 Interrupt Flag (bit b6)

CA2 (CB2) Established as Input (b5 = 0): Goes high on active transition of CA2 (CB2); Automatically cleared by MPU Read of Output Register A(B). May also be cleared by hardware Reset.

CA2 (CB2) Established as Output (b5 = 1): IRQA(B)2 = 0, not affected by CA2 (CB2) transitions.

Determines Whether Data Direction Register Or Output Register is Addressed

b2 = 0 : Data Direction Register selected.

b2 = 1 : Output Register selected.

CA2 (CB2) Established as Output by b5 = 1

b5	b4	b3
1	0	

(Note that operation of CA2 and CB2 output functions are not identical).

► CA2

b3 = 0 :   Read Strobe With CA1 Restore

CA2 goes low on first high-to-low E transition following an MPU Read of Output Register A; returned high by next active CA1 transition.

b3 = 1 :   Read Strobe with E Restore

CA2 goes low on first high-to-low E transition following an MPU Read of Output Register A; returned high by next high-to-low E transition.

► CB2

b3 = 0 :   Write Strobe With CB1 Restore

CB2 goes on low on first low-to-high E transition following an MPU Write into Output Register B; returned high by the next active CB1 transition.

b3 = 1 :   Write Strobe With E Restore

CB2 goes low on first low-to-high E transition following an MPU Write into Output Register B; returned high by the next low-to-high E transition.

b5	b4	b3
1	1	

► Set/Reset CA2 (CB2)

CA2 (CB2) goes low as MPU writes b3 = 0 into Control Register.

CA2 (CB2) goes high as MPU writes b3 = 1 into Control Register.

CA2 (CB2) Established as Input by b5 = 0

b5	b4	b3
0		

► CA2 (CB2) Interrupt Request Enable/Disable

b3 = 0 :   Disables IRQA(B) MPU Interrupt by CA2 (CB2) active transition.[1]

b3 = 1 :   Enables IRQA(B) MPU Interrupt by CA2 (CB2) active transition.

1. IRQA(B) will occur on next (MPU generated) positive transition of b3 if CA2 (CB2) active transition occurred while interrupt was disabled.

► Determines Active CA2 (CB2) Transition for Setting Interrupt Flag IRQA(B)2 — (bit b6)

b4 = 0 :   IRQA(B)2 set by high-to-low transition on CA2 (CB2).

b4 = 1 :   IRQA(B)2 set by low-to-high transition on CA2 (CB2).

FIGURE 3-4.1.2-3: PIA Control Register Format

Each Control Register has two interrupt request flags, b_7 = IRQA(B)1 and b_6 = IRQA(B)2; they are set by transitions on the CA1(CB1) and CA2(CB2) control lines and can be read by an MPU read Control Register operation. The status of the interrupt flags cannot be altered by an MPU write instruction, that is, IRQA(B)1 and IRQA(B)2 are Read Only with respect to the MPU. They are indirectly reset to zero each time the MPU reads the corresponding Output Register or can be cleared with the hardware $\overline{\text{Reset}}$.

Bits b_0 and b_1 of the Control Registers determine the CA1(CB1) operating mode. A "one" written into b_1 by the MPU will cause subsequent positive-going transitions of the CA1(CB1) input to set IRQA(B)1; if $b_1 = 0$, negative-going transitions on CA1(CB1) cause IRQA(B)1 to set. If $b_0 = 1$ when the IRQA(B)1 flag goes high, the PIA's external interrupt request line, IRQA(B), immediately goes low, providing a hardware interrupt signal to the MPU. The external interrupt is disabled if $b_0 = 0$ when the internal interrupt is set by CA1(CB1). If b_0 is later set by an MPU Write Control Register operation, the disable is immediately released and a pending external interrupt request will occur.

When $b_5 = 0$, b_3 and b_4 of the Control Register perform similarly to b_0 and b_1, controlling the $\overline{\text{IRQA(B)}}$2 interrupt via the CA2(CB2) input. The IRQA(B) interrupt terminal, when enabled, responds to either IRQA(B)1 or IRQA(B)2.

If $b_5 = 1$, CA2(CB2) acts as an output and will function in one of three modes. If b_4 is also equal to one, CA2(CB2) serves as a program-controlled set/reset output to the peripheral and follows b_3 as it is changed by MPU Write Control Register operations. If $b_4 = 0$ when $b_5 = 1$, CA2(CB2) can be used in either a pulse-strobed or handshake mode. Operation of the two sections differ slightly for these two operating modes. In the handshake mode ($b_3 = 0$) CA2 is taken low by the negative transition of the MPU Enable Pulse following an MPU Read Output Register operation and returns high when IRQA1 is next set by CA1. This, in effect, tells the peripheral it has been read and allows it to acknowledge via CA1. The "B" Side operation is similar except that CB2 is taken low following an MPU Write Output Register operation and returned high by the next CB1 transition; this tells the peripheral it has been written into and allows it to respond via CB1.

In the pulse-strobed mode ($b_3 = 1$), CA2 is again set low by a Read Output Register command, but is now returned high by the negative transition of the next MPU originated Enable Pulse. CB2 operation is similar except that an MPU Write Operation initiates the pulse. Relative timing waveforms for the strobe control modes are shown in Figures 3-4.1.2-4 and 3-4.1.2-5. The use of A side for Read and B side for Write in those figures is not meant to imply that the A and B sides must be used only for peripheral data in and out, respectively. However, the strobe modes are implemented only as shown, i.e., a strobe is not generated by an A side Write or a B side Read. Strobes can be generated for these cases by including "dummy" instructions in the program. For example, an A side Write instruction can be followed immediately by an A side dummy Read to generate the strobe. Similarly, a B side Read can be followed by a dummy Write.

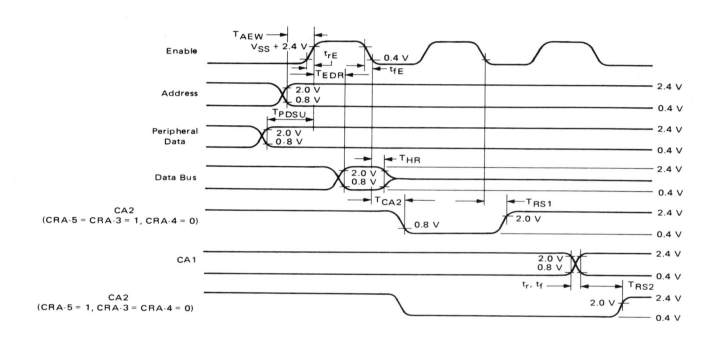

Loading = 30 pF and one TTL load for PA0-PA7, PB0-PB7, CA2, CB2
= 130 pF and one TTL load for D0-D7, IRQA, IRQB)

Characteristic	Symbol	Min	Typ	Max	Unit
Delay Time, Address valid to Enable positive transition	T_{AEW}	180	—	—	ns
Delay Time, Enable positive transition to Data valid on bus	T_{EDR}	—	—	395	ns
Peripheral Data Setup Time	T_{PDSU}	300	—	—	ns
Data Bus Hold Time	T_{HR}	10	—	—	ns
Delay Time, Enable negative transition to CA2 negative transition	T_{CA2}	—	—	1.0	μs
Delay Time, Enable negative transition to CA2 positive transition	T_{RS1}	—	—	1.0	μs
Rise and Fall Time for CA1 and CA2 input signals	t_r, t_f	—	—	1.0	μs
Delay Time from CA1 active transition to CA2 positive transition	T_{RS2}	—	—	2.0	μs
Rise and Fall Time for Enable input	t_{rE}, t_{fE}	—	—	25	ns

FIGURE 3-4.1.2-4: Read Timing Characteristics

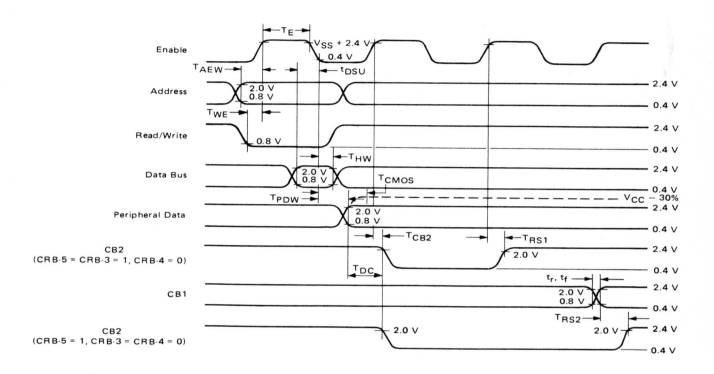

Characteristic	Symbol	Min	Typ	Max	Unit
Enable Pulse Width	T_E	0.470	—	25	μs
Delay Time, Address valid to Enable positive transition	T_{AEW}	180	—	—	ns
Delay Time, Data valid to Enable negative transition	T_{DSU}	300	—	—	ns
Delay Time, Read/Write negative transition to Enable positive transition	T_{WE}	130	—	—	ns
Data Bus Hold Time	T_{HW}	10	—	—	ns
Delay Time, Enable negative transition to Peripheral Data valid	T_{PDW}	—	—	1.0	μs
Delay Time, Enable negative transition to Peripheral Data Valid, CMOS ($V_{CC} - 30\%$) PA0-PA7, CA2	T_{CMOS}	—	—	2.0	μs
Delay Time, Enable positive transition to CB2 negative transition	T_{CB2}	—	—	1.0	μs
Delay Time, Peripheral Data valid to CB2 negative transition	T_{DC}	0	—	1.5	μs
Delay Time, Enable positive transition to CB2 positive transition	T_{RS1}	—	—	1.0	μs
Rise and Fall Time for CB1 and CB2 input signals	t_r, t_f	—	—	1.0	μs
Delay Time, CB1 active transition to CB2 positive transition	T_{RS2}	—	—	2.0	μs

FIGURE 3-4.1.2-5: Write Timing Characteristics

3-4.1.3 **Addressing and Initialization:**

Chapters 6 and 7 of this manual include numerous examples of PIA addressing and initialization, however, some basic considerations are discussed in the following paragraphs. As indicated in Section 3-4.1.1, the MPU addresses the PIA via the five chip select and register select inputs and bit 2 of the Control Registers. The correspondence between internal registers and the address inputs is shown in Figure 3-4.1.3-1.

$\overline{CS2}$	CS1	CSϕ	RS1	RSϕ	b2	
ϕ	1	1	ϕ	ϕ	ϕ	Data Direction Register A (PIADRA)
ϕ	1	1	ϕ	ϕ	1	Output Register A (PIAORA)
ϕ	1	1	ϕ	1	X	Control Register A (PIACRA)
ϕ	1	1	1	ϕ	ϕ	Data Direction Register B (PIADRB)
ϕ	1	1	1	ϕ	1	Output Register B (PIAORB)
ϕ	1	1	1	1	X	Control Register B (PIACRB)
X	X	ϕ	X	X	X	PIA Not Selected
X	ϕ	X	X	X	X	PIA Not Selected
1	X	X	X	X	X	PIA Not Selected

X = Doesn't Matter

FIGURE 3-4.1.3-1: PIA Register Addressing

Addressing a PIA can be illustrated in conjunction with the simple system configuration shown in Figure 3-4.1.3-2[6]. The method shown is typical for assigning mutually exclusive memory addresses to the family devices without using additional address decode logic. The connections shown in Figure 3-4.1.3-2 assign memory addresses as follows:

RAM	0000 – 007F
PIA	4004 – 4007
ACIA	4008 – 4009
ROM	C000 – C3FF

(Hexadecimal notation)

In most cases, the desired I/O configuration and Control Register modes are established as part of an initialization sequence. The steps involved depend on the particular application but can be clarified by means of a specific example.

Assume that a PIA is to be used as the interface between two peripherals. When interrupted by a positive transition on a control line, the MPU is to fetch 8 bits of data from Peripheral #1 and then send an acknowledgement pulse. The MPU must be able to transfer a byte of data to Peripheral #2 and receive acknowledgement that it was accepted. Peripheral #2 must be provided with a control signal indicating that there is data ready for it.

A suitable hardware configuration is shown in Figure 3-4.1.3-3. Peripheral Lines PA0-PA7 are assigned to "read" Peripheral #1 and, hence, must be established as inputs. CA1 provides the interrupt input and must be conditioned to recognize incoming positive transitions. CA2 will be used to signal that data has been read, hence, it must be established as an output using the pulse strobe mode, i.e., reading PIAORA[7] will automatically transmit a pulse to the peripheral.

Peripheral Lines PB0-PB7 are assigned for transmitting data to Peripheral #2 and, hence, must be established as outputs. CB2 will be used as an output for signalling that there is data ready. CB1 will be

---

[6] Figure 3-4.1.3-2 is identical to Figure 1-1.2-1 and is discussed in Section 1-1.2 of Chapter 1.

[7] In order to use symbolic labels instead of absolute addresses in the initialization program, the labels introduced in Figure 3-4.1.3-1 will be used to refer to PIA registers.

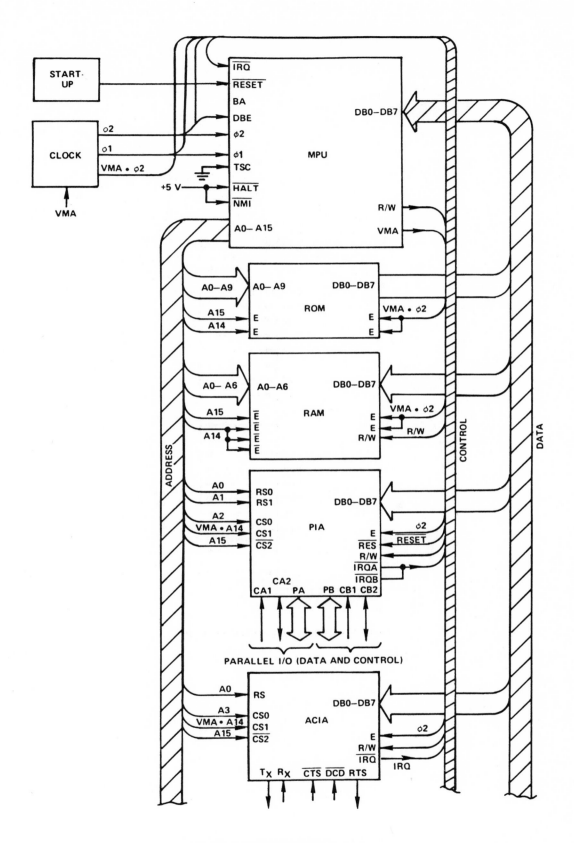

FIGURE 3-4.1.3-2: Family Addressing

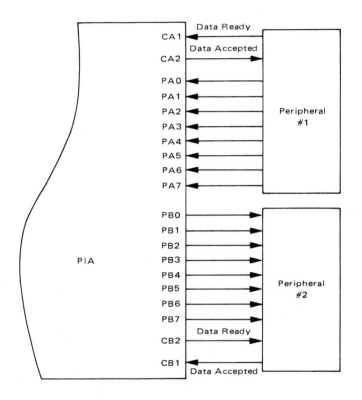

FIGURE 3-4.1.3-3: Typical I/O Configuration

conditioned to accept a negative transition acknowledgement signal from Peripheral #2. CB2 is to be restored by that transition.

If it is known that a hardware system $\overline{\text{Reset}}$ is to be applied prior to initializing, all PIA register bits will be zero initially and the following sequence can be used:

```
10   LDAA   #$2F     SELECT ORA; SET MODE CONTROL
20   STAA   PIACRA     FOR "A" SIDE
30   COM    PIADRB   ESTABLISH PB0-PB7 AS OUTPUTS
40   LDAA   #$24     SELECT ORB; SET MODE CONTROL
50   STAA   PIACRB     FOR "B" SIDE
```

The constant[8] $2F = 00101111$ loaded into the A Control Register by Instruction 20 has the following effect: b0 = 1 enables a CA1 interrupt; b1 = 1 selects positive transition for interrupt recognition; b2 = 1 selects ORA (the initial zeros in DDRA establish PA0-PA7 as inputs); b3 = 1, b4 = 0 selects read strobe with E restore; b5 = 1 establishes CA2 as an output; b6 and b7 are don't cares since MPU cannot write into those two positions:

b7	b6	b5	b4	b3	b2	b1	n0	
0	0	1	0	1	1	1	1	= 2F (Hex)

Instruction 30 writes "ones" into the B Data Direction Register, thus establishing PB0-PB7 as outputs. The constant loaded into the B Control Register by instruction 50 has the following effect: b0 = 0 disables $\overline{\text{IRQB}}$ interrupt by CB1 transition (it is assumed that the MPU will read flag bit b7 to check for acknowledgement rather than allowing an interrupt); b1 = 0 selects recognition of negative transition on CB1 for setting flag bit 7; b2 = 1 selects ORB; b3 = 0, b4 = 1 selects Write strobe with CB1 restore; b5 = 1 establishes CB2 as an output; b6 and b7 are don't cares:

b7	b6	b5	b4	b3	b2	b1	b0	
0	0	1	0	0	1	0	0	= 24 (Hex)

If there is no assurance that the PIA internal register bit positions are initially zero prior to initialization, the following sequence can be used:

```
10   CLRA              SELECT
20   STAA   PIACRA       DATA DIRECTION REGISTER A
30   STAA   PIACRB        AND DATA DIRECTION REGISTER B.
40   STAA   PIADRA     ESTABLISH PA0-PA7 AS INPUTS.
50   LDAA   #$2F       SELECT ORA; SET MODE
60   STAA   PIACRA        CONTROL FOR "A" SIDE.
70   LDAA   #$FF       ESTABLISH
80   STAA   PIADRB        PB0-PB7 AS OUTPUTS.
90   LDAA   #$24       SELECT ORB; SET MODE
100  STAA   PIACRB        CONTROL FOR "B" SIDE.
```

Note that if the initialization sequence is started from a known hardware clear only half as many instructions are required.

---

[8]Refer to Figure 3-4.1.2-3 for derivation of the Control Register words.

3-4.1.4 System Considerations:

The information provided in the preceding paragraphs has been limited to only the more obvious characteristics of the PIA. The features described greatly simplify I/O processing, as will be seen in the examples of later chapters. There are several general techniques worth considering as a system is configured.

The fact that the PIA registers are treated as memory combined with the fact that many of the MPU's instructions (CLR, ASL, COM, TST, etc) operate directly on memory makes possible a variety of I/O techniques. This characteristic should be given careful attention when hardware/software tradeoffs are being considered.

The flexibility inherent in being able to change the I/O direction of individual peripheral lines under program control was not adequately stressed in the initialization discussion. A detailed example making use of this feature to decode a switch matrix is included in Section 5-1.1.1.

Only a simple case of address assignment was considered. Other approaches may lead to a more efficient system. As an example, consider the memory allocation that results from applying A0, and A1 of the address bus to RS0 and RS1, respectively:

RS1 (A1)	RS0 (A0)	
0	0	PIAORA
0	1	PIACRA
1	0	PIAORB
1	1	PIACRB

Here the registers alternate between output and Control[9] Registers. If A0 is connected to RS1 and A1 to RS0, the following result is obtained:

RS1 (A0)	RS0 (A1)	
0	0	PIAORA
1	0	PIAORB
0	1	PIACRA
1	1	PIACRB

Notice that the output registers are now in adjacent memory locations. This configuration can be used to advantage in applications where 16 bits must be brought into memory. With both the A and B sides established as input ports, the LDX and STX instructions can be used to efficiently transfer two bytes at a time. A specific example of this technique is described in Section 5-4. If this allocation is selected, initialization routines such as the first example of Section 3-4.1.3 can also be simplified:

```
10  LDX     #$2F24    ESTABLISH CONTROL MODES
20  STX     PIACRA    FOR BOTH SIDES.
```

In this sequence, the single instruction STX causes the appropriate constant to be loaded into both Control Registers.

---

[9]This assumes that b2 of the Control Registers has been set to select the Output Registers.

3-4.2 MC6850 ASYNCHRONOUS COMMUNICATIONS INTERFACE ADAPTER

3-4.2.1 Input/Output Configuration

The MC6850 Asynchronous Communications Interface Adapter (ACIA) provides a means of efficiently interfacing the MPU to devices requiring an asynchronous serial data format. The ACIA includes features for formatting and controlling such peripherals as Modems, CRT Terminals, and teletype printer/readers. An Input/Output Diagram of the MC6850 is shown in Figure 3-4.2.1-1.

Data flow between the MPU and the ACIA is via 8 bi-directional lines, DB0 through DB7, that interface with the MPU Data Bus. The direction of data flow is controlled by the MPU via the Read/Write input to the ACIA.

The "MPU side" of the ACIA also includes (see Figure 3-4.1.3-2) three chip select lines, CS0, CS1, and $\overline{CS2}$, for addressing a particular ACIA. An additional addressing input, Register Select (RS), is used to select specific registers within the ACIA. The MPU can read or write into the internal registers by addressing the ACIA via the system Address Bus using these four input lines. From the MPU's addressing point of view, each ACIA is simply two memory locations that are treated in the same manner as any other read/write memory.

The MPU also provides a timing signal to the ACIA via the Enable input. The Enable (E) pulse is used to condition the ACIA's internal interrupt control circuitry and for the timing of status/control changes. Since all data transfers take place during the $\phi2$ portion of the clock cycle, $\phi2$ is applied as the E signal.

The "Peripheral side" of the ACIA includes two serial data lines and three control lines. Data is transmitted and received via the Tx Data output and Rx Data inputs, respectively. Control signals Clear-To-Send ($\overline{CTS}$), Data Carrier Detect ($\overline{DCD}$), and Request-To-Send ($\overline{RTS}$) are provided for interfacing with Modems such as the MC6860. Two clock inputs are available for supplying individual data clock rates to the receiver and transmitter portions of the ACIA.

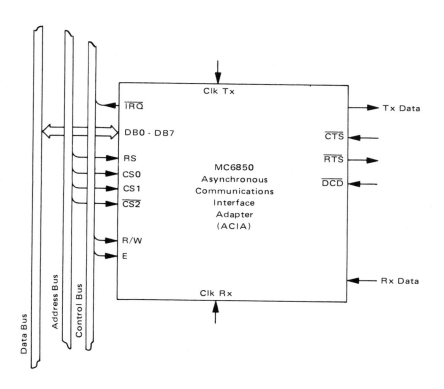

FIGURE 3-4.2.1-1: MC6850 ACIA I/O Diagram

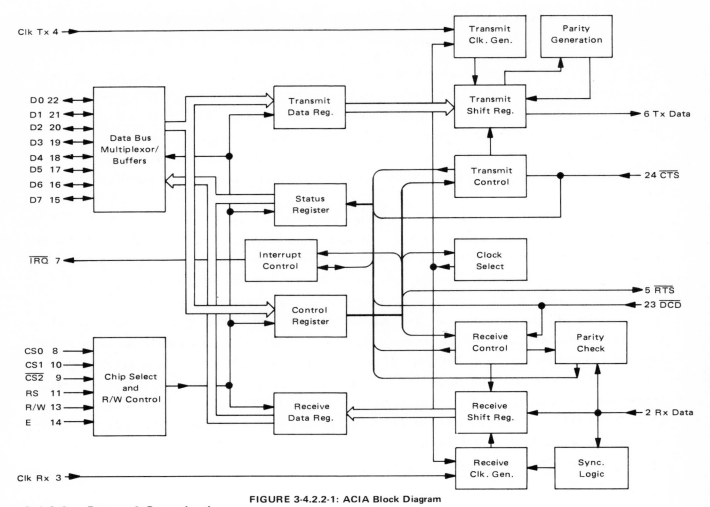

FIGURE 3-4.2.2-1: ACIA Block Diagram

3-4.2.2   **Internal Organization**

An expanded Block Diagram of the ACIA is shown in Figure 3-4.2.2-1. While the ACIA appears to the MPU as two addressable memory locations, internally there are four registers, two that are Write Only and two that are Read Only. The Read Only registers are for status and received data and the Write Only registers are for ACIA control and transmit data.

The Status Register format and a summary of the status bits is shown in Figure 3-4.2.2-2. The first two bits b0 and b1 indicate whether the Receiver Data Register is full (RDRF) or if the Transmit Data Register is empty (TDRE). b0 will go high when Rx data has been transferred to the Receiver Data Register (RDR). b0 will go low on the trailing edge of the Read Data command (reading the Receiver Data Buffer) or by a master reset command from bits b0 and b1 of the Control Register.

Status bit b1 (Tx Data Register Empty) will go high when a transmitter data transfer has taken place indicating that the Transmit Data Register (TDR) is available for new data entry from the MPU Bus. Bit b1 will return low on the trailing edge of a write data command. b1 will be held low if Clear-To-Send is not received from a peripheral device ($\overline{CTS}$ = ''1'')

Status bits b2 (Data Carrier Detect) and b3 (Clear-To-Send) are flag indicators from an external modem. Bit b2 ($\overline{DCD}$) will be high when the received carrier at the modem has been lost (ACIA's $\overline{DCD}$ input is high). Bit b2 will remain high until the interrupt is cleared by reading the Status Register and the Receiver Data Register. Bit b3 ($\overline{CTS}$) is low during reception of a Clear-To-Send command from a modem or other peripheral device.

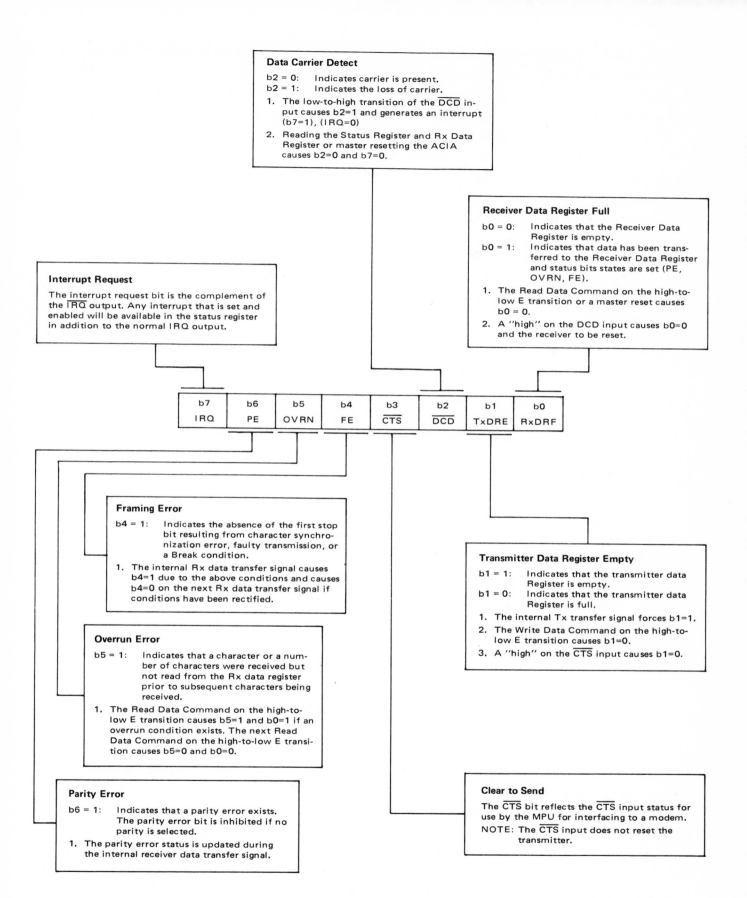

Data Carrier Detect

b2 = 0:   Indicates carrier is present.
b2 = 1:   Indicates the loss of carrier.

1. The low-to-high transition of the $\overline{DCD}$ input causes b2=1 and generates an interrupt (b7=1), (IRQ=0)

2. Reading the Status Register and Rx Data Register or master resetting the ACIA causes b2=0 and b7=0.

Receiver Data Register Full

b0 = 0:   Indicates that the Receiver Data Register is empty.

b0 = 1:   Indicates that data has been transferred to the Receiver Data Register and status bits states are set (PE, OVRN, FE).

1. The Read Data Command on the high-to-low E transition or a master reset causes b0 = 0.

2. A "high" on the DCD input causes b0=0 and the receiver to be reset.

Interrupt Request

The interrupt request bit is the complement of the $\overline{IRQ}$ output. Any interrupt that is set and enabled will be available in the status register in addition to the normal IRQ output.

b7	b6	b5	b4	b3	b2	b1	b0
IRQ	PE	OVRN	FE	$\overline{CTS}$	$\overline{DCD}$	TxDRE	RxDRF

Framing Error

b4 = 1:   Indicates the absence of the first stop bit resulting from character synchronization error, faulty transmission, or a Break condition.

1. The internal Rx data transfer signal causes b4=1 due to the above conditions and causes b4=0 on the next Rx data transfer signal if conditions have been rectified.

Transmitter Data Register Empty

b1 = 1:   Indicates that the transmitter data Register is empty.

b1 = 0:   Indicates that the transmitter data Register is full.

1. The internal Tx transfer signal forces b1=1.

2. The Write Data Command on the high-to-low E transition causes b1=0.

3. A "high" on the $\overline{CTS}$ input causes b1=0.

Overrun Error

b5 = 1:   Indicates that a character or a number of characters were received but not read from the Rx data register prior to subsequent characters being received.

1. The Read Data Command on the high-to-low E transition causes b5=1 and b0=1 if an overrun condition exists. The next Read Data Command on the high-to-low E transition causes b5=0 and b0=0.

Parity Error

b6 = 1:   Indicates that a parity error exists. The parity error bit is inhibited if no parity is selected.

1. The parity error status is updated during the internal receiver data transfer signal.

Clear to Send

The $\overline{CTS}$ bit reflects the $\overline{CTS}$ input status for use by the MPU for interfacing to a modem.

NOTE: The $\overline{CTS}$ input does not reset the transmitter.

FIGURE 3-4.2.2-2: ACIA Status Register Format

Bit b4 (Framing Error) will be high whenever a data character is received with an improper start/stop bit character frame. The framing error flag b4 is cleared by the next data transfer signal if the condition causing the framing error has been rectified. Bit b5 (Receiver Overrun) being high indicates that the Receiver Data Register has not been read prior to a new character being received by the ACIA. This bit is cleared by reading the Receiver Data Register. Status Register bit b6 (Parity Error) is set whenever the number of high ("1's") in the received character does not agree with the preselected odd or even parity. Bit b7 (Interrupt Request) when high indicates the ACIA is requesting interrupt to the MPU via the ACIA $\overline{\text{IRQ}}$ output and may be caused by b0 or b1 or b2 being set. All of the Status Register bits (except b3) will be cleared by an ACIA Master Reset.

The Control Register is an eight bit write only buffer which controls operation of the ACIA receiver, transmitter, interrupt enables, and the modem Request-To-Send control line. The Control Register format and a summary of its features is shown in Figure 3-4.2.2-3.

Control bits b0 and b1 select a Master Reset function for the ACIA when both bits are high and selects different clock divide ratios for the transmitter and receiver sections for the other combinations:

b1 (CDS2)	b0 (CDS1)	Clock Division
0	0	÷ 1
0	1	÷ 16
1	0	÷ 64
1	1	Master Reset

The next 3 control bits, b2, b3, and b4, are provided for character length, parity, and stop bit selection. The encoding format is as follows:

b4 (WS3)	b3 (WS2)	b2 (WS1)	Character Frame
0	0	0	7 Bit + Even Parity + 2 Stop Bits
0	0	1	7 Bit + Odd Parity + 2 Stop Bits
0	1	0	7 Bit + Even Parity + 1 Stop Bit
0	1	1	7 Bit + Odd Parity + 1 Stop Bit
1	0	0	8 Bit + No Parity + 2 Stop Bits
1	0	1	8 Bit + No Parity + 1 Stop Bit
1	1	0	8 Bit + Even Parity + 1 Stop Bit
1	1	1	8 Bit + Odd Parity + 1 Stop Bit

The ACIA transmitter section is controlled by control bits b5 (TC1) and b6 (TC2). The four combinations of these two inputs provide transmission of a break command, Modem Request-To-Send ($\overline{\text{RTS}}$) command, and a transmitter inhibit/enable for the ACIA Interrupt Request output. When both b5 and b6 are low, the Request-To-Send ($\overline{\text{RTS}}$) output will be active low and the transmitter data register empty flag is inhibited to the ACIA's Interrupt Request ($\overline{\text{IRQ}}$) output. If b5 is high and b6 is low the $\overline{\text{RTS}}$ output remains active low but the transmit IRQ input is enabled. To turn off the $\overline{\text{RTS}}$ output b6 should be high and b5 low. This selection also inhibits the transmitter interrupt input to the $\overline{\text{IRQ}}$ output. When both b5 and b6 of the control register are high, Request-To-Send is on ($\overline{\text{RTS}}$) = 0, $\overline{\text{IRQ}}$ is inhibited for the transmitter, and a break is transmitted (a space).

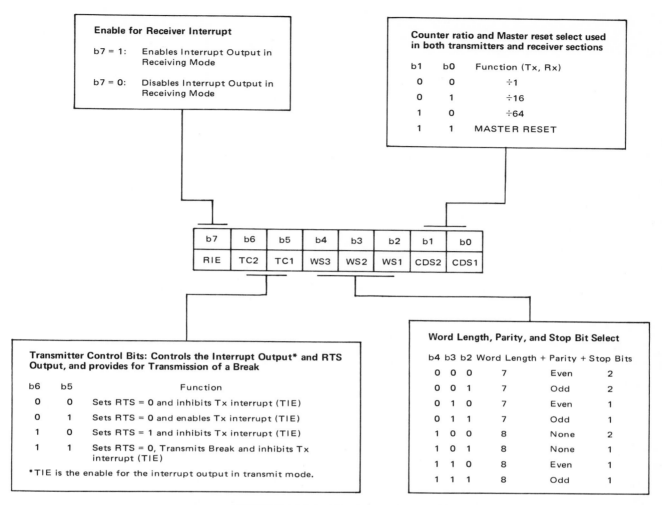

FIGURE 3-4.2.2-3: ACIA Control Register Format

Bits b7 controls the Receiver Interrupt Enable to the $\overline{\text{IRQ}}$ output. When b7 is high $\overline{\text{IRQ}}$ will indicate an interrupt request of the Receiver Data Register is Full (RDRF).

3-4.2.3 Addressing and Initialization

A specific example of ACIA usage is shown by the application described in Section 5-3, however, some basic considerations are discussed in the following paragraphs. As indicated in Section 3-4.1.2, the MPU addresses the ACIA via the chip select and register select inputs from the Address Bus. The correspondence between internal registers and the address inputs is shown in Figure 3-4.2.3-1.

With the chip selects properly enabled and RS = 0, either the Status or Control Register will be selected, depending on the current state of the Read/Write line: R/W = 0 = Write, Control Register is selected;

CS2	CS1	CS0	RS	R/W	
0	1	1	0	0	Control Register
0	1	1	0	1	Status Register
0	1	1	1	0	Transmit Data Register
0	1	1	1	1	Receive Data Register
X	X	0	X	X	ACIA Not Selected
X	0	X	X	X	ACIA Not Selected
1	X	X	X	X	ACIA Not Selected

X = Don't Care

FIGURE 3-4.2.3-1: ACIA Register Addressing

R/W = 1 = Read, Status Register is selected. Similarly, when RS = 1, either the Receive Data Register (R/W = 1 = Read) or the Transmit Data Register (R/W = 0 = Write) is selected.

Addressing the ACIA can be illustrated in conjunction with the simple system configuration shown in Figure 3-4.1.3-2[10]. The method shown is typical for assigning mutually exclusive memory addresses to the family devices without the use of additional decode logic. The connections shown assign memory addresses as follows:

RAM	0000 – 007F
PIA	4004 – 4007
ACIA	4008 – 4009
ROM	C000 – C3FF

(Hexadecimal notation)

As voltage is applied to the ACIA during the power-on sequence, its internal registers are cleared to zero[11] by circuitry within the ACIA to prevent spurious outputs. This initial condition means that interrupts are disabled, IRQ to the MPU is high (no interrupt request), and the Ready-To-Send, $\overline{RTS}$, output is high. The first step in preparation for using the ACIA must be a master reset via bits b0 and b1 of the Control Register, that is, the MPU must write ones into those positions. Once reset, the ACIA operating mode is established by writing the appropriate data into the Control Register.

3-4.2.4 System Considerations

The ACIA is used primarily to transfer serial data between the microprocessor and real time peripheral devices such as teletypes, CRT terminals, etc. The most common data format used for the transfer of real-time data is the asynchronous data format. Use of this format is generally limited to low transmission rates — below 1200 bps or 120 char/sec. For example, the maximum transmission rate of a teletype is 10 char/sec. Here, the transmission of data to the MPU depends on the operator's dexterity of depressing a key on the keyboards. Since the transmission of data is dependent on the operator, gaps (non transmission of data) between data characters occur as a general rule.

In the transmission of asynchronous data, there is no pre-synchronized clock provided along with the data. Also, the gaps between data characters in this transmission mode requires that synchronization be re-established for each character. Therefore, the receiving device must be capable of establishing bit and

---

[10] Figure 3-4.1.3-1 is identical to Figure 1-1.2-1 and is discussed in Section 1-1.2 of Chapter 1.

[11] If external high signals are present on the $\overline{DCD}$ and $\overline{CTS}$ inputs, their respective bits, b2 and b3, in the Status Register will also be high.

character synchronization from the characteristics of the asynchronous format. Each character consists of a specified number of data bits preceded by a start bit and followed by one or more stop bits as shown in Figure 3-4.2.4-1.

These start and stop elements do not contain any information and they actually slow down the effective transmission rate. Since the asynchronous format is used in real time systems, the effect of the start and stop bits on the transmission rate is negligible. The purpose of the start bit is to enable a receiving system to synchronize its clock to this bit for sampling purposes and thereby establish character synchronization. The stop bit is used as a final check on the character synchronization.

Since the MPU processes eight bit parallel bytes that do not include start and stop elements, received serial data in an asynchronous format must be converted to parallel form with the start and stop elements stripped from the character. Likewise, in order to transmit serial data the parallel data byte from the MPU must be converted to serial form with the start and stop elements added to the character. This serial-to-serial/parallel-to-parallel conversion is the primary function of the ACIA.

Desired options such as variable clock divider ratios, variable word length, one or two stop bits, odd or even parity, etc. are established by writing an appropriate constant into the ACIA's Control Register. The combination of options selected depends on the desired format for a particular application. The general characteristics of data flow through the ACIA are described in the following paragraphs.

A typical transmitting sequence consists of reading the ACIA status register either as a result of an interrupt or in the ACIA's turn in a polling sequence. A character may be written into the Transmit Data Register if the status read operation has indicated that the Transmit Data Register is empty. This character is transferred to a shift register where it is serialized and transmitted from the Tx Data output preceded by a start bit and followed by one or two stop bits. Internal parity (odd or even) can be optionally added to the character and will occur between the last data bit and the first stop bit. After the first character is written in the data register, the Status Register can be read again to check for a Transmit Data Register Empty condition and current peripheral status. If the register is empty, another character can be loaded for transmission even though the first character is in the process of being transmitted. This second character will be automatically transferred into the shift register when the first character transmission is completed. The above sequence may be continued until all the characters have been transmitted.

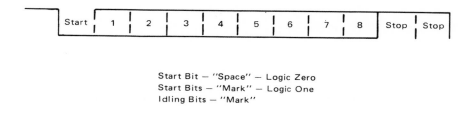

Start Bit — "Space" — Logic Zero
Start Bits — "Mark" — Logic One
Idling Bits — "Mark"

FIGURE 3-4.2.4-1: Asynchronous Data Format

Data is received from a peripheral by means of the Rx Data input. A divide by one clock ratio is provided for an external clock that is synchronized to its data; the divide by 16 and 64 ratios may be used for internal synchronization. Bit synchronization in the divide by 16 and 64 modes is obtained by detecting the leading mark-to-space transition of the start bit. False start bit detection capability insures that a full half bit of a start bit has been received before the internal clock is synchronized to the bit time. As a character is being received, parity (odd or even) will be checked and the possible error indication will be available in the status register along with framing error, overrun error, and receiver data register full. In a typical receiving sequence, the Status Register is read to determine if a character has been received from a peripheral. If the receiver data register is full, the character is placed on the Data Bus when the MPU reads the ACIA Receive Data Register. The status register can be read again to determine if another character is available in the receiver data register. The receiver is also double buffered so that a character can be read from the data register as another character is being received in the shift register. The above sequence may be continued until all characters have been received.

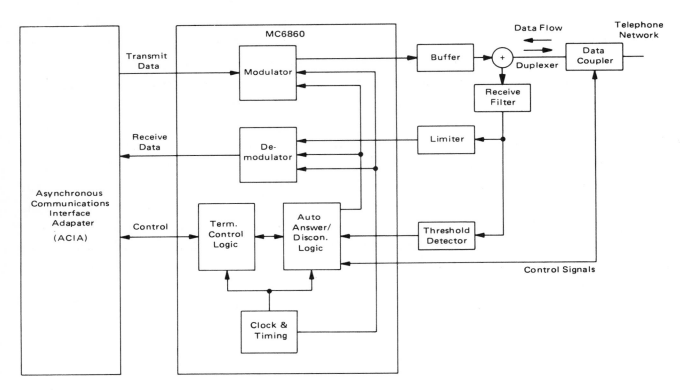

FIGURE 3-4.3.1-1: Typical MC6860 System Configuration

3-4.3   MC6860 LOW SPEED MODEM

3-4.3.1   Input/Output Configuration

The MC6860 Modem provides a very effective method of interfacing a MPU based system, via a MC6850 ACIA, to a telephone network as shown in Figure 3-4.3.1-1. The modem provides full automatic answer/originate and initiate disconnect capability under MPU program control thru the ACIA. Data may be asynchronously sent and received over the telephone network at data rates up to 600 bits per second.

The Input/Output configuration of the MC6860 when used with the MC6850 ACIA and the MC6800 MPU family is shown in Figure 3-4.3.1-2. Data flow from the terminal side of the modem enters in serial digital format via the transmit data line of the modem. It is then digitally processed by the modulator section and exits the telephone network side of the modem via the transmit carrier line. This digitized sinewave FSK signal is post filtered by an output buffer/low pass filter. The filtered analog sinewave passes through a line duplexer to the telephone line via a data coupler.

The returning analog signal from the remote modem at the other end of the telephone line passes through the data coupler and duplexer and is applied to a bandpass filter/amplifier. The receive bandpass filter bandlimits the incoming signal to remove noise and adjacent transmit channel interference. After being bandlimited the analog signal is full limited to a 50% duty cycle TTL level signal by the input limiter. This digital signal is the receive carrier that is applied to the modem. The output signal from the bandpass filter is also routed to a threshold detector to determine if the input signal to the limiter is above the minimum detectable signal level presented to the modem. When the signal input level exceeds the bias point of the threshold detector, the detector's output goes low at the threshold input pin to the MC6860 modem indicating that carrier is present.

A complete listing and functional description of all I/O pins for the MC6860 (Figure 3-4.3.2-1) is provided in the following:

Data Terminal Ready ($\overline{\text{DTR}}$)

The Data Terminal Ready signal must be low before the modem function will be enabled. To initiate a disconnect, $\overline{\text{DTR}}$ is held high for 34 msec minimum. A disconnect will occur 3 seconds later.

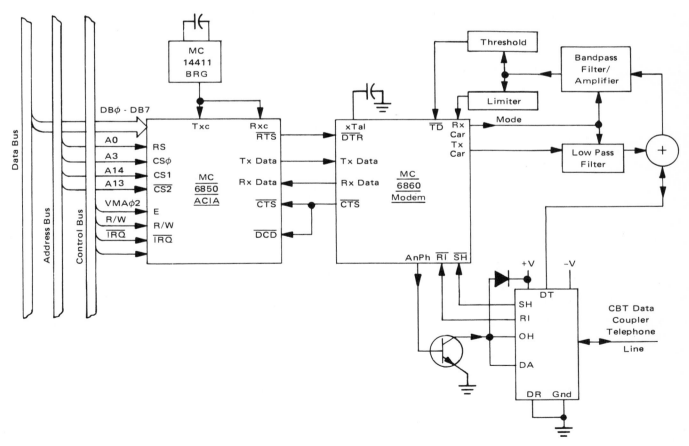

FIGURE 3-4.3.1-2: I/O Configuration For MC6860 Modem

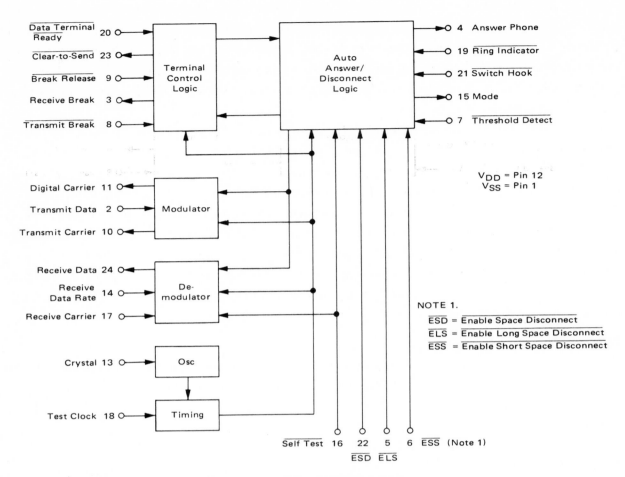

FIGURE 3-4.3-2-1: MC6860 Modem Block Diagram

NOTE 1.
$\overline{ESD}$ = Enable Space Disconnect
$\overline{ELS}$ = Enable Long Space Disconnect
$\overline{ESS}$ = Enable Short Space Disconnect

Clear-To-Send ($\overline{CTS}$)

A low on the $\overline{CTS}$ output indicates the Transmit Data input has been unclamped from a steady Mark, thus allowing data transmission.

Ring Indicator ($\overline{RI}$)

The modem function will recognize a receipt of a call from the CBT if at least 20 cycles of the 20-47 Hz ringing signal are present. The CBS $\overline{RI}$ signal must be level-converted from EIA RS-232 levels before interfacing it with the modem function. The receipt of a call from the CBS is recognized if the $\overline{RI}$ signal is present for at least 51 msec. This input is held high except during ringing. A $\overline{RI}$ signal automatically places the modem function in the Answer Mode.

Switch Hook ($\overline{SH}$)

$\overline{SH}$ interfaces directly with the CBT and via a EIA RS-232 level conversion for the CBS. An $\overline{SH}$ signal automatically places the modem function in the Originate Mode.

$\overline{SH}$ is low during origination of a call. The modem will automatically hang up 17 seconds after the release of $\overline{SH}$ if the handshaking routine between the local and remote modem has not been accomplished.

Threshold Detect ($\overline{\text{TD}}$)

This input is derived from an external threshold detector. If the signal level is sufficient, the $\overline{\text{TD}}$ input must be low for 20μs at least once every 32 msec to maintain normal operation. An insufficient signal level indicates the absence of the Receive Carrier; an absence for greater than 32 msec will not cause channel establishment to be lost; however, data during this interval will be invalid.

Answer Phone (An Ph)

Upon receipt of Ring Indicator or Switch Hook signal and Data Terminal Ready, the Answer Phone output goes high $[(\overline{\text{SH}} + \overline{\text{RI}}) \bullet \overline{\text{DTR}}]$. This signal drives the base of a transistor which activates the Off Hook (OH) and Data Transmission (DA) control lines in the data coupler. Upon call completion, the Answer Phone signal returns to a low level.

Mode

The Mode output indicates the Answer (low) or Originate (high) status of the modem. This output changes state when a Self Test command is applied.

Transmit Break ($\overline{\text{Tx Brk}}$)

The Break command is used to signal the remote modem to stop sending data.

A Transmit Break (low) greater than 34 msec forces the modem to send a continuous space signal for 233 msec. Transmit Break must be initiated only after $\overline{\text{CTS}}$ has been established. This is a negative edge sense input. Prior to initiating $\overline{\text{Tx Brk}}$, this input must be held high for a minimum of 34 msec.

Receive Break (Rx Brk)

Upon receipt of a continuous 150 msec space, the modem automatically clamps the Receive Break output high. This output is also clamped high until Clear-To-Send is established.

Break Release ($\overline{\text{Brk R}}$)

After receiving a 150 msec space signal, the clamped high condition of the Receive Break output can be removed by holding Break Release low for at least 20 μs.

Transmit Data (Tx Data)

Transmit Data is the binary information presented to the modem function for modulation with FSK techniques. A high level represents a Mark.

Receive Data (Rx Data)

The Receive Data output is the data resulting from demodulating the Receive Carrier. A Mark is a high level.

Receive Data Rate (Rx Rate)

The demodulator has been optimized for signal-to-noise performance at 300 bps and 600 bps. The Receive Data Rate input should be low for 0-600 bps and should be high for 0-300 bps.

Digital Carrier (FO)

A test signal output is provided to decrease the chip test time. The signal is a square wave at the transmit frequency.

Transmit Carrier (Tx Car)

The Transmit Carrier is a digitally-synthesized sinewave derived from the 1.0 MHz crystal reference. The frequency characteristics are as follows:

Mode	Data	Transmit Frequency	Accuracy*
Originate	Mark	1270 Hz	−0.15 HZ
Originate	Space	1070 Hz	+0.09 Hz
Answer	Mark	2225 Hz	−0.31 Hz
Answer	Space	2025 Hz	−0.71 Hz

*The reference frequency tolerance is not included.

The proper output frequency is transmitted within the 3.0 μs following a data bit change with no more than 2.0 μs phase discontinuity. The typical output level is 0.35 V (RMS) into a 200 k-ohm load impedance.

The second harmonic is typically 32 dB below the fundamental.

Receive Carrier (Rx Car)

The Receive Carrier is the FSK input to the demodulator. The local Transmit Carrier must be balanced or filtered out prior to this input, leaving only the Receive Carrier in the signal. The Receive Carrier must also be hard limited. Any half-cycle period greater than or equal to 429 ± 1.0 μs for the low band or 235 ± 1.0 μs for the high band is detected as a space.

Enabled Space Disconnect ($\overline{\text{ESD}}$)

When $\overline{\text{ESD}}$ is strapped low and $\overline{\text{DTR}}$ is pulsed to initiate a disconnect, the modem transmits a space for either 3 seconds or until a loss of threshold is detected, whichever occurs first. If $\overline{\text{ESD}}$ is strapped high, data instead of a space is transmitted. A disconnect occurs at the end of 3 seconds.

Enable Short Space Disconnect ($\overline{\text{ESS}}$)

$\overline{\text{ESS}}$ is a strapping option which, when low, will automatically hang up the phone upon receipt of a continuous space for 0.3 seconds. *$\overline{\text{ESS}}$ and $\overline{\text{ELS}}$ must not be simultaneously strapped low*.

Enable Long Space Disconnect ($\overline{\text{ELS}}$)

ELS is a strapping option which, when low, will automatically hang up the phone upon receipt of a continuous space for 1.5 seconds.

Crystal (Xtal)

A 1.0-MHz crystal with the following parameters is required to utilize the on-chip oscillator. A 1.0-MHz square wave can also be fed into this input to satisfy the clock requirement.

Mode:	Parallel
Frequency:	1.0 MHz ±0.1%
Series Resistance:	750 ohms max
Shunt Capacitance:	7.0 pF max
Temperature:	0-70°C
Test Level:	1.0 mW
Load Capacitance:	13 pF

When utilizing the 1.0-MHz crystal, external parasitic capacitance, including crystal shunt capacitance, must be ≤9 pF at the crystal input.

Test Clock ($\overline{\text{TST}}$)

A test signal input is provided to decrease the test time of the chip. In normal operation this input *must be strapped low*.

Self Test ($\overline{\text{ST}}$)

When a low voltage level is placed on this input, the demodulator is switched to the modulator frequency and demodulates the transmitted FSK signal. Channel establishment, which occurred during the initial handshake, is not lost during self test. The Mode Control output changes state during $\overline{\text{Self Test}}$, permitting the receive filters to pass the local Transmit Carrier.

INPUTS			OUTPUT
ST	SH	RI	Mode
H	L	H	H
H	H	L	L
L	L	H	L
L	H	L	H

MODE CONTROL TRUTH TABLE

3-4.3.2 Internal Organization

The MC6860 Modem may be broken down into internal functional sections as shown in Figure 3-4.3.2-1. The terminal control logic and auto answer/disconnect logic sections are referred to as the supervisory control section. This section contains digital counters which provide the required time out intervals and necessary control gating logic. This provides logic outputs Clear-To-Send and Answer Phone from inputs Ring Indicator, Switch Hook, and Data Terminal Ready. Also the control section has some local strapping options available on pins 5, 6, and 22. These options provide time outs for line hang-up or termination of the data communication channel.

The oscillator/timing blocks accept a 1.0 MHz clock into pin 13 either from an external clock source or by connecting a 1.0 MHz crystal between pin 13 and ground. A test clock input is provided to allow more rapid testing of the MC6860 timing chains used for various timeouts. This input must be strapped low during normal operation.

The modulator section takes the input digital data and converts it to one of two FSK tones for transmission over the telephone network. There are two tones for transmission and two tones used for reception during full depulx operation. During data transmission from the call origination modem the transmit tones are: 1270 Hz for a Mark and 1070 Hz for a Space. This originating modem will receive two frequencies in the high band which are: 2225 Hz for a Mark and 2025 Hz for a space. If the local modem answers the data call it will transmit in the high band 2225/2025 Hz and receive in the low band 1270/1070 Hz. The modulator section generates these frequencies digitally by synthesizing a sinewave with an 8 step D to A available on pin 10 and a digital square wave output at the above frequencies available on pin 11.

The demodulator accepts a 50% duty cycle TTL level square wave derived from amplifying, filtering, and limiting the incoming line FSK analog signal. The binary data is recovered from the FSK signal by detecting when the signal has a zero crossing and digitally using post detection techniques to discriminate between the two incoming mark/space tones. A receive data rate input (pin 14) is used to optimize the post detection filter at either 300 or 600 bits per second.

3-4.3.3 Handshaking and Control

The supervisory control section of the modem can function in four different modes. Two are associated with data communication channel initialization (Answer Mode and Originate Mode) and two are for channel termination or hang-up (Automatic Disconnect and Initiate Disconnect).

Answer Mode

Automatic answering is first initiated by a receipt of a Ring Indicator ($\overline{\text{RI}}$) signal. This can be either a low level for at least 51 msec as would come from a CBS data coupler, or at least 20 cycles of a 20-47 Hz ringing signal as would come from a CBT data coupler. The presence of the Ring Indicator signal places the modem in the Answer Mode; if the Data Terminal Ready line is low, indicating the communication terminal is ready to send or receive data, the Answer Phone output goes high. This output is designed to drive a transistor switch which will activate the Off Hook (OH) and Data Transmission (DA) relays in the data coupler. Upon answering the phone the 2225-Hz transmit carrier is turned on.

The originate modem at the other end detects this 2225-Hz signal and after a 450 msec delay (used to disable any echo suppressors in the telephone network) transmits a 1270-Hz signal which the local answering modem detects provided the amplitude and frequency requirements are met. The amplitude threshold is set external to the modem chip. If the signal level is sufficient the $\overline{\text{TD}}$ input should be low for 20 μs at least once every 32 msec. The absence of a threshold indication for a period greater than 51 msec denotes the loss of Receive Carrier and the modem begins hang-up procedures. Hang-up will occur 17 seconds after $\overline{\text{RI}}$ has been released provided the handshaking routine is not re-established. The frequency tolerance during handshaking is ± 100 Hz from the Mark frequency.

After the 1270-Hz signal has been received for 150 msec, the Receive Data is unclamped from a Mark condition and data can be received. The Clear-To-Send output goes low 450 msec after the receipt of carrier and data presented to the answer modem is transmitted.

Automatic Disconnect

Upon receipt of a space of 150 msec or greater duration, the modem clamps the Receive Break high. This condition exists until a Break Release command is issued at the receiving station. Upon receipt of a 0.3 second space, with Enable Short Space Disconnect at the most negative voltage (low), the modem automatically hangs up. If Enable Long Space Disconnect is low, the modem requires 1.5 seconds of continuous space to hang up.

Originate Mode

Upon receipt of a Switch Hook ($\overline{\text{SH}}$) command the modem function is placed in the Originate Mode. If the Data Terminal Ready input is enabled (low) the modem will provide a logic high output at Answer Phone. The modem is now ready to receive the 2225-Hz signal from the remote answering modem. It will continue to look for this signal until 17 seconds after SH has been released. Disconnect occurs if the handshaking routine is not established.

Upon receiving 2225 ± 100 Hz for 150 msec at an acceptable amplitude, the Receive Data output is unclamped from a Mark condition and data reception can be accomplished. 450 msec after receiving a 2225-Hz signal, a 1270-Hz signal is transmitted to the remote modem. 750 msec after receiving the 2225-Hz signal, the Clear-To-Send output is taken low and data can now be transmitted as well as received.

Initiate Disconnect

In order to command the remote modem to automatically hang up, a disconnect signal is sent by the local modem. This is accomplished by pulsing the normally low Data Terminal Ready into a high state for greater than 34 msec. The local modem then sends a 3 second continuous space and hangs up provided the Enable Space Disconnect is low. If the remote modem hangs up before 3 seconds, loss of Threshold Detect will cause loss of Clear-To-Send, which marks the line in Answer Mode and turns the carrier off in the Originate Mode.

If $\overline{ESD}$ is high the modem will transmit data until hang-up occurs 3 seconds later. Transmit Break is clamped 150 msec following the Data Terminal Ready interrupt.

Each of the four above operational modes are shown in Figures 3-4.3.3-1 through 3-4.3.3-4.

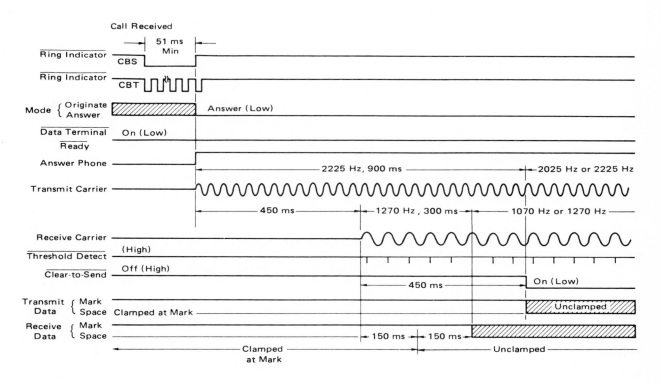

FIGURE 3-4.3.3-1: Answer Mode

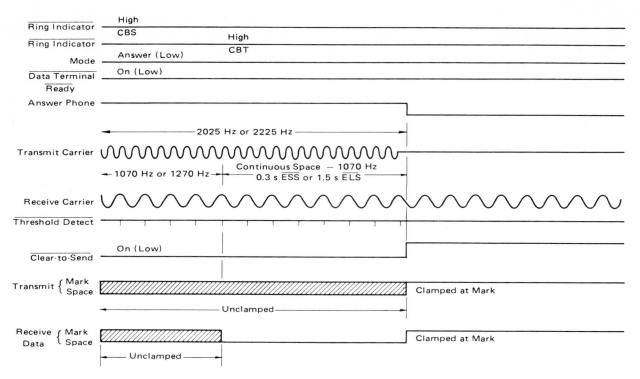

FIGURE 3-4.3.3-2: Automatic Disconnect - Long or Short Space

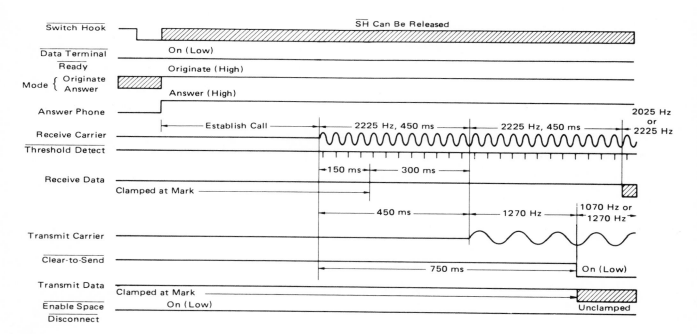

FIGURE 3-4.3.3-3: Originate Mode

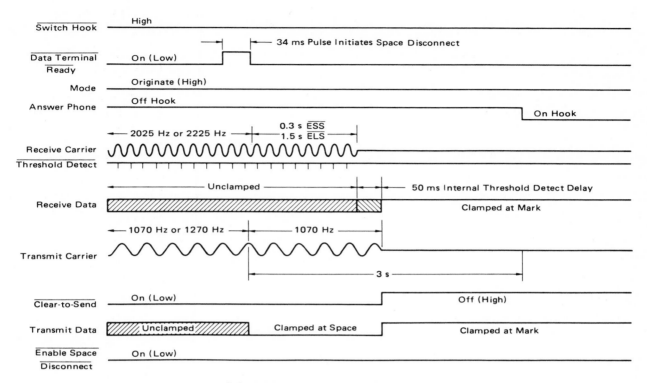

FIGURE 3-4.3.3-4: Initiate Disconnect

The term Direct Memory Access (DMA) is applied to a variety of techniques for speeding up overall system operation by loading and unloading memory faster than can be done using an MPU control program. DMA is often described as a means of allowing fast peripherals (perhaps another Microprocessor), to access the system memory without "bothering" the MPU. However, most DMA procedures do interfere with normal operation to some extent. The capability for handling the various techniques is an often used figure of merit for evaluating Microprocessors.

The MC6800's supervisory control features permit any of three commonly used DMA techniques to be used; (1) Transfer data with MPU halted; (2) Transfer data on burst basis (cycle stealing) with MPU running; (3) Transfer data synchronously with MPU running. Methods for implementing each of these techniques are described in Section 4-2.2 therefore, only qualitative descriptions are included here.

The simplest procedure for DMA merely uses the $\overline{\text{Halt}}$ control to shut the MPU down while the DMA takes place. In the Halt state, the MC6800 effectively removes itself from the Address and Data Buses by putting all buffers in the high impedence off state. This method has the disadvantage that it can take a relatively long time for the MPU to "vacate" the buses. The MC6800 is designed to finish executing its current instruction before entering the Halt or Wait state; the resulting delay depends on which instruction is being executed and may be as much as 13 machine (clock) cycles. However, due to its simplicity this is the preferred method if the delay can be tolerated and long transfers are required.

In contrast to this, the Three-State Control (TSC) may be used to obtain DMA control within 500 nanoseconds of initiation but must be used only for short transfers. Activation of TSC puts the MPU's buffers in the high impedence off state. This technique has the disadvantage that activation of TSC should be synchronized with the $\phi1$ clock and both clocks must be "frozen" ($\phi1$ high, $\phi2$ low) for the duration of the DMA. Due to the MPU's address and R/W refresh requirements, the clocks can only be frozen for a maximum of 5 microseconds, thus limiting the duration of the transfer.

A third method can be used that is completely transparent to the MPU. This technique takes advantage of the fact that MPU data transfers take place only during $\phi2$ of the clock cycle. If the DMA control signals are properly synchronized and the memory is fast enough, DMA can be accomplished during $\phi1$ of each clock cycle.

Each of these three methods is described in greater detail in Section 4-2.2. It should be noted that the faster methods impose additional external hardware requirements on the system.

The techniques described above of course do not exhaust all methods for performing DMA. As an additional example, DMA can be program controlled in the sense that a control program and hence the MPU can be used to establish the memory area to be used and to grant permission for the DMA. In this case the DMA circuitry is treated as another peripheral from which status and control signals can be passed through a PIA. This technique is also outlined in Section 4-2.2.

CHAPTER 4

4   M6800 FAMILY HARDWARE CHARACTERISTICS

There are four classes of control signals which control the execution of the MC6800 MPU. The first pair of control signals is the two phase clock $\phi 1$ and $\phi 2$ which time the entire MPU system. The second pair of signals, $\overline{\text{HALT}}$ and Bus Available (BA), are used to stop program execution and free up the Address and Data Bus for other uses such as a DMA channel. The interrupt signals make the MPU responsive to outside control and are listed in decreasing order of priority: $\overline{\text{RESET}}$, Non-Maskable Interrupt $\overline{(\text{NMI})}$ and Maskable Interrupt $\overline{(\text{IRQ})}$. The Three-State Control (TSC) and Data Bus Enable (DBE) control lines provide a way to momentarily remove the MPU from the busses and can be used for implementing a burst type DMA channel.

4-1   CLOCK CIRCUITRY FOR THE MC6800 MPU

4-1.1   Clock Requirements and Circuitry

Figure 4-1.1-1 is a summary of the MC6800 Microprocessor clock waveform requirements. The $\phi 1$ and $\phi 2$ clock inputs require complementary 5 volt non-overlapping clocks. The clock inputs of the MPU appear primarily capacitive being 110 pf typical and 160 pf maximum plus 100 μa of leakage. Provision is made in the specification for the undershoot and overshoot that will result from the generation of a high speed transistion into a capacitive load.

The clock specifications which constrain the clock driver the most are the rise and fall times required to meet the pulse widths at the maximum operating frequency of 1 MHz, the non-overlapping requirement, and the logic level requirements of Vss + 0.3 volts and Vcc −0.3 volts. The clock buffer circuit that drives the MPU clock inputs must be designed to meet the rise and fall time requirements as well as the logic level requirements. The non-overlapping requirement of the clock signals can be met by the design of the control logic which drives the buffers. A clock buffer, the MPQ6842*, will guarantee the clock designer the speed and saturation voltages necessary to design the clock circuit to meet the MPU clock requirements. Relevant specifications of the MPQ6842 for this design are detailed in Figure 4-1.1-2. Note that the VcE (SAT)'s, rise and fall times are specified to meet this clock driver requirement.

Figure 4-1.1-3 is a circuit designed with TTL logic devices and the MPQ6842 buffer to meet the MPU clock requirements while operating from a single +5 volt supply. The oscillator can be any source with a maximum frequency of 1 MHz, TTL logic levels and 50% duty cycle. This oscillator signal source could vary from a commercial oscillator such as a K1100A available from Motorola's Component Product Department,[1] to a signal derived from a higher frequency signal already available in the system. The TTL gates shown are standard MC3000 and MC3001 (74H00 and 74H08) which were chosen for their speed and drive characteristics. The discrete buffers require good "1" level pullup and drive capability which is provided by the MC3001. The circuit was constructed on a wire wrap board and tested on an EXORciser.[2] Good power and ground distribution practice was followed but no special care was taken in parts layout.

---

[1]2553 N. Edgington, Franklin Park, Illinois 60131, 312-451-1000
[2]A system prototyping tool for the M6800 Microprocessor family.

*To be introduced first quarter 1975.

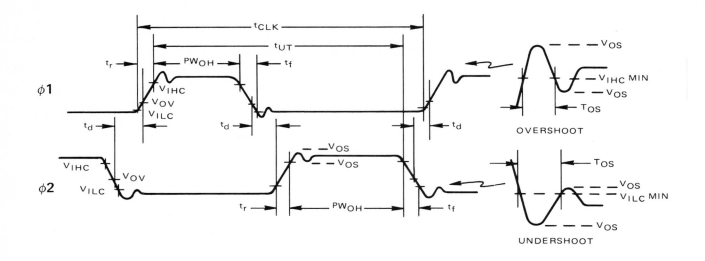

CHARACTERISTIC	SYMBOL	MIN	TYP	MAX	UNITS
Input High Voltage $\phi 1$, $\phi 2$	V_{IHC}	V_{CC}-0.3	—	V_{CC} + 0.1	V_{dc}
Input Low Voltage $\phi 1$, $\phi 2$	V_{ILC}	V_{SS}-0.1	—	V_{SS} + 0.3	V_{dc}
Clock Overshoot/Undershoot	V_{OS}				V_{dc}
Input High Voltage		V_{CC}-0.5		V_{CC} + 0.5	V_{dc}
Input Low Voltage		V_{SS}-0.5		V_{SS} + 0.5	
Input Leakage Current $\phi 1$, $\phi 2$					
(V_{IN} = 0 to 5.25 V, V_{CC} = MAX)	I_{IN}	—	—	100	μa
Capacitance					
(V_{IN} = 0, T_A = 25°C, f = 1.0MHz)	C_{IN}	80	120	160	pf
Frequency of Operation	f	0.1	—	1.0	MHz
Clock Timing					
Cycle Time	t_{cyc}	1.0	—	10	μs
Clock Pulse Width					
(Measured at V_{CC}-0.3 V) $\phi 1$	PW_{OH}	430	—	4500	ns
$\phi 2$		450	—	4500	ns
Rise and Fall Times $\phi 1$, $\phi 2$ (Measured between V_{SS} + 0.3 V and V_{CC}-0.3 V)	t_r, t_f	5	—	50	ns
Delay Time or Clock Overlap (Measured at V_{OV} = V_{SS} + 0.5 V)	t_d	0	—	9100	ns
Overshoot/Undershoot Duration	t_{OS}	0	—	40	ns
Clock High Times	t_{UT}	940	—	—	ns

FIGURE 4-1.1-1 MPU Clock Waveform Specifications

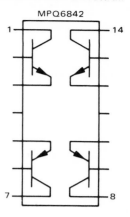

DEVICE CHARACTERISTICS: T = 25°C, V_{CC} = 5.00 VDC

Characteristic	Symbol	Measurement Levels	Min	Typ	Max	Units
Propagation Delay	T_{PD}	50% Points TP1 to TP3 50% Points TP2 to TP4	— —	5 5	15 15	nsec nsec
Rise Time	t_r	0.3 V to 4.7 V TP3 and TP4	5	20	25	nsec
Fall Time	t_f	4.7 V to 0.3 V TP3 and TP4	5	15	25	nsec
Collector-Emitter Saturation Voltage	$V_{CE(sat)}$	I_C = 0.5 ma, I_B = 0.05 ma T = 0°C to 70°C	—	0.10	0.15	VDC

TEST CIRCUIT

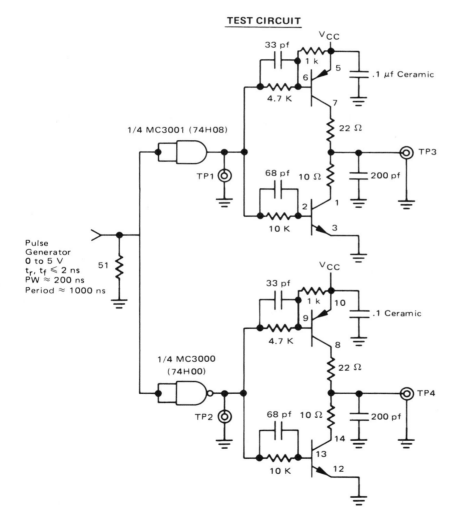

NOTES:
1. Unless otherwise noted, all resistors carbon composition ¼ W ±5%, all capacitors dipped mica ±2%.
2. Use short interconnect wiring with good power and ground busses.
3. TP1→TP4 are coaxial connectors to accept scope probe tip and provide a good ground.
4. Device under test is MPQ6842.
5. 200 pf load includes strays plus scope probe capacitance.

FIGURE 4-1.1-2. MPQ6842 Clock Buffer

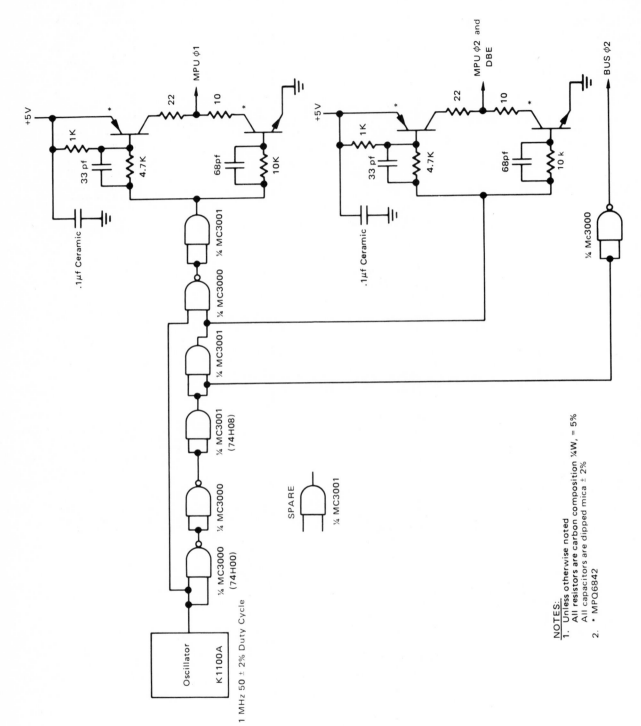

FIGURE 4-1.1-3 MPU Clock Circuit

NOTES:
1. Unless otherwise noted
   All resistors are carbon composition ¼W, = 5%
   All capacitors are dipped mica ± 2%
2. * MPQ6842

4-4

Waveforms typical of the circuit in Figure 4-1.1-3 at T =20°C and V_{CC} = 5.00 volts are shown in Figure 4-1.1-4. Figure 4a and 4b depict the logic levels and pulse widths achieved by this circuitry with V_{CC} and GND as reference levels. Figure 4c superimposes the two clock waveforms so that their phase relationship can be seen. Figure 4d shows the phase relationship of BUS $\phi2$ and MPU $\phi2$. Figures 4e and 4f examine the non-overlap regions as well as rise and fall times typical of this clock drive circuit. Table 4-1.1-1 presents test data taken over a voltage range of 4.75 volts to 5.25 volts and over a temperature range of 0°C to 70°C. Note the stability of these measured parameters and that the logic levels achieved will provide noise margin on the system clocks. Both $\phi1$ and $\phi2$ clock high times were designed to be about 20 ns wider than the minimum required by the MPU ($\phi1$ − 430 ns, $\phi2$ − 450 ns) to provide system margin. Rise and fall times were minimized to provide maximum clock high times consistent with non-critical circuit layout considerations. The overlap margin shown easily meets the MPU requirement of 0 ns at 0.5 volts but will decrease as the capacitive loading increases. The MPU tested for this data had a clock input capacitance on the order of the 110 pf typical value.

Test Conditions	MPU $\phi1$					MPU $\phi2$					Non-Overlap Region	
	PW	RT	FT	"1" LL*	"0" LL*	PW	RT	FT	"1" LL*	"0" LL*	$\phi1\downarrow$ to $\phi2\uparrow$	$\phi2\downarrow$ to $\phi1\uparrow$
T = 20°C												
V_{CC} = 4.75 V	460 ns	15 ns	10 ns	4.75 V	0.1 V	465 ns	15 ns	10.5 ns	4.75 V	0 V	10.5 ns	12 ns
V_{CC} = 5.00 V	460	16	11	5.00	0.1	465	16	10	5.00	0	10	11
V_{CC} = 5.25 V	460	16	11	5.25	0.1	465	16	11	5.25	0	9.5	10.5
V_{CC} = 5.00 V, C_L = 210 pf	450	21	15.5	5.00	0.1	460	22	15	5.00	0	2	5.5
T = 70°C												
V_{CC} = 4.75 V	460	15	12	4.75	0.1	465	16	12	4.75	0	9	10.5
V_{CC} = 5.00 V	460	16	12	5.00	0.1	465	16	12	4.75	0	8.5	10
V_{CC} = 5.25 V	455	17	12.5	5.25	0.1	465	17	13	5.25	0	8	9
T = 0°C												
V_{CC} = 4.75 V	460	14	10	4.75	0.1	465	15	10.5	4.75	0	11	12
V_{CC} = 5.00 V	460	15	10	5.00	0.1	465	15	10	5.00	0	10.5	11.5
V_{CC} = 5.25 V	460	15	10.5	5.25	0.1	465	15	10	5.25	0	10	10.5

*Resolution of this measurement ≈ ±50 mv

LEGEND:

PW:	Pulse width measured at V_{CC} − 0.3 V
RT:	Rise time measured from 0.3 V to V_{CC} − 0.3 V
FT:	Fall time measured from V_{CC} − 0.3 V to 0.3 V
"0" LL:	Zero logic level
"1" LL:	One logic level
Non-Overlap:	Measured from 0.5 volt levels

TABLE 4-1.1-1. Performance of Circuit in Figure 4-1.1-3

In many systems, especially in the breadboard and evaluation stage, it may be desirable to have the flexibility to vary the system clock to test the effects on data throughput, real time operation with interrupts or to help diagnose a system timing problem. In these applications, or in those not requiring crystal oscillator stability, an even simpler clock circuit can be used. A pair of cross coupled monostable multivibrators with individual pulse width adjustments can be used as the clock oscillator with the previously described clock driver. This approach is shown in Figure 4-1.1-5. The non-overlapping clock is generated by the propagation delays through the monostable multivibrators. Figure 4-1.1-6 shows waveforms resulting from this circuit. Table 4-1.1-2 shows test data taken of this circuit over the voltage and temperature range driving a typical MPU (C_L ≈ 110 pf). Note the small variations in the pulse widths.

Test Conditions	MPU φ1					MPU φ2					Non-Overlap Region	
	PW	RT	FT	"1" LL*	"0" LL*	PW	RT	FT	"1" LL*	"0" LL*	φ1↓ to φ2↑	φ2↓ to φ1↑
T = 20°C												
V_CC = 4.75 V	470 ns	11 ns	11.5 ns	4.75 V	0.1 V	450 ns	12 ns	12 ns	4.75 V	0 V	12 ns	11 ns
V_CC = 5.00 V	470	12.5	13	5.00	0.1	460	13	12.5	5.00	0	11	9.5
V_CC = 5.25 V	470	13	12	5.25	0.1	460	13.5	12.5	5.25	0	10	9
T = 70°C												
V_CC = 4.75 V	455	12.5	13.5	4.75	0.1	450	13	13	4.75	0	11	10
V_CC = 5.00 V	455	13	14	5.00	0.1	450	14	14	5.00	0	10	9
V_CC = 5.25 V	455	13	14.5	5.25	0.1	450	14	14	5.25	0	8.5	7
T = 0°C												
V_CC = 4.75 V	473	12	12	4.75	0.1	470	12	12	4.75	0	11	11
V_CC = 5.00 V	475	12	12	5.00	0.1	470	12.5	12	5.00	0	9	11
V_CC = 5.25 V	475	12.5	12.5	5.25	0.05	473	12.5	12	5.25	0	9	8

*Resolution of this measurement ≈ ±50 mv

LEGEND:

PW: Pulse width measured at $V_{CC} - 0.3$ V

RT: Rise time measured from 0.3 V to $V_{CC} - 0.3$ V

FT: Fall time measured from $V_{CC} - 0.3$ V to 0.3 V

"0" LL: Zero logic level

"1" LL: One logic level

Non-Overlap: Measured from 0.5 volt points

TABLE 4-1.1-2. Performance of Circuit in Figure 4-1.1-5

The fast rise and fall times produced by this circuitry and the highly capacitive loads require some care in layout to avoid excessive ringing and/or pulse distortion. While no particular care was taken in the construction of the wirewrap test boards other than placing all of the discretes into one header board, the following construction guidelines are recommended. Wide power and ground lines (50-100 mils) should be used to provide low impedance voltage and ground sources. The clock driver should be physically located as near the MPU as possible to avoid ringing down long lines. Close proximity of the clock circuitry to the MPU allows common power and ground connections so that any noise appears common mode rather than differential to the MPU and clock driver. Finally, it is recommended that the MPU φ2 clock signal not be used to clock any device other than the MPU so that it is not distributed all over the system with the possibility of picking up noise and causing reflections. The circuits shown in this section provide an additional buffer for the other φ2 loads in the system to isolate MPU φ2 from all the other φ2 loads.

For further discussion on clock generators for the MC6800 including interface with dynamic and slow memories, the reader is referred to Section 4-2.5.1.

4-1.1.2 Clock Module

A hybrid clock module is being developed by the Communications Division of Motorola[1] for the M6800 Microprocessor family. This module is composed of a crystal oscillator and associated buffering circuitry to provide either 1 MHz or user specified frequency operation of the M6800 family. Provision is made within this module for cycle stealing in order to interface with dynamic memory (see Section 4-2.5.1) or implement a DMA channel (see Section 4-2.2.2). The module is designed to provide a MEMORY READY

[1]Component Products, 2553 N. Edgington St., Franklin Park, Illinois 60131, 312-625-0020

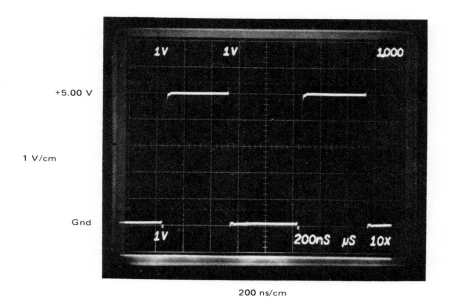

200 ns/cm

FIGURE 4-1.1-4a MPU ϕ1 Clock

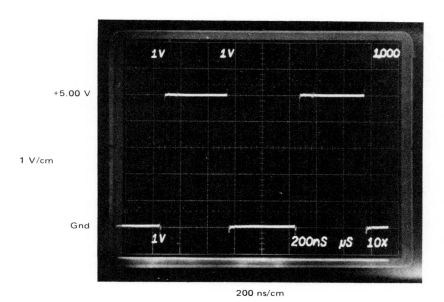

200 ns/cm

FIGURE 4-1.1-4b. MPU ϕ2 Clock

φ1   φ2

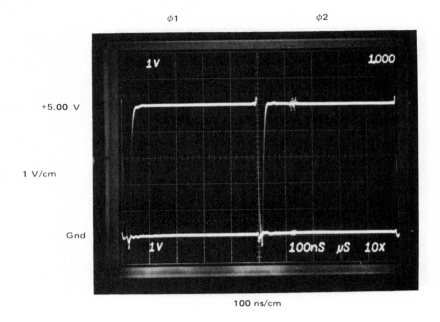

100 ns/cm

FIGURE 4-1.1-4c. MPU φ1 and φ2 Clocks

Bus φ2: 4V Pulse   MPU φ2: 5 V Pulse

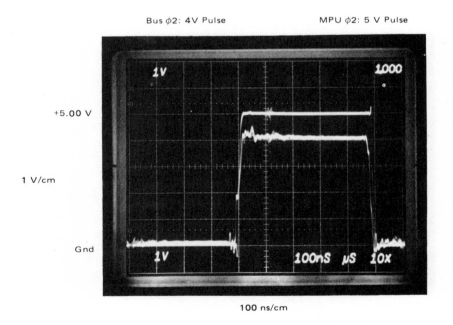

100 ns/cm

FIGURE 4-1.1-4d. MPU φ2 Clock and Bus φ2

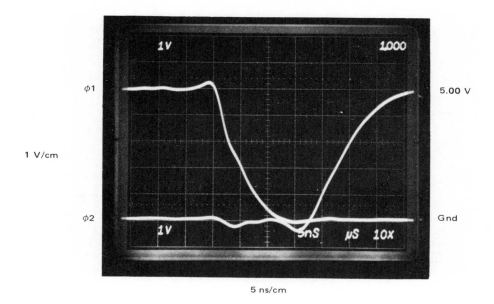

5 ns/cm

FIGURE 4-1.1-4e. MPU Clock Non-Overlap Region

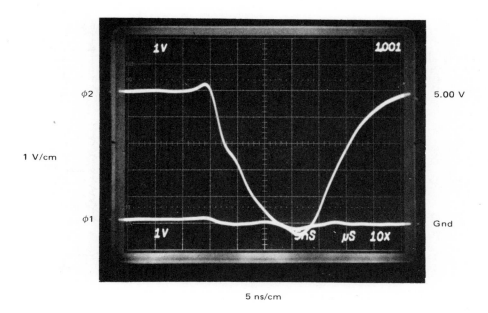

5 ns/cm

FIGURE 4-1.1-4f. MPU Clock Non-Overlap Region

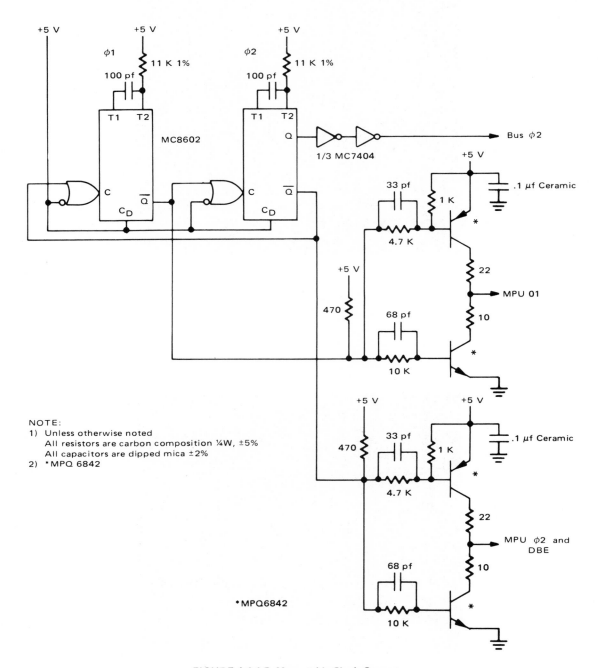

FIGURE 4-1.1-5. Monostable Clock Generator

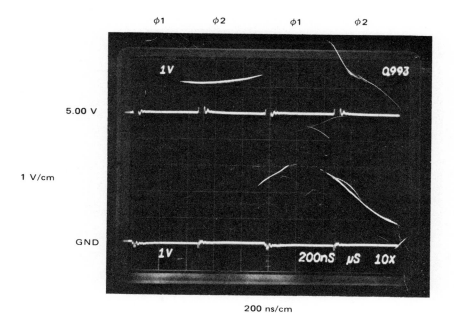

200 ns/cm

FIGURE 4-1.1-6a. MPU Clock Waveforms

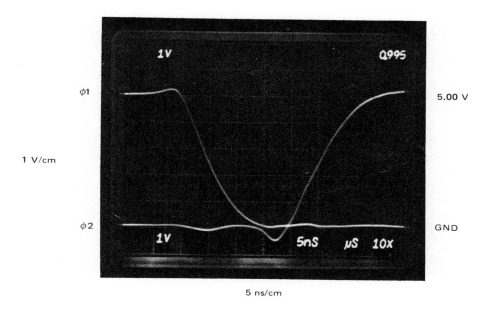

5 ns/cm

FIGURE 4-1.1-6b. MPU Clock Non-Overlap Region

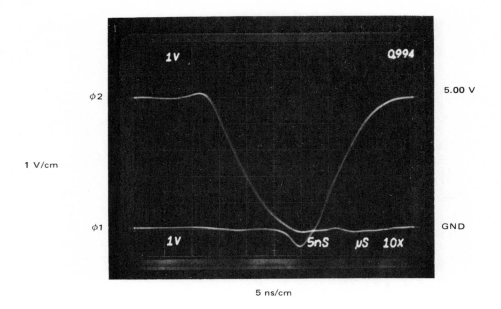

5 ns/cm

FIGURE 4-1.1-6c. MPU Clock Non-Overlap Region

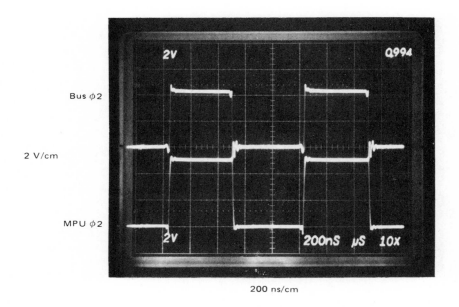

200 ns/cm

FIGURE 4-1.1-6d. MPU φ2 Clock and Buss φ2

function in order to interface with slow memories (see Section 4-2.5.1). Those interested in this device should contact their Motorola salesman for further details.

4-1.2   HALTING THE MC6800 AND SINGLE INSTRUCTION EXECUTION

The $\overline{\text{HALT}}$ line provides an input to the MPU to allow control of program execution by an outside source. If $\overline{\text{HALT}}$ is high, the MPU will execute; if it is low, the MPU will go to a halted or idle mode. A response signal, Bus Available (BA) provides an indication of the MPU's current status. When BA is low, the MPU is in the process of executing the control program; if BA is high, the MPU has halted and all internal activity has stopped. When BA is high, the Address Bus, Data Bus, and R/W line will be in a high impedance state, effectively removing the MPU from the system bus. VMA is forced low so that the floating system bus will not activate any device on the bus that is enabled by VMA.

While the MPU is halted, all program activity is stopped and, if either a $\overline{\text{NMI}}$ or $\overline{\text{IRQ}}$ interrupt occurs, it will be latched into the MPU and acted on as soon as the MPU is taken out of the halted mode. If a $\overline{\text{RESET}}$ command occurs while the MPU is halted, the following states occur: VMA-low, BA-low (while $\overline{\text{RESET}}$ is low), Data Bus-high impedance, R/W-Read state (while $\overline{\text{RESET}}$ is low), and the Address Bus will contain the reset address FFFE (while $\overline{\text{RESET}}$ is low). As soon as the HALT line goes high, the MPU will go to locations FFFE and FFFF for the address of the reset routine.

Figure 4-1.2-1 shows the timing relationships involved when halting the MPU and executing a single instruction. Both of the instructions illustrated are single byte, 2 cycles, such as CLRA and CLRB. The MPU always halts after completing execution of an instruction when $\overline{\text{HALT}}$ is low. If $\overline{\text{HALT}}$ is low within 100 nsec after the leading edge of $\phi 1$ in the last cycle of an instruction (point A in the figure) then the MPU will halt at the end of the current instruction. The fetch of the OP code by the MPU is the first cycle of an instruction. If $\overline{\text{HALT}}$ had not been low at point A but went low during $\phi 2$ of that cycle, the MPU would have halted after completion of the next instruction after instruction X. BA will go high within 470 nsec of the leading edge of the next $\phi 2$ clock after the last instruction cycle executed. At this point in time, VMA is low and the R/W line, Address Bus, and the Data Bus are in the high impedance state.

To single cycle the MPU, $\overline{\text{HALT}}$ must be brought high for one MPU cycle and then returned low as shown at (B). Again, the transitions of $\overline{\text{HALT}}$ must occur within 100 nsec of the leading edge of $\phi 1$. BA will go low within 300 nsec of the leading edge of the next $\phi 1$ indicating that the Address Bus Data Bus, VMA and R/W lines are back on the bus. A single byte, 2 cycle instruction, such as CLRB is used for this example also. During the first cycle, the instruction Y is fetched from address M+1. BA returns high 470 nsec after $\phi 2$ on the last cycle indicating the MPU is off the bus. If instruction Y had more than two cycles, the width of the BA's low time would have been increased proportionally.

4-1.3   MC6800 RESET AND INTERRUPT CONTROLS

The $\overline{\text{RESET}}$ input is used to reset and start the MPU from a power down condition resulting from a power failure or initial start-up of the processor. This input can also be used to reinitialize the machine at any time after start up. If a positive edge is detected on this input, this will signal the MPU to begin the restart sequence. During the reset sequence, all of the higher order address lines will be forced high. The contents of the last two locations (FFFE, FFFF) in memory will be loaded into the program counter to point to the reset program. During the reset routine, the interrupt mask bit is set and must be reset by an Instruction in the initializing program before the MPU can be interrupted by $\overline{\text{IRQ}}$. While $\overline{\text{RESET}}$ is low (assuming 8 clock cycles

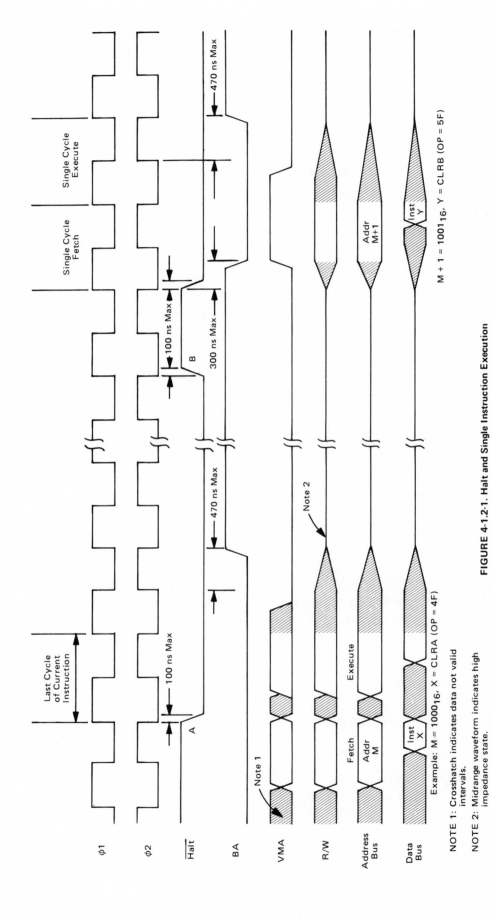

FIGURE 4-1.2-1. Halt and Single Instruction Execution

NOTE 1: Crosshatch indicates data not valid intervals.

NOTE 2: Midrange waveform indicates high impedance state.

Example: M = 1000₁₆, X = CLRA (OP = 4F)
M + 1 = 1001₁₆, Y = CLRB (OP = 5F)

4-14

have occurred) the MPU output signals will be in the following states: VMA-low, BA-low, Data Bus-high impedance, R/W (Read State) and the Address Bus will contain the reset address FFFE.

Figure 4-1.3-1 illustrates a power up sequence using the $\overline{\text{RESET}}$ control line. After the power supply reaches 4.75 volts, eight clock cycles are required for the processor to stabilize in preparation for restarting. During these eight cycles, VMA will be in an indeterminate state so any devices that are enabled by VMA which could accept a false write during this time (such as a battery backed RAM) must be disabled until VMA is forced low after 8 cycles. $\overline{\text{RESET}}$ can go high asynchronously with the system clock, however, its rise time must be less than 500 nsec. If $\overline{\text{RESET}}$ is high at least 200 nsec before the leading edge of $\phi1$ in any given cycle, then the restart sequence will begin in that cycle as shown in Figure 4-1.3-1. The $\overline{\text{RESET}}$ control line may also used to reinitialize the MPU system at any time during its operation. This is accomplished by pulsing $\overline{\text{RESET}}$ low for the duration of at least three complete $\phi2$ pulses. The $\overline{\text{RESET}}$ pulse can be completely asynchronous with the MPU system clock.

The MC6800 is capable of handling two types of interrupts, maskable $(\overline{\text{IRQ}})$ and non-maskable $(\overline{\text{NMI}})$. The handling of these interrupts by the MPU is the same with the exception that each has its own vector address. The behavior of the MPU when interrupted by these two types of interrupts falls into two categories as shown in Figure 4-1.3-2. Figure 4-1.3-2a details the MPU response to an interrupt while the MPU is executing the control program. The interrupt shown could be either an $\overline{\text{IRQ}}$ or $\overline{\text{NMI}}$ and can be asynchronous with respect to $\phi1$. The Interrupt is shown going low 200 nsec before the leading edge of $\phi1$ in cycle #2 which is the first cycle of an instruction (OP code fetch). This instruction is not executed but instead the Program Counter, Index Register, Accumulators, and the Condition Code Register are pushed onto the stack. The Interrupt Mask is then set to prevent further IRQ interrupts. The address of the interrupt service routine is then fetched from FFFC, FFFD, for a NMI interrupt and from FFF8, FFF9 for an IRQ interrupt. Upon completion of the interrupt service routine, the execution of RTI will pull the PC, X, ACCUMULATORS, and CCR off of the stack.

Figure 4-1.3-2b is a similar interrupt sequence except, in this case, a WAIT instruction has been executed in preparation for the interrupt. This technique speeds up the MPU's response to the interrupt because the stacking of the PC, X, ACCUMULATORS, and the CCR is already done. While the MPU is waiting for the Interrupt, Bus Available will go high indicating the following state of the control lines: VMA-low, Address Bus-R/W-Data Bus all in the high impedance state. After the interrupt occurs, it is serviced as previously described.

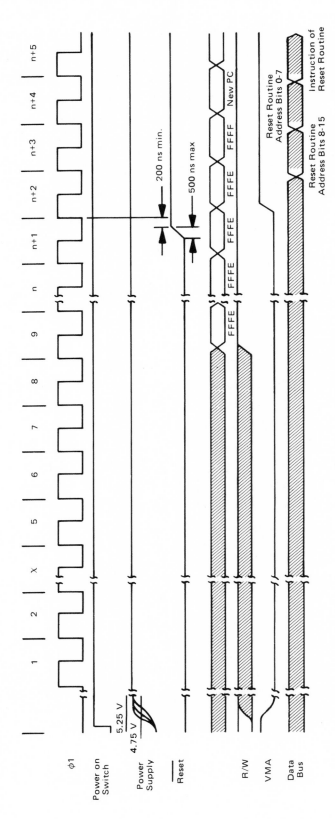

FIGURE 4-1.3-1. $\overline{\text{RESET}}$ Timing

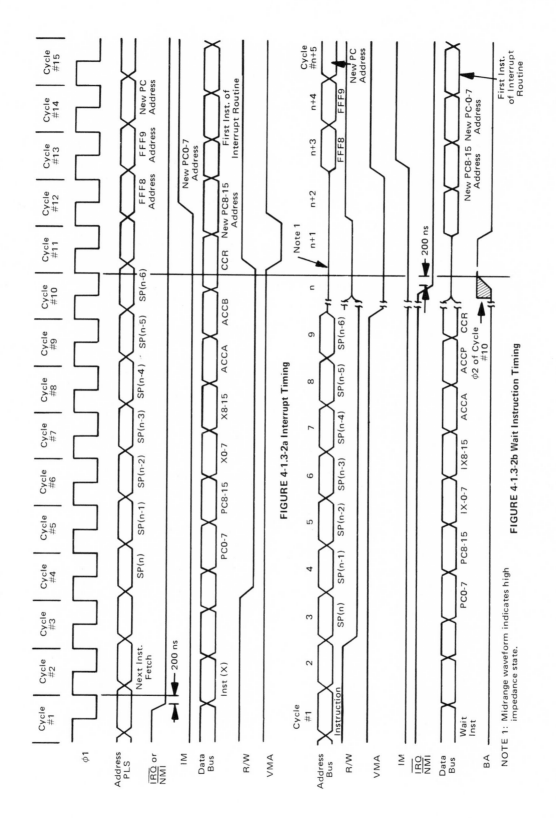

FIGURE 4-1.3-2a Interrupt Timing

FIGURE 4-1.3-2b Wait Instruction Timing

NOTE 1: Midrange waveform indicates high
impedance state.

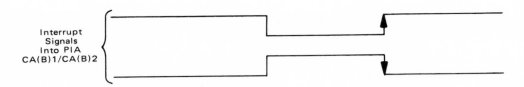

FIGURE 4-1.3-3. Interrupt signal Format

INTERRUPT ENABLING DURING HALT AND/OR WAI

While there are nominally no restrictions on the format of interrupt signals into CA1, CA2, CB1, and CB2 of the PIA, there are certain combinations of system situations that require special consideration. Assume that the interrupt signal format follows one of the cases shown in Figure 4-1.3-3 and that the PIA has been conditioned by the MPU to recognize the transition polarity represented by the "trailing edge" of the interrupt pulse.

The design of the PIA is such that at least one E pulse must occur between the inactive and active edges of the input signal if the interrupt is to be recognized. Relative timing requirements are shown in Figure 4-1.3-4. Note that an internal enable signal that is initiated by the first positive transition of E following the inactive edge of the input signals is included.

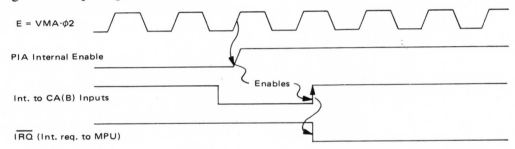

FIGURE 4-1.3-4: Interrupt Enabling

When the MPU has been halted either by hardware control or execution of the Wait For Interrupt (WAI) instruction, its VMA output goes low. Since VMA is normally used to generate the Enable signal (E = VMA•ϕ2) either of these two conditions temporarily eliminates the E signal. The effect of this on the trailing edge interrupt format is shown in Figure 4-1.3-5 where it is assumed that VMA went low and eliminated the Enable pulses before the PIA's interrupt circuitry was properly conditioned to recognize the active transition. It should be noted that this condition occurs only when an active transition is preceded by an inactive transition and there are no intervening E pulses.

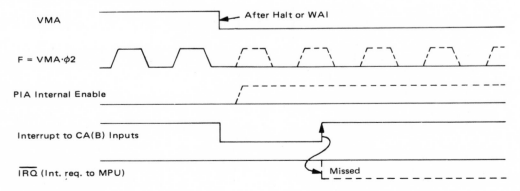

FIGURE 4-1.3-5. Interrupt not properly enabled

If this combination occurs during system operation, valid interrupts will be ignored. Either of two simple precautions can be adopted. If the format of the interrupt signals is up to the designer, the potential problem can be avoided by not using the pulse-with-trailing-edge-interrupt format.

If this format is compulsory, the Chip Select signal can be generated by ANDing VMA and one of the PIA's chip select inputs as shown in Figure 4-1.3.6, while the $\phi2$ clock is used to enable the PIA.

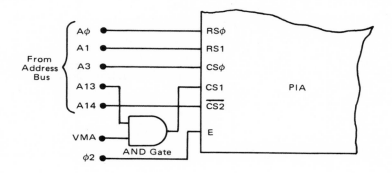

FIGURE 4-1.3-6. Alternate Enable Generation

4-1.4 THREE-STATE CONTROL LINE OPERATION

When the Three-State Control (TSC) line is a logic one, the Address Bus and the R/W line are placed in a high impedance state. VMA and BA are forced low whenever TSC = "1" to prevent false reads or writes on any device enabled by VMA. BA is low to indicate that the bus is not available for long term use. While TSC is held high, the $\phi1$ and $\phi2$ clocks must be held high and low, respectively, in order to delay program execution (this is required because of the bus lines being in the high impedance state). Since the MPU is a dynamic device, the clocks can be stopped for no more than 4.5 μsec without destroying data within the MPU.

Figure 4-1.4-1 shows the effect of TSC on the MPU. TSC must have its transitions within 50 nsec of the leading edge of $\phi1$ while holding $\phi1$ high and $\phi2$ low as shown. Within 500 nsec of TSC going high, the Address Bus, and R/W line will reach the high impedance state with VMA being forced low. In this example, the Data Bus is also in the high impedance state while $\phi2$ is being held low because DBE is controlled by $\phi2$. At this point in time, a DMA transfer could occur as explained in Section 4-2.2.2.

When TSC is returned low, the MPU's Address and R/W lines return to the bus within 500 nsec. Because it is too late in cycle number 5 to access memory, this cycle is a dead cycle used for synchronization and program execution resumes in cycle 6.

4.1.5 M6800 FAMILY INTERFACE AND ENABLING CONSIDERATIONS

The specifications of the M6800 family allow easy interfacing with other family members and with TTL systems. All logic levels (with the exception of the clocks) are TTL compatible with the outputs having a fanout of 1 7400 TTL load and 130 pf shunt capacitance at a 1.0 MHz clock rate. TTL logic level compatibility allows the system designer access to a whole realm of standard interface and memory devices to complement the M6800 family.

The limiting factor on size in building a M6800 system without buffering will usually be the loading on the data bus. Data bus loading by family devices in the high impedance state is 10 μa of leakage current with 10 pf of capacitance each for the PIA and ACIA and 15 pf of capacitance each for the MPU, RAM, and ROM.

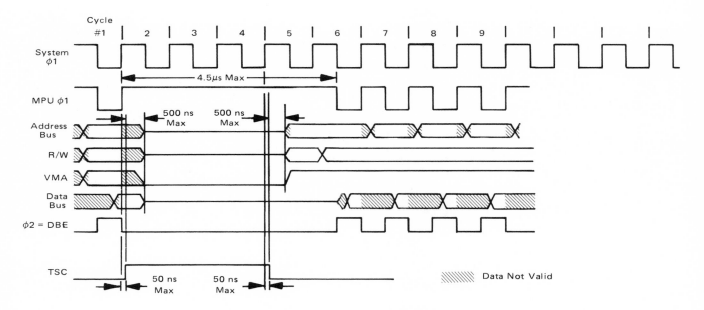

FIGURE 4-1.4-1. Three-State Control Timing

Each family device can source 100 μa and drive a 130 pf load at rated speed (refer to the family data sheets for more detail), thus, the data bus fanout varies from 7 to 10 family parts when assuming 25-30 pf of stray capacitance. Once the system becomes larger than the 7 to 10 family parts of a minimum system, Bus Extenders (BEX) are necessary in order to increase the fanout.

Figure 4-1.5-1 shows a generalized block diagram of a buffered M6800 system. The different modules shown could be composed of family members (PIA, ACIA, 128 X 8 RAM, and 1K X 8 ROM) or other devices such as 4K RAMS (for large memory arrays) or bipolar PROMs (for bootstrap loaders). Bus drivers and receivers are available which provide a fanout on the order of 50 receivers for each driver, providing almost unlimited system expansion.

The buffers shown are used on the unidirectional lines, i.e., Address, R/W, VMA and φ2 clock. Devices used for this function can vary from MC7404 hex buffers for a fanout of 10 to Bus Interface devices such as the MC8T97* which can provide fanout on the order of 50 MC8T97 receivers from one MC8T97 driver. These buffer devices may have three state capability but unless the bus is needed for something like a DMA channel, the buffers can remain enabled all the time. Devices that can be used for the bidirectional data transceivers are the MC8T26* and the MC8833*. The data transceiver at the MPU should be controlled by the following signals, φ2, VMA, and R/W. φ2 and VMA can be used to enable the data transceivers only during the data transfer portion of the cycle and only on memory reference cycles. The R/W line is used to control the direction of the data transfer. The data transceivers for each module are enabled by these same signals plus an additional signal which selects one module from the others. This additional signal can be derived from a full decode of the Address Bus or it could be as simple as one of the high order address lines in an abbreviated address decoding method as described in Section 1-1.2.

Figure 4-1.5-2 is an example of a buffered system using MC8T97 buffers and MC8T26 data transceivers. In this example, all MC8T97s are enabled permanently because they are used with unidirectional lines and no DMA channel is included. The drivers from the MPU could be disabled to allow control of the bus by a DMA channel. The MC8T26 is used as the data bus transceiver in Figure 4-1.5-2. The enabling logic

---

*To be introduced third quarter, 1975.

shown places the transceiver in the mode of normally driving the bus except during $\phi2$ of a valid read cycle in which case the driver is disabled and the receiver enabled. The logic of the data transceivers for the module enables the receiver and disables the driver except during $\phi2$ of a valid read cycle for that module (For a valid read cycle, the receiver is disabled and the driver enabled). The ADDR input to this logic is used to enable only one driver of the modules on the bus at any one time and is dependent on the address decoding method used.

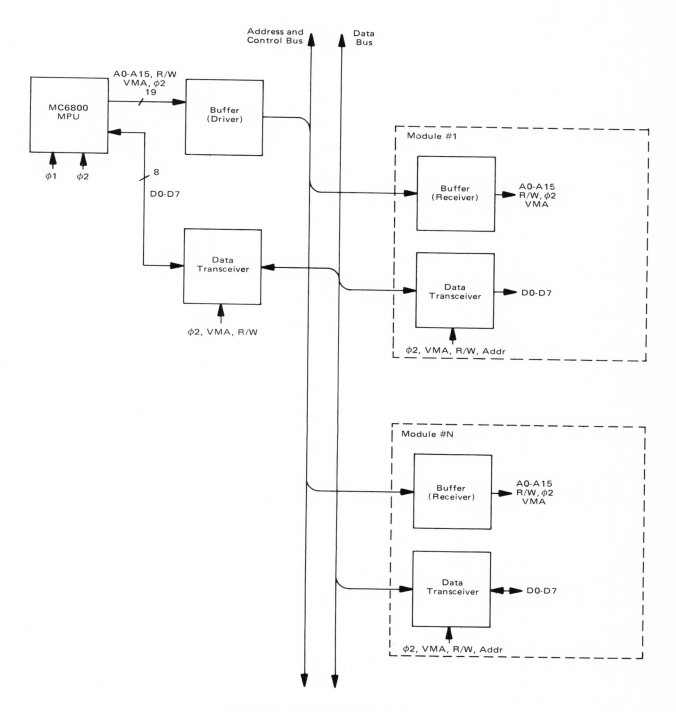

FIGURE 4-1.5-1. Buffered M6800 System

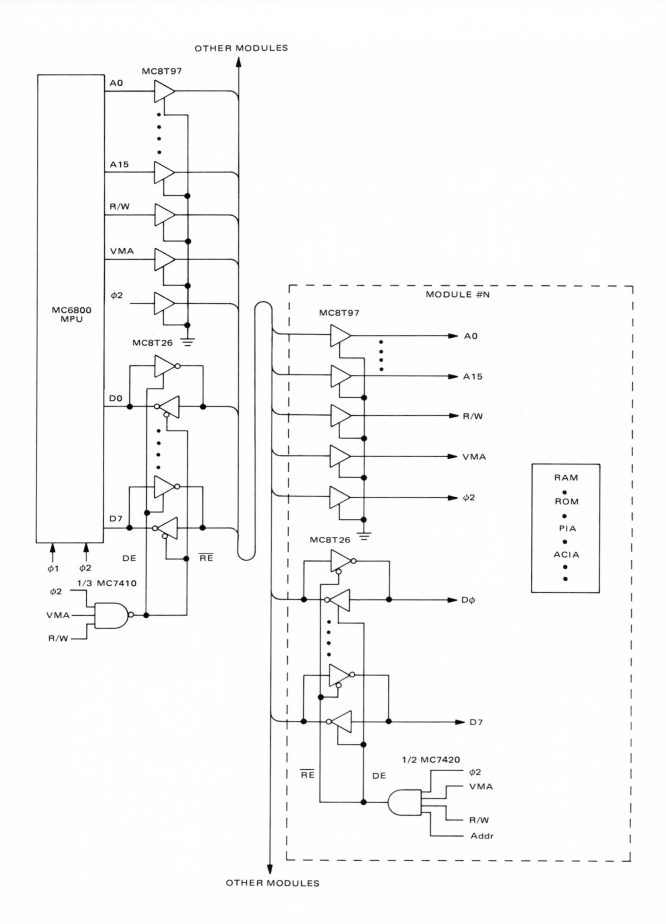

FIGURE 4-1.5.2. M6800 Bus Expansion Example

Enabling Considerations of Module Devices

VMA, R/W, and $\phi2$ are all available to enable RAMs, ROMs, and PIA/ACIAs. In some cases, it may be desirable to eliminate one of these enabling signals so that the enable input is available for address decoding. The following discussion indicates which control signals could be deleted for a given device and the effects on the system operation:

ROM

R/W and $\phi2$ can be used to enable the ROMs without using the VMA signal. Not using the VMA signal means that the ROM may be enabled during a non-memory reference read cycle (VMA would be low but since it is not used, the ROM may be enabled). A false read of the ROM will have no effect on the system and if the non-memory reference cycle had been a write, then the R/W signal would have disabled the ROM.

RAM

VMA can be left off as an enable to a RAM if the MPU will not be halted, the WAI instruction not used, or if the TSC will not be used. Either of these conditions cause the Address lines and the R/W lines to float which could produce a false write into RAM if not prevented by VMA. During normal operation of the MPU, only one instruction, TST, causes a false write to memory (i.e., the R/W line going low without VMA going high). This instruction does not pose a problem because it first reads the memory and then rewrites the same data. If VMA was used to enable the RAM, this false write would not occur, however, since the memory is rewritten with the same data, no problem occurs by not using VMA as an enable.

PIA/ACIA

All three signals must be used to enable or select a PIA or ACIA. Both of these devices automatically clear the Interrupt Flags when the MPU reads the PIA or ACIA data registers so that a false read of a PIA or ACIA may cause an interrupt on CA1, CB1, CA2, or CB2 to be missed. In addition, it is suggested that VMA•$\phi2$ not be used as an Enable signal for a PIA because, if the machine is halted, VMA is forced low removing the clocks from the PIA. Without the Enable input to the PIA, an external interrupt may not be recognized.[1] $\phi2$ should be used for the PIA Enable signal so that the PIA Enable clock always occurs whether or not the MPU is halted. VMA may then be taken directly to Chip Select inputs or be gated with address signals to the Chip Select inputs.

[1]Refer to Section 4-1.3 for a complete explanation.

4-2.1   **INTERRUPT PRIORITY CIRCUITRY**

The interrupt control features of the MC6800 are described in Sections 3-2 & 3-3. The software polling and prioritizing methods discussed there are adequate for most applications. However, in systems having several interrupts that must be handled quickly on a priority basis, hardware prioritizing circuitry can be used to advantage.

The prioritizing method recommended in Chapter 3 is shown in more detail in the block diagram of Figure 4-2.1-1. With this technique, each interrupting device is assigned a separate ROM location which is used to store the starting address of a service routine. After the MPU recognizes an interrupt, external circuitry selects the interrupt that is to be serviced and directs the MPU to the proper location in memory.

The MPU responds to an $\overline{\text{IRQ}}$ by trying to fetch the $\overline{\text{IRQ}}$ vector address from locations FFF8 and FFF9. However, some of the address lines are no longer tied directly to memory but go instead to a 1-of-2 Data Selector. The other set of inputs to the Data Selector is generated by a Priority Encoder that outputs a binary number corresponding to the highest priority interrupt signal present at the time the interrupt is recognized by the MPU.

Detection of addresses FFF8 and FFF9 by the INTERRUPT ADDRESS DECODE circuitry then causes the outputs of the Priority Encoder to be substituted for part of the normal address. Hence, even though the MPU outputs FFF8 and FFF9, other locations are read by the MPU.

4-2.1.1   **8-Level Prioritizing**

Specific circuitry for prioritizing eight interrupts is shown in Figure 4-2.1.1-1. The interrupting

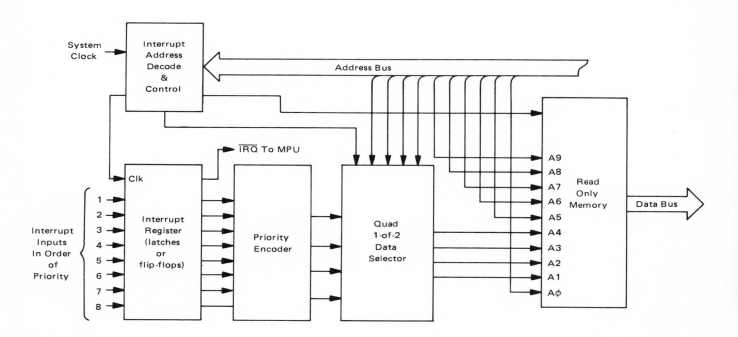

FIGURE 4-2.1-1. 8-level Priority Interrupt Configuration Block Diagram

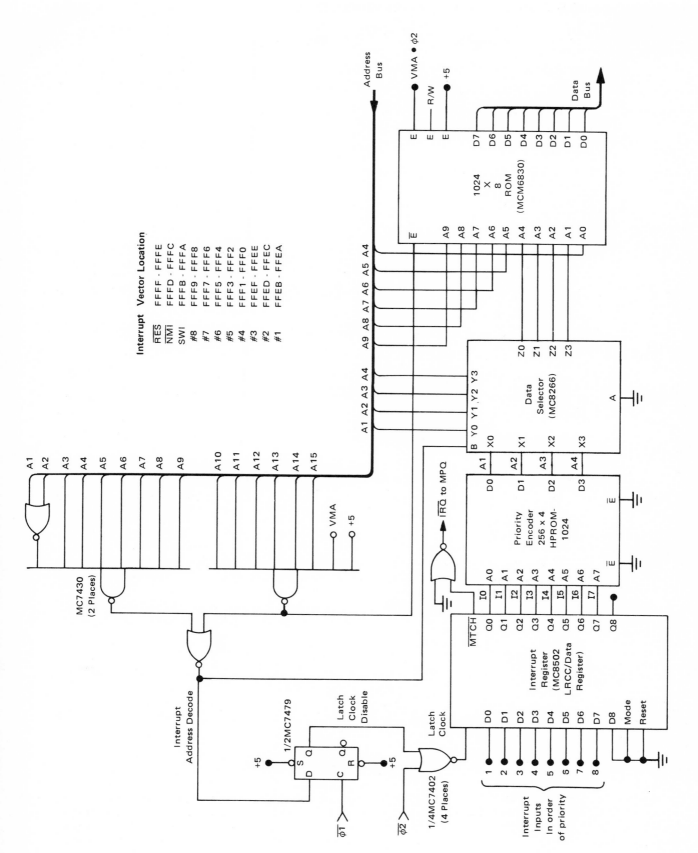

FIGURE 4-2.1.1-1. 8 Level Hardware Prioritized Interrupt Logic

Interrupt	Vector Location
RES	FFFF - FFFE
NMI	FFFD - FFFC
SWI	FFFB - FFFA
#8	FFF9 - FFF8
#7	FFF7 - FFF6
#6	FFF5 - FFF4
#5	FFF3 - FFF2
#4	FFF1 - FFF0
#3	FFEF - FFEE
#2	FFED - FFEC
#1	FFEB - FFEA

4-25

signals are tied to the D inputs of an MC8502.[1] In the absence of interrupts, all the inputs are low and the $\overline{\text{IRQ}}$ line to the MPU is high. One or more interrupts going high causes $\overline{\text{IRQ}}$ to go low (following the next positive transition of $\phi2$), thus initiating an $\overline{\text{IRQ}}$.

After setting the Interrupt Mask and stacking its contents, the MPU responds in the normal manner by outputting FFF8 and FFF9 onto the Address Bus where it is decoded by the INTERRUPT ADDRESS DECODE circuitry. The resulting decode pulses are shown in the relative timing diagram of Figure 4-2.1.1-2.

The INTERRUPT DECODE signal causes the MC8266 Data Selector to select the Priority Encoder outputs for addressing inputs A1 through A4 of the ROM. If any address other than FFF8 or FFF9 is on the Address Bus, INTERRUPT ADDRESS DECODE is low and the normal A1-A4 address lines are routed to the ROM.

The INTERRUPT ADDRESS DECODE signal is also used in generating the LATCH CLOCK DISABLE signal. When the INTERRUPT DECODE pulses are not present, the contents of the D flip-flops in the Interrupt Register are updated by each negative transition of $\phi2$. During retrieval of the current interrupt vector, further changes on the interrupt inputs are shut out by disabling the LATCH CLOCK. The clock is disabled by the presence of the INTERRUPT DECODE signal on the D input of the LATCH CLOCK Disable flip-flop which causes the disable signal to go high on the next negative transition of $\phi1$.

On the negative transition of $\phi1$ following the FFF9 decode pulse the D input to the disable flip-flop will again be low, the disable signal will go low, and sampling of the interrupts will be resumed.

When no interrupts are present, all inputs to the Interrupt Register/Priority Encoder are low and $\overline{\text{IRQ}}$ is high. With one or more of the interrupt inputs high, the Priority Encoder translates the highest priority input into a corresponding 4-bit output. The priority is an indicated in Table 4-2.1.1-1; I0 is the highest, I1 is second highest, etc. The response of the Priority Encoder to various combinations of interrupts is shown in Table 4-2.1.1-1.

The A1-A4 outputs corresponding to each priority are obtained by encoding a 256 X 4 PROM with the desired results.[2] The code is determined by where the vectors are to be located in memory. In this case, the

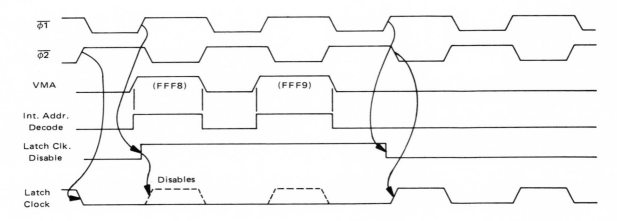

FIGURE 4-2.1.1-2. Prioritizing Interrupt Circuitry Relative Timing

---

[1]The MC8502 Longitudinal Redundancy Check/Data Register is a dual-mode circuit developed for use in 9-channel magnetic tape systems. It contains nine flip-flops and logic to detect an all zeros condition. All nine flip-flops have common reset, clock, and mode control inputs. Each flip-flop may operate either as a Toggle (mode control high) or D (mode control low) flip-flop. The flip-flops are edge-triggered and are updated on the negative edge of the clock input. An all zero condition in the register is indicated by a low state at the Match output.

[2]A complete code listing is shown in Table 4-2.1.1-2.

$\overline{\text{IRQ}}$ vectors are contiguous with the RES, NMI, and SWI vectors as shown in Figure 4-2.1.1-3. The code that must be generated by the Priority Encoder to accomplish this is enclosed by dashed lines in the Figure.

If a conventional 8-input priority encoder such as the MC9318 (see next section) was used only five interrupts could be implemented without additional address decoding. This is due to the fact that three of its inputs would, if active, cause the addresses for RES, NMI, and SWI to be accessed by an $\overline{\text{IRQ}}$. Use of the PROM allows any desired code and, hence, any memory locations to be selected.

In this example, addressing is shown for an MCM6830 1024 X 8 ROM assigned memory locations FF00 to FFFF with the interrupt vectors located at the top of memory. If no interrupts are being processed, lines A0 through A9 of the Address Bus select individual ROM locations in the usual manner. A suitable chip enable for locating the ROM at FFXX is developed by decoding A10-A15 and tying it to an $\overline{\text{E}}$ on the ROM. The chip enable requires no additional logic since A10-A15 must be decoded for the interrupt circuitry anyway.

Interrupt Priority	D0	D1	D2	D3	D4	D5	D6	D7	A4	A3	A2	A1	IRQ	Vector Location
1 (Highest)	1	X	X	X	X	X	X	X	1	1	0	0	0	FFF8 - FFF9
2	0	1	X	X	X	X	X	X	1	0	1	1	0	FFF6 - FFF7
3	0	0	1	X	X	X	X	X	1	0	1	0	0	FFF4 - FFF5
4	0	0	0	1	X	X	X	X	1	0	0	1	0	FFF2 - FFF3
5	0	0	0	0	1	X	X	X	1	0	0	0	0	FFF0 - FFF1
6	0	0	0	0	0	1	X	X	0	1	1	1	0	FFEE - FFEF
7	0	0	0	0	0	0	1	X	0	1	1	0	0	FFEC - FFED
8 (Lowest)	0	0	0	0	0	0	0	1	0	1	0	1	0	FFEA - FFEB
	0	0	0	0	0	0	0	0	0	0	0	0	1	

X = Doesn't matter

TABLE 4-2.1.1-1. 8-Level Priority Circuitry Truth Table

4-2.1.2 13-level Prioritizing

For the 8-level prioritizing circuitry described in the preceding section, the vector addresses were located near the top of a block of memory assigned locations FF00 to FFFF. This required decoding address lines A10-A15; in addition, for purposes of illustration, the Interrupt Address Decode signal was generated by doing a complete decode of the Address Bus.

In a typical application, the block memory assignments may be different and the decoding can be simplified. This is illustrated in Figure 4-2.1.2-1 where the specific circuitry for prioritizing 13 levels of interrupt is shown. The addressing follows the example of Section 1-1.2.1 and assigns the ROM to memory locations C000 through C3FF by tying address lines A14 and A15 to chip enables on the ROM.

The requirements for decoding the $\overline{\text{IRQ}}$ Interrupt Address Decode signal are determined by the following considerations:

(1) When the MPU places addresses on the Address Bus during interrupt sequences the vector data is fetched from the memory locations that *respond* to those addresses even though they are not actually locations FFF8 through FFFF. For example, if the MPU outputs the address FFFF (all ones) while fetching the vector data for a $\overline{\text{Reset}}$, in this case it is actually addressing memory locations C3FF in the ROM since the A15 and A14 "ones" on the chip enable selects the particular ROM and the X3FF portion of the address is determined by the ones on A0-A9.

ADDR	I8	I7	I6	I5	I4	I3	I2	I1	A4	A3	A2	A1
0	0	0	0	0	0	0	0	0	0	0	0	0
1	0	0	0	0	0	0	0	1	1	1	0	0
2	0	0	0	0	0	0	1	0	1	0	1	1
3	0	0	0	0	0	0	1	1	1	1	0	0
4	0	0	0	0	0	1	0	0	1	0	1	0
5	0	0	0	0	0	1	0	1	1	1	0	0
6	0	0	0	0	0	1	1	0	1	0	1	1
7	0	0	0	0	0	1	1	1	1	1	0	0
8	0	0	0	0	1	0	0	0	1	0	0	1
9	0	0	0	0	1	0	0	1	1	1	0	0
10	0	0	0	0	1	0	1	0	1	0	1	1
11	0	0	0	0	1	0	1	1	1	1	0	0
12	0	0	0	0	1	1	0	0	1	0	1	0
13	0	0	0	0	1	1	0	1	1	1	0	0
14	0	0	0	0	1	1	1	0	1	0	1	1
15	0	0	0	0	1	1	1	1	1	1	0	0
16	0	0	0	1	0	0	0	0	1	0	0	0
17	0	0	0	1	0	0	0	1	1	1	0	0
18	0	0	0	1	0	0	1	0	1	0	1	1
19	0	0	0	1	0	0	1	1	1	1	0	0
20	0	0	0	1	0	1	0	0	1	0	1	0
21	0	0	0	1	0	1	0	1	1	1	0	0
22	0	0	0	1	0	1	1	0	1	0	1	1
23	0	0	0	1	0	1	1	1	1	1	0	0
24	0	0	0	1	1	0	0	0	1	0	0	1
25	0	0	0	1	1	0	0	1	1	1	0	0
26	0	0	0	1	1	0	1	0	1	0	1	1
27	0	0	0	1	1	0	1	1	1	1	0	0
28	0	0	0	1	1	1	0	0	1	0	1	0
29	0	0	0	1	1	1	0	1	1	1	0	0
30	0	0	0	1	1	1	1	0	1	0	1	1
31	0	0	0	1	1	1	1	1	1	1	0	0
32	0	0	1	0	0	0	0	0	0	1	1	1
33	0	0	1	0	0	0	0	1	1	1	0	0
34	0	0	1	0	0	0	1	0	1	0	1	1
35	0	0	1	0	0	0	1	1	1	1	0	0
36	0	0	1	0	0	1	0	0	1	0	1	0
37	0	0	1	0	0	1	0	1	1	1	0	0
38	0	0	1	0	0	1	1	0	1	0	1	1
39	0	0	1	0	0	1	1	1	1	1	0	0
40	0	0	1	0	1	0	0	0	1	0	0	1
41	0	0	1	0	1	0	0	1	1	1	0	0
42	0	0	1	0	1	0	1	0	1	0	1	1
43	0	0	1	0	1	0	1	1	1	1	0	0
44	0	0	1	0	1	1	0	0	1	0	1	0
45	0	0	1	0	1	1	0	1	1	1	0	0
46	0	0	1	0	1	1	1	0	1	0	1	1
47	0	0	1	0	1	1	1	1	1	1	0	0
48	0	0	1	1	0	0	0	0	1	0	0	0
49	0	0	1	1	0	0	0	1	1	1	0	0
50	0	0	1	1	0	0	1	0	1	0	1	1
51	0	0	1	1	0	0	1	1	1	1	0	0
52	0	0	1	1	0	1	0	0	1	0	1	0
53	0	0	1	1	0	1	0	1	1	1	0	0
54	0	0	1	1	0	1	1	0	1	0	1	1
55	0	0	1	1	0	1	1	1	1	1	0	0
56	0	0	1	1	1	0	0	0	1	0	0	1
57	0	0	1	1	1	0	0	1	1	1	0	0
58	0	0	1	1	1	0	1	0	1	0	1	1
59	0	0	1	1	1	0	1	1	1	1	0	0
60	0	0	1	1	1	1	0	0	1	0	1	0
61	0	0	1	1	1	1	0	1	1	1	0	0
62	0	0	1	1	1	1	1	0	1	0	1	1
63	0	0	1	1	1	1	1	1	1	1	0	0
64	0	1	0	0	0	0	0	0	0	1	1	0
65	0	1	0	0	0	0	0	1	1	1	0	0
66	0	1	0	0	0	0	1	0	1	0	1	1
67	0	1	0	0	0	0	1	1	1	1	0	0
68	0	1	0	0	0	1	0	0	1	0	1	0
69	0	1	0	0	0	1	0	1	1	1	0	0
70	0	1	0	0	0	1	1	0	1	0	1	1
71	0	1	0	0	0	1	1	1	1	1	0	0
72	0	1	0	0	1	0	0	0	1	0	0	1
73	0	1	0	0	1	0	0	1	1	1	0	0
74	0	1	0	0	1	0	1	0	1	0	1	1
75	0	1	0	0	1	0	1	1	1	1	0	0
76	0	1	0	0	1	1	0	0	1	0	1	0
77	0	1	0	0	1	1	0	1	1	1	0	0
78	0	1	0	0	1	1	1	0	1	0	1	1
79	0	1	0	0	1	1	1	1	1	1	0	0
80	0	1	0	1	0	0	0	0	1	0	0	0
81	0	1	0	1	0	0	0	1	1	1	0	0
82	0	1	0	1	0	0	1	0	1	0	1	1
83	0	1	0	1	0	0	1	1	1	1	0	0
84	0	1	0	1	0	1	0	0	1	0	1	0
85	0	1	0	1	0	1	0	1	1	1	0	0
86	0	1	0	1	0	1	1	0	1	0	1	1
87	0	1	0	1	0	1	1	1	1	1	0	0
88	0	1	0	1	1	0	0	0	1	0	0	1
89	0	1	0	1	1	0	0	1	1	1	0	0
90	0	1	0	1	1	0	1	0	1	0	1	1
91	0	1	0	1	1	0	1	1	1	1	0	0
92	0	1	0	1	1	1	0	0	1	0	1	0
93	0	1	0	1	1	1	0	1	1	1	0	0
94	0	1	0	1	1	1	1	0	1	0	1	1
95	0	1	0	1	1	1	1	1	1	1	0	0
96	0	1	1	0	0	0	0	0	0	1	1	1
97	0	1	1	0	0	0	0	1	1	1	0	0
98	0	1	1	0	0	0	1	0	1	0	1	1
99	0	1	1	0	0	0	1	1	1	1	0	0
100	0	1	1	0	0	1	0	0	1	0	1	0
101	0	1	1	0	0	1	0	1	1	1	0	0
102	0	1	1	0	0	1	1	0	1	0	1	1
103	0	1	1	0	0	1	1	1	1	1	0	0
104	0	1	1	0	1	0	0	0	1	0	0	1
105	0	1	1	0	1	0	0	1	1	1	0	0
106	0	1	1	0	1	0	1	0	1	0	1	1
107	0	1	1	0	1	0	1	1	1	1	0	0
108	0	1	1	0	1	1	0	0	1	0	1	0
109	0	1	1	0	1	1	0	1	1	1	0	0
110	0	1	1	0	1	1	1	0	1	0	1	1
111	0	1	1	0	1	1	1	1	1	1	0	0
112	0	1	1	1	0	0	0	0	1	0	0	0
113	0	1	1	1	0	0	0	1	1	1	0	0
114	0	1	1	1	0	0	1	0	1	0	1	1
115	0	1	1	1	0	0	1	1	1	1	0	0
116	0	1	1	1	0	1	0	0	1	0	1	0
117	0	1	1	1	0	1	0	1	1	1	0	0
118	0	1	1	1	0	1	1	0	1	0	1	1
119	0	1	1	1	0	1	1	1	1	1	0	0
120	0	1	1	1	1	0	0	0	1	0	0	1
121	0	1	1	1	1	0	0	1	1	1	0	0
122	0	1	1	1	1	0	1	0	1	0	1	1
123	0	1	1	1	1	0	1	1	1	1	0	0
124	0	1	1	1	1	1	0	0	1	0	1	0
125	0	1	1	1	1	1	0	1	1	1	0	0
126	0	1	1	1	1	1	1	0	1	0	1	1
127	0	1	1	1	1	1	1	1	1	1	0	0
128	1	0	0	0	0	0	0	0	0	1	0	1
129	1	0	0	0	0	0	0	1	1	1	0	0
130	1	0	0	0	0	0	1	0	1	0	1	1
131	1	0	0	0	0	0	1	1	1	1	0	0
132	1	0	0	0	0	1	0	0	1	0	1	0
133	1	0	0	0	0	1	0	1	1	1	0	0
134	1	0	0	0	0	1	1	0	1	0	1	1
135	1	0	0	0	0	1	1	1	1	1	0	0
136	1	0	0	0	1	0	0	0	1	0	0	1
137	1	0	0	0	1	0	0	1	1	1	0	0
138	1	0	0	0	1	0	1	0	1	0	1	1
139	1	0	0	0	1	0	1	1	1	1	0	0
140	1	0	0	0	1	1	0	0	1	0	1	0
141	1	0	0	0	1	1	0	1	1	1	0	0
142	1	0	0	0	1	1	1	0	1	0	1	1
143	1	0	0	0	1	1	1	1	1	1	0	0
144	1	0	0	1	0	0	0	0	1	0	0	0
145	1	0	0	1	0	0	0	1	1	1	0	0
146	1	0	0	1	0	0	1	0	1	0	1	1
147	1	0	0	1	0	0	1	1	1	1	0	0
148	1	0	0	1	0	1	0	0	1	0	1	0
149	1	0	0	1	0	1	0	1	1	1	0	0
150	1	0	0	1	0	1	1	0	1	0	1	1
151	1	0	0	1	0	1	1	1	1	1	0	0
152	1	0	0	1	1	0	0	0	1	0	0	1
153	1	0	0	1	1	0	0	1	1	1	0	0
154	1	0	0	1	1	0	1	0	1	0	1	1
155	1	0	0	1	1	0	1	1	1	1	0	0
156	1	0	0	1	1	1	0	0	1	0	1	0
157	1	0	0	1	1	1	0	1	1	1	0	0
158	1	0	0	1	1	1	1	0	1	0	1	1
159	1	0	0	1	1	1	1	1	1	1	0	0
160	1	0	1	0	0	0	0	0	0	1	1	1
161	1	0	1	0	0	0	0	1	1	1	0	0
162	1	0	1	0	0	0	1	0	1	0	1	1
163	1	0	1	0	0	0	1	1	1	1	0	0
164	1	0	1	0	0	1	0	0	1	0	1	1
165	1	0	1	0	0	1	0	1	1	1	0	0
166	1	0	1	0	0	1	1	0	1	0	1	1
167	1	0	1	0	0	1	1	1	1	1	0	0
168	1	0	1	0	1	0	0	0	1	0	0	1
169	1	0	1	0	1	0	0	1	1	1	0	0
170	1	0	1	0	1	0	1	0	1	0	1	1
171	1	0	1	0	1	0	1	1	1	1	0	0
172	1	0	1	0	1	1	0	0	1	0	1	0
173	1	0	1	0	1	1	0	1	1	1	0	0
174	1	0	1	0	1	1	1	0	1	0	1	1
175	1	0	1	0	1	1	1	1	1	1	0	0
176	1	0	1	1	0	0	0	0	1	0	0	0
177	1	0	1	1	0	0	0	1	1	1	0	0
178	1	0	1	1	0	0	1	0	1	0	1	1
179	1	0	1	1	0	0	1	1	1	1	0	0
180	1	0	1	1	0	1	0	0	1	0	1	0
181	1	0	1	1	0	1	0	1	1	1	0	0
182	1	0	1	1	0	1	1	0	1	0	1	1
183	1	0	1	1	0	1	1	1	1	1	0	0
184	1	0	1	1	1	0	0	0	1	0	0	1
185	1	0	1	1	1	0	0	1	1	1	0	0
186	1	0	1	1	1	0	1	0	1	0	1	1
187	1	0	1	1	1	0	1	1	1	1	0	0
188	1	0	1	1	1	1	0	0	1	0	1	0
189	1	0	1	1	1	1	0	1	1	1	0	0
190	1	0	1	1	1	1	1	0	1	0	1	1
191	1	0	1	1	1	1	1	1	1	1	0	0
192	1	1	0	0	0	0	0	0	0	1	1	0
193	1	1	0	0	0	0	0	1	1	1	0	0
194	1	1	0	0	0	0	1	0	1	0	1	1
195	1	1	0	0	0	0	1	1	1	1	0	0
196	1	1	0	0	0	1	0	0	1	0	1	0
197	1	1	0	0	0	1	0	1	1	1	0	0
198	1	1	0	0	0	1	1	0	1	0	1	1
199	1	1	0	0	0	1	1	1	1	1	0	0
200	1	1	0	0	1	0	0	0	1	0	0	1
201	1	1	0	0	1	0	0	1	1	1	0	0
202	1	1	0	0	1	0	1	0	1	0	1	1
203	1	1	0	0	1	0	1	1	1	1	0	0
204	1	1	0	0	1	1	0	0	1	0	1	0
205	1	1	0	0	1	1	0	1	1	1	0	0
206	1	1	0	0	1	1	1	0	1	0	1	1
207	1	1	0	0	1	1	1	1	1	1	0	0
208	1	1	0	1	0	0	0	0	1	0	0	0
209	1	1	0	1	0	0	0	1	1	1	0	0
210	1	1	0	1	0	0	1	0	1	0	1	1
211	1	1	0	1	0	0	1	1	1	1	0	0
212	1	1	0	1	0	1	0	0	1	0	1	1
213	1	1	0	1	0	1	0	1	1	1	0	0
214	1	1	0	1	0	1	1	0	1	0	1	1
215	1	1	0	1	0	1	1	1	1	1	0	0
216	1	1	0	1	1	0	0	0	1	0	0	1
217	1	1	0	1	1	0	0	1	1	1	0	0
218	1	1	0	1	1	0	1	0	1	0	1	1
219	1	1	0	1	1	0	1	1	1	1	0	0
220	1	1	0	1	1	1	0	0	1	0	1	1
221	1	1	0	1	1	1	0	1	1	1	0	0
222	1	1	0	1	1	1	1	0	1	0	1	1
223	1	1	0	1	1	1	1	1	1	1	0	0
224	1	1	1	0	0	0	0	0	0	1	1	1
225	1	1	1	0	0	0	0	1	1	1	0	0
226	1	1	1	0	0	0	1	0	1	0	1	1
227	1	1	1	0	0	0	1	1	1	1	0	0
228	1	1	1	0	0	1	0	0	1	0	1	1
229	1	1	1	0	0	1	0	1	1	1	0	0
230	1	1	1	0	0	1	1	0	1	0	1	1
231	1	1	1	0	0	1	1	1	1	1	0	0
232	1	1	1	0	1	0	0	0	1	0	0	1
233	1	1	1	0	1	0	0	1	1	1	0	0
234	1	1	1	0	1	0	1	0	1	0	1	1
235	1	1	1	0	1	0	1	1	1	1	0	0
236	1	1	1	0	1	1	0	0	1	0	1	0
237	1	1	1	0	1	1	0	1	1	1	0	0
238	1	1	1	0	1	1	1	0	1	0	1	1
239	1	1	1	0	1	1	1	1	1	1	0	0
240	1	1	1	1	0	0	0	0	1	0	0	0
241	1	1	1	1	0	0	0	1	1	1	0	0
242	1	1	1	1	0	0	1	0	1	0	1	1
243	1	1	1	1	0	0	1	1	1	1	0	0
244	1	1	1	1	0	1	0	0	1	0	1	0
245	1	1	1	1	0	1	0	1	1	1	0	0
246	1	1	1	1	0	1	1	0	1	0	1	1
247	1	1	1	1	0	1	1	1	1	1	0	0
248	1	1	1	1	1	0	0	0	1	0	0	1
249	1	1	1	1	1	0	0	1	1	1	0	0
250	1	1	1	1	1	0	1	0	1	0	1	1
251	1	1	1	1	1	0	1	1	1	1	0	0
252	1	1	1	1	1	1	0	0	1	0	1	0
253	1	1	1	1	1	1	0	1	1	1	0	0
254	1	1	1	1	1	1	1	0	1	0	1	0
255	1	1	1	1	1	1	1	1	1	1	0	0

TABLE 4-2.1.1-2 PROM Coding for Priority Encoder

(2) During system operation, the unused lines A11 and A12 will be high only when the MPU is processing an interrupt; otherwise the address generated would be outside (below) the highest system assignment.

(3) If one of the lines A11-A13 is included in the decode, the MPU's response to an $\overline{IRQ}$ can be decoded by distinguishing between XXX8 and XXX9 and the other fourteen possibilities that can be generated by A1 through A4.

The resulting decode requirement is simply $\overline{A1}\cdot\overline{A2}\cdot A3\cdot A13$, as shown in Figure 4-2.1.2-1. INTERRUPT ADDRESS DECODE will be high only when the MPU has put FFF8 or FFF9 on the Address Bus.

Operation of the clock disable and data selection control for the 13-level circuitry is identical to that described in the preceeding section for the 8-level case. However, a different priority encoding method that uses two cascaded MC9318 8-input Priority Encoders is shown (this technique can be extended to any required

ADDRESS BUS   A15 A14 A13 A12 A11 A10 A9 A8 A7 A6 A5 A4 A3 A2 A1 A0
(VMA • A15 • A14 • A13 • A12 • A11 • A10)

ROM Connection	Ē	A9	A8	A7	A6	A5	A4	A3	A2	A1	A0		
	0	1	1	1	1	1	1	1	1	1	1	FFFF	$\overline{RES}$
	0	1	1	1	1	1	1	1	1	1	0	FFFE	
	0	1	1	1	1	1	1	1	1	0	1	FFFD	$\overline{NMI}$
	0	1	1	1	1	1	1	1	1	0	0	FFFC	
	0	1	1	1	1	1	1	1	0	1	1	FFFB	SWI
	0	1	1	1	1	1	1	1	0	1	0	FFFA	
	0	1	1	1	1	1	1	1	0	0	1	FFF9	1
	0	1	1	1	1	1	1	1	0	0	0	FFF8	
	0	1	1	1	1	1	1	0	1	1	1	FFF7	2
	0	1	1	1	1	1	1	0	1	1	0	FFF6	
	0	1	1	1	1	1	1	0	1	0	1	FFF5	3
	0	1	1	1	1	1	1	0	1	0	0	FFF4	
	0	1	1	1	1	1	1	0	0	1	1	FFF3	4
	0	1	1	1	1	1	1	0	0	1	0	FFF2	
	0	1	1	1	1	1	1	0	0	0	1	FFF1	5
	0	1	1	1	1	1	1	0	0	0	0	FFF0	
	0	1	1	1	1	1	0	1	1	1	1	FFEF	6
	0	1	1	1	1	1	0	1	1	1	0	FFEE	
	0	1	1	1	1	1	0	1	1	0	1	FFED	7
	0	1	1	1	1	1	0	1	1	0	0	FFEC	
	0	1	1	1	1	1	0	1	0	1	1	FFEB	8
	0	1	1	1	1	1	0	1	0	1	0	FFEA	

FIGURE 4-2.1.1-3. Interrupt Vector Memory Allocation

number of priority levels). The five additional interrupt register stages are obtained by using the ninth flip-flop in the MC8502 and an MC4015 Quad D Flip-Flop.

The characteristics of the MC9318 Priority Encoder introduce several other minor differences between the 13-level and 8-level circuits. Their operation requires active low input signals, hence the interrupts must be active low. The OUT of the lowest priority MC9318 stage can be used to generate $\overline{IRQ}$. EOUT of the highest priority stage (E'OUT in Figure 4-2.1.2-1) is used for the fourth bit, A4.

The resulting truth table for this configuration is shown in Figure 4-2.1.2-2. The "substitute partial

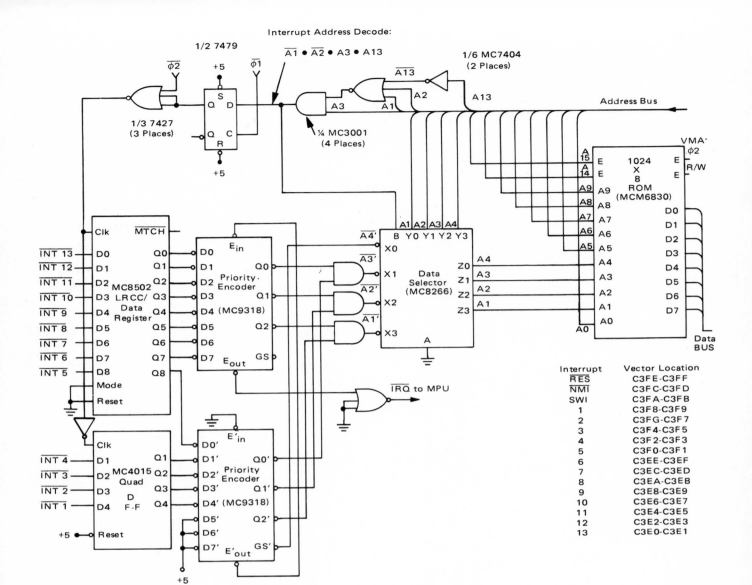

Interrupt Address Decode:

$\overline{A1} \bullet \overline{A2} \bullet A3 \bullet A13$

FIGURE 4-2.1.2-1. 13—Level Hardware Prioritized Interrupt Logic

Interrupt	Vector Location
$\overline{RES}$	C3FE-C3FF
$\overline{NMI}$	C3FC-C3FD
SWI	C3FA-C3FB
1	C3F8-C3F9
2	C3FG-C3F7
3	C3F4-C3F5
4	C3F2-C3F3
5	C3F0-C3F1
6	C3EE-C3EF
7	C3EC-C3ED
8	C3EA-C3EB
9	C3E8-C3E9
10	C3E6-C3E7
11	C3E4-C3E5
12	C3E2-C3E3
13	C3E0-C3E1

$\overline{INT}$	D7'	D6'	D5'	D4'	D3'	D2'	D1'	D0'	D7	D6	D5	D4	D3	D2	D1	D0	G'S (A4')	$\overline{A3}$	$\overline{A2}$	$\overline{A1}$	$\overline{E_{out}}$ $\overline{IRQ}$	A4	A3	A2	A1	
1	1	1	1	0	X	X	X	X	X	X	X	X	X	X	X	X	0	0	1	1	0	1	1	0	0	C3F8-C3F9
2	1	1	1	1	0	X	X	X	X	X	X	X	X	X	X	X	0	1	0	0	0	1	0	1	1	C3F6-C3F7
3	1	1	1	1	1	0	X	X	X	X	X	X	X	X	X	X	0	1	0	1	0	1	0	1	0	C3F4-C3F5
4	1	1	1	1	1	1	0	X	X	X	X	X	X	X	X	X	0	1	1	0	0	1	0	0	1	C3F2-C3F3
5	1	1	1	1	1	1	1	0	X	X	X	X	X	X	X	X	0	1	1	1	0	1	0	0	0	C3F0-C3F1
6	1	1	1	1	1	1	1	1	0	X	X	X	X	X	X	X	1	0	0	0	0	0	1	1	1	C3EE-C3EF
7	1	1	1	1	1	1	1	1	1	0	X	X	X	X	X	X	1	0	0	1	0	0	1	1	0	C3EC-C3ED
8	1	1	1	1	1	1	1	1	1	1	0	X	X	X	X	X	1	0	1	0	0	0	1	0	1	C3EA-C3EB
9	1	1	1	1	1	1	1	1	1	1	1	0	X	X	X	X	1	0	1	1	0	0	1	0	0	C3E8-C3E9
10	1	1	1	1	1	1	1	1	1	1	1	1	0	X	X	X	1	1	0	0	0	0	0	1	1	C3E6-C3E7
11	1	1	1	1	1	1	1	1	1	1	1	1	1	0	X	X	1	1	0	1	0	0	0	1	0	C3E4-C3E5
12	1	1	1	1	1	1	1	1	1	1	1	1	1	1	0	X	1	1	1	0	0	0	0	0	1	C3E2-C3E3
13	1	1	1	1	1	1	1	1	1	1	1	1	1	1	1	0	1	1	1	0	0	0	0	0	0	C3E0-C3E1
	1	1	1	1	1	1	1	1	1	1	1	1	1	1	1	1	1	1	1	1	1	0	0	0	0	

X = Doesn't Matter

FIGURE 4-2.1.2-2. Truth Table, 13-Level Priority Circuitry

[1]The MC4015 contains 4 type D flip-flops. All four flip-flops have common resets and common positive edge triggered clocks.

addresses'' that are selected during processing of an $\overline{IRQ}$ are shown in the memory map of Figure 4-2.1.2-3. Note that low signals on inputs D5', D6' and D7' of the high priority encoder stage would generate addresses in the range C3FA- C3FF. As mentioned in the preceding section, this would cause accessing of the locations reserved for $\overline{RES}$, NMI, and SWI vectors so those encoder inputs are not used.

This method can be expanded as required. For example, 21 levels could be obtained by adding one additional MC8502 register stage, one more MC9318 Priority Encoder, and one more bit of data selection. Three-input AND gates would be required for combining the encoder outputs.

ROM Connection	A15 E	A14 E	A13	A12	A11	A10	A9 A9	A8 A8	A7 A7	A6 A6	A5 A5	A4 A4	A3 A3	A2 A2	A1 A1	A0 A0		
	1	1					1	1	1	1	1	1	1	1	1	1	C3FF	$\overline{RES}$
	1	1	−	−	−	−	1	1	1	1	1	1	1	1	1	0	C3FE	
	1	1	−	−	−	−	1	1	1	1	1	1	1	1	0	1	C3FD	$\overline{NMI}$
	1	1	−	−	−	−	1	1	1	1	1	1	1	1	0	0	C3FC	
	1	1	−	−	−	−	1	1	1	1	1	1	1	0	1	1	C3FB	SWI
	1	1	−	−	−	−	1	1	1	1	1	1	1	0	1	0	C3FA	
	1	1	−	−	−	−	1	1	1	1	1	1	1	0	0	1	C3F9	INT 1
	1	1	−	−	−	−	1	1	1	1	1	1	1	0	0	0	C3F8	
	1	1	−	−	−	−	1	1	1	1	1	1	0	1	1	1	C3F7	2
	1	1	−	−	−	−	1	1	1	1	1	1	0	1	1	0	C3F6	
	1	1	−	−	−	−	1	1	1	1	1	1	0	1	0	1	C3F5	3
	1	1	−	−	−	−	1	1	1	1	1	1	0	1	0	0	C3F4	
	1	1	−	−	−	−	1	1	1	1	1	1	0	0	1	1	C3F3	4
	1	1	−	−	−	−	1	1	1	1	1	1	0	0	1	0	C3F2	
	1	1	−	−	−	−	1	1	1	1	1	1	0	0	0	1	C3F1	5
	1	1	−	−	−	−	1	1	1	1	1	1	0	0	0	0	C3F0	
	1	1	−	−	−	−	1	1	1	1	1	0	1	1	1	1	C3EF	6
	1	1	−	−	−	−	1	1	1	1	1	0	1	1	1	0	C3EE	
	1	1	−	−	−	−	1	1	1	1	1	0	1	1	0	1	C3ED	7
	1	1	−	−	−	−	1	1	1	1	1	0	1	1	0	0	C3EC	
	1	1	−	−	−	−	1	1	1	1	1	0	1	0	1	1	C3EB	8
	1	1	−	−	−	−	1	1	1	1	1	0	1	0	1	0	C3EA	
	1	1	−	−	−	−	1	1	1	1	1	0	1	0	0	1	C3E9	9
	1	1	−	−	−	−	1	1	1	1	1	0	1	0	0	0	C3E8	
	1	1	−	−	−	−	1	1	1	1	1	0	0	1	1	1	C3E7	10
	1	1	−	−	−	−	1	1	1	1	1	0	0	1	1	0	C3E6	
	1	1	−	−	−	−	1	1	1	1	1	0	0	1	0	1	C3E5	11
	1	1	−	−	−	−	1	1	1	1	1	0	0	1	0	0	C3E4	
	1	1	−	−	−	−	1	1	1	1	1	0	0	0	1	1	C3E3	12
	1	1	−	−	−	−	1	1	1	1	1	0	0	0	1	0	C3E2	
	1	1	−	−	−	−	1	1	1	1	1	0	0	0	0	1	C3E1	13
	1	1	−	−	−	−	1	1	1	1	1	0	0	0	0	0	C3E0	

FIGURE 4-2.1.2-3. Interrupt Vector Memory Allocation.

4-2.2   DIRECT MEMORY ACCESS (DMA)

In this section, three methods of implementing DMA using the MC6800 microprocessor are discussed along with the advantages and disadvantages of each method. The methods range from completely halting the processor in order to do the DMA transfer, to ''sandwiching'' in the DMA transfer during an MPU cycle without reducing throughput or increasing execution time appreciably.

4-2.2.1 DMA Transfers by Halting Processor

A block diagram of a minimum system configured for a DMA channel is shown in Figure 4-2.2.1-1. This system is shown with only four family parts for simplicity in demonstrating the DMA concept and can be expanded to a larger system without affecting the DMA methods discussed here. The DMA interface consists of a 16-bit address bus, an 8-bit bi-directional data bus, and the following control signals ϕ2, BA or DMA GRANT, $\overline{VMA}$, $\overline{HALT}$ or $\overline{DMA\ REQUEST}$, and R/W. The ϕ2 clock occurs whether the MPU is halted or not and is used to synchronize the DMA data.

The Bus Available (BA) signal from the MPU goes to a logic "1" when the MPU has halted and all three-state lines are in the high impedance state. The $\overline{VMA}$ signal is from an open collector gate and is high when the MPU is halted. This signal can be wire-ORed with an external signal from the DMA circuitry to enable the RAM during a DMA transfer. The $\overline{HALT}$ ($\overline{DMA\ REQUEST}$) signal from the DMA circuitry commands the MPU to halt and place all three-state lines in the high impedance state. The R/W line is a command signal from the DMA channel to control the direction of transfer through the DMA interface. For this system to operate correctly, the DMA circuitry connected to the MPU's Address Bus, Data Bus, and R/W line must have three-state outputs which are in the high impedance state when BA is low and the MPU is controlling the Address, Data, and Control Busses. The address assignment of this system is given in Table 4-2.2.1-1.

A timing diagram of the DMA/MPU interface using this technique is presented in Figure 4-2.2.1-2. A DMA transfer is initiated by the DMA channel pulling the $\overline{HALT}$ ($\overline{DMA\ REQUEST}$) low. $\overline{HALT}$ must go low synchronously with ϕ1. The negative transition of $\overline{HALT}$ must not occur during the last 250 nsec of ϕ1 for proper MPU operation to occur. It is suggested that $\overline{HALT}$ be brought low coincident with the rising edge of ϕ1. The MPU always completes the current instruction before halting. If the $\overline{HALT}$ line is low within 100 nsec after the leading edge of the ϕ1 in the last cycle of an instruction, the MPU will halt at the end of that instruction (this case is shown in Figure 4-2.2.1-2). If the $\overline{HALT}$ line goes low after this 100 nsec region from the leading edge of ϕ1 in the last cycle of an instruction, then the MPU will not halt at the end of the current instruction but will halt at the end of the next instruction.

SELECTION ADDRESS BITS		DEVICE	ADDRESS	AMOUNT OF MEMORY
A15	A14			
1	1	ROM	C000-C3FF	1024 Bytes
0	0	RAM	0000-007F	128 Bytes
0	1	PIA	4000-4003	4 Bytes

TABLE 4-2.2.1-1. Address Assignment

What this means to the DMA channel is that the time from the $\overline{HALT}$ line going low to the MPU halting and producing a BA (DMA GRANT) will be variable depending on what instruction is being executed at the time $\overline{HALT}$ goes low and in which cycle of that instruction HALT goes low. Since the $\overline{HALT}$ ($\overline{DMA\ REQUEST}$) signal will probably be asynchronous with respect to the instruction currently being executed, this will result in a variable time delay from $\overline{HALT}$ going low to BA (DMA GRANT) responding by going high. The minimum time delay between $\overline{HALT}$ and BA is shown in Figure 4-2.2.1-2 as being two cycles which would be 2 μseconds at the maximum clock rate of 1 MHz. The maximum time delay would occur if the $\overline{HALT}$ line goes low on the first cycle of a long instruction such as Software Interrupt (SWI), which is 12 cycles long. Added to

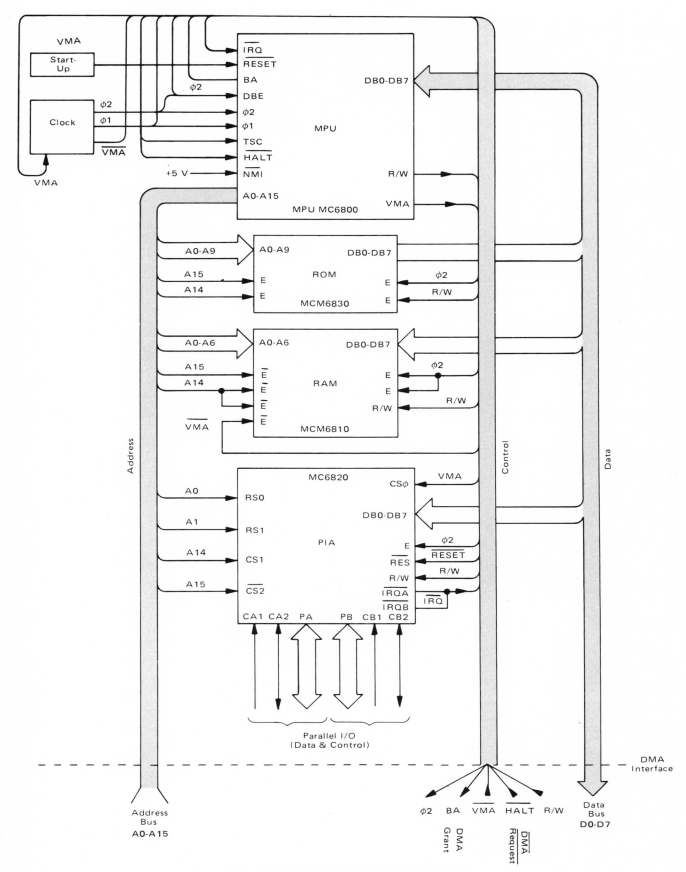

FIGURE 4-2.2.1-1. DMA Transfers by Halting Processor

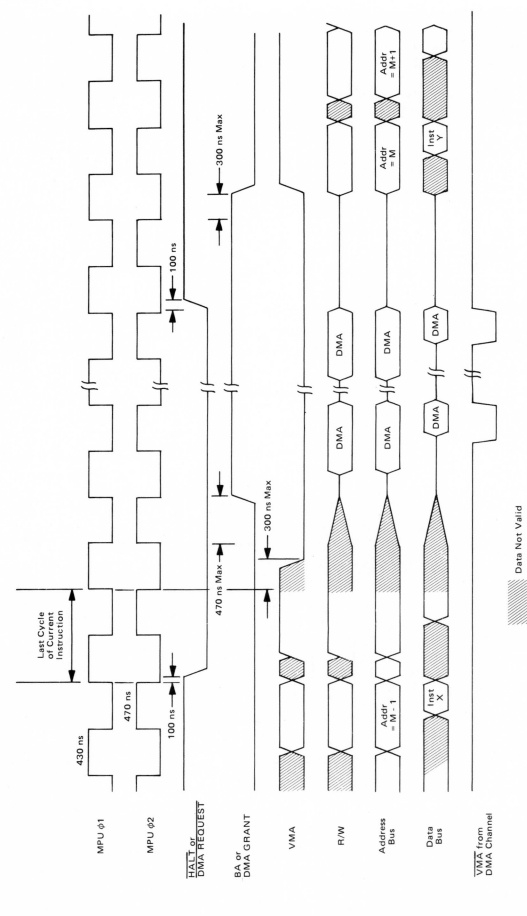

FIGURE 4-2.2.1-2. Timing of DMA Transfers by Halting the Microprocessor

the twelve cycles required to complete SWI is the one cycle required for the MPU's address, data and R/W signals to go into the high impedance state. In summary then, the delay time for the BA signal to go high after $\overline{HALT}$ goes low (assuming it occurs within 100 nsec of the leading edge of $\phi1$) will vary from two to thirteen machine cycles. This delay must be taken into account in the design of the DMA channel, however, it should not present a significant problem in most systems.

The other signals shown in Figure 4-2.2.1-2 indicate the response of the MPU to the $\overline{HALT}$ command. The VMA signal is forced low within 300 nsec of the leading edge of the $\phi1$ signal that occurs after the last instruction cycle has been completed. This signal going low will prevent false reads or writes to memory or peripherals on the MPU bus as the address and R/W lines go into the high impedance state. VMA from the MPU will remain low as long as the MPU is halted. The address, R/W, and data lines will be in the high impedance state when BA reaches the logic "1" state, indicating that DMA transfers can begin. Addresses, R/W commands, and Data to or from the DMA interface are shown in the timing diagram synchronized with $\phi2$ to indicate the DMA transfers. The MPU can remain in the halted mode indefinitely placing no constraints on the length of the DMA transfer.

Note that the RAM is enabled by $\overline{VMA}$ which is the output of an open collector inverting gate with VMA (from the MPU) as its input. This $\overline{VMA}$ signal is provided to the DMA interface so that the RAM can be enabled during the DMA transfer. During the transition into the $\overline{DMA}$ mode, the VMA signal from the MPU was forced low (forcing $\overline{VMA}$ high) to disable the RAM in order to protect it from false writes or reads as the address and R/W lines went into a high impedance condition. During DMA transfers, the $\overline{VMA}$ signal is wire-ORed with a DMA controller signal to enable the RAM. In order to exit the DMA mode, the $\overline{HALT}$ line is switched high (synchronously with the leading edge of $\phi1$), the BA signal returns low and the MPU resumes control. When BA returns low, it is required that the DMA channel's address, R/W and data lines be in the high impedance state and that $\overline{VMA}$ from the DMA channel be high so as not to affect MPU operation.

4-2.2.2   DMA Transfers by Cycle Stealing

The previous section discussed the transfer of DMA information by completly halting the MPU which stops program execution. This section discusses a technique of DMA transfer which slows down program execution during DMA transfer but does not completely stop execution. The basic technique is to "steal" MPU clock cycles for a DMA transfer; this results in a apparently lower clock rate and, therefore, slower program execution during the DMA transfer.

The block diagram of Figure 4-2.2.2-1 uses the same minimum system concept as was used in Section 4-2.2.1 to illustrate this DMA technique. The DMA Interface using this technique is composed of the following signals: a 16-bit Address Bus, an 8-bit Data Bus, CLOCK, $\overline{VMA}$, Three-State Control (TSC), and Read/Write (R/W). The CLOCK signal is an uninterrupted system clock that is used to synchronize DMA data transfers with the execution of the MPU. The $\overline{VMA}$ signal frrom the DMA interface is wire-ORed with the VMA signal generated in the clock circuitry to enable the RAM for either MPU access or a DMA transfer. The Three-State Control (TSC) or DMA ENABLE signal causes the address bus and the R/W signal to go into the high impedance state and forces the VMA signal low. This signal can also "stretch" the $\phi1$ and $\phi2$ clock signals. The Read/Write (R/W) line controls the direction of the data in or out of the DMA Interface. The Address Bus, Data Bus, and R/W signals at the DMA Interface must have three-state outputs so that when TSC is low, the DMA signals will not interfere with normal MPU execution.

A timing diagram of the DMA/Microprocessor interface using this technique is shown in Figure 4-2.2.2-2. Assume that the clock rate is initially adjusted to 1 μsec and that the MPU is executing the control

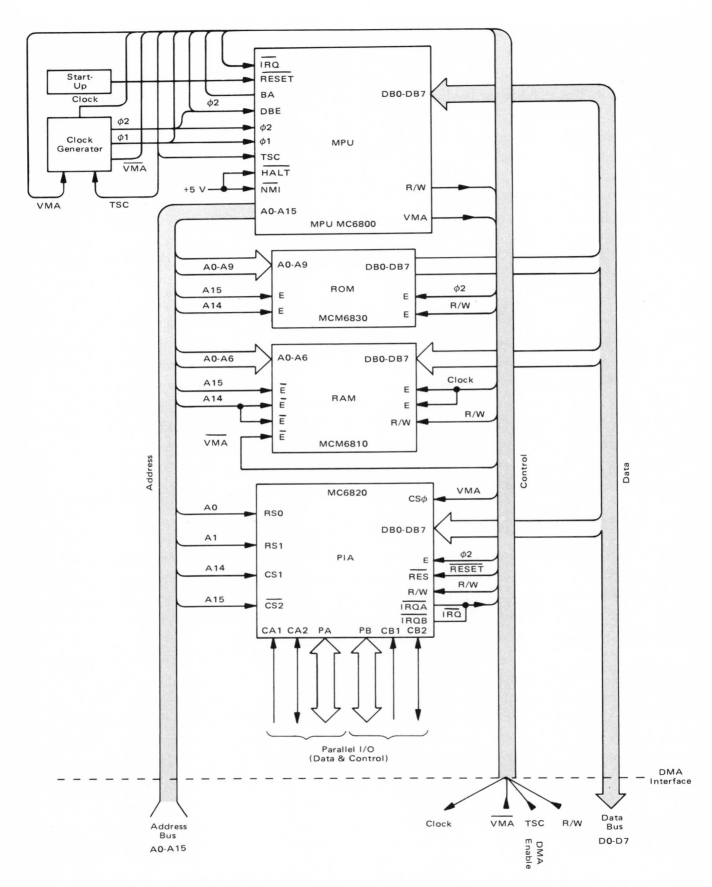

FIGURE 4-2.2.2-1. Block Diagram of DMA Transfers by Cycle Stealing

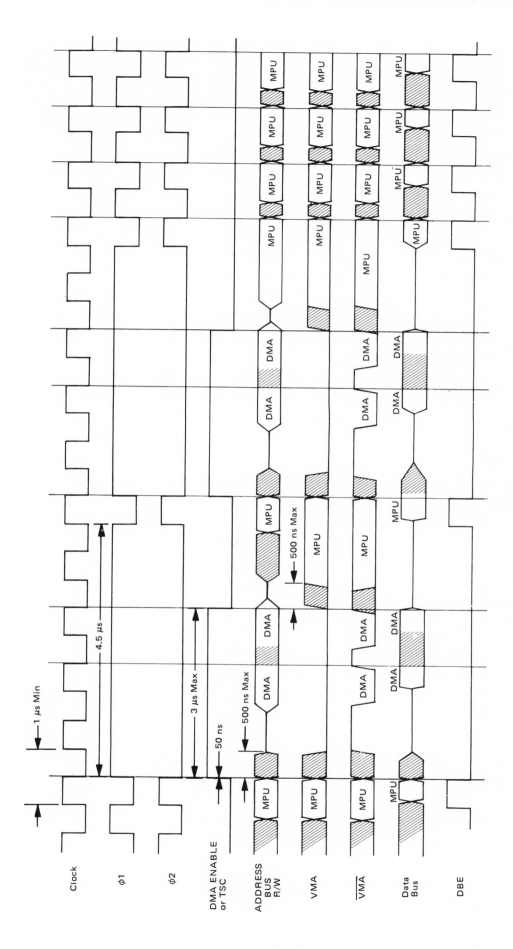

FIGURE 4-2.2.2-2 Timing of DMA Transfers by Cycle Stealing

4-37

program. In order to initiate a DMA transfer, the DMA controller takes the DMA ENABLE (TSC) line to a logic "1" within 50 nsec of the leading edge of the $\phi 1$ clock. This signal goes to the TSC input of the MPU to command the Address Bus and the R/W line into the high impedance state. This will occur within 500 nsec of the rising edge of the TSC signal. The DMA ENABLE signal also goes to the clock generating circuitry to control the $\phi 1$ and $\phi 2$ clocks to the MPU as shown in Figure 4-2.2.2-2. $\phi 1$ must be held in the high state while DMA ENABLE is high and for one CLOCK cycle after DMA ENABLE goes low. $\phi 2$ is held in the low state while DMA ENABLE is high and for one CLOCK cycle after DMA ENABLE goes low. Neither $\phi 1$ nor $\phi 2$ to the MPU can be held high for longer than 4.5 μsec because of the need to refresh dynamic registers within the MPU. This constraint places a maximum time limit on DMA ENABLE being high of 3 μsec using this technique, so that the $\phi 1$ high time will not be greater than 4.5 μsec. DMA ENABLE may occur on the leading edge of any $\phi 1$ signal and MPU execution will be stopped regardless of the instruction currently being executed. This feature provides a fast and constant response of the MPU to the DMA ENABLE line.

The DMA address, R/W, and data signals can be placed on the MPU bus 500 nsec after DMA ENABLE (TSC) goes high (this is the time required for the MPU outputs to go to the high impedance state). In order to maintain a fully synchronous system, the DMA data is shown transferred during the CLOCK high time in Figure 4-2.2.2-2. The signal labeled VMA is from the MPU and is forced low when TSC is high. VMA is the output of a three-state or open collector inverter which normally follows $\overline{\text{VMA}}$ but can be pulled low by the DMA controller to enable the RAMs during the DMA transfer. DBE of the MPU is driven by the $\phi 2$ clock and enables the MPU data buffers only during the MPU cycles.

In the timing diagram, only two DMA transfers (of two bytes each) are shown before the full execution rate of the MPU is resumed for simplicity in drawing the figure. There is no limit to the number of DMA transfers that can be made using this technique, which can range from one byte transfers (by shortening the DMA ENABLE high time to 2 μsec and only pulsing it once) to a continuous average DMA transfer rate of one byte every 2.5 μsec (by pulsing DMA ENABLE high for 3 μsec at a periodic rate of 5.0 μs). By using the continuous DMA transfer mode, one can handle a DMA channel with a maximum date rate of one byte every 2.5 μs and still execute the control program at a minimum rate of one cycle every 5.0 μs.

4-2.2.3 **Multiplexed DMA/MPU Operation**

This method of implementing DMA results in the highest DMA transfer rate and, at the same time, allows the highest MPU execution rate when compared to the previous DMA techniques discussed, but requires higher speed memories.

A block diagram of this technique is shown in Figure 4-2.2.3-1. The three-state buffers and transceivers shown are enabled when the control signals are high and provide the high speed multiplexing required to transfer DMA data to the memory during $\phi 1$ and to allow MPU access during $\phi 2$. The signals at the DMA INTERFACE are the following: 16 bit Address bus, 8-bit bidirectional Data Bus, Read/Write (R/W), Valid Memory Address (VMA), DMA SYNCH and the DMA CLOCK.

Figure 4-2.2.3-2 is a timing diagram of a multiplexed DMA/MPU operation. C1 and C2 are positive enables for the three-state buffers and transceivers and bracket the $\phi 1$ and $\phi 2$ signals so that the buffers are out of the high impedance state before either $\phi 1$ or $\phi 2$ goes high. The MPU operation has been slowed down to a 1.2 μs clock rate in order to show the timing requirements for a specific memory, the MCM6605; in general, the MPU clock rate will have to be adjusted for the speed of the memory devices dused. This timing diagram assumes that the memory cycle is equal to or less than 560 nsec. During $\phi 1$, the buffers associated with C1 are

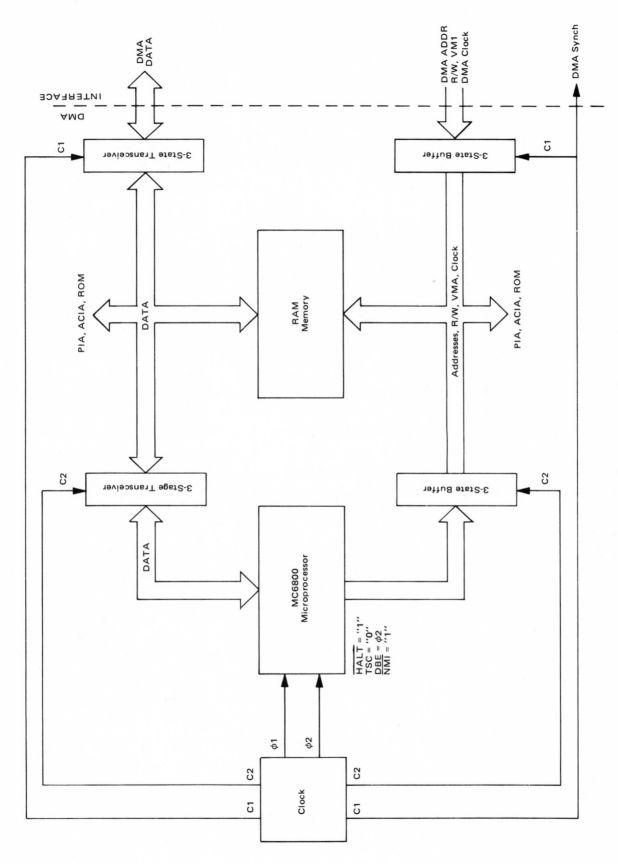

FIGURE 4-2.2.3-1. Multiplexed DMA/MPU Operation

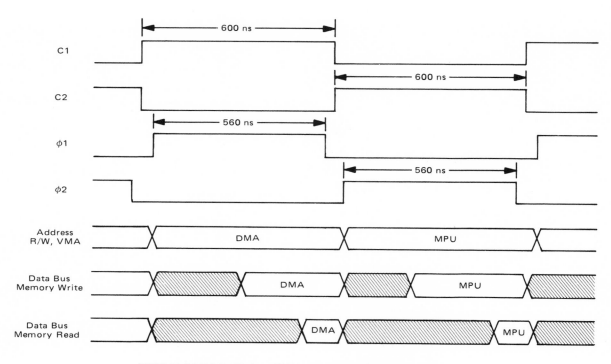

FIGURE 4-2.2.3-2. Timing of Multiplexed DMA/MPU Operation

enabled and the buffers associated with C2 are strobed into the high impedance state. The DMA SYNCH signal (C1) causes the DMA channel to place valid addresses, R/W, VMA and Data signals on the DMA INTER-FACE. When C2 goes high, the buffers from the DMA Interface are switched to the high impedance state and the MPU buffers are strobed on, applying the MPU's address, R/W, and VMA signals (which become valid during $\phi 1$) to the memory. The Data Bus signals from the MPU are applied to the memory at the leading edge of C2, however, the Data Bus signals do not become valid until 200 nsec after the leading edge of $\phi 2$.

By multiplexing in this manner, the MPU will have one $\phi 2$ cycle every 1.2 μs and the DMA channel can have access to the memory every 1.2 μs during $\phi 1$. This concept is not limited to DMA channels alone. For example, a multiprocessing system with two MPU's accessing one memory system could be implemented by connecting another MPU to the DMA INTERFACE. The second MPU will execute during the high portion of $\phi 1$ in place of the areas marked DMA on Figure 4-2.2.3-2.

Figure 4-2.2.3-3 details the timing interface with a memory device that is capable of meeting the speed requirements dictated by a 560 nsec memory system cycle time. This memory device is the MCM6605, a 4K X 1 dynamic RAM, which has an access time of 210 nsec and a Write Cycle Time of 490 nsec. Only the timing for the MPU data transfer is shown, however, the same timing would apply during $\phi 1$ for a DMA transfer. The address bus becomes valid 30 nsec (the delay of the bus buffers and transceivers in responding to the C2 signal) after the leading edge of C2. Addresses will remain valid until after $\phi 2$'s negative edge, however, they are only required for 60 nsec after the leading edge of CE to the memory as they are latched on the memory device. 100 nsec is allocated for delays in the memory system to receive the address, drive the memory array, and decode and drive the R/W and $\overline{CS}$ inputs of the memory array.

The CE signal is created from $\phi 2$ when the memory system has been selected by the Address Bus, and is delayed 180 nsec from the leading edge of $\phi 2$. The CE signal remains high until the trailing edge of $\phi 2$, creating a 380 nsec CE pulse which is 50 nsec longer than the 330 nsec minimum specification of the MCM6605.

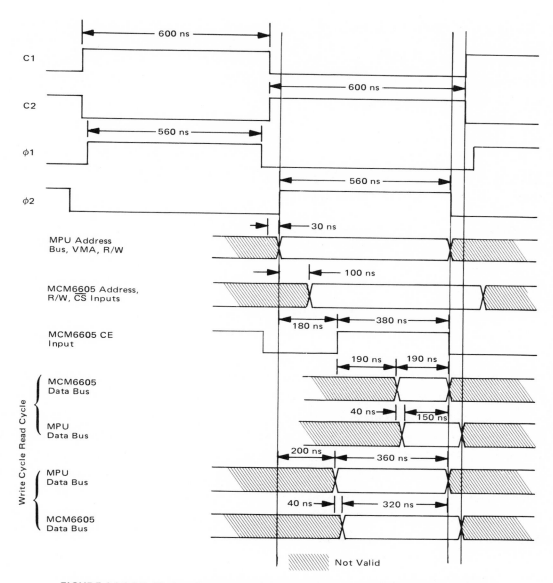

FIGURE 4-2.2.3-3. Timing of Multiplexed DMA/MPU Operation Using MCM6605 4k RAM

During a Read cycle, data is specified to be valid 190 nsec after the leading edge of the CE signal, assuming that the addresses are valid 20 nsec before the CE signal (which is the case here). Assuming a 40 nsec delay between the data lines of the memory array and the MPU data bus results in 150 nsec of valid data before the trailing edge of $\phi 2$. This exceeds the MPU requirement of 100 nsec by 50 nsec. In a Write cycle, the data is valid on the MPU Data Bus within 200 nsec of the leading edge of $\phi 2$. Again, assuming a 40 nsec delay between the MPU data bus and the data lines of the memory array results in 320 nsec of valid data before the trailing edge of CE. This exceeds the minimum D_{IN} stable requirement of the 4K RAM (160 nsec) by a factor of 2.

This timing has been based on the MCM6605, which is one of the faster MOS memories available. Even with this memory, the processor is required to run slightly slower to avoid exceeding the memory's speed. Many other timing diagrams could be drawn for the variety of memory devices available but the exact system implementation depends on the following considerations: DMA channel speed requirement, MPU execution rate requirement, and the speed of memory devices available.

4-2.2.4 Summary of DMA Techniques

Table 4-2.2.4-1 summarizes the DMA techniques previously discussed plus a comparison with a technique of bringing the data in through a PIA under software control, which is described in Section 5-4 on the Floppy Disk Controller design.

TECHNIQUE	MAX DMA CHANNEL RATE	MPU PROGRAM EXECUTION RATE	HARDWARE COMPLEXITY
Halt Processor	1 byte/1μs[1]	0	Lowest
Cycle Steal	1 byte/2.5μs	1 cycle/5μs	Medium
Multiplexed DMA	1 byte/1.2μs	1 cycle/1.2μs	Highest
Software/PIA	1 byte/14 μs	Dedicated to service DMA Channel	Lowest

[1] Limited only by memory speed.

TABLE 4-2.2-4.-1: Summary of DMA Techniques

The first DMA technique is to halt the processor and transfer the DMA data at the maximum rate the memories can handle. This technique has the advantage of requiring the least amount of hardware of the techniques discussed, but has the disadvantage of stopping program execution. The second technique of cycle stealing is a compromise between DMA transfer rate, MPU execution rate, and hardware complexity. The MPU execution time and the DMA transfer rate can be maximized using the third technique with an increase of system hardware complexity and memory speed by using a multiplexing technique for DMA. The Software/ PIA technique is based on the data being brought into memory through a PIA or ACIA interface under MPU software control. Using this technique, the MPU can be used at full capacity to service a data channel with a date rate of approximately 1 byte every 14 μs.

This brief description of DMA techniques is intended to provide a basic understanding of how the various control signals of the MPU can be used to implement a DMA channel. Each system design will involve different tradeoffs in order to satisfy the specific system requirements.

4-2.3 AUTOMATIC RESET AND SINGLE CYCLE EXECUTION CIRCUITRY

In an MPU based system where a manual reset is not desirable (manual reset can be accomplished with a switch and a debounce circuit), such as a remote peripheral controller, an automatic $\overline{\text{RESET}}$ signal must be provided. A circuit designed to accomplish this must satisfy the two start up criteria:

(1) It must insure that the power supply to the MPU has reached the minimum required operating voltage of 4.75 Vdc.

(2) The $\overline{\text{RESET}}$ line must then be held low for a *minimum* of 8 complete clock periods.

Of the many ways in which these criteria can be met, the circuit shown in Figure 4-2.3-1 is among the cheapest and simplest.

The MC1455 TIMER MODULE provides the delay necessary to complete a minimum of 8 clock cycles with the R_2C_2 time constant after the R_1C_1 time constant input has triggered the device insuring that V_{CC}

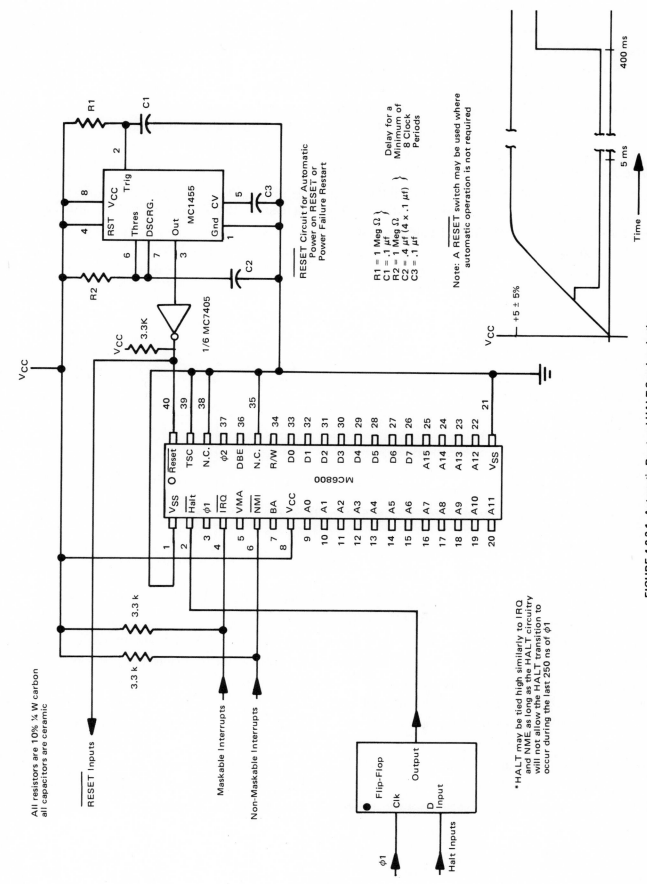

FIGURE 4-2.3-1. Automatic Reset and HALT Synchronization

4-43

has reached the minimum level. The particular RC values shown were chosen to be used with a crystal oscillator clock circuit which has a start-up time of approximately 100 ms. A 400 ms time out was used to cover the tolerances of the components used with room to spare. In an application requiring minimum reset delay, a counter could be used to determine when the 8 clock cycles were complete.

The interrupt inputs, $\overline{\text{IRQ}}$ and $\overline{\text{NMI}}$, need not be tied high if they are not used due to internal pull up resistors, but greater noise immunity will be had if they are tied high with a 5.1KΩ resistor. In wired-or interrupt applications, a pull up resistor of 3.3KΩ will provide optimum device operation.

The $\overline{\text{HALT}}$ input must not make a transition during the last 250 ns of $\phi1$. If this input is to be used in applications requiring the MPU status be saved (most applications), it must be synchronized with the leading edge of $\phi1$ or the trailing edge of $\phi2$. A flip-flop will accomplish this synchronization, or the circuitry generating the $\overline{\text{HALT}}$ request may use the system clock and not require extra hardware. This input also may be wire-ORed using an external 3.3KΩ pull up resistor.

Single instruction operation, which is useful during debug, is accomplished by holding the $\overline{\text{HALT}}$ high for one $\phi1$ clock cycle (Figure 4-2.3-2).

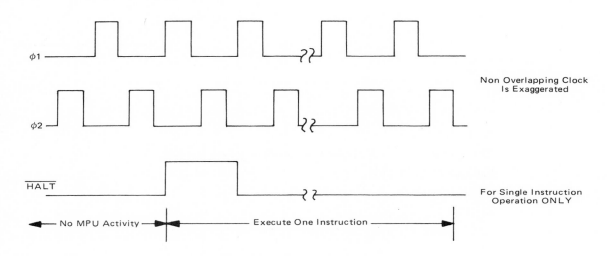

FIGURE 4-2.3-2. Single Instruction Timing

The circuit and timing diagrams of Figure 4-2.3-3 show how the single instruction execution can be accomplished in conjunction with the $\overline{\text{HALT}}$ input restrictions.

When the GO/HALT switch (S2) is in the GO position, A will be low after the first $\phi1$ clock causing the $\overline{\text{HALT}}$ input to be high. When the GO/HALT switch (S2) is in the HALT position, A will be high after the first $\phi1$ clock. Since S1's normal position causes C to be low, signal B will be high. A and B high cause the $\overline{\text{HALT}}$ to go low halting MPU activity.

When S1 is pushed, C goes high allowing the next positive $\phi1$ transition to clock F1. Since the J and K inputs of F1 are 1 and 0 respectively, this clock will cause D to go high and B to go low. The J and K inputs of F1 are now both 1. The next positive $\phi1$ transition will cause D to go low and B to go high clocking F2. J of F1 now goes low. With both J and K of F1 low, any further clock transitions will cause no change in the outputs until C is again made to go low. A and B are NANDed to produce the $\overline{\text{HALT}}$ input signal.

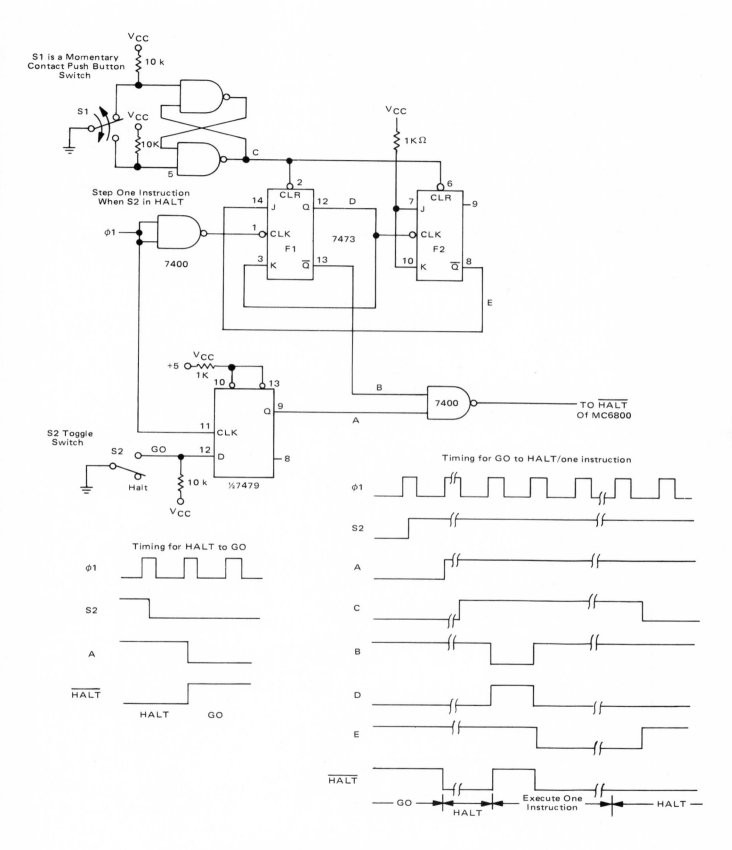

FIGURE 4-2.3-3. Single Cycle Instruction Execution

4-2.4 INTERVAL TIMER

A hardware interval timer circuit can be used to provide the MPU system with timing interrupts that are under program control. This allows the system to perform other functions while long critical timing functions, e.g., disk head step time during seek, printer line feed solenoid hold period, cassette gap and record length, etc., are performed by the interval timer. An interval timer using an MC6820 PIA to interface to TTL timing circuitry shown in Figure 4-2.4-1.

Table 4-2.4-1 shows how the interval timer of Figure 4-2.4-1 is programmed. An 8 bit binary count (COUNT) is preset into the MC74455 up/down counter from Output Register B of the controlling PIA (If a MC74454 counter was used, a 2-digit BCD value may be used). The counter then counts this value down to zero using the clock rate provided by the programmable divider circuits. When the counter reaches 0, the $\overline{SEO}$' output triggers the CB1 input of the PIA generating an interrupt to the operating system.

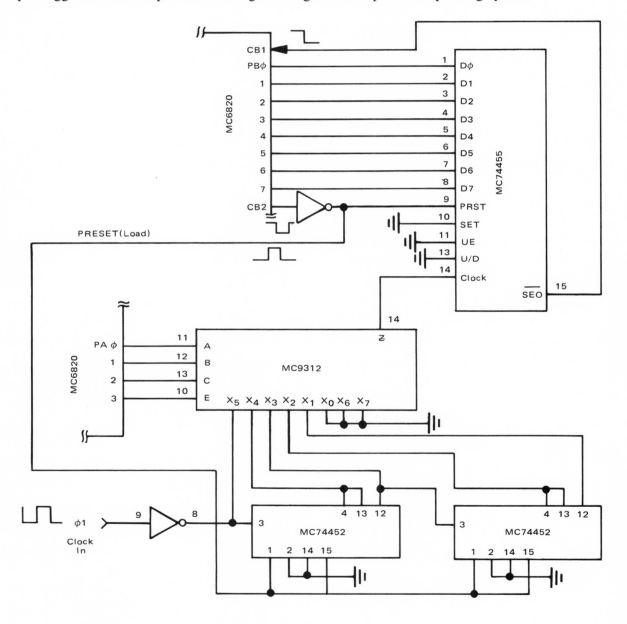

FIGURE 4-2.4-1. Interval Timer

| PA0-PA3 | | | | CLOCK FREQ | INTERVAL TIMER DELAY |
b3	b2	b1	b0		
0	0	0	0	0	—
0	0	0	1	100 Hz	COUNT X 10 ms
0	0	1	0	1 KHz	COUNT X 1 ms
0	0	1	1	10 KHz	COUNT X 100μs
0	1	0	0	100 KHz	COUNT X 10μs
0	1	0	1	1 MHz	COUNT X 1μs
0	1	1	0	0	—
0	1	1	1	0	—
1	0	0	0	0	—

Count = Binary Value of PB0 — PB7

```
01800                        •  Interval Timer 8-Bit Prescale Constants
01800         0005   01US     EQU    5        1   Microsecond Clock
01800         0004   010US    EQU    4       10   Microsecond Clock
01800         0003   0100US   EQU    3      100   Microsecond Clock
01800         0002   01MS     EQU    2        1   Millisecond Clock
01800         0001   010MS    EQU    1       10   Millisecond Clock

01801                        •  Interval Timer 16-Bit Prescale Constants
01801         0500   S1US     EQU    1280     1   Microsecond Clock
01801         0400   S10US    EQU    1024    10   Microsecond Clock
01801         0300   S10PUS   EQU    768    100   Microsecond Clock
01801         0200   S1MS     EQU    512      1   Millisecond Clock
01801         0100   S10MS    EQU    256     10   Millisecond Clock
01900  5000                   ORG    15000   10   Millisecond Clock
```

TABLE 4-2.4-1. Interval Timer Programming Chart

The programmable divider uses the PA0-PA2 lines of the PIA to control the MC9312 8-channel data selector which acts as a single pole 8 position switch. A 4 decade divider chain is provided by the 2-MC74452 dual decade counters. The input clock (ϕ1, nominally 1 MHz) and all 4 decade outputs (100 KHz, 10KHz, 1 KHz, 100 Hz) are provided as inputs to the data selector. Table 4-2.4-1 shows the various data selector output frequencies and the resulting delay generated. The binary value of COUNT is preset into the MC74454 counter as the starting point of the count down. The counter counts down at the rate determined by the code in PA0-PA3 until the zero state is reached at which time $\overline{SE0}$ goes low causing a MPU interrupt. A one written in b$_3$ of Peripheral Register A causes PA3 to go high, disabling the clocks to the MC74455 and the interval timer. The timer may also be disabled by selecting a grounded input code on the 9312 as noted by "0" clock frequency in Table 4-2.4-1.

Figure 4-2.4-2 shows examples of software control of the interval timer hardware in Figure 4-2.4-1. In these examples, it is assumed that the PIA's are already intialized to provide PB0-PB7 and PA0-PA3 as data output lines (ones in the Data Direction Registers). In the first example, the control registers for the A and B sides of the PIA are initialized to provide access to Peripheral Register B, to provide a negative pulse on CB2 when the B Data Register is written into, and to cause an interrupt on the $\overline{IRQ}$ line when CB1 sees a negative transition. Control Register A is set up to provide access to Peripheral Register A. The clock rate of 1 millisecond is binary 0010 or decimal 2 from Table 4-2.4-1 and is stored in XP2DRA (Peripheral Data Register A) which outputs 0010 on PA0-PA3 selecting the clock rate. The counter value of decimal 236 is stored into XP2DRB (Peripheral Data Register B) causing binary 1110 1100 to appear on PB0-PB7 and CB2 to pulse low,

```
                    .
                    .
                    .
** 236 MS TIME OUT USING 8 BIT PRESCALE
        LDAA    #%00101101      PRB ACCESS, CB2 PULSE LOW, CB1 ↓
        STA     XP2CRB          STORE IN CONTROL REGISTER B
        LDAA    #%00000100      PRA ACCESS
        STA     XP2CRA          STORE IN CONTROL REGISTER A
        LDAA    #C1MS           CLOCK RATE
        LDAB    #236            COUNTER VALUE
        STAA    XP2DRA          OUTPUT RATE TO PA0-PB3
        STAB    XP2DRB          OUTPUT COUNTER VALUE TO PB0-PB7
C1MS  EQU     2               1 MILLISECOND CLOCK RATE
                    .
                    .
                    .
** 236 MS TIME OUT USING 16 BIT PRESCALE
        LDAA    #$0010101       PRB ACCESS, CB2 PULSE LOW, CB1 ↓
        STA     XP2CRB          STORE IN CONTROL REGISTER B
        LDX     #S1MS+236       LOAD INDEX REGISTER WITH S1MS+236
        STX     SP2DRA          RATE TO PA0-PA3, VALUE TO PB0-PB7
S1MS  EQU     512             1 MILLISECOND CLOCK RATE
                    .
                    .
                    .
                    .
                    .
```

FIGURE 4-2.4-2. Timer Software Examples

thereby, presetting the MC74455 counter. CB1 is monitoring the $\overline{SE0}$ output of the counter waiting for a low transition indicating that the counter has reached the zero state, resulting in the required 236 msec delay.

The second example uses different software code to arrive at the same result. The initialization of the PIA's is the same as discussed previously. In this case, the index register is used to form a 16-bit word which is then loaded into PRA and PRB. Address line A0 is connected to RS1 and A1 is connected to RS0 of the PIA so that PRA and PRB are consecutive memory locations. The 16-bit word is formed by loading the sum of S2MS and decimal 236 into the index register. Note that S1MS always will occupy XH and the offset (which has to be less than 255) will always occupy XL of the index register. By storing this value to XP2DRA (Peripheral Register A), S1MS will be loaded into PRA and 236 will be loaded into PRB (the next memory location). This technique of connecting the PIA for adjacent Peripheral Reg. locations and using the Index instructions to store two bytes at a time produces the same result as the previous example with less code.

4-2.5   MEMORY SYSTEM DESIGN

4-2.5.1   Interfacing the MC6800 with Slow and Dynamic Memories

There are many different system configurations utilizing the MC6800 microprocessor (MPU) with memories that are not a part of the M6800 family. In many applications, the most cost effective system will use memories that are slower than the 575 ns access time required by the MC6800 running at maximum speed or will be of the dynamic type so that the refresh requirement of the memory will have to be handled by the system.

The purpose of this section is to discuss methods of operating the MC6800 with these two classes of memories and to describe the operation of the MC6800 in relationship to memory usage in enough detail so that the user can develop system configurations using slow and/or dynamic memories.

The MC6800 microprocessor uses two non-overlapping clocks to time the execution of the program by the MPU. Figure 4-2.5.1-1 details the specification of the clock requirements for the M6800 family. The use of dynamic registers inside of the MC6800 places the following timing restriction on the clock waveforms. The clocks can be held in one state for a maximum of 5 μs without loss of the information contained in the dynamic registers.

In Figures 4-2.5.1-2 and 4-2.5.1-3 are the timing diagrams of a M6800 Read and Write cycle. As can be seen from these timing diagrams, during $\phi1$ control lines (address, R/W and VMA) are placed valid on the MPU bus and during $\phi2$, data is transferred between the MPU and memories or peripherals.

The minimum cycle time is 1.0 μsec and the following control signals are valid 300 nsec after the leading edge of $\phi1$: R/W (TASR), address lines (TASC), and VMA (TVSC). During a read cycle, the data must be valid on the data bus 100 nsec (TDSU) before the trailing edge of $\phi2$, allowing 575 nsec for memory or peripheral access time (TACC) assuming a rise time on the clock waveform of 25 nsec. During a write cycle, the timing is the same for the control signals; the MPU places data to be written on the data bus within 200 nsec (TASD) after the leading edge of $\phi2$ and will hold the data valid for a minimum of 10 nsec (TH) after the trailing edge of $\phi2$. This produces a minimum of 280 nsec (470 + 10 − 200) of valid data (TDATA VALID) available to be written into the memory or peripheral. Many memory or peripheral devices including the M6800 family devices can meet this timing requirement and their use poses no problems.

SLOW MEMORY INTERFACE

The following discussion will describe some techniques that can be used to interface the MC6800 with memories or peripherals that have an access time slower than 575 nsec and/or require data valid during a write operation for longer than 280 nsec. The basic technique of using the MC6800 with slower memories is to lengthen or stretch $\phi2$, the data transfer portion of the MPU cycle. $\phi2$ can be stretched to a maximum of 5.0 μsec, allowing use of memories with an access time of 5,105 nsec (575 + 5000 −470) and a write data valid time of 4,810 nsec (280 + 5000 − 470). Operation of the MPU at these speeds is slow enough for the vast majority of memory or peripheral devices on the market today. Operation with a slower device than can be accomplished by stretching $\phi2$ to 5 μsec is possible by using the interrupt feature of the MC6820 Peripheral Interface Adapter and treating the extremely slow memory as one would a slow peripheral.

There are two ways to implement the stretching of $\phi2$ to accommodate slower memories. The first and the simplest method is to stretch $\phi2$ every cycle regardless of whether the current cycle is an access to slow memory or not. $\phi2$ should be lengthened by the amount the access time of the slowest peripheral or memory exceeds 575 nsec (TACC of 6800). Examples are shown in Figures 4-2.5.1-4 and 4-2.5.1-5 for a slow memory with access time of 1000 nsec with $\phi2$ increased by 425 nsec (1000-575). The cycle time of the MPU has now become 1.425 μsec, resulting in slower program execution by about 30% due to the slow memory. The advantage of this approach is that it is the simplest to implement in hardware (only a change in the clock waveforms is required). The disadvantage is the reduction of execution time and corresponding reduction in data throughout.

If the MPU is servicing several slow peripherals, the reduction in MPU speed may not affect system operation. However, in many systems such as real time control, the MPU speed is critical to system operation and a 30% reduction would be undesirable. The second method of operation with slow memories that has a

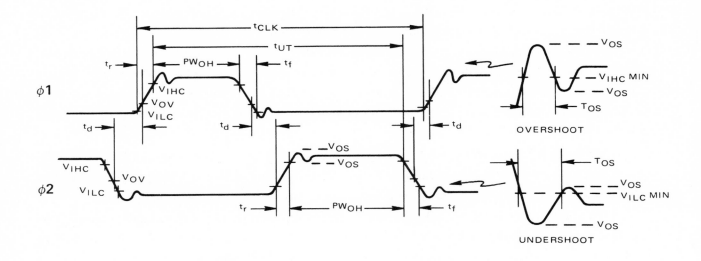

CHARACTERISTIC	SYMBOL	MIN	TYP	MAX	UNITS
Input High Voltage $\phi1$, $\phi2$	V_{IHC}	Vcc-0.3	—	Vcc + 0.1	Vdc
Input Low Voltage $\phi1$, $\phi2$	V_{ILC}	Vss-0.1	—	Vss + 0.3	Vdc
Clock Overshoot/Undershoot	V_{OS}				Vdc
Input High Voltage		Vcc-0.5	—	Vcc = 0.5	Vdc
Input Low Voltage		Vss-0.5		Vss + 0.5	
Input Leakage Current $\phi1$, $\phi2$ (V_{IN} = 0 to 5.25 V, Vcc = MAX)	I_{IN}	—	—	100	μa
Capacitance (V_{IN} = 0, T_A = 25°C, f = 1.0MHz)	C_{IN}	80	120	160	pf
Frequency of Operation	f	0.1	—	1.0	MHz
Clock Timing					
Cycle Time	t_{cyc}	1.0	—	1.0	μs
Clock Pulse Width					
(Measured at Vcc-0.3 V) $\phi1$	PW_{OH}	430	—	4500	ns
$\phi2$		450	—	4500	ns

Rise and Fall Times $\phi1$, $\phi2$
        (Measured between
        Vss + 0.3 V and Vcc-0.3 V)
	t_r, t_f	5	—	50	ns

Delay Time or Clock Overlap (Measured at V_{OV} = Vss + 0.5 V)	t_d	0	—	9050	ns
Overshoot/Undershoot Duration	t_{OS}	0	—	40	ns
Clock High Times	t_{UT}	940	—	—	ns

FIGURE 4-2.5.1-1. MPU Clock Waveform Specifications

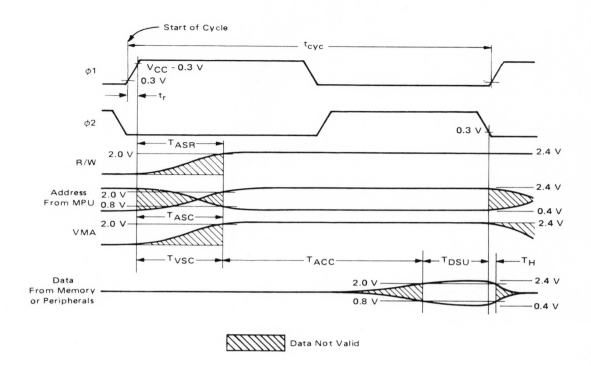

FIGURE 4-2.5.1-2. Read Data From Memories or Peripherals

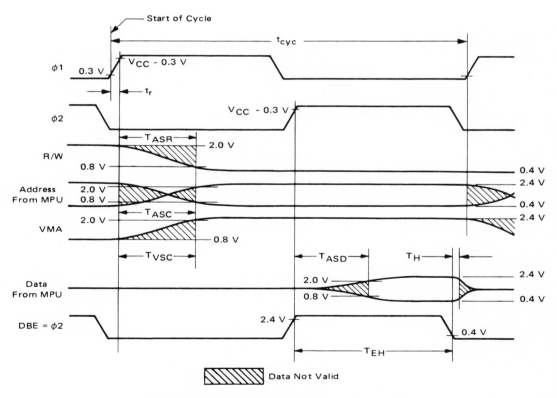

FIGURE 4-2.5.1-3. Write Data to Memories or Peripherals

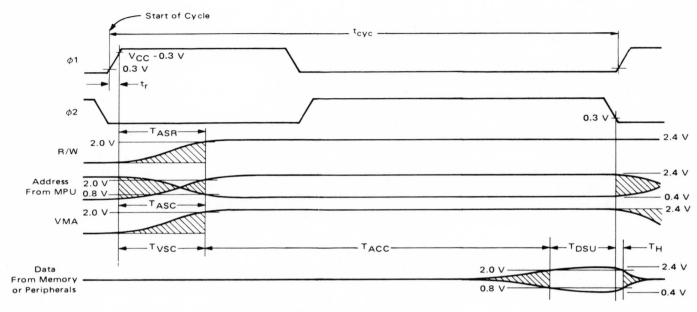

Data Not Valid

$$t_{cyc} = 1.425 \, \mu s \qquad \phi 1 \, PW_{OH} = 430 \, ns \, Min$$
$$T_{ASA} = T_{ASC} = T_{VSC} = 300 \, ns \, Min \qquad \phi 1 \, PW_{OH} = 895 \, ns \, Min$$
$$T_{ACC} = 1.0 \, \mu s \, Max$$
$$T_{DSU} = 100 \, ns \, Min$$

FIGURE 4-2.5.1-4. Read Cycle With 1.0 μs Memory

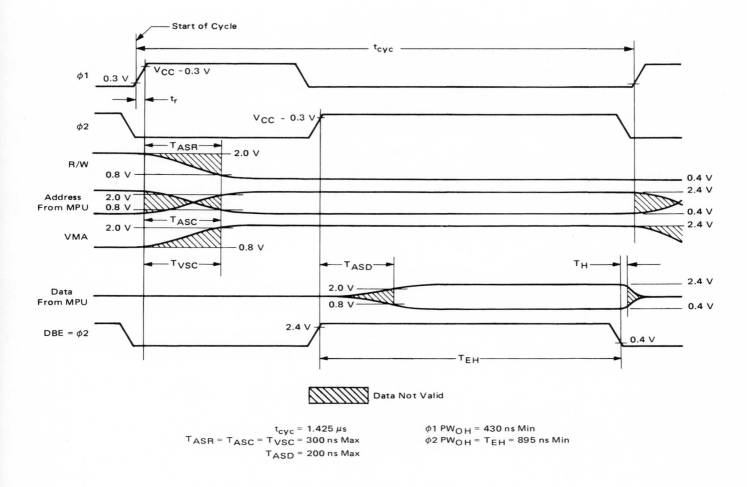

t_{cyc} = 1.425 μs

T_{ASR} = T_{ASC} = T_{VSC} = 300 ns Max

T_{ASD} = 200 ns Max

ϕ1 PW_{OH} = 430 ns Min

ϕ2 PW_{OH} = T_{EH} = 895 ns Min

FIGURE 4-2.5.1-5. Write Cycle With 1.0 μs Memory

smaller reduction in MPU execution time involves the use of a Memory Ready concept. In this configuration, a MEMORY READY signal is used between the slow memory and the MPU clock circuitry to indicate that a slow memory has been accessed. This signal goes low long enough for data to become valid out of the slow memory. While MEMORY READY is low, ϕ2, is stretched or lengthened as shown in Figure 4-2.5.1-6. This technique only slows execution of the processor when the slow memory is being accessed. The amount by which the throughput of the MPU is reduced due to the slow memory is directly proportional to the number of slow memory accesses and can be evaluated for each system configuration. Memory devices do not inherently provide a MEMORY READY type signal; this signal must be generated by the interface circuitry associated with the slow memory system.

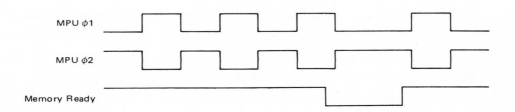

FIGURE 4-2.5.1-6. Effect of MEMORY READY on Clock Signals

A block diagram of a generalized MPU to memory interface is shown in Figure 4-2.5.1-7. The address and control signals are shown buffered from the MPU bus to increase fanout (in a small system, this may not be required). The low order address lines (A0 to A9 for a 1K memory) and the R/W signal are routed to the memory devices directly. The high order address lines, VMA, and $\phi 2$ are decoded to select this memory system using the Chip Select input of the memory devices. All high order address lines may be decoded, however, in many small systems, this decoding logic may be eliminated by selecting the memory devices with only one or two of the high order address bits. By not decoding all address lines, multiple areas of the 65K address map are selected at the same time requiring careful assignment of addresses for memory and peripherals (see the minimum system discussion in Chapter 1 for further explanation). The data buffers may be required for

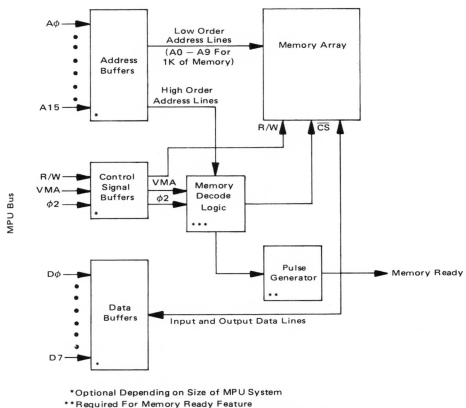

*Optional Depending on Size of MPU System
**Required For Memory Ready Feature
***Can Be Replaced by Multiple Chip Select Inputs on Memory Devices

FIGURE 4-2.5.1-7. General MPU to MEMORY INTERFACE

system fanout considerations or may be required to combine the separate data input and data output lines found on many memory devices into bidirectional data lines as required by the MPU. If the memory devices chosen are not fast enough to meet the MPU timing requirements at maximum operating frequency of 1 MHz, pulse generating circuitry can be added to provide the MEMORY READY signal. This signal can be triggered by the Chip Select decoding logic to stretch $\phi 2$ of the current cycle long enough to allow proper operation of the slow memory devices.

DYNAMIC MEMORY INTERFACE

All dynamic memories have the basic characteristic that they require periodic refreshing of their data storage elements (usually capacitors). Most dynamic memory devices handle this refresh requirement by performing 32 or 64 refresh cycles every 2 msec. During these refresh cycles, the memory is not available for a Read or Write cycle from the system bus (by MPU or DMA). The "memory busy" period for most dynamic memory devices is of short duration, normally 1-5% of the total time.

The simplest method for handling this refresh requirement is to steal MPU cycles in order to refresh the memory. The effect of the stolen processor cycles on system operation is to slow program execution or data throughput. Figure 4-2.5.1-8 shows the dynamic memory interface and the clock waveforms associated with a cycle steal configuration. During $\phi1$, address control signals are set valid by the MPU in preparation for the

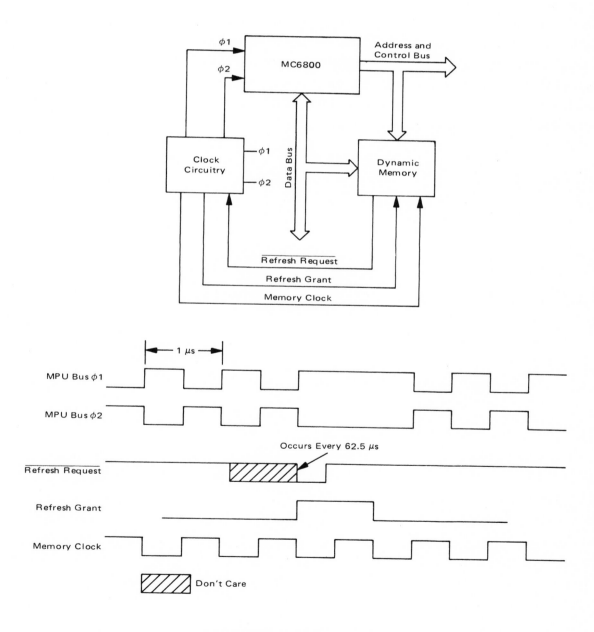

FIGURE 4-2.5.1-8. Dynamic Memory Interface

4-55

data transfer during $\phi2$. By stretching or lengthening the $\phi1$ portion of the cycle, program execution is delayed, allowing memory refresh to take place. Circuitry in the memory system controller multiplexes in the refresh addresses and controls the memory R/W and $\overline{CS}$ lines to provide proper signals for the refresh cycle. For a dynamic memory that requires 32 cycles of refresh every 2 msec and with the MPU running at the maximum clock rate of 1 μsec, the reduction in MPU speed due to clock stealing would be $\dfrac{32 \times 1\ \mu sec\ (100)}{2\ msec} = 1.6\%$.

In most systems, this reduction in program execution time would not affect system performance.

In some systems, the design constraints may be such that a reduction in program execution time due to memory refresh requirements cannot be tolerated. For these types of systems, a "hidden" refresh configuration may be used. The place to hide or perform the memory refresh independent of MPU program execution time is during $\phi1$ as no data is being transferred between the MPU and memory or peripherals. This technique places the additional constraint on the dynamic memory system of being able to perform a complete refresh cycle during $\phi1$ (430 ns minimum) and a complete Read or Write cycle during $\phi2$ (470 ns minimum) if the MPU is to operate at full speed. Using this concept only 32 of the $\phi1$ periods every 2 msec are used for refreshing (for the dynamic memory discussed earlier) leaving the other $\phi1$ time periods open for other uses. One use would be for a DMA transfer from some external source. In this mode, DMA and memory refresh would share the $\phi1$ portion of the cycle while the MPU would have access to the memory during $\phi2$ portion of the cycle. See Section 4-2.2 for a further discussion of DMA techniques.

CLOCK CIRCUITRY FOR SLOW AND DYNAMIC MEMORIES

The circuitry to modify the clock signals to interface the M6800 with dynamic and slow memories as described above can be evolved from the clock circuitry described in Section 4-1.1.1. Figure 4-2.5.1-9 illustrates a previous clock circuit (Figure 4-1.1.1-3) with a crystal stabilized source which has been extended to include interface signals for dynamic ($\overline{\text{REFRESH REQUEST}}$ and REFRESH GRANT) and slow memories (MEMORY READY). Note that the only extra parts required are a MC7479 dual latch, MC7404 hex inverter, and a pair of 10K ohm pull-up resistors. The state of $\overline{\text{REFRESH REQUEST}}$ is sampled during the leading edge of $\phi1$ and, if it is low, the $\phi1$ and $\phi2$ clocks to the MPU are held in the high and low states respectively for at least one full clock cycle. A high REFRESH GRANT signal is issued to indicate to the dynamic memory system that this cycle is a refresh cycle. Upon receipt of the REFRESH GRANT signal, the memory system controller sets $\overline{\text{REFRESH REQUEST}}$ back high which is clocked through on the next leading edge of $\phi1$, thereby restoring the system back to normal operation. The MEMORY READY line is sampled on the leading edge of $\phi2$ and, if low, the MPU $\phi1$ and $\phi2$ clocks are held in the low and high states, respectively. The clocks will be held in these states until the MEMORY READY line is brought high by the slow memory controller, allowing the slow memory controller to determine the amount by which $\phi2$ is stretched. Figures 4-2.5.1-10a, b show the effect of REFRESH REQUEST and MEMORY READY signals on the MPU clocks. Note that the REFRESH REQUEST signal is asynchronous with the MPU clocks as it is generated by the refresh oscillator in the dynamic memory controller. Figures 4-2.5.11a, b shows the phase relationship between MPU $\phi2$, BUS $\phi2$, and DYNAMIC MEMORY CLOCK. Note that BUS $\phi2$ and MPU $\phi2$ are in phase and that DYNAMIC MEMORY CLOCK leads MPU $\phi2$ to help offset delays added by the memory system controller in decoding the level shifting this signal onto the memory array.

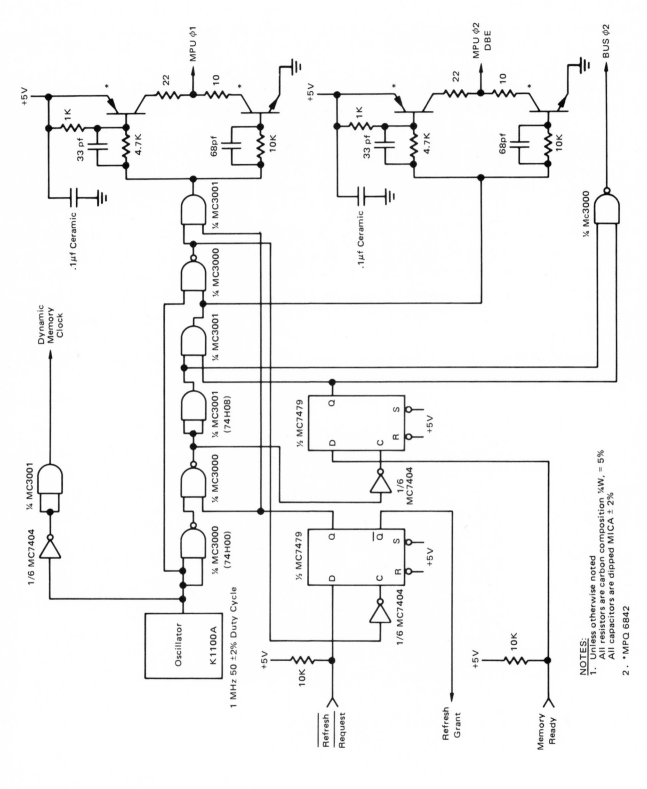

FIGURE 4-2.5.1-9. MPU Clock Circuitry with Interface for Slow and Dynamic Memory

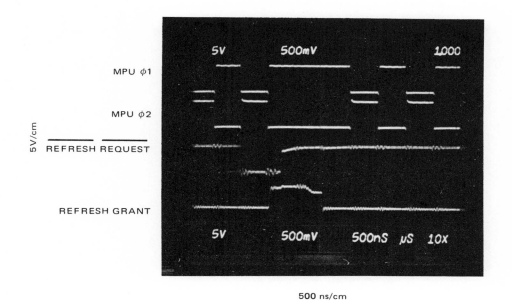

500 ns/cm

(a)

MPU Clocks, REFRESH REQUEST, REFRESH GRANT

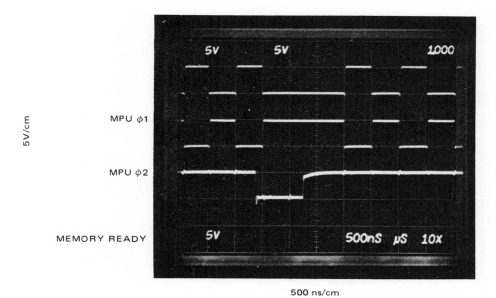

500 ns/cm

(b)

MPU Clocks, MEMORY READY

FIGURE 4-2.5.1-10: MPU Clock Circuitry

Mem Clk: 4 V Pulse   MPU φ2: 5 V Pulse

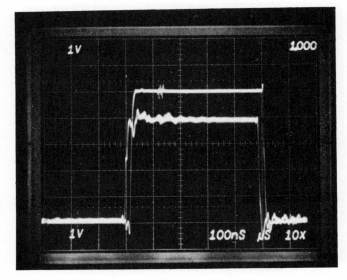

100 ns/cm

(a)

Dynamic Memory Clock and MPU 02

Bus φ2: 4 V Pulse   MPU φ2: 5 V Pulse

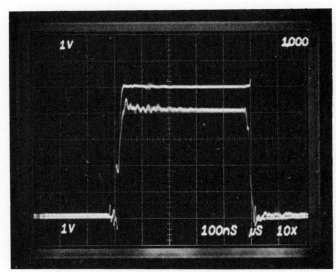

100 ns/cm

(b)

Bus φ2 and MPU φ2

FIGURE 4-2.5.1-11: MPU Clock Circuitry

The circuit in Figure 4-2.5.1-12 shows how the MEMORY READY concept can be added to the cross coupled monostable clock generator of Figure 4-1.1.1-5. The MEMORY READY feature is incorporated into this circuit by switching an additional timing resistor in or out of the $\phi2$ pulse width generator. By selection of the timing resistors for $\phi1$ and $\phi2$, all combinations of $\phi1$, $\phi2$, and stretched $\phi2$ pulse width can be generated.

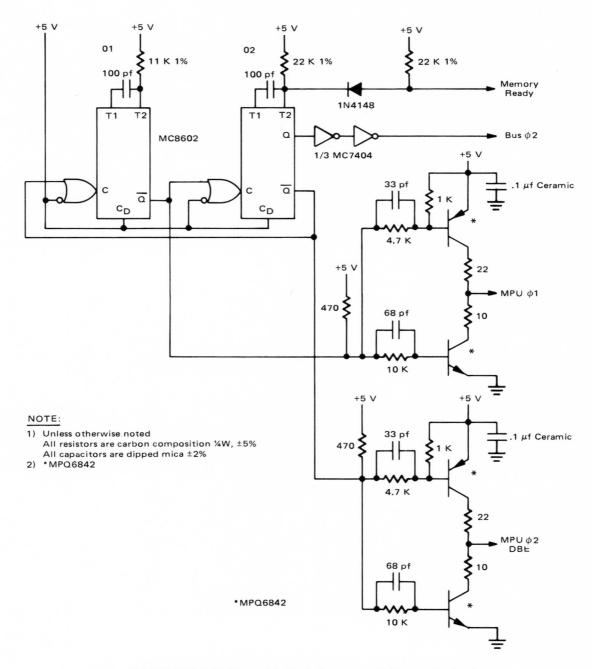

FIGURE 4-2.5.1-12. Monostable Clock Generator with Memory Ready

4-2.5.2 **2K X 8 RAM Memory Design Example**

This section will describe the design of a memory system for the MC6800 microprocessor using memory devices that are not a part of the MPU family but that are cost-effective choices in many MPU based system designs. The intent is to demonstrate the ease with which memory systems can be designed around the MC6800 because of its straightforward architecture. The MPU signals to be considered in the memory system design are the clock signals (ϕ_1 and ϕ_2), the 16 bit Address Bus, the 8-bit bidirectional Data Bus and the control signals: Valid Memory Address (VMA), Read/Write (R/W), and clock control signals such as MEMORY READY, $\overline{\text{REFRESH REQUEST}}$ or REFRESH GRANT if they are required.

The MCM6602, 1K X 1 static RAM, can be a cost-effective choice for MPU memory systems in the size range of 1K bytes up to about 8K bytes. Below 1K bytes, memory systems composed of the MCM6810 will probably be the cost effective choice. Memory systems larger than 8K bytes will probably use a 4K RAM such as the MCM6605 in order to be cost effective. In this section, the detailed design of a 2K X 8 memory system is described for the MC6800 MPU using sixteen MCM6602 L-1 N-channel static MOS RAMs. This memory system is available from Motorola as a component module of the EXORciser.

The 2K Static Memory System (illustrated in Figure 4-2.5.2-1) receives the 16 address bits A0 through A15, the ϕ_2 timing signal, the 8 bit bidirectional data bus, VMA (Valid Memory Address) signal, and a R/W (Read/Write) command during each MPU memory operation. The system address lines connect to the address bus interface and the ϕ_2, VMA, and R/W inputs from the MPU connect to the control bus interface. Data lines connect to the Data Bus Interface.

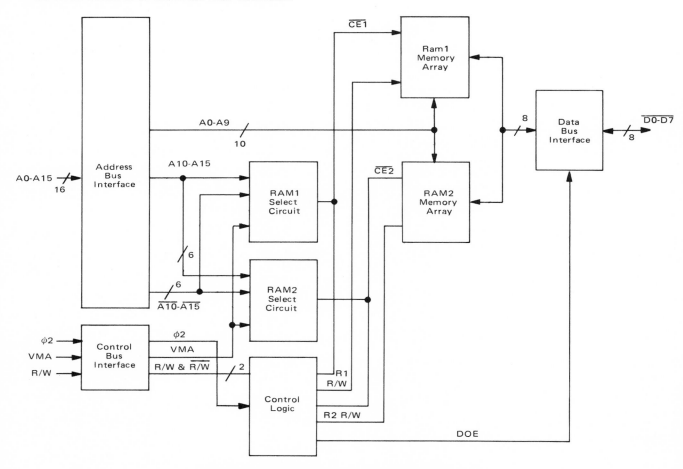

FIGURE 4-2.5.2-1. 2k X 8 Memory System Block Diagram

The address bus interface, after buffering the inputs, applies the ten address bits A0 through A9 to the RAM 1 and RAM 2 memory blocks. (Refer to Figure 4-2.5.2-2, the Schematic Diagram) The address bus interface, at the same time, applies the six address bits A10 through A15 with their complements to the RAM 1 and RAM 2 select circuits. The control bus interface applies the VMA signal to the RAM 1 and RAM 2 select circuits and $\phi2$ with the R/W signal and its complement to the control logic. The two RAM select circuits decode the address bits and determine whether the MPU is addressing their respective RAM memory block. Since the two RAM select circuits and the RAM memory blocks are identical, only the RAM 1 select circuit and the RAM 1 memory block will be discussed in detail.

The RAM 1 select circuit consists of two base memory address switches and a decoding circuit. The address switches allow the 2K X 8 of memory to be allocated as two independent 1K X 8 blocks any where in the system's 65K memory field. The base address switches select the base memory address for the RAM 1 memory block and the decoding circuit determines when its memory is being addressed. The RAM 1 select circuit, on determining that its memory is being addressed, couples a $\overline{\text{CE1}}$ (Chip Enable 1) signal to the RAM 1 memory block and to the control logic. The RAM 1 memory block, consisting of eight 1K X 1 bit MOS static RAM chips, is then enabled to perform a memory read or memory write operation.

During a memory read operation, the control bus interface receives a high level R/W signal and applies this signal with its complement to the control logic. The control logic now transfers a high level R1 R/W (Read Memory 1 Read/Write) pulse to the RAM 1 memory block and couples a DOE (Data Output Enable) signal to the data bus interface. The high level R1 R/W pulse instructs the RAM 1 memory block to perform a memory read operation (providing the address select signal, $\overline{\text{CE1}}$, is low) and the DOE signal instructs the data bus interface to transfer the memory's output to the MPU via the system bus.

During a memory write operation, the control bus interface receives a low level R/W signal and the data bus interface receives the eight data bits D0 through D7. The control bus interface applies the low level R/W signal and its complement to the control logic and the data bus interface applies the data bits to the RAM memory blocks. The control logic now reads the position of the RAM 1 RAM/ROM switch and determines whether the RAM 1 memory block is protected or may be written into. When this RAM/ROM switch is in the ROM position, the switch inhibits the control logic from initiating a memory write operation. When the switch is in the RAM position, however, it enables the control logic to generate a 470 nsec low level R1 R/W pulse. This low level pulse instructs the RAM 1 memory block to perform a memory write operation and to store the data it receives from the data bus interface. (If the address select signal (CE1) is low).

The following paragraphs discuss the operation of the various circuits contained on the 2K Static RAM Module. Refer to the module's block diagram in Figure 4-2.5.2-1 and schematic diagram in Figure 4-2.5.2-2 as required.

The address bus interface, consisting of U1 through U4, receives and buffers the 16 MPU address bits A1 through A15. Address bits A0 through A9 are applied to the RAM 1 and RAM 2 memory blocks. The address bus interface applies the six address bits A10 through A15 and their complements to the RAM 1 and RAM 2 select circuits. The control bus interface, U5, receives and buffers the $\phi2$, the VMA, and the R/W signals. The control bus interface couples the $\phi2$ and VMA signals to the RAM 1 and RAM 2 select circuits and applies the R/W signal and its complement to the control logic circuit. U1 through U5 are MC8T26* bus receivers which provide very light loading on the MPU bus so that the fanout is not reduced appreciably. The loading of these devices is $-200\ \mu a$ for a logic 0 and $+20\ \mu a$ for a logic 1.

The RAM 1 and RAM 2 select circuits decode the address bits and determine whether the MPU is addressing their respective RAM memory blocks. Since the two RAM select circuits are identical, only the

*To be introduced third quarter, 1975.

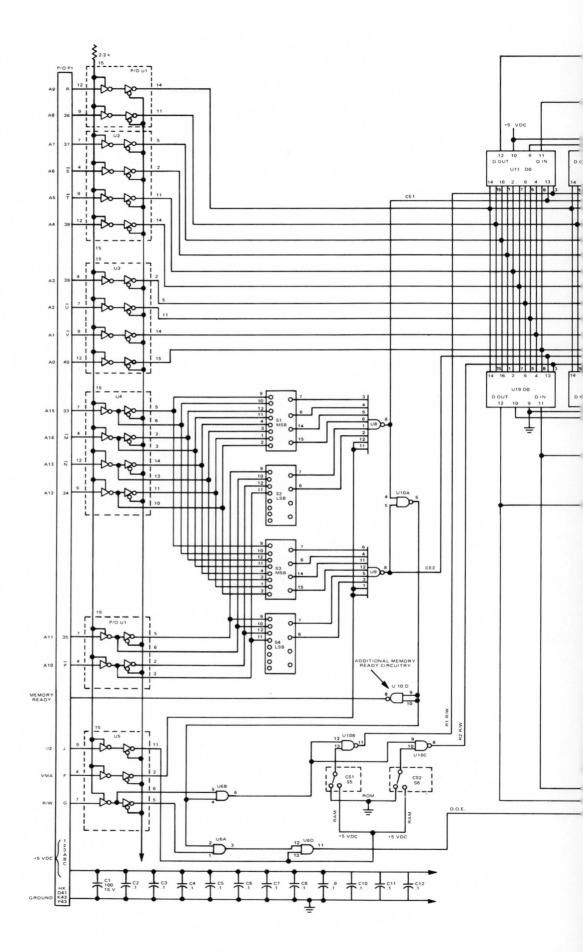

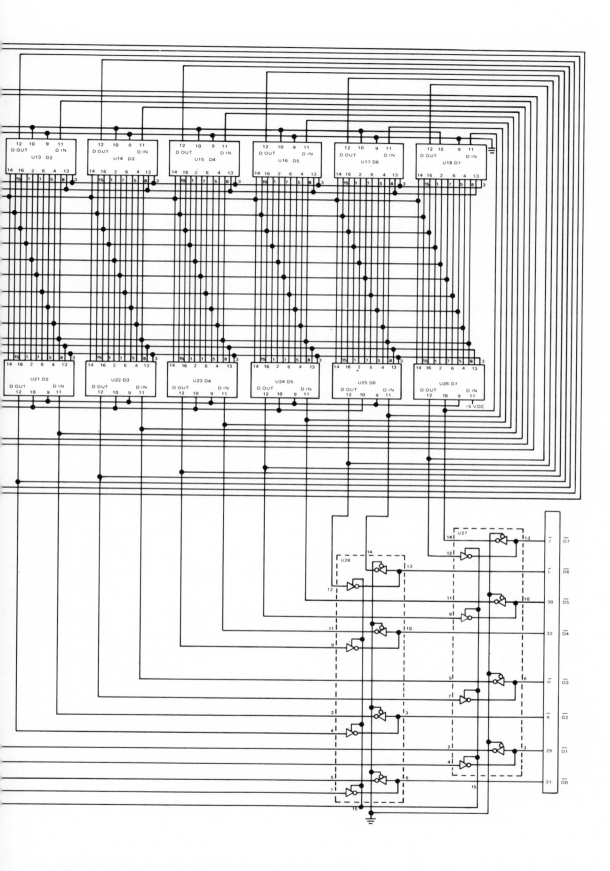

FIGURE 4-2.5.2-2 2K x 8 Memory System Schematic Diagram

4-65

RAM 1 select circuit is discussed in detail with the RAM 2 select circuit components identified parenthetically after the RAM 1 select circuit components.

The RAM 1 select circuit consists of the two switches S1 and S2 (S3 and S4) along with gate U8 (U9). Switches S1 and S2 (S3 and S4) are set during use and, through their switching of bits A10 through A15, select the base memory address for their respective memory block. The position of each switch determines whether the switch is coupling the address bit or its complement to gate U8 (U9). Gate U8 (U9), on receiving a VMA signal, decodes the switches outputs and determines whether the MPU is addressing its memory block. If its memory block is being addressed, U8 (U9) couples a $\overline{CE1}$ ($\overline{CE2}$) signal to the RAM 1 memory block (RAM 2 memory block) and to gate U10A of the control logic circuit.

The control logic circuit decodes the $\overline{CE1}$ ($\overline{CE2}$) signal, the R/W, the $\phi2$ clock signal, and the position of the RAM/ROM switches to determine whether to read data from, to write data into, or to inhibit the write function of the selected RAM memory block. Each time one of the RAM select circuits determines that the MPU is addressing its RAM memory block, this circuit causes gate U10A to couple a high level to gates U6A and U6B. During a memory read operation, the control bus interface applies a high level R/W pulse to gate U6A and $\overline{R/W}$ to gate U6B. Gate U6A is enabled by U10A when either memory is selected and with gate U6D applies the DOE Data Out Enable signal to the data bus interface. The low level R/W pulse to U6B inhibits this gate. The output of gate U6B remains low and forces gates U10B and U10C to continue holding the R1 R/W and R2 R/W signals high. The high level R1 R/W and R2 R/W signals instruct the enabled RAM memory block to perform a memory read operation.

During a memory write operation, the control bus interface applies a low level R/W pulse to gate U6A and $\overline{R/W}$ to gate U6B. Gate U6A is now inhibited from generating a DOE signal. The high level $\overline{R/W}$ pulse to U6B enables this gate and gates U10B and 10C. Gates U10B and U10C decode their RAM/ROM switches and determine whether the selected RAM memory block is to perform a memory write operation. If the RAM/ROM switch to the selected RAM memory block (switch S5 for the RAM 1 memory block and switch S6 for the RAM 2 memory block) is in the ROM position, the low level from this switch inhibits its respective gate from going low. If, on the other hand, the RAM/ROM switch is in the RAM position, the $\phi2$ pulse is coupled to U10B and U10C to generate a low going write pulse. This low level pulse instructs the enabled RAM memory block to perform a write operation.

The RAM 1 and RAM 2 memory blocks consist of eight 1024 X 1 bit memory chips. The ten address bits A0 through A9 and the output of its RAM select circuit determine when the MPU is addressing this memory block. The control logic determines whether data is to be written into or read from the selected RAM memory block.

The data bus interface, consisting of U27 and U28, provides a two-way data transfer of data bits D0 through D7 between the MPU and the 2K Static RAM Memory. These integrated circuits provide TTL compatible inputs and three-state outputs. When the MPU has selected one of the module's RAM memory blocks during a memory read operation, the data bus interface receives a high level DOE signal and is enabled to transfer data from the 2K Static RAM. At all other times, these outputs are in the high impedance state.

The timing diagram of Figure 4-2.5.2-3 shows a Read operation of the memory system design in Figure 4-2.5.2-2 operating with the MPU's control lines and busses driving the memory board directly. The waveforms assume a delay of 20 nsec through the driver portion and 18 nsec through the receiver portion of the MC8T26. The control lines R/W, Address, and VMA are specified to be valid within 300 nsec after the leading edge of $\phi1$ (TASR, TASC, and TVSC). The delay from the address bus of the MPU to the address inputs of the MCM6602 is composed of a receiver and a driver portion of a MC8T26 in series. This time totals $20 + 18 = 38$

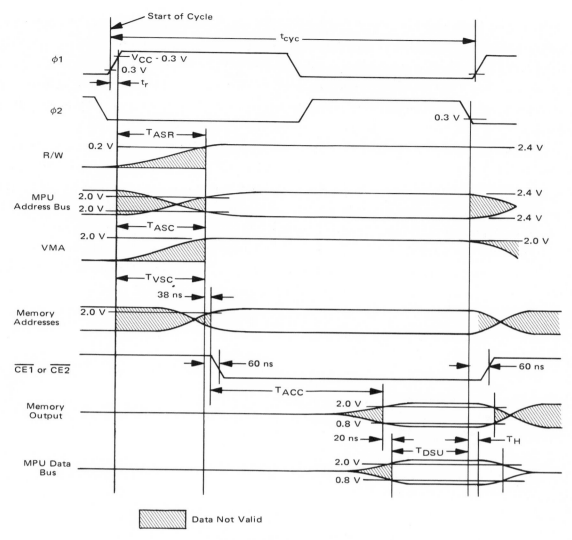

Start of Cycle

MPU/2k X 8 Memory Read Cycle

FIGURE 4-2.5.2-3

nsec. At this point in time, the addresses on the memory devices are valid and the access time can begin. The access time of the MCM6602L-1 is 500 nsec maximum, that is, data out of the RAMs during a read cycle is valid 500 nsec after the addresses are valid. The data encounters an MC8T26 driver delay of 20 nsec before reaching the MPU data bus. The data set up requirement of the MPU is 100 nsec before the falling edge of $\phi 2$. By using the above data, the margin in this system when operating at the maximum MPU clock period of 1000 nsec can be calculated as follows (refer to Figure 4-2.5.2-3):

tr	25 nsec
T_{ASR}	300 nsec
MC8T26	38 nsec
T_{ACC}	500 nsec
MC8T26	20 nsec
T_{DSU}	100 nsec
T_{CYCLE}	983 nsec

Since this is 17 nsec less than the minimum MPU clock period of 1000 nsec, this MPU/memory system configuration has a margin of 17 nsec during a read cycle. The $\overline{CE}$ signals are enabled by decoding the upper address lines, A10-A15, in gates U8 and U9. Since the addresses are valid during $\phi 1$, the $\overline{CE}$ signals become the inversion of VMA when the correct addresses are decoded. The $\overline{CE}$ signals will be held low past the falling edge of $\phi 2$ due to the holding effect of bus capacitance and the delay into the next $\phi 1$ for the MPU to set new addresses.

The write cycle of this system may be analyzed in the same manner using the timing diagram shown in Figure 4-2.5.2-4. The control signals from the MPU (Addresses, VMA, and R/W) become valid within 300 nsec after the leading edge of $\phi 1$. The $\overline{CE}$ signals are delayed from the address and VMA valid points by a receiver and driver section of the MC8T26 and the delay of the MC7430 Nand gate. This delay is $18 + 20 + 22 = 60$ nsec. Assuming that the RAM/ROM switch is in the RAM position, the R/W pulse on the memory devices is $\phi 2$ delayed by a receiver and driver of the MC8T26 plus the delay of U10 (MC7400). This time is $(18 + 20 + 22)$ also 60 nsec producing a write pulse skewed from $\phi 2$ as shown. The data hold requirement of 100 nsec for the MC6602 is met by extending Data Bus Enable (DBE) beyond the trailing edge of $\phi 2$ to hold the data on the

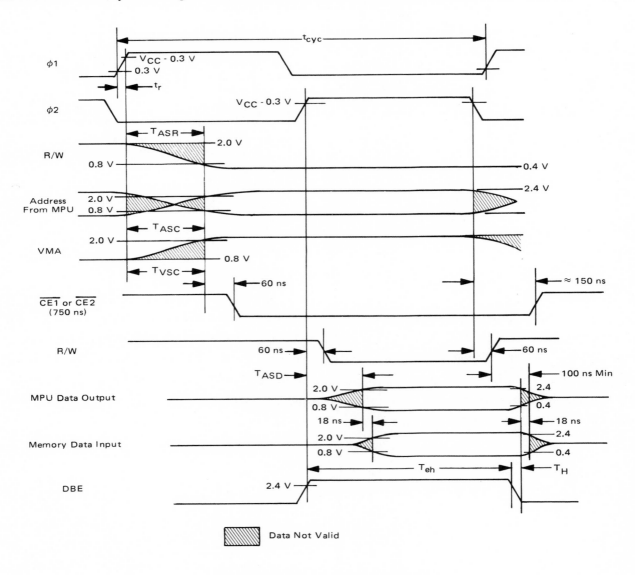

FIGURE 4-2.5.2-4. MPU/2 k x 8 Memory Write Cycle

bus valid. Memories of this type vary in their data setup requirement (t_{DW}) from 150 ns to 330 ns depending on manufacturer. The MCM6602L-1 as well as the 2102 types have the 330 ns requirement. In order to meet this requirement the $\phi2$ pulse width required can be calculated as follows (see Figure 4-2.5.2-4):

$$\phi2 \text{ PW} = \text{T}_{ASD} + 18 \text{ ns} + t_{DW} - 60 \text{ ns.}$$
$$\phi2 \text{ PW} = 200 + 18 + 330 - 60 = 488 \text{ ns.}$$

In many system designs, it may be cost effective to design this memory system with the MCM6602L which has an access time of 1 μs. This slower memory can be handled using one of the two methods discussed in Section 4-2.5.1. The first method is to stretch $\phi2$ every processor cycle to accommodate the slow memory as detailed in Figures 4-2.5.1-4 and 4-2.5.1-5. The other method is to use the Memory Ready concept. This can be accomplished as simply as the following: Assume that the clock circuitry used for the MPU is as shown in Figure 4-2.5.1-9. A low level on the MEMORY READY line will stretch $\phi2$ for that cycle. The time constants of the U1-B monostable can be adjusted to provide the correct $\phi2$ width during normal operation (470 nsec) and to provide the correct width (895 nsec for T$_{ACC}$ = 1 μsec) when the MEMORY READY line is low indicating a slow memory access. The additional circuitry required in the 2K memory system of Figure 4-2.5.2-2 to implement MEMORY READY consists of one inverter. The output of U10A goes high 360 nsec after the leading edge of $\phi1$ if this memory is addressed. The inverse of this signal, called MEMORY READY, controls the clock circuit of Figure 4-2.5.1-9. These signals are shown in Figure 4-2.5.2-3.

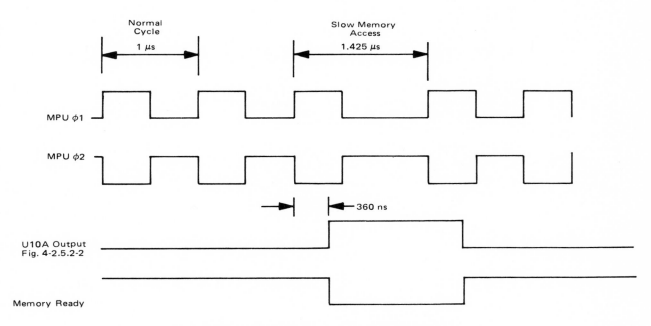

FIGURE 4-2.5.2-5. 2 k X 8 Memory System with Memory Ready

4-2.5.3   8K X 8 Non-Volatile RAM Deisgn Example

Many system designs can be optimized by using the high bit density and low cost/bit offered by dynamic memories (i.e., those that store information on a capacitor which must periodically be recharged or refreshed). At this time, the 4K X 1 dynamic RAM is the most cost effective choice for large memory systems ($\geq$4K bytes). Because these memories are dynamic and require refreshing, the system designer must handle the dynamic memory slightly differently than static memories. Refer to Section 4-2.5.1 for a discussion of techniques and clock circuitry used for interfacing the MPU with dynamic memories.

This section describes the design of a 8192 byte Non-Volatile memory system for an MPU based system using dynamic 4K RAMs and CMOS control logic. This system was designed to be an add-on memory for the EXORciser,* a System Development Tool in the M6800 Microprocessor family.

MEMORY DEVICE DESCRIPTION

The memory device used in this system is the MCM6605L-1, a 4096 word X 1 bit, dynamic Random Access Memory (RAM). The dynamic characteristic of this memory device requires that refreshing of the memory cells be performed at periodic intervals in order to retain the stored data. This device was chosen for the following features: high bit density per chip and correspondingly low price per bit, standby mode with low power dissipation, TTL compatability of inputs and outputs, and speed characteristics compatible with microprocessors and the EXORciser.

Figure 4-2.5.3-1 is a functional block diagram of the MCM6605L-1. The single external Chip

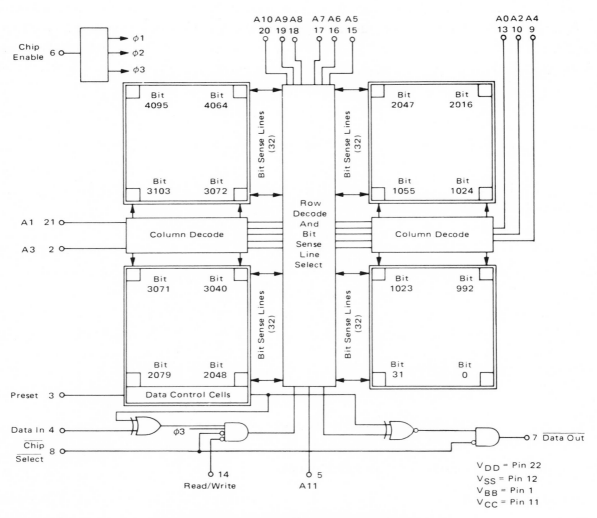

FIGURE 4-2.5.3-1. MCM6605 4 k RAM Block Diagram

---

*Trademark of Motorola, Inc.

Enable clock starts an internal three phase clock generator which controls data handling and routing on the memory chip. The lower 5 address lines (A0 to A4) control the decoding of the 32 columns and the upper 7 address lines control the decoding of the 128 rows within the memory chip. The $\overline{\text{Chip Select}}$ $\overline{(\text{CS})}$ input is used for memory expansion and controls the I/O buffers: when $\overline{\text{CS}}$ is low the data input and output are connected to the memory data cells and when $\overline{\text{CS}}$ is high, the data input is disconnected and the data output is in the high impedance state. Refreshing is required every 2 ms and is accomplished by performing a write cycle with $\overline{\text{CS}}$ high on all 32 columns selected by A0 through A4. The read/write line controls the generation of the internal $\phi 3$ signal which transfers data from the bit sense lines into storage.

All inputs and outputs with the exception of the high level Chip Enable signal are TTL compatible and the outputs feature 3-state operation to facilitate wired-or operation. The Chip Enable signal has GND and +12V as logic levels. Power requirements are typically 330 mw per device in the active mode from +12V, +5V, and −5 volt power supplies and 2.6 mw in standby with refresh from the +12V and −5 volt power supplies (the +5V supply powers the output buffers and is not required during standby operation).

Memory timing is outlined in Figure 4-2.5.3-2 and operates as follows for a read cycle (2a). The Chip Enable line is brought high after the correct addresses are set up, which starts the internal three phase clock and latches the addresses into an internal register. $\overline{\text{Chip Select}}$ must be brought low in order to connect the data input and output to the data cells and the Read/Write line must be brought high to inhibit the $\phi 3$ cycle which writes data into the storage cells. A write cycle (2b) occurs in exactly the same manner as a read cycle except that the R/W line is placed in the Write mode, which gates the input data onto the bit sense lines, and enables a $\phi 3$ cycle to write into the data cells.

A write and a refresh cycle are the same with the exception of $\overline{\text{Chip Select}}$, which is held high for a refresh cycle and low for a write cycle.

The Read-Modify-Write cycle is a read followed by a write within the same CE cycle. $\overline{\text{CS}}$ is brought low shortly after the leading edge of CE and R/W is held high long enough for the $\overline{\text{Data Out}}$ to become valid. The R/W line can then be strobed low for a minimum write time to enter the Data In (which has been placed on the input) into the data cells.

By holding the $\overline{\text{Chip Select}}$ high during refresh, the input data is inhibited from modifying the bit sense lines and the original data is returned to the data cells during $\phi 3$ of the cycle. This refreshing action recharges the storage cells and must be done at least every two milliseconds if the memory is to retain the information. The fact that the data is stored on a capacitor in a dynamic memory (rather than an "ON" transistor in a static memory) requires that the capacitor be recharged periodically. This capacitive storage produces a low power standby mode of operation where only refreshing takes place, which is the foundation of this low current drain non-volatile memory design. The memory device typically dissipates 330 mw in the active mode but only 2.6 mw in the standby mode (refreshing only).

MEMORY SYSTEM DESIGN REQUIREMENTS

This memory system was designed with the following major design goals:

First, non-volatility for a period of time in the range of 7 to 10 days from a reasonable sized battery. It is also desirable for the system to operate from one battery voltage during the standby mode to simplify the battery requirements. Second, the memory size was desired to be 8K bytes on a PC card easily expandable upward and addressable in 4K byte blocks. Third, the memory system must be able to interface with the MC6800 microprocessor which has a basic cycle time of 1 μsec. Fourth, the memory system controller must handle all refresh requirements in a manner as invisible as possible to microprocessor operation.

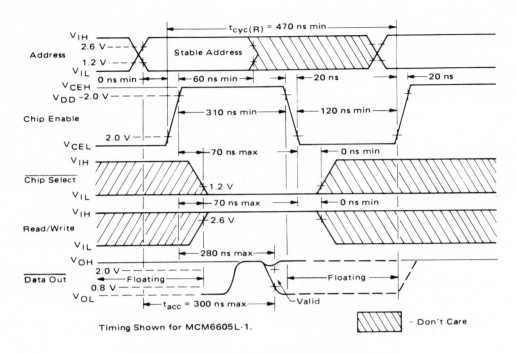

FIGURE 4-2.5.3-2a. Read Cycle Timing (Minimum Cycle)

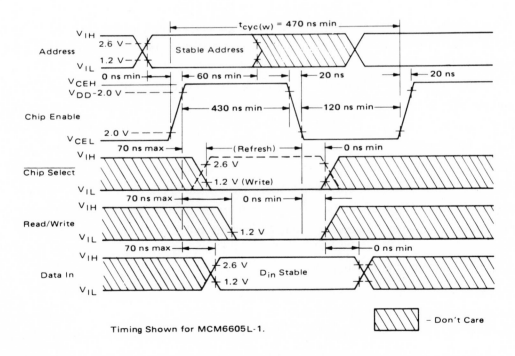

FIGURE 4-2.5.3-2b. Write and Refresh Cycle Timing (Minimum Cycle)

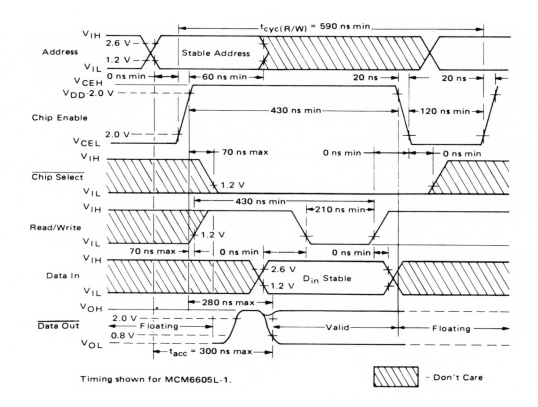

FIGURE 4-2.5.3-2c. Read-Modify-Write Timing (Minimum Cycle)

MEMORY SYSTEM DESCRIPTION

A block diagram of the memory system is shown in Figure 4-2.5.3-3. This system can be split into three main sections as follows. The first section is comprised of the address buffers, Read/Write and Chip Select decoding logic. The second section consists of the data bus buffering and the memory array. The memory array consists of sixteen memory devices (4K words X 1 bit) organized into two rows of 4096 bytes each. The third section consists of the refresh and control logic for the memory system. This logic provides the timing of the refresh handshaking, request for refresh, generation of the refresh addresses, synchronization of the POWERFAIL signal, multiplexing of the external MEMORY CLOCK with the internal clock (used during standby), and generation of the −5 volt supply on the board by a charge pump method.

Figure 4-2.5.3-4 is a worst case timing diagram of the read and write cycles of the EXORciser and the 4K memory system. The timing is composed of two phases. During phase 1 ($\phi1$) addresses are setup and during phase 2 ($\phi2$) data is transferred. Figure 4-2.5.3-5 is a timing diagram of the memory system in standby showing refresh cycles only. This timing analysis will be referred to in the following discussions of the memory control circuitry.

ADDRESS BUFFERS AND DECODING

Figure 4-2.5.3-6 is a schematic of the address buffers, decoding logic, and refresh address multiplexer. Address and data lines from the EXORciser are buffered from the capacitance of the memory array in order to provide a small load to the bus. Since the addresses are valid on the EXORciser bus 300 nsec into $\phi1$, 200 nsec is available to setup the address on the memories. The worst case input capacitance on the address

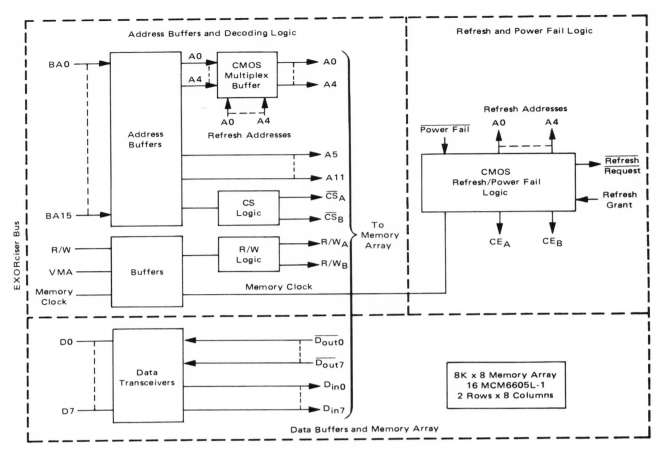

FIGURE 4-2.5.3-3. Non-Volatile Memory System Block Diagram

lines of the MCM6605 is 5 pf/input. A system of 16 memory devices (8K bytes) presents a total capacitive load on the address lines of only 100 pf (20 pf stray capacitance). Since 200 nsec is available to set up the addresses on the memory devices, no high current buffers are required to drive the memories. For address lines A5 through A11 the output of the MC8T26 address receiver drives the address lines directly. A0 through A4 must be multiplexed with the refresh addresses so that all 32 columns will be refreshed every 2 msec. Because of the requirement of low current drain in the standby mode, an MM80C97* CMOS buffer with a 3-state output is used to meet the multiplexing requirement. The buffers have sufficient current drive capability to drive the address line's capacitance within 100 nsec. An open collector TTL gate (MC7406) is used to translate to +12 volt CMOS levels. A0 through A4 are driven with GND and 12 volt logic levels so that +5 volts is not required in the standby mode.

The high order address lines (A12-A15) are used to decode one 4K block of memory out of the 16 total possible blocks in the 65K address map. The addresses and their complements are routed through hexidecimal switches to MC7430 Nand gates in order to create a $\overline{CS}$ signal for each 4K bytes of memory. By rotating the hexidecimal switches (S3 and S4), all combinations of true and complement addresses can be routed to the Nand gates, thereby selecting one of the sixteen 4K blocks. VMA and $\overline{REFA}$ are also inputs to these Nand gates VMA is a Valid Memory Address signal on the bus indicating that the address lines are valid and $\overline{REFA}$ is a control signal indicating that a refresh cycle is taking place. During a refresh cycle $\overline{REFA}$ goes low forcing $\overline{CSA}$ and $\overline{CSB}$ high (a refresh cycle for the memory devices is a write cycle with the Chip Select

*To be introduced as MC14503, third quarter 1975

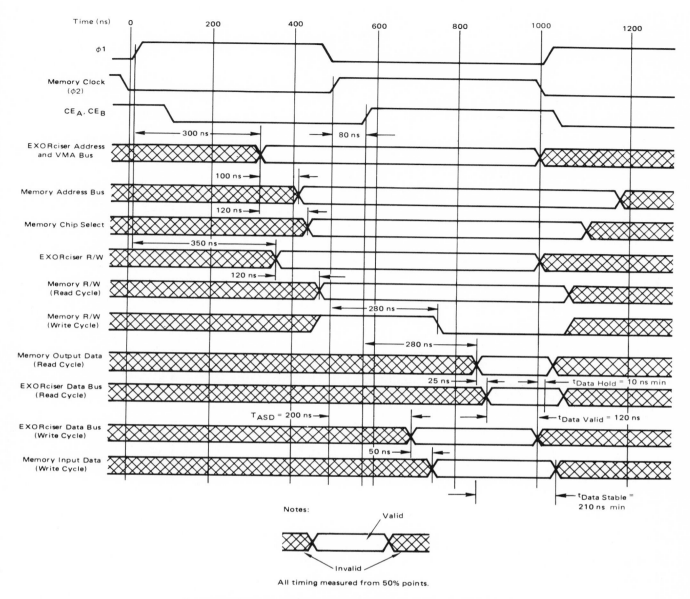

Notes:

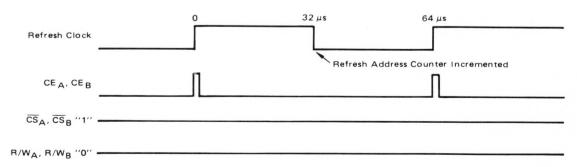

All timing measured from 50% points.

FIGURE 4-2.5.3-4. EXORciser/4K Memory System Timing Diagram

FIGURE 4-2.5.3-5. Memory Timing in Standby Mode

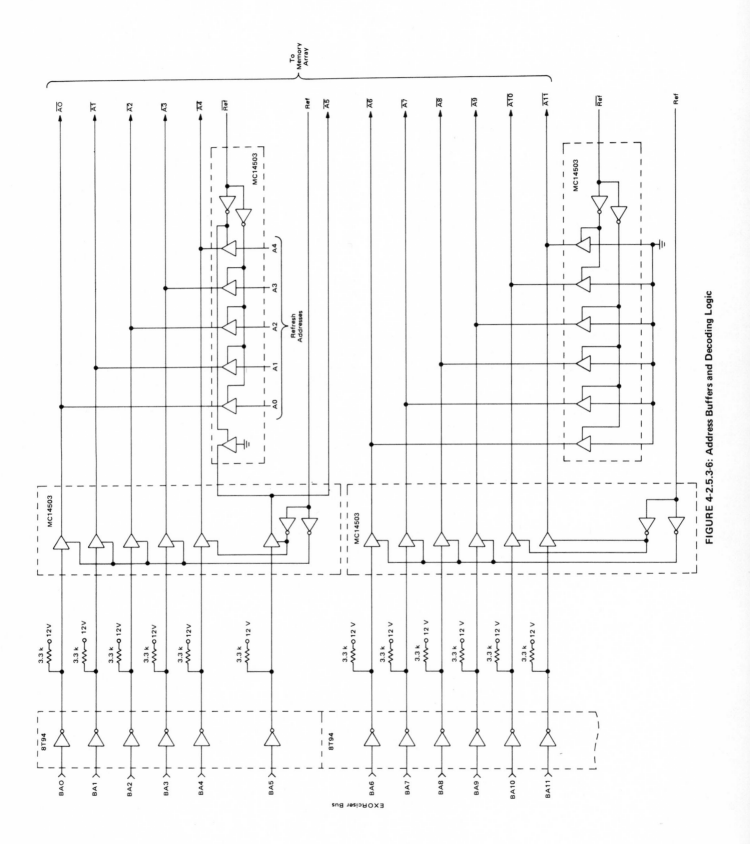

FIGURE 4-2.5.3-6: Address Buffers and Decoding Logic

4-76

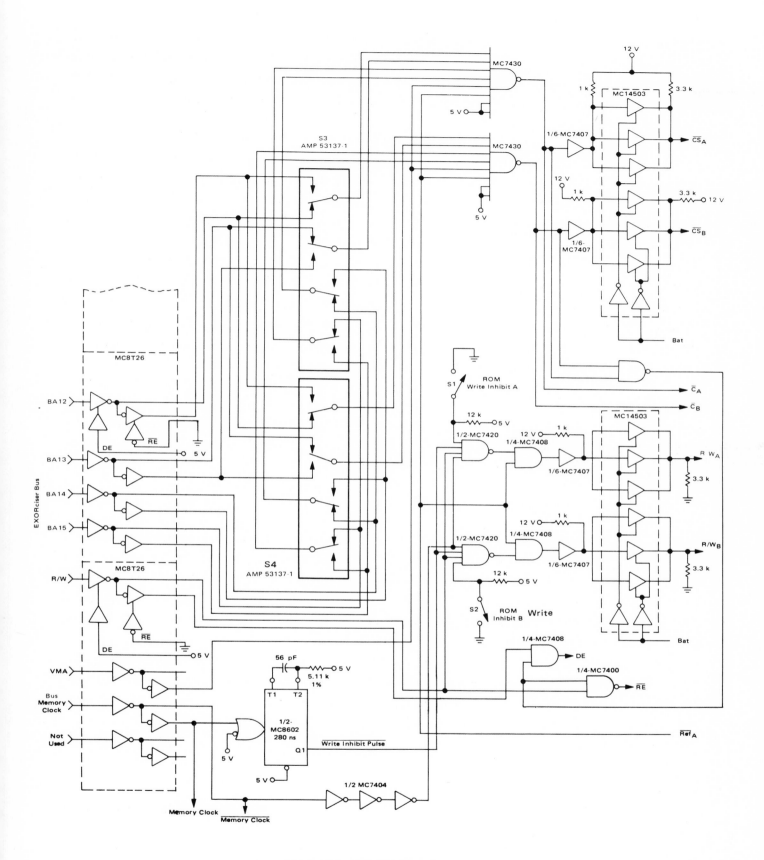

FIGURE 4-2.5.3-6. Address Buffers and Decoding Logic
(continued from preceding page)

4-77

held high). The output of the MC7430 is translated to 12 volt CMOS levels with the open collector gates and buffered with the MM80C97 3-state buffer. The capacitive loading on each set of 3 paralleled drivers is 60 pf allowing $\overline{\text{Chip Select}}$ to be decoded and valid 120 nsec after addresses are valid on the data bus. During the standby mode (BAT = ''1'') the CMOS buffer is disabled allowing the 3.3K ohm resistors to pull $\overline{\text{CSA}}$ and $\overline{\text{CSB}}$ high for continuous refreshing.

The Read/Write signal is received by an MC8T26 and then decoded in the following manner. A write inhibit feature is provided using switches S1 and S2 for each 4K byte block of memory so that in a ROM simulation application, the memory can be protected from inadvertant writes due to programming or operator errors. The Ready-Modify-Write cycle of the MCM6605 is used in this application because it requires a shorter data valid time ($T_{\text{Data Stable}}$) than a normal write cycle (See Figure 4-2.5.3-2b and 4-2.5.3-2c). This feature is desirable because the EXORciser places valid data on the bus for the last 300 nsec of a Write cycle. In order to delay the write pulse to the memory array until the data is valid on the Data Inputs of the memory array, a write inhibit pulse is combined with the EXORciser's R/W signal in the MC7420 Nand gates. This write inhibit pulse is generated by the MC8602 monstable multivibrator triggered from the leading edge of the memory clock (MEM CLOCK) bus signal. The effect of this added delay can be seen from Figure 4-2.5.3-4 when comparing the memory array's R/W line for a read and a write cycle. Note that for a write cycle, the R/W of the memory array is inhibited from dropping to the Write mode until memory input data is valid.

The refresh control signal ($\overline{\text{REFA}}$) is combined with the output of the MC7420 in a MC7408 AND gate in order to force a write signal on the memory array's R/W lines while in a refresh cycle. Translation and buffering is accomplished in a similar manner to that for the Chip Select signals. When in the standby mode (BAT = ''1'') the MM80C97 buffers are disabled allowing the 3.3K resistor to establish a zero level on the R/W line of the memory array for continuous refreshing.

DATA BUFFERS AND MEMORY ARRAY

The EXORciser data bus is bidirectional while the MCM6605 memory has separate data inputs and outputs. The MC8T26* data bus receiver/driver buffers the capacitance of the memory array (very low, about 30 pf per data line) and combines the Data Input and $\overline{\text{Data Output}}$ of the memory array into one bidirectional bus as shown in Figure 4-2.5.3-7. The $\overline{\text{Data Out}}$ of the memory devices is inverted from the Data In requiring an extra inverter (MC7404) in the data path when working with a non-inverting bus (i.e., the data is returned to the bus in the same sense it was received).

During a memory write cycle, the data is valid on the data bus 200 nsec (T_{ASD}) after the leading edge of $\phi2$. With a 50 nsec delay through the bus translators, the data setup requirement of the memories (210 nsec) is easily met (See Figure 4-2.5.3-4). A memory read cycle requires a data setup time on the data bus of 120 nsec. The access time of the memory from the leading edge of the CE signal plus the bus transceiver delay of 305 nsec is compatible with this setup time.

REFRESH AND CONTROL LOGIC

The refresh control logic shown in Figure 4-2.5.3-8 handles the refreshing of the memory during both operating and standby modes. The timing is shown in Figure 4-2.5.3-9.

The refresh timing is controlled by an astable multivibrator constructed with a MC3302 comparator. This device was chosen for its low current consumption (1.5 ma max) and single supply voltage operation, both

*To be introduced third quarter 1975

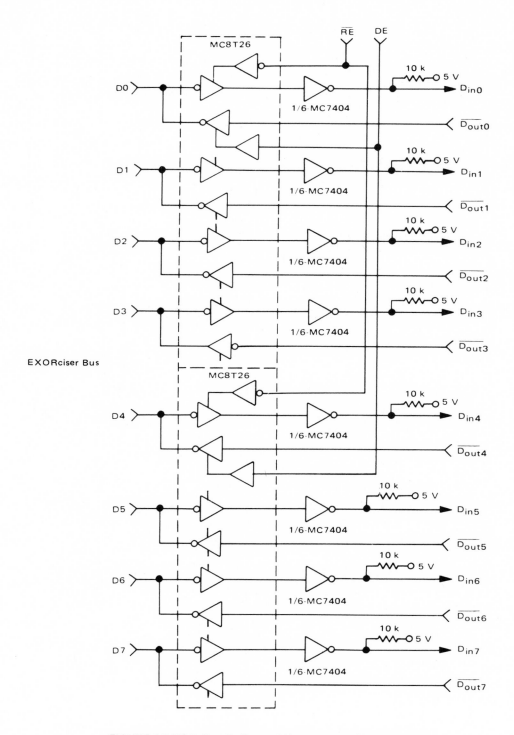

FIGURE 4-2.5.3-7. Data Buffers and Memory Array (Sheet 1 of 2)

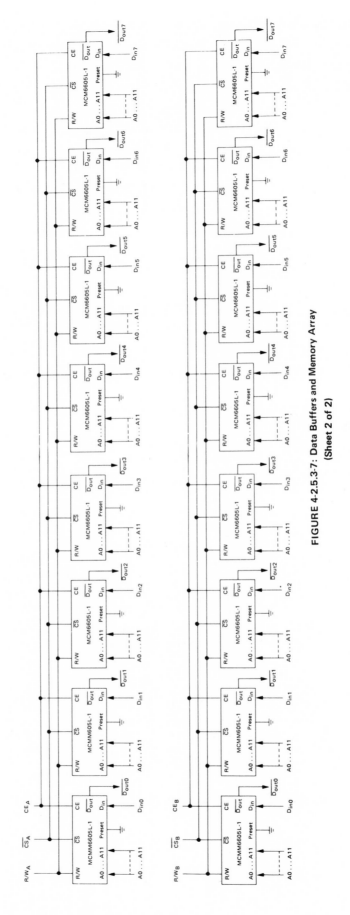

FIGURE 4-2.5.3-7: Data Buffers and Memory Array
(Sheet 2 of 2)

important for battery operation. The refresh requirement of 32 refresh cycles every 2 msec is handled by stealing cycles from the processor. This cycle stealing results in a 1.6% slower program execution rate than the basic microprocessor clock frequency. During the refresh cycle, the clocks to the microprocessor are "stretched" during the $\phi1$ high and the $\phi2$ low times by 1 μsec as shown in Figure 4-2.5.3-9. During this 1 μsec period, the memory executes a refresh cycle. In order to minimize the effects of memory refresh on microprocessor program execution the 32 refresh cycles are distributed over the 2 msec period, one occuring every 62.5 μsec. Refresh could be done in a burst of 32 cycles every 2 msec but this would cause a larger gap in program execution which in this case was undesirable.

The MC3302 produces the 62.5 μsec signal to time the refresh requirement and also is used in the generation of the -5 VDC supply required by the MCM6605 memory. Since these functions are required in the standby mode, which is powered by the battery, a CMOS buffer is used in a charge pump circuit to minimize current drain from the battery. This charge pump creates -5 VDC at 3 ma from the $+12$ volt battery to satisfy the bias requirements of the memory devices.

The REFRESH CLOCK is used to increment the address counter (MC14024) and to clock the refresh handshaking logic (MC14027). REFRESH REQUEST goes low on the leading edge of the REFRESH

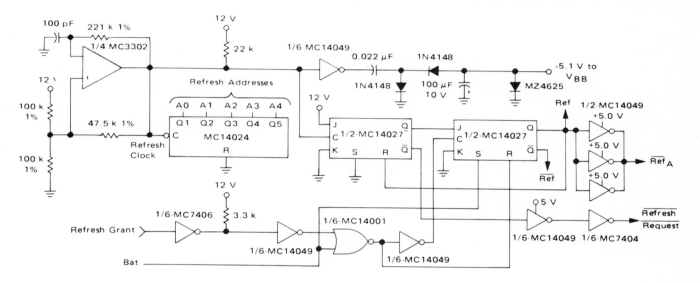

FIGURE 4-2.5.3-8. Refresh Control Logic

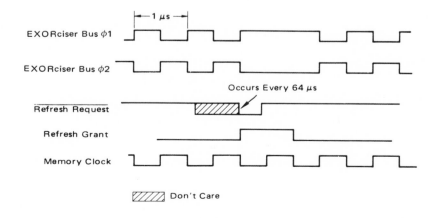

FIGURE 4-2.5.3-9. Refresh Timing

CLOCK thus requesting a refresh cycle. Logic in the clock generation circuitry stretches the high portion of $\phi1$ and the low portion of $\phi2$ while sending back a REFRESH GRANT signal. This stretching of the $\phi1$ signal delays program execution during this cycle. The leading edge of REFRESH GRANT starts the refresh cycle and cancels $\overline{\text{REFRESH REQUEST}}$. The trailing edge of REFRESH GRANT returns the refresh logic to the normal state and the memory is ready for a memory access. The trailing edge of the REFRESH CLOCK then increments the refresh counter in preparation for the next refresh cycle.

Decoding of the memory clock (CEA and CEB) and the circuitry to synchronize the $\overline{\text{POWERFAIL}}$ signal is shown in Figure 4-2.5.3-10 with the timing given in Figure 4-2.5.3-11.

The memory device clock (CEA and CEB) during standby is generated by a monostable multivibrator (MC14528) and buffered from the memory array by three MM80C97 buffers in parallel. This clock is multiplexed with the $\overline{\text{MEMORY CLOCK}}$ by use of the 3-state feature of the MM80C97. The $\overline{\text{MEMORY CLOCK}}$ (used during normal operation) is translated to 12 volt levels by use a MC3460 clock driver.* Decoding of the CE signals (i.e., only clocking the memory bank addressed) to conserve power is accomplished by internal logic within the MC3460.

Since the $\overline{\text{POWERFAIL}}$ signal will occur asynchronously with both the $\overline{\text{MEM CLOCK}}$ and the refreshing operation (REF CLOCK), it is necessary to synchronize the $\overline{\text{POWERFAIL}}$ signal to the rest of the system in order to avoid aborting a memory access cycle or a refresh cycle. An MC14027 dual flip flop is used as the basic synchronization device. The leading edge of the REFRESH CLOCK triggers a 3 μsec monostable multivibrator which is used as a refresh pretrigger. The trailing edge of this pretrigger triggers a 500 nsec monostable which creates the CE pulse during standby operation. The 3 μsec pretrigger signal is used to direct set half of the MC14027 flip-flop, the output of which then inhibits a change over from the standby to the operating modes (or vice versa). This logic prevents the system from aborting a refresh cycle should the $\overline{\text{POWERFAIL}}$ signal change states just prior to or during a refresh cycle. The trailing edge of the 500 nsec monostable clears the MC14027 flip-flop enabling the second flip-flop in the package. The state of $\overline{\text{POWERFAIL}}$ and POWERFAIL is applied to the K and J inputs, respectively, of this second flip-flop and is synchronized by clocking with $\overline{\text{MEM CLOCK}}$.

The outputs of this flip-flop, labeled BAT and $\overline{\text{BAT}}$, lock the system into the refresh mode and multiplexes in the internal clock for standby operation when BAT = ''1''.

SYSTEM PERFORMANCE

Figure 4-2.5.3-12 is a photograph of the breadboard of this dynamic memory system. This breadboard was interfaced with an EXORciser system and tested using a comprehensive memory test program written in-house.

Figure 4-2.5.3-13 is a photograph of waveshapes associated with alternate reads and writes in one 4K bank of the memory system. Included also is the simple MC6800 program used to generate these waveforms. This type of operation produces repetitive signals on the memory board in order to aid troubleshooting. Note the refresh cycle sandwiched in amongst the read and write cycles and that the decoding of the CE signals produces no clocks on CEA (accesses are to bank B), except during refresh.

Figure 4-2.5.3-14 shows the printed circuit memory array used to interconnect the memories. The addresses are bused between the 4K memory chips in the horizontal direction. Data lines are bused in the vertical direction. The MCM6605 4K RAM has power and ground pins on the corners of the package allowing

*To be introduced first quarter 1975

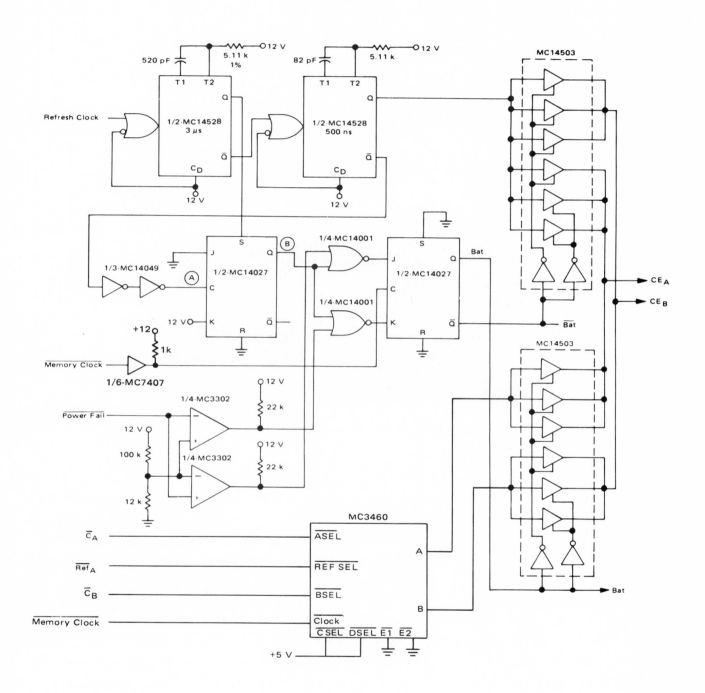

FIGURE 4-2.5.3-10. Power Fail Logic and Chip Enable Driver

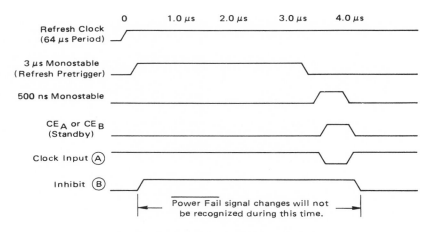

FIGURE 4-2.5.3-11. Power Up/Down Synchronization

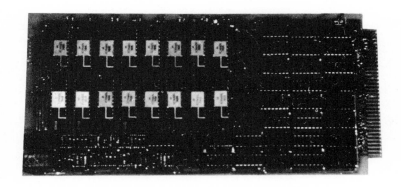

FIGURE 4.2.5.3-12. Memory System Breadboard

wide, low impedance power and ground interconnects within the memory array. Decoupling capacitors were used as follows within the memory array: +12 volt — one 0.1 μf ceramic per package, +5 volt — one 0.01 μf ceramic for every three packages, and −5 volt — one 0.01 μf ceramic for every three packages. Figure 4-2.5.3-15 is a photograph showing the ripple on the power supplies in the memory array caused by accesses to one 4K byte bank of memory as shwon in the photograph. The +12 volt line supplies the most current to the array and is the one on which the most care in decoupling (wide PC lines and distributed capacitance) should be taken. Placement of the V$_{DD}$ pin on the corner of the package gives the designer the option to do this easily.

The dc power dissipation of this memory system is shown in Table 4-2.5.3-1. Of these current drains, the most critical to non-volatile operation is the current requirement in the Standby mode where the current would probably be supplied from a battery. A breakdown of the typical current required from +12 volts to maintain the memory in the Standby mode is shown in Table 4-2.5.3-2.

By using CMOS for the refresh logic and capacitance drivers, a dynamic memory, and a low current refresh oscillator; the standby current has been reduced to a level that can be supplied easily by a battery. Table 3 is a brief list of various capacity 12 volt batteries that could be used to power a system of this type in the Standby mode. Support time runs from one-half to 35 days and can be made as long as desired if sufficient battery capacity is available.

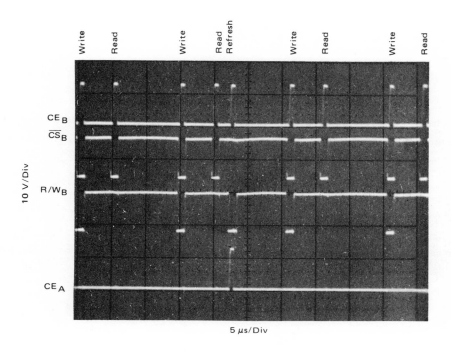

FIGURE 4.2.5.3-13. Alternate Read and Write Memory Accesses

M6800 Program to Generate Waveforms Shown

Address	Data	Mnemonic	Comment
0000 0001	B6 55	LDA #$55	Load data to be written (55)
0002 0003 0004	B7 30 00	STA A $3000	Store data in address 3000_{16}
0005 0006 0007	F6 30 00	LDA B $3000	Read data from address 3000_{16}
0008 0009 000A	7E 00 02	JMP $0002	Loop back

TABLE 4.2.5.3-1 8K x 8 Non-Volatile Memory System Power Requirements (1-MHz EXORciser Clock Rate)

Mode	Power Supply*	Current	
		Typical	Maximum
Operating	+12 V**	100 mA	300 mA
	+5 V	600 mA	860 mA
Standby	+12 V	14 mA	20 mA
	+5 V	No +5 V Supply required	

*5 V supply is not listed because it is generated on the board from +12 V

**Because memory is dynamic, the +12 V current requirement is dependent on rate of memory access.

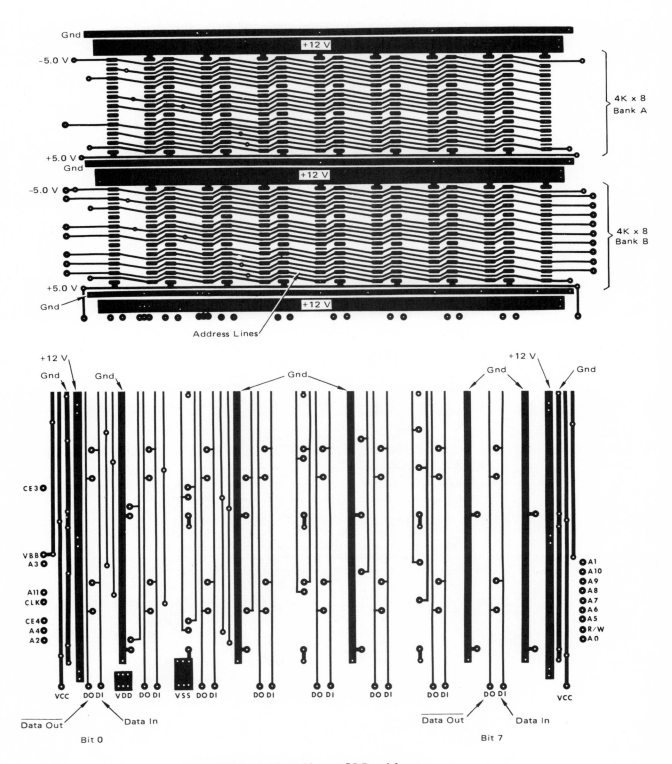

FIGURE 4-2.5.3-14. Memory PC Board Array

Circuit Section	Typical Current
+12 V Current (V_{DD})	5 mA
Charge Pump	3 mA
Comparator	2 mA
Capacitance Drivers	4 mA
Total	14 mA

TABLE 4.2.5.3-2 Standby Mode Current Allocation

Battery	AH	Size (L x W x H)	Weight	Support Time*
Globe GC 12200	20	6.9" x 6.5" x 4.9"	16.75 lbs.	35 days (850 hrs)
Globe GC 1245-1	4.5	6" x 2.5" x 4"	4.51 lbs.	8 days (192 hrs)
Globe GC 1215-1	1.5	7" x 1.3" x 2.6"	1.51 lbs.	2.6 days (63.75 hrs)
Burgess MP 202	0.6	3.4" x 1.4" x 2.3"	11.6 oz.	1.25 days (30 hrs)
Burgess 12.0V 225 Bh	0.225	3.5" H x 1" Diam.	4.65 oz.	.47 days (11.25 hrs)

*Assumes 20 ma average current drain (14 ma for memory and 6 ma for powerfail detection circuitry) and a battery voltage range during discharge of from 13 to 11 volts.

TABLE 4-2.5.3-3. Battery Characteristics

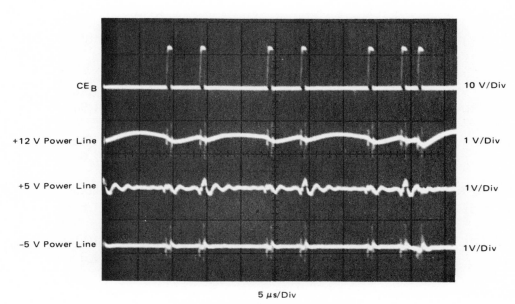

FIGURE 4.2.5.3-15 Power Line Ripple

4-2.5.4   Design Considerations When Using Non-Family Memories with the MC6800

The previous sections have discussed general interfacing with slow and dynamic memories and two design examples using the MCM6602 1K X 1 static RAM and the MCM6605 4K X 1 dynamic RAM. In this section, the general interface characteristics of the M6800 family will be discussed as well as methods for interfacing with various classes of memory devices. The categories of memories to be discussed are the following: Bipolar PROMS/ROMS, MOS PROMS/ROMS, Bipolar RAMS, and MOS RAMS.

Table 4-2.5.4-1 lists the relevant characteristics of the M6800 family parts to be considered when interfacing with each other or with non-family parts. In most small systems, the limiting factor will be the data bus load exceeding 130 pf maximum capacitance and/or 1 TTL (7400) load. Depending on the mix of PIA/ACIA and memories, the fanout can be 7 to 10 family parts before buffering is required.

BIPOLAR PROMS/ROMS

The PROMS available in bipolar technology are constructed with nichrome or poly silicon links which can be "blown" or programmed in the field to provide a custom program for small quantity, quick turn around, requirements. In many cases, a pin for pin equivalent is available in a mask programmable ROM for large quantity usages of a known bit pattern. Common memory organizations available are 64 X 8, 256 X 4, 512 X 4, and 512 X 8 from several manufacturers. Because these devices are constructed in bipolar TTL technology, their speed is much greater than required by the MPU. A typical device of this type will have a

DEVICE	C_{IN}	C_{OUT}	I_{IN}	I_{DATA}* (3 st)	I_{DATA} (drive)
MC6800 MPU	10 pf logic 15 pf data	12 pf logic 15 pf data	2.5μa	10μa	-100μa 1.6 ma +130 pf
MCM6810 RAM (128 X 8)	7.5 pf	15 pf	2.5μa	10μa	-100μa 1.6 ma +130 pf
MCM6605 RAM MCM6815 RAM (4K X 1)	5 pf	5 pf	10μa	10μa	-100μa 2 ma + 50 pf
MC6820 PIA	7 pf logic 10 pf data	10 pf	2.5μa	10μa	-100μa 1.6 ma +130 pf
MCM6830 ROM (1K X 8)	7.5 pf	15 pf	2.5μa	10μa	-100μa 1.6 ma +130 pf
MCM6832 ROM (2K X 8)	8 pf	10 pf	10μa	10μa	-40μa 1.6 ma +30 pf
MC6850 ACIA	7 pf logic 10 pf data	10 pf	2.5μa	10μa	-100μa 1.6 ma +130 pf

*Current leakage on data bus in high impedance state is into the device.

TABLE 4-2.5.4-1. MPU Family Interface Chart

maximum access time of 70 nsec from address valid while the MPU only requires 575 nsec access time when operating at full speed. Because of their programmability, these types of devices find use in system prototypes, bootstrap loaders, and system debug packages. Devices of these types are the MCM5003 PROM and its mask programmable equivalent, the MCM4003.

Interfacing with these devices requires buffers for the MPU because each bipolar PROM/ROM is one unit TTL load. Since the MPU has TTL levels on all inputs and outputs, no level translation is necessary. Timing interface between the MPU operating at full speed and these TTL memories can be accomplished easily because the TTL memories are much faster.

MOS PROMS/ROMS

The mask programmable MOS ROMS are both P-channel and N-channel with the newer faster devices being N-channel. Memory organizations commonly available at 1K X 8 and 2K X 8. Most of these ROMS require multiple power supplies with $+12V$, $+5V$, $-3V$, or $+5V$, $-12V$, being common. Current requirements on the non$-3V$ supply voltages are in many cases low so that charge pump techniques can be used. The majority of these devices are TTL compatible on the inputs and outputs making MPU interfacing easy. Because of the MOS technology, these devices all present light loads on their inputs usually 10 μa leakage and 5-10 pf shunt capacitance and, therefore, can be interfaced without buffering up to 130 pf + 1 TTL load. Those parts with an access time of longer than 575 nsec will require usage of the slow memory techniques described in Section 4-2.5.1 in order to operate with an MPU at a 1 MHz clock rate. These devices vary in speed from 350 nsec to 1800 nsec depending on manufacturer and process type. Devices of this type are the MCM6830 and the MCM6832.

The PROMS available in MOS technology are electrically programmable and erasable by exposure to ultraviolet light. Device organizations available are 256 X 8 with 512 X 8 under development. Inputs and outputs are TTL compatible with the use of pull up resistors on the inputs and access times range from 500 nsec to 2.5 μsec. Input loading is on the order of 1-5 μa and 15 pf. A MPU system operating at full speed may require the slow memory techniques described in Section 4-2.5.1 to operate with the devices.

DYNAMIC MOS RAMS

These devices are available in P-channel in a 1K X 1 organization with the newer devices being N-channel and 4K X 1 organization. Their dynamic characteristics require that periodic refreshing of the memory take place. The number of refresh cycles varies from 16 to 64 every 1 or 2 ms. Several ways to handle this refresh requirement in the MPU system were described in Section 4-2.5.1. The access time of these devices is usually less than 500 nsec resulting in easy timing interface with the MPU at full speed. Inputs and outputs of most of these devices are TTL compatible with input loading being typically 10 μa leakage and 5 pf shunt capacitance. These devices typically require a clock signal which can be derived from the $\phi2$ MPU clock signal. A design of a memory system for the MPU using dynamic memories is detailed in Section 4-2.5.3. Devices of this type are the MCM6605 and the MCM6815.

STATIC MOS RAMS

Static RAMS do not require refreshing and as such are simple to interface into a MPU system. In N-channel MOS technology, the common organizations are 128 X 8, 256 X 4, and 1024 X 1. The inputs and outputs are TTL level compatible with the input loading on the order of 10 μa and 5-10 pf Output drive capability typically is one TTL gate and 100 pf shunt capacitance. These devices operate from a single 5 volt power supply with access times between 200 and 1000 nsec.

Example of this type of device are the MCM6810 and the MCM6602. A design of a static memory design for the MPU using the MCM6602 is detailed in Section 4-2.5.2

CHAPTER 5

5. PERIPHERAL CONTROL TECHNIQUES

The MC6800's general I/O handling capability is described in detail in Chapter 3 of this manual. This Chapter further demonstrates the I/O characteristics of the M6800 system by applying them to a variety of specific peripheral control problems. The emphasis here is on control of the peripherals; system integration procedures are described in Chapter 6.

The development of both hardware and software is described for representative peripherals in the following categories:

(1) Input devices such as keyboards and label scanning wands;

(2) Output devices such as visual displays and hard-copy printers;

(3) Data interchange devices such as teletype terminals, tape cassettes, and floppy disks. Where appropriate, the possible hardware/software trade-offs and their effect on system efficiency and cost are discussed. However, the main objective was to minimize the external conventional circuit requirements by using the MC6820 PIA and the MC6850 ACIA family interface devices. The PIA and ACIA are described in detail in Sections 3-4.1 and 3-4.2, respectively, of Chapter 3.

5-1 DATA INPUT DEVICES

5-1.1 KEYBOARDS FOR MANUAL ENTRY OF DATA

Keyboards represent particularly good examples of the hardware/software tradeoffs that should be considered when configuring a system. They can be obtained from original equipment manufacturing (OEM) sources with widely varying amounts of electronics provided.

At one extreme is the fully decoded[1] keyboard complete with multiple key rollover protection[2] and a strobe signal for indicating that data is available. Use of these units with an MPU results in the simplest interface and also requires a minimum control program.

At the opposite extreme is the keyboard with no electronics at all; only the terminals of the individual key switches are provided. With this type, the designer may choose to add a full complement of external electronics, do a partial decode, or let the MPU perform the complete task in software.

Representative examples of each approach are described in the following paragraphs. In each case, the MC6820, Peripheral Interface Adapter (PIA), is used for interfacing to the MC6820 Microprocessor.

5-1.1.1 Decoded Keyboard for a POS Terminal

A MICROSWITCH 26SW3-1 POS Keyboard was selected for use with the Transaction Terminal described in Chapter 6. A schematic representation of the key configuration is shown in Figure 5-1.1.1-1. The function keys CODE ENTRY, SUBTOTAL ($+$), SUBTOTAL ($-$), and CLEAR each provide a logic level out when depressed. The remaining keys are decoded, that is, closure generates a 6-bit code word accompanied by

---

[1] Each switch closure is converted to a unique code word.

[2] The first of near-simultaneous closures is selected.

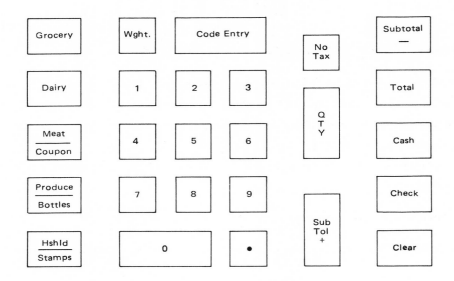

FIGURE 5.1.1.1-1 POS Keyboard Configuration

Key Function	Key Number	b7	b6	b5	b4	b3	b2	b1	b0
					Code	to PIA			
0	43	0	0	0	0	0	0	0	0
1	13	0	0	0	0	0	0	0	1
2	14	0	0	0	0	0	0	1	0
3	15	0	0	0	0	0	0	1	1
4	23	0	0	0	0	0	1	0	0
5	24	0	0	0	0	0	1	0	1
6	25	0	0	0	0	0	1	1	0
7	33	0	0	0	0	0	1	1	1
8	34	0	0	0	0	1	0	0	0
9	35	0	0	0	0	1	0	0	1
. (Demical pt.)	45	0	0	0	0	1	0	1	0
Grocery	1	0	0	0	0	0	0	0	1
Dairy	11	0	0	0	0	0	0	1	0
Meat/Coupon	21	0	0	0	0	0	0	1	1
Produce/Bottles	31	0	0	0	0	0	1	0	0
Hshld/Stamps	41	0	0	0	0	0	1	0	1
Weight	3	0	0	1	0	0	0	0	0
No Tax	7	0	0	1	0	0	0	1	1
Quantity	17	0	0	1	0	0	1	1	1
Total	20	0	0	1	0	1	0	1	0
Cash	30	0	0	1	0	1	1	1	1
Check	40	0	0	1	1	0	0	1	1
Code Entry	5	0	1	Will be holding					
Subtotal (−)	10	1	0	data from					
Subtotal (+)	37	1	1	previous entry					
Clear	50			[C2 interrupt]					
		0	0	0	1	1	0	0	0
Strobe	—			[C1 interrupt]					

1. Strobe will be high while any key is closed

FIGURE 5.1.1.1-2 Keyboard Coding/PIA Interface

a strobe pulse. The code generated by the keyboard is shown in Figures 5-1.1.1-2. That Figure also shows the interconnection to an MC6820 PIA as represented schematically in Figure 5-1.1.1-3.

For system purposes, it was decided that any key closure should cause an interrupt via the PIA's CA1 Input. The interrupt was generated by using a Quad Exclusive OR gate package to combine the four function key outputs and the STROBE signal. The CLEAR signal was also required as a separate interrupt and is, hence, applied to the CA2 Interrupt Input. The remaining three function outputs, CODE ENTRY, SUBTOTAL (+), and SUBTOTAL (−), were decoded by using two 2-input NAND gates applied to PA6 and PA7 of the PIA.

Operation of the system executive program described in Chapter 6 is largely determined by data that is input through this keyboard. However, the control program for the actual capture of the data is relatively simple. When the MPU is ready to accept manually entered data, it polls the keyboard PIA interrupt flag bits until an input is detected. A Flowchart and an Assembly Listing of the relevant portion of the executive program[3] are shown in Figures 5-1.1.1-4 and 5-1.1.1-5, respectively.

After recognizing an interrupt, the MPU checks for a keyboard closure by testing flag bits 6 and 7 of the keyboard PIA's Control Register. These bits would have been set by transitions on CA1 or CA2. If neither is set, the MPU branches to check for a Wand interrupt service request. If one is set, the MPU tests for a CLEAR closure (bit 6) and, if it is present, branches to the CLEAR service routine. If the CLEAR flag is not set, the MPU assumes bit 7 was set and proceeds with the keyboard service routine.

This sequence is typical for encoded keyboards. Aside from the interrupt service housekeeping, capturing the data consists of nothing more than the MPU "reading" a PIA Data Register as it would any other memory location.

[3] See Section 6-4.2.4 of Chapter 6 for the relationship to the remainder of the executive program.

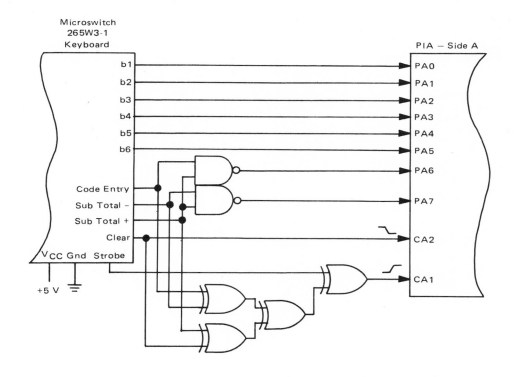

FIGURE 5-1.1.1-3 Keyboard/PIA Hardware Interface

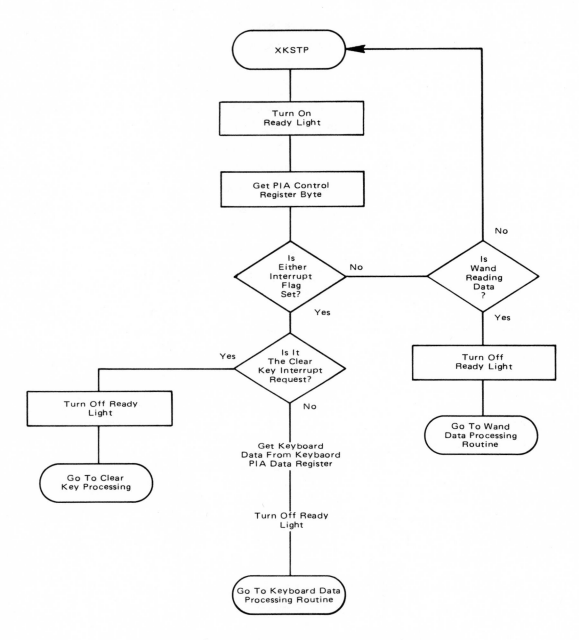

FIGURE 5-1.1.1-4 Flow Chart for Keyboard Service Routine

```
00072 A1C3 01          XKSFTP NOP
00074 A1C4 0F                 SEI
00076 A1C5 01                 NOP
00078 A1C6 01                 NOP
00080 A1C7 F6 C010           LDA B  XP2DRA     TURN ON READY LIGHT
00090 A1CA CA F0            ORA B  #$F0       SET PA-6
00100 A1CC F7 C010           STA B  XP2DRA
00110 A1CF 0E               CLI                ENABLE INTERRUPTS
00120                 ◆ KEYBOARD REQUEST ?
00130 A1D0 B6 8009          LDA A  XP3CRA     READ KEYBOARD PIA CONTROL
00140 A1D3 85 C0            BIT A  #$C0       CHECK CRA7,CRA6
00150 A1D5 27 19            BEQ    XK1065     IF NO REQUEST, CHECK WAND
00160 A1D7 85 40            BIT A  #$40       CHECK FOR CLEAR KEY
00170 A1D9 27 07            BEQ    XK1040     IF NO, CONTINUE KYBD SERVIC
00180 A1DB 86 18            LDA A  #$18       IF YES, LOAD CLEAR CODE
00190 A1DD F6 8008          LDA B  XP3DRA     CLEAR INTERRUPT
00200 A1E0 20 03            BRA    XK1045
00210 A1E2 B6 8008 XK1040 LDA A  XP3DRA     LOAD KYBD DATA/CLEAR INTERR
00220 A1E5 F6 C010 XK1045 LDA B  XP2DRA     TURN OFF READY LIGHT
00230 A1E8 C4 BF            AND B  #$BF       CLR PA-6
00240 A1EA F7 C010           STA B  XP2DRA
00250 A1ED BD A203          JSR    XKKYIN     GO TO KYBD ROUTINE,ACCA=DAT
00260                 ◆
00270                 ◆ WAND SERVICE REQUEST?
00280                 ◆
00290 A1F0 B6 C010 XK1065 LDA A  XP2DRA     IS WAND ON SPACE, B7=0?
00310 A1F3 2B CE            BMI    XKSFTP     IF NOT LOOP BACK
00320 A1F5 F6 C010           LDA B  XP2DRA     TURN OFF READY LIGHT
00330 A1F8 C4 BF            AND B  #$BF       CLR PA-6
00340 A1FA F7 C010           STA B  XP2DRA
00350 A1FD BD B60C          JSR    XKWAND     OTHERWISE, GO TO WAND ROUTI
00360 A200 7E A1C3          JMP    XKSFTP
```

FIGURE 5-1.1.1-5 Keyboard Service Assembly Listing

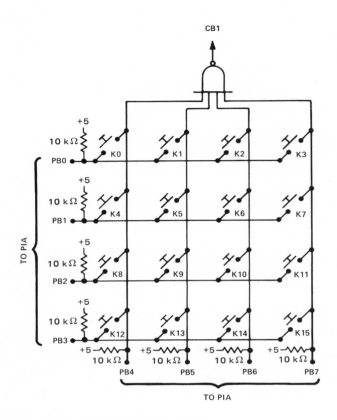

FIGURE 5-1.1.2-1: Keyboard/PIA Interface

5-1.1.2 Non Encoded Keyboard

An example of capturing data from a keyboard with no external electronics is shown in Figure 5-1.1.2-1 where half of a PIA being used to interface with a sixteen function keyboard connected in a matrix configuration. The row lines of the matrix are connected to PB0 through PB3, the column lines to PB4 through PB7. A suitable keyboard control Flowchart is shown in Figure 5-1.1.2-2. The corresponding Assembly Listing is shown in Figure 5-1.1.2-4.

An initialization sequence uses the Data Direction Register, DDR, to establish the Row lines (PB0–PB3) as outputs and the Column lines (PB4–PB7) as inputs. In addition, ones are written into the Column section and zeros are written into the Row section, leading to the situation shown in Figure 5-1.1.2-4.

Any key closure will now couple a Row zero through the key switch, causing one of the Column lines to go low and generate a CB1 interrupt via the 4-input NAND gate. A typical case (K6 closed) is illustrated in Figure 5-1.1.2-5.

The programmable features of the PIA can be used to generate a simple program for capturing the data. Refer to the Flow Chart and Assembly Listing of Figures 5-1.1.2-2 and 5-1.1.2-3, respectively as additional aids to understanding. The MPU, as its first step in servicing the keyboard, reads Peripheral Interface Register B (PIRB), thus clearing the interrupt (b7 of Control Register B) and storing the current contents of PIRB in accumulator A. Note that because of the initial conditions, the word stored in ACCA must be one of the four[4] shown in Figure 5-1.1.2-6 depending on which column the closure was in.

The MPU, using the DDR as in the Initialization sequence, next reverses the I/O relationship of the column and row lines, that is, PB0–PB3 are established as inputs and PB4–PB7 as outputs (see Figure

---

[4]This assumes only one key was closed. Multiple key closures will be discussed in a later paragraph.

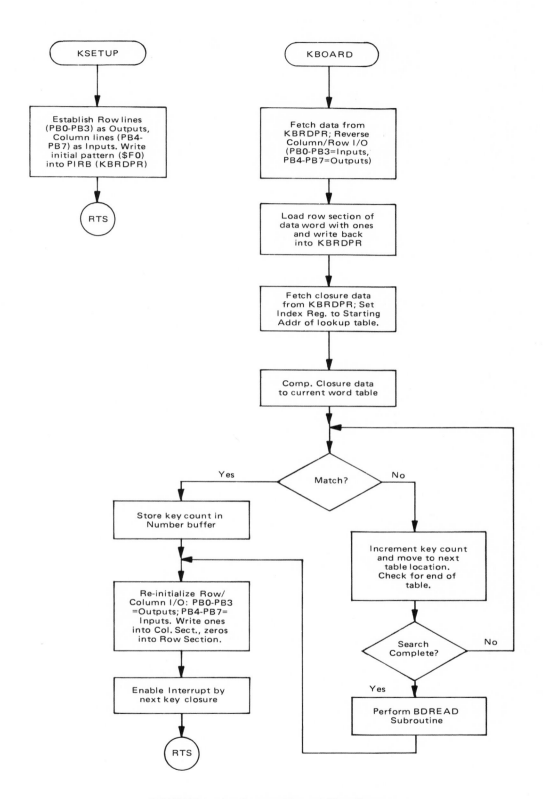

FIGURE 5-1.1.2-2 Keyboard Control Flow Chart

```
00001                         NAM     KBOARD
00010               *THIS PROGRAM CAUSES THE MC6800 MICROPROCESSOR
00020               *TO CAPTURE KEY CLOSURES ON A 16 KEY KEYBOARD
00030               *AND PLACE THE BINARY EQUIVALENT IN A BUFFER
00040               *NAMED NBRBUF. THE B SIDE OF AN MC6820 PIA
00050               *IS USED TO ENTER THE DATA.
00070                         OPT     M
00080  0100                   ORG     $100
00090  0100 B6 800A KYBOAR LDA A     KBRDPR     READ THE PIA PERIPH REG.
00100  0103 96 04          LDA A     #$04       LOAD ACCB WITH 00000100
00110  0105 F7 8008         STA B     KBRDCR     SELECT DATA DIR REG
00120  0108 C6 F0           LDA B     #$F0       SELECT PB0-PB3 AS INPUTS AN
00130  010A F7 8009         STA B     KBRDDR     *PB4-PB7 AS OUTPUTS.
00140  010D 5F             CLR B
00150  010E 8A 0F           ORA A     #$0F       LOAD B0-B3 OF ACCA WITH ONE
00160  0110 B7 800A         STA A     KBRDPR     WRITE BACK INTO PERIPH REG
00170  0113 B6 800A         LDA A     KBRDPR     FETCH CLOSURE DATA.
00180  0116 FE 0143         LDX     KTABLE     POINT TO TBL STRT ADDR
00190  0119 A1 00   LOOKUP CMP A     X          DATA = CURRENT TABLE VALUE?
00200  011B 27 09           BEQ     STASH      *YES, GO PUT DATA IN BUFFER
00210  011D 5C             INC B              *NO, ADVANCE NBR COUNT AND
00220  011E 08             INX                *MOVE TO NEXT TABLE LOCATIO
00230  011F 8C 0152         CPY     #TBLEND    SEARCH COMPLETE?
00240  0122 26 F5           BNE     LOOKUP     *NO,GO TO LOOKUP,CONT SRCH
00250  0124 8D 1B           BSR     BDREAD     *YES,GO TO BADREAD RTN
00260  0126 97 F0   STASH STA A     NBRBUF     STORE KEY NUMBER.
00270  0128 8D 07           BSR     KSETUP     GO RE-INITIALIZE
00280  012A C6 03           LDA B     #$03       ENABLE N/T CLOSURE INTRPT
00290  012C F7 8008         STA B     KBRDCR     *
00300  0130 3B       KEXIT RTI                RETURN TO MAIN PROGRAM.
00320  0131 C6 04   KSETUP LDA B     #$04       LD CONTROL REG WTH PATTERN
00330  0133 F7 8008         STA B     KBRDCR     *TO SELECT DIRECTION REG.
00340  0136 C6 0F           LDA B     #$0F       SELECT PB0-PB3 AS OUTPUTS
00350  0138 F7 8009         STA B     KBRDDR     *AND PB4-PB7 AS INPUTS
00360  013B C6 F0           LDA B     #$F0       WRITE 11110000 PATTERN INTO
00370  013D F7 8008         STA B     KBRDCR     *PERIPHERAL REGISTER.
00380  0140 39             RTS                RETURN TO MAIN PROGRAM
00400  0141 20 EE   BDREAD BRA     KSETUP     DUMMY BDREAD PROGRAM
00410  0143 EE       KTABLE FCB       $EE,$DE,$BE,$7E,$ED,$DD,$BD,$7D,$EB
       0144 DE
       0145 BE
       0146 7E
       0147 ED
       0148 DD
       0149 BD
       014A 7D
       014B EB
00420  014C DB               FCB       $DB,$BB,$7B,$E7,$D7,$B7
       014D BB
       014E 7B
       014F E7
       0150 D7
       0151 B7
00430  0152 77       TBLEND FCB       $77
00440      8008     KBRDCR EQU       $8008
00450      8009     KBRDDR EQU       $8009
00460      800A     KBRDPR EQU       $800A
00470      00F0     NBRBUF EQU       $00F0
00480               END
```

FIGURE 5-1.1.2-3: Keyboard Control Assembly Listing

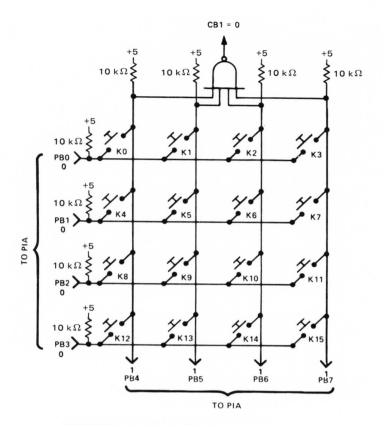

FIGURE 5-1.1.2-4: Initial PIA I/O Configuration

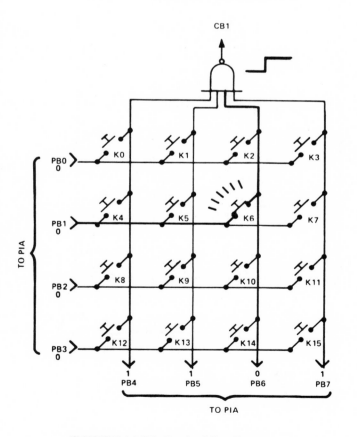

FIGURE 5-1.1.2-5: Result of Key Closure

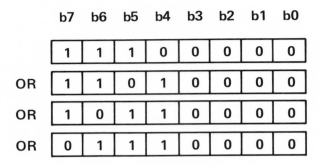

	b7	b6	b5	b4	b3	b2	b1	b0
	1	1	1	0	0	0	0	0
OR	1	1	0	1	0	0	0	0
OR	1	0	1	1	0	0	0	0
OR	0	1	1	1	0	0	0	0

FIGURE 5-1.1.2-6: Contents of Accumulator A

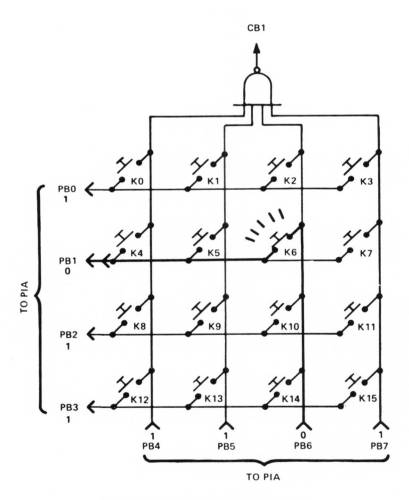

FIGURE 5-1.1.2-7: I/O Conditions Reversed

5-1.1.2-7). ACCB is used in order to avoid disturbing the contents of ACCA. The ORAA instruction is then used to replace the row bit positions with ones (see Figure 5-1.1.2-8) and the resulting word is written back into PIRB.

The time required for the MPU to perform the steps just described is very short compared to typical minimum switch closure times. Therefore, the switch is still closed and the conditions are as shown in Figure 5-1.1.2-7. The column zero that was preserved and written back into PIRB is coupled through the still closed switch and applies a low signal to a row input now established as an input. PIRB is immediately re-read back into ACCA by the MPU. For a single key closure, the word thus captured must be one of the sixteen stored in memory locations 0143 to 0152 in the Assembly Listing of Figure 5-1.1.2-3. The first four values are also illustrated in Figure 5-1.1.2-9.

The MPU sequentially compares the contents of ACCA to the lookup table (stored in ROM) containing the words until a match is obtained. ACCB is incremented following each comparison; when the match occurs, a binary number corresponding to the key number is stored in ACCB and is available for transfer to a buffer location in RAM.

If a match is obtained, the MPU stores the key count, re-initializes the PIA, and returns from the service routine interrupt. If no match is obtained, it is assumed that the data is bad and a Bad Read subroutine is called. Since only data corresponding to valid single key closures is stored in the lookup table, this approach automatically takes care of both multiple key closures and inadvertent noise.

The specific action to be taken following a bad read is not shown since it depends on the particular application. In many practical designs, affirmative action such as an audible approval tone is taken following the entry of good data. The Bad Read subroutine in this case would merely disable the approval sequence. A different routine would be used in designs requiring positive indication (blinking light, tone, etc.) of bad data. In either case, the Bad Read sequence should end with a return from subroutine instruction, RTS, so that the PIA will be properly re-initialized.

Many mechanical switches exhibit contact bounce when they are initially closed. A bad read will result if the MPU reads PIRB during one of the bounce intervals. This problem can be avoided by inserting a suitable delay routine (see Section 2-2 for examples) as the initial steps of the keyboard service routine. The duration of the bounce varies with switch design but is normally in the range of one millisecond or less. The keyboard manufacturer should be able to provide specific information.

The extension of this procedure to larger keyboards is straight forward. For instance, a sixty-four key matrix could be implemented using both halves of a PIA and similar programming techniques.

	b7	b6	b5	b4	b3	b2	b1	b0
ACCA	1	0	1	1	0	0	0	0
CONSTANT = 0F	0	0	0	0	1	1	1	1
ORA #0F	1	0	1	1	1	1	1	1

FIGURE 5-1.1.2-8: Generation of Output Word

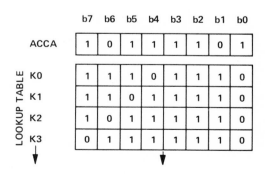

	b7	b6	b5	b4	b3	b2	b1	b0
ACCA	1	0	1	1	1	1	0	1
K0	1	1	1	0	1	1	1	0
K1	1	1	0	1	1	1	1	0
K2	1	0	1	1	1	1	1	0
K3	0	1	1	1	1	1	1	0

FIGURE 5-1.1.2-9: Lookup Table

5-1.2 SCANNING WAND FOR CAPTURING DATA FROM PRINTED SYMBOLS

The use of scanning techniques to retrieve information from machine readable labels, badges, credit cards, etc., is gaining acceptance in a wide variety of business machine applications. This is due in large part to the development and acceptance of industry-wide standards. The simultaneous growth of systems based on microprocessors will give additional impetus to this trend.

Few tasks are as made-to-order for an MPU as the conversion of scanned data to a usable format. The specifications for both magnetic and optical recording formats were designed to allow for either mechanical or manual capture techniques. In addition, it was desirable for the labels to be humanly readable and verifiable in case of equipment failure. The net result is that emphasis is given to the human aspects of the problem rather than simplification of the electronics involved.

5-1.2.1 Universal Product Code (UPC) Symbol

The grocery industry's Universal Product Code (UPC) symbol is an excellent example of the genre. Labels similar to the example shown in Figure 5-1.2.1-1 are beginning to appear on virtually every kind of retail grocery product. They are intended to facilitate the use of automatic checkstand equipment and are the result of an industry-wide effort to improve productivity in the grocery industry[1]. The symbol is optimized for ease of printing, reading, and manually checking results. The symbol is designed to minimize the cost of marking by the manufacturers and their suppliers. The symbol size is infinitely variable to accommodate the ranges in quality achievable by various printing processes. It can be uniformly magnified or reduced from the nominal size without significantly affecting the degree to which it can be scanned. An example of the human orientation is indicated by the error check calculation described in Section 5-1.2.5. The error check is an involved addition, multiplication, and modulo-ten reduction, a formidable task for conventional digital IC's, but relatively simple for people (and microprocessors).

A suitable control method depends on both the characteristics of the symbol and the scanning technique that is used. The symbol is designed for use with either fixed position scanners (label passes by on a conveyor belt) or handheld wands. The "wandable" approach will, in general, be more difficult to implement since allowance must be made for variable human scanning techniques. The control program described in this section is suitable for either but was developed specifically for use with handheld wands.

A 10-digit numbering system was adopted by the grocery industry for product identification. Each participating supplier is issued a 5-digit manufacturer's identification number. The remaining 5 digits are assigned to generic product categories, that is, tomato soup, canned peas, tissue paper, etc., each have specific numbers regardless of brand name. This 10-digit number[2] is combined with error checking features and encoded into a symbol similar to that shown in Figure 5-1.2.1-2.

The standard symbol consists of a series of parallel light and dark bars of different widths. The symbol will be referred to as the "bar code" to distinguish it from the "UPC code" that it represents. The basic characteristics of the bar code are summarized in Figures 5-1.2.1-2 and 5-1.2.1-3 and the following list of features from the UPC specification:

---

[1] Information concerning the UPC symbol described in this Section is from the *UPC Symbol Specification* obtained from: Distribution Number Bank, 1725 K Street N.W., Washington, D.C. (Telephone — (202)833-1134), Administrator of the Universal Product Code and UPC Symbol for the Uniform Grocery Product Code Council.

[2] Although the symbol is primarily designed for these 10-digit codes, it also includes growth capacity for longer codes to facilitate future compatibility in other distribution industries.

FIGURE 5-1.2.1-1 UPC Symbol from Box of Kleenex[1] Tissues
Registered trademark of Kimberly-Clark Corp., Neenah, Wis.

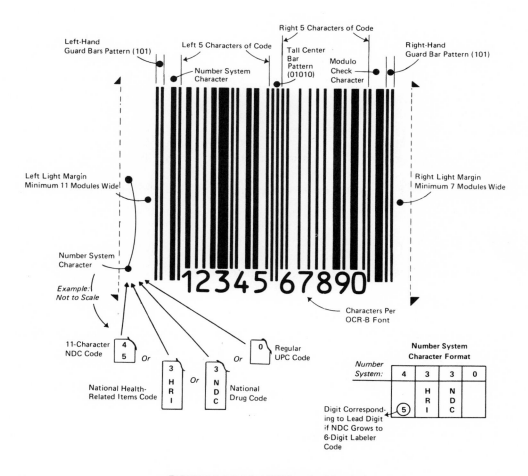

FIGURE 5-1.2.1-2: UPC Standard Symbol

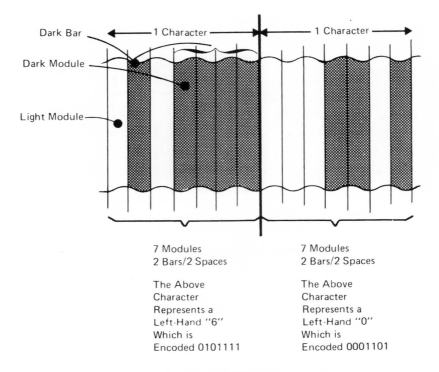

Dark Bar

Dark Module

Light Module

1 Character

1 Character

7 Modules
2 Bars/2 Spaces

The Above
Character
Represents a
Left-Hand "6"
Which is
Encoded 0101111

7 Modules
2 Bars/2 Spaces

The Above
Character
Represents a
Left-Hand "0"
Which is
Encoded 0001101

FIGURE 5-1.2.1-3: UPC Character Structure

- Series of light and dark parallel bars (30 dark and 29 light for any 10-character code) with a light margin on each side.

- Overall shape is rectangular.

- Each character or digit of a code is represented by 2 dark bars and 2 light spaces.

- Each character is made up of 7 data elements; a data element hereinafter will be called a "module."

- A module may be dark or light.

- A bar may be made up of 1, 2, 3, or 4 dark modules, as shown in Figure 5-1.2.1-3.

- Each character is independent.

- The symbol also includes two characters beyond the 10 needed to encode the UPC.

  — One character, a modulo check character (see Section 5-1.2.5 for details) is embedded in the right-most position of the symbol to insure a high level of reading reliability. (See Figure 5-1.2.1-2.)

  — Another character, embedded in the left-most position of the symbol, shows which number system a particular symbol encodes. Concurrent number sets are used to accommodate such things as meat and produce without the need to set aside code numbers in the UPC.

- The symbol prevents tampering. Unauthorized addition of lines is readily detectable by scanning devices. In the same way, poor printing will not result in scanning devices reading a wrong number. This is facilitated by multiple error-detecting features which allow scanner designers to build equipment to automatically detect and reject a very poorly printed symbol or one that has been tampered with.

- The symbol also incorporates and presents the code number in a human-readable form.

The nominal dimensions of a typical symbol (as printed on a product) are shown in Figure 5-1.2.1-4. The dark and light bars are built up from nominal 0.0130-inch modules, however, some of the characters involve undersize dark bars and oversize light spaces. There are 95 modules in the symbol itself and 18 modules in the white marginal guard bands.

Starting at the left side of the symbol, it is encoded first with "guard bars", then a number system character ("0" in the figure) followed by five UPC characters on the left side of the center "guard bars." To the right of the center bars is the remaining five UPC characters followed by a modulo ten check character. Finally, the same guard bar pattern is repeated on the right-hand side.

NOTES
1. (6X) .0910 MAY VARY ±.0005 FROM X-X ⎫ TOLERANCES APPLY
2. (6X) .0910 MAY VARY ±.0005 FROM Y-Y ⎬ TO ARTWORK ONLY
3. NUMBERS ARE OCR-B

FIGURE 5-1.2.1-4: Nominal Dimensions of Printed UPC Symbol

On the left-to-right basis, each character on the left side of the center bars begins with a light space and ends with a dark bar; characters to the right of the center bars begin with a dark bar and end with a light space. Dark modules represent 1's while light modules represent 0's. The number of dark modules per character on the left side is always three or five; the number of dark modules is always two or four for right-hand characters. Encoding is identical for all similar characters on a given side of the symbol, whether it is a number system character, UPC Character, or check character. The first two bars at either end encode the guard bar pattern, 101. The guard bars in the center encode as 01010. The corresponding encodation for the characters is summarized in Figure 5-1.2.1-5.

Since the UPC number encoded in the symbol does not include price information, the primary objective is to recover the 10-digit number and store it in RAM where it can be used by a price lookup routine. As is usually the case in MPU-based systems, stripping of the extraneous information, performing error checks and recovering the data can be accomplished in a variety of ways. A software oriented approach was selected in this case; external hardware processing is held to a minimum.

Decimal Value	Left Characters (Odd Parity — O)	Right Characters (Even Parity — E)
0	0001101	1110010
1	0011001	1100110
2	0010011	1101100
3	0111101	1000010
4	0100011	0011100
5	0110001	0001110
6	0101111	1010000
7	0111011	1000100
8	0110111	1001000
9	0001011	1110100

FIGURE 5.1.2.1-5 Encoding For UPC Characters

5-1.2.2 Hardware Requirements

For the wand used in this application, the data is captured by using a photo-cell to detect the variation in reflectivity as a light source as passed across the light (high reflectivity) and dark (low reflectivity) areas on the symbol. Circuitry suitable for recovering the resulting analog signal is shown in Figure 5-1.2.2-1. Two MC1747 Dual Operational Amplifiers are used to amplify and condition the photo-cell output. The conditioned output provides a TTL level logic "1" while the wand is scanning black and a logic "0" while scanning white. This is all the external hardware that is required; the MPU can perform all additional processing.

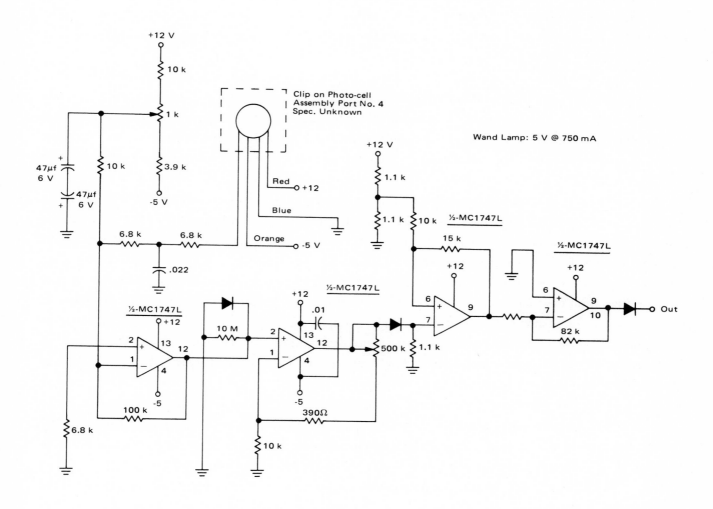

FIGURE 5-1.2.2-1 UPC Wand Signal Conditioning Circuitry

5-1.2.3 Data Recovery Technique

The output of the conditioning circuitry is effectively an asynchronous waveform with a widely variable and unknown data rate. An initial decision must be made as to what synchronization techniques will be used and what range of scanning rates can be expected. Lacking more specific information, it was deemed reasonable to expect rates from one-half inch per second to fifty inches per second.

Having a uniform constant pattern at the beginning and middle of each scan suggests that data recovery could be accomplished as follows: (1) Assume that the data rate is constant; (2) use the known initial guard bar pattern to establish a sampling rate; (3) use that rate to sample the data at the expected midpoint of each module for the next six characters; (4) use the middle guard bar to update the sampling rate; (5) sample the last six characters at the expected module midpoints.

A second data recovery method that does not require a synchronization technique could also be used: (1) Again assume a reasonably constant data rate during the scan; (2) measure and store in memory the time between transitions for an entire scan; (3) calculate the total time and divide it by the known number of modules per symbol (95) to determine an "average" module time; (4) use this and a comparison of "bar widths" (time between adjacent transitions) to one another; (5) use ratios established by (4) to determine bit patterns for each character.

An analysis of the expected rate variations, symbol printing tolerances, and computing complexity indicated that either of these two methods would lead to marginal results. A major difficulty lies in the way the module patterns for the individual characters are specified (see Figure 5-1.2.3-1). It is important to note that the dimensional specifications for each character are referenced to the edge of the pattern *nearest* the *middle* of the symbol. This means that left-hand characters are specified from their right edge and the right-hand characters are specified from their left edge. In addition, a printing tolerance (see Figure 5-1.2.3-2) is specified that swamps the tolerances shown in Figure 5-1.2.3-1. For example, the artwork tolerance of ± 0.0002 inches is lost in the tolerance of 0.013 ± 00397 inches that is permitted for printing a nominal module width. The net result is that legitimate symbols can have both undersize and oversize bars. This is illustrated in Figure 5-1.2.3-3, where a worst case situation for a left-hand "zero" is shown.

There, the right-hand black bar could be only 0.010 inches wide and still be in tolerance. Since the specification requires that the combination of the right-hand bar and the adjacent white bar be 0.0260 ± 0.0002 inches, this implies that the white bar could be 0.016 inches wide and still be in tolerance. Variations of this magnitude were observed when actual symbols on a variety of products were examined.

When the allowable dimensional variations across an entire symbol are considered, neither of the two methods proposed would give reliable results. The procedure finally selected incorporates features from both methods.

5-1.2.4 WAND/MPU Interface

Obtaining a record of the time between transitions is the first step in capturing the data. This raises the question of how the waveform recovered by the wand is to be entered into the MPU system. Since it is a

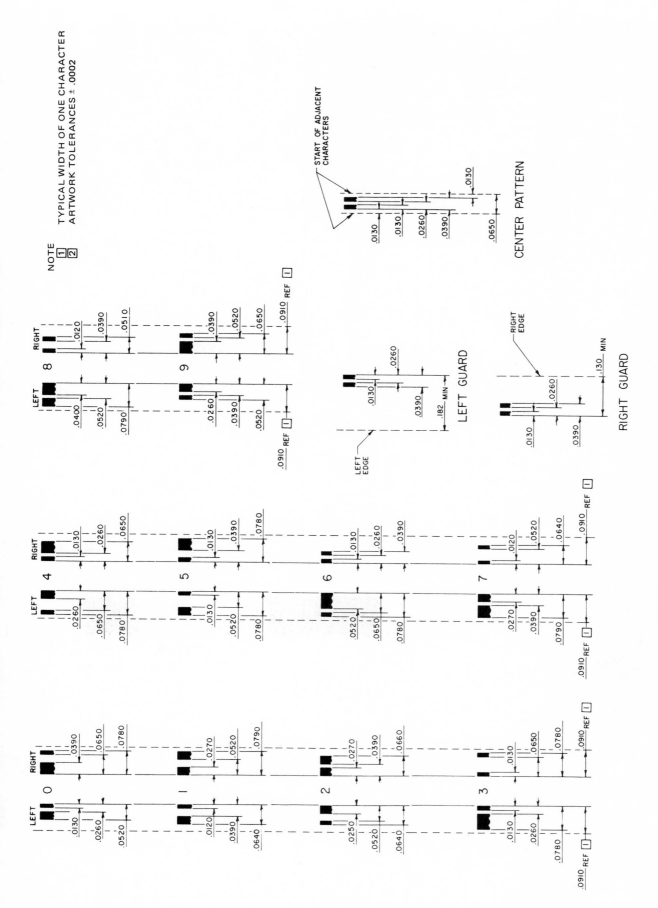

FIGURE 5-1.2.3-1: Dimensioning for Standard Symbol Characters

Module Width (Thousandths of an Inch)	Magnification Factor	Total Bar-Width Tolerance (Thousandths of an Inch)
11	.85	± 2
12	.92	± 3
13	1.00	± 3.97
14	1.08	± 4.4
15	1.15	± 4.9
16	1.23	± 5.4
17	1.30	± 5.8
18	1.38	± 6.3
19	1.46	± 6.8
20	1.54	± 7.2
21	1.62	± 7.7
22	1.69	± 8.2
23	1.77	± 8.6
24	1.84	± 9.1
25	1.92	± 9.6

FIGURE 5.1.2.3-2 UPC Symbol Printing Tolerances

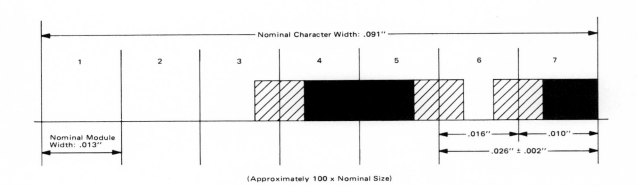

(Approximately 100 x Nominal Size)

FIGURE 5-1.2.3-3 Worst Case Printing Tolerances for "Lefthand 0".

serial stream and there are no handshaking requirements, only a single PIA input to the MPU is involved. The data can be introduced either through an interrupt line[CA(B)1,CA(B)2] or one of the data lines, PA(B)0— –PA(B)7. Input through a data line was selected based on the system flow shown in Figure 5-1.1.4-1. The wand is assumed to be one of the two manual input devices (the other is a keyboard) to a transaction terminal. The terminal's executive program enters a polling loop when it is willing to accept data[3]. This approach assumes that both devices will not be in use at the same time, hence, there is no need to handle the incoming data on an interrupt driven basis.

---

[3]The relationship of the wand routines to system flow is duscussed in greater detail in Section 6-4.2.4.

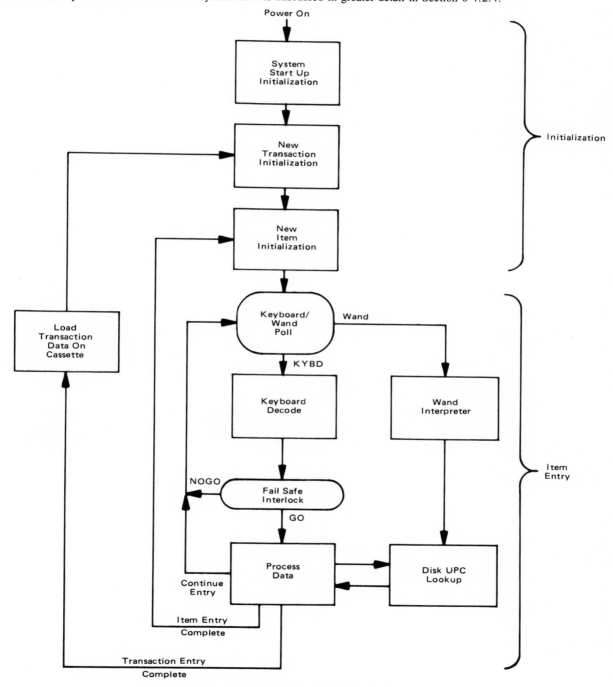

FIGURE 5-1.2.4-1: Transaction Terminal Flow Diagram

5-1.2.5 Data Recovery Control Program

3   The encoded wavefore enters the MPU via the seventh bit, PB7, on the B side of the Wand PIA. Selecting bit 7, the sign bit, provides the simplest means of testing to see if the current status of the waveform is one or zero.

Recovery of the UPC data consists of the following steps:

(1) Initialization — XKIWND — (Figures 5-1.2.5-1 and 5-1.2.5-2) Clears the various memory locations that will be used for buffers and data storage. This routine is entered each time a UPC Code is to be read.

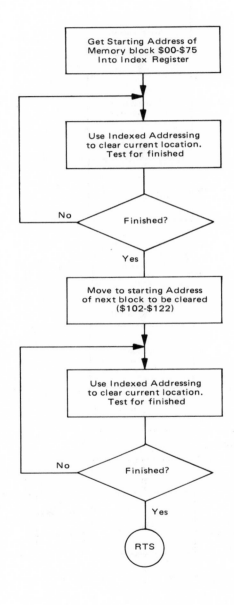

FIGURE 5-1.2.5-1 Flow Chart for XKIWND Initialization Routine

```
00010                          NAM     WKIWND
00020  B5EB                     ORG     $B5EB

00031  B5EB  CE  000D           LDX     #$0D        GET STRTNG ADDR OF BUFFER

00040  B5EE  6F  00     WCLRBL   CLR     X           CLEAR CURRENT LOCATION
00050  B5F0  08                  INX                 MOVE TO NEXT LOCATION
00060  B5F1  8C  0076            CPX     #$76        FINISHED?
00070  B5F4  26  F8              BNE     WCLRBL      NO, CONTUE;YES,GO NXT BLK
00080  B5F6  CE  0102            LDX     #$102       GET STRT ADDR OF NXT BLOCK

00100  B5F9  6F  00     WCLRB2   CLR     X           CLEAR CURRENT LOCATION
00110  B5FB  08                  INX                 MOVE TO NXT LOCATION
00120  B5FC  8C  0123            CPX     #$123       FINISHED?
00130  B5FF  26  F8              BNE     WCLRB2      NO, CONTINUE SEARCHING
00140  B601  39                  RTS                 YES, RETURN TO EXECUTIVE
```

FIGURE 5-1.2.5-2: XKIWND Assembly Listing

(2) Data Recovery — YKWAND — (Figure 5-1.2.5-3 and 5-1.2.5-4) This routine is entered from the executive's Keyboard/Wand Interrogation loop. The Interrogation loop continually tests bit 7 of XP4DRB, the PIA Data Register until a "zero" is encountered. The zero is assumed to result from reading the high reflectivity white space caused by the wand passing across the white guard band at the edge of a symbol. The wand output will normally be high at other times. For example, the wand just laying on a counter is equivalent to reading "black" or some other low reflectivity surface. The objective of YKWAND is to measure the time between transitions and store the results in RAM memory.

(3) Data Processing — WSORT — (Figures 5-1.2.5-5 and 5-1.2.5-6) The objective of WSORT is to reduce the timing data captured during YKWAND to set up UPC characters in binary format.

There are several additional routines associated with recovering the data: WERCHK tests the data to see if it is a valid UPC number by performing an error check based on the check character included in the symbol; (2) WBCDPK converts the data into packed BCD (two digits per byte), the format required for the price look-up routine; (3) WBADRD, the error processing routine, may be called for a variety of reasons during execution of YKWAND, WSORT, WCDTST, or WPACK. Each of these routines include validation tests and will call WBADRD if a bad read occurs. The action to be taken following a bad read depends on the particular application and may be performed by either the MPU or the human operator. Therefore, no specific WBADRD routine is included in this description. The system described in Chapter 6 generates an audible "approval" tone for "good data." In this case, the WBADRD routine could be nothing more than a deletion of the approval tone, indicating that either another scan or manual entry is required.

Details of the YKWAND routine are shown in the Flow Chart and Assembly Listing of Figures 5-1.2.5-3 and 5-1.2.5-4, respectively. Following entry from the Keyboard/Wand Interrogation Loop, bit 7 of the PIA Register (XP4DRB) is again tested to insure that the data is still low. If the entry was caused by a short

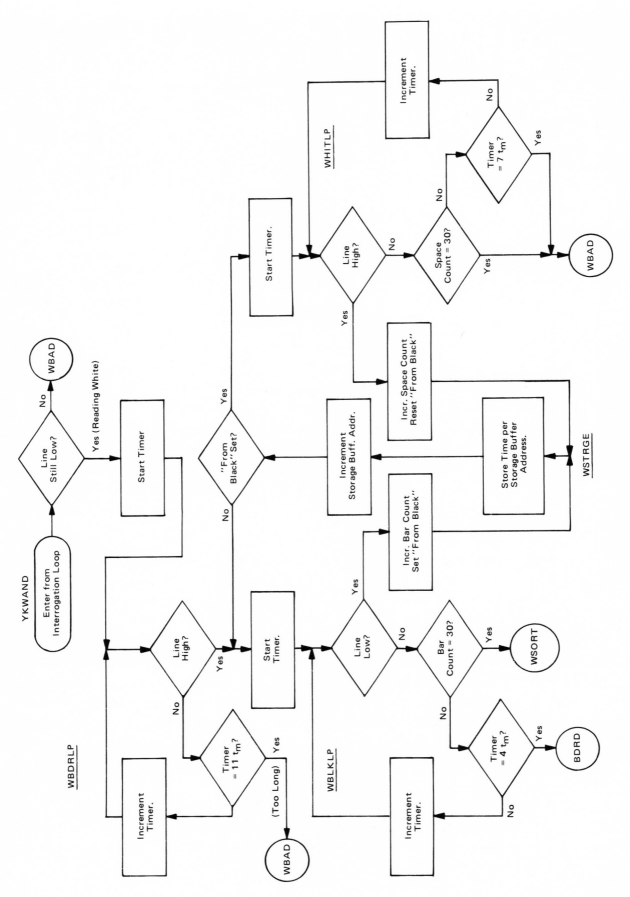

Figure 5-1.2.5-3 Flow Chart for YKWAND Routine

5-24

```
00010                              NAM    XKWAND
00010                              OPT    LIST
00010                       •   NAME:  XKWAND
00020                       •   REV:    12/13/74
00030  B60C                        ORG    $B60C
00040                       •
00050                       •••••••••••••••••••   WAND ROUTINE   ••••••••••••••
00060                       •
00080                       •
00090  B60C 7E B610  XKWAND JMP    YKWAND    ENTRY POINTS
00095  B60F 39       XKIWND RTS               NO INITIALIZATION
00280                       •
00290                       •              •   SECTION "XKWAND"   •
00300                       •
00310                       •       THIS PART OF THE ROUTINE IS THE
00320                       •       DATA GATHERING SECT. OF XKWAND.
00330                       •       IT READS THE UPC CODED LABEL
00340                       •       AS 60 BLACK AND WHITE BARS AND
00350                       •       STORES THE SCANNING TIME OF EACH
00360                       •       BAR OR SPACE IN LOCATIONS $00-$75
00370                       •
00380  B610 7F 0106  YKWAND CLR    WBRCNT
00381  B613 7F 0104         CLR    WFLAG
00382  B616 7F 0105         CLR    WSPCNT
00383  B619 7F 0114         CLR    WSBFAD
00384  B61C 7F 0115         CLR    WSBFAD+1
00390  B61F F6 C010         LDA B  XP2DRA    LINE LOW, SPACE?
00400  B622 2B 30           BMI    WBAD      NO: ERROR
00420                       •
00430  B624 CE 0000         LDX    #$0000    YES
00440  B627 F6 C010  WBDRLP LDA B  XP2DRA    LINE HIGH, BAR?
00460  B62A 2B 08           BMI    WBLKLP    YES: TO TIMING BAR LOOP
00470                       •
00480                       •       SET MAXIMUM TIME ALLOWED ON BORDER
00490                       •
00500  B62C 8C FF00         CPX    #$FF00    NO:  GUARD BAND DELAY
00510  B62F 27 23           BEQ    WBAD      TOO LONG ON GUARD BAND: ERR
00520  B631 08              INX
00530  B632 20 F3           BRA    WBDRLP    LOOP BACK
```

FIGURE 5-1.2.5-4: YKWAND Assembly Listing (Sheet 1 of 2)

```
00540                    ◆
00550  B634 CE 0000 WBLKLP LDX      #$0000      BLACK BAR TIMING LOOP
00560  B637 F6 C010 WBLKL1 LDA B    XP2DRA      LINE LOW, SPACE?
00580  B63A 2A 0F          BPL      WHS1        YES:   END LOOP
00590  B63C B6 0106        LDA A    WBRCNT      NO
00600  B63F 81 1E          CMP A    #$1E        BAR COUNT = 30?
00610  B641 27 4E          BEQ      WSORT       YES:   END SCAN
00620                    ◆
00630                    ◆         SET MAXIMUM TIME ALLOWED ON BLK BAR
00640                    ◆
00650  B643 8C 0B29        CPX      #$0B29      NO,TIMER = 4XU?
00660  B646 27 0C          BEQ      WBAD        YES
00670  B648 08             INX                  NO
00680  B649 20 EC          BRA      WBLKL1      LOOP BACK
00690                    ◆
00700  B64B 7C 0106 WHS1   INC      WBRCNT      INC BAR COUNT
00710  B64E 7C 0104        INC      WFLAG       SET "FROM BLACK" FLAG
00720  B651 7E B675        JMP      WSTRGE
00730                    ◆
00740  B654 3F      WBAD   SWI
00750                    ◆
00760  B655 CE 0000 WHITLP LDX      #$0000      WHITE BAR TIMING LOOP
00770  B658 F6 C010 WHITL1 LDA B    XP2DRA      LINE HIGH, BAR?
00790  B65B 2B 0F          BMI      WHS2        YES:   END LOOP
00800  B65D B6 0105        LDA A    WSPCNT      NO
00810  B660 81 1E          CMP A    #$1E        SPACE COUNT = 30?
00820  B662 27 F0          BEQ      WBAD        YES, TOO MANY SPACES:   ERRO
00830                    ◆
00840                    ◆         SET MAXIMUM TIME ALLOWED ON WHITE BAR
00850                    ◆
00860  B664 8C 1400        CPX      #$1400      NO,TIMER=7XU?
00870  B667 27 EB          BEQ      WBAD        YES
00880  B669 08             INX                  NO
00890  B66A 20 EC          BRA      WHITL1
00900                    ◆
00910  B66C 7C 0105 WHS2   INC      WSPCNT      INC SPACE COUNT
00920  B66F 7F 0104        CLR      WFLAG       RESET "FROM BLACK" FLAG
00930  B672 7E B675        JMP      WSTRGE
00940                    ◆
00950  B675 FF 0102 WSTRGE STX      WDUMBF      LOAD A AND B
00960  B678 FE 0114        LDX      WSBFAD      WITH CONTENTS OF
00970  B67B B6 0102        LDA A    WDUMBF      INDEX REG. (TIMER)
00980  B67E F6 0103        LDA B    WDUMBF+1
00990  B681 A7 00          STA A    X
01000  B683 E7 01          STA B    $1,X        STORE TIMER IN STORAGE BUFF
01020  B685 08             INX                  INCREMENT STORAGE
01030  B686 08             INX                  BUFFER ADDRESS
01040  B687 FF 0114        STX      WSBFAD
01050  B68A 7D 0104        TST      WFLAG       TEST FLAG
01060  B68D 27 A5          BEQ      WBLKLP      JUMP TO CORRECT
01070  B68F 20 C4          BRA      WHITLP      TIMING LOOP
```

FIGURE 5-1.2.5-4: YKWAND Assembly Listing (Sheet 2 of 2)

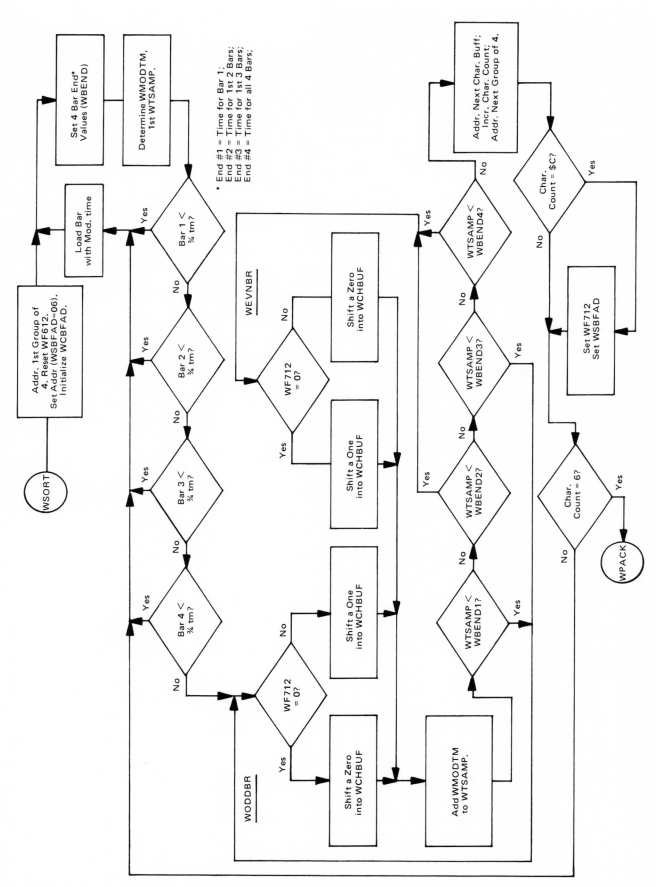

FIGURE 5-1.2.5-5 Flow Chart for WSORT Routine

```
01320                    ◆
01330                    ◆
01340                    ◆                    ◆ SECTION "WSORT"  ◆
01350                    ◆
01360                    ◆
01370                    ◆          THIS PART OF THE ROUTINE USES
01380                    ◆          THE DATA IN RAM $00-$75 AND
01390                    ◆          DECIPHERS IT INTO 12 7-BIT
01400                    ◆          BINARY WORDS WHICH ARE CODED
01410                    ◆          AS ONE OF THE UPC CHARACTER
01420                    ◆          CODES AND LOADED INTO WSTGBF
01430                    ◆          A 12 BYTE BUFFER
01440                    ◆
01450  B691 CE 0006 WSORT  LDX     #6          INIT DATA TO START
01451  B694 FF 0114        STX     WSBFAD      AFTER GUARD BARS
01470  B697 7F 0104        CLR     WF712       RESET FLAG 7-12
01480  B69A CE 0116        LDX     #WSTGBF      INIT CHARACTER BUFFER
01490  B69D FF 0102        STX     WCBFAD      ADDRESS
01530  B6A0 7F 0106        CLR     WCHRCT      CLEAR CHARACTER COUNT
01540                    ◆
01550  B6A3 FE 0114 WSRTLP LDX     WSBFAD      SET WBEND# VALUES
01560  B6A6 A6 00         LDA A    X
01570  B6A8 E6 01         LDA B    $1,X
01580  B6AA B7 0108       STA A    WBEND1
01590  B6AD F7 0109       STA B    WBEND1+1
01600  B6B0 EB 03         ADD B    $3,X
01610  B6B2 A9 02         ADC A    $2,X
01620  B6B4 B7 010A       STA A    WBEND2
01630  B6B7 F7 010B       STA B    WBEND2+1
01640  B6BA EB 05         ADD B    $5,X
01650  B6BC A9 04         ADC A    $4,X
01660  B6BE B7 010C       STA A    WBEND3
01670  B6C1 F7 010D       STA B    WBEND3+1
01680  B6C4 EB 07         ADD B    $7,X
01690  B6C6 A9 06         ADC A    $6,X
01700  B6C8 B7 010E       STA A    WBEND4
01710  B6CB F7 010F       STA B    WBEND4+1
01720                    ◆
01730  B6CE 97 D6         STA A    XKDVND      SET DIVIDEND
01740  B6D0 D7 D7         STA B    XKDVND+1
01750  B6D2 86 07         LDA A    #$07
01760  B6D4 97 D5         STA A    XKDVSR      SET DIVISOR
01770  B6D6 BD BA53       JSR      XKDIVD      DIVIDE BY 7
01780  B6D9 D6 D9         LDA B    XKQUOT+1     RECOVER ANSWER
01790  B6DB 7F 0110       CLR      WMODTM      LOAD MODULE TIME BUF.
01800  B6DE F7 0111       STA B    WMODTM+1
01810  B6E1 4F            CLR A                DIVIDE BY 2
01820  B6E2 56            ROR B
01830  B6E3 B7 0112       STA A    WTSAMP      LOAD SAMP. TIME BUF.
01840  B6E6 F7 0113       STA B    WTSAMP+1     WITH INIAL VALUE
```

FIGURE 5-1.2.5-6: WSORT Assembly Listing (Sheet 1 of 3)

```
01850              ♦
01860              ♦          ADJUSTMENT TEST: IS ONE OF THE
01870              ♦          BARS OR SPACES TOO NARROW?
01880              ♦
01890 B6E9 B6 0113          LDA A   WTSAMP+1
01900 B6EC 44               LSR A
01910 B6ED BB 0113          ADD A   WTSAMP+1    CALCULATE 3/4 OF MODULE T
01920 B6F0 B7 0107          STA A   W34MOD      STORE FOR USE
01930              ♦
01940 B6F3 FE 0114          LDX     WSBFAD
01950 B6F6 F6 0111          LDA B   WMODTM+1
01960 B6F9 B6 0107          LDA A   W34MOD
01970              ♦
01980              ♦          IF ANY BAR IS TOO NARROW,THE NOMINAL
01990              ♦          MODULE WIDTH IS USED TO REPLACE IT,
02000              ♦          THIS ALLOWS FOR MORE ACCURATE DATA PROC.
02020 B6FC 6D 00            TST     X           CHECK FIRST BAR
02030 B6FE 26 08            BNE     WCMP1
02040 B700 A1 01            CMP A   $1,X
02050 B702 25 04            BCS     WCMP1
02060 B704 E7 01            STA B   $1,X
02070 B706 20 9B            BRA     WSRTLP
02080 B708 6D 02   WCMP1    TST     $2,X        CHECK SECOND BAR
02090 B70A 26 08            BNE     WCMP2
02100 B70C A1 03            CMP A   $3,X
02110 B70E 25 04            BCS     WCMP2
02120 B710 E7 03            STA B   $3,X
02130 B712 20 8F            BRA     WSRTLP
02140 B714 6D 04   WCMP2    TST     $4,X        CHECK THIRD BAR
02150 B716 26 08            BNE     WCMP3
02160 B718 A1 05            CMP A   $5,X
02170 B71A 25 04            BCS     WCMP3
02180 B71C E7 05            STA B   $5,X
02190 B71E 20 83            BRA     WSRTLP
02200 B720 6D 06   WCMP3    TST     $6,X        CHECK FOURTH BAR
02210 B722 26 09            BNE     WODDBR
02220 B724 A1 07            CMP A   $7,X
02230 B726 25 05            BCS     WODDBR
02240 B728 E7 07            STA B   $7,X
02250 B72A 7E B6A3          JMP     WSRTLP
02260              ♦
02270              ♦
02280 B72D FE 0102 WODDBR   LDX     WCBFAD      LOADING LOOP 1
02290 B730 68 00            ASL     X
02300 B732 7D 0104          TST     WF712
02310 B735 27 10            BEQ     WHS8
02320 B737 6C 00            INC     X
02330 B739 20 0C            BRA     WHS8
02340              ♦
02350 B73B FE 0102 WEVNBR   LDX     WCBFAD      LOADING LOOP 2
02360 B73E 68 00            ASL     X
02370 B740 7D 0104          TST     WF712
02380 B743 26 02            BNE     WHS8
02390 B745 6C 00            INC     X
```

FIGURE 5-1.2.5-6: WSORT Assembly Listing (Sheet 2 of 3)

```
02400                      ◆
02410  B747 B6 0112  WHS8   LDA A   WTSAMP     UPDATE SAMP. TIME
02420  B74A F6 0113         LDA B   WTSAMP+1
02430  B74D FB 0111         ADD B   WMODTM+1
02440  B750 B9 0110         ADC A   WMODTM
02450  B753 B7 0112         STA A   WTSAMP
02460  B756 F7 0113         STA B   WTSAMP+1
02470                      ◆
02480  B759 B6 0112         LDA A   WTSAMP     FIRST TEST
02490  B75C F6 0113         LDA B   WTSAMP+1
02500  B75F B1 0108         CMP A   WBEND1
02510  B762 25 C9           BCS     WODDBR     IF TSAMP<END1
02520  B764 26 05           BNE     WHS9       IF TSAMP>END1
02530  B766 F1 0109         CMP B   WBEND1+1
02540  B769 25 C2           BCS     WODDBR     IF TSAMP<END1
02550  B76B B1 010A  WHS9   CMP A   WBEND2
02560  B76E 25 CB           BCS     WEVNBR     IF TSAMP<END2
02570  B770 26 05           BNE     WHS10      IF TSAMP>END2
02580  B772 F1 010B         CMP B   WBEND2+1
02590  B775 25 C4           BCS     WEVNBR     IF TSAMP<END2
02600  B777 B1 010C  WHS10  CMP A   WBEND3
02610  B77A 25 B1           BCS     WODDBR     IF TSAMP<END3
02620  B77C 26 05           BNE     WHS11      IF TSAMP>END3
02630  B77E F1 010D         CMP B   WBEND3+1
02640  B781 25 AA           BCS     WODDBR     IF TSAMP<END3
02650  B783 B1 010E  WHS11  CMP A   WBEND4
02660  B786 25 B3           BCS     WEVNBR     IF TSAMP<END4
02670  B788 26 05           BNE     WHS13      IF TSAMP>END4
02680  B78A F1 010F         CMP B   WBEND4+1
02690  B78D 25 AC           BCS     WEVNBR     IF TSAMP<END4
02700                      ◆
02710  B78F 7C 0103  WHS13  INC     WCBFAD+1    ADDRESS NEXT CHAR. BUF.
02720  B792 7C 0106         INC     WCHRCT     INC. CHAR. COUNT
02730  B795 B6 0115         LDA A   WSBFAD+1    ADDRESS NEXT GROUP OF
02740  B798 8B 08           ADD A   #$08       FOUR STRGE. BUF.
02750  B79A B7 0115         STA A   WSBFAD+1
02760                      ◆
02770  B79D B6 0106         LDA A   WCHRCT
02780  B7A0 81 06           CMP A   #$06       BEGINNING 7 TH CHAR.?
02790  B7A2 26 08           BNE     WHS14      NO
02800  B7A4 7C 0104         INC     WF712      YES,SET FLAG FOR 7-12
02810  B7A7 86 40           LDA A   #$40       SKIP OVER GUARD BARS
02820  B7A9 B7 0115         STA A   WSBFAD+1
02830                      ◆
02840  B7AC B6 0106  WHS14  LDA A   WCHRCT
02850  B7AF 81 0C           CMP A   #$0C       FINISHED 12 TH CHAR.?
02860  B7B1 27 03           BEQ     WHS15      YES
02870  B7B3 7E B6A3         JMP     WSRTLP     NO,LOOP BACK
02880  B7B6 20 00   WHS15   BRA     WPACK      GO TO PACKING SECT.
02890                      ◆
02900                      ◆
```

FIGURE 5-1.2.5-6: WSORT Assembly Listing (Sheet 3 of 3)

"noise" pulse on the data line, the program causes the MPU to exit to the bad read routine, WBADRD. If the line is still low, indicating that the wand is passing over a white space, the MPU enters a delay loop, WBDRLP, to wait for the expected first white-to-black transition.

Exit from the loop occurs when the first black guard bar is encountered or after too much time has passed for the white space to be a symbol border. The count loaded into the Index Register determines a number of passes through the 23 microsecond waiting loop and hence the maximum time that will be spent on white before exiting to the bad read routine. The required time is derived from the slowest allowed scan rate and the nominal dimensions of the symbol. A minimum scan rate of one-half inches per second was deemed reasonable for this application. The nominal module width of 0.013 inches yields a time per module, t_m, width of 0.13 inches/o.5 inches per second = 0.026 seconds at the slowest scan rate. The white guard bar is specified to be at least eleven modules wide, hence, the waiting time should be at least (.026) (11) = 0.286 seconds. The program causes the MPU to wait approximately 1.5 seconds before exiting in order to allow for operator variance at the beginning of a scan.

The next section of the program is used to determine the elapsed time between transitions during a scan. The first low-to-high (white-to-black) transition following the white border cuases the MPU to enter the Black Bar Timing Loop, WBLKLP. The symbol consists of 30 black bars and 30 white bars (the last white bar is the white border at the end of a scan). The program alternates between WBLKLP and a similar White Bar Timing Loop, WHITLP. The elapsed times are stored in sixty memory locations for later use by the WSORT processing routine. The Index Register and a 35 microsecond timing loop are used to measure the elapsed time until the next transition.

The WBLKLP loop will cause an exit to the bad read routine if the elapsed time becomes greater than what is anticipated for the maximum black bar width of 4 modules at the slowest scan rate. This is monitored by comparing the number of passes through the 35 microsecond loop to $0B9B, corresponding to (.026) (4) = 0.104 seconds.

When the subsequent black-to-white transition occurs, the current bar count, WBRCNT, is increased by one, a flag indicating "From Black" is set, and the current time between transitions is stored. Since the count in the Index Register may be as large as $0B9A, two bytes or storage are required for each timeout (maximum single byte storage is $FF). The storage segment of the program, WSTRGE, is entered from both the Black Bar Timing Loop and the White Bar Timing Loop and causes the current elapsed time to be stored in the appropriate buffer.

The time to be stored (current contents of the Index Register) is temporarily placed in RAM locations WDUMBF and WDUMBF+1. The current storage buffer address, WSBFAD, points to the storage address and is loaded into the Index Register. The indexed addressing mode is used to retrieve the time from WDUMBF and WDUMBF+1 and store it in the proper storage buffer location. The Index Register is advanced to the next storage address and placed in WSBFAD for use during the next storage cycle. Control is returned to the proper timing loop by testing the "From Black" flag.

The White Bar Timing Loop, WHITLP, functions similarly to WBLKLP except that it measures the time between black-to-white and white-to-black transitions. If a white bar count of 30 is encountered, the program exits to WBADRD since a black bar count of 30 should have been reached on the previous pass through WBLKLP. A time in excess of seven module units. corresponding to the maximum anticipated for a white (right-hand) border, will also cause an exit to WBADRD. The white bar count is increased by one and the "From Black" flag is cleared prior to branching to WSTRGE.

The WSORT section of the program recovers the 12 UPC characters by operating on the black and white timing measurements that were captured and stored as the wand scanned the symbol. The process is based on the following assumption: since the nominal width of a given character within the symbol is only 0.091 inches, the per character scan rate should be very nearly constant. The format of the black bar — white bar pattern is specified. Each of the 12 UPC characters are known to consist of 7 modules encoded as 2 white and 2 black bars. The WSORT procedure uses these facts to generate a sampling procedure for recovering the data.

The bar times (from the storage buffer) for each character are used to compute a total time for that character. This time is then divided by seven to obtain an "average time per module." Due to the allowable variations in the symbol, each module should be sampled within ±10% of its midpoint for reliable results. Therefore, the average module width is used to generate a series of sampling times that occur near the expected center of each character's seven modules. The sample times then used to test the bar times and determine the bit pattern of the character.

A Flow Chart and an Assembly Listing of the WSORT program are shown in Figures 5-1.2.5-5 and 5-1.2.5-6, respectively. The recovery process is best explained with the aid of a representative example. Assume that the times recorded in memory locations $0006 through $000D of the storage buffer are as follows:

Memory Location	Contents
$0006	$ 00
$0007	$ 29
$0008	$ 00
$0009	$ C6
$000A	$ 00
$000B	$ 1E
$000C	$ 00
$000D	$ 30

These locations contain the timing information for the first character to be scanned following the 101 guard bar pattern (the guard bar data is in locations $0000 through $0005 and is not used in this sequence). Note that for this example the even positions, $0006, $0008, etc., all contain zero. This simply indicates that none of the times between transitions were long enough to require the second byte of storage. From the data, the bar pattern times are:

	$29	C6	1E	30	(Hexadecimal)
or:	41	198	30	48	(Decimal)

After an initialization sequence, the program starting at WSRTLP, establishes the Bar End values by computing accumulative totals and storing them in buffers as:

WBEND1	WBEND2	WBEND3	WBEND4	
41	239	269	317	(Decimal)

The total, 317 in this case, is then divided by seven to obtain an average module time (the division is performed by a subroutine located elsewhere in system memory). The result, 45, is stored in buffer WMODTM and the first sampling time, one-half of WMODTM, is obtained as WTSAMP = 22. The MPU next performs a sequence to determine if any of the bars are too narrow for accurate data recovery. The procedure assumes that each bar must be at least three-quarters of the nominal calculated width of 45 or ¾(45) = 33:

$$41 > 33$$
$$198 > 33$$
$$30 < 33$$
$$48 > 33$$

If all the bars are greater than ¾ of the nominal bar width, the program branches to the next main sequence, WODDBR. If, as in the case of the third bar in this example, some of the bars are undersize, they are replaced with the nominal value and the checking procedure is repeated until all bars are at least the nominal width. For example, this leads to:

41	198	(45)	48
		30	

with new values:

WBEND1: 41
WBEND2: 239
WBEND3: 284
WBEND4: 332
WMODTM: 47
WTSAMP: 23
¾(WMODTM): 33

and the test is now satisfied by all four bars.

By repeatedly increasing the initial sample time by WMODTM, a set of sampling times are generated that can be compared to the Bar End values in order to determine which bars are currently being sampled. For the example:

$23 <$ WBEND $= 41$; therefore, in 1st Bar.
$41 < 23 + 47 = 70) <$ WBEND2 $= 239$;
$41 < 70 + 47 = 117 < 239$;
$41 < 164 < 239$; $\qquad$ therefore, in 2nd Bar.
$41 < 211 < 239$;
$239 < 258 <$ WBEND3 $= 284$; therefore, in 3rd Bar.
$284 < 305 <$ WBEND4 $= 332$; therefore, in 4th Bar.
$332 < 352$; therefore, beyond last Bar.

Since the symbol and code are defined such that the first module of a character (scanning from either direction) is a zero, the result of this sequence indicated that the UPC code for this character is 0111101, or from Figure 5-1.2.1-5, the decimal value is "3." Note that it was assumed that the code was a left-hand character implying a left-to-right sweep since the character was recovered immediately followed the initial guard bar pattern. The program as shown in Figure 5-1.2.5-6 is for left-to-right scans only. A simple parity check is adequate to determine whether left or right hand characters are being read since each side has opposite parity.

The data for all 12 characters is recovered in this fashion and stored in consecutive RAM buffer locations. At this point, the data is still encoded in the UPC format of Figure 5-1.2.1-5. The UPC code follows no simple algorithm and, hence, must be converted to weighted binary before error check calculations can be made.

The Flow Chart and Assembly Listing for WCNVRT, a suitable conversion routine, is shown in Figures 5-1.2.5-7 and 5-1.2.5-8, respectively. The conversion routine uses a table look-up procedure. Code words corresponding to each of the ten UPC characters is stored in a permanent table in ROM (see Figure 5-1.2.5-9). The MPU tests each recovered data byte against the values in the table until a match is obtained. When this occurs, the current UPC data is replaced with its weighted binary equivalent. Since the desired equivalent is weighted binary, it can be generated by using accumulator B as a counter that tracks with the UPC look-up table position. When a match results, the value that is to be substituted is then available in the B accumulator. Note that while there are two sets of codes, left-hand and right-hand, for the UPC characters, only one table is required. This is due to one's complement relationship of the two sets. The look-up table contains the left-hand set. If the MPU tests a given data byte against all ten left-hand words without obtaining a match, it then complements each bit of the UPC data and goes through the look-up table again. If no match is obtained after a second pass, the program causes an exit to WBADRD. When all twelve characters have been successfully converted, the MPU proceeds to the next sequence, an error calculation to determine if the data represents a valid UPC number.

The Error Check Character included in the symbol was originally obtained by applying the following steps to the UPC number:

Step 1. Starting at the left, sum up all the characters in the odd positions (that is, first on the left, third from the left, etc.), starting with the number system character.

Step 2. Multiply the sum obtained in Step 1 by 3.

Step 3. Again starting at the left, sum all the characters in the even positions.

Step 4. Add the product of Step 2 to the sum of Step 3.

Step 5. The modulo-10 check character value is the smallest number which when added to the sum of Step 4 produces a multiple of 10.

The error check routine, WERCHK, applies this algorithm to the first eleven digits of the recovered data and checks the result against the recovered check character. The Flow Chart and Assembly Listing are shown in Figures 5-1.2.5-10 and 5-1.2.5-11, respectively.

The error check is performed by duplicating the steps taken during the original generation of the check character and comparing the result to the recovered check character. The modulo-10 result for Step 5 is obtained by repeated subtraction of 10 until the result is less than or equal to zero. If no match is obtained the program exits to WBADRD. If the test is satisfied, the program proceeds to the last step in the sequence, placement of the 10-digit UPC number in five bytes of RAM as packed BCD characters.

The Flow Chart and Assembly Listing for the packing routine, WBCDPK, are shown in Figures 5-1.2.5-12 and 5-1.2.5-13, respectively. The packing order is indicated in Figure 5-1.2.5-9.

5-1.2 PRINTER CONTROL

A great many different printers are in use; they range from the slow but economical devices for

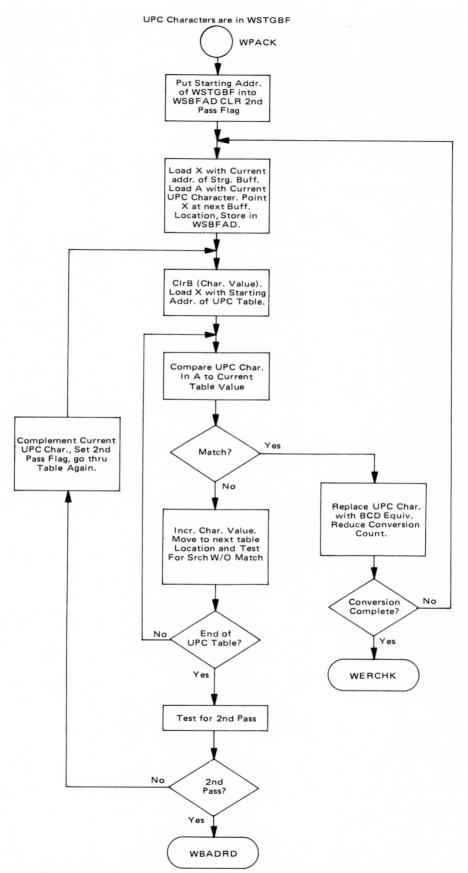

Figure 5-1.2.5-7 Flow Chart for WCNVRT UPC to BCD Conversion Routine

```
00010                               NAM     WCNVRT
00020  B7B7                         ORG     $B7B7

00040  B7B7  CE 0116   WCNVRT  LDX     #WSTGBF     GET STARTING ADDRESS OF
00050  B7BA  FF 0114           STX     WSBFAD      STRGE BUFF INTO BUF ADDR &
00060  B7BD  86 0C             LDA A   #$0C        LOAD WSPCNT WITH # OF
00070  B7BF  B7 0112           STA A   WSPCNT      CHARS. TO BE CONVERTED

00090  B7C2  7F 0110   WNXTCH  CLR     WFLAG       CLEAR 2ND PASS FLAG
00100  B7C5  A6 00             LDA A   X           GET CURRENT UPC CHARACTER
00110  B7C7  08                INX                 POINT TO NEXT UPC LOCATION
00120  B7C8  FF 0114           STX     WSBFAD      AND STORE IN BUFFER

00140  B7CB  5F        WPASS2  CLR B               INITIALIZE CHAR BCD VALUE
00150  B7CC  CE B7F1           LDX     #WPCTBL     GET START ADDR OF UPC TABL

00170  B7CF  A1 00     WCMPRE  CMP A   X           UPC CHAR MATCH TBLE CHAR?
00180  B7D1  26 0C             BNE     WNXLOC      NO, CONTINUE SEARCH
00190  B7D3  FE 0114           LDX     WSBFAD      GET CURRENT ADDR FROM BUF
00200  B7D6  E7 00             STA B   X           YES, REPLACE UPC WITH BCD E
00210  B7D8  7A 0112           DEC     WSPCNT      REDUCE CONVERSION COUNT
00220  B7DB  27 20             BEQ     WBCDPK      IF DONE, EXIT TO WBCDPK
00230  B7DD  20 E3             BRA     WNXTCH      IF NOT, GET NEXT CHAR

00250  B7DF  08        WNXLOC  INX                 MOVE TO NEXT UPCTBL LOCATIO
00260  B7E0  5C                INC B               INCREASE BCD CHAR VALUE
00270  B7E1  9C B7F1           CPX     #WPCTBL     SEARCHED ENTIRE TABLE?
00280  B7E4  26 E9             BNE     WCMPRE      NO, CONTINUE THRU TABLE
00290  B7E6  7D 0110           TST     WFLAG       YES, SEE IF ON SECOND PASS
00300  B7E9  26 06             BNE     WBADRD      2 PASSES WTH NO MTCH = BADR
00310  B7EB  43                COM A               1ST PASS, COMPLEMENT UPC CH
00320  B7EC  7C 0110           INC     WFLAG       SET 2ND PASS FLAG
00330  B7EF  20 DA             BRA     WPASS2      GO THROUGH TABLE AGAIN
00340        B7F1      WBADRD  EQU     *
00341        0114      WSBFAD  EQU     $0114
00342        0116      WSTGBF  EQU     $0116
00343        0112      WSPCNT  EQU     $0112
00344        0110      WFLAG   EQU     $0110
00345  B7F1  19        WPCTBL  FCB     $19,$13,$16,$01,$0E,$07,$08,$02
       B7F2  13
       B7F3  16
       B7F4  01
       B7F5  0E
       B7F6  07
       B7F7  08
       B7F8  02
00346  B7F9  04                FCB     $04,$1A
       B7FA  1A
```

FIGURE 5-1.2.5-8: WCNVRT Assembly Listing

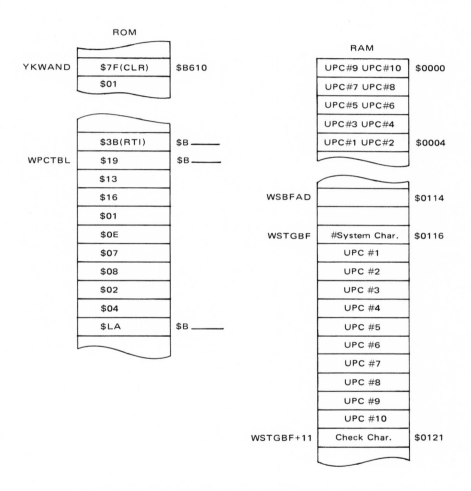

FIGURES 5-1.2.5-9 XKWAND Table and Buffer Memory Allocation.

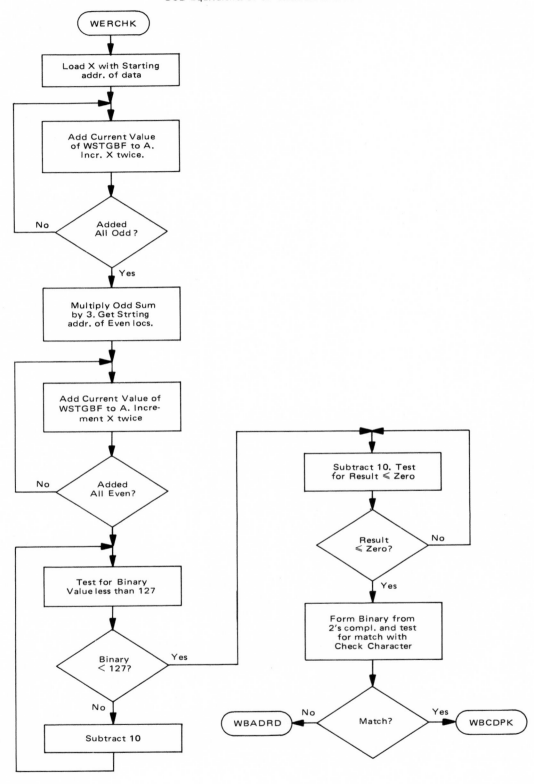

FIGURE 5-1.2.5-10 Flowchart for WERCHK Error Check

```
00010                         NAM     WERCHK
00020  B7FE                   ORG     $B7FE

00040  B7FE  CE  0115  WERCHK  LDX     #WSTGBF    GET STRING ADDR OF ODD
00050  B801  4F                CLR  A             LOCATIONS; CLEAR A.

00070  B802  AB  00   WSTEP1  ADD  A  X          ADD FROM CURRENT ODD LOCATI
00080  B804  08                INX                MOVE TO NEXT LOCATION
00090  B805  08                INX
00100  B806  8C  0122          CPX     #WSTGBF+12   ADDED ALL ODD LOCATIONS
00110  B809  26  F7            BNE     WSTEP1     IF NO CONTNUE;IF YES,GO STE

00120  B80B  16       WSTEP2  TAB                MULTIPLY STEP1 RESULT
00130  B80C  1B                ABA                BY THREE. LEAVE RESULT
00140  B80D  1B                ABA                IN ACCA
00150  B80E  CE  0117          LDX     #WSTGBF+1   GET EVEN STRING ADDR

00170  B811  AB  00   WSTEP3  ADD  A  X          ADD FROM CURRENT LOCATION
00180  B813  08                INX                MOVE TO NEXT LOCATION
00190  B814  08                INX
00200  B815  8C  0116          CPX     #WSTGBF    ADDED ALL EVEN LOCATIONS?
00210  B818  26  F7            BNE     WSTEP3     IF NO,CONTNUE; IF YES, GO S

00230  B81A  40       WSTEP4  TST  A             GREATER THAN 127 BINARY?
00240  B81B  2A  04            BPL     WMOD10     NO, CONTINUE MODULO CALC.
00250  B81D  80  0A            SUB  A  #10        YES, SUBTRACT 10,CHECK
00260  B81F  20  F9            BRA     WSTEP4     FOR STILL >127

00280  B821  80  0A   WMOD10  SUB  A  #10        SUBTRACT 10
00290  B823  2E  FC            BGT     WMOD10     KEEP SUBBING UNTIL 0 OR
00300  B825  40                NEG  A             FORM BINARY FROM 2'S COMPLE
00310  B826  B1  0121          CMP  A  WSTGBF+11   MATCH WITH CHK CHAR?
00320  B829  26  C6            BNE     WBADRD     NO, GO BADREAD; YES, CONTIN
```

FIGURE 5-1.2.5-11: WERCHK Assembly Listing

```
00001                          NAM     WBCDPK
00002  B82C                     ORG     $B82C

00010  B82C  0F        WBCDPK   SEI
00020  B82D  BF  0114           STS     WSBFAD    SAVE CURRENT SP
00030  B830  8E  0004           LDS     #$0004    POINT STK AT PACKING LOC
00040  B833  CE  0117           LDX     #WSTGBF+1    GET STRING ADDR OF UNPAC

00060  B836  A6  00    WPAKLP   LDA  A  X         GET CURRENT ODD BCD CHAR
00070  B838  48                 ASL  A            SHIFT ODD CHAR TO
00080  B839  48                 ASL  A            UPPER FOUR BITS OF
00090  B83A  48                 ASL  A            CURRENT LOCATION
00100  B83B  48                 ASL  A
00110  B83C  A4  01             AND  A  1,X       PACK CURRENT EVEN CHAR
00120  B83E  36                 PSH  A            PUSH INTO PACKING LOCATION
00130  B83F  08                 INX              MOVE TO NEXT ADDR
00140  B840  08                 INX              BUFFER LOCATION
00150  B841  8C  0121           CPX     #WSTGBF+11    PACKING COMPLETE?
00160  B844  26  F0             BNE     WPAKLP    NO, CONTINUE PACKING
00170  B846  BE  0114           LDS     WSBFAD    YES, RESTORE SP AND
00180  B849  0E                 CLI              RETURN TO EXECUTIVE
00190  B84A  39                 RTS
```

FIGURE 5-1.2.5-13: WBCDPK Assembly Listing

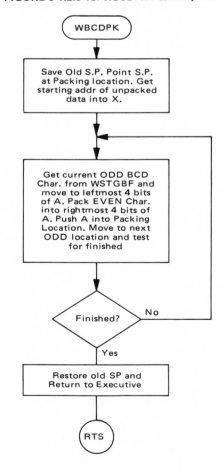

FIGURE 5-1.2.5-12 WBCDPK Flowchart for WBCDPK Packing Routine

printing out supermarket receipts, to the super-machines capable of printing 1200 132-character lines per minute. The broadest common ground for printers and microprocessors appears to be in the medium to low speed printing applications.

Medium performance is taken here to include auxiliary printers used with terminals or small computing systems printing up to a maximum of 200 132-character lines/minute. The gamut of printers spanning the medium to low speed range includes: electronic discharge printers, thermal printers, chain printers, drum printers, matrix printers, serial printers, etc., with types and speed ranges available for almost any conceivable application.

High performance microprocessors like the MC6800 provide an efficient means for controlling the higher speed printers and in the lower speed applications, additional functions can be combined with the controller function to produce a more cost-effective system.

Designing the microprocessor into the controlling system allows hardware (logic)/software (programming) tradeoffs to be made to satisfy the specific system requirements. For example, in the high speed printers, additional logic might be required if the desired data transfer rate is to be met even though the MPU is only used for printer control.

At the other end of the spectrum, using one of the newer high performance MPUs as a dedicated controller for a slower printer amounts to gross overkill. More often the relationship is similar to that shown in Figure 6-4.1-1, a generalized diagram of an MPU based transaction terminal described in Chapter 6. In applications of this type, the printer is merely one of several peripherals and its control is a relatively minor task that involves a small percentage of the MPU's attention.

It is in applications such as this that the real value of an MPU shows. They permit the designer to reduce a relatively complex system to a number of manageable tasks. Service routines are developed for the various peripherals and a suitable executive control program then ties the system together.

In a typical case, there are several factors to be considered in the development of a peripheral control routine. The device selected must, of course, satisfy the basic system requirements such as speed, reliability, etc. Beyond that, some devices of the same class are more amenable to MPU control than others. Some of these factors are illustrated in the following paragraphs where the development of hardware and software for a representative low speed printer application is discussed.

5-2.1.1   SEIKO AN-101F Operating Characteristics

A SEIKO AN-101F printer was selected as the hard copy output device for the transaction terminal design described in Chapter 6. The SEIKO AN-101F Printer employs a continually rotating print drum mechanism using what is referred to as the flying printer technique. The printing principle of the mechanism is indicated schematically in Figure 5-2.1.1-1.

The print drum and the ratchet shaft are geared together and rotate continuously in the direction shown. During a non-print condition, the right end of the trigger lever is removed from the ratchet's pawl locus by the downward force of the trigger lever spring. In the non-printing condition, the trigger magnet is not actuated and the hammers are lifted upward to a neutral position by the hammer lever springs.

When actuated, the trigger magnet's actuating lever forces the opposite end of the trigger lever into the locus of the ratchet pawl. During its next rotation, the pawl will engage the right end of the trigger lever causing a downward motion to the right hand end of the hammer. The hammer thus strikes through the inked ribbon and paper, causing the character then under the hammer to be printed.

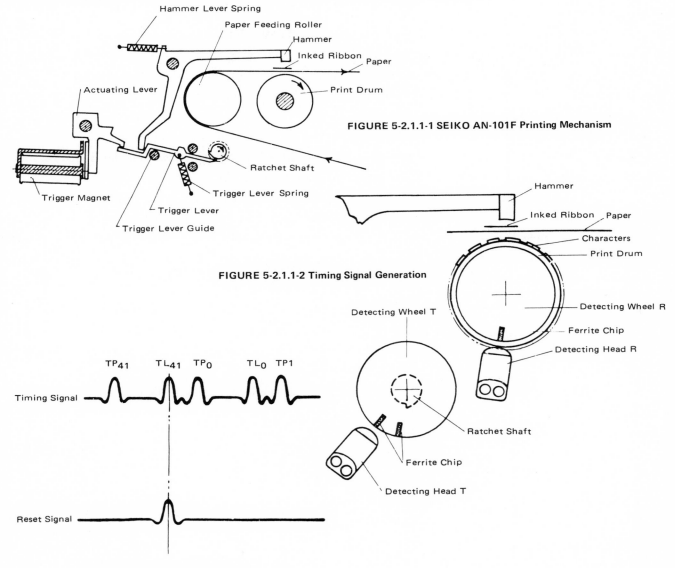

FIGURE 5-2.1.1-1 SEIKO AN-101F Printing Mechanism

FIGURE 5-2.1.1-2 Timing Signal Generation

FIGURE 5-2.1.1-3 Timing Signals

Any of 42 characters (alphanumeric plus special characters *, $, ', -, ., and /) may be printed in a 21-column format. Each column position has a complete character set spaced evenly around the drum. Because of a 42:1 gear ratio, the ratchet rotates 42 times for each complete drum rotation. Hence, each character of the set is positioned under a print hammer once during every rotation of the drum.

From this brief description of the printer mechanisms characteristics, it is evident that the control circuitry must actuate the hammers at just the right time if printing is to occur. Timing signals are generated electromagnetically by means of detection heads and ferrite magnets associated with the ratchet shaft and drum (See Figures 5-2.1.1-2 and 5-2.1.1-3).

Rotation of the ratchet shaft generates signals TP and TL for each of the 42 characters. TP provides timing for energizing the trigger magnets, TL for de-energizing. A reset signal R is generated by each complete rotation of the drum. The resulting waveform for a complete drum rotation is illustrated in Figure 5-2.1.4-1.

5-2.1.2 Printer Hardware/Software Tradeoffs

It is at this point that a designer must start considering trade-offs in order to arrive at the most effective design. A suitable peripheral device has been selected and its characteristics have been studied. In this case, the manufacturer provides a suggested controller design that can be implemented (exclusive of Trigger Magnet drive circuitry) with 16-20 SSI and MSI integrated circuits. If this approach is adopted, the MPU merely monitors status and transfers data bytes to the controller at the proper time.

At the other extreme, the MPU could assume as much of the control function as possible and eliminate all of the external conventional circuits. When overall system timing permits it, this is usually the most cost effective approach.

There may be reason to adopt some intermediate approach. For example, a sixteen column format was required for the application described here. The required information for identifying one of the sixteen items can be handled by four encoded bits. The design could have been implemented using 4 PIA data lines and external decode circuitry. However, it was decided to assign each column its own PIA data line, using up the data capability of one PIA but requiring little external circuitry (See Figure 5-2.1.3-1). Had there been four "spare" PIA lines elsewhere in the system, the alternate approach would have been given greater consideration.

As a further consideration in the trade-off area, note that while only 16 columns are used in this design, the AN-101F has 21 columns available. If all 21 were to be used, the designer could decide between using five more PIA lines as opposed to an external 5-bit shift register. Unless there happened to be 5 "spare" PIA lines somewhere, the relative cost would probably dictate using the shift register.

Selection of a particular configuration is, of course, not made in pure hardware vacuum. Knowledge concerning the MPU's capability to handle the control problem heavily influences the method that is finally selected.

5-2.1.3 Printer I/O Configuration

As is generally the case with MPU based designs, there are numerous ways to solve a given problem. The method to be discussed here was selected to satisfy three basic objectives: (1) Use minimum external electronics; (2) Use the timing signals provided with no additional external processing other than pulse shaping; (3) Minimize the time in which the MPU must be involved with printer control activity. The hardware configuration selected is shown in Figure 5-2.1.3-1.

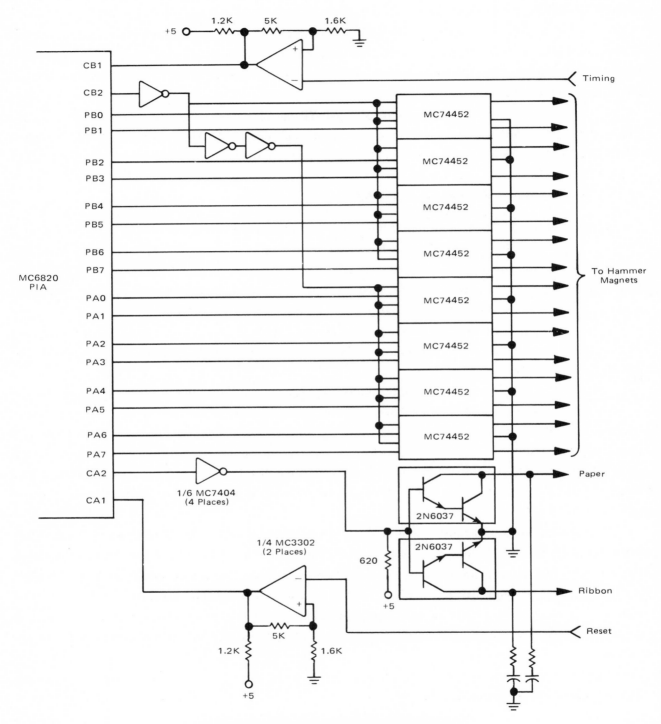

FIGURE 5-2.1.3-1: SEIKO Printer Circuit Requirements

As indicated in the earlier discussion of hardware/software trade-offs, each hammer driver is controlled by one of the PIA's sixteen data lines. These lines are the outputs of Registers ORA and ORB in the PIA which are regarded as memory locations by the MPU; hence, the MPU can enable the activation of a particular column hammer by setting the appropriate bit position in the memory locations assigned to ORA and ORB.

During initialization, CB2 is established as an output and is used by the MPU to strobe the enabled hammer drivers at the proper time. At the end of a print cycle, the printer's paper and ribbon must be advanced. This requires a 36 msec pulse which is generated by the control program and is applied through CA2 which is also established as an output during initialization.

After being shaped and inverted by the MC3302 Comparators, the printer timing and reset pulses are applied to the CB1 and CA1 inputs, respectively. It is by means of these signals and the MC6800 interrupt structure that the Printer "tells" the MPU it requires servicing. Part of the printer control program's function is to establish suitable interrupt modes using the PIA Control Registers.

As an example, in the control sequence described below, negative transitions on the CB1 timing input during a print cycle must cause the MPU to service the printer. The MPU sets this up by writing $b0 = 1$ and $b1 = 0$ into Control Register B during initialization. The subsequent timing transitions then cause the PIA to issue an Interrupt Request to the MPU via the system $\overline{IRQ}$ line.

The MPU responds by interrupting its current activity (the MPU's internal registers are saved on a "stack" so that the task may be resumed later) and fetches the starting address of an executive service routine from a memory location permanently assigned to the Interrupt Request. The service routine directs the MPU to "poll" its peripherals by testing the flag bits in the PIA Control Registers to see which one needs servicing. Flag bit b7 of the printer PIA's Control Register was set by the same transition that caused the interrupt. When the MPU finds this flag set, it jumps out of the polling routine to an appropriate printer control program.

5-2.1.4 **Printer Control Program**

The basic task, or algorithm, of the control program is to examine the text of the message to be printed and make sure that the appropriate bits in the PIA's Output Registers, ORA and ORB, are set at the proper time. The details of timing and program flow are shown in Figures 5-2.1.4-2 through 5-2.1.4-7.

Understanding of the operation is aided by regarding the time for one print drum rotation as forty-two equal intervals, t_0 through t_{41}. With this in mind, note that all similar characters in the text are printed simultaneously, i.e., all 0's are printed during t_0, all 1's during t_1, etc. For example, if the text requires the letter C in columns 3 and 9 (as in Figure 5-2.1.4-1), column hammers 3 and 9 must be engaged during the time interval t_{12} during which all C's are under the hammers.

Following each "TL" interrupt, the MPU examines the entire message to see if there are any characters to be printed during the next time interval. The text to be printed may be either a "canned" message stored in ROM or variable information generated by the executive program and stored in RAM. Messages are stored in memory in 16-byte blocks with each memory position corresponding to a printer column position. Prior to calling the printer, the executive program loads the starting address of the message to be printed into a buffer. The printer routine then uses this address in conjunction with the MPU's indexed addressing mode to locate the desired message; this technique permits using the same subroutine for all of the system printer requirements.

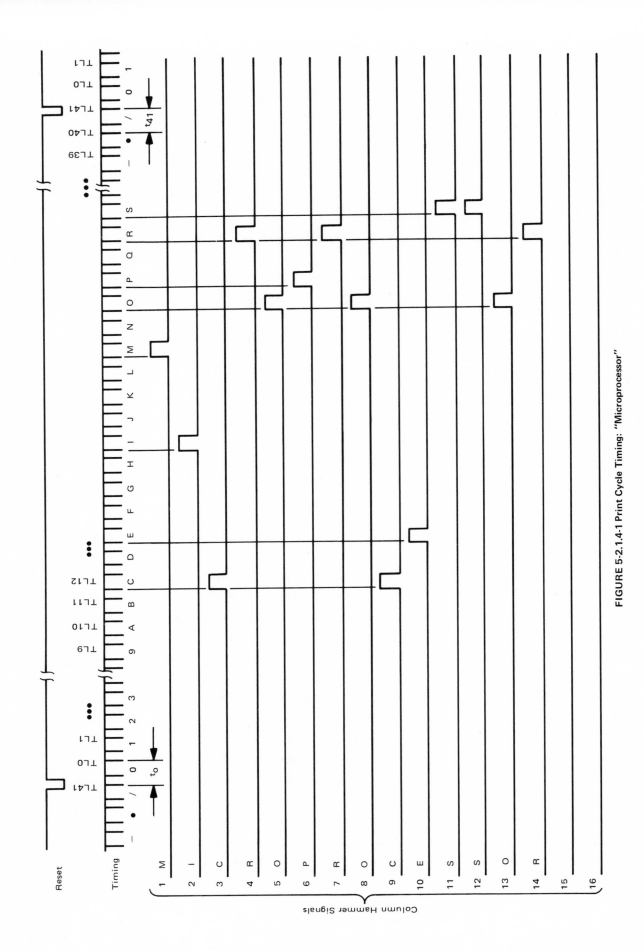

FIGURE 5-2.1.4-1 Print Cycle Timing: "Microprocessor"

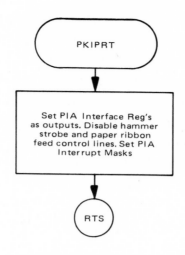

RTS = Return from Subroutine
R = Reset Timing Pulse

(a)

```
00280                   ◆◆ INITIALIZE PRINTER PIA
00300 7C4C 7F 8009 PKIPRT CLR     XP1CRA
00310 7C4F 7F 800B        CLR     XP1CRB
00320 7C52 4F             CLR A
00330 7C53 43             COM A
00340 7C54 B7 8008        STA A   XP1DRA    SET PIA DATA LINES AS OUT
00350 7C57 B7 800A        STA A   XP1DRB
00360 7C5A 86 3C          LDA A   #$3C      SET PIA CONTROL REGSTRS TO
00370 7C5C B7 8009        STA A   XP1CRA    DISABLE OUTPUTS
00380 7C5F B7 800B        STA A   XP1CRB    AND SET INTRPT MASKS
00390 7C62 B6 8008        LDA A   XP1DRA    READ DATA RGSTRS TO CLEAR
00400 7C65 F6 800A        LDA B   XP1DRB    INTRPTS AND FLAGS
00410 7C68 39             RTS
```

(b)

FIGURE 5-2.1.4-2: Initialization

A 42-byte Character File corresponding to the printer's character set is stored[1] in ROM in the same sequence as it appears on the printer drum. As each TL interrupt is serviced, the Character File Pointer is incremented pointing to the address of the next character on the drum.

The MPU then compares every character of the text to the current Character File character, keeping a running column count as it does so. Each bit position in the PIA Output Registers is set or cleared depending on whether or not the respective text characters matched the Character File characters.

The flow charts and control programs that resulted are shown in Figures 5-2.1.4-2 through 5-2.1.4-6. The control problem was broken into four tasks: (1) Initialization; (2) Printer Enable; (3) Reset Service Routine; (4) Print Service Routine.

The Initialization routine, PKIPRT[2], defines the housekeeping tasks that are routinely taken care of by the executive program during system power-up.

Referring to Figure 5-2.1.4-2(b), lines 300 and 310 clear CRA and CRB (XPICRA, XPICRB) setting $b_2 = 0$ so that DDRA and DDRB can be addressed. Lines 320–350 store ones in all of the DDR bits defining the 16 data lines of ORA and ORB as outputs. Lines 360–380 load the control registers with the hexadecimal (HEX) value 3C resulting in the control lines being defined as shown below:

	b_7	b_6	b_5	b_4	b_3	b_2	b_1	b_0
CRA(B)	0	0	1	1	1	1	0	0

3   C

$b_0 = 0$ IRQ interrupts are disabled.

$b_1 = 0$ CA1, CB1 are established as negative edge sensitive inputs

$b_2 = 1$ ORA, ORB are now selected

$b_3 = 1$

$b_4 = 1$ } CA2, CB2 are established as outputs which follow b_3; they are now high.

$b_5 = 1$

With CA2 and CB2 high, all the driver circuits are disabled since one input of each driver AND gate is held low (see Figure 5-2.1.4-1). Note that CA2 and CB2 are inverted prior to reaching the AND gates.

Lines 390 and 400 are "dummy reads" of ORA and ORB which clear the IRQ flags that may have been set and insure that the IRQA(B) lines are high, i.e., inactive. Line 410 returns control to the executive program.

The Printer Enable routine, PKNTRL, is called by the executive program whenever a line of text is to be printed (refer to Figure 5-2.1.4-3(b). Since the printer drum is continuously generating reset pulses at CA1, the IRQA flag will be set but the IRQA line will be inactive (it was disabled during initialization by setting $b_0 = 0$). In order to insure that the next reset pulse starts the print cycle instead of the CA1 interrupt enable, the IRQA flag is cleared by a dummy read of ORA (XPICRA) prior to enabling CA1, lines 490–510.

The "printer done" flag (#$29) is cleared by another service routine before returning to the main program. Subsequent interrupts generated by the printer will cause the line of text to be printed with further control by the executive program unnecessary.

---

[1] Both Character File data and message characters are stored in memory using ASCII code. Any convenient code could be used, however, in this application, the ASCII message format is required by other peripherals in the system.

[2] Labels appearing in the following discussion conform to a format adopted for the Transaction Terminal system. In complex systems, it is advisable to sacrifice some mnemonic meaningfulness in favor of system documentation requirements.

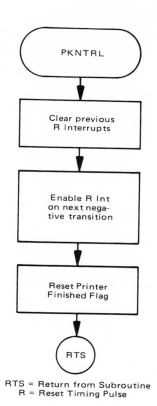

RTS = Return from Subroutine
R = Reset Timing Pulse

(a)

```
00430                          ** PRINT 16 CHARACTERS BEGINNING AT THE MEM ADD
00440                          ** STORED IN PVTXBF (C7,C8) ON ONE LINE
00450                          ** JSR PKNTRL TO START, INTRPTS WILL SYNC REMAININ
00460                          ** OPERATIONS.   CB2: HAMMER ENABLE, CA2: PPR/RBN
00470                          ** FEED, CA1: RESET INTRPT, CB1: TIMING INTRPT..
00490  7C69  B6 8008   PKNTRL  LDA A    XP1DRA    CLR PREV. RESET INTRPTS
00500  7C6C  86 3D             LDA A    #$3D      SET CA1 TO INTRPT ON NEXT
00510  7C6E  B7 8009           STA A    XP1CRA    NEG TRANSI OF RESET
00520  7C71  86 29             LDA A    #$29
00530  7C73  BD 6309           JSR      XKRSTF    CLEAR PRINTER DONE FLAG
00540  7C76  39                RTS                RETURN - WAIT FOR START INT
```

(b)

FIGURE 5-2.1.4-3 Printer Enable

When the CA1 input is triggered by the printer reset pulse, the MPU interrupt sequence directs processing control to the PRNTIR routine (Figure 5-2.1.4-4(b)). Since the IRQ flag and line are active, they must be disabled prior to exiting from the routine in order to allow further interrupts. Line 590 reads ORA (XP1DRA) to accomplish this as the first instruction. Lines 600–620 test b_1 of CRA to determine whether the CA1 input was positive or negative edge sensitive:

(A) If $b_1 = 0$, CA1 was a negative transition and the program branches to PKSCN1. Lines 780 and 790 set CRA to 3C as was done in the initialization routine to mask or disable the CA1 interrupt input. The starting address of the printer character file, PCKF00, is stored by lines 800–810 for use during the first scan loop. Lines 820–840 clear the previous timing interrupts and set CRB to allow the next negative CB1 transition to interrupt the MPU. The RTI instruction at line 850 returns the MPU to the status that existed at the time the interrupt occurred and program execution continues from there.

(B) If $b_1 = 1$, CA1 was positive signalling the end of the printing cycle. The routine disables the line, CA1, the hammer strobe and the interrupts CA1, CB1, CB2, with lines 630–640 by setting CRA(B) to 3C. The next two lines store 34 in CRA clearing b_3 and making CA2 go low. A delay loop is then generated with lines 670–720. Accumulators A and B are loaded with the values 48 and A6. Accumulator B is then decremented (A6 times) to zero each time Accumulator A is decremented once. When Accumulator A is zero (≈ 36 ms), the program jumps out of the delay loop and stops the paper ribbon feed by loading CRA with 3C (b_3 = 1) making CA2 go high. Note that the delay loop accumulator values depend on the system clock frequency; here, 1 MHz.

The printer done flag (#$29) is then set by a jump to another service subroutine before returning to the program flow where the interrupt occurred.

The printer timing signals are asynchronous with respect to the MPU clock. Hence, if the printer interrupt is enabled immediately following an interrupt, it could take nearly two full print drum rotations or approximately 1.5 seconds to print a line of text. This is a relatively long period in terms of MPU processing time; if the printer required continuous control during this period, it would be impractical in many applications. Fortunately, the printer signals may be used in an interrupt driven approach that will be clarified as more control program is described.

The printer interrupt service routines are designed so that the MPU can resume other system tasks shortly after each printer interrupt is serviced. The relationship between the printer signals and MPU activity is shown in Figure 5-2.1.4-5. The approximate time in which the MPU is busy servicing the printer is indicated by the cross-hatched area following each allowed interrupt. Using this interrupt driven approach involves the MPU for less than 30 msec out of each 850 msec print cycle.

The majority of this time is used during the Print Service routine, PRNTIT (Figure 5-2.1.4-6). Printer operation requires that the selected print hammers be engaged only during the time between TP_n and TL_n (See Figure 5-2.1.4-1). The PRNTIT routine selects the hammers that are required during a given interval and causes them to engage and disengage at the required times. Most of the processing time (approximately 0.6 msec following each TL pulse) is spent determining which hammers should be engaged during the next interval.

Referring again to Figure 5-2.1.4-5, TL_{41} will be the first CB1 transition after PRNTIR has enabled CB1 to be negative edge sensitive. TL_{41} will cause the IRQB line to go low interrupting the MPU in the same manner as before, except that this time the IRQB flag is set by CB1. The interrupt sequence will jump to PRNTIT (Figure 5-2.1.4-6) instead of PRNTIR.

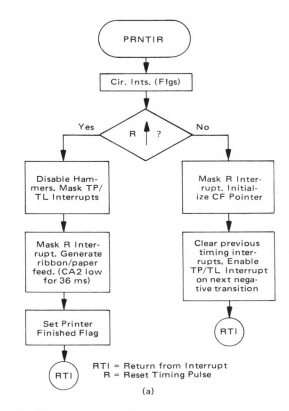

RTI = Return from Interrupt
R = Reset Timing Pulse

(a)

```
560                 ●● INTRPT VECTORED HERE IF CA1 INTRPT
570                 ●● SCAN TEXT FOR FIRST CHAR OR MAKE PPR/RBN FEED
590  7C77 B6 8008  PRNTIR  LDA A   XP1DRA  CLR INTRPT AND FLAG
600  7C7A B6 8009          LDA A   XP1CRA  TEST IF CA1 POS OR NEG
610  7C7D 85 02            BIT A   #$02    INTRPT
620  7C7F 27 1F            BEQ     PKSCN1  NEG, GO INT'L SCAN LOOP
630  7C81 C6 3C            LDA B   #$3C    TRUE, PPR/RBN FEED
640  7C83 F7 800B          STA B   XP1CRB  DISABLE HAMMERS;INTRPT MASKED
650  7C86 86 34            LDA A   #$34
660  7C88 B7 8009          STA A   XP1CRA  START PPR/RBN FEED;INTRPT M
670  7C8B 86 48            LDA A   #$48    DELAY LOOP = 36 MILLISECOND
680  7C8D C6 92    PKTG01  LDA B   #$92    #CYCLES=ACCA((ACCB)3+5)
690  7C8F 5A       PKTG02  DEC B           FOR A 1MHZ CLOCK
700  7C90 26 FD            BNE     PKTG02  LET ACCA = $48
710  7C92 4A              DEC A            ACCB = $A6
720  7C93 26 F8            BNE     PKTG01  LOOP
730  7C95 86 3C            LDA A   #$3C    STOP PPR/RBN FEED;INTRPT MSKD
740  7C97 B7 8009          STA A   XP1CRA
750  7C9A 86 29            LDA A   #$29
760  7C9C BD 6303          JSR     XKSETF  SET PRINTER DONE FLAG 29
770  7C9F 3B               RTI             RETURN
780  7CA0 86 3C    PKSCN1  LDA A   #$3C    MSAK CA1 INTRPT
790  7CA2 B7 8009          STA A   XP1CRA
800  7CA5 CE 7EB8          LDX     #PKCF00  INT'L CF POINTER
810  7CA8 DF D7            STX     PVXBFR
820  7CAA F6 800A          LDA B   XP1DRB  CLR PREV TIMING INTRPTS
830  7CAD C6 3D            LDA B   #$3D    SET CB1 TO INTRPT ON NEXT
840  7CAF F7 800B          STA B   XP1CRB  NEG TIMING PULSE
850  7CB2 3B               RTI             RETURN
```

(b)

FIGURE 5-2.1.4-4 Reset Service

5-51

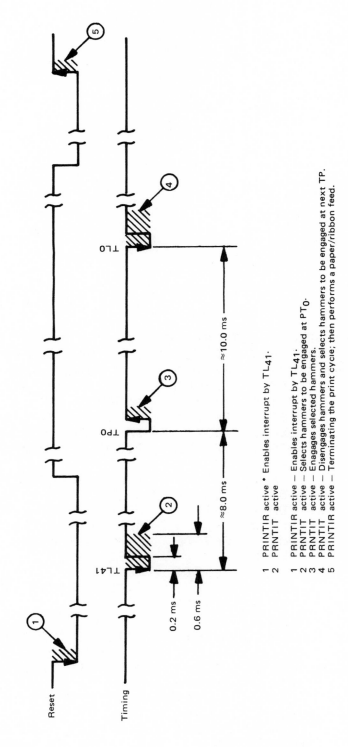

1   PRINTIR active * Enables interrupt by TL_{41}.
2   PRNTIT active

1   PRINTIR active — Enables interrupt by TL_{41}.
2   PRNTIT   active — Selects hammers to be engaged at PT_0.
3   PRNTIT   active — Enagages selected hammers.
4   PRNTIT   active — Disengages hammers and selects hammers to be engaged at next TP.
5   PRINTIR active — Terminating the print cycle; then performs a paper/ribbon feed.

FIGURE 5-2.1.4-5 Printer Loading of MPU Activity

5-52

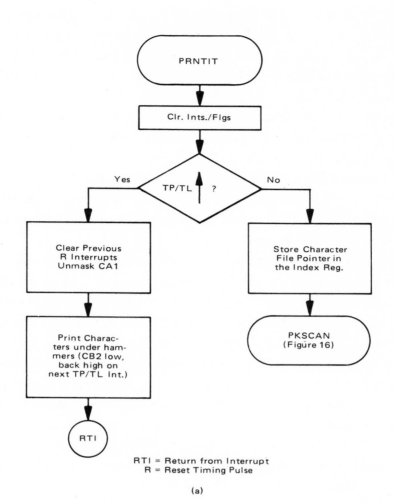

RTI = Return from Interrupt
R = Reset Timing Pulse

(a)

```
 870                    ◆◆  INTRPT VECTORED HERE IF CB1 INTRPT
 880                    ◆◆  PRINT CHAR UNDER HAMMERS OR SCAN TEXT
 900 7CB3 F6 800A PRNTIT  LDA B  XP1DRB    CLR INTRPT AND FLAG
 910 7CB6 F6 800B         LDA B  XP1CRB    TEST IF CB1 IS A POS
 920 7CB9 C5 02           BIT B  ⊕$02      OR NEG INTRPT
 930 7CBB 27 13           BEQ    PKSCN2    NEG, GO SCAN
 940               ◆                       POSITIVE, PRINT
 950 7CBD B6 8008         LDA A  XP1DRA    CLR PREV RESET INTRPT
 960 7CC0 86 3F           LDA A  ⊕$3F      SET CA1 TO INTRPT ON NEXT
 970 7CC2 B7 8009         STA A  XP1CRA    POS TRANS OF RESET PULSE
 980 7CC5 C6 25           LDA B  ⊕$25      PRINT CHAR NOW UNDER HAMMA
 990 7CC7 F7 800B         STA B  XP1CRB    CB2 LOW, HI NEXT NEG CB
1000 7CCA D6 DA           LDA B  BF1DRB    GET SIDE B OUTPUT INFO
1010 7CCC F7 800A         STA B  XP1DRB    STORE IT AND START PRINT
1020 7CCF 3B              RTI              RETURN - WAIT FOR NEXT
1030 7CD0 DE D7 PKSCN2    LDX    PVXBFR    LOAD CURRENT CF POINTER
```

(b)

FIGURE 5-2.1.4-6 Print Service

Again the first thing done is to clear the IRQB flag and the $\overline{\text{IRQ}}$ line by reading ORB (XP1DRB). Then lines 910–930 test b_1 of CRB to determine whether the CB1 input was positive or negative edge sensitive.

(A) If $b_1 = 0$, CB1 was a negative transition and the program branches to PKSCN2 (line 1030) which loads the index register with the current character file (CF) address pointer. The scan loop follows and will be discussed later.

(B) If $b_1 = 1$, CB1 was a positive transition, i.e., a TP timing pulse. This means that the hammers must now be strobed. Before this is done, CA1 is cleared and enabled (lines 950–970) to allow the next positive reset transition at CA1 to signal the end of the print cycle. The hammer strobe is then armed to be set low on the next write in ORB by storing #$25 in CRB (lines 980 and 990). This combination of b_3, b_4, and b_5 also returns CB2 high on the next CB1 interrupt at TL. The 8 data bits set by the previous scan loop for the B side outputs are then stored in ORB (lines 1000 and 1010) causing CB2 to go low. The strobe inputs on the driver AND gates go high activating those hammers whose data lines have been set high.

Line 1020 returns control to the place the interrupt occurred. The scan loop, PSKCAN (Figure 5-1.2.4-7), is the actual data processing section of the program. The column counter (Accumulator B) is cleared and the current character file character stored in the test buffer (lines 1410–1430). The next character file character address is then stored (lines 1440–1450) for initializing the next loop. The first text character address is loaded into the index register before starting the scanning process.

The first instruction in the actual loop (line 1470) compares the column count with #$10 (decimal 16) to see if the last text character has been checked. If it has, the program enables an interrupt by the next positive timing pulse transition (lines 1490–1510) and returns control to the executive program. If the last character has not been tested, the program branches to PVNXT1. Line 1520 loads accumulator A (ACCA) with the text character corresponding to the present column counter value. This is then compared with the current character file (CF) character (lines 1530 and 1540) with the carry bit being set if they match (line 1550), cleared if they don't (line 1570). The carry is then saved by the TPA instruction so that it will not be destroyed by the following test. Lines 1550 and 1600 determine which output register is to be operated on. If the column count is ⩾8, ORA; if <8, ORB. In either case the carry bit is restored by the TAP instruction (line 1610 for side B, 1640 for side A) before it is shifted into ORA or the ORB buffer, BFIDRB, using the ROL instructions on line 1620 for side B and line 1650 for side A, (since a write into ORB is required to activate CB2, the data is stored in a buffer until time for hammer activation). Figure 5-2.1.4-8 is the schematic representation of the ROL instruction. As the scan progresses, the bits are shifted from right to left. At the end of the loop, the bits representing the character to be printed will be shifted into the position indicated in Figure 5-2.1.4-9. When the shift has been completed, the column counter and text address pointers are incremented (lines 1660 and 1680), then a branch is executed to the start of the loop.

The control operation just described might appear at first glance to be a slow and cumbersome approach. However, it should be kept in mind that during an actual print operation, less than 4% (30 msec out of 850 msec) of the MPU's capability is used.

This combined with the fact that only twenty conventional integrated circuits are being replaced seems to indicate that the control of printers of this class is a trivial task for high performance microprocessors. The proper perspective in this situation is to remember that the MPU is controlling 7–10 other peripheral devices while also performing the executive function and that the control of the printer is accomplished with a minimum of additional expense in hardware (200 bytes of ROM) and engineering development time.

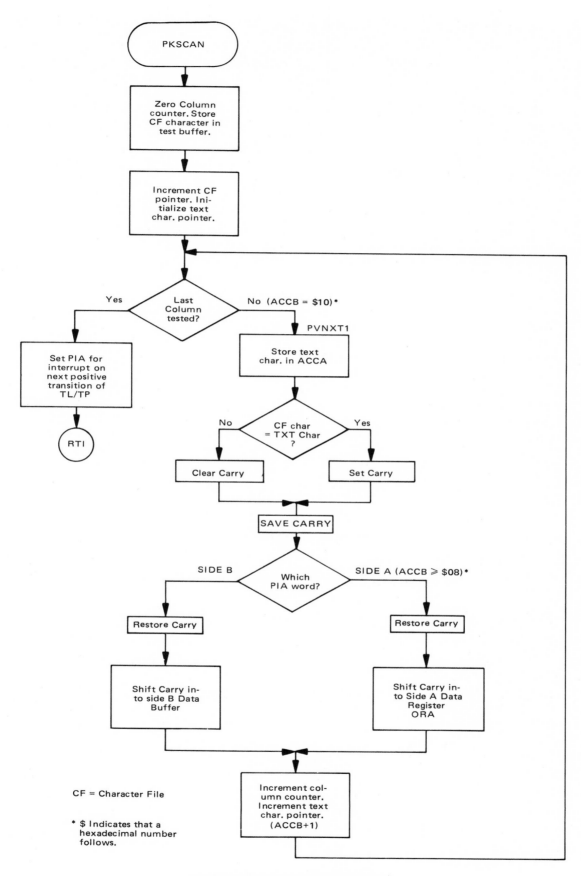

FIGURE 5-2.1.4-7(a): PKSCAN Flow Chart

```
01390                          ** SCAN TEXT FOR CURRENT CHAR AND SET OUTPUT LINES
01410  B9B8 5F         PKSCAN  CLR  B              ZERO COLUMN COUNTER
01420  B9B9 A6 00              LDA  A    X
01430  B9BB B7 0123            STA  A    PVCFBF     STORE CF CHAR IN TST BUF
01440  B9BE 08                 INX
01450  B9BF FF 0121            STX       PVXBFR     STORE NEXT CF ADDRESS
01460  B9C2 FE 011F            LDX       PVTXBF     GET TEXT CHAR ADDRESS
01470  B9C5 C1 10      PKCLOP  CMP  B    #$10       HAS LAST TEXT COLUMN
01480  B9C7 26 06              BNE       PVNXT1     BEEN TESTED
01490  B9C9 86 3F              LDA  A    #$3F       SET CB1 TO INTRPT ON NEXT
01500  B9CB B7 C00B            STA  A    XP1CRB     POS TRANS OF TIMING PULSE
01510  B9CE 3B                 RTI                  YES, RETURN
01520  B9CF A6 00      PVNXT1  LDA  A    X          STORE TX CHAR IN ACCA
01530  B9D1 B1 0123            CMP  A    PVCFBF     DOES TEXT MATCH
01540  B9D4 26 03              BNE       PVNXT2     CURRENT CF CHARACTER
01550  B9D6 0D                 SEC                  YES, SET CARRY
01560  B9D7 20 01              BRA       PVNXT3
01570  B9D9 0C        PVNXT2  CLC                  NO, CLEAR CARRY
01580  B9DA 07        PVNXT3  TPA                  SAVE CARRY
01590  B9DB C1 08             CMP  B    #08       WHICH PIA SIDE?
01600  B9DD 2C 05             BGE       PVNXT4
01610  B9DF 06               TAP                  SIDE B:  GET CARRY
01620  B9E0 79 0124          ROL       BF1DRB     SHFT C INTO PRNT BUFFER
01630  B9E3 20 04            BRA       PVNXT7     CONTINUE
01640  B9E5 06        PVNXT4  TAP                  SIDE A:  GET CARRY
01650  B9E6 79 C008          ROL       XP1DRA     SHFT C INTO PIA ORA
01660  B9E9 5C        PVNXT7  INC  B              INCREMENT COLUMN CTR
01670  B9EA 08               INX                  INCREMENT TEXT POINTER
01680  B9EB 20 D8            BRA       PKCLOP
```

FIGURE 5-2.1.4-7(b): PKSCAN Assembly Listing

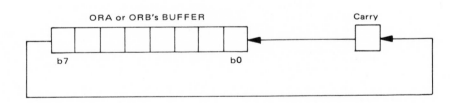

FIGURE 5-2.1.4-8: Roll Left Operation on PIA Registers

PRINTER COL. #	19	18	17	16	15	14	13	12	11	10	9	8	7	6	5	4
OUTPUT FORMAT		M	I	C	R	O	P	R	O	C	E	S	S	O	R	
COLUMN COUNTER	0	1	2	3	4	5	6	7	8	9	A	B	C	D	E	F
PIA OUTPUT LINE	PB7	PB6	PB5	PB4	PB3	PB2	PB1	PB0	PA7	PA6	PA5	PA4	PA3	PA2	PA1	PA0
TEXT BUFFER ADDR.	+0	1	2	3	4	5	6	7	8	9	10	11	12	13	14	15

FIGURE 5-2.1.4-9: Printer Column/Text Buffer Relationship

5-2.2 BURROUGHS SELF-SCAN DISPLAY CONTROL

Interfacing displays such as the Burroughs Self-Scan Model SSD 1000-0061 Gas Discharge Display (with memory) to the MC6800 MPU can be done using half of one PIA. The display has a sixteen position, single row array with a 64 character repertoire.

Each character is entered in the right most position, and is shifted left upon entry of another character. When the display has filled to sixteen characters, the left most position will be shifted off the display as subsequent characters are shifted into the right most position. The display is also equipped with a "backspace" (effectively a right shift) and "clear" capability for flexible error correction. Additional characteristics of the display are shown in Figure 5-2.2-1.

The PIA/DISPLAY Interface is shown in Figure 5-2.2-2. The "B" side of the PIA is used to connect both control and data signals, leaving the "A" side available for another peripheral. During initialization, the PB0 through PB7 lines are established as outputs; CA1 is an interrupt input and CB2 is a strobe output. Data can be transferred from the MPU to the display using a single instruction, STAA PIADRB, where the data was in accumulator A and the "B" Data Register address was equated to the label PIADRB during assembly. This instruction transfers the next character to the display and simultaneously generates a "data present" pulse. The MPU can then resume other tasks until it is interrupted by a "data taken" pulse from the display.

5-3.1 INTRODUCTION TO DATA COMMUNICATIONS

The following sections contain the hardware and software requirements for a teletype connected directly to the ACIA and for a teletype connected to the ACIA through a pair of modems. The modems enable data stored at a remote site to be transmitted over the telephone lines to an MPU system. Therefore, the only major difference in the software required for the two systems is the modem control functions. For the software examples, data from a teletype tape is stored into memory under MPU control. After the complete message is stored in memory, the data is transferred to a Burroughs Self-scan Display for viewing purposes. The data contained on the tape is stored by program control in memory locations that are specified by the address field on the tape. Data received from the teletype is in the format shown in Figure 5-3.1-1, which is consistent to that used in other MPU software packages. The records consist of a header record (S0), data record (S1), and an end of file record (S9). A data record begins with an S1 preamble, followed by the byte count in that record, the beginning address to store data, the data and the checksum (one's complement of the summation of 8-bit bytes). Since an error could occur in the reception of the data, the data is repeated several times on tape and an S8 is used to indicate the end of tape. Examples of the TTY/ACIA and MODEM/ACIA are shown in Figure 5-3.1-2.

5-3.1.1 TTY To ACIA Hardware

The hardware requirements to interface a teletype to the MPU system include the Asynchronous Communications Interface Adapter (ACIA) and some form of voltage to current interface circuit or RS232C type interface. The current interface circuits may vary to suit the particular teletype used within the data system. Two of the most common methods of receiving data from a teletype are from a teletype keyboard or teletype paper tape reader. Also, the paper tape reader can have either manual or automatic control. The automatic paper tape reader turns on and off by internally decoding words received on the serial input line. A "DC1" Control word turns the reader "on" while a "DC3" Control word turns the reader "off;" DC1 and DC3 control words

INPUTS (Figures 3 and 5)

Data Input
Positive logic (a high is written into memory as "1"). Data may not be changed during the period in which the WRITE cycle line is in the logic "1" state.

Data Present Pulse
A logical "0" causes the INPUT DATA to be written into memory. Minimum pulse width is 1.0 us. This function is triggered on the high-to-low transitional edge.

Clear Pulse
A logical "0" clears the memory. Minimum duration for the SSD1000-0041 is 33 us. Minimum duration for the SSD1000-0061 is 66 us.

Blank Disable
A logical "1" blanks the display. This input does not affect the memory portion of the system.

Back Space
A logical "0" causes a left-to-right shift of one character. Minimum pulse width is 1.0 us. This function is triggered on the high-to-low transitional edge.

OUTPUTS (Figure 3)

Write Cycle
A logical "1" appears at this output during the WRITE CYCLE beginning with the negative edge of the DATA PRESENT pulse and ending with the DATA TAKEN pulse.

Data Taken
A logical "0" pulse occurs when INPUT DATA is written into memory or when BACK SPACE occurs. New data may be entered no less than 100 ns following the low-to-high transition of the DATA TAKEN pulse.

REQUIRED DRIVE SIGNALS

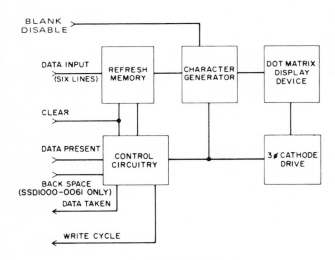

BLOCK DIAGRAM

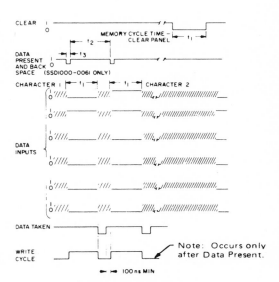

TIMING DIAGRAM

BINARY INPUT	CHAR.	BINARY INPUT	CHAR.
0	@	32	(BLANK)
1	A	33	!
2	B	34	"
3	C	35	#
4	D	36	$
5	E	37	%
6	F	38	&
7	G	39	/
8	H	40	<
9	I	41	>
10	J	42	·
11	K	43	+
12	L	44	,
13	M	45	−
14	N	46	.
15	O	47	/
16	P	48	Ø
17	Q	49	1
18	R	50	2
19	S	51	3
20	T	52	4
21	U	53	5
22	V	54	6
23	W	55	7
24	X	56	8
25	Y	57	9
26	Z	58	
27	[	59	
28	\	60	<
29	]	61	=
30	{	62	>
31	}	63	?

TRUTH TABLE

FIGURE 5-2.2-1: Burroughs Self-Scan Display Characteristics

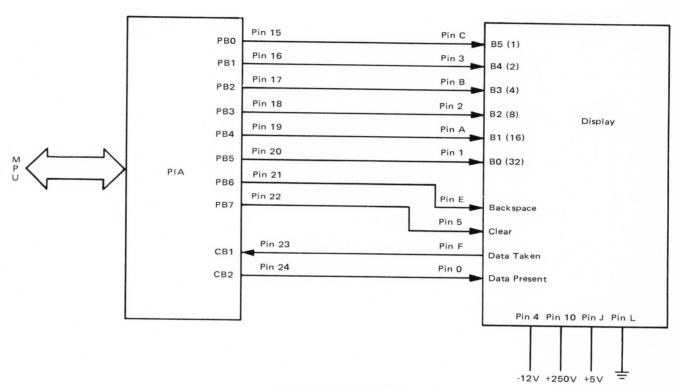

FIGURE 5-2.2-2: PIA/Burroughs Display Interface

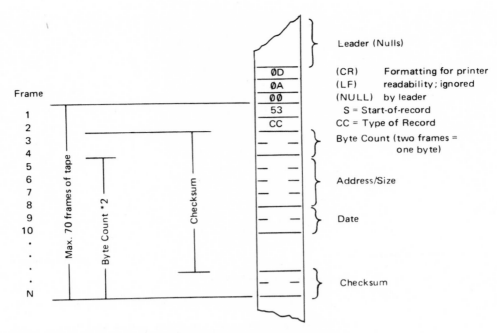

Leader (Nulls)

(CR) Formatting for printer
(LF) readability; ignored
(NULL) by leader
S = Start-of-record
CC = Type of Record
Byte Count (two frames = one byte)
Address/Size
Date
Checksum

Frames 3 through N are hexadecimal digits (in 7-bit ASCII) which are converted to BCD. Two BCD digits are combined to make one 8-bit byte.

The checksum is the one's complement of the summation of 8-bit bytes.

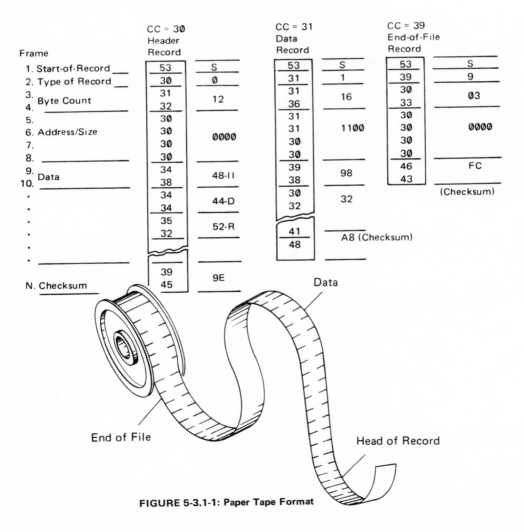

FIGURE 5-3.1-1: Paper Tape Format

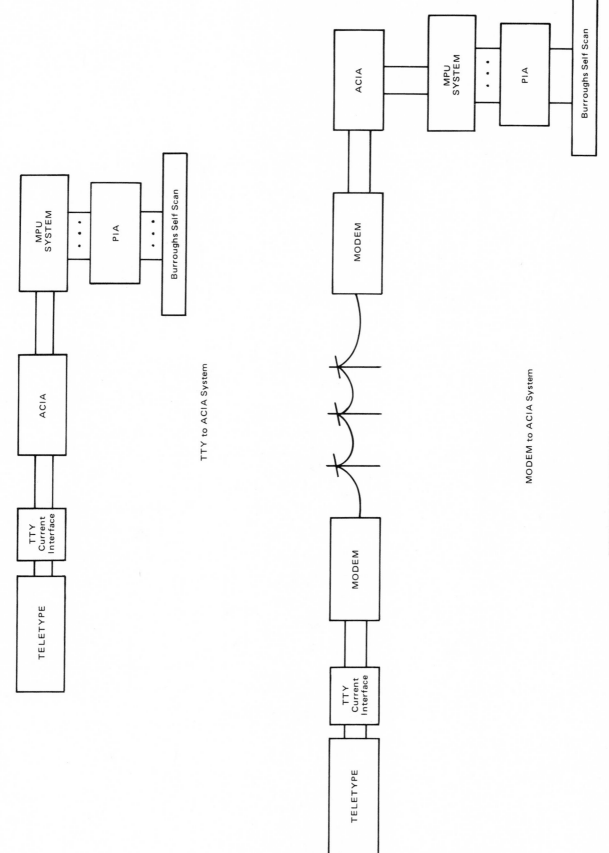

TTY to ACIA System

MODEM to ACIA System

FIGURE 5-3.1-2 TTY/ACIA and MODEM/ACIA Systems

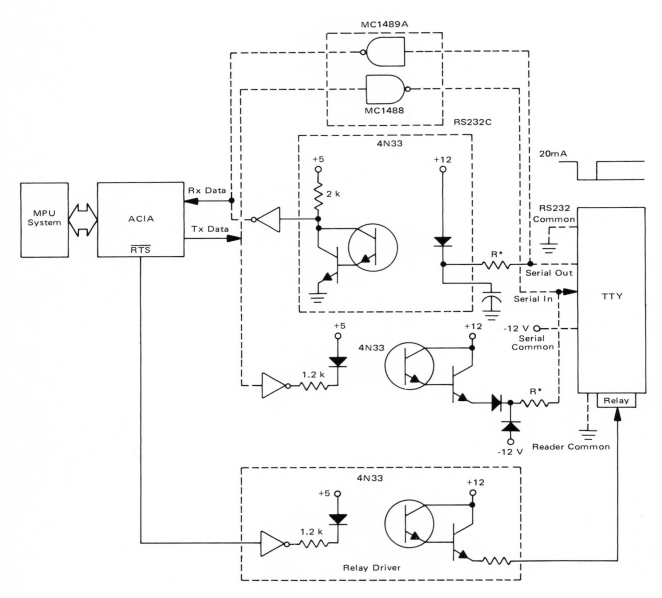

FIGURE 5-3.1.1-1 MPU to TTY Interface

are teletype requirements. The manual paper tape reader requires an externally provided relay to turn the reader on and off via the ACIA. For the system shown in Figure 5-3.1.1-1, the Request to Send ($\overline{RTS}$) output of the ACIA is used to control the relay; the $\overline{RTS}$ output is normally used for interfacing to a modem. There are separate data lines for serial-in and serial-out data transfer from the teletype which connect to the transmit data output and receive data input of the ACIA via the interface circuits. The current/voltage options for the serial-in and serial-out data lines of the teletype are (1) 20 ma, (2) 60 ma, or (3) RS232C. Typical interface circuits for options 1 and 3 are shown in Figure 5-3.1.1-1. The 4N33 optical coupler can provide the 20 ma requirement, and the MC1488 and MC1489A line driver/receiver provide the RS232C specifications. Communication between the teletype and other devices is accomplished with an asynchronous data format. This format requires that the data bits are preceded by a START bit (space) and followed by 1 or more STOP bits (mark). The teletype requires a minimum of 1½ STOP bits for completion of mechanical operations within the teletype.

5-3.1.2 TTY To ACIA Software

The flow diagram and assembled program for the communications routine are shown in Figure 5-3.1.2-1 and 5-3.1.2-2 respectively. The shaded areas in these figures represent requirements for using a modem and therefore would be deleted in a program that does not utilize a modem. Referring to the assembled program and flow diagram, the internal power-on reset of the ACIA is released by master resetting the ACIA via the control register. Then, the control register of the ACIA is set for word length, parity, etc. If at any time a power-fail occurs, these two steps must be repeated to initialize the ACIA. Next, in lines 150–200 the PIA is initialized to receive data from the MPU System and output this data to the Burroughs Self-Scan display.

Line 240 turns on the teletype by the control character "DC1." If a relay is being used to turn the reader on instead of a control character, the $\overline{RTS}$ output of the ACIA could have been used to control the relay.

Line 260 initializes a memory location that stores error conditions from the data that is received.

Lines 280–370 ignores all data that is on the tape until an S1, S9, or S8 indication is found. An S1 indicates a data record as shown in Figure 5-3.1-1, and the following is performed on the data record in lines 400–590. The memory location for accumulating a checksum is cleared. Next, the number of bytes in the data record (minus two for the byte count) is stored in memory. The next four bytes on the tape represent the beginning address for the data and these four bytes are loaded into two consecutive addresses. Line 480 loads the X register with the two consecutive addresses making a 16-bit address.

In lines 520–590 the remaining data in the record is stored in consecutive addresses beginning at the address specified on the tape. A byte count of zero indicates the end of the record and the checksum is checked for a data error indication. The final checksum is generated by adding the accumulated checksum to the checksum (1's complement) at the end of the record and incrementing the total by one resulting in all zero's with a carry. If the checksum does not equal zero, the error memory location is loaded with a one at line 580.

The remaining data records are handled as above until the end of file (S9) is read. Then, at line 600–620 the error memory location is checked for an error indication. If an error was stored in this location, the routine looks for a duplicate of the message on the tape and processes data as before. If data is read into the MPU without any errors the tape reader is turned off by a "DC3" control word at line 680. Again, if a teletype with a relay is used, the $\overline{RTS}$ output of the ACIA could be used to turn off the relay. In lines 810–970 the data is fetched from memory and displayed at a program controlled rate on the Burroughs self-scan display.

The input and output of characters through the ACIA is done by the subroutine contained in lines 980–1300. Beginning at line 980, the status of the receiver data register is checked until a full condition exists.

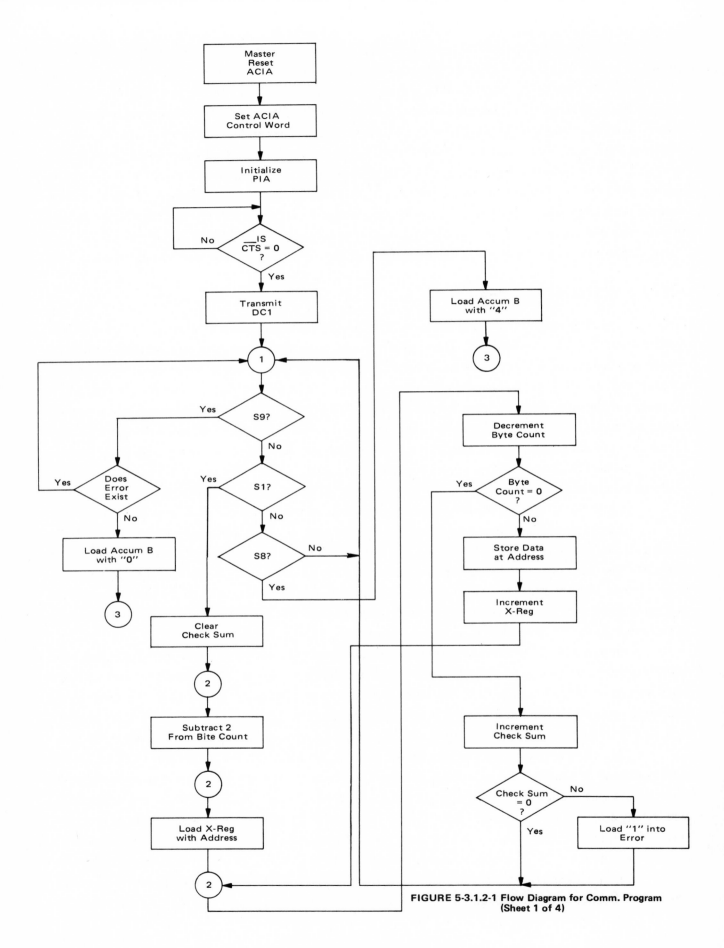

FIGURE 5-3.1.2-1 Flow Diagram for Comm. Program (Sheet 1 of 4)

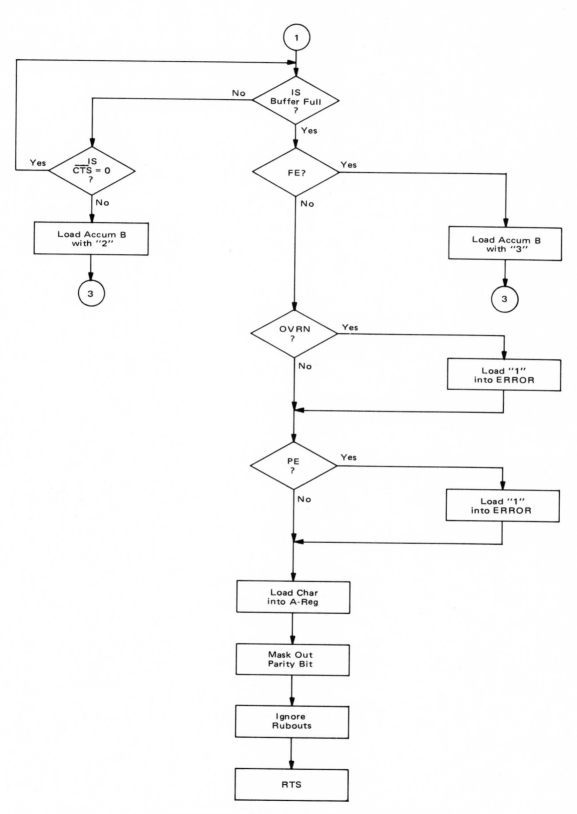

FIGURE 5-3.1.2-1 Flow Diagram for Comm. Program;
(Sheet 2 of 4)

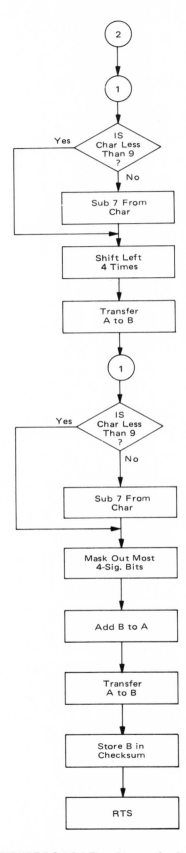

FIGURE 5-3.1.2-1 Flow Diagram for Comm. Program
(Sheet 3 of 4)

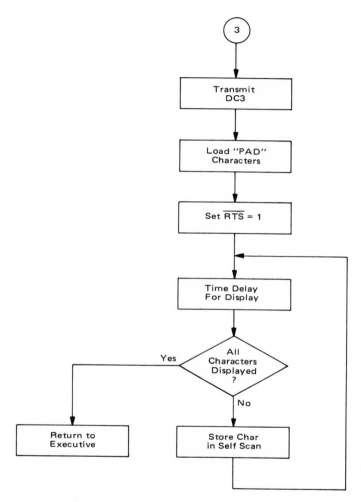

FIGURE 5-3.1.2-1 Flow Diagram for Comm. Program (Sheet 4 of 4)

```
00050         8200    CC100   EQU     $8200       ACIACS
00060         8201    CC110   EQU     CC100+1      ACIADA
00070         8023    PIAC    EQU     $8023       PIA
00080         8022    PIADI   EQU     $8022
00090 0200                    ORG     $200
00100                         *ENTER POWER ON
00110 0200 86 B3    CK140     LDA A   #$B3        MASTER RESET,RTS=0
00120 0202 B7 8200            STA A   CC100
00130 0205 86 A9              LDA A   #$A9        CONTROL WORD
00140 0207 B7 8200            STA A   CC100
00150 020A 86 23              LDA A   #$23
00160 020C B7 8023            STA A   PIAC
00170 020F 86 FF              LDA A   #$FF
00180 0211 B7 8022            STA A   PIADI
00190 0214 86 2C              LDA A   #$2C
00200 0216 B7 8023            STA A   PIAC
00210 0219 B6 8200  CK180     LDA A   CC100       CTST
00220 021C 84 08              AND A   #$08
00230 021E 26 F9              BNE     CK180
00240 0220 86 11              LDA A   #$11        DC1
00250 0222 B7 8201            STA A   CC110
00260 0225 86 00    CK254     LDA A   #0          INITIALIZE ZERO
00270 0227 B7 0328            STA A   CK3820
00280 022A BD 02C4  CK260     JSR     CK2000      INPUT CHAR
00290 022D 81 52              CMP A   #'R         S?
00300 022F 26 F9              BNE     CK260
00310 0231 BD 02C4            JSR     CK2000
00320 0234 81 39              CMP A   #'9         S9
00330 0236 27 3F              BEQ     CK700
00340 0238 81 31              CMP A   #'1         S1?
00350 023A 27 08              BEQ     CK380
00360 023C 81 39              CMP A   #'8         S8?
00370 023E 26 EA              BNE     CK260
00380 0240 C6 04              LDA B   #$4
00390 0242 20 5C              BRA     CK740
00400 0244 7F 0326  CK380     CLR     CK3800      ZERO CKSM
00410 0247 BD 0301            JSR     CK3000
00420 024A 80 02              SUB A   #2
00430 024C B7 0327            STA A   CK3810      BYTE COUNT
00440 024F BD 0301  CK420     JSR     CK3000      READ 2 FRAMES
00450 0252 B7 0329            STA A   CK3830
00460 0255 BD 0301            JSR     CK3000
00470 0259 B7 032A            STA A   CK3840
00480 025B FE 0329            LDX     CK3830      ADDRESS
00490 025E BD 0301  CK470     JSR     CK3000
00500 0261 7A 0327            DEC     CK3810
00510 0264 27 05              BEQ     CK530
00520 0266 A7 00              STA A   X           STORE DATA
```

FIGURE 5-3.1.2-2 Assembled Data Comm Program (Sheet 1 of 3)

```
00530  0268  09              INX
00540  0269  20 F3           BRA     CK470       NEXT CHAR
00550  026B  7C 0326  CK530  INC     CK3800
00560  026E  27 BA           BEQ     CK260
00570  0270  86 01           LDA A   #1
00580  0272  B7 0328         STA A   CK3820
00590  0275  20 B3           BRA     CK260
00600  0277  B6 0328  CK700  LDA A   CK3820      CHECK ERROR
00610  027A  27 02           BEQ     CK730
00620  027C  20 A7           BRA     CK254
00630  027E  C6 00    CK730  LDA B   #0
00640  0280  B6 8200  CK740  LDA A   CC100
00650  0283  47              ASR A
00660  0284  47              ASR A
00670  0285  24 F9           BCC     CK740
00680  0287  86 93           LDA A   #$93        DC3
00690  0289  B7 8201         STA A   CC110
00700  028C  B6 8200  CK751  LDA A   CC100
00710  028F  47              ASR A
00720  0290  47              ASR A
00730  0291  24 F9           BCC     CK751
00740  0293  B7 8201         STA A   CC110
00750  0296  B6 8200  CK756  LDA A   CC100
00760  0299  47              ASR A
00770  029A  47              ASR A
00780  029B  24 F9           BCC     CK756
00790  029D  86 43    CK760  LDA A   #$43        RTS=1
00800  029F  B7 8200         STA A   CC100
00810  02A2  CE 0000  START  LDX     #$0
00820  02A5  C6 4F    BEG1   LDA B   #$4F        COUNT
00830  02A7  86 FF    TIME2  LDA A   #$FF
00840  02A9  4A       TIME1  DEC A
00850  02AA  26 FD           BNE     TIME1
00860  02AC  5A              DEC B
00870  02AD  26 F8           BNE     TIME2
00880  02AF  A6 00    BEG    LDA A   X
00890  02B1  08              INX
00900  02B2  31 EA           CMP A   #$EA
00910  02B4  26 01           BNE     NEXT
00920  02B6  39              RTS                 END OF PROGRAM
00930  02B7  B7 8022  NEXT   STA A   PIADI
00940  02BA  F6 8023  NEXT1  LDA B   PIAC
00950  02BD  C4 80           AND B   #$80
00960  02BF  27 F9           BEQ     NEXT1
00970  02C1  7E 02A5         JMP     BEG1
00980  02C4  B6 8200  CK2000 LDA A   CC100       INPUT CHAR
00990  02C7  47              ASR A
01000  02C8  25 02           BCS     CK2100      BF
01010  02CA  84 04           AND A   #$04        CTS?
01020  02CC  27 F6           BEQ     CK2000
01030  02CE  C6 02           LDA B   #$2
01040  02D0  20 CB           BRA     CK760
```

FIGURE 5-3.1.2-2 Assembled Data Comm Program (Sheet 2 of 3)

```
01050  02D2  47        CK2100  ASR  A
01060  02D3  47                ASR  A
01070  02D4  47                ASR  A
01080  02D5  47                ASR  A
01090  02D6  24 04             BCC      CK2170
01100  02D8  C6 03             LDA B    #$3            FE
01110  02DA  20 A4             BRA      CK740
01120  02DC  47        CK2170  ASR  A                  OVRN
01130  02DD  24 05             BCC      CK2210
01140  02DF  86 02             LDA A    #2
01150  02E1  B7 0328           STA A    CK3820
01160  02E4  47        CK2210  ASR  A                  PE
01170  02E5  24 05             BCC      CK2250
01180  02E7  86 03             LDA A    #3
01190  02E9  B7 0328           STA A    CK3820
01200  02EC  B6 8201  CK2250   LDA A    CC110          LOAD CHAR
01210  02EF  84 7F             AND A    #$7F
01220  02F1  81 7F             CMP A    #$7F           IGNORE RUBOUTS
01230  02F3  27 CF             BEQ      CK2000
01240  02F5  F6 8200  CK2280   LDA B    CC100          ECHO CHAR
01250  02F8  57                ASR  B
01260  02F9  57                ASR  B
01270  02FA  24 F9             BCC      CK2280
01280  02FC  B7 8201           STA A    CC110
01290  02FF  5F                CLR  B
01300  0300  39                RTS
01310  0301  8D C1    CK3000   BSR      CK2000
01320  0303  81 39             CMP A    #$39           BELOW 9
01330  0305  2F 02             BLE      CK3040
01340  0307  80 07             SUB A    #7             ASCII TO HEX
01350  0309  48       CK3040   ASL  A
01360  030A  48                ASL  A
01370  030B  48                ASL  A
01380  030C  48                ASL  A
01390  030D  B7 032B           STA A    CK3850
01400  0310  8D B2             BSR      CK2000         2ND CHAR
01410  0312  81 39             CMP A    #$39
01420  0314  2F 02             BLE      CK3130
01430  0316  80 07             SUB A    #7
01440  0318  84 0F    CK3130   AND A    #$0F           MASK TO 4 BITS
01450  031A  F6 032B           LDA B    CK3850
01460  031D  1B                ABA
01470  031E  16                TAB
01480  031F  FB 0326           ADD B    CK3800
01490  0322  F7 0326           STA B    CK3800
01500  0325  39                RTS
01510  0326  0001     CK3800   RMB      1              CHECKSUM
01520  0327  0001     CK3810   RMB      1              BYTECT
01530  0328  0001     CK3820   RMB      1              ERROR
01540  0329  0001     CK3830   RMB      1              XHI
01550  032A  0001     CK3840   RMB      1              XLOW
01560  032B  0001     CK3850   RMB      1
```

FIGURE 5-3.1.2-2 Assembled Data Comm Program
(Sheet 3 of 3)

Then the remaining status bits (framing, overrun, and parity error) are checked for an error condition on the received character. If a framing error condition exists, indicating a possible loss of character synchronization, the program is terminated. The fact that an overrun or parity error occurred is stored and the program continues to receive characters. The character is loaded into the A-register of the MPU from the ACIA in line 1200. In lines 1240 to 1280, the received character is transmitted back to the source. This is accomplished by checking the status of the transmitter and when empty the character is loaded into the transmitter data register.

The characters stored on tape are in ASCII notation but represent hexadecimal numbers; the alpha-numeric representation for 0–15 in hexadecimal is 0–9, A–F (10–15). Therefore, the eight bit ASCII notation must be converted to a four bit binary number (0000–1111). For the ASCII characters 0–9, the four least significant bits are equivalent to the binary representation 0000–1001. For the ASCII characters A–F, subtracting 7 from the ASCII character results in the four least significant bits being equivalent to binary representation 1010–1111. In lines 1310–1490, ASCII characters are converted to four bit binary numbers and then two 4-bit numbers are stored in an eight bit register.

5-3.1.3 ACIA to Modem HARDWARE

The MPU system can communicate over the telephone lines to a remote peripheral by utilizing a modem and an ACIA as shown in Figure 5-3.1.3-1. The modem takes serial digital data and converts it to an analog signal for transmission over the telephone lines. Incoming data in analog form from the remote modem is converted to serial digital form by the on-site modem. The ACIA provides the MPU with the ability to control the handshaking requirements of the modem. The first step requires that the Data Terminal Ready ($\overline{\text{DTR}}$) input be "low" to enable the modem to complete the handshaking. Response by the remote modem to the on-site modem completes the handshaking and results in a "low" logic level from the Clear to Send ($\overline{\text{CTS}}$) output of the modem. After handshaking has been completed, the remote and on-site systems can transmit and receive data. When communications is lost between the modems, the $\overline{\text{CTS}}$ output returns "high."

In the transmitter portion of the ACIA, the Transmitter Data Register Empty (TxDRE) flag and associated interrupt ($\overline{\text{IRQ}}$), are enabled when both the $\overline{\text{CTS}}$ and Transmitter Interrupt Enable (TIE) functions are enabled. In the receiver portion of the ACIA, the Receiver Data Register Full (RxDRF) flag and associated interrupt ($\overline{\text{IRQ}}$) are enabled when both the Data Carrier Detect ($\overline{\text{DCD}}$) and Receiver Interrupt Enable (RIE) functions are enabled; the low to high transition of the $\overline{\text{DCD}}$ input with RIE enabled generates an interrupt ($\overline{\text{IRQ}}$). Since the MC6860 modem does not have a Data Carrier Detect output, the $\overline{\text{DCD}}$ and $\overline{\text{CTS}}$ inputs of the ACIA can be tied together which results in an interrupt ($\overline{\text{IRQ}}$) being generated when communications is lost.

Used separately, the $\overline{\text{DCD}}$ and $\overline{\text{CTS}}$ inputs of the ACIA allow the use of higher performance modems. For example, a high-performance modem will transmit on one pair of wires and receive on another pair referred to as a four-wire modem system. As in the low speed modem system, the MPU, via the ACIA, generates a $\overline{\text{DTR}}$ and after a time delay, the $\overline{\text{CTS}}$ output of the high-performance modem goes "low." The transmitter can start transferring data immediately after $\overline{\text{CTS}}$ goes "low." After the on-site modem receives the carrier frequency from the remote modem, the $\overline{\text{DCD}}$ output goes "low" and data can be received. The transmit and receive lines of the modem are completely independent of each other which, for example, allows transmission to the remote site when the other line is down.

5-3.1.4 ACIA To Modem Software

The program used to receive data from a teletype with the addition of the modem control functions is

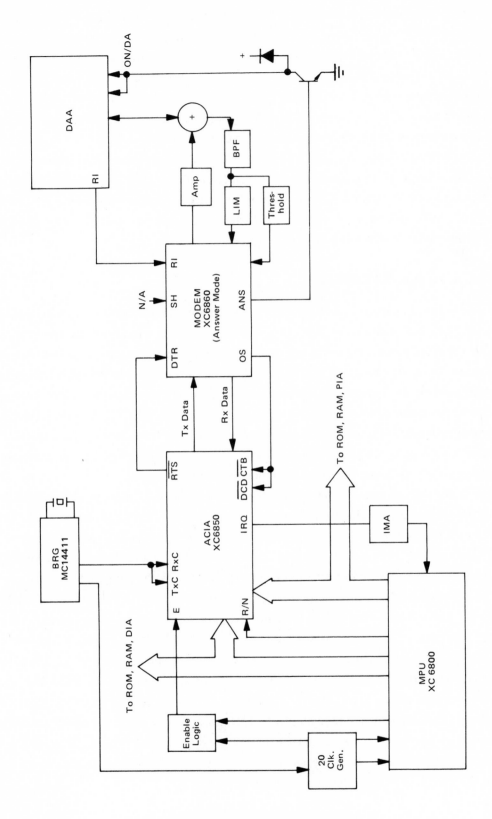

FIGURE 5-3.1.3-1 MPU to Remote Site

used for the following explanation. The local modem is initially enabled by writing a control word into the ACIA as shown in line 130. This control word sets the $\overline{RTS}$ output of the ACIA "low" and in turn enables the Data Terminal Ready ($\overline{DTR}$) input of the modem. In lines 210 to 230, the completion of the handshaking between the remote and local modem (indicated by a "low" on the $\overline{CTS}$ bit) is checked until established. Also, during the reception of characters the status of $\overline{CTS}$ is checked as shown in lines 1010 to 1020 to insure that the program does not remain in an endless loop if the transmission lines go "down." At the end of the program the modem is disabled in line 790 by writing a control word into the ACIA to set the $\overline{RTS}$ output "high." This immediately terminates transmission from the modem.

To insure that the last character to be transmitted is received at the remote site, two "pad" characters must be inserted between the last character and the control word ($\overline{RTS} = 1$) as shown in lines 700–780. This enables the last character to be completely transmitted prior to disabling the modem.

5-3.2   TAPE CASSETTE SUBSYSTEM

This section describes the design of an MPU based Tape Cassette Subsystem. The scope is limited to the control of a single transport operated in a bit serial format.

The technique used may be extended to the control of multiple transports, however, this requires some additional hardware (multiplexers for data lines and either an encoder to encode additional control and status lines, or half of another PIA). A similar approach may be used when data is transferred in parallel format. This will require additional data lines (8 lines instead of one). The additional data lines could be bidirectional PIA lines, programmable to be outputs during write, inputs during read. Note also that if data is transferred in parallel, the MPU can handle the faster data transfer rates resulting from use of more than one transport. In multiple transport applications, the system will also require additional lines to monitor tape drive status signals such as "READY" and "BUSY" that provide an indication of whehter the selected transport is available or busy.

In a typical tape subsystem, many functions must be performed, however, only the following basic routines are described in this section.

(1) Search to a given record.

(2) Stop in an interrecord gap.

(3) Write (Fwd).

(4) Read (Fwd).

(5) Write filemark.

5-3.2.1 HARDWARE DESCRIPTION

Tape Transport Description

The data recorded on the tape conforms to the A.N.S.I. "Specification For Information Interchange" (X3B1/579 — September 14, 1972). The data recording format is shown in Figure 5-3.2.1-1 below. A block recording format is used with each data block consisting of: (A) a preamble (1 byte); (B) data (4-256 bytes) including the Cyclic Redundancy Check Character (2 bytes); and a (C) postamble (1 byte).

The Tape Transport that was used has an adjustable capstan controlled Read/Write speed which was set at 15 ips. The search speed was adjusted for an average speed of 100 ips. The pinch roller engagement time is 30 msec (max). Disengagement time is 20 msec. The tape acceleration time is 20 msec to stabilized speed. Speed stability is within the A.N.S.I. specifications. Photo-detectors are used for sensing End Of Tape (EOT) and Beginning Of Tape (BOT). The transport is provided with both a Cassette-In-Place sensor and a File-Protect sensor (also called a Write-Protect sensor). A single Read/Write head is used which is also used to write gaps in erase polarity.

Four control lines are provided for the control of tape motion and to select a given transport. These are:

(1) SELECT/NOT SELECT

(2) STOP/GO

(3) FORWARD/REVERSE

(4) SEARCH/REWIND or READ/WRITE SPEED

Since in the present subsystem only a single tape drive is used, the select line is not used. The interfaces between the PIA, the tape drive, and the control electronics are shown in Figure 5-3.2.1-2.

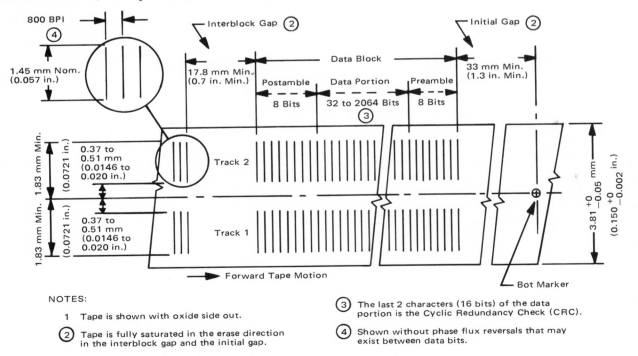

NOTES:

1. Tape is shown with oxide side out.

② Tape is fully saturated in the erase direction in the interblock gap and the initial gap.

③ The last 2 characters (16 bits) of the data portion is the Cyclic Redundancy Check (CRC).

④ Shown without phase flux reversals that may exist between data bits.

FIGURE 5-3.2.1-1. Recording Format 800 BPI

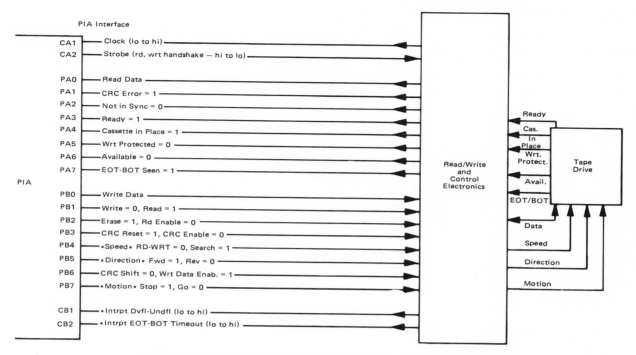

FIGURE 5-3.2.1-2. PIA, Tape Drive and Read/Write Control Electronics Interface

READ/WRITE Electronics Description

The data to be recorded on the tape is presented to the tape transport in Non-Return-to-Zero (NRZ) format but is recorded in Phase Encoded (PE) format. The data conversion is performed by the logic shown in Figure 5-3.2.1-3. The timing diagram for the conversion from NRZ to PE format is shown in Figure 5-3.2.1-4.

Write data (or CRC Data) is gated through a data selector to flip-flop FF1 which provides a one-bit storage. This storage is necessary because in P.E. format, a phase transition is required whenever the next data bit is the same as the current bit. The exclusive-OR gate compares the next bit with the current bit, and provides a high level to FF2 at phase time whenever the two are equal. The 12KHz clock is low at data time, and provides a high level to FF2 input at data time. Thus, FF2 always toggles at data time and also toggles at phase time if the next data bit is the same as the current data bit.

The Write data is also sent through a Cyclic Redundancy Check Character Generator (MC8503 CRCC Generator). The CRCC is appended to the data block and the CRC data passes through the same circuitry as the Write data for conversion to the P.E. format for recording. The timing for this operation is also detailed in Figure 5-3.2.1-4. Both the preamble and the postamble are 8-bit patterns of alternating ones and zeros (01010101-M.S. bit). (This can be used to establish the data rate during data recovery since there is a single transition per bit). During the Write operation, the CRC Generator is enabled after the preamble data has been written. The CRC Generator remains enabled throughout the data block. At the end of the data block, the CRC Data is shifted out of the generator into the Write circuitry.

The read-write head is switched to carry the write current from FF2, via three-state gates enabled by the Read-Write Line (PB1). The series resistors R adjust the write current to a nominal value of 4 ma.

During a Read operation (Ref. Figures 5-3.2.1-3 and 5-3.2.1-5), the write circuits are disabled, and one end of the read head is switched to ground via a three-state gate. The other end passes the read signals onto the read circuits which amplify and convert the read signals to logic levels in P.E. format. The P.E. read data goes to the Phase Locked Loop data recovery circuit which decodes the data and clock signals. The P.E. data also goes to a monostable multivibrator which is used to detect gaps during a search operation.

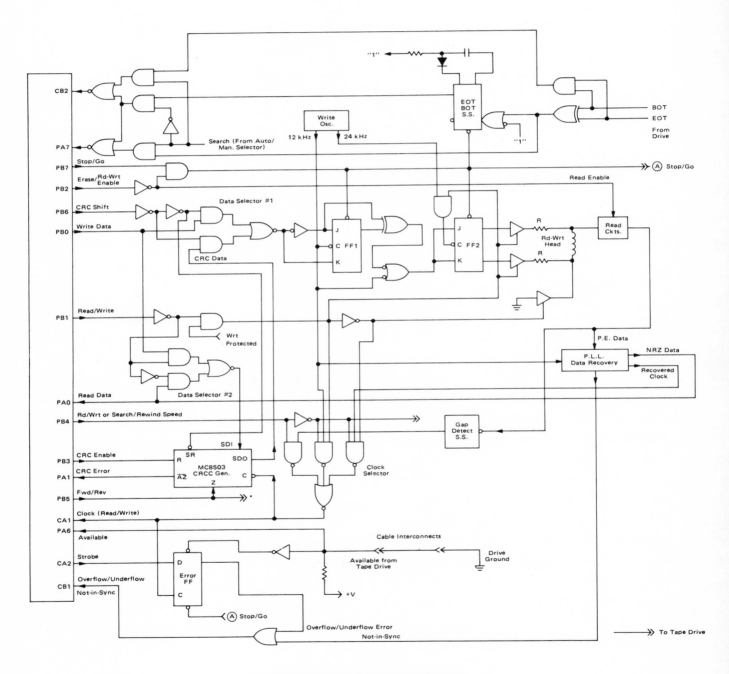

FIGURE 5-3.2.1-3: Read-Write Circuitry

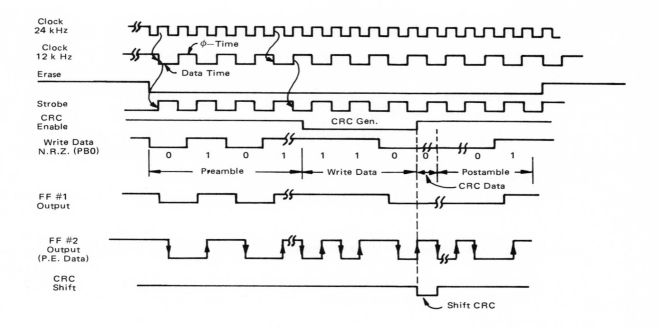

FIGURE 5-3.2.1-4. Write Operation Timing and Format Conversion

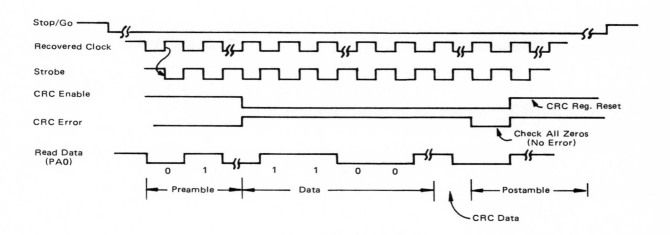

FIGURE 5-3.2.1-5. Read Operation Timing

The Read data goes to the PIA directly (PA0) while the recovered clock goes to the PIA (CA1) via the clock selector circuit. The clock selector selects between the read and write clock during a read or write operation. During a search operation, the gap-detector retriggerable single shot output is substituted for the read-write clock.

During a Read operation, the CRC Generator is turned on after the preamble has been read and remains on throughout the data block, including the appended CRC character. At the end of the CRC character the CRC Error line is examined to see if it is low (all zeros line out of the MC8503, CRC Generator). If the data has been read correctly, the line will be low. (For additional details on the use of the CRCC Generator see the Applications Section of the MC8503 Data Sheet.)

An UNDERFLOW-OVERFLOW Error interrupt is provided in order to abort the current operation in the event of such an error. The interrupt signal is generated when the MPU fails to either write or read data after every clock pulse during the write or read operation. The error flip-flop output should always be high. The normal response to a clock pulse on the clock line (CA1) is to provide a strobe by reading the data and clearing the flag set by the clock pulse.

Status Signals from Transport and Electronics

The tape transport contains two microswitches, one to sense the presence of a tape cassette in place, and the other to see if the write protect tab is removed. If the tab is removed, the tape is "Write-protected", and hardware logic disables the write circuitry (the three-state gates at the output of the write flip-flop are turned off, and the clock to the write flip-flop is gated off.) These two signals are available at the PIA interface, and the MPU checks them prior to issuing any "motion" commands.

The Available signal from the electronics and tape drive is essentially a ground-loop which checks whether all of the cables interconnecting the PIA to the electronics and drive are in place. If a cable is disconnected, the group loop is not completed and a high logic level will be present at the PIA interface.

The EOT/BOT sensor on the tape drive provides a transition when the EOT or BOT is seen. During a Read or Write Operation, this transition triggers a single shot whose output appears at CB2 and PA7 of the PIA (Figure 5-3.2.1-6). The single-shot period is set to a time such that one complete record may be read or written. If the single shot times out, then it will generate an interrupt to the MPU system via the PIA, and will stop the tape transport. This hardware controlled stop is a safety feature, and prevents damage to the tape cassette if there is system failure. Normally, the MPU examines the EOT/BOT line at the end of each record being read or written. If the EOT/BOT transition has occurred, the MPU will stop the transport (and this will reset the single-shot). During a Search Operation if EOT or BOT is seen an interrupt is generated to the PIA immediately. Note that the EOT/BOT signal is used both as a status signal (on PA7) and as an interrupt signal (CB2). This allows the MPU to read the EOT/BOT status before system operation is interrupted. If tape is at Clear Leader, then PA7 will remain low when the speed select line (PB4) is at a Search Speed (high).

The Phase-Locked-Loop (PLL) Data Recovery circuit is shown in Figure 5-3.2.1-7. The first PE transition after Read is enabled sets the First Bit Detector flip-flop, FF2. P.E. Data is clocked into a two bit shift register (FF3 and FF4) by the PLL clock (Fout). Each time there is a transition on the P.E. data line, a pulse, one VCM period in duration is generated from the exclusive OR gate tied to the outputs of the two bit shift register. The VCM also clocks a window counter whose carry-out output (TC = 1 during count $F) generates the read clock which clocks the Read Data to the PIA (PA0). The time during which the Q3 output of the counter is high (count 8 through $F) is defined as the data window (or data time). If a P.E. transition occurs during the data window, it is gated through to the Preset Enable (PE) input of the counter, and presets the counter to the middle

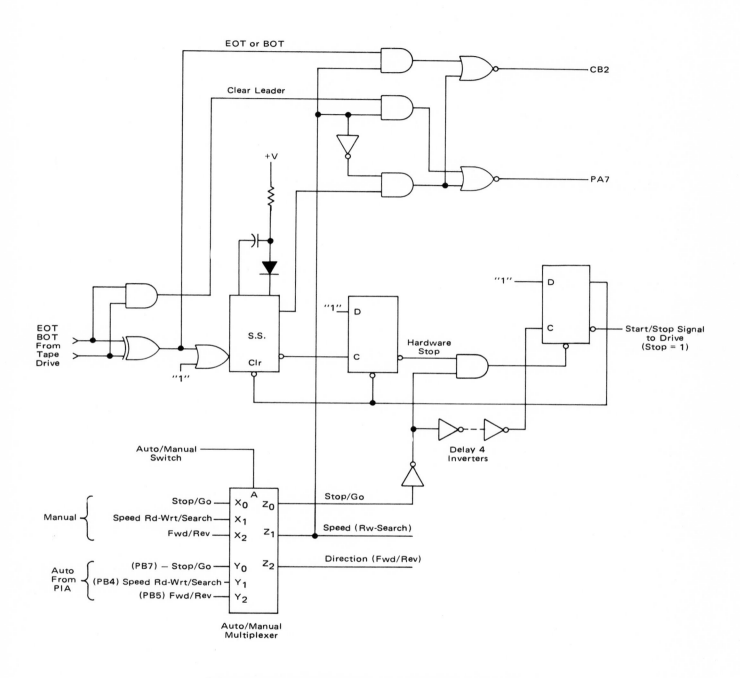

FIGURE 5-3.2.1-6. EOT/BOT Circuitry with Hardware Safety Feature

5-79

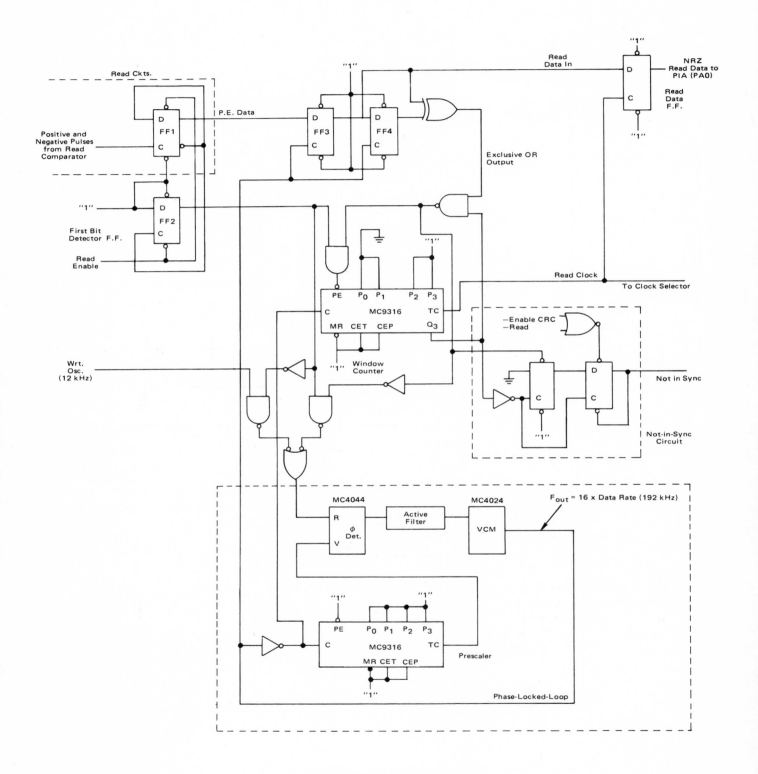

**FIGURE 5-3.2.1-7: Phase Locked Loop
Data Recovery**

5-80

of the data window (count of $C). The timing diagram in Figure 5-3.2.1-8 shows nominal system operation after the preamble has been read and the system is in exact lock. If the P.E. transitions occur anywhere within the ''data window'', the P.L.L. system will track them and adjust its output frequency accordingly. P.E. transitions during window-counter counts of 0 to 7 will be gated off because the Q3 output will be low. Thus, only the data transitions affect the P.L.L. system frequency. For additional details of P.L.L. data recovery, see Section 5.4 (Floppy Disk). Additional details on the design of the P.L.L. system are described in Motorola's *Phase Locked-Loop Systems Data Book* and Application Note AN-535, ''Phase Locked Loop Design Fundamentals.'' These publications may be obtained by writing to the Literature Distribution Center, Motorola Semiconductor Products, Inc., P. O. Box 20912, Phoenix, Arizona 85036.

The Not-In-Sync circuit checks to see if a data transition occurred during the data window. (The circuit is enabled after the preamble has been read, and remains enabled throughout the data record via the Enable CRC line.) If there is no P.E. transition within the ''data window'', the Not-In-Sync latch is set. The Not-In-Sync signal is ORed with the Overflow/Underflow signal, and generates an interrupt to the PIA (on line CB1).

An Auto/Manual multiplexer (see Figure 5-3.2.1-6) is used to allow tape motion operation either under MPU or manual control. Manual operation is useful during program and system debugging.

A complete logic diagram of the tape-cassette Read-Write and Control circuitry that was used is shown in Figure 5-3.2.1-9.

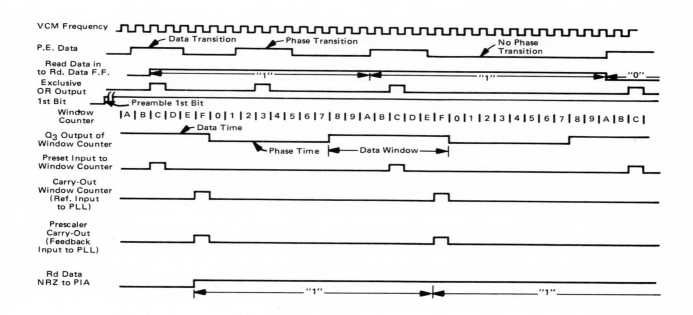

FIGURE 5-3.2.1-8. Read Data Recovery Timing (After Preamble, with Loop in Lock)

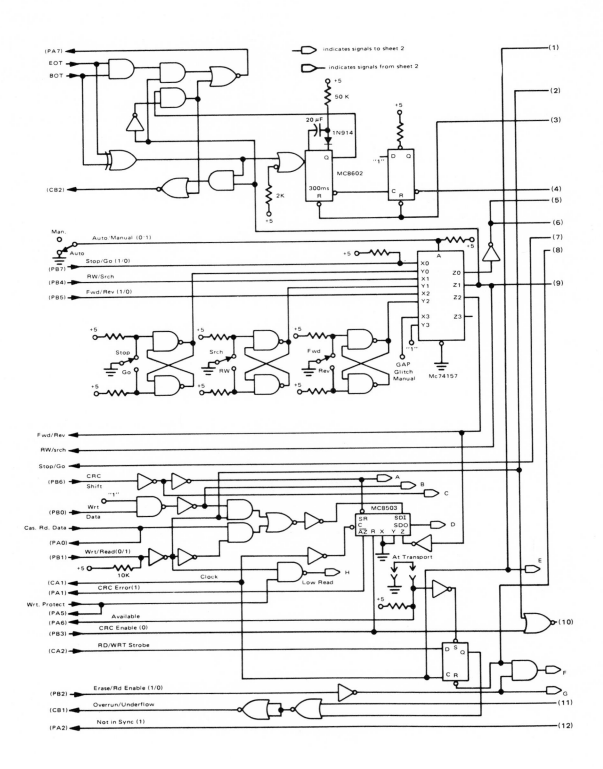

FIGURE 5-3.2.1-9: Cassette Serial Read/Write and Control Logic (Sheet 1 of 3)

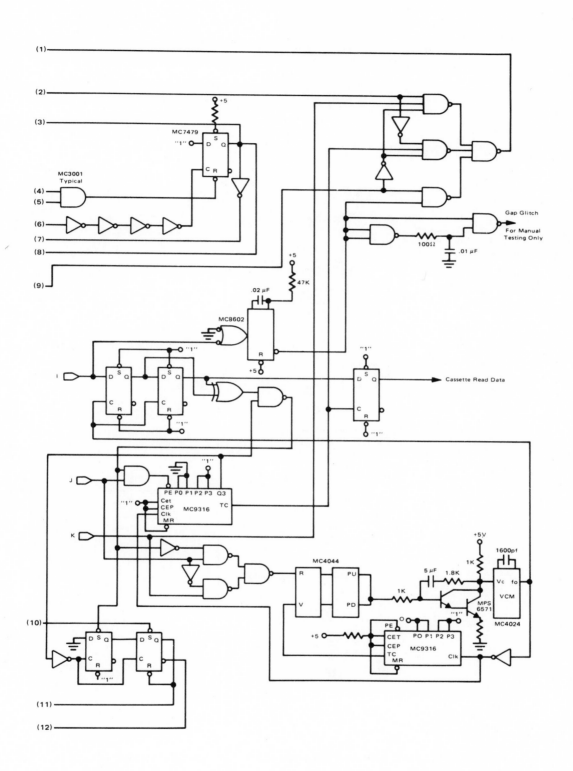

FIGURE 5-3.2.1-9: Cassette Serial Read/Write and Control Logic (Sheet 2 of 3)

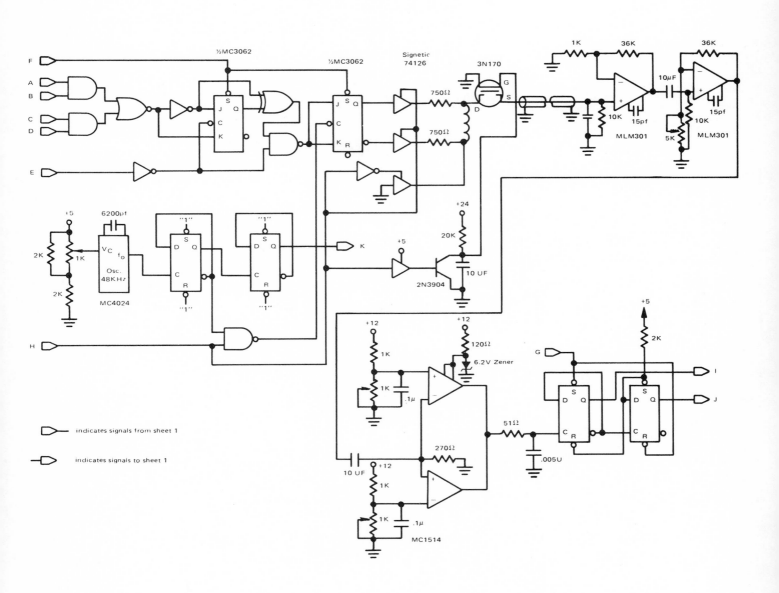

FIGURE 5-3.2.1-9: Cassette Serial Read/Write and Control Logic (Sheet 3 of 3)

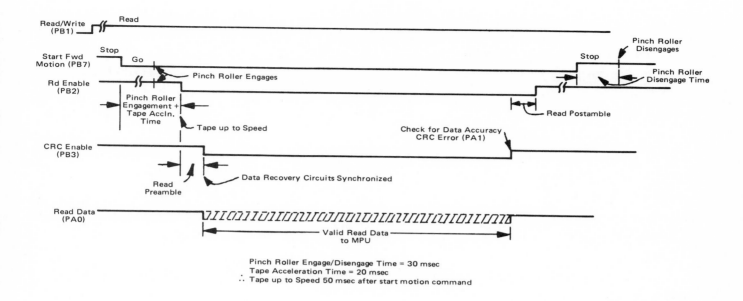

FIGURE 5-3.2.1-10. Read Operation Sequence Timing

For MPU controlled operation, the Auto/Manual switch is placed in the Auto position. Tape Motion and Read/Write functions are then controlled via the PIA interface. For example, if it is desired that the tape be moved forward at Read/Write speed, the interface at the PIA must be set to:

Data Reg. B	7	6	5	4	3	2	1	0
	0	X	1	0	X	X	X	X
	GO		FWD	RD/WRT				

where X denotes a "don't care" condition

e.g.	0	0	1	0	0	0	0	0

If the binary word 00100000 is present at the interface, then the tape will move in a forward direction at Read/Write speed. Similarly if the binary word 00000000 is present at PB0-7, then the tape will move in a reverse direction at Read/Write Speed.

Examples of other basic tape motion commands are shown below:

Operation	Required PIA Word								Example								HEX
	7	6	5	4	3	2	1	0 PB	7	6	5	4	3	2	1	0	EQUIV.
STOP	1	X	X	X	X	X	X	X	1	0	0	0	0	0	0	0	80
Motion-Fwd-RD.WRT.SPD.	0	X	1	0	X	X	X	X	0	0	1	0	1	0	1	0	2A
Motion-Rev-RD.WRT.SPD.	0	X	0	0	X	X	X	X	0	0	0	0	1	0	1	0	0A
Motion-Fwd-SEARCH SPD.	0	X	1	1	X	X	X	X	0	0	1	1	1	0	1	0	3A
Motion-Rev-SEARCH SPD.	0	X	0	1	X	X	X	X	0	0	0	1	1	0	1	0	1A

For a typical read operation, the MPU issues a sequence of commands to the circuitry via the PIA. The sequence may be depicted by the timing diagram of Figure 5-3.2.1-10. The tape motion command initiates motion in the forward direction at Read/Write Speed. The MPU then allows sufficient time for the pinch roller to engage the capstan and for the tape to come up to stable Read/Write speed. The MPU next reads the preamble (by counting eight P.E. transitions) and then enables the CRC generator. It is assumed that by this time the P.L.L. read circuitry is in lock and has begun to successfully track the data rate variations. The MPU begins to transfer data in bit serial form to the Read/Write Data Buffer in the MPU system. If any read errors occur due to loss of synchronization in the P.L.L. circuits or due to overflow, the hardwired logic generates an interrupt to the MPU system via the PIA.

In the description of the above sequence, only the PIA B side interface operation has been discussed. Typically, the MPU performs other operations, such as initializing the PIA so that it can communicate with the read/write and control electronics; checking to see if the tape drive is available for the desired operation; enabling the EOT/BOT and Read Error interrupts; and using an Interval Timer to generate the required delays for allowing the tape to come up to speed. These additional operational details are discussed within the software documentation.

The Write operation sequence is illustrated in Figure 5-3.2.1-11. Tape motion is started in the Erase mode, and a start-gap is written. The Start-Gap duration is slightly longer than the total time it takes for pinch roller engagement and for the tape to come up to stable speed. The MPU then disables the Erase mode and enables write data to be gated to the P.E. write circuits. After the preamble word has been transferred, the CRC is enabled (so that it accumulates the checksum). The CRC remains enabled till the data from the MPU has been transferred. Next, the CRC is shifted out to the Write circuitry followed by the postamble word from the MPU. The MPU then issues a stop command and allows the stop-gap to be written by keeping the write current on until the tape stops. At this time, the tape drive is placed in a Read-Forward Mode (PB1 = 1; PB5 = 1; PB7 = 1) if no other records are to be written.

Start, Stop, and Interblock Gaps

An Interblock gap is defined as the distance between two successive blocks of data, and it is specified by the A.N.S.I. specification, referenced earlier, to have a nominal length of 20.3 mm (0.8 in) with a minimum length of 17.8 mm (0.7 in) and a maximum length of 500 mm (19.7 in). Any gap in excess of 500 mm (19.7 in) is considered to be end of data.

From a study of the tape drive specifications, a tape motion velocity profile may be generated (see Figure 5-3.2.1-12) and used to calculate Start, Stop, and Interblock gap lengths. With reference to Figure 8, note that tape motion begins 30 msec after the motion command is issued and reaches stable speed 20 msec

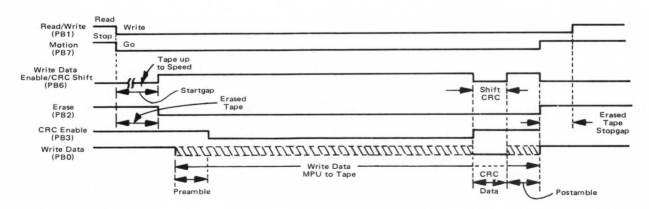

FIGURE 5-3.2.1-11. Write Operation Sequence

later. This is the Startgap delay. Since the tape is actually moving for only the last 20 msec of the start gap delay, the Physical Startgap corresponds to the length of tape moved during the Startgap delay. If desired, a longer Startgap may be written by continuing in Erase even after stable tape speed has been reached. Similarly, the Physical Stopgap is the length of tape moved after the Stop command and until tape motion actually stops. If desired, a longer Stop-Gap may be written by enabling Erase at the end of data, prior to issuing a Stop command.

Two operations are performed at Search speed: (1) Rewinding tape; (2) Searching to a given record on tape.

Typically, tape is rewound at Search speed until the BOT marker is seen and then moved forward at Read/Write speed to the *Load Point*. The Load Point (Figure 5-3.2.1-13) is the logical beginning of tape and establishes the reference point from which record counts are kept. The Load Point is located in the Initial Gap between the BOT marker hole and the first record to be written or read.

Note that when rewinding tape to Load Point, the BOT marker is encountered twice, and this must be accounted for in the MPU control program for this operation.

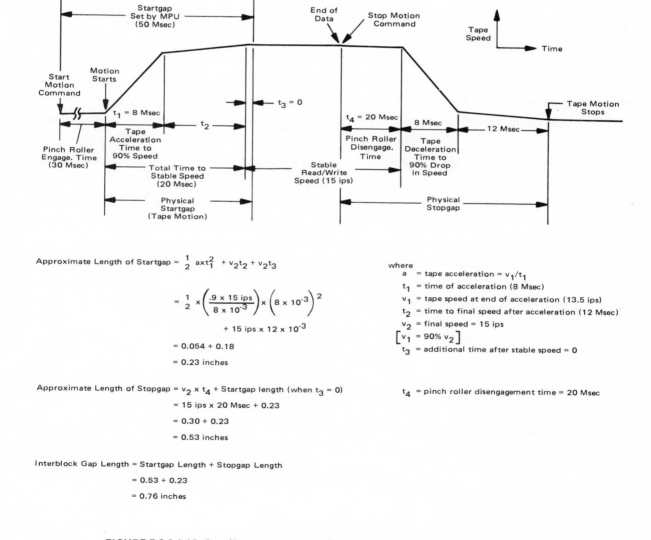

Approximate Length of Startgap = $\frac{1}{2} a x t_1^2 + v_2 t_2 + v_2 t_3$

$$= \frac{1}{2} \times \left(\frac{.9 \times 15 \text{ ips}}{8 \times 10^{-3}}\right) \times \left(8 \times 10^{-3}\right)^2$$

$$+ 15 \text{ ips} \times 12 \times 10^{-3}$$

$$= 0.054 + 0.18$$

$$= 0.23 \text{ inches}$$

where
a = tape acceleration = v_1/t_1
t_1 = time of acceleration (8 Msec)
v_1 = tape speed at end of acceleration (13.5 ips)
t_2 = time to final speed after acceleration (12 Msec)
v_2 = final speed = 15 ips
$\left[v_1 = 90\% \ v_2\right]$
t_3 = additional time after stable speed = 0

Approximate Length of Stopgap = $v_2 \times t_4$ + Startgap length (when t_3 = 0)

$$= 15 \text{ ips} \times 20 \text{ Msec} + 0.23$$

$$= 0.30 + 0.23$$

$$= 0.53 \text{ inches}$$

t_4 = pinch roller disengagement time = 20 Msec

Interblock Gap Length = Startgap Length + Stopgap Length

$$= 0.53 + 0.23$$

$$= 0.76 \text{ inches}$$

FIGURE 5-3.2.1-12: Start/Stop and Interblock Gaps Derived from the Tape Velocity Profile

To search to a given record, the MPU counts the interrecord gaps while moving the tape at Search Speed. Since the tape is moving at a much faster speed during Search, it is necessary to slow down the tape to a Read/Write speed prior to getting to the desired record to enable the tape to stop within the required Interrecord gap. For example, to read or write the 15th record, tape is moved at search speed until the 13th Inter-Record Gap (I.R.G.) and then switched to a Read/Write speed until the 14th I.R.G. is reached before a stop command is issued. (It may not be necessary to stop the tape in the I.R.G. prior to reading or writing the 15th record. The two operations may be performed sequentially without issuing the stop command.)

5-3.2.2 SOFTWARE DESCRIPTION

The Tape Cassette Subsystem uses a 256-byte Data Buffer for storage of Read and Write data and 20 bytes of storage for flags and variables. The variables determine the direction and speed of tape motion, the number of records being written, and other similar directive commands to the subsystem.

At Power-On, the Tape PIA is initialized so that the A-side is defined as inputs and the B-side is defined as outputs, and the tape is moved to the Load Point. An Interval Timer is used to generate the delays needed during tape operations.

Move to Load Point

When a tape cassette is inserted in the Drive, it may be at Clear Leader either on the BOT or EOT end, or it may be in the "Middle" of the tape between the BOT and EOT markers. A number of different schemes may be used to move the tape to the Load Point. The method used may be either completely automatic or require some operator intervention. The Rewind to Load Point operation described here assumes that the tape has, at some prior time, been advanced past the BOT marker and it is desired to rewind the tape to the Load Point. (This operation is distinguished from the Load Forward operation where the tape has been rewound to Clear Leader and needs to be moved forward to the Load Point. The Load Forward operation requires that the tape be moved forward until the BOT is seen and then advanced past the BOT to the Load Point. To enable the MPU to determine if the tape has been rewound to clear leader, where both EOT and BOT sensors will be triggered, it may be desirable to bring the EOT and BOT lines as separate inputs to the PIA interface. It is also possible to generate a Clear Leader status signal from the EOT and BOT sensors.) The flow chart for the System Integration of the Rewind to Load Point operation is shown in Figure 5-3.2.2-1. Additional details are shown in the Flow Chart and Assembly Listing of Figures 5-3.2.2-2 and 5-3.2.2-3, respectively.

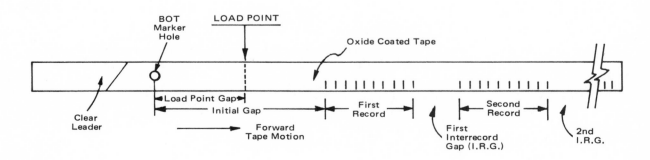

FIGURE 5-3.2.1-13. Load Point

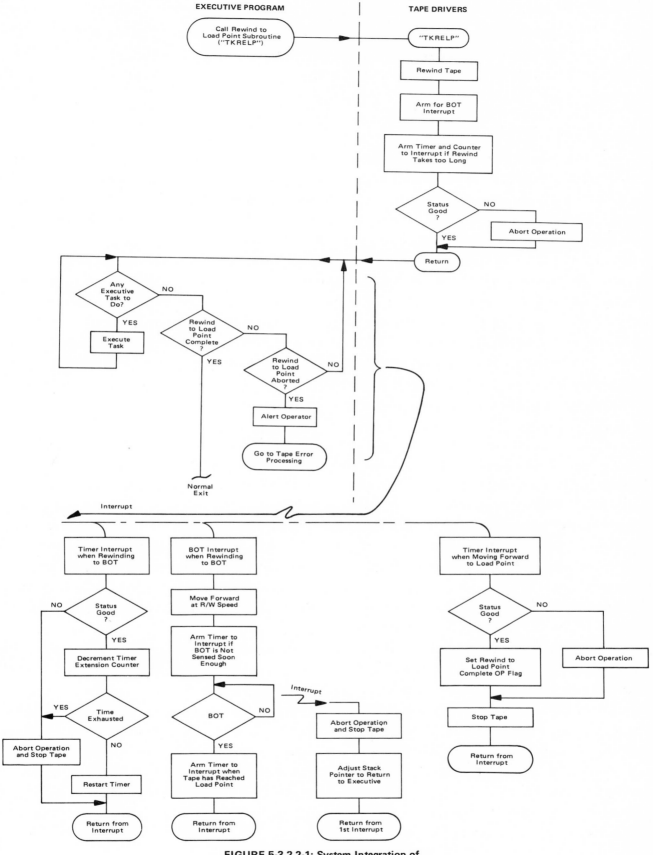

FIGURE 5-3.2.2-1: System Integration of Rewind to Load Point

Write Routine

The Write Routine consists of three subroutines, TKWRT1, TKWRT2, and TKWRT8. TKWRT1 is used to write the Startgap, TKWRT2 is used to write one complete record (Preamble, Data, CRCC, and Postamble), and TKWRT8 is used to write the Stopgap. If more than one record is to be written, tape motion is not stopped in the Interrecord Gaps.

The Executive Program determines the ending address of the Data Buffer and stores the address in the end address buffer TKDATA.

There are three possible sources of Interrupts during the execution of the Write program. They are: (1) Underflow Interrupt, (2) EOT Interrupt, and (3) Interval Timer Interrupt. The Underflow Interrupt occurs if the MPU does not provide the next Data Bit when it is requested by the Write Clock transition on the CA1 Interrupt input to the PIA. The operation will then be aborted by the MPU. The EOT interrupt should not normally occur during the Write operation since the EOT single-shot period is set to a time greater than the length of one record. The hardware design is such than even if an EOT transition is seen on starting Write motion, there is enough time to complete that record before being interrupted by the EOT single-shot. The MPU, via the Executive Program, checks if EOT was seen and alerts the operator to insert a new tape cassette into the drive when necesary. If no Write Clock is present, then the Write Operation is aborted after a time slightly longer than the length of one record. This results in one record being erased. It may be desirable to set a shorter time period (e.g., a time equal to two bit times or 166.6 milliseconds) to abort the Write operation. The details of the Write Operation are shown in the Flow Charts of Figures 5-3.2.2-4 and 5-3.2.2-5 and in the accompanying Assembly Listing of Figure 5-3.2.2-6.

Read Forward Routine

The Read Forward Routine consists of four subroutines: TKRD00,TKRD02, TKRD09, and TKRDST. TKRD00 is used to check tape status and to bring the tape up to speed if the status is good. The Tape Status check consists of checking for Tape Available, Ready, Cassette in Place, In Sync, EOT Seen, and CRCC Error. Whenever the tape is stopped, the hardware sets the In Sync and CRCC Error status bits to a good status. This allows a single Read Status Check subroutine, TKRDST, to be used both while the tape is stopped and while it is in motion. TKRD02 is the basic Read Routine which reads the Data portion of a record including the two bytes of CRCC. (Data is transferred to the Read Data Buffer in serial format). The CRCC is checked at the end of the Data portion, and appropriate operation codes are set to inform the Executive of the operation status. TKRD09 is used to stop the tape motion and store ending status.

The details of the Read operation are described in the Flow Chart and Assembly Listing of Figures 5-3.2.2-7 and 5-3.2.2-8, respectively. There are three possible sources of Interrupts during the execution of the Read program. They are: (1) Overflow Interrupt, (2) EOT Interrupt, and (3) Interval Timer Interrupt. The Overflow interrupt occurs if the MPU does not read the next Data Bit when its presence is indicated by the Read Clock transition on the CA1 Interrupt input to the PIA. The operation will then be aborted by the Overflow Interrupt. The EOT interrupt should not normally occur during the Read operation since the EOT single-shot period is set to a time greater than the length of one record. This implies that even if an EOT transition is seen on starting Read motion, there is enough time to complete that record before being interrupted by the EOT single-shot. If no Read Clock is present, then the Read Operation is aborted after a time corresponding approximately to the length of one record.

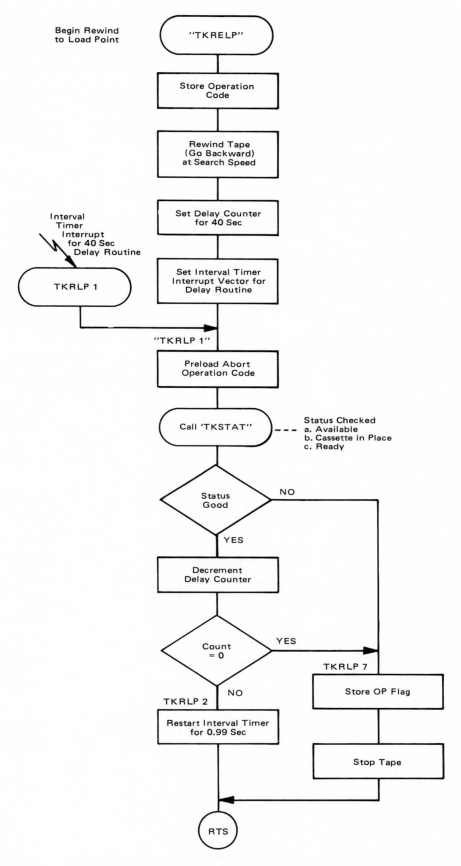

FIGURE 5-3.2.2-2: Move to Load Point Flow Chart (Sheet 1 of 2)

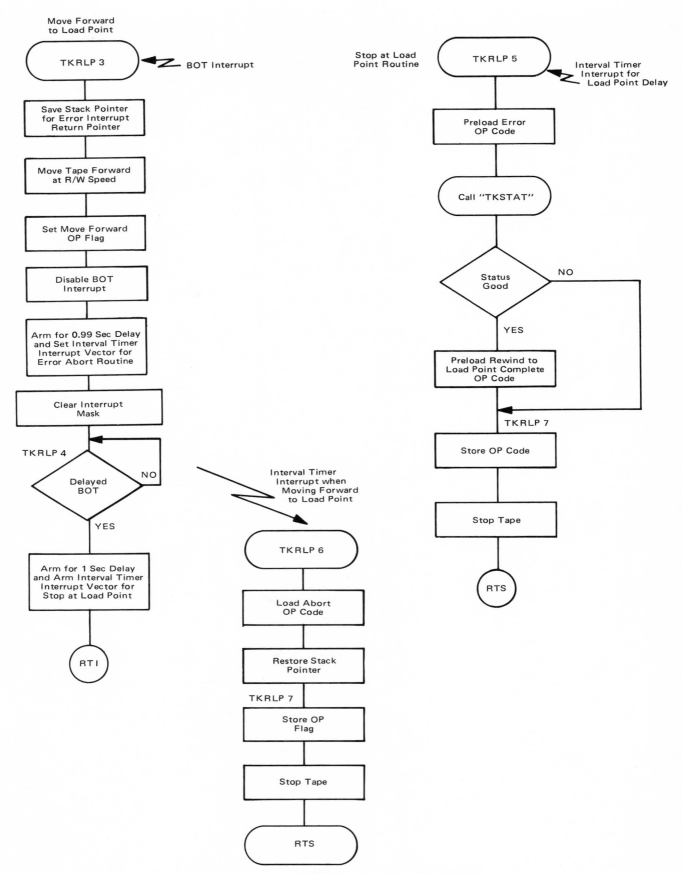

FIGURE 5-3.2.2-2: Move to Load Point Flow Chart (Sheet 2 of 2)

```
00010                    NAM    TKRELP
00020                    OPT    S
00030           ◆ REV 0.6 AS OF 1-2-75
00040           ◆
00060           ◆◆REWIND TO LOAD-POINT SUBROUTINE◆◆INTRPT-DRIVEN◆◆

00080           ◆ THIS SUBROUTINE MOVES THE TAPE FROM
00090           ◆ BETWEEN THE BOT AND EOT MARKERS, TO THE
00100           ◆ LOAD- POINT. IT REWINDS THE TAPE AT SEARCH
00110           ◆ SPEED TO THE BOT MARKER AND THEN MOVES
00120           ◆ FORWARD PAST THE BOT MARKER TO THE LOAD-POINT.

00140           ◆ THE INTERVAL TIMER IS USED TO ABORT
00150           ◆ THE OPERATION IF NO BOT INTERRUPT IS SEEN
00160           ◆ DURING THE TIME IT SHOULD TAKE TO REWIND
00170           ◆ THE TAPE FROM EOT. THIS TIME IS APPROXIMATELY
00180           ◆ 40 SECONDS (AT 100 I.P.S.).
00190           ◆ NOTE THAT THE DRIVER PROGRAM MUST ENSURE
00200           ◆ THAT THE INTERVAL TIMER IS AVAILABLE FOR
00210           ◆ USE BY THIS SUBROUTINE. SINCE THE MAXIMUM
00220           ◆ DELAY FROM THE INTERVAL TIMER IS 990 MSECS.
00230           ◆ A DELAY COUNTER TVDLYC IS USED TO COUNT TO
00240           ◆ THE REQUIRED DELAY TIME. THE INTERVAL TIMER IS
00250           ◆ RESTARTED AND ALLOWED TO INTERRUPT THE MPU UNTIL
00260           ◆ THE DELAY COUNT IS COMPLETE.

00280           ◆ ERROR SUBROUTINES TO STOP INTERVAL TIMER
00290           ◆ AND SET OPERATION STATUS FLAGS.
00300           ◆ OPERATION STATUS FLAGS IN TVOPST
00310           ◆ AS FOLLOWS
00320           ◆
00330           ◆ BIT 7 - 0 =COMPLETE; 1=INCOMPLETE
00340           ◆ BIT 6 - 0 =NO ERR. ; 1=ERROR
00350           ◆ BIT 5 - 0 =BACKWARD; 1= FWD DIRCTN.
00360           ◆ BIT 4 - 0 =NO ERASE; 1=ERASE
00370           ◆ BIT 3 - 0 =RD-WRT SP 1=SEARCH SPD.
00380           ◆ BIT 2 - 0 =NO WRITE; 1=WRITE
00390           ◆ BIT 1 - 0 =NO READ ; 1=READ
00400           ◆ BIT 0 - 0 =STOP    ; 1=GO


00420           ◆ THE OPERATION STATUS CODES USED ARE
00430           ◆ AS FOLLOWS
00440           ◆
00450           ◆

00470           ◆   REWIND TO B.O.T. IN PROGRESS    10001001
00480           ◆   REWIND TO B.O.T. ABORT          11001001
00490           ◆   MOVE FWD TO L.PT. IN PROGRESS   10100001
00500           ◆   MOVE FWD TO B.O.T. ABORT        11100001
00510           ◆   MOVE FWD TO L.PT. ABORT         11100000
00520           ◆   REWIND TO LOAD PT. COMPLETE     00100000
```

FIGURE 5-3.2.2-3. Move to Loadpoint Assembly Listing (Sheet 1 of 4)

```
00540  0010                        ORG      $10

00560                       ◆ VARIABLES USED BY THE ROUTINE

00580  0010  0001    TVOPST  RMB      1          OPERATION STATUS BUFF.
00590  0011  0002    IVSERV  RMB      2          INTRPT SERVICE ADDR. BUFF.
00600  0013  0001    TVSTAT  RMB      1          TAPE STATUS BYTE BUFF.
00610  0014  0001    TVDLYC  RMB      1          DELAY COUNTER
00615  0015  0002    TVSVSP  RMB      2          STACK POINTER STORE

00630                       ◆ CONSTANTS USED BY ROUTINE

00650        C010     XP2DRA  EQU      $C010      ITIMER PIA ADDR & CONTRL
00660        C011     XP2DRB  EQU      $C011
00670        C012     XP2CRA  EQU      $C012
00680        C013     XP2CRB  EQU      $C013
00690        1000     XP5DRA  EQU      $1000      TAPE PIA ADDR & DATA
00700        1001     XP5DRB  EQU      $1001
00710        1002     XP5CRA  EQU      $1002
00720        1003     XP5CRB  EQU      $1003
00730        0100     S10MS   EQU      256        10 MILLISECOND CLOCK
00740  0300                        ORG      $300

00770                       ◆ BEGIN REWIND TO LOAD POINT ROUTINE

00790  0300  C6 89    TKRELP  LDA B    #%10001001   OPERATION IN PROGRESS
00800  0302  D7 10            STA B    TVOPST     STORE OPERATION STATUS
00810  0304  86 0F            LDA A    #%00001111   SRCH-RWND CNTRL. WD.
00820  0306  B7 1001          STA A    XP5DRB     REWIND AT SRCH. SPD.
00830  0309  86 29            LDA A    #41        SET DELAY CNTR TO ,
00840  030B  97 14            STA A    TVDLYC     COUNT 40 DELAY INTERVALS.
00850  030D  CE 0312          LDX      #TKRLP1
00860  0310  DF 11            STX      IVSERV     SET  RETRN ADDR FOR ITIMER
00880                       ◆ SUBROUTINE TO CHECK IF DELAY COUNT IS COMPLETE
00890                       ◆ THIS SUBROUTINE IS INTERRUPT DRIVEN.
00900                       ◆ IF THE DELAY COUNT IS COMPLETE THEN THE
00910                       ◆ PROGRAM WILL CONTINUE WITH THE REST
00920                       ◆ OF THE LOAD-POINT ROUTINE. IF THE DELAY
00930                       ◆ IS NOT COMPLETE, THE PROGRM WILL SET THE
00940                       ◆ SAME INTRPT SERVICE ADDRESS,RESTART
00950                       ◆ THE INTERVAL TIMER AND RETURN.

00970  0312  C6 C9    TKRLP1  LDA B    #%11001001   ERROR INCOMPLETE FLAG
00980  0314  BD 0365          JSR      TKSTAT     CHK. STATUS
00990  0317  26 44            BNE      TKRLP7
01000  0319  7A 0014          DEC      TVDLYC     DECREMENT DELAY COUNTER
01010  031C  27 3F            BEQ      TKRLP7     DELAY COUNT COMPLETE ?

01030                       ◆ NOTE : SINCE THE INTRPT. SERVICE RTN. STOPS
01040                       ◆          THE TIMER, IT MUST BE RESTARTED EACH TIME

01060  031E  CE 0199  TKRLP2  LDX      #S10MS+$99   DELAY\990 MSEC.
01070  0321  FF C010          STX      XP2DRA     SET & START ITIMER
01080  0324  39               RTS                 RETRN FROM SUBROUTINE
```

FIGURE 5-3.2.2-3. Move to Loadpoint Assembly Listing (Sheet 2 of 4)

```
01100                           **SUBRTN TO MOVE TO LOAD POINT AFTER
01110                            * REWINDING TO BOT.**
01120                            * THE PROGRAM GETS TO THIS POINT FROM
01130                            * A BOT INTRPT.

01150  0325 C6 2E    TKRLP3 LDA B  #%00101110    RD. FWD. CNTRL. WD.
01160  0327 F7 1001         STA B  XP5DRB    MOVE FWD AT RD-WRT SPEED
01165  032A 9F 15           STS    TVSVSP    SAVE STACK POINTER
01170  032C C6 A1           LDA B  #%10100001    MOVE-FWD- IN PROG.
01180  032E D7 10           STA B  TVOPST    STORE OPERATION STATUS
01190  0330 C6 04           LDA B  #%00000100    DISABLE TAPE INTRPTS.
01200  0332 F7 1003         STA B  XP5CRB
01210  0335 CE 0359         LDX    #TKRLP6
01220  0338 DF 11           STX    IVSERV    SET RETRN ADDR FOR ITIMER
01230  033A 8D E2           BSR    TKRLP2    ARM TIMER FOR 990 MS
01235  033C 0E              CLI              CLEAR INTERRUPT MASK
01240  033D B6 1000  TKRLP4 LDA A  XP5DRA    LOAD STATUS WORD
01250  0340 2A FB           BPL    TKRLP4    MOVE FWD UNTIL BOT SEEN
01260  0342 CE 034E         LDX    #TKRLP5
01270  0345 DF 11           STX    IVSERV    SET RETRN ADDR FOR ITIMER
01280  0347 CE 0199         LDX    #$10MS+$99    STARTGAP DELAY TO LD.PT
01290  034A FF C010         STX    XP2DRA    SET & START TIMER
01300  034D 3B              RTI              RETURN TO HOST PROGRAM


01320                            * STOP AT LOAD POINT SUBROUTINE

01340  034E C6 E0    TKRLP5 LDA B  #%11100000    PRELOAD ERR. CODE
01350  0350 BD 0365         JSR    TKSTAT    CHK ENDING STATUS
01360  0353 26 08           BNE    TKRLP7
01370  0355 C6 20           LDA B  #%00100000    MOVE TO LD. PT. DONE
01380  0357 20 04           BRA    TKRLP7


01400                            * INTERVAL TIMER ERROR INTERRUPT ENTRY POINT
01410                            * WHEN MOVING FORWARD TO B.O.T.

01430  0359 C6 E1    TKRLP6 LDA B  #%11100001    ERROR ON MOVE FORWARD.
01435  035B 9E 15           LDS    TVSVSP    RESTORE STACK POINTER

01450                            * EXIT FROM INTERVAL TIMER INTERRUPT

01470  035D D7 10    TKRLP7 STA B  TVOPST    STORE OPERATION STATUS
01480  035F 86 EE           LDA A  #%11101110    RD-FWD-STOP CNTRL. WD.
01490  0361 B7 1001         STA A  XP5DRB    STOP TAPE
01500  0364 39              RTS              RETURN
```

FIGURE 5-3.2.2-3. Move to Loadpoint Assembly Listing (Sheet 3 of 4)

```
01530                    ** STATUS CHECK SUBROUTINE   **

01550              * THIS SUBROUTINE CHECKS THE CURRENT STATUS
01560              * OF THE TAPE WHICH IS AVAILABLE AT PA0-PA7.
01570              * THE STATUS IS COMPARED WITH THE EXPECTED
01580              * GOOD STATUS (AVAIL.,CAS. IN PLACE, RDY.)
01590              * AND THE RESULT OF THE COMPARISON IS SAVED
01600              * IN THE TAPE STATUS BUFFER TVSTAT.

01620 0365 B6 1000 TKSTAT LDA A  XP5DRA    READ THE STATUS; CLR FLAGS
01630 0368 84 D8          AND A  #%11011000   MASK OUT UNWANTED BITS
01640 036A 88 18          EOR A  #%00011000   TAPE AVAIL RD WD
01650 036C 97 13          STA A  TVSTAT    SAVE ERROR STATUS
01660 036E 39             RTS              RETURN


01680                     END


SYMBOL TABLE


IVSERV 0011 S10MS  0100 TKRELP 0300 TKRLP1 0312 TKRLP2 031E
TKRLP3 0325 TKRLP4 033D TKRLP5 034E TKRLP6 0359 TKRLP7 035D
TKSTAT 0365 TVDLYC 0014 TVOPST 0010 TVSTAT 0013 TVSVSP 0015
XP2CRA C012 XP2CRB C013 XP2DRA C010 XP2DRB C011 XP5CRA 1002
XP5CRB 1003 XP5DRA 1000 XP5DRB 1001
```

FIGURE 5-3.2.2-3. Move to Loadpoint Assembly Listing (Sheet 4 of 4)

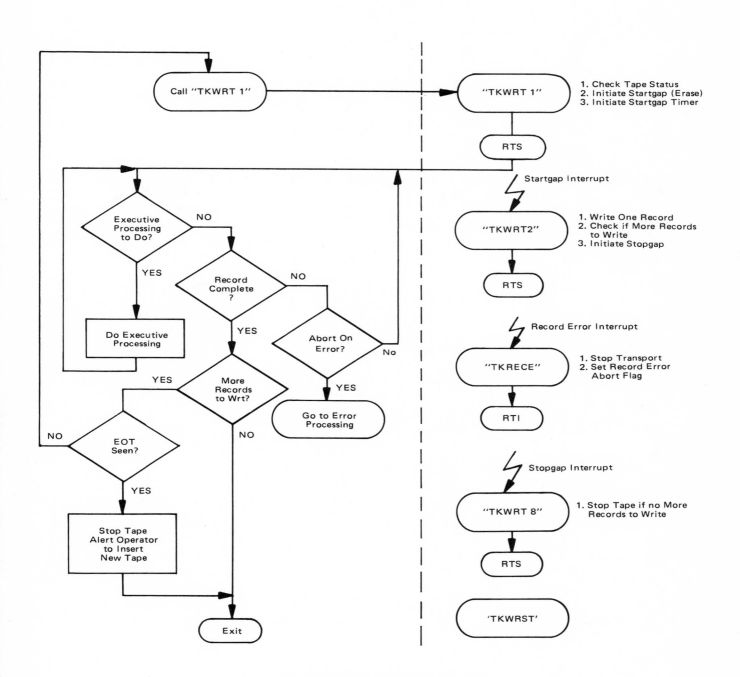

FIGURE 5-3.2.2-4: System Integration of Write Routine

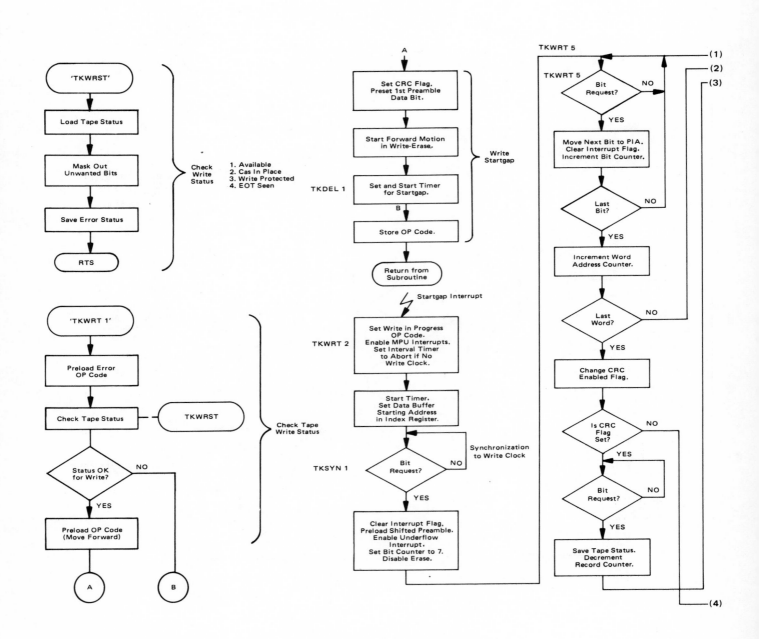

FIGURE 5-3.2.2-5 Flow Chart of Write Routine (Sheet 1 of 2)

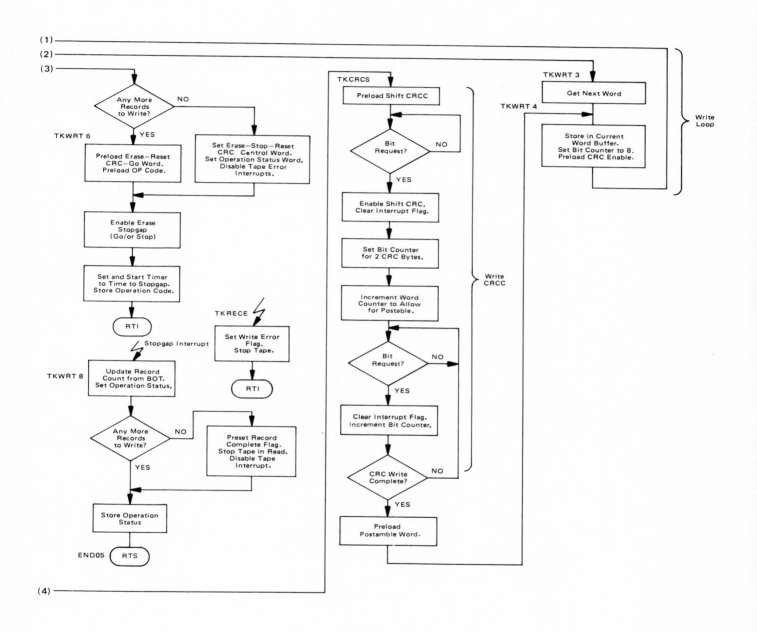

FIGURE 5-3.2.2-5 Flow Chart of Write Routine (Sheet 2 of 2)

```
00010                          NAM    TKWRT1
00020              * REV 0.13 AS OF 1-3-75
00030              *
00040                          OPT    S
00060              **WRITE SUBROUTINE**INTRPT-DRIVEN**

00080              * THIS SUBROUTINE IS USED TO WRITE
00090              * VARIABLE LENGTH RECORDS.
00100              * EACH RECORD CONSISTS OF A 1-BYTE PREAMBLE,
00110              * FROM 4-256 BYTES OF DATA (WHICH INCLUDES
00120              * A 2-BYTE CRCC, AND A 1-BYTE POSTAMBLE.

00140              * THE STARTING ADDRESS OF THE DATA
00150              * BUFFER IS DEFINED BY TKDATA. THE
00160              * ENDING ADDRESS STORED IN TVDATA DEFINES
00170              * THE NUMBER OF BYTES IN THE NEXT RECORD.
00180              * THE ENDING ADDRESS IS DETERMINED AS
00190              * (TKDATA+TVDATL) WHERE TVDATL HOLDS
00200              * THE NUMBER OF WORDS IN THE NEXT RECORD.
00210              * THE TKWRT1 PROGRAM  MOVES DATA STORED
00220              * BETWEEN THE ADDRESSES TKDATA AND TVDATA.
00230              * A STARTGAP OF ERASED TAPE IS WRITTEN PRIOR
00240              * TO THE FIRST BIT OF PREAMBLE AND A STOPGAP
00250              * OF ERASED TAPE IS WRITTEN AT THE END OF THE
00260              * LAST BIT OF THE POSTAMBLE. DURING THE STOPGAP
00270              * THE WRITE CURRENT REMAINS ON UNTIL TAPE
00280              * MOTION HAS STOPPED. AN INTERVAL TIMER IS USED
00290              * FOR STARTGAP AND STOPGAP TIMING AND TO
00300              * ABORT THE WRITE OPERATION IF NO WRITE CLOCK
00310              * IS PRESENT. THE OPERATION IS ABORTED
00320              * AFTER A DURATION CORRESPONDING APPROX.
00330              * TO THE LENGTH OF ONE RECORD.

00350              * IF MORE THAN ONE RECORD IS TO BE WRITTEN
00360              * THE WRITE (ERASE) CURRENT IS TURNED ON
00370              * BUT A STOP COMMAND IS NOT ISSUED DURING
00380              * THE STOPGAP. THE STARTGAP OF THE NEXT
00390              * RECORD IS WRITTEN AS THE CONTINUATION
00400              * OF THE PRECEDING STOPGAP.

00420              * THE OPERATION STATUS CODES USED ARE
00430              * AS FOLLOWS (USE THE TABLE GIVEN IN THE
00440              * TKRELP ROUTINE FOR FURTHER DETAILS ON
00450              * ON THE OPERATION STATUS FLAGS):

00470              * BAD TAPE STATUS                11100000
00480              * WRITE ERASE IN PROG.           10110101
00490              * ERASE STOP IN PROG.            10110100
00500              * WRT. DATA COMPL.-STOP          00100010
00510              * WRT.DATA COMPL.-ERASE-GO       00110101
00520              * WRT. ERR. -NO CLOCK            11100100
```

FIGURE 5-3.2.2-6. Write Routine Assembly Listing (Sheet 1 of 6)

```
00540  0020                          ORG      $20
00560                         * VARIABLES USED BY ROUTINE
00580  0020  0001    TVCRCF  RMB      1          CRC ENABLED FLAG
00590  0021  0002    IVSERV  RMB      2          INTRPT SERVICE ADDR. BUFF
00600  0023  0001    TVRECC  RMB      1          RECORD COUNT FROM BOT
00610  0024  0001    TVSTAT  RMB      1          STATUS BYTE
00620  0025  0002    TVDATL  RMB      2          NO. OF WORDS IN RECORD
00630  0027  0100    TKDATA  RMB      256        RD-WRT BUFFER
00640  0127  0002    TVLWA   RMB      2          LAST WORD ADDR OF DATA BUFF
00650  0129  0001    TVCDAT  RMB      1          CURRENT DATA-WORD BUFF
00660  012A  0001    TVOPST  RMB      1          OPERATION STAT. BUFF.
00670  012B  0001    TORECC  RMB      1          NO. OF RECORDS TO RD OR WRT
00680  012C  0002    TVDATA  RMB      2          (TKDATA + TVDATL) ADDRESS
00730                         * CONSTANTS USED BY ROUTINE
00750        C010    XP2DRA  EQU      $C010      ITIMER PIA ADDR & CONTRL
00760        C011    XP2DRB  EQU      $C011
00770        C012    XP2CRA  EQU      $C012
00780        C013    XP2CRB  EQU      $C013
00790        1000    XP5DRA  EQU      $1000      TAPE TAPE PIA ADDR &DATA
00800        1001    XP5DRB  EQU      $1001
00810        1002    XP5CRA  EQU      $1002
00820        1003    XP5CRB  EQU      $1003
00830        0100    $10MS   EQU      256        10 MILLISECOND CLOCK
00860                         *** PIA INTERFACE DEFINITION***********************
00870                         *
00880                         * OUTPUTS- WRT DATA AND CONTROL
00890                         *
00900                         * PB0 - WRITE DATA
00910                         * PB1 - WRITE =0 , READ = 1
00920                         * PB2 - ERASE =1 , RD ENABLE =0
00930                         * PB3 - CRC RESET = 1 ,CRC ENABLE = 0
00940                         * PB4 -**SPEED** RD-WRT = 0 ,SEARCH =1
00950                         * PB5 -**DIRECTION** FWD =1 ,REV =0
00960                         * PB6 - CRC SHIFT = 0 ,WRT DATA ENABLE =1
00970                         * PB7 -**MOTION** STOP = 1, GO = 0
00980                         *
00990                         * INPUTS -RD DATA AND STATUS
01000                         *
01010                         * PA0 - READ DATA
01020                         * PA1 - CRC ERROR =1
01030                         * PA2 - NOT IN SYNC = 0
01040                         * PA3 - READY =1
01050                         * PA4 - CASSETTE IN PLACE = 1
01060                         * PA5 - WRT PROTECTED = 0
01070                         * PA6 - AVAILABLE = 0
01080                         * PA7 - EOT-BOT SEEN = 1
01090                         *
01100                         * CA1 - CLOCK (LOW TO HIGH)
01110                         * CA2 - STROBE (RD WRT HANDSHAKE- HIGH TO LOW)
01120                         *
01130                         * CB1 - *INTRPT* OVFL-UNDFL (LOW TO HIGH)
01140                         * CB2 = *INTRPT* EOT-BOT TIMEOUT (LOW TO HIGH)
```

FIGURE 5-3.2.2-6. Write Routine Assembly Listing (Sheet 2 of 6)

```
01170                    ◆◆◆  WRITE START GAP (INTERVAL TIMER USED)

01190                    ◆ CHECK TAPE STATUS FOR WRITE

01210  0400 C6 E0   TKWRT1 LDA B  #%11100000    PRELOAD ERR.OPCODE
01220  0402 BD 04F2         JSR    TKWRST    CHECK TAPE STAT. FOR WRT.
01230  0405 26 16          BNE    TKWR01
01240  0407 C6 B5          LDA B  #%10110101    WRT-ERASE IN PROG.
01250  0409 86 FF          LDA A  #$FF
01260  040B 97 20          STA A  TVCRCF    SET CRC FLAG
01270  040D 86 6C          LDA A  #%01101100    GO-FWD-ERASE CNTRL. WD.

01290                    ◆ NOTE PB0=0 FIRST PRAMBLE BIT PRESET.

01310  040F B7 1001        STA A  XP5DRB    MOVE FWD IN ERASE
01320  0412 CE 0421  TKDEL1 LDX    #TKWRT2
01330  0415 DF 21          STX    IVSERV    RTRN. ADDR FOR INTRPT.
01340  0417 CE 0105        LDX    #S10MS+$05    STARTGAP DELAY (50 MS)
01350  041A FF C010        STX    XP2DRA    SET & START ITIMER
01360  041D F7 012A  TKWR01 STA B  TVOPST    STORE OPERATION STATUS
01370  0420 39            RTS              RETURN FROM SUBROUTINE


01390                    ◆ WRITE DATA SUBROUTINE

01410                    ◆ MPU INTRPTS. ARE ENABLED FOR POSSIBLE
01420                    ◆ EOT OR ERROR ABORT INTRPTS.



01440                    ◆ WRITE DATA SUBROUTINE

01460  0421 0E     TKWRT2 CLI              ENABLE INTRPTS TO MPU
01470  0422 86 A4          LDA A  #%10100100    WRT-IN-PROG. OPCODE
01480  0424 B7 012A        STA A  TVOPST    STORE OPERATION STATUS
01490  0427 CE 04E7        LDX    #TKRECE    SET RETRN FOR RECORD ERR.
01500  042A DF 21          STX    IVSERV    NO CLOCKS.
01510                    ◆ SET TIMER TO ABORT OPERATION IF NO WRITE
01520                    ◆ CLOCK IS PRESENT.
01530  042C CE 0122        LDX    #S10MS+$22    REC. LENGTH (220 MSEC)
01540  042F FF C010        STX    XP2DRA    SET & START ITIMER
01550                    ◆◆WRITE PREAMBLE
01560                    ◆ NOTE THAT A SHIFTED PREAMBLE IS LOADED
01570                    ◆ INTO THE CURRENT WORD BUFFER SINCE
01580                    ◆ THERE IS A 1-BIT DELAY IN THE HARDWARE.
01590                    ◆ THE FIRST BIT OF THE PREAMBLE IS PRESET AND
01600                    ◆ THE BIT COUNTER IS SET TO 7 FOR THE
01610                    ◆ PREAMBLE.
01620                    ◆ EACH DATA BYTE TO BE WRITTEN IS TRANSFERRED
01630                    ◆ FROM THE DATA BUFFER INTO THE CURRENT WORD
01640                    ◆ BUFFER.
01650  0432 CE 0027        LDX    #TKDATA    STARTING ADDR OF DATA BUFF
```

FIGURE 5-3.2.2-6. Write Routine Assembly Listing (Sheet 3 of 6)

```
01660  0435 09                  DEX              ACCOUNT FOR PREAMBLE BYTE
01670                     ◆ SYNCHRONIZATION TO WRITE CLOCK
01680  0436 F6 1002 TKSYN1 LDA B   XP5CRA
01690  0439 2A FB           BPL     TKSYN1    POLL FOR BIT REQ
01700                     ◆
01710  043B F6 1000         LDA B   XP5DRA    CLR INTRR FLAG
01720  043E C6 55           LDA B   #%01010101   LOAD SHIFTED PREAMBLE
01730  0440 F7 0129         STA B   TVCDAT    STORE IN CURRENT WORD BUFF.
01740  0443 C6 0F           LDA B   #%00001111   ENABLE UNDERFLOW INTERR
01750  0445 F7 1003         STA B   XP5CRB
01760  0448 C6 F9           LDA B   #0-7     SET BIT CNTR TO 7
01770  044A 86 68           LDA A   #%01101000   SET ERASE LINE PB2=0
01780  044C B7 1001         STA A   XP5DRB    DISABLE ERASE
01790  044F 20 28           BRA     TKWRT5


01810                     ◆ SHIFT CRCC LOOP
01820  0451 86 20  TKCRCS LDA A   #%00100000   PRELOAD SHIFT CRCC
01830  0453 F1 1002 TKCRC3 CMP B   XP5CRA
01840  0456 2B FB           BMI     TKCRC3    POLL FOR BIT REQUEST
01850  0458 B7 1001         STA A   XP5DRB    ENABLE SHIFT CRCC
01860  045B F5 1000         BIT B   XP5DRA    CLR INTRR FLAG
01870  045E C6 F1           LDA B   #0-15    SET BIT CNTR FOR 2 CRC BYTE
01880  0460 08              INX              INC. WD. CNTR. FOR POSTAMBL
01890  0461 F5 1002 TKCRC4 BIT B   XP5CRA
01900  0464 2A FB           BPL     TKCRC4    POLL FOR BIT REQUEST
01910  0466 F5 1000         BIT B   XP5DRA    CLR INTRR FLAG
01920  0469 5C              INC B            INCREMENT BIT CNTR
01930  046A 26 F5           BNE     TKCRC4    CRCC SHIFT DONE ?
01940  046C 86 AA           LDA A   #%10101010   PRELOAD POSTAMBLE BYTE
01950  046E 20 02           BRA     TKWRT4
01960                     ◆ BASIC WRITE LOOP
01970                     ◆
01980  0470 A6 00  TKWRT3 LDA A   0,X      GET NEXT DATA WORD
01990  0472 B7 0129 TKWRT4 STA A   TVCDAT    MOVE DATA TO CURRENT WD BUF
02000  0475 C6 F8           LDA B   #0-8     SET BIT CNTR TO 8 BITS
02010  0477 86 60           LDA A   #%01100000   WRT-FWD-GO CNTRL. WD.


02030  0479 F5 1002 TKWRT5 BIT B   XP5CRA
02040  047C 2A FB           BPL     TKWRT5    POLL FOR BIT REQUEST
02050  047E 46              ROR A            PURGE OLD DATA BIT
02060  047F 76 0129         ROR     TVCDAT    SHIFT NEW BIT TO CARRY
02070  0482 49              ROL A            CARRY TO DATA BIT POSITION
02080  0483 B7 1001         STA A   XP5DRB    NEW BIT TO PIA
02090  0486 F5 1000         BIT B   XP5DRA    CLR INTRR FLAG
02100  0489 5C              INC B            INCREMENT BIT CNTR
02110  048A 26 ED           BNE     TKWRT5    IF NOT DONE GET NEXT BIT
02120  048C 08              INX              INC. WD. ADDR. CNTR.
02130  048D BC 012C         CPX     TVDATA    COMP. FOR END ADDR.
02140  0490 26 DE           BNE     TKWRT3    LAST WORD ?
02150  0492 7C 0020         INC     TVCRCF    CHANGE CRC ENABLED FLAG
```

FIGURE 5-3.2.2-6. Write Routine Assembly Listing (Sheet 4 of 6)

```
02160  0495  27 BA              BEQ    TKCRCS
02170                     ••• WRITE STOP GAP (INTERVAL TIMER USED)
02180  0497  F1 1002  TKSYN2 CMP B  XP5CRA
02190  049A  2B FB              BMI    TKSYN2    POLL FOR BIT REQUEST
02200  049C  F6 1000            LDA B  XP5DRA    CHK STATUS FOR EOT/BOT
02210  049F  D7 24             STA B  TVSTAT    SAVE TAPE STATUS
02220  04A1  7A 012B            DEC    TORECC    DECREMENT RECORD COUNTER
02230  04A4  26 0C              BNE    TKWRT6    BRANCH TO NO-STOP-ERASE
02240  04A6  8A 8C              ORA A  #%10001100   CLR.CRC-ERASE-STP WORD
02250  04A8  C6 B4              LDA B  #%10110100   ERASE-STOP IN PROG.
02260  04AA  FE 340C            LDX    $340C     SETUP CONTROL REGS. TO ,
02270  04AD  FF 1002            STX    XP5CRA    DISABLE ERROR INTERR
02280  04B0  20 04              BRA    TKWRT7    BRANCH TO STOP-ERASE
02290  04B2  8A 0C   TKWRT6 ORA A  %00001100    GO-ERASE-RESET CRC
02300  04B4  C6 B5              LDA B  #%10110101   WRT-ERASE IN PROG.
02310  04B6  B7 1001  TKWRT7 STA A  XP5DRB
02320  04B9  CE 04C8            LDX    #TKWRT8   SET INTRPT SERV ADDR
02330  04BC  DF 21              STX    IVSERV
02340  04BE  CE 0102            LDX    #$10MS+$02   STOPGAP DELAY 20 MSEC.
02350  04C1  FF C010            STX    XP2DRA    START INTVL TIMER
02360  04C4  F7 012A            STA B  TVOPST    STORE OPERATION STATUS
02370  04C7  39                RTS              RETURN FROM SUBROUTINE
02400                     • IF NO OTHER RECORDS TO BE WRITTEN,THEN
02410                     • TURN OFF WRITE CURRENT AND RESET FOR
02420                     • READ-FWD. IF MORE RECORDS TO BE WRITTEN
02430                     • THEN LEAVE WRITE (ERASE) CURRENT ON
02440                     • AND RETURN FOR THE NEXT RECORD.
02460  04C8  7C 0023  TKWRT8 INC    TVRECC    UPDATE RECORD CNTR FROM BOT
02470  04CB  C6 35              LDA B  #%00110101   RECD. CMPL.-ERASE-GO
02480  04CD  B6 012B            LDA A  TORECC    CHK IF RECORDS DONE
02490  04D0  26 11              BNE    END05
02500  04D2  C6 22              LDA B  #%00100010   RECD. CMPL.-STOP
02510  04D4  86 EE              LDA A  #$EE      PRELOAD RDFWD STOP WD
02520  04D6  B7 1001            STA A  XP5DRB    STOP TAPE IN RD FWD
02530  04D9  86 04              LDA A  #$04
02540  04DB  F7 1003            STA B  XP5CRB    DISABLE TAPE PIA INTRPTS.
02550  04DE  86 2C              LDA A  #$2C
02560  04E0  B7 C013            STA A  XP2CRB    DIABLE INTVL TIMER INTRPTS.
02570  04E3  F7 012A  END05  STA B  TVOPST    STORE OPERATION STATUS
02580  04E6  39                RTS              RETURN FROM SUBROUTINE
02590                     • ERROR INTRPT ROUTINE
02600                     •
02610                     • SET ERROR ABORT FLAG & RETURN TO EXEC
02620  04E7  96 EE   TKRECE LDA A  $EE       PRELOAD READ FWD CONTROL WO
02630  04E9  B7 1001            STA A  XP5DRB    STOP TAPE
02640  04EC  86 E4              LDA A  #%11100100   WRT.ERR.-INCOMPLETE
02650  04EE  B7 012A            STA A  TVOPST    SAVE IN STATUS BUFF.
02660  04F1  39                RTS              RETURN FROM SUBROUTINE
```

FIGURE 5-3.2.2-6. Write Routine Assembly Listing (Sheet 5 of 6)

```
02680                    ◆ WRITE STATUS CHECK SUBROUTINE

02700  04F2  B6 1000  TKWRST  LDA A  XP5DRA    READ TAPE STATUS
02710  04F5  84 FC            AND A  #%11111100   MASK UNWANTED BITS
02720  04F7  88 1C            EOR A  #%00011100   COMPARE WITH GOOD STAT.
02730  04F9  97 24            STA A  TVSTAT    SAVE ERROR STATUS
02740  04FB  39               RTS              RETRN FROM SUBROUTINE
 02750                        END
```

SYMBOL TABLE

```
END05   04E3  IVSERV  0021  S10MS   0100  TKCRC3  0453  TKCRC4  0461
TKCRC5  0451  TKDATA  0027  TKDEL1  0412  TKRECE  04E7  TKSYN1  0436
TKSYN2  0497  TKWR01  041D  TKWRST  04F2  TKWRT1  0400  TKWRT2  0421
TKWRT3  0470  TKWRT4  0472  TKWRT5  0479  TKWRT6  04B2  TKWRT7  04B6
TKWRT8  04C8  TORECC  012B  TVCDAT  0129  TVCRCF  0020  TVDATA  012C
TVDATL  0025  TVLWA   0127  TVOPST  012A  TVRECC  0023  TVSTAT  0024
XP2CRA  C012  XP2CRB  C013  XP2DRA  C010  XP2DRB  C011  XP5CRA  1002
XP5CRB  1003  XP5DRA  1000  XP5DRB  1001
```

FIGURE 5-3.2.2-6. Write Routine Assembly Listing (Sheet 6 of 6)

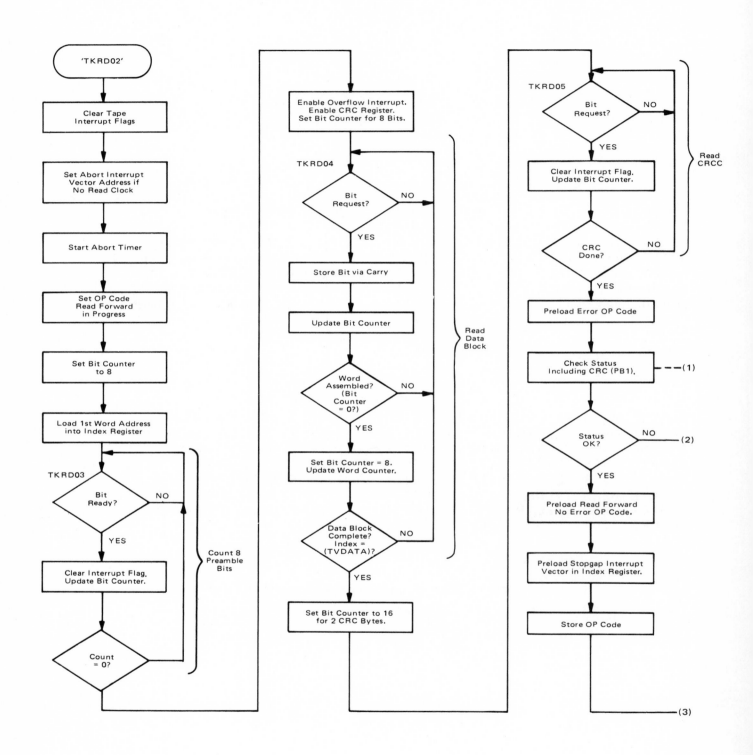

FIGURE 5-3.2.2-7: Flow Chart of Read Routine (Sheet 1 of 2)

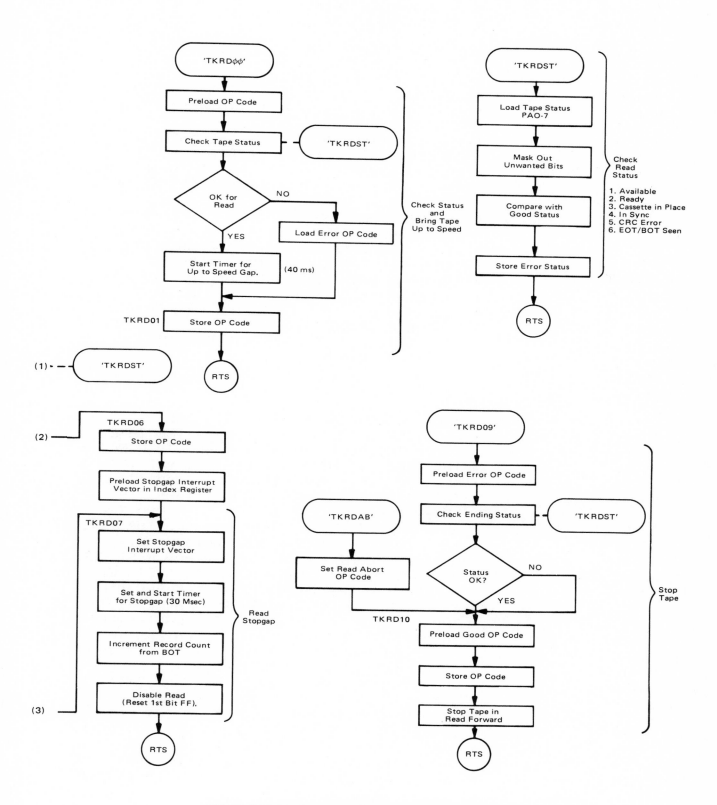

FIGURE 5-3.2.2-7: Flow Chart of Read Routine (Sheet 2 of 2)

```
00010                          NAM     TKREAD
00020         ◆  REV 0.07 AS OF 1-2-75
00030                          OPT     S
00040         ◆

00060         ◆◆ READ FORWARD SUBROUTINE◆◆
00070         ◆
00080         ◆ THIS SUBROUTINE IS USED TO READ FORWARD
00090         ◆ ONE VARIABLE LENGTH RECORD.
00100         ◆ THE STARTING ADDRESS OF THE DATA
00110         ◆ BUFFER IS DEFINED BY TKDATA. THE
00120         ◆ ENDING ADDRESS STORED IN TVDATA DEFINES
00130         ◆ THE NUMBER OF BYTES IN THE NEXT RECORD.
00140         ◆
00150         ◆ AN INTERVAL TIMER IS USED TO GENERATE
00160         ◆ THE STARTGAP AND STOPGAP DELAYS AND TO
00170         ◆ ABORT THE OPERATION IF NO READ CLOCK IS
00180         ◆ SEEN OVER THE LENGTH OF A RECORD.
00190         ◆ THE INTERVAL TIMER IS USED IN THE
00200         ◆ FOLLOWING SEQUENCE:
00210         ◆  A. 40 MSEC.  TO ALLOW THE TAPE TO
00220         ◆     COME UP TO SPEED.
00230         ◆  B. 300 MSEC.  TO ABORT OPERATION
00240         ◆     IF NO READ CLOCKS
00250         ◆  C. 30 MSEC. TO ALLOW TAPE TO MOVE
00260         ◆     INTO STOPGAP
00270         ◆
00280         ◆ TAPE MOTION IS STARTED WITH THE
00290         ◆ READ CIRCUITS DISABLED. WHEN THE TAPE
00300         ◆ IS UP TO SPEED (APPROXIMATELY 40 MSECS.)
00310         ◆ THE READ CIRCUITS ARE ENABLED AND THE
00320         ◆ MPU LOOKS FOR THE FIRST BIT TRANSITION.
00330         ◆ THE FIRST BIT TRANSITION SWITCHES THE
00340         ◆ REFERENCE INPUT OF THE P.L.L. FROM THE
00350         ◆ WRT. OSC. TO  THE READ DATA AND THE P.L.L.
00360         ◆ BEGINS TO TRACK THE READ DATA. THE 8 BITS
00370         ◆ OF THE PREAMBLE ARE COUNTED AND USED FOR
00380         ◆ BYTE ALIGNMENT. THE P.L.L. IS DESIGNED
00390         ◆ TO LOCK TO THE DATA WITHIN THE PREAMBLE
00400         ◆ BITS. CRCC ACCUMULATION IS STARTED WITH
00410         ◆ THE FIRST DATA BIT. DATA IS TRANSFERRED
00420         ◆ IN BIT SERIAL FORMAT AND ASSEMBLED INTO
00430         ◆ BYTES IN THE DATA BUFFER.  THE LAST TWO
00440         ◆ BYTES OF THE DATA PORTION OF THE RECORD
00450         ◆ ARE THE CRC BYTES. THESE ARE NOT SHIFTED
00460         ◆ INTO THE DATA BUFFER BUT THEY ARE
00470         ◆ ACCUMULATED IN THE CRCC GENERATOR. AT
00480         ◆ THE END OF THE CRCC BYTES, THE CRC ERROR
00490         ◆ LINE IS EXAMINED TO SEE IF THE DATA
00500         ◆ WAS READ CORRECTLY. STATUS FLAGS ARE SET
00510         ◆ AT THE END OF EACH OPERATION STEP BEFORE
```

FIGURE 5-3.2.2-8. Read Routine Assembly Listing (Sheet 1 of 5)

```
00520                       ◆ RETURNING TO THE EXECUTIVE.
00530                       ◆
00540                       ◆ THE OPERATION STATUS CODES USED ARE
00550                       ◆ AS FOLLOWS (USE THE TABLE GIVEN IN THE
00560                       ◆ TKRELP ROUTINE FOR FURTHER DETAILS ON
00570                       ◆ ON THE OPERATION STATUS FLAGS):
00580                       ◆
00590                       ◆ MOVE FWD IN PROGRESS-(10100001)
00600                       ◆ READ FWD IN PROGRESS-(10100011)
00610                       ◆ READ ERROR INCOMPL. -(11100011)
00620                       ◆ RD. ERR. ENDG. STAT.-(11100010)
00630                       ◆ READ RECORD COMPL.  -(00100010)


00650  0020                          ORG     $20


00670  0020 0001    TVCRCF RMB      1         CRC ENABLED FLAG
00680  0021 0002    IVSERV RMB      2         INTRPT SERVICE ADDR. BUFF
00690  0023 0001    TVRECC RMB      1         RECORD COUNT FROM BOT
00700  0024 0001    TVSTAT RMB      1         STATUS BYTE
00710  0025 0002    TVDATL RMB      2         VARIABLE LENGTH BUFF
00720  0027 0001    TVCDAT RMB      1         CURRENT DATA-WORD BUFF
00730  0028 0001    TVOPST RMB      1         OPERATION STAT. BUFF.
00740  0029 0002    TVDATA RMB      2         (TKDATA + TVDATL) ADDRESS


00760                       ◆ DATA BUFFER STORAGE
00770  0400                          ORG     $400
00780  0400 0100    TKDATA RMB      256       RD-WRT BUFFER


00800                       ◆ CONSTANTS USED BY ROUTINE

00820       0100    TKDATL EQU     $0100      FIXED LENGTH BUFF 256 BYTES
00830       C010    XP2DRA EQU     $C010      ITIMER PIA ADDR & CONTRL
00840       C011    XP2DRB EQU     $C011
00850       C012    XP2CRA EQU     $C012
00860       C013    XP2CRB EQU     $C013
00870       1000    XP5DRA EQU     $1000      TAPE TAPE PIA ADDR &DATA
00880       1001    XP5DRB EQU     $1001
00890       1002    XP5CRA EQU     $1002
00900       1003    XP5CRB EQU     $1003
00910       0100    S10MS  EQU     256        10 MILLISECOND CLOCK

00930  0600                          ORG     $600
```

FIGURE 5-3.2.2-8. Read Routine Assembly Listing (Sheet 2 of 5)

```
00950                         ◆ MOVE TAPE UPTO SPEED SUBROUTINE

00970  0600  C6 E2   TKRD00  LDA B  #%11100010    ERROR OP-CODE
00980  0602  BD 06B2          JSR    TKRDST    CHK. READ STATUS
00990  0605  26 17            BNE    TKRD01
01000  0607  CE 0621          LDX    #TKRD02    SET RD ENABLE RETRN ADDR
01010  060A  DF 21            STX    IVSERV
01020  060C  C6 0C            LDA B  #%00001100
01030  060E  F7 1003          STA B  XP5CRB    ENABLE EOT INTRPT.
01040  0611  86 2E            LDA A  #%00101110    MOVE-FWD CNTRL. WD.
01050  0613  B7 1001          STA A  XP5DRB    START MOVING UPTO SPEED
01060  0616  C6 A1            LDA B  #%10100001    MOVE-FWD IN PROG.
01070  0618  CE 0104          LDX    #S10MS+$04    40 MSEC UPTO SPD. DELAY
01080  061B  FF C010          STX    XP2DRA    SET & START ITIMER.
01090  061E  D7 28   TKRD01  STA B  TVOPST    STORE OPERATION STATUS
01100  0620  39               RTS


01120                         ◆ READ DATA SUBROUTINE


01140  0621  FE 1000  TKRD02  LDX    XP5DRA    CLR TAPE   INTRPT. FLAGS
01150  0624  CE 06AE          LDX    #TKRDAB    SET RD ABORT RET ADDRES
01160  0627  DF 21            STX    IVSERV
01170  0629  CE 0130          LDX    #S10MS+$30    RECRD. LENGTH 300 MSEC.
01180  062C  FF C010          STX    XP2DRA    SET & START ITIMER.
01190                         ◆ ENABLE READ (LOOK FOR FIRST BIT)
01200  062F  86 2A            LDA A  #%00101010    READ-FWD CNTRL. WD.
01210  0631  B7 1001          STA A  XP5DRB    CONTINUE MOTION IN RD
01220  0634  C6 A3            LDA B  #%10100011    RD-FWD IN PROG.
01230  0636  D7 28            STA B  TVOPST    STORE OPERATION STATUS
01240  0638  C6 F8            LDA B  #0-8    SET BIT CNTR
01250  063A  CE 0400          LDX    #TKDATA    LOAD FIRST WORD ADDR.


01270                         ◆ READ PREAMBLE
01280  063D  F5 1002  TKRD03  BIT B  XP5CRA
01290  0640  2A FB            BPL    TKRD03    POLL FOR BIT REQ
01300  0642  F5 1000          BIT B  XP5DRA
01310  0645  5C               INC B            UPDATE BIT CNTR
01320  0646  26 F5            BNE    TKRD03


01340                         ◆ READ DATA
01350  0648  C6 0F            LDA B  #%00001111    ENABL OVERFLO INTRPT.
01360  064A  F7 1003          STA B  XP5CRB
01370  064D  84 F7            AND A  #%11110111    ENABLE CRC REG
01380  064F  B7 1001          STA A  XP5DRB
01390  0652  C6 F8            LDA B  #0-8    SET BIT CNTR
01400  0654  F5 1002  TKRD04  BIT B  XP5CRA
01410  0657  2A FB            BPL    TKRD04    POLL FOR BIT RDY REQ
01420  0659  B6 1000          LDA A  XP5DRA    GET NEXT BIT
01430  065C  46               ROR A            SHIFT BIT TO CARRY
```

FIGURE 5-3.2.2-8. Read Routine Assembly Listing (Sheet 3 of 5)

```
01440  065D 69 00           ROR      0,X         STORE BIT IN DATABUFF.
01450  065F 5C              INC B                UPDATE BIT CNTR
01460  0660 26 F2           BNE      TKRD04
01470  0662 C6 F8           LDA B    #0-8        SET BIT CNTR
01480  0664 08              INX                  INCREMENT WORD CNTR
01490  0665 8C 0029         CPX      #TVDATA     COMPARE LAST WD ADDR.
01500  0668 26 EA           BNE      TKRD04      LAST WORD ?
01510  066A C6 F0           LDA B    #0-16       SET BIT CNTR FOR CRC
01520  066C F5 1002 TKRD05  BIT B    XP5CRA
01530  066F 2A FB           BPL      TKRD05      POLL FOR BIT REQ
01540  0671 B6 1000         LDA A    XP5DRA      CLR INTRPT. FLAG &RD STATUS
01550  0674 5C              INC B                UPDATE BIT CNTR
01560  0675 26 F5           BNE      TKRD05

01580                       ◆ CHECK STATUS FOR AVAIL.,CAS. IN PLACE,
01590                       ◆ READY, IN SYNC, AND CRC ERR.
01600  0677 C6 E3           LDA B    #%11100011   PRELOAD ERR.OP CODE
01610  0679 BD 06B2         JSR      TKRDST   CHK. READ STATUS
01620  067C 26 09           BNE      TKRD06
01630  067E C6 A3           LDA B    #%10100011   RD-FWD-IN PROG.
01640  0680 CE 069D         LDX      #TKRD09   SET ITIMER RETRN. ADDR.
01650  0683 D7 28           STA B    TVOPST   STORE OPER. STAT.
01660  0685 20 05           BRA      TKRD07
01670  0687 D7 28   TKRD06  STA B    TVOPST   STORE OPERATION STATUS
01680                       ◆  READ STOP GAP
01690  0689 CE 06A6         LDX      #TKRD10   SET ITIMER RETRN. ADDR.
01700  068C DF 21   TKRD07  STX      IVSERV
01710  068E CE 0103         LDX      #S10MS+$03   30 MSEC STOPGAP
01720  0691 FF C010         STX      XP2DRA   SET & START ITIMER.
01730  0694 7C 0023         INC      TVRECC   INC. RECRD. COUNT FROM BOT
01740  0697 86 2E           LDA A    #%00101110   MOVE -FWD-CNTRL.  D.
01750                       ◆ NOTE: RD DISABLED (PB2=1) RESETS
01760                       ◆       1ST BIT FLIP-FLOP.
01770  0699 B7 1001         STA A    XP5DRB   RESETS 1ST BIT FF
01780  069C 39              RTS                RTRN FROM SUBRTN


01800                       ◆ STOP TAPE IN INTERRECORD GAP
01810                       ◆

01830  069D C6 E2   TKRD09  LDA B    #%11100010   RD-ERR. END. STAT.
01840  069F BD 06B2         JSR      TKRDST   CHK ENDING STATUS
01850  06A2 26 02           BNE      TKRD10
01860  06A4 C6 22           LDA B    #%00100010   READ RECORD DONE
01870  06A6 D7 28   TKRD10  STA B    TVOPST   STORE OPERATION STATUS
01880  06A8 86 EE           LDA A    #%11101110   RD-FWD-STOP CNTRL. WD.
01890  06AA B7 1001         STA A    XP5DRB   STOP TAPE
01900  06AD 39              RTS                RETRN FROM SUBRTN
```

FIGURE 5-3.2.2-8. Read Routine Assembly Listing (Sheet 4 of 5)

```
01920                           ◆ READ ABORT SUBROUTINE

01940  06AE  C6 E2   TKRDAB  LDA B  #%11100010    RD-ABORT-OPCODE
01950  06B0  20 F4           BRA    TKRD10     STOP TAPE IN RECORD GAP


01970                           ◆◆STATUS CHECK SUBROUTINE ◆◆◆◆◆
01980                           ◆
01990                           ◆ THIS SUBROUTINE CHECKS THE CURRENT STATUS
02000                           ◆ OF THE TAPE WHICH IS AVAILABLE AT PA0-PA7.
02010                           ◆ THE STATUS IS COMPARED WITH THE EXPECTED
02020                           ◆ GOOD STATUS ( AVAIL.,CAS. IN PLACE,RDY.,
02030                           ◆ IN SYNC,AND CRC ERR.) AND THE RESULT
02040                           ◆ OF THE COMPARISON IS SAVED IN THE TAPE
02050                           ◆ STATUS BUFFER TVSTAT.

02070                           ◆ CHECK TAPE STATUS SUBROUTINE


02090  06B2  B6 1000  TKRDST  LDA A  XP5DRA     READ TAPE STATUS;CLR FLAGS
02100  06B5  84 DE            AND A  #%11011110    MASKOUT UNWANTED BITS
02110  06B7  88 1C            EOR A  #%00011100    TAPE AVAIL RD WD
02120  06B9  97 24            STA A  TVSTAT     SAVE ERROR STATUS
02130  06BB  39               RTS               RETRN FROM SUBRTN
02140                          END
```

SYMBOL TABLE

```
IVSERV  0021  S10MS   0100  TKDATA  0400  TKDATL  0100  TKRD00  0600
TKRD01  061E  TKRD02  0621  TKRD03  063D  TKRD04  0654  TKRD05  066C
TKRD06  0687  TKRD07  068C  TKRD09  069D  TKRD10  06A6  TKRDAB  06AE
TKRDST  06B2  TVCDAT  0027  TVCRCF  0020  TVDATA  0029  TVDATL  0025
TVOPST  0028  TVRECC  0023  TVSTAT  0024  XP2CRA  C012  XP2CRB  C013
XP2DRA  C010  XP2DRB  C011  XP5CRA  1002  XP5CRB  1003  XP5DRA  1000
XP5DRB  1001
```

FIGURE 5-3.2.2-8. Read Routine Assembly Listing (Sheet 5 of 5)

5-4.1 INTRODUCTION

The floppy disk is fast becoming an important storage media. The promise of low cost and direct access has encouraged minicomputer users to select the floppy disk for mini-mass storage requirements. As microprocessing systems enter the marketplace, proposed applications for the floppy disk broaden to include the "less-than-mini" market. These new applications include:

- Program loaders for intelligent terminals and larger systems
- Key-to-disk keypunch replacement
- Price look-up and credit card verification files for POS systems
- Message buffers for communications systems.

In these applications, the floppy disk will contend with cassettes and paper tape. The attractiveness of floppy disk over other means of mass storage rests in:

- Cost per bit of usable storage
- Cost of the floppy disk subsystem
- Reliability and maintainability
- Ease of media handling and transportability
- Compatibility of recorded data with other systems, large or small.

The purpose of this section is to show techniques for controlling a floppy disk with the MC6800 microprocessor. Because the floppy disk data rates lie at the extreme high end of the MC6800's data handling capability, this section also serves to demonstrate optimization techniques that can be used in applications other than the floppy disk.

The floppy disk itself (often referred to as a diskette) is a removable magnetic storage media which is permanently contained in a paper envelope. The diskette drive is a low cost peripheral which performs the electro-mechanical and read/write functions necessary to record and recover data on the diskette. Reprints from the reference manuals for the CALCOMP 140, Orbis Systems Model 74 and Shugart SA 900 floppy disk drives are appended to this section. Familiarity with floppy disk terminology, operations and specifications will be of value in understanding the design techniques illustrated in this section.

Data is recorded serially on the floppy disk. Due to the high serial data rates, it is necessary to use auxiliary logic for the serial/parallel conversion, data recovery, and data error checking when interfacing the floppy disk to the M6800 system. The hardware which performs this function is usually called a *formatter*. The formatter also serves as a buffer between the M6800 system and the disk (Figure 5-4.1-1).

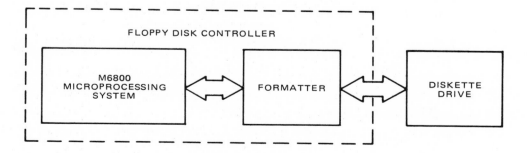

FIGURE 5-4.1-1. M6800/Floppy Disk Subsystem

The purpose of the M6800 system and the formatter is to control the diskette drive. Therefore, the combination of the M6800 SYSTEM and FORMATTER blocks in Figure 5-4.1-1 is referred to as the Floppy Disk Controller. As used here, the term "controller" includes not only the system hardware, but also those microprocessing system programs which directly or indirectly control the diskette drive. The program routines for the floppy disk are often referred to as floppy disk *drivers* or *control modules*. A more complete diagram of the controller is depicted in Figure 5-4.1-2.

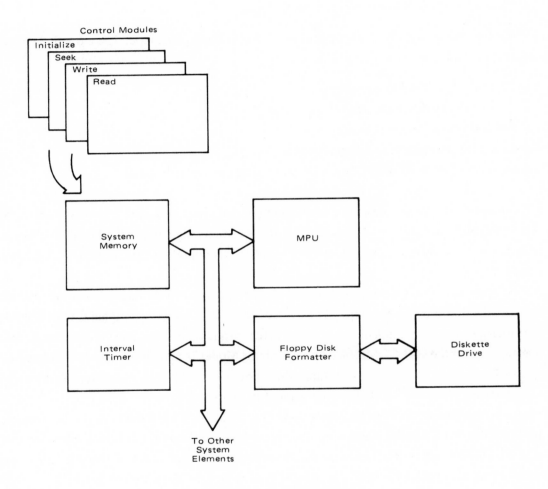

FIGURE 5-4.1-2. Floppy Disk System

5-4.2 OVERALL CONSIDERATIONS

The content of the blocks shown in Figure 5-4.1-2 is the subject of this section. However, before describing the system, it is of interest to discuss the tradeoffs involved in microprocessor-based floppy disk controllers. The decision to design a floppy disk controller using the M6800 system depends upon:

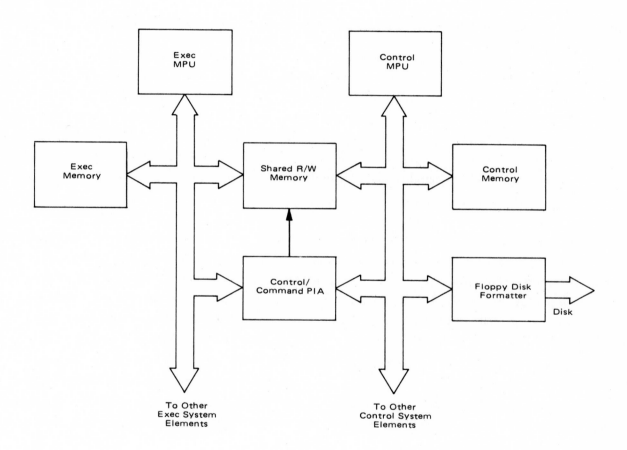

FIGURE 5-4.2-2. Multiple MPU System

(1) The way the disk system will be used in the overall system;

(2) The cost difference between the alternative design methods (such as hardwired logic); and,

(3) Both the short term and long term goals with respect to the use of the disk subsystem.

Due to the high data rates of the floppy disk, the microprocessor is, in effect, busy 100% of the time during data handling. This means no other microprocessor peripherals can be serviced while in a disk read or write operation. This is true provided that the transfer of data is controlled by the microprocessor and not via some type of Direct Memory Access (DMA) hardware.

Since no other peripherals can be serviced, interrupts generated by the other system elements must be disabled during disk read or write operations. Allowances must be made in the system design to permit 100% system dedication to floppy disk during read and write operations. This can be accomplished in three ways:

(1) If feasible, design the system such that other peripherals will not need service during floppy disk data transfer time. An example of this is a serial task system where each system task is executed in sequence with no overlap (Figure 5-4.2-1).

(2) Dedicate a microprocessor to handle peripherals which never interfere with disk operations and assign the disk to that microprocessor. This microprocessor would then be a peripheral control processor which is subservient to an executive processor (Figure 5-4.2-2). The executive processor could be another micro, a mini or even a large processor.

(3) Dedicate a microprocessor to the disk subsystem.

Alternatives (1) and (2) can represent significant cost savings over a hardwired logic disk controller because the M6800 hardware is shared by the other system peripherals. In alternative (3) the cost of the M6800 parts is directly attributable to the disk system. A dedicated full capability floppy disk subsystem would require a minimum of the MC6800 MPU, 1K of program storage (usually ROM), 256 bytes of RAM, two PIA's for formatter interface, one half a PIA for the interval timer, one half a PIA for interface to the external world, system clock logic, and approximately 40 SSI and MSI IC's for the formatter. This is compared to approximately 180 SSI and MSI IC's in a hardwired logic design of the controller plus the interface in the executive processor system. Depending on the system design goals, it is possible that the dedicated MPU based design can be more expensive than hardwired logic. Of course, the MPU based design is much more flexible and can be programmed to have a higher level of "intelligence" than its hardwired logic counterpart. If the system has a potential to grow (long term consideration), or if there is a need to design a flexible floppy disk system, a dedicated MPU based design would be a wise decision.

The design described here is limited to non-DMA design, that is, all data transfer is under program control via the MPU. The design discussion will cover methods of R/W head electro-mechanical control (seek operation), write, read, and a specific application called UPC lookup. In this manual, the various routines have not been completely integrated as an operating system, that is, the discussion does not completely link the routines together nor does it include error or malfunction processing.

Single diskette drive formatter logic is described in this section. Expansion of the subsystem to multiple drive control is dependent on the specific floppy disk drive's interface. For example, the Shugart SA 900 interface is designed for "radial" interconnection (Figure 5-4.2-3). In the "radial" interface, all interconnections are dedicated to specific drives.

The CAL-COMP 140 interface is designed for "daisy chain" interconnection (Figure 5-4.2-4). In

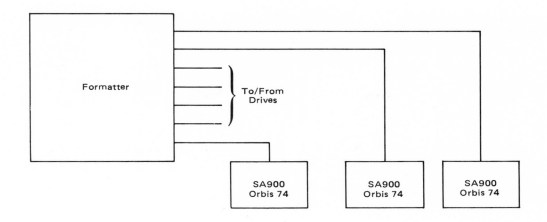

FIGURE 5-4.2-3. Radial Interface

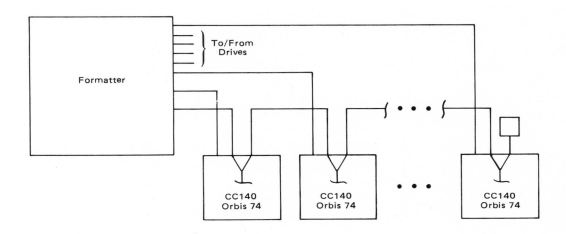

FIGURE 5-4.2-4. Daisy Chain Interface

the "daisy chain" configuration, some of the lines are shared and some are dedicated while the Orbis 74 allows for either configuration.

Each type of interface has its advantages. The "radial" interface isolates (buffers) each drive but the "daisy chain" interface requires less system hardware.

The single drive formatter described in this section is designed to interface to either the Shugart SA 900 ("radial") or the CALCOMP 140 ("Daisy chain") interface. The Orbis 74 will operate in both modes. On earlier Model 74's a minor modification must be made to generate the ERASE GATE signal. Because more than one model of diskette drive can be connected certain interface signals are controlled which may not be required by one or the other diskette drive.

The IBM 3740 recording format has been chosen for this design description. Appendix 5-4.D is a description of the recording formats commonly used in floppy disk applications. (Courtesy of Shugart Associates).

The limited scope of this Section is not intended to imply that the MC6800 can not be used in other floppy disk applications. The techniques are general enough to aid the systems designer in most floppy disk applications.

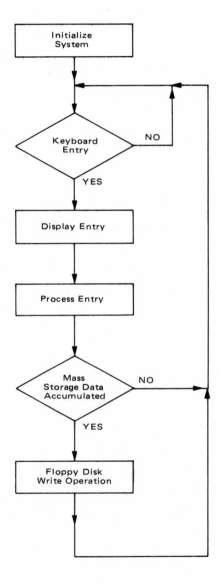

FIGURE 5-4.2-1. Example of a Serial Task System

5-4.3 SYSTEM HARDWARE/SOFTWARE INTERFACE

Figure 5-4.3-1 is a functional block diagram which shows all the signal lines between the floppy disk system and the PIAs. Note that two PIA's are used to control the disk system. The following is a brief description of the signals. More detailed descriptions from a programming view follow the brief descriptions.

PIA #1 is used primarily as a data buffer. Peripheral Register A is the WRITE CLOCK buffer register for write operations and the READ DATA gate for read operations. Peripheral Register B is the WRITE DATA buffer for write operations and is used as a status signal gate for read operations. The four read status signals which are routed to PIA #1, Peripheral Port B are:

PB0 + 1ST BIT
PB3 − CRC=00
PB6 − INDEX CLOCK MARK
PB7 − ID/DATA MARK

NOTE: The + signifies the signal is active in the high logic level when the − signifies low logic level is active.

PIA #1 peripheral ports A & B are used as both inputs (read operation) and outputs (write operation). Because all data field write operations must be preceded by a read ID field operation, the Direction Registers must be restored to all "0's" in preparation for a read operation.

CA1 and CA2 of PIA #1 are used to synchronize the timing of the program to the data rate during read or write operations. CA1 is a service request line. In the read operation a positive transition of the CA1 line indicates that a complete 8-bit byte has been assembled and is present at the A port. In the write operation a positive transition of CA1 means that the clock and data patterns in Peripheral Registers A & B have been moved to the external parallel-to-serial shift registers and the Peripheral Registers can now be updated.

Data synchronization is controlled by polling for Interrupt Flag #1. An active transition of the CA1 line causes Interrupt Flag #1 of Control Register A to be set to a "1". It takes the MPU a minimum of 8 cycles to recognize that the flag has been set (if the PIA is located in the extended address range $0100 to $FFFF). After the flag is recognized by the MPU, write or read data is transferred to or from the PIA. At a 1 MHz MPU clock rate, there is a minimum 8 microseconds delay between recognition of the service request and servicing the PIA.

The BYTE READY/BYTE REQUEST CA1 signal is one bit period in duration. It goes low at the beginning of the last serial bit time of a byte, then returns high at the beginning of the next serial byte (Figure 5-4.3-2). Due to the 8 microsecond program delay, the interrupt flag could be set at the beginning of the last bit period even though the data won't be ready until the end of that period. This lookahead technique can provide additional processing time in critical timing areas of the program.

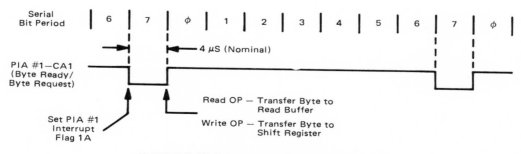

FIGURE 5-4.3-2. Byte Ready/Request Interface

5-119

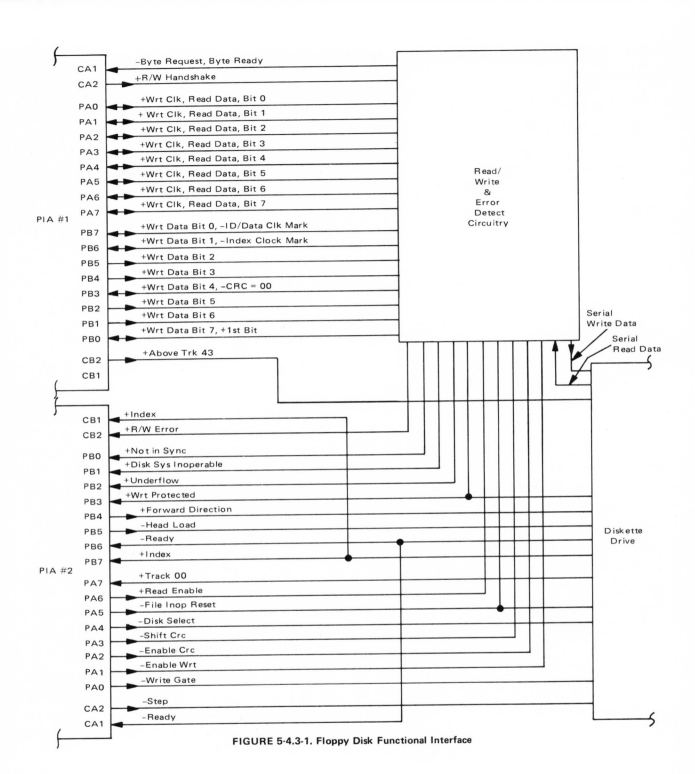

FIGURE 5-4.3-1. Floppy Disk Functional Interface

5-120

The CA2 line is the MPU's response to the disk system indicating that the service request at CA1 has been accepted. It is used to signal overrun errors for the read operation and underflow errors for the write operation. The CA1/CA2 operation of PIA #1 is a handshake mode of operation in which CA2 is set high on an active transition of CA1 and returned low by a MPU read instruction (LDA, BIT, etc).

CB2 of PIA #1 is a control signal called "ABOVE TRK 43" that is used only in write operations. When recording data on a diskette track greater than 43, this line is raised high. This signal is used by the CALCOMP 140 and Orbis 74 to control the write current amplitude on inner tracks in order to reduce the effects of a phenomena called "bit shift."[1]

PIA #2 is used as a control, status and interrupt interface. The control signals are:

PA0	−	WRITE GATE
PA1	−	ENABLE WRITE
PA2	−	ENABLE CRC
PA3	−	SHIFT CRC
PA4	−	DISK SELECT (CALCOMP 140 ONLY)
PA5	−	FILE INOP RESET
PA6	+	READ ENABLE
PB4	+	FORWARD DIRECTION
PB5	−	HEAD LOAD
CA2	−	STEP

The status signals are:

PA7	+	TRACK 00
PB0	+	NOT IN SYNC
PB1	+	DISK SYSTEM INOPERABLE
PB2	+	UNDERFLOW/OVERRUN
PB3	+	WRITE PROTECTED
PB6	−	READY
PB7	+	INDEX

The interrupt signals are:

CA1	−	READY
CB1	+	INDEX
CB2	+	R/W ERROR

The use of the control, status and interrupt signals is described with the appropriate operation.

The following is a general summary of PIA Control Register and Peripheral Register assignments in the floppy disk programs as seen by the operating programs. Refer to Section 3-4 of Chapter 3 for additional information on PIA operation.

---

[1]The bit density of the diskette increases as the radius of the track location decreases. This means that the magnetic flux reversal of the bit being written affects the bit that had just been written. The magnetic field generated by the R/W head is approximately proportional to the amount of current in the head. The ABOVE TRK 43 signal causes less current to pass through the R/W head thereby reducing the intensity of the magnetic field. This signal is not used by the Shugart SA 900 Diskette Drive.

FP1CRA —PIA #1, Control Register A; Address $8082;

b7   b0

| | | | | | |0|0|

Describes CA1 operation. CA1 is the input signal BYTE REQUEST for Write Operations and BYTE READY for Read Operations. Interrupt Flag #1 (Bit 7, FPICRA) is set to a ''1'' by a high-to-low transition of the BYTE REQUEST/BYTE READY signal. Interrupts to the MPU from Interrupt Flag #1 are disabled.

b7   b0

| | |1|0|0| | | |

Describes CA2 operation during data transfer programs. CA2 is the output signal R/W HANDSHAKE. When BYTE REQUEST/BYTE READY (CA1) makes a high-to-low transition, CA2 responds with a low-to-high transition. The CA2 output is restored low by a Read Peripheral Register A (DP1PRA) instruction such as:

    LDAA FP1PRA

or   BITB FP1PRA.

During data transfer, the program must execute a Read FP1PRA instruction before the next BYTE REQUEST/BYTE READY high-to-low transition at CA1 or an Underflow (WRITE OP)/Overrun (READ OP) error latch will be set.

b7   b0

| | |1|1|0| | | |

Describes CA2 operation when not transferring data. This Control Register bit configuration holds R/W Handshake (CA2) low when not transferring data to prevent the UNDERFLOW/OVERRUN latch from being set.

FP1PRA — PIA #1, Peripheral Register A; Address $8080;

Write Operation:

b7   b0

| WRITE CLOCK |

$0 < PA > 7$, Write Clock Buffer;

For a Write Operation, these PIA lines are defined as outputs. Peripheral Register A stores the clock pattern to be recorded on disk.

Read Operation:

b7   b0

| READ DATA | |

$0 < PA > 7$, Read Data;

For a read operation, these lines are defined as inputs. The PIA lines P0-P7 are the parallel read data lines.

FP1PRB — PIA #1, Peripheral Register B; Address $8081

Write Operation:

b7   b0

| | WRITE DATA | |

$0 < PB > 7$, Write Data Buffer;

For a write operation, these lines are defined as outputs. Peripheral Register B stores the data pattern to be recorded on disk.

Read Operation:

b7   b0

| 0 | 0 | | | 0 | | | 1 |

For a read operation, these lines are defined as inputs.

PB0, +1ST BIT;

b7   b0

| | | | | | | | 1 |

1ST BIT is a read status signal which latches when a "1" data bit has been detected in the serial read data. The 1ST BIT latch is enabled and cleared by the ENABLE CRC control signal.

b7   b0

| | | | | 0 | | | |

PB3, −CRC = 00;

CRC = 00 is a Read Data validity error check. CRC = 00 goes low for one byte period after a record has been read if there were no read errors detected.

b7   b0

| | 0 | | | | | | |

PB6, −INDEX CLOCK MARK;

INDEX CLOCK MARK goes low for one byte time during a read operation when the serial data stream contains $D7 in the clock bits. This unique pattern is recorded 46 bytes after the INDEX signal and is referred to as "Soft Index."

b7   b0

| 0 | | | | | | | |

PB7, −ID/DATA CLOCK MARK;

ID/DATA CLOCK MARK goes low for one byte time during a read operation when the special clock pattern $C7 is detected. When this signal occurs, it means the next BYTE READY signal (CA1) is for the first data byte of the record.

P1CRB — PIA #1, Control Register B; Address $8083;

b7   b0

| | | 1 | 1 | 1 | | | |

CB2 is used as an output to generate the ABOVE TRACK 43 control signal. When the disk track address is greater than 43, the CB2 line is set high.

b7   b0

| | | 1 | 1 | 0 | | | |

When the track address is less than 43, CB2 is restored low. During a write operation, the ABOVE TRACK 43 signal controls the write current amplitude.

b7   b0

| | | | | 1 | | |

Select PIA #1 Peripheral Register B;

b7   b0

| | | | | 0 | | |

Select PIA #1 Direction Register B

FP2CRA — PIA #2, Control Register A; Address $8042

b7   b0

| | | | | | 0 | 1 |

CA1 is programmed to generate an MPU interrupt when the diskette drive goes from a Not Ready to Ready status during initialization.

b7   b0

| | | | | | 1 | 1 |

When in a data transfer operation CA1 is programmed to generate an MPU Error Interrupt when the drive goes Not Ready.

b7   b0

| | | | | | 1 | 0 |

When not in a data transfer operation, the Ready Interrupt is disabled.

b7   b0

| | 1 | 0 | 1 | | | |

CA2 is the output control signal STEP. During a seek operation, the R/W Head is moved one track by pulsing the STEP signal (CA2). When in the seek operation, the step pulse is generated by reading PIA #2 Peripheral Register A (FP2PRA).

b7   b0

| | 1 | 1 | 1 | | | |

When not in the seek operation, the STEP signal is held high.

b7   b0

| | | | 1 | | |

Select PIA #2 Peripheral Register A;

b7   b0

| | | | 0 | | |

Select PIA #2 Direction Register A;

FP2PRA — PIA #2, Peripheral Register A; Address $8040;

b7   b0

| | | | | | | 0 |

PA0, −WRITE GATE (output);

WRITE GATE turns the diskette drive's write current on.

b7   b0

| | | | | | 0 | |

PA1, −ENABLE WRITE (output);

ENABLE WRITE switches the formatter hardware to write mode.

```
b7          b0
| | | | | |0| | |
```
PA2, −ENABLE CRC (output);

Write Operation:

ENABLE CRC gates the Polynomial CRC Generator on. ENABLE CRC is set low during the byte time in which the address mark is moved to the write buffer.

Read Operation:

When ENABLE CRC is set low, the read operation begins. The CRC Polynomial Generator is gated on automatically at 1st bit time. Raising ENABLE CRC high resets the Formatter read circuits.

```
b7          b0
| | | |0| | | |
```
PA3, −SHIFT CRC (output);

SHIFT CRC is used during write operation. SHIFT CRC is set low the byte time after the last data byte is moved to the write buffer. This causes the accumulated CRC bytes to be appended to the serial write data stream. SHIFT CRC must be held low for two byte times.

```
b7          b0
| | |0| | | | |
```
PA4, −DISK SELECT (output);

DISK SELECT enables the diskett drive's interface.

```
b7          b0
| |0| | | | | |
```
PA5, −FILE INOPERABLE RESET (output);

FILE INOPERABLE RESET clears any latched error conditions. If the error condition is "hard", i.e., present at time of reset, the error latch will not reset.

```
b7          b0
| |1| | | | | |
```
PA6, +READ ENABLE (output);

READ ENABLE enables the NOT IN SYNC error latch to be set in the event serial read data synchronization is lost. READ ENABLE is raised high during a read operation after the desired address mark is recognized by the program.

```
b7          b0
|1| | | | | | |
```
PA7, +TRACK 00 (input);

TRACK 00 is a diskette drive status signal which goes high when the R/W head is at Track 00.

FP2PRB — PIA #2, Peripheral Register B; Address $8041;

```
b7          b0
| | | | | | | |1|
```
PB0, +NOT IN SYNC (input);

NOT IN SYNC is an error latch signal which is set when a zero bit is detected in the clock pattern being read. The NOT IN SYNC error latch cannot be set when READ ENABLE is low.

b7   b0

| | | | | | |1| |

PB1, +DISK SYSTEM INOPERABLE (input);

DISK SYSTEM INOPERABLE is the logical OR of FILE INOPERABLE from the diskette drive and ENABLE WRITE if the drive WRITE PROTECTED status is active. This signal is an error latch output which means that the disk system is unsafe to use.

Note: Unsafe in this context means recorded data may be destroyed.

b7   b0

| | | | | |1| | |

PB2, +UNDERFLOW/OVERRUN (input);

UNDERFLOW/OVERRUN is an error latch which is set when the microprocessing system did not respond to the disk system BYTE REQUEST/BYTE READY in time. This indicates that data has been lost. The PIA #1 CA1 & CA2 handshake mode of operation govern the timing of this error condition.

b7   b0

| | | | |1| | | |

PB3, +WRITE PROTECTED (input);

WRITE PROTECTED is a diskette drive status signal which indicates that a write operation should not be attempted. An error condition will result if ENABLE WRITE or WRITE GATE is made active while the drive is write protected.

b7   b0

| | | |1| | | | |

PB4, +FORWARD DIRECTION (output);

When high, FORWARD DIRECTION will cause the R/W head to move toward the center (increasing track address) of the disk with a step pulse. When low, the R/W head will move away (toward TRACK 00) from the hub with a step pulse.

b7   b0

| | |0| | | | | |

PB5, −HEAD LOAD (output).

When low, the R/W head contacts the diskette recording surface.

b7   b0

| |0| | | | | | |

PB6, −READY (input).

READY is a diskette drive status signal which indicates that the drive is ready to be operated.

b7   b0

|1| | | | | | | |

PB6, +INDEX (input).

INDEX is a pulse of approximately 450 microseconds in duration which occurs once every revolution (167 milliseconds). INDEX indicates the beginning of a track.

FP2CRB — PIA #2, Control Register B. Address $8043.

b7   b0

						1	1

During write data operations, the leading edge of INDEX implies a WRITE ERROR.

b7   b0

						1	0

During the format write operation, the leading edge of INDEX is the initial timing reference. The INDEX interrupt is disabled in the format write and when not in a data write operation.

b7   b0

	0	0	1				

R/W ERROR interrupt is enabled during data transfer operation. R/W ERROR is the logical OR of NOT IN SYNC, DISK SYSTEM INOPERABLE and UNDERFLOW/OVERRUN. During data transfer operations, a low to high transition on CB2 generates an MPU interrupt. The interrupt program then aborts the data transfer operation.

b7   b0

	0	0	0				

When not in a data transfer operation, the interrupt is disabled.

b7   b0

					1		

Select PIA #2 Peripheral Register B.

b7   b0

					0		

Select PIA #2 Direction Register B.

5-4.4   DISK PROGRAM ROUTINE LINKING CONTROL

The programs listed in this section operate under a supervisory (host) program. In order to enable the host program to determine the operational status of the floppy disk, three bytes of RAM storage are maintained by the floppy disk drivers.

The first byte, called FVDELT, defines how far away the R/W head is from the desired track location (Table 5-4.4-1).

TRACK DELTA CODES

0XXXXXXX   HEAD NOT ON DESIRED TRACK

00000000   HEAD SETTLING ON DESIRED TRACK

11111111   SEEK NOT IN PROGRESS (I.E., COMPLETED OR ABORTED)

TABLE 5-4.4-1. 'FVDELT' Ram Location

The second byte (Figure 5-4.4-2) is the overall ending status of the last disk operation executed. Operation status is stored in RAM location FVABOR. The codes are used by the executive and error processing routines to determine the major state of the disk system. FVABOR is also tested in the interrupt poll routine to determine if an interrupt occurred during a floppy disk Read or Write operation. If an interrupt occurs during floppy disk read or write, the normal interrupt poll is not executed. Instead a special disk interrupt routine is executed that aborts the disk routine that was interrupted.

FVABOR	OPERATION CODE
00010000	SEEK IN PROGRESS
01010000	SEEK ABORTED
00010010	SEEK COMPLETED
00010001	RESTORE IN PROGRESS
01010010	RESTORE ABORTED
00010010	RESTORE COMPLETED
01111111	SEEK VERIFY ABORT
10001000	READ IN PROGRESS
01001000	READ ABORT BY PROGRAM
01101000	READ ABORT BY INTERRUPT
00001010	READ COMPLETE
10000100	WRITE IN PROGRESS
01000100	WRITE ABORT BY PROGRAM
01100100	WRITE ABORT BY INTERRUPT
00000110	WRITE COMPLETE
10001100	WRITE FORMAT IN PROGRESS
01001100	WRITE FORMAT ABORT BY PROGRAM
01101100	WRITE FORMAT ABORT BY INTERRUPT
00001110	WRITE FORMAT COMPLETE

TABLE 5-4.4-2. 'FVABOR' Ram Location

The third byte is the error status code. Any bit set to a "1" in this code indicates a disk system malfunction has occurred. When a disk subsystem error is detected, an error code which describes the cause of the error is stored in RAM location FVSTAT. (Table 5-4.4-3).

BIT POSITION	MEANING
BIT 0	READ OPERATION — NOT IN SYNC IN A READ OPERATION "NOT IN SYNC" MEANS THE DATA RECOVERY CIRCUITS ARE NOT SYNCHRONIZED TO THE SERIAL DATA.
BIT 1	DISK SYSTEM INOPERABLE THIS SIGNAL IS AN OR OF THE FOLLOWING ERROR CONDITIONS.
BIT 2	OVERRUN/UNDERFLOW
BIT 3	WRITE OPERATION — WRITE PROTECTED
BIT 4	READ OPERATION — CRC NOT EQUAL TO 00
BIT 5	NOT HEAD LOAD
BIT 6	NOT READY
BIT 7	WRITE OPERATION — INDEX

TABLE 5-4.4-3. 'FVSTAT' Ram Location

5-4.5 SEEK AND RESTORE OPERATIONS

The floppy disk records data on 77 circular tracks numbered 00 - 76. In order to access a certain record, the R/W head must first be locked in position at the track which contains that record. The operation which performs the head movement function is called a seek operation. For the floppy disk, a seek is executed by stepping the head one track at a time. The timing between steps is controlled from an interval timer.

The restore operation is similar to the seek operation. The main difference between seek and restore is that a restore operation always moves the R/W head to track 00. After the seek operation has completed, the only way to verify that the proper track has been accessed is to read the track address of the ID field. When track 00 is accessed, the diskette drive generates a TRACK 00 status signal from an electrical/mechanical sensor. The restore operation is completed when the TRACK 00 signal goes active.

Figure 5-4.5-1 is a partial system flow chart which shows how the floppy disk seek routines might integrate into the system program. Referring to the flow chart, entry into the disk routines is controlled by a host program — sometimes referred to as an executive program.

The seek function is divided into two parts, the SEEK INITIALIZATION routine and the INTER-RUPT DRIVEN SEEK routine.

The SEEK INITIALIZATION routine is entered by the host program. The routine calculates the number of tracks and direction the head must move, sets up the disk control signals, and generates the first interval timer interrupt to begin head movement.

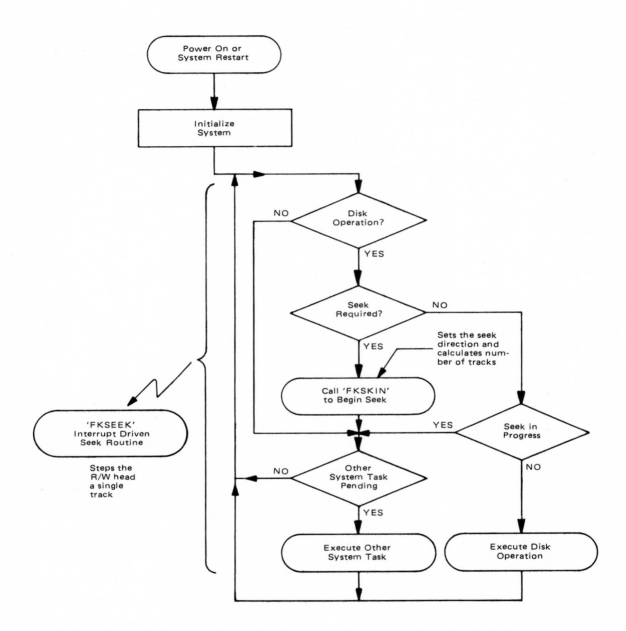

FIGURE 5-4.5-1. Typical Host/Floppy Disk Program Interaction

Head movement from track to track is controlled by the INTERRUPT DRIVEN SEEK program routine. This routine is interrupt driven by the interval timer. Because the actual seek is interrupt driven, the host program is free to execute other routines while the seek is in progress. The interval timer is set to 9.9 milliseconds for each step of the seek. However, the interrupt poll plus additional processing time causes the time between steps to be closer to 10 milliseconds. When the seek is completed, a seek complete indicator flag is set. It is the responsibility of the host program to test this flag before advancing to a disk read or write operation.

For seek and restore control, the MC6800 interfaces to the diskette drive via a PIA as shown in Figure 5-4.5-2. The two control signals DIRECTION and STEP govern head movement from track to track. The diskette drive specifications also require that the HEAD LOAD signal be active and WRITE GATE signal be inactive during head movement. The status signal, TRACK 00, is active when the head is located at the outermost track.

The STEP signal clocks a three bit left/right rotating shift register. The DIRECTION signal controls the direction of bit rotation in the shift register. The outputs of the shift register enable DC current through two of three windings of a three-phase stepper motor (Figure 5-4.5-2). The repetition rate of the STEP pulse is determined by the minimum time it takes the motor to rotate one-third of a turn.

The seek and restore operations are further clarified by the flow charts of Figures 5-4.5-3 & 5-4.5-4. The Assembly Listings are included as Figures 5-4.5-5 & 5-4.5-6.

A review of the seek initialization routine shows that the current track memory location "FVCTRK" is stored in positive binary notation for a forward seek and negative notation for a reverse seek. Then in the interrupt driven seek routine "FVCTRK" is incremented to update the current track location.

One of the primary reasons to use floppy disk as a storage media instead of another type of media such as tape cassette is improved data access time. By definition, access time include:

(a) seek-time — the time for the R/W head positioner to move from its present location to the newly specified location (10 milliseconds/track);

(b) settle time — the time for the positioner to settle onto the new track (10 milliseconds from last step pulse); and

(c) latency time — the time required for the diskette to rotate to the desired position (83.3 milliseconds, average).

The diskette spins at the fixed rate of 167 milliseconds per revolution. On the average, the data will be one half of a revolution — 83.3 milliseconds — away from the head. This is known as average latency time. While there is no way to decrease latency time of a disk system, there are ways to improve overall seek time.

Consider a system in which a single record must be accessed from a large number of records. An example of this type of system is a grocery store price lookup in a point-of-sale terminal. The lookup begins when a commodity with the UPC bar code imprinted on it is scanned. Then the resultant numerical UPC code is decoded to the floppy disk track number where the price data is recorded. A seek operation then moves the R/W head to that track.

The seek portion of data access time is the number of tracks times approximately 10 milliseconds. Accessing the track where the price information is located can be considered to be a random access seek. If the head were initially located at a central track in the price lookup area, then the average and maximum seek times would be minimized. This means that after each price lookup operation, a seek back to the central track would be initiated. Since a seek is interrupt driven, the operation is essentially transparent to the host program. Further, returning the head to a central track can be considered a low priority operation. If the host program

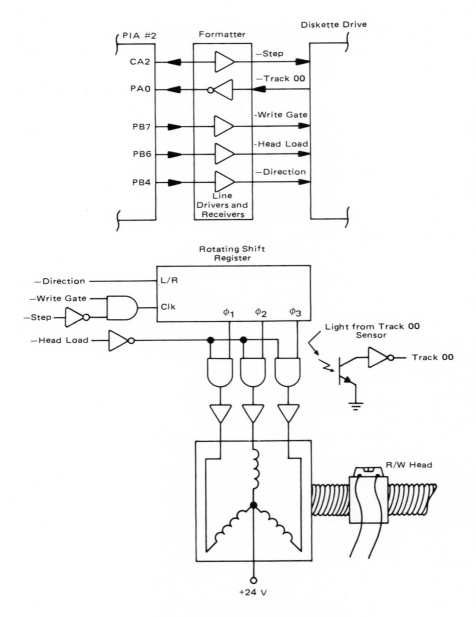

FIGURE 5-4.5-2. Seek/Restore Interface

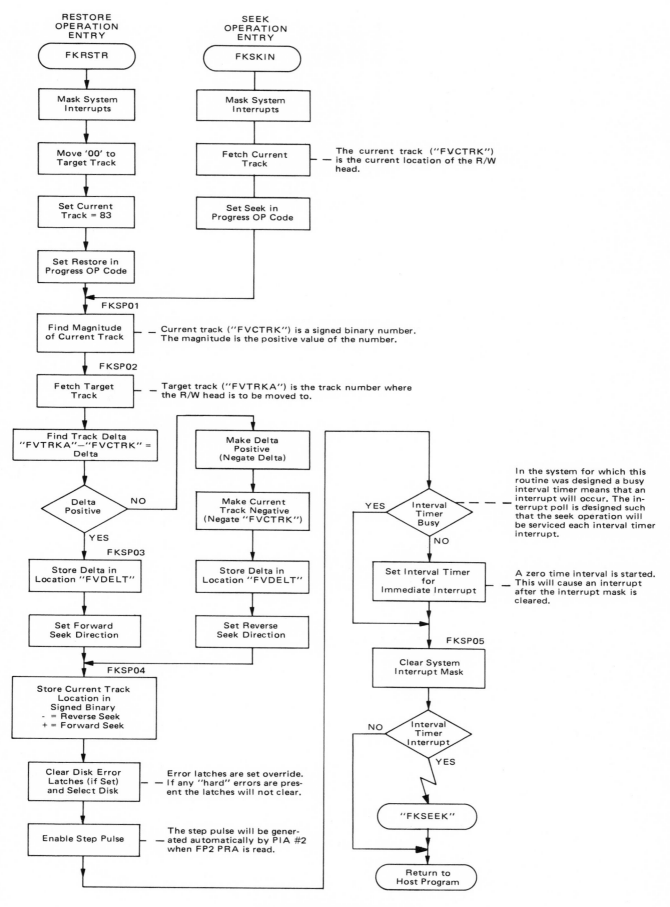

FIGURE 5-4.5-3. 'FKSKIN' Flow

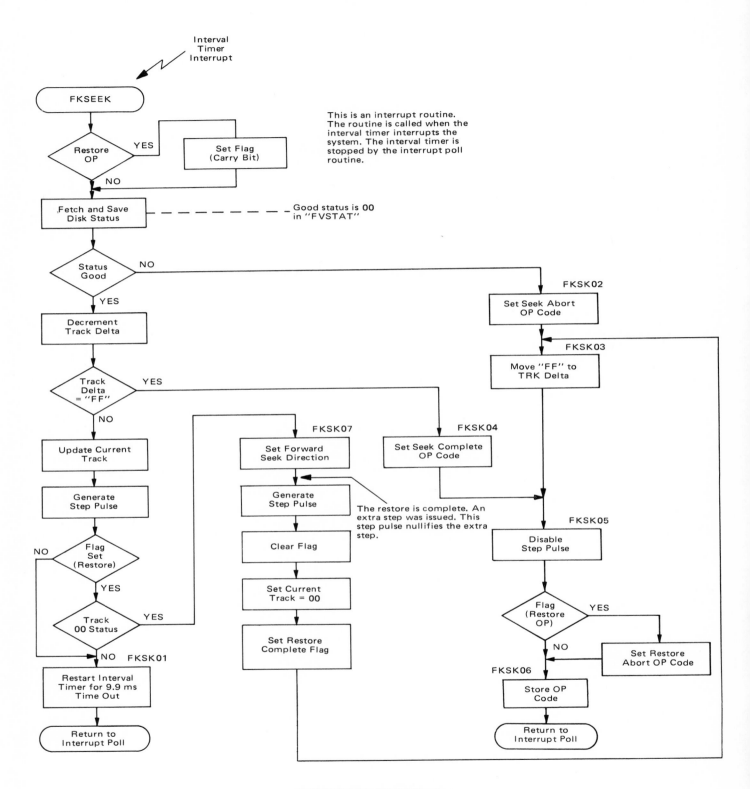

FIGURE 5-4.5-4. 'FKSEEK' Flow

```
02070                    *  SEEK/RESTORE PREPARATION ROUTINE


02090               *   THIS ROUTINE PREPARES THE DISKETTE DRIVE
02100               *  AND RAM LOCATIONS FOR A SEEK OR RESTORE
02110               *  OPERATION. FOR A RESTORE OPERATION THE CURRENT
02120               *  TRACK ADDRESS ("FVCTRK") IS PRESET TO 83 AND
02130               *  THE TARGET TRACK ADDRESS ("FVTRKA") IS
02140               *  CLEARED TO 00. FOR A SEEK OPERATION THE
02150               *  CURRENT TRACK VALUE IS DETERMINED BY THE LAST
02160               *  SEEK OR RESTORE OPERATION. THE TRACK DELTA
02170               *  ("FVDELT") IS CALCULATED BY SUBTRACTING THE
02180               *  CURRENT TRACK FROM THE TARGET TRACK AND
02190               *  CONVERTING THE SIGNED BINARY RESULT TO A
02200               *  POSITIVE BINARY NUMBER.

02220               *  THE DIRECTION OF THE SEEK IS DETERMINED BY
02230               *  SIGN OF THE TRACK DELTA BEFORE IT IS CONVERTED
02240               *  TO A POSITIVE BINARY NUMBER. IF THE SIGN IS
02250               *  NEGATIVE THE SEEK IS REVERSE (TOWARD TRK 00).

02270               *  TO INITIATE THE INTERRUPT DRIVEN SEEK ROUTINE
02280               *  A DUMMY INTERVAL TIMER INTERRUPT IS GENERATED
02290               *  IF THE TIMER IS NOT BUSY.  IF THE TIMER IS
02300               *  BUSY IT IS ASSUMED THAT THE INTERRUPT WILL
02310               *  OCCUR WHEN THE TIMER RUNS OUT, SO A DUMMY
02320               *  INTERVAL TIMER INTERRUPT IS NOT GENERATED.
02330               *  THUS INTERFERENCE WITH CONCURRENT OPERATIONS
02340               *  USING THE TIMER IS ELIMINATED, I.E. THE SEEK
02350               *  WILL NOT BEGIN UNTIL THE TIMER IS AVAILABLE.
```

TABLE 5-4.5-5. Seek/Restore Preparation Routine (Sheet 1 of 3)

```
02380                           * RESTORE OPERATION ENTRY = "FKRSTR"


02400  5061 0F        FKRSTR SEI                 MASK SYSTEM INTERRUPTS
02410  5062 7F 0004          CLR    FYTRKA       TARGET TRACK = 00
02420  5065 C6 53            LDA B  #83          PRELOAD ARTIFICIAL CURR TRK
02430  5067 86 11            LDA A  #%00010001   PRELOAD RESTORE OP CODE
02440  5069 20 05            BRA    FKSP01


02460                           * SEEK OPERATION ENTRY = "FKSKIN"


02480  506B 0F        FKSKIN SEI                 MASK SYSTEM INTERRUPTS
02490  506C D6 03            LDA B  FYCTRK       FETCH CURRENT TRACK
02500  506E 86 10            LDA A  #%00010000   PRELOAD SEEK OP CODE
02510  5070 97 00     FKSP01 STA A  FYABOR       STORE OP CODE
02520  5072 5D              TST B
02530  5073 2A 01           BPL    FKSP02        BRANCH IF "FYCTRK" POSITIVE
02540  5075 50              NEG B                MAKE "FYCTRK" POSITIVE

02560                           * SINCE "DYCTRK" IS IN SIGNED BINARY FORMAT IT
02570                           * IS NECESSARY TO CONVERT IT TO POSITIVE BEFORE
02580                           * CALCULATING THE TRACK DELTA.

02600  5076 96 04     FKSP02 LDA A  FYTRKA       FETCH TARGET TRACK
02610  5078 10              SBA                  CALCULATE TRACK DELTA
02620  5079 2A 07           BPL    FKSP03        BRANCH IF DELTA POSITIVE
02630  507B 40              NEG A                MAKE DELTA POSITIVE
02640  507C 50              NEG B                NEGATE CURRENT TRK ADDR.

02660                           * "FYCTRK" IS A NEGATIVE BINARY NUMBER IF THE
02670                           * SEEK IS REVERSE

02690  507D 97 02            STA A  FYDELT       STORE TRACK DELTA
02700  507F 4F              CLR A                PRELOAD REVERSE DIRECTION
02710  5080 20 04           BRA    FKSP04
02720  5082 97 02     FKSP03 STA A  FYDELT       STORE TRACK DELTA
02730  5084 86 10            LDA A  #%00010000   PRELOAD FORWARD DIRECT.
02740  5086 B7 8041   FKSP04 STA A  FP2PRB       SET DISK DIRECTION
02750  5089 D7 03            STA B  FYCTRK       STORE CURRENT TRK ADDRESS
02760  508B 8D 16            BSR    FKERST       RESET DISK ERROR LATCHES
02770  508D 86 24            LDA A  #%00100100
02780  508F B7 8042          STA A  FP2CRA       ENABLE STEP PULSE
02790  5092 B6 8010          LDA A  FP3PRA       FETCH TIMER STATUS
02800  5095 85 07            BIT A  #%00000111   MASK NON-TIMER STATUS
02810  5097 26 08            BNE    FKSP05       BRANCH IF TIMER BUSY
02820  5099 8A 05            ORA A  #C1US
02830  509B B7 8010          STA A  FP3PRA       -START INTERVAL TIMER
02840  509E 7F 8011          CLR    FP3PRB       -FOR IMMEDIATE INTERRUPT
02850  50A1 0E        FKSP05 CLI                 CLEAR SYSTEM INTERRUPT MASK
02860  50A2 39              RTS                  RETURN TO HOST PROGRAM
```

TABLE 5-4.5-5. Seek/Restore Preparation Routine (Sheet 2 of 3)

```
02890                         *   THIS ROUTINE RESETS THE DISKETTE DRIVE
02900                         * ERROR LATCHES AND SELECTS THE DRIVE.

02920 50A3 86 0F   FKERST LDA A   #%00001111
02930 50A5 B7 8040        STA A   FP2PRA    RESET ERROR LATCHES
02940 50A8 86 2F          LDA A   #%00101111
02950 50AA B7 8040        STA A   FP2PRA    REMOVE RESET & SELECT DRIVE
02960 50AD BC 8040        CPX     FP2PRA    CLEAR ERROR INTERRUPT FLAGS

02980                     * THE "CPX" INSTRUCTION PERFORMS A DUMMY READ
02990                     * TO "FP2PRA & FP2PRB" TO CLEAR THE PIA
03000                     * INTERRUPT FLAGS.

03020 50B0 39            RTS
```

TABLE 5-4.5-5. Seek/Restore Preparation Routine (Sheet 3 of 3)

```
00580                    *INTERRUPT DRIVEN SEEK/RESTORE ROUTINE

00600                    *   THIS ROUTINE EXECUTES A ONE TRACK STEP OF
00610                    * A SEEK OR RESTORE SEQUENCE. THE DISKETTE
00620                    * DRIVE MOVES THE HEAD ONE TRACK POSITION
00630                    * EACH TIME THE STEP SIGNAL IS PULSED.
00640                    * ENTRY INTO THIS ROUTINE IS GOVERNED BY
00650                    * INTERRUPTS FROM THE INTERVAL TIMER. THE
00660                    * TIMER IS PRESET TO 9.9 MILLISECONDS FOR
00670                    * EACH STEP.  THE NUMBER OF TRACKS THE HEAD
00680                    * MUST MOVE FOR A SEEK OPERATION IS STORED
00690                    * IN RAM LOCATION "FVDELT." FOR A RESTORE
00700                    * OPERATION "FVDELT" IS PRESET TO 83 TO INSURE
00710                    * THAT THE MAXIMUM NUMBER OF TRACKS (77) CAN
00720                    * BE STEPPED. WHEN THE SEEK OR RESTORE IS
00730                    * COMPLETED OR ABORTED "FVDELT" IS SET TO
00740                    * ALL ONES. WHILE THE SEEK IS IN PROGRESS
00750                    * BIT 7 OF "FVDELT" IS ZERO.

00770                    * RAM LOCATION "FVCTRK" CONTAINS THE CURRENT
00780                    * TRACK ADDRESS OF THE HEAD. THE VALUE
00790                    * "FVCTRK" IS IN SIGNED BINARY FORMAT.
00800                    * IF THE SEEK DIRECTION IS FORWARD
00810                    * (FROM TRACK 00) "FVCTRK" IS A POSITIVE
00820                    * BINARY NUMBER, I.E. BIT 7 IS ZERO. IF
00830                    * THE SEEK DIRECTION IS REVERSE (TOWARD
00840                    * TRACK 00) "FVCTRK" IS A NEGATIVE BINARY
00850                    * NUMBER, I.E. BIT 7 IS A ONE.

00870                    * DISK STATUS IS CHECKED EACH STEP. IF
00880                    * THE STATUS IS GOOD AND THE SEEK OR
00890                    * RESTORE IS NOT COMPLETE THE INTERVAL TIMER
00900                    * IS RESTARTED TO TIME OUT THE NEXT STEP.
00910                    * AN EXCEPTION TO THE ABOVE IS IF SEEK
00920                    * COMPLETE IS DETECTED ("FVDELT" BIT 7=1)
00930                    * DURING A RESTORE OPERATION THE TIMER IS NOT
00940                    * RESTARTED AND THE RESTORE OPERATION IS
00950                    * ABORTED. IF SEEK COMPLETE, RESTORE COMPLETE
00960                    * OR A STATUS ERROR IS DETECTED THE TIMER
00970                    * IS NOT RESTARTED.
```

TABLE 5-4.5-6. Interrupt Driven Seek/Restore Routine (Sheet 1 of 4)

```
00990                    * AN OPERATION/ABORT FLAG IS MAINTAINED
01000                    * IN RAM LOCATION "FYABOR" AS FOLLOWS:
01010                    *     0001000X  SEEK/RESTORE IN PROGRESS
01020                    *     0101000X  SEEK/RESTORE ABORTED
01030                    *     0001001X  SEEK/RESTORE COMPLETE
01040                    *       X=0  SEEK OPERATION
01050                    *       X=1  RESTORE OPERATION
```

TABLE 5-4.5-6. Interrupt Driven Seek/Restore Routine (Sheet 2 of 4)

```
01080 5000 96 00   FKSEEK LDA A   FYABOR      FETCH OP CODE
01090 5002 46              ROR A               IF RESTORE OP, CARRY=1
01100 5003 C6 62           LDA B   #%01100010   SET STATUS MASK
01110 5005 F4 8041         AND B   FP2PRB      FETCH MASKED STATUS
01120 5008 D7 01           STA B   FYSTAT      STORE ERROR STATUS
01130 500A 26 16           BNE     FKSK02      BRANCH IF ERROR

01150              * ERROR STATUS CHECKED:
01160              *    BIT 1 = DISK SYSTEM INOPERABLE
01170              *    BIT 5 = NOT HEAD LOAD
01180              *    BIT 6 = NOT READY

01200 500C 7A 0002         DEC     FYDELT      DECREMENT TRK DELTA
01210 500F 2B 19           BMI     FKSK04      BRANCH IF SEEK COMPLETE
01220 5011 7C 0003         INC     FYCTRK      UPDATE CURRENT TRK
01230 5014 B6 8040         LDA A   FP2PRA      FETCH CONTROL WORD

01250              * READING THE DISK CONTROL WORD FP2PRA
01260              * AUTOMATICALLY GENERATES THE STEP
01270              * PULSE.

01290 5017 24 02           BCC     FKSK01      BRANCH IF NOT RESTORE OP
01300 5019 2B 1D           BMI     FKSK07      BRANCH IF TRK 00

01320              * RESTORE OPERATION IS COMPLETE
01330              * WHEN TRACK 00 IS DETECTED.

01350 501B CE 0363  FKSK01 LDX     #S100US+99
01360 501E FF 8010         STX     FP3PRA      REARM TIMER FOR 9.9MS
01370 5021 39              RTS                 RETURN TO INTERRUPT POLL




01390              * ERROR DETECTED IN STATUS

01410 5022 86 50   FKSK02 LDA A   #%01010000   PRELOAD SEEK ABORT FLAG
01420 5024 C6 FF   FKSK03 LDA B   #$FF
01430 5026 D7 02          STA B   FYDELT      RESTORE TRK DELTA
01440 5028 20 02          BRA     FKSK05      GO TO EXIT PREPARATION
```

TABLE 5-4.5-6. Interrupt Driven Seek/Restore Routine (Sheet 3 of 4)

```
01470                          * SEEK COMPLETE DETECTED

01490 502A 86 12       FKSK04 LDA A  #%00010010   PRELOAD SEEK COMPL FLAG
01500 502C C6 3C       FKSK05 LDA B  #%00111100
01510 502E F7 8042            STA B  FP2CRA    DISABLE STEP PULSE
01520 5031 24 02              BCC    FKSK06    BRANCH IF NOT RESTORE
01530 5033 86 51              LDA A  #%01010001   PRELOAD RESTORE ABORT

01550                          * RESTORE OP IN PROGRESS IS INDICATED WHEN
01560                          * THE CARRY BIT IS SET. BECAUSE THE TRACK
01570                          * DELTA IS SET TO A HIGH VALUE (83) PRIOR
01580                          * TO BEGINNING A RESTORE OPERATION AN ERROR
01590                          * IS IMPLIED IF SEEK COMPLETE IS DETECTED.
01600                          * BEFORE TRACK 00 STATUS IS SENSED.
01610                          * ALSO THIS PATH IS TAKEN IF DISK STATUS IS
01620                          * BAD DURING A RESTORE OPERATION.

01640 5035 97 00       FKSK06 STA A  FYABOR    SET OP/ABORT FLAG WORD
01650 5037 39                 RTS              RETURN TO INTERRUPT POLL




01670                          * RESTORE OPERATION COMPLETE

01690 5038 86 10       FKSK07 LDA A  #%00010000
01700 503A B7 8041            STA A  FP2PRB    SET FORWARD DIRECTION
01710 503D B6 8040            LDA A  FP2PRA    GENERATE STEP PULSE

01730                          * THE FORWARD STEP IS USED TO RESTORE THE HEAD
01740                          * STEPPER MOTOR TO TRACK 00 PHASE.

01760 5040 0C                 CLC              CLEAR RESTORE OP FLAG
01770 5041 7F 0003            CLR    FYCTRK    SET CURRENT TRK TO 00
01780 5044 86 13              LDA A  #%00010011   RESTORE COMPLETE FLAG
01790 5046 20 DC              BRA    FKSK03    GO TO RESTORE EXIT PREP
```

TABLE 5-4.5-6. Interrupt Driven Seek/Restore Routine (Sheet 4 of 4)

EXAMPLE: SEEK FORWARD

CURRENT TRACK = 33   "FVCTRK" = 0010 0001
TARGET TRACK = 36   "FVTRKA" = 0010 0100
                            "FVDELT" = 0000 0011

VALUE AFTER INTERRUPT SERVICE

	INTERRUPT	"FVCTRK"	"FVDELT"
DUMMY =	#1	0010 0010	0000 0010
	#2	0010 0011	0000 0001
	#3	0010 0100	0000 0000
	#4	0010 0100	1111 1111

EXAMPLE: SEEK BACKWARD

CURRENT TRACK = 33   "FVCTRK" = 1101 1111
TARGET TRACK = 29   "FVTRKA" = 0001 1101
                            "FVDELT" = 0000 0100

VALUE AFTER INTERRUPT SERVICE

	INTERRUPT	"FVCTRK"	"FVDELT"
DUMMY =	#1	1110 0000	0000 0011
	#2	1110 0001	0000 0010
	#3	1110 0010	0000 0001
	#4	1110 0011	0000 0000
	#5	1110 0011	1111 1111

1110 0011 NEGATED = 0001 1101 = 29

TABLE 5-4.5-7. Seek Examples

must call or execute a critical time dependent operation during the return seek, the interval timer interrupt can be masked off at the PIA. This would prevent interference from the seek operation.

In some systems, it is desirable to issue a new seek before the last seek has completed. For example, a new price lookup may be issued while the head is returning to the central track. To account for this possibility, the SEEK INITIALIZATION routine masks system interrupts to take control of the RAM locations used by FKSEEK. (NOTE: In some systems, it may be more desirable to disable the interval timer interrupt and allow other system interrupts.) Also, before generating the first interval timer interrupt, it is determined whether or not the timer is being used. If the timer is busy, control is immediately returned to the host program and the seek is deferred. This extra processing insures that interval timer operation is not interfered with whether the timer is being used for the last step of the former seek operation or for some other purpose.

The safety circuits in the diskette drive should prevent destruction of data during head movement. Therefore, checking the disk status during seek may be considered unnecessary in some systems. If an error is detected by the FKSEEK routine, the seek operation aborts and an appropriate error flag is stored in RAM.

5-4.6   READ OPERATION

An IBM 3740 compatible floppy disk system records data at 250 K bits/second or 4 microseconds/bit. Because the serial data rate is too high for the MC6800 MPU to handle directly, a hardware/software tradeoff must be made.

Since the MC6800 is an 8-bit parallel processor, its reasonable to see if a program can be written to handle the data in 8 bit bytes. In order to do this the worst case byte data rate must be determined. The nominal data rate is $250 \div 8 = 31.25$ K bytes/second or 32 microseconds/byte.

Conceivably, the system could record (write) data with the disk running at one rotational speed tolerance, then try to read the data back with the diskette at the other tolerance extreme. This difference represents the worst case tolerance of the floppy disk read rate. Both the microprocessor program and the data recovery circuits must be capable of operating within the max/min extremes.

The worst case speed tolerances can be derived by assuming a 2.5% speed variation from nominal, both upward and downward. Then the worst case data rate extremes can be calculated as:

MAX	MIN

$$\frac{31.25(1 + .025)}{(1 - .025)} = 32.85\text{KB} \qquad \frac{31.25(1 - .025)}{(1 + .025)} = 29.73\text{KB}$$

$$= 30.44\mu\text{s/B} \qquad\qquad = 33.74\mu\text{s/B}$$

The above MAX/MIN read data rates account only for a $\pm$ 2.5% diskette speed variation. Other factors must also be considered. Variations in the microprocessor clock rate, MPU clock cycle stealing for dynamic memory refresh, and the disk write oscillator frequency variations are other factors which affect the systems ability to successfully read data.

The frequency deviations of the MPU clock and the write oscillator can be minimized by using stable oscillators. However, if cycle stealing is necessary to refresh dynamic memory the time lost for refresh must be accounted for in the programs which control the transfer of data.

For purposes of this design description, the $\pm$ 2.5% speed variation is conservative enough to account for small frequency deviations in the MPU clock and write oscillator. A complete analysis of the system including memory refresh time can be made using the techniques outlined in Section 2-3. The memory refresh can be treated mathematically as secondary peripheral service requests which must be serviced in an interlaced manner with floppy disk service requests. The analysis of the floppy disk service programs may be all that is necessary if the "time available" figure from the analysis ensures that there is sufficient time to refresh the memory. The data transfer routines in this section were analyzed using a one microsecond out of 50 (worst case) RAM memory refresh cycle.

Other important design requirements due to the worst case read data rate are data capture time and the ability of the data recovery system to remain locked to the bit data rate through the missing clocks of address marks. This requirement is further discussed in Section 5-4.6.2, Data Recovery.

In summary, the key to writing the read programs and designing the read circuits is to work within the framework of the worst case specifications of the entire system. The hardware and software development can not be treated separately if the optimum system is to be designed. The analytical tools techniques of Section 2-3 can be used to find the best hardware/software tradeoffs and prove the feasibility of the final design before it is committed to hardware. An example of the analysis is shown for the write operation in Section 5-4.7, Write Operation.

5-4.6.1 The Read Operation Interface

Figure 5-4.6.1-1 is a block diagram which shows the major formatter functions used in a read operation.

When ENABLE WRITE is not active, the formatter circuits are in the Read mode of operation. When WRITE GATE is not active to the selected diskette, the drive SERIAL READ DATA is present. The SERIAL READ DATA signal contains both clock and data information. This signal is routed to the Data and Clock Recovery block of Figure 5-4.6.1-1. The outputs of the recovery block are separated serial NRZ data, a clock that is synchronized to the data and serial NRZ clock information, and another clock that is synchronized to the recovered clock pattern. To prevent confusion with the term "clock" the synchronizing clock signals are referred to as DATA TIME and CLOCK TIME. The data recovery system is described in Section 5-4.6.2.

The Read Data Logic block (Figure 5.4.6.3-1) contains the serial to parallel shift register, a read data buffer register, the bit counter (used to determine the byte boundaries) and the CRC polynomial generator (used for detection of read errors). Detailed description of the Read Data Logic is in section 5.4.6.3.

The Read Clock Logic block of Figure 5-4.6.1-1 contains the clock shift register and the decode of the clock portion of the data, deleted data, ID and index address marks as shown in Figure 5-4.6.1-2. Another signal developed in this block is called IN SYNC. Since the clock pattern is all "1's" except during an address mark the first position of the clock shift register in Figure 5-4.6.1-2 should be high except at mark time. Therefore, once an address mark has been detected, a low out of the first shift register position means the data recovery system is not locked to the data rate. When this signal goes low during the data portion of an ID or Data Field the system is said to be not in sync.

The IN SYNC signal is routed to the Error Detect Logic block (Figure 5-4.6.1-3). This block contains error latches which when set generate an interrupt to the M6800 system.

The NOT IN SYNC latch is set when the IN SYNC signal goes low (as previously discussed) if the ENABLE READ signal from PIA #2 is high. The Read routine raises ENABLE READ after an address mark is detected.

The OVERRUN/UNDERFLOW latch is set when the Read routine does not respond to the last BYTE READY service request before new data overruns the data in the read buffer register. This operation was discussed in section 5-4.3.

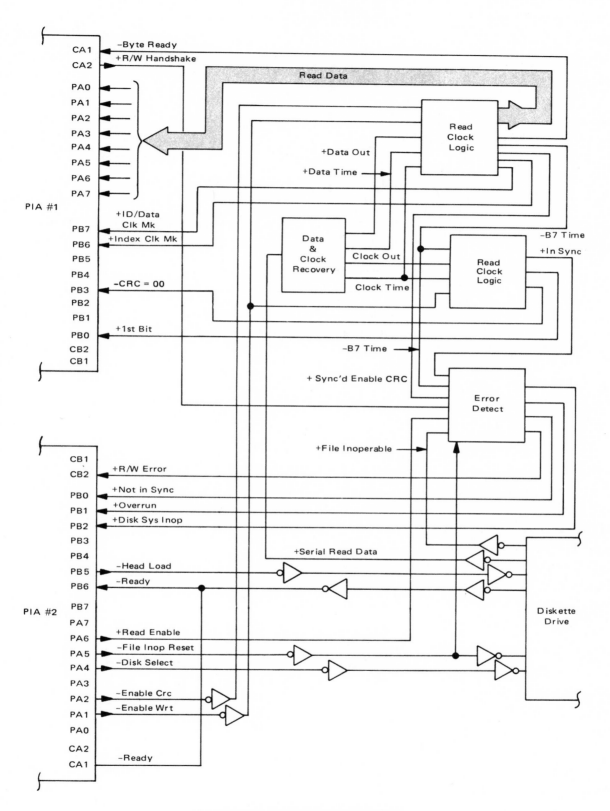

FIGURE 5-4.6.1-1. Read Operation Interface

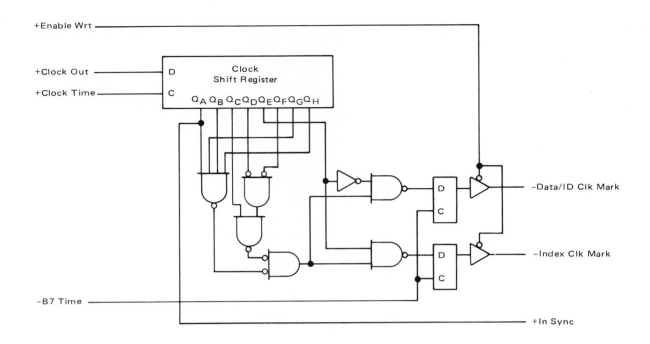

FIGURE 5-4.6.1-2. Read Clock Logic

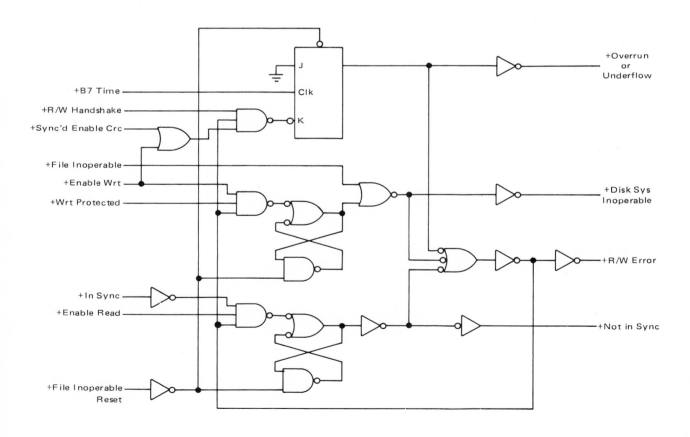

FIGURE 5-4.6.1-3. Error Detect Logic

5-146

The third error latch is OR'd with the diskette drive status signal FILE INOPERABLE (see appendix 5.4.B). The output signal is called DISK SYS INOPERABLE. Further discussion of this latch will be found in section 5-4.7.3, Write Operation Formatter Error Detect Logic.

Although the error programs are not included in this Manual, one observation of diagnostic aids is appropriate at this time. Many of the floppy disk system detectable malfunctions are of a "snowball" nature. That is, one malfunction causes the next. The error detect logic of Figure 5-4.6.1-3 inhibits secondary error trapping by blocking the set mechanisms of the error latches after any one of the error latches or FILE INOPERABLE goes active. This means that diagnostic programs would be able to detect the original cause of the malfunction.

5-4.6.2 **Data Recovery**

The data recovery system of Figure 5-4.6.2-1 is designed to generate a synchronized clock from the diskette drive's raw digitized data. Other goals of the design shown in Figure 5-4.6.2-1 are:

(1) Separate and recover *both* clock and data bits from the serial data stream.
(2) Generate a continuous clock even when clocks are missing, i.e., address marks.
(3) Track the long term changes in data rate but not the short term data rate changes.

The MC4044/4024 Phase Lock Loop (PLL) is the heart of the data recovery system. In this system the MC4024 Voltage Controlled Multivibrator (VCM) is phase and frequency locked to 16 times the data rate. Each record is preceded by a preamble of all zero's which the PLL uses to lock to the data rate. Mathematical analysis of the PLL system is not treated in this section, however, equations for the 4044/4024 PLL system are treated in Motorola's *Phase-Locked Loop Systems Data Book* and Application Note AN-535, *Phase-Locked Loop Design Fundamentals*. These publications may be obtained by writing to the Literature Distribution Center, Motorola Semiconductor Products Inc., P. O. Box 20912, Phoenix, Arizona 85036.

Figure 5-4.6.2-2 is a timing diagram of the data recovery system shown in Figure 5-4.6.2-1. This timing diagram is idealized for illustrative purposes. Raw digitized read data enters the system as a series of pulses. Each pulse toggles a flip-flop, forming the signal READ DATA ÷ 2. The output of the divide by two flip/flop is clocked into a two bit shift register by the MC4024 VCM's frequency output. Each time the divide by two flip/flop output switches, a pulse one VCM period in duration is generated from the exclusive OR gate tied to the output of the two bit shift register. Thus each pulse of serial read data generates a single pulse of one VCM period in duration.

The VCM frequency also clocks a counter called the window counter. When the VCM is locked to the serial data rate, the decoded output of the window counter generates a waveform called DATA TIME which is nominally high 10/16ths of a bit cell (count "6" to count "F")[1]. When the PLL system is in lock the clock bit occurs between count "6" and count "F". When DATA TIME is high, the pulse generated by the exclusive OR presets the window counter to "B." If the VCM is in perfect lock with the data as in Figure 5-4.6.2-2, the window counter is being advanced to "B" at the time of the exclusive OR pulse. If the VCM is running slower than the data rate, the window counter will be at a count less than "B." Or if the VCM is running faster than the window counter the count will be greater than "B." These cases are shown in Figures 5-4.6.2-3 and 5-4.6.2-4, respectively. Due to presetting of the window counter to "B" when DATA TIME is high, the data window (when DATA TIME is low) tracks the preceding clock bit. Likewise the R input to the MC4044 phase detector tracks the preceding clock bit.

---

[1]Hexadecimal notation is used in reference to the window counter. The counter has a range 0-15 in decimal which corresponds to 0-F in hexadecimal.

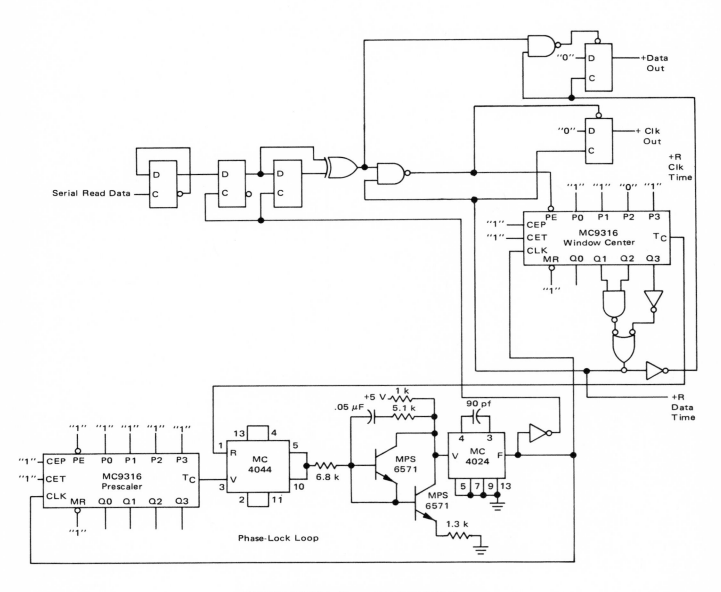

FIGURE 5-4.6.2-1. Floppy Disk IBM 3740 Format Data and Clock Recovery

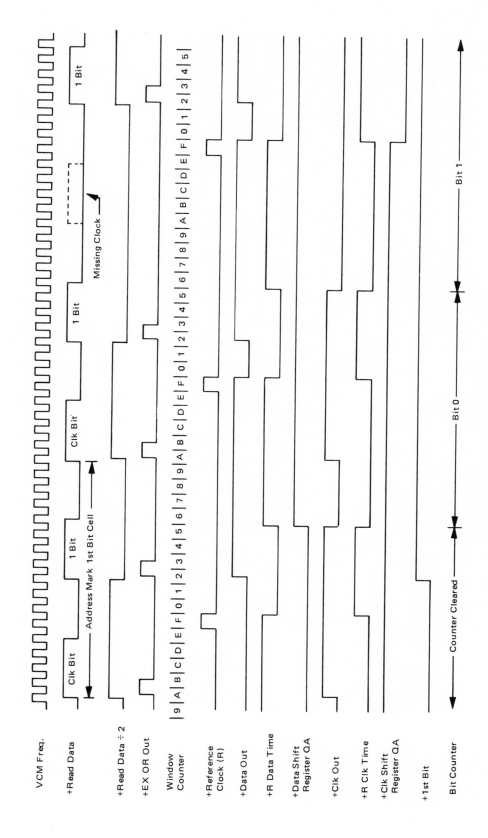

FIGURE 5-4.6.2-2: Data and Clock Recovery Timing

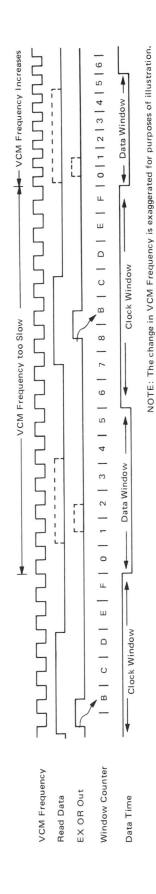

FIGURE 5.4.6.2-3. VCM Frequency Slower than Data Rate

NOTE: The change in VCM Frequency is exaggerated for purposes of illustration.

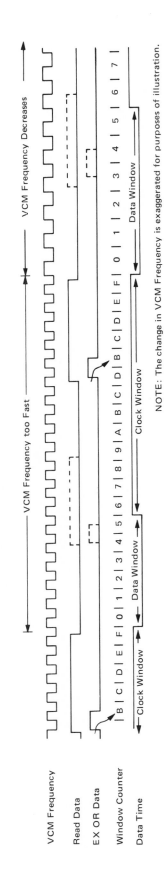

FIGURE 5.4.6.2-4. VCM Frequency Faster than Data Rate

NOTE: The change in VCM Frequency is exaggerated for purposes of illustration.

The PLL reference frequency (R input to MC4044) is the carry out of the window counter. The reference frequency of the system is beat against the VCM frequency divided by sixteen which is applied to the MC4044 V input. When the VCM frequency is too slow the window counter carry out occurs before the VCM ÷ 16 carry out. This results in a "pump up" error voltage signal which causes the voltage at the VCM input to rise and the VCM frequency to increase. Likewise, when the VCM frequency is too fast a "pump down" error voltage causes the frequency to decrease.

The "pump up" and "pump down" error voltages are filtered before being applied to the VCM input. The filter is designed to reduce the effects of the error voltage and gain long term stability. This results in a data recovery system tradeoff — long term stability causes long "capture time."

Long term stability is required to enable the system to remain in the lock frequency range when clock bits are missing, i.e., during address marks. When a missing clock is encountered in the serial data stream, the window counter is not preset to "B" when DATA TIME is high. Thus the window counter is not corrected. During this time the window counter acts like a flywheel generating the R input to the MC4044 from the carry out signal. The PLL system tends to drift upward in frequency. *But, because the active filter was designed with a low leakage the increase in frequency is kept within lock range.* The system in Figure 5-4.6.2-1 is designed to drift through three consecutive missing clock bits.

The tradeoff for long term stability is a longer capture time. Capture time refers to the amount of time it takes the PLL system to lock to the data rate from an out of lock condition. Figure 5-4.6.2-5 is a representation of the system response for worst case out of lock condition. The figure is a plot of the voltage input to the MC4024 VCM. At 4.1 volts the VCM output is at the nominal data frequency. Above 4.1 volts the VCM

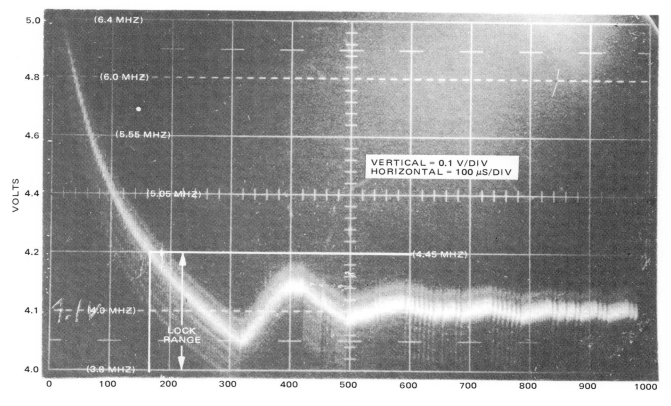

NOTE: "Grass" pulses are pump up/pump down error voltages.

FIGURE 5-4.6.2-5. PLL Response — Worst Case Capture Time

5-151

frequency is higher than nominal and below 4.1 volts the frequency is lower than nominal. Figure 5-4.6.2-6 is a plot of VCM frequency versus voltage input.

The design goal for the floppy disk was to insure that the capture time did not exceed six bytes. For the worst case read data rate, six byte times is approximately 180 μs (assuming 30 μs/byte worst case). Six byte times was chosen because it is the minimum write gate turn on time prior to a data record field.

Once the VCM is locked to the data rate, the window counter's 10/16 decode is used as a bit clock. In Figure 5-4.6.2-1, each pulse out of the exclusive OR when DATA TIME is high presets the clock out flip/flop. When DATA TIME is low, the pulse presets the data out flip/flop. On the rising edge of DATA TIME the content of the data out flip/flop is moved into the data shift register. The content of the clock out flip/flop is moved into the clock shift register on the falling edge of DATA TIME.

The data recovery signal is not gated on or off. During write the serial read data from the drive contains no data pulses. Therefore, the MC4024 VCM frequency tends to rise to approximately 6 MHZ. It is not necessary to get a nominal frequency into the R input of the MC4044 phase detector to keep the frequency down, but the designer should be aware of the 6 MHZ signal presence during write to ensure that noise is not picked up in the system.

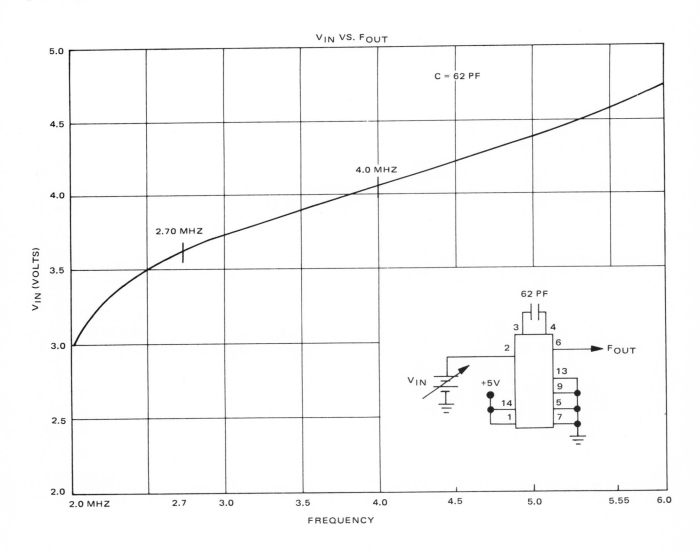

FIGURE 5-4.6.2-6 MC4024 Voltage vs. Frequency for Floppy Disk Data Recovery

5-4.6.3 Read Data Logic

Figure 5-4.6.3-1 is a logic diagram of the read data logic. Figure 5-4.6.3-2 is a timing diagram which shows the signal timing relationship when a read operation is begun.

The data recovery circuits are always active. When WRITE GATE is not active to the selected drive, SERIAL READ DATA is fed to the data recovery circuits. When the recovery circuits are locked to the incoming data, a clock called R DATA TIME which has a nominal period of 4 microseconds is fed to the Read Data Logic.

A read operation is begun when the program activates the signal ENABLE CRC (PA2 of PIA #2). ENABLE CRC removes the reset to the 1ST BIT latch and the bit counter control flip/flop. The 1ST BIT latch sets when the first "1" bit occurs on the DATA OUT line. The DATA OUT line goes high when a "1" bit is present. The bit counter control flip/flop is set at R DATA TIME after the first "1" bit is present on the DATA OUT line.

The MC8503 CRC polynomial generator is enabled when the 1ST BIT latch is set. The read error polynomial check begins to accumulate on the next R DATA TIME clock. The polynomial accumulates throughout the read operation. The routine keeps track of the number of bytes transferred and, at the end of the record, checks the CRC = 00 status. The CRC = 00 status signal is stable for one byte period (approx. 32 microseconds). Description of the CRC polynomial generator and its application to floppy disk may be found in the MC8503 data sheet and Appendix 5-4.D of this section of the applications manual.

The bit counter is held cleared until after the first "1" bit is clocked into the data shift register. Subsequent clocks then clock the bit counter. The bit counter is an eight bit counter which generates a pulse one bit period in duration once every eight bits.

The value of the count when the pulse is generated is 7. If ENABLE CRC was asserted during a gap the first "1" bit on DATA OUT is the first bit of an address mark byte. Then count 7 of the bit counter occurs at bit 7 time (B7 TIME) of each data byte. At the end of B7 TIME the parallel data is transferred from the shift register to a read data buffer register. The output of the read data buffer register is routed to PA0-PA7 of PIA #1. Data is moved into the M6800 system by executing an LDA instruction from Peripheral Register A of PIA #1.

B7 TIME is also BYTE READY time for a read operation. The leading edge of BYTE READY sets an interrupt flag in PIA #1 to indicate to the program that the read buffer has new data.

If ENABLE CRC was not asserted during a gap (i.e., in a record field) the first "1" bit will still set the 1ST BIT latch and start the bit counter as before. However, the first byte transferred to the read buffer register and the clock pattern decode (see Figure 5-4.6.1-2) will not indicate the presence of an address mark. In that case the program will remove ENABLE CRC to restore the Read Data Logic and then reassert ENABLE CRC to search for an address mark again. This process is repeated until the desired address mark is found or the read operation is aborted.

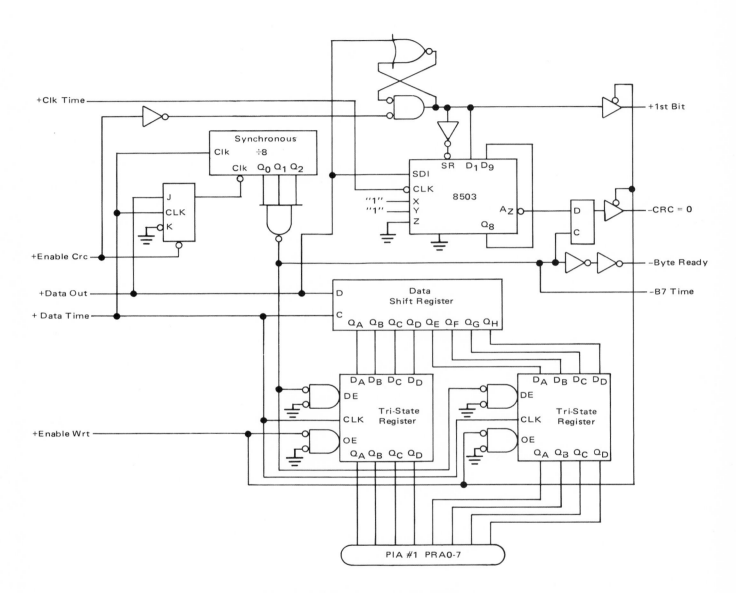

**FIGURE 5-4.6.3-1. Read Data Logic (Read Shift Register,
Read Buffer, Bit Counter and CRC Check)**

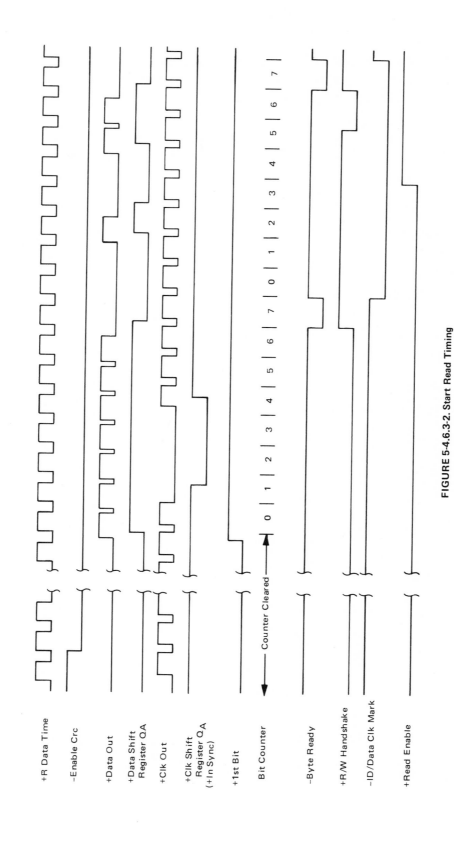

FIGURE 5-4.6.3-2. Start Read Timing

+R Data Time

−Enable Crc

+Data Out

+Data Shift
Register Q$_A$

+Clk Out

+Clk Shift
Register Q$_A$
(+In Sync)

+1st Bit

Bit Counter

−Byte Ready

+R/W Handshake

−ID/Data Clk Mark

+Read Enable

Counter Cleared

0 | 1 | 2 | 3 | 4 | 5 | 6 | 7 | 0 | 1 | 2 | 3 | 4 | 5 | 6 | 7 |

5-4.6.4 Read Operation Program Routine

The read operation is controlled by the routine listed in Figure 5-4.6.4-1. A flow chart of the program routine is shown in Figure 5-4.6.4-2. This routine is used to execute a general read operation of an ID or Data record. By "a general read operation" it is meant that the routine obtains the data from the diskette and stores the data in RAM. Other "non-general" types of read operations would perform more specific tasks than that stated above. An example of a "tailored" read operation is the UPC Lookup operation which is the subject of section 5-4.8.

A detailed explanation of the operation is included with the program listing. The following is an explanation of some of the less straight-forward characteristics of the read program.

The read program of Figure 5-4.6.4-1 can be used to execute either an ID field or data field read operation. The differences between an ID and data field read operation:

(1) The number of bytes in the field
    a. ID field = 7 bytes
    b. Data field (fixed format) = 131 bytes
(2) The data portion of the address mark
    a. ID field = $FE
    b. Data field = $FB
(3) The time interval over which the read operation should be completed.

These three differences are accounted for by requiring the following RAM locations to be initialized to desired values prior to execution of the read routine:

(1) Byte counter = "FVBCNT"
    a. ID field, "FVBCNT" = 256-4
    b. Data field, "FVBCNT" = 256-128
(2) Address mark = "FVDMRK"
    a. ID field, "FVDMRK" = $FE
    b. Data field, "FVDMRK" = $FB
(3) Interval time = "FVTIME"
    The value of FVTIME is dependent on the host system requirements.

Note that the byte counter, "FVBCNT," is shown as a number subtracted from 256. "256-4" is decimal notation of an 8-bit negative binary number which has the magnitude of 4.

First, the magnitude is the number of bytes between the address mark and the first CRC byte (see Appendix 5-4.D), i.e., the usable data portion of the physical record. The read program of Figure 5-4.6.4-1 does not use the byte counter for keeping track of the address mark byte and the two CRC bytes.

Second, the number of bytes is represented as a negative binary number to take advantage of MC6800 MPU characteristics. In eight bit signed binary numbers a negative value from -1 to -128 has the characteristic that the high order bit position (bit 7) is a "1". Because the maximum byte count for the usable data portion of the data field is 128, the byte counter will have a "1" in bit 7 throughout the data transfer. "FVBCNT" is the initial byte count which is loaded into accumulator B prior to entering the basic read loop of the read program. Then accumulator B is incremented each time a byte of data is transferred. When accumulator B rolls over to all zeros the basic read loop is exited.

```
06600                      * FLOPPY DISK READ ROUTINE

06620                      * THIS ROUTINE READS AND STORES ONE ID OR ONE
06630                      * DATA RECORD.

06650                      * THE READ DATA RATE IS GOVERNED PRIMARILY BY
06660                      * THE ROTATIONAL SPEED OF THE DISKETTE. THE
06670                      * WORST CASE READ DATA RATE IS DETERMINED BY
06680                      * ALLOWING FOR THE ACCUMULATION OF THE
06690                      * ROTATIONAL SPEED ERROR DURING THE WRITE
06700                      * OPERATION PLUS THE SPEED ERROR DURING THE READ
06710                      * OPERATION. THE DESIGN CRITERION OF THIS ROUTINE
06720                      * IS TO OPERATE AT MAX/MIN DATA RATES OF:
06730                      *      29.75 TO 34.25 MICROSECONDS/BYTE

06750                      * SYNCHRONIZATION OF PROGRAM TIMING TO THE READ
06760                      * DATA RATE IS ACCOMPLISHED BY WAITING UNTIL BYTE
06770                      * READY OCCURS. BYTE READY IS RECOGNIZED BY THE
06780                      * PROGRAM WHEN THE CA1 INPUT TO PIA #1 MAKES A
06790                      * HIGH TO LOW TRANSITION AND SETS BIT 7 OF
06800                      * CONTROL REGISTER A (INTERR FLAG #1) TO A ONE.
06810                      * THE INTERRUPT FLAG IS POLLED FOR BY THE PROGRAM.
06820                      * AFTER BYTE READY IS RECOGNIZED THE DATA IS
06830                      * FETCHED FROM THE PIA. MOVING THE DATA FROM
06840                      * THE PIA TO THE MPU AUTOMATICALLY CLEARS THE
06850                      * INTERRUPT FLAG.

06870                      * THE INTERVAL TIMER IS USED TO ABORT THE READ
06880                      * OPERATION IF THE READ IS NOT COMPLETED BEFORE
06890                      * THE TIME SPECIFIED IN "FYTIME" IS EXHAUSTED.
06900                      * OTHER ERROR INTERRUPTS INCLUDE:
06910                      *      A.   SYSTEM INOPERABLE
06920                      *      B.   OVERRUN
06930                      *      C.   NOT READY

06950                      * DATA IS STACKED INTO A BUFFER AREA
06960                      * SPECIFIED BY THE CONTENTS OF "FYDADR." WHEN
06970                      * THE READ OPERATION IS COMPLETE THE ADDRESS OF
06980                      * THE LAST DATA BYTE IS TRANSFERRED TO THE INDEX
06990                      * REGISTER.

07010                      * ACCUMULATOR B IS USED AS THE DATA BYTE COUNTER
07020                      * IN THE READ ROUTINE. THE INITIAL BYTE COUNT
07030                      * MUST BE STORED IN "FYBCNT." THIS VALUE IS
07040                      * REQUIRED TO BE IN NEGATIVE BINARY FORMAT.
07050                      * USING THE IBM 3740 FORMAT, THE DATA RECORD IS
07060                      * 128 BYTES. THEREFORE THE BYTE COUNTER WILL HAVE
07070                      * A "1" IN BIT 7 THROUGHOUT DATA TRANSFER. THE "1"
07080                      * IN BIT 7 ENABLES ACCUMULATOR B TO BE USED AS A
07090                      * BIT TEST MASK FOR BYTE READY AS WELL AS A BYTE
07100                      * COUNTER.
```

TABLE 5-4.6.4-1. Floppy Disk Read Routine (Sheet 1 of 5)

```
07120          * AN OPERATION/ABORT FLAG IS MAINTAINED IN RAM
07130          * LOCATION "FYABOR" AS FOLLOWS:
07140          *     10001000   READ OPERATION IN PROGRESS
07150          *     01001000   READ OPERATION ABORTED BY PROGRAM
07160          *     01101000   READ OPERATION ABORTED BY INTERRUPT
07170          *     00001010   READ OPERATION COMPLETE
```

TABLE 5-4.6.4-1. Floppy Disk Read Routine (Sheet 2 of 5)

```
07200 51E5 86 88    FKREAD LDA A  #%10001000   -PRESET READ IN
07210 51E7 97 00           STA A  FYABOR   ----PROGRESS OP CODE
07220 51E9 BD 50A3         JSR    FKERST

07240               * "FKERST" IS A DISK SYSTEM ERROR LATCH RESET
07250               * SUBROUTINE. THIS ROUTINE ALSO SELECTS THE
07260               * DISKETTE DRIVE AND CLEARS PIA #2 ERROR
07270               * INTERRUPT FLAGS.

07290 51EC 86 E6           LDA A  #%11100110   SET ERROR STATUS MASK
07300 51EE B4 8041         AND A  FP2PRB   FETCH MASKED STATUS
07310 51F1 26 74           BNE    FKRD09   BRANCH IF ERROR

07330               * ERROR STATUS CHECKED
07340               *    BIT 0 = NOT IN SYNC
07350               *    BIT 1 = DISK SYSTEM INOPERABLE
07360               *    BIT 2 = OVERRUN
07370               *    BIT 5 = NOT HEAD LOADED
07380               *    BIT 6 = NOT READY

07400 51F3 9F 08           STS    FYSVSP   SAVE STACK POINTER
07410 51F5 9E 07           LDS    FYDADR   POINT TO DATA STACK
07420 51F7 CE 3F1E         LDX    #$3F1E
07430 51FA FF 8042         STX    FP2CRA   ENABLE ERROR INTERRUPTS
07440 51FD DE 09           LDX    FYTIME   FETCH TIMER VARIABLE
07450 51FF FF 8010         STX    FP3PRA   START INTERVAL TIMER
07460 5202 CE 3E16         LDX    #3E16    PRELOAD DISABLE INTERRUPTS
07470 5205 D6 05           LDA B  FYBCNT   LOAD BYTE COUNTER
07480 5207 86 24           LDA A  #%00100100
07490 5209 B7 8082         STA A  FP1CRA   ENABLE R/W HANDSHAKE
07500 520C 86 2B    FKRD01 LDA A  #%00101011   PRELOAD ENABLE CRC
07510 520E F5 8080         BIT B  FP1PRA   CLR BYTE RDY INTERR FLAG
07520 5211 B7 8040         STA A  FP2PRA   ENABLE CRC

07540               * FOR A READ OPERATION "ENABLE CRC" ARMS THE
07550               * READ CIRCUITS TO SYNCHRONIZE TO THE FIRST
07560               * "1" DATA BIT DETECTED.

07580 5214 96 05           LDA A  FYDMRK   PRELOAD DATA MARK
07590 5216 76 8081  FKRD02 ROR    FP1PRB   MOVE 1ST BIT TO CARRY
07600 5219 24 FB           BCC    FKRD02   WAIT UNTIL 1ST BIT
07610 521B F5 8082  FKRD03 BIT B  FP1CRA
07620 521E 2A FB           BPL    FKRD03   WAIT FOR BYTE READY
07630 5220 B1 8080         CMP A  FP1PRA   COMPARE MARK PATTERN
07640 5223 26 05           BNE    FKRD04   BRANCH IF NOT MARK
07650 5225 F5 8081         BIT B  FP1PRB
07660 5228 2A 07           BPL    FKRD05   BRANCH IF ID/DATA MRK
07670 522A 86 2F    FKRD04 LDA A  #%00101111
07680 522C B7 8040         STA A  FP2PRA   DROP ENABLE CRC
07690 522F 20 DB           BRA    FKRD01   DO AGAIN,LOOK FOR 1ST BIT
```

TABLE 5-4.6.4-1. Floppy Disk Read Routine (Sheet 3 of 5)

```
07710 5231 86 6B    FKRD05 LDA A  #%01101011
07720 5233 B7 8040          STA A  FP2PRA    RAISE READ ENABLE

07740               * "READ ENABLE" ENABLES THE NOT IN SYNC
07750               * ERROR DETECTION LOGIC. "NOT IN SYNC" IS A
07760               * LATCHED ERROR SIGNAL WHICH IS SET WHEN THE
07770               * CLOCK RECOVERY CIRCUITS DO NOT
07780               * DETECT A "1" BIT AT CLOCK TIME AND "READ
07790               * ENABLE" IS SET.


07810               * THE FOLLOWING SERIES OF INSTRUCTIONS IS THE
07820               * BASIC READ LOOP

07840 5236 F5 8082  FKRD06 BIT B  FP1CRA
07850 5239 2A FB           BPL    FKRD06    WAIT FOR BYTE READY
07860 523B B6 8080         LDA A  FP1PRA    GET DATA & CLR INTERR FLAG
07870 523E 36              PSH A            STORE DATA
07880 523F 5C              INC B            UPDATE BYTE COUNTER
07890 5240 26 F4           BNE    FKRD06    LOOP UNTIL LAST BYTE


07910 5242 F1 8082  FKRD07 CMP B  FP1CRA
07920 5245 2B FB           BMI    FKRD07    WAIT FOR 1ST CRC BYTE RDY

07940               * ACCUMULATOR B IS 00 AT THIS TIME. THE "CMPB"
07950               * AND "BMI" INSTRUCTIONS TEST THE BYTE READY
07960               * INTERRUPT FLAG (FP1CRA, BIT 7). IF THE FLAG IS
07970               * A ""0" THE PROGRAM LOOPS BACK TO "FKRD07."

07990 5247 F5 8080         BIT B  FP1PRA    CLEAR INTERRUPT FLAG
08000 524A 86 2F           LDA A  #%00101111   PRELOAD STOP READ
08010 524C C6 08           LDA B  #%00001000   LOAD TST CRC MASK
08020 524E F1 8082  FKRD08 CMP B  FP1CRA
08030 5251 2B FB           BMI    FKRD08    WAIT FOR 2ND CRC BYTE
08040 5253 F4 8081         AND B  FP1PRB    FETCH CRC STATUS
08050 5256 B7 8040         STA A  FP2PRA    STOP READ
08060 5259 FF 8042         STX    FP2CRA    DISABLE INTERRUPTS
08070 525C 7F 8010         CLR    FP3PRA    STOP INTERVAL TIMER
08080 525F 86 34           LDA A  #%00110100
08090 5261 B7 8082         STA A  FP1CRA    TURN OFF R/W HANDSHAKE
08100 5264 30              TSX              XFER DATA POINTER TO INDEX
08110 5265 9E 09           LDS    FYSYSP    RESTORE STACK POINTER
```

TABLE 5-4.6.4-1. Floppy Disk Read Routine (Sheet 4 of 5)

```
08130  5267 D7 01    FKRD09 STA B    FYSTAT    STORE ERROR STATUS
08140  5269 27 02           BEQ      FKRD10    SKIP IF NO READ ERROR
08150  526B C6 42           LDA B    #%01000010   SET OP CODE MODIFIER
08160  526D C8 0A    FKRD10 EOR B    #%00001010   GENERATE ENDING OP CODE
08170  526F D7 00           STA B    FYABOR    STORE OP/ABORT CODE

08190                * THE OP/ABORT CODE IS GENERATED FROM THE
08200                * VALUE OF ACCUMULATOR B. IF ANY ERROR
08210                * STATUS IS PRESENT B IS NON ZERO. IN THAT CASE
08220                * THE OP CODE MODIFIER IS SET. IF NO ERROR STATUS
08230                * EXISTS ACCUMULATOR B IS ZERO. THEN:

08250                *              ERROR         NO ERROR
08260                *            --------        --------
08270                *    B =     01000010        00000000
08280                *  EOR B =   00001010        00001010
08290                *            --------        --------
08300                *  CODE =    01001000        00001010

08320  5271 39              RTS              RETURN TO HOST PROGRAM
```

TABLE 5-4.6.4-1. Floppy Disk Read Routine (Sheet 5 of 5)

The above is one use of accumulator B. Because accumulator B has a "1" in bit 7 throughout data transfer it can also be used as a bit test mask for the BYTE READY interrupt flag. Just prior to new data being available the BYTE READY signal sets bit 7 of PIA #1 control register A. To synchronize the program timing to the read data rate the following instruction sequence is used:

```
FKRD5   BIT B  FP1CRA
BPL     FKRD5
```

The BIT B instruction is an AND operation which affects only the condition code register bits. Since bit 7 of accumulator B is a "1", the sign bit (Bit N) of the condition code register is "1" if the BYTE READY interrupt flag is set and a "0" if the flag is not set. The BPL instruction will cause the program to loop until BYTE READY occurs.

This programming technique enables accumulator B to serve double duty — byte counter and interrupt flag test mask. Using this technique results in time savings during program execution. In contrast, another way to perform the same interrupt mask test is as follows:

```
FKRD5   TST    FP1CRA
BMI     FKRD5
```

Although this instruction sequence performs the same task as the prior sequence in the same number of control memory bytes, it takes two MPU cycles longer to execute. This means there would be two less cycles of time available at the beginning and the end of the basic read loop to do necessary housekeeping tasks.

The interval timer is used to abort a read operation if the program should hang up in an infinite loop due to hardware malfunction. When searching for a specific data record, the ID field must first be read to determine where the R/W head is relative to the desired data sector. In this case, the interval timer could be programmed to abort the read operation after the worst case time between any two ID Fields has elapsed. Or the timer could be set up to abort the operation after one revolution of the diskette. The choice of how to use an interval timer or even not to use a timer at all depends upon total system requirements.

If a variable interval timer is used, the abort time for a read data field operation after the proper sector has been located is the maximum time it should take to fully execute the read routine. Allowing for 17 bytes of prerecord gap plus 131 bytes of data field and interval timer accuracy, the timer should be initialized to:

$$17 + 131 = 148 \text{ byte times}$$
$$\text{or} \quad 148 \text{ bytes} \times 33.74 \text{ } \mu\text{s/BYTE(MAX)} + 1.0 \text{ ms} = 5.1 \text{ ms}$$

In the floppy disk routine, the data is stored in RAM using the PSH instruction. The stack pointer must be set up prior to executing the read program. One cautionary note should be made:

Because an error interrupt can occur any time the PIA interrupts are enabled, an additional seven bytes of storage must be allotted for the data storage area. This ensures that if an interrupt occurs there will be no over write of RAM data.

Figure 5-4.6.4-3 is a system flow chart which shows how the read program routine integrates into a typical M6800 system. The labels used are:

FKSKIN — Seek Initialization Routine
FKSEEK — Interrupt Driven Seek Routine
FKREAD — Read Routine
FKWRIT — Write Routine

Note that FKREAD is called by the supervisor in both floppy disk read and write operations. In Figure 5-4.6.4-3 all read and write operations are said to be sector oriented. That is, a read or write data operation begins only after the desired sector has been located. FKREAD is used to read ID records prior to reading or writing the data record. To determine if the desired sector has been located after a sector read operation, the data is pulled from the stack and compared against the desired track and sector address. If the track address does not match, it is assumed that a seek error has occurred. If the sector address does not match, the read ID is repeated until the proper sector is located.

Because the orientation of the R/W head is not known at the beginning of the sector search the worst case is assumed. That is, it is conceivable that one full diskette rotation is required before the desired sector is located. Prior to the first read ID record the interval timer variable is set to 180 milliseconds. Then after each ID record, is passed 6 milliseconds is subtracted from the interval timer variable. If there are no hardware malfunctions, 30 ID records will have been read before an interval timer interrupt aborts the search ID operation.

Each time a CRC error is encountered a read error counter is incremented. This information is used in error processing to determine if a retry should be attempted.

Note that if an error interrupt occurs, the program is not returned to by a RTI instruction. This is typical of time critical operations. Once a timing is lost due to a malfunction, the error processing routines determine what must be done to recover from the situation.

5-4.7 WRITE OPERATION

An IBM 3740 compatible floppy disk system records data at 250 K bits/second or 4 microseconds/ bit. As in the read operation, the serial data rate is too fast for the MC6800 system to handle. So the formatter logic performs the function of converting the 8-bit parallel write data to serial data to be recorded on the diskette.

The write data rate is not subject to the rotational speed variations of the diskette since it is controlled by a fixed write oscillator (1.0 MHz). Therefore, the variations in write data rate are a function of oscillator frequency specifications.

Because the write frequency range is small, the MC6800 system clock frequency specifications must also be considered in calculating program timing requirements for the write operation. One way to minimize variations is to use the MC6800 1.0 MHz oscillator as the floppy disk system's write oscillator. In this case theMC6800 system and floppy disk system are synchronized and the net frequency error for a write operation is zero. Then all timing can be calculated in MC6800 cycles where 32 cycles is equal to one byte. The total system is synchronous as long as there is no cycle stealing from the MPU as is the case when dynamic RAM is used in system memory. In a synchronous system, the write program can be optimized by taking advantage of the fact that all timing can be calculated in terms of cycles. This case will not be documented in this Section.

The more general case is when the write oscillator is separate from the MC6800 system clock or when the oscillators are common but dynamic RAM memory refresh steals MPU cycles. These are examples of asynchronous control of the floppy disk. The programs and hardware described in this section are designed to operate under these conditions.

Three factors affect program timing:

(1) Write Data Rate

(2) MC6800 Clock Rate

(3) Memory Refresh Rate

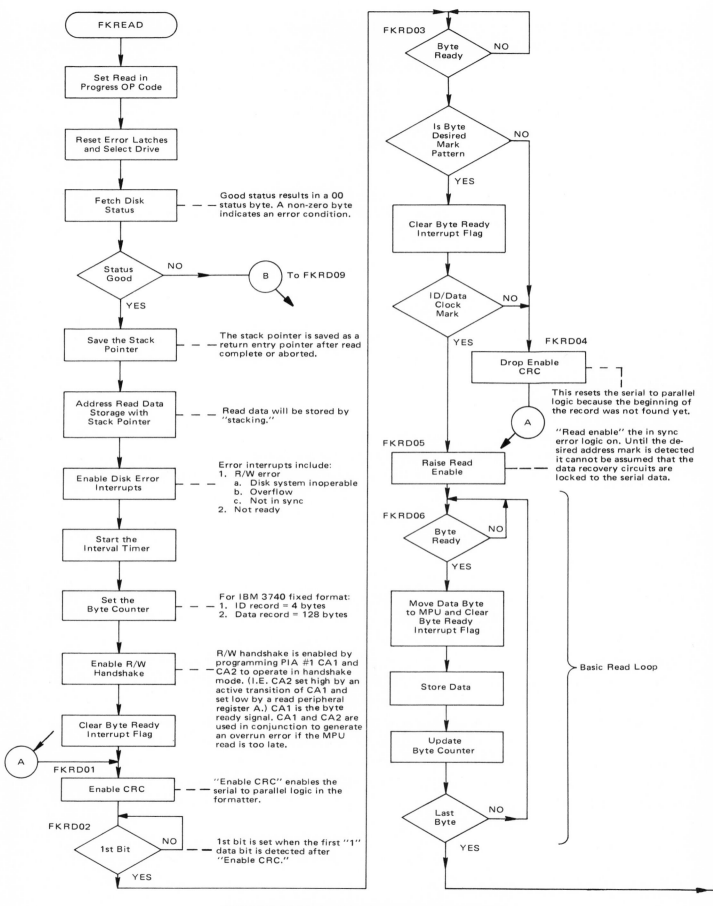

FIGURE 5-4.6.4-2: Read Routine Flow Chart (Sheet 1 of 2)

5-164

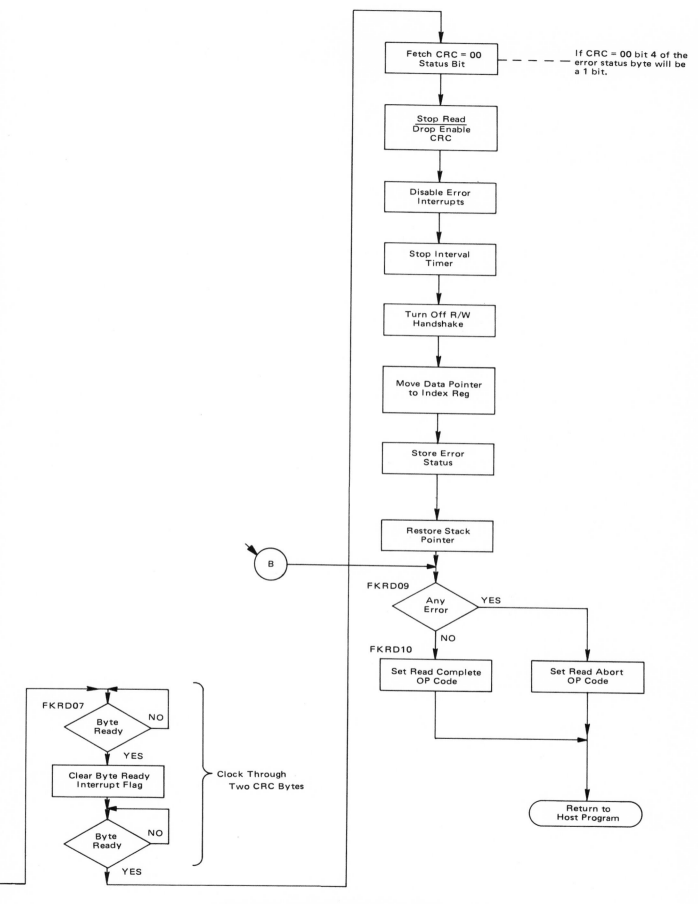

FIGURE 5-4.6.4-2: Read Routine Flow Chart (Sheet 2 of 2)

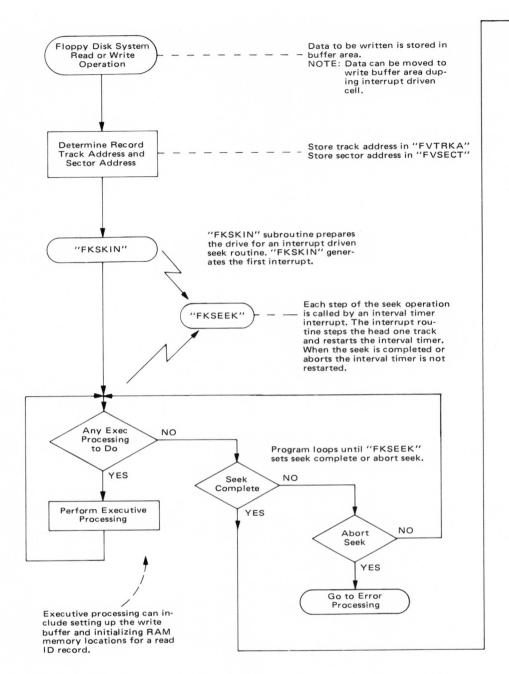

Floppy Disk System
Read or Write
Operation — — — — — — — Data to be written is stored in
buffer area.
NOTE: Data can be moved to
write buffer area dup-
ing interrupt driven
cell.

Determine Record
Track Address and
Sector Address — — — — — — Store track address in "FVTRKA"
Store sector address in "FVSECT"

"FKSKIN" — "FKSKIN" subroutine prepares
the drive for an interrupt driven
seek routine. "FKSKIN" generates the first interrupt.

"FKSEEK" — — Each step of the seek operation
is called by an interval timer
interrupt. The interrupt routine steps the head one track
and restarts the interval timer.
When the seek is completed or
aborts the interval timer is not
restarted.

Any Exec
Processing
to Do — NO

YES

Perform Executive
Processing

Seek
Complete — NO

YES

Program loops until "FKSEEK"
sets seek complete or abort seek.

Abort
Seek — NO

YES

Go to Error
Processing

Executive processing can include setting up the write
buffer and initializing RAM
memory locations for a read
ID record.

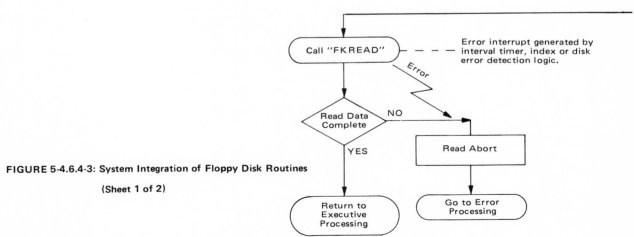

Call "FKREAD" — — — Error interrupt generated by
interval timer, index or disk
error detection logic.

Error

Read Data
Complete — NO

YES

Read Abort

FIGURE 5-4.6.4-3: System Integration of Floppy Disk Routines

(Sheet 1 of 2)

Return to
Executive
Processing

Go to Error
Processing

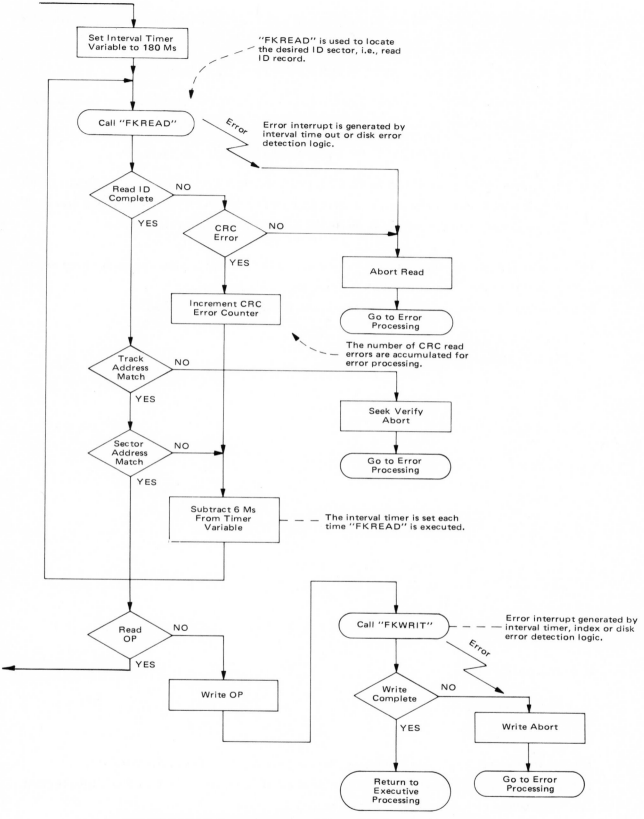

FIGURE 5-4.6.4-3: System Integration of Floppy Disk Routines (Sheet 2 of 2)

The following labels appear within the flowchart:

Set Interval Timer Variable to 180 Ms

"FKREAD" is used to locate the desired ID sector, i.e., read ID record.

Call "FKREAD"

Error

Error interrupt is generated by interval time out or disk error detection logic.

Read ID Complete — NO / YES

CRC Error — NO / YES

Abort Read

Go to Error Processing

Increment CRC Error Counter

The number of CRC read errors are accumulated for error processing.

Track Address Match — NO / YES

Seek Verify Abort

Go to Error Processing

Sector Address Match — NO / YES

Subtract 6 Ms From Timer Variable

The interval timer is set each time "FKREAD" is executed.

Read OP — NO / YES

Write OP

Call "FKWRIT"

Error interrupt generated by interval timer, index or disk error detection logic.

Error

Write Complete — NO / YES

Write Abort

Return to Executive Processing

Go to Error Processing

(1) Assume that the floppy disk write oscillator is accurate to 0.1%. Then the worst case write data rate extends over:

$$31.968\mu s/\text{BYTE} \leqslant \text{WRITE RATE} \leqslant 32.032\mu s/\text{BYTE}$$

(2) Assume that the MC6800 write oscillator is also accurate to 0.1%. Then the worst case MC6800 clock rate extends over:

$$0.999\mu s/\text{cycle} \leqslant \text{CLOCK RATE} \leqslant 1.001\mu s/\text{cycle}$$

(3) Finally assume the dynamic memory refresh steals one clock cycle out of 50 (for a memory with 32 cycle refresh this corresponds to a memory refresh rate of $32 \times 50 = 1.6$ ms at a $1\mu s$ clock rate). Dynamic memory refresh is discussed is Section 4-2.5.1 of this manual.

The memory refresh and write rate can be treated as a two service request system for purposes of calculations. Explanation of this type of calculation is the subject of Section 2-3.

In the maximum worst case memory refresh uses $1.001\mu s$ out of $50.05\mu s$.

Let $T20 = 49.95\mu s$

$\quad\quad T21 = \quad .999\mu s$

For the floppy disk

$\quad\quad T10 = 31.968\mu s$

From Section 2-3.

$$\frac{T11}{T10} + \frac{T21}{T20} \leqslant 1$$

$$\frac{T11}{31.968} + \frac{1}{50} \leqslant 1 \quad \text{NOTE:} \quad \frac{.999}{49.95} = \frac{1.001}{50.05} = \frac{1}{50}$$

$$T11 \leqslant 31.328\mu s$$

at $1.001\mu s/\text{MPU Cycle}$

$$\frac{31.328}{1.001} \leqslant 31.297 \text{ MPU cycles/byte}$$

This means that the write data processing must not exceed 31 MPU cycles per byte.

The preceding analysis shows the effect of system specifications on the floppy disk write program. The write data loop section of the program must not exceed 31 cycles.

Suppose, however, the dynamic refresh rate requirement was one out of 32 MC6800 clocks for a memory with 64 cycles refresh this corresponds to a refresh rate of 32 x 64 = 2.048 ms at a $1\mu s$ clock rate. The analysis in this case shows:

$$T11 \leqslant 30.969$$

or in terms of MPU cycles:

30.93 MPU cycles/byte

This means that, given these specifications, a write data loop of 30 cycles is maximum. In this case a 31 cycle write data loop can not be guaranteed to work.

The final case to be considered is:

(a) The write oscillator is derived from the 1 MHz MPU clock

(b) The dynamic refresh is one out of 32 MPU cycles (worst case).

In this case the data rate tolerance is the same as the MPU clock tolerance. If the clock tolerance is 1.0% then the write data rate range is:

$$31.68\mu s/\text{Byte} \leqslant \text{WRITE RATE} \leqslant 32.32\mu s/\text{Byte}$$

From section 2-3.

$$\frac{T11}{32} + \frac{1}{32} = 1$$

$$T11 = 31.3 \text{ MPU cycles}$$

Because the clock sources are common the tolerances are cancelling. The resultant maximum execution time can be written in MPU cycles.

Other requirements outlined in Section 2-3, must also be met to ensure successful operation. As in the case of the Read Operation in Section 5-4.6, the key to programming and designing the data handling hardware is to work within the framework of the worst case specifications of the system — both the MPU and the floppy disk, as well as any other system components (i.e. dynamic memory).

5-4.7.1 The Write Operation Interface

Figure 5-4.7.1-1 is a block diagram which shows the major formatter functions used in a write operation.

In a write operation, PIA #1 is programmed as an output port. Both the clock pattern and data pattern are supplied by the MC6800 system.

Before beginning the write operation, the ABOVE TRK 43 signal is set or cleared by the program. If the program determines that the track location is greater than 43 the signal is raised high. ABOVE TRK 43 is used by some models of diskette drives to control the write current on inner tracks.

A write operation is begun by making ENABLE WRT active to the formatter. This signal conditions the formatter circuits to begin accepting data and clock information from PIA #1. the ENABLE WRT signal also permits the BYTE REQUEST to pulse the CA1 input of PIA #1 once every eight bit times.

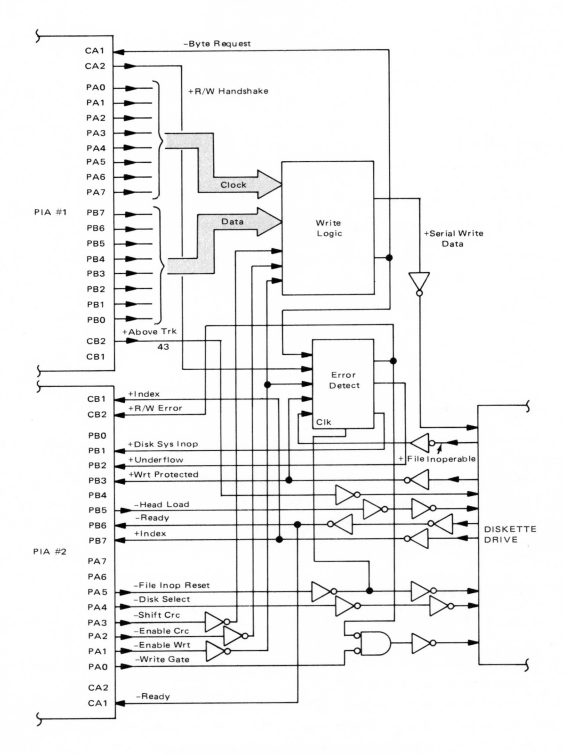

FIGURE 5-4.7.1-1. Write Operation Interface

Serial data is gated into the diskette drive when WRITE GATE is made active.

In a write operation, a gap of all zeros is written in accordance with the IBM 3740 format. Then an address mark is written with a special clock pattern. The address mark is followed by 128 bytes of data (data field) or a 4 bytes of data. (ID field) and 2 CRC bytes.

ENABLE CRC is made active by the program at address mark time.

After the last byte of data has been transferred by the program, the SHIFT CRC is made active. SHIFT CRC is dropped two byte times after it is raised. This causes the 2 byte CRC code to be appended to the data record.

One byte time after the 2nd CRC byte, all the write control lines are dropped. The sequence diagram of the write control signals is shown in Figure 5-4.7.1-2.

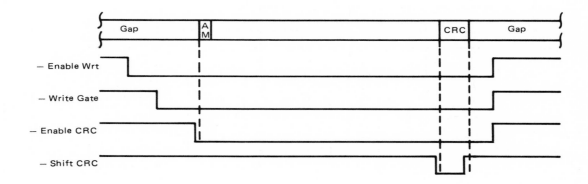

FIGURE 5-4.7.1-2. Write Control Signal Sequence

Other control signals required to be active for a write operation are DISK SELECT (required for some models of Diskette Drives) and HEAD LOAD.

The FILE INOP reset is used to clear any error conditions detected by the logic.

The operation of CA1 & CA2 of PIA #1 (BYTE REQUEST & R/W HANDSHAKE) is described in Section 5-4.3.

The status signals which describe the operating condition of the floppy disk system during the write operation are also described in Section 5-4.3.

5-4.7.2 Formatter Write Logic

The formatter's write logic is shown in Figure 5-4.7.2-1. Timing diagrams for the beginning and ending of a write operation are shown in Figures 5-4.7.2-2 and 5-4.7.2-3.

ENABLE WRT enables the write logic by removing the reset to the bit counter, enabling the parallel load to the clock and data shift registers, and removing the reset to the serial data flip/flop. The write oscillator advances the bit counter and shifts the shift registers every $4\mu s$. At bit counter 7 time the shift registers are loaded with PIA #1 data. Note that the clock shift register and data shift register are 180° out of phase. The data shift register is loaded on the trailing edge of bit 7 time (or leading edge of bit 0 time) and the clock shift register is loaded in the middle of bit 7 time.

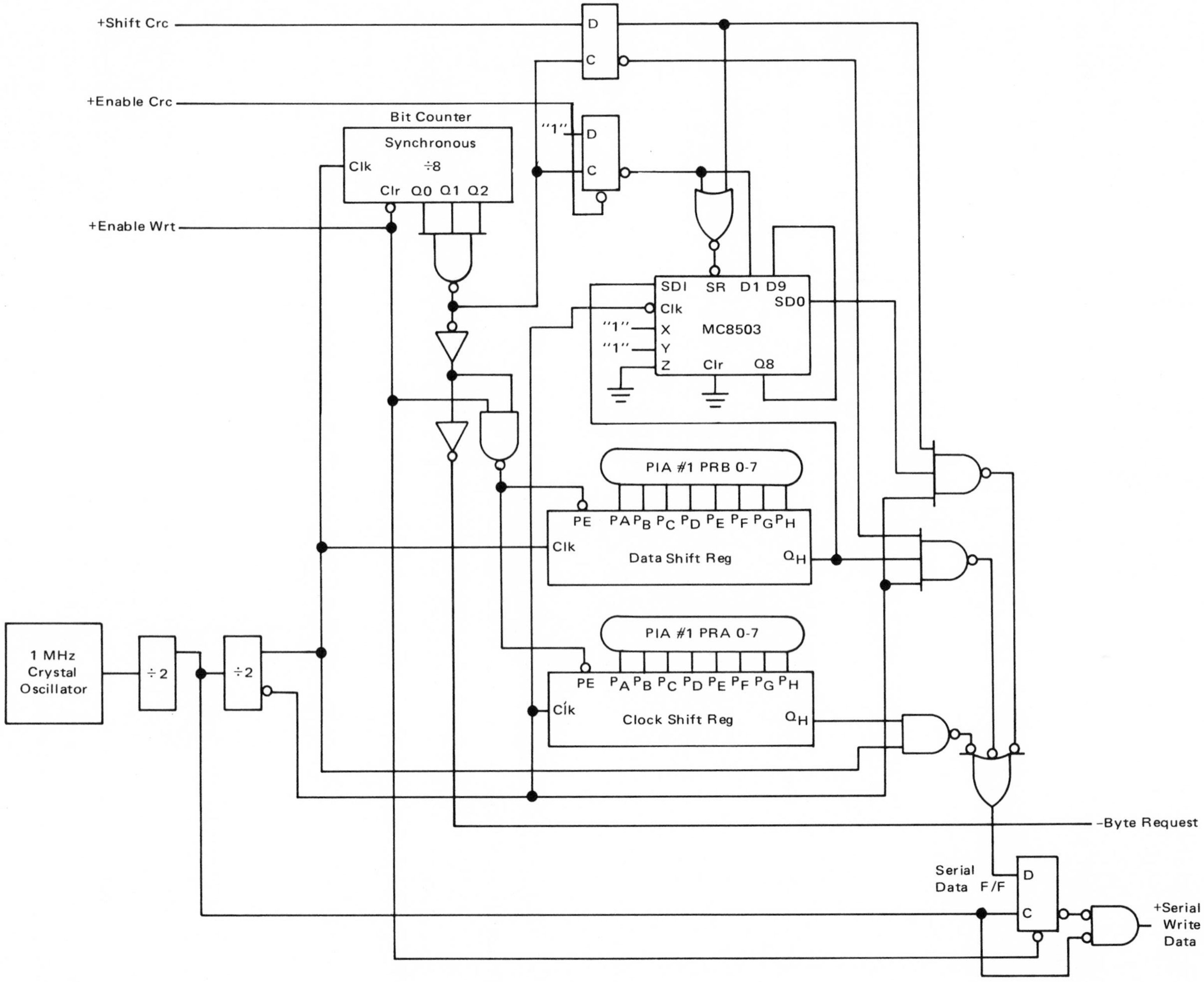

FIGURE 5-4.7.2-1. Floppy Disk Write Logic

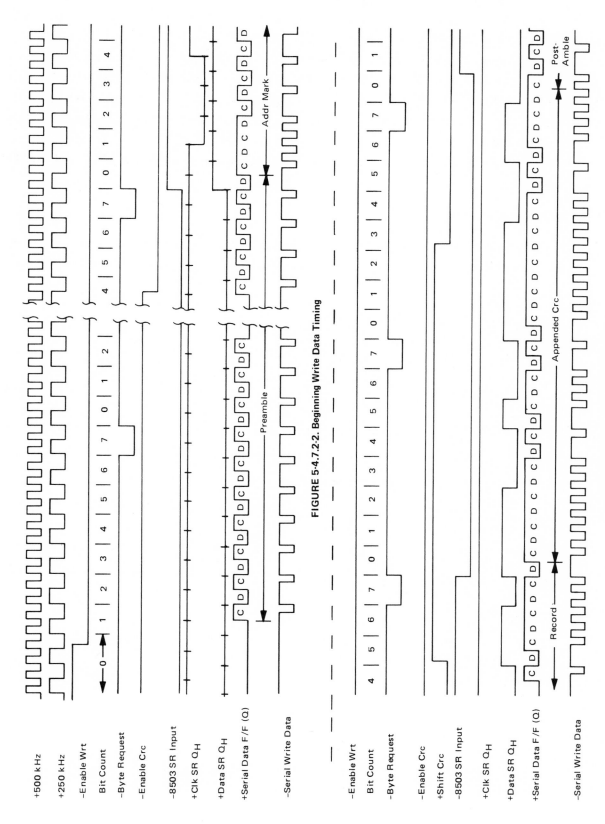

FIGURE 5-4.7.2-2. Beginning Write Data Timing

FIGURE 5-4.7.2-3. Append CRC Timing

Serial data in digital frequency modulation format is generated by the serial data flip/flop and a NOR gate. The flop/flop is clocked at twice the bit rate. The serial clock and data patterns are moved into the flip/flop on alternate half bit cells. The resulting serial data output is gated by the 2x bit rate clock to develop a digital frequency modulated serial data stream.

After the program moves the address byte into PIA #1, the ENABLE CRC is made active. Then at the trailing edge of the next bit 7 time the MC8503 Polynomial Generator is enabled. A CRC check polynomial is generated until the SHIFT CRC signal is activated by the program. At the trailing edge of bit 7 time the accumulated CRC character is serially gated into the serial data flip/flop in place of the data pattern. 16 bits of CRC are appended to the end of the data before the program drops SHIFT CRC.

One byte time after the CRC pattern is recorded the program drops ENABLE WRT. and WRITE GATE.

5-4.7.3 Formatter Error Detect Logic

The Error Detect Logic in Figure 5-4.7.3-1 traps logical malfunctions which could occur in the diskette drive or formatter logic. When an error condition is trapped, an interrupt (R/W ERROR) is made active

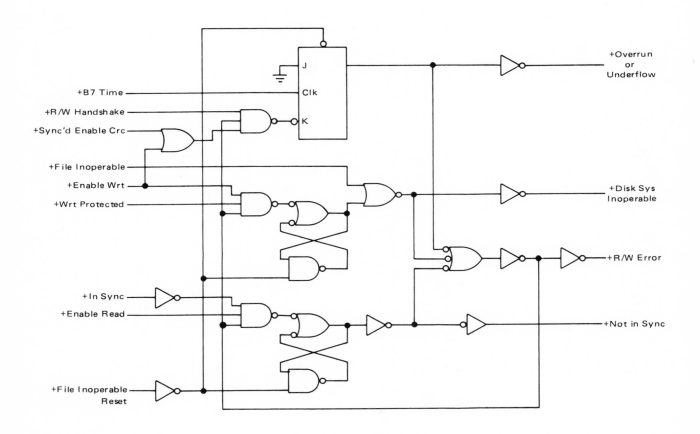

FIGURE 5-4.7.3-1. Error Detect Logic

5-174

to the MC6800 system via PIA #2. The trapped conditions are:

    (1) OVERRUN/UNDERFLOW

    (2) DISK SYSTEM INOPERABLE

    (3) NOT IN SYNC

The OVERRUN/UNDERFLOW flip/flop is set when the write program does not respond to the last BYTE REQUEST service request before the next BYTE REQUEST (i.e. the data is not refreshed in PIA #1). This operation is discussed in section 5-4.3.

The DISK SYSTEM INOPERABLE signal is active when the diskette drive status signal FILE INOPERABLE (See appendix 5-4.A, 5-4.B & 5-4.C) or when WRITE ENABLE and WRITE PROTECTED set the error latch in Figure 5-4.7.3-1.

The Error Detect Logic is designed such that when any error condition is detected the R/W ERROR signal inhibits the setting of other error latches. Thus, the original cause of the failure is preserved for diagnostic purposes.

When an error condition is detected, the drive control signal WRITE GATE is disabled to prevent any further loss of data.

5-4.7.4 Write Operation Program Routine

The write operation is controlled by the routine listed in Figure 5-4.7.4-1. A flow chart of the program is shown in Figure 5-4.7.4-2. This routine is used only to execute a write data record field. The index address mark and ID record fields are written under control of a special program called Format Write. Deleted data address marks are also written under control of the Format Write routine. The Format Write routine is not shown in this Manual.

A detailed explanation of the operation is included with the program listing. As in the case of the read operation, error interrupts abort the write operation. The error recovery routines are not included in this Section. The following is an explanation of some of the unique characteristics of the write program.

Index Error — The IBM 3740 format is such that the index pulse should not be detected until after the 26th record is recorded. Therefore, if index is encountered, the write operation is aborted by an index interrupt.

Basic Write Loop — In Section 5-4.7 the timing considerations of the write operation were described. The following is the write data loop:

			CYCLES
FKWRD06	LDAA	FKDATA,X	5
FKWR07	BIT B	FP1CRA	4
	BPL	FKWR07	4
	STAA	FP1PRB	5
	BIT B	FP1PRA	4
	DEX		4
	BNE	FKWR06	4
			30 Cycles

```
08350          * FLOPPY DISK WRITE DATA ROUTINE


08370          * THIS ROUTINE OBTAINS BYTE PARALLEL DATA FROM
08380          * RAM STORAGE AND MOVES THE DATA TO THE DISK
08390          * FORMATTER. DATA IS THEN WRITTEN ON THE DISKETTE
08400          * IN SERIAL.

08420          * A CRYSTAL OSCILLATOR IS USED TO GENERATE THE
08430          * WRITE FREQUENCY. THEREFORE, THE WRITE DATA
08440          * RATE WILL DEVIATE ONLY SLIGHTLY. THIS ROUTINE
08450          * WILL OPERATE WITH AS MUCH AS + OR - 5%
08460          * FREQUENCY DEVIATION.

08480          * DATA IS MOVED FROM MEMORY USING INDEXED MODE
08490          * ADDRESSING. THIS ROUTINE USES THE INDEX REGISTER
08500          * AS BOTH A MEMORY ADDRESS REGISTER AND AS A
08510          * BYTE COUNTER. BECAUSE OF THE TIMING REQUIREMENTS
08520          * OF THE FLOPPY DISK THE INDEX REGISTER IS TESTED
08530          * FOR ZERO TO DETERMINE THE END OF THE DATA
08540          * TRANSFER. TESTING FOR ZERO PLACES ADDRESSING
08550          * CONSTRAINTS ON THE LOCATION OF THE WRITE DATA
08560          * STORAGE AREA. THE HIGHEST ADDRESS OF THIS AREA
08570          * IS DETERMINED BY ADDING THE MAXIMUM OFFSET
08580          * VALUE TO THE DATA LENGTH:
08590          *     MAX ADDRESS = 255 (OFFSET) + 128 (DATA)
08600          *                 = 383

08620          * THE INTERVAL TIMER IS ARMED TO INTERRUPT THE
08630          * SYSTEM AFTER 4.6 MILLISECONDS  THIS INSURES
08640          * THAT IF THERE IS A HARDWARE MALFUNCTION THE
08650          * ONLY RECORD AFFECTED IS THAT ONE WHICH WAS TO
08660          * BE WRITTEN.

08680          * OTHER ERROR INTERRUPTS INCLUDE:
08690          *     A. SYSTEM INOPERABLE
08700          *     B. UNDERFLOW
08710          *     C. INDEX
08720          *     D. NOT READY

08740          * THE "ABOVE TRK 43" SIGNAL IS SET TO A "1" OR
08750          * "0" PRIOR TO BEGINNING THE DATA TRANSFER. THE
08760          * RAM LOCATION "FVTRKA" IS USED TO DETERMINE THE
08770          * PRESENT LOCATION OF THE HEAD.
```

TABLE 5-4.7.4-1. Floppy Disk Write Data Routine (Sheet 1 of 5)

```
08790                * SYNCHRONIZATION OF THE WRITE DATA RATE TO THE
08800                * PROGRAM IS ACCOMPLISHED BY WAITING UNTIL A BYTE
08810                * REQUEST OCCURS. THIS WAIT LOOP CONSISTS OF
08820                * TESTING BIT 7 OF PIA #1 CONTROL REGISTER A
08830                * AND LOOPING BACK TO TEST THE BIT AGAIN IF IT
08840                * HAD BEEN "0." AFTER A "1" BIT IS DETECTED
08850                * A DATA BYTE IS MOVED TO THE PIA. AFTER
08860                * THE BYTE HAS BEEN MOVED A DUMMY READ CLEARS
08870                * THE INTERRUPT FLAG. FAILURE TO EXECUTE THE
08880                * DUMMY READ BEFORE THE NEXT BYTE REQUEST WILL
08890                * CAUSE AN UNDERFLOW ERROR SIGNAL TO LATCH.

08910                * WHEN THE WRITE ROUTINE IS COMPLETED OR ABORTED
08920                * THE PIA'S ARE RETURNED TO READ MODE.



08940                * AN OPERATION/ABORT FLAG IS MAINTAINED IN RAM
08950                * LOCATION "FVABOR" AS FOLLOWS:
08960                *    10000100 WRITE OPERATION IN PROGRESS
08970                *    01000100 WRITE OPERATION ABORTED BY PROGRAM
08980                *    01100100 WRITE OPERATION ABORTED BY INTERRUPT
08990                *    00000110 WRITE OPERATION COMPLETE
```

TABLE 5-4.7.4-1. Floppy Disk Write Data Routine (Sheet 2 of 5)

```
09020  5272  86 EF      FKWRIT  LDA A  #%11101111   SET STATUS MASK
09030  5274  B4 8041            AND A  FP2PRB       FETCH MASKED STATUS
09040  5277  97 01             STA A  FYSTAT       STORE ERROR STATUS
09050  5279  27 05             BEQ    FKWR01       BRANCH IF STATUS GOOD

09070                   * ERROR STATUS CHECKED:
09080                   *    BIT 0 = NOT IN SYNC
09090                   *    BIT 1 = DISK SYSTEM INOPERABLE
09100                   *    BIT 2 = UNDERFLOW
09110                   *    BIT 3 = WRITE PROTECTED
09120                   *    BIT 5 = NOT HEAD LOADED
09130                   *    BIT 6 = NOT READY
09140                   *    BIT 7 = INDEX

09160  527B  86 44              LDA A  #%01000100
09170  527D  97 00              STA A  FYABOR       STORE ABORT CODE
09180  527F  39                 RTS                 RETURN TO HOST PROGRAM

09200  5280  9F 09      FKWR01  STS    FYSYSP       SAVE STACK POINTER
09210  5282  86 84              LDA A  #%10000100
09220  5284  97 00              STA A  FYABOR       STORE WRITE OP CODE
09230  5286  CE FF00            LDX    #$FF00
09240  5289  FF 8080            STX    FP1PRA       MOVE GAP PATTERN TO PIA

09260                   * "FF" IS MOVED TO FP1PRA AND "00" IS MOVED TO
09270                   * FP1PRB. "FF" IS THE GAP CLOCK PATTERN AND
09280                   * "00" IS THE GAP DATA PATTERN.

09300  528C  86 AD              LDA A  #%10101101
09310  528E  B7 8040            STA A  FP2PRA       ENABLE WRITE

09330                   * "ENABLE WRITE" GATES THE FORMATTER WRITE
09340                   * CIRCUITS ON. BECAUSE "WRITE GATE" IS OFF THE
09350                   * SERIAL DATA IS NOT TRANSFERRED TO THE DRIVE.
09360                   * ALSO, THE READ STATUS SIGNALS WHICH ARE ROUTED
09370                   * TO PIA #1 ARE SWITCHED TO A HIGH IMPEDANCE
09380                   * STATE BY "ENABLE WRITE" IN PREPARATION TO
09390                   * CHANGING THE PIA #1 I/O LINES FROM INPUTS TO
09400                   * OUTPUTS.

09420  5291  CE 3030            LDX    #$3030
09430  5294  FF 8082            STX    FP1CRA       SELECT DIRECTION REGS
09440  5297  CE FFFF            LDX    #$FFFF
09450  529A  FF 8080            STX    FP1PRA       DEFINE PIA #1 LINES OUTPUTS
```

TABLE 5-4.7.4-1. Floppy Disk Write Data Routine (Sheet 3 of 5)

```
09470 529D C6 34          LDA B  #%00110100   PRELOAD FP1CRA CONTROL
09480 529F 86 29          LDA A  #43
09490 52A1 91 04          CMP A  FYTRKA   TEST TRK ADDR > 43
09500 52A3 22 02          BHI    FKWR02   BRANCH IF > 43
09510 52A5 86 23          LDA A  #43-8
09520 52A7 88 13  FKWR02  EOR A  #%00010011   FORM TRK > 43 CONTR WOR
09530 52A9 B7 8083        STA A  FP1CRB   SET ABOVE TRK 43

09550                   * THE TRK > 43 CONTROL WORD IS GENERATED FROM THE
09560                   * VALUE 43 AS FOLLOWS:

09580                   *                  TRK > 43              TRK =/< 43
09590                   *                  --------              --------
09600                   *    43 =          00101011    43-8 =    00100011
09610                   *   EOR#           00010111              00010111
09620                   *                  --------              --------
09630                   *   FP1CRB         00111100              00110100

09650                   * IF THE TRACK IS GREATER THAN 43 THE CB2 SIGNAL
09660                   * OF PIA #1 IS SET TO A HIGH. ALSO PERIPHERAL
09670                   * REGISTER B IS SELECTED BY BIT 2.

09690 52AC F7 8082        STA B  FP1CRA   SELECT PERIPHERAL REG A
09700 52AF C6 FB          LDA B  #256-5   SET BYTE COUNTER = 5
09710 52B1 86 24          LDA A  #%00100100   PRELOAD R/W HANDSHAKE
09720 52B3 CE 032E        LDX    #S100US+46
09730 52B6 FF 8010        STX    FP3PRA   ARM TIMER FOR 4.6 MS
09740 52B9 CE C7FB        LDX    #$C7FB   PRELOAD ADDRESS MARK
09750 52BC 7A 8040        DEC    FP2PRA   SET WRITE GATE

09770                   * SERIAL WRITE DATA IS GATED INTO THE DRIVE AT
09780                   * THIS TIME.

09800 52BF F5 8080        BIT B  FP1PRA   CLR BYTE REQUEST
09810 52C2 B7 8082        STA A  FP1CRA   SET R/W HANDSHAKE
09820 52C5 86 A8          LDA A  #%10101000   PRELOAD ENABLE CRC
09830 52C7 F5 8082 FKWR03 BIT B  FP1CRA
09840 52CA 2A F9          BPL    FKWR03   WAIT FOR BYTE REQUEST
09850 52CC F5 8080        BIT B  FP1PRA   CLR INTERRUPT FLAG
09860 52CF 5C             INC B           UPDATE BYTE COUNTER
09870 52D0 26 F5          BNE    FKWR03   LOOP UNTIL LAST GAP BYTE
09880 52D2 F1 8082 FKWR04 CMP B  FP1CRA
09890 52D5 2B F9          BMI    FKWR04   WAIT FOR BYTE REQUEST
09900 52D7 FF 8080        STX    FP1PRA   MOVE ADDR MARK TO PIA
09910 52DA B7 8040        STA A  FP2PRA   ENABLE CRC
09920 52DD F5 8080        BIT B  FP1PRA   CLEAR INTERRUPT FLAG
09930 52E0 86 FF          LDA A  #$FF     PRELOAD CLK PATTERN
09940 52E2 F6 017F        LDA B  FKDATA+128   GET 1ST DATA BYTE
09950 52E5 CE 007F        LDX    #127     LOAD BYTE COUNTER
09960 52E8 B5 8082 FKWR05 BIT A  FP1CRA
09970 52EB 2A F9          BPL    FKWR05   WAIT FOR BYTE REQUEST
09980 52ED B7 8080        STA A  FP1PRA   MOVE CLK PATTERN TO PIA
```

TABLE 5-4.7.4-1. Floppy Disk Write Data Routine (Sheet 4 of 5)

FLDISK

```
09990  52F0  F7 8081          STA  B   FP1PRB      MOVE 1ST BYTE TO PIA
10000  52F3  F5 8080          BIT  B   FP1PRA      CLR INTERRUPT FLAG
10010  52F6  C6 A0            LDA  B   #%10100000    PRELOAD SHIFT CRC

10030                   * THE FOLLOWING SERIES OF INSTRUCTIONS IS THE
10040                   * BASIC WRITE LOOP.

10060  52F8  A6 FF     FKWR06 LDA A   FKDATA,X     FETCH NEXT DATA BYTE
10070  52FA  F5 8082   FKWR07 BIT B   FP1CRA
10080  52FD  2A F9            BPL      FKWR07       WAIT FOR BYTE REQUEST
10090  52FF  B7 8081          STA A   FP1PRB        MOVE DATA TO PIA
10100  5302  F5 8080          BIT B   FP1PRA        CLR INTERRUPT FLAG
10110  5305  09               DEX                   DECREMENT BYTE COUNTER
10120  5306  26 F0            BNE      FKWR06        LOOP UNTIL LAST BYTE

10140  5308  F7 8040          STA B   FP2PRA        SHIFT CRC
10150  530B  F5 8082   FKWR08 BIT B   FP1CRA
10160  530E  2A F9            BPL      FKWR08        POLL FOR 1ST CRC BYTE
10170  5310  F5 8080          BIT B   FP1PRA        CLR INTERRUPT FLAG
10180  5313  7F 8081          CLR      FP1PRB        MOVE "00" TO DATA PIA
10190  5316  86 AD            LDA A   #%10101101    PRELOAD DROP WRITE GATE
10200  5318  C6 A8            LDA B   #%10101000    PRELOAD STOP SHIFT CRC
10210  531A  F5 8082   FKWR09 BIT B   FP1CRA
10220  531D  2A F9            BPL      FKWR09        POLL FOR 2ND CRC BYTE
10230  531F  F5 8080          BIT B   FP1PRA        CLR INTERRUPT FLAG
10240  5322  F7 8040          STA B   FP2PRA        STOP SHIFT CRC
10250  5325  CE 3E16          LDX      #$3E16        PRELOAD DISABLE INTERRUPTS
10260  5328  C6 AF            LDA B   #%10101111    PRELOAD STOP WRITE
10270  532A  F5 8082   FKWR10 BIT B   FP1CRA
10280  532D  2A F9            BPL      FKWR10        POLL FOR LAST BYTE REQUEST
10290  532F  FF 8042          STX      FP2CRA        DISABLE INTERRUPTS
10300  5332  CE 3030          LDX      #$3030        -GATE R/W HANDSHAKE OFF
10310  5335  FF 8082          STX      FP1CRA        - AND SELECT DIRECT. REG.
10320  5338  B7 8040          STA A   FP2PRA        DROP WRITE GATE

10340                   * "WRITE GATE" IS DROPPED 30 TO 38 MICROSECONDS
10350                   * AFTER THE LAST BYTE REQUEST. THIS ENSURES THAT
10360                   * THE LAST CRC BYTE HAS PASSED THE TRIMMER ERASE
10370                   * COIL IN THE R/W HEAD.

10390  533B  7F 8010          CLR      FP3PRA        STOP INTERVAL TIMER
10400  533E  CE 0000          LDX      #0
10410  5341  FF 8080          STX      FP1PRA        CHANGE PIA #1 TO INPUTS
10420  5344  CE 3434          LDX      #$3434
10430  5347  FF 8082          STX      FP1CRA        RESELECT PERIPHERAL REG.
10440  534A  F7 8040          STA B   FP2PRA        DROP ENABLE WRITE

10460                   * PIA #1 IS NOW IN READ MODE.

10480  534D  86 06            LDA A   #%00000110

10490  534F  97 00            STA A   FYABOR        SET WRITE COMPLETE FLAG
10500  5351  39               RTS                   RETURN TO HOST PROGRAM
10520                   END
```

TABLE 5-4.7.4-1. Floppy Disk Write Data Routine (Sheet 5 of 5)

Note that under the system specifications described in Section 5-4.7 the above instruction series is guaranteed to operate within system timing requirements.

Note that in the write loop, the index register is used as a data storage pointer.

Because of this, restrictions are placed on the storage location of the recovered data. The data must be stored in the memory address range 0-383. This is due to the fact that if an address greater than 383 were used a CPX instruction would have to be added to the loop as in the following example:

			CYCLES
FKWR06	LDAA	FKDATA,X	5
FKWR07	BIT B	FP1CRA	4
	BPL	FKWR07	4
	STAA	FP1PRB	5
	BITB	FP1PRA	4
	DEX		4
	CPX	#FKLADR+1	3
	BNE	FKWR06	4

33 Cycles

Clearly, 33 cycles at $1.0\mu s$/cycle will not transfer $32\mu s$/byte data. The example program will not work.

The upper storage address of 383 is calculated by adding the maximum value of index offset (255) to the number of bytes to be transferred (128). Using the maximum offset, the write data would be stored in addresses 256 through 383 inclusive. Because this address range does not interfere with the direct addressing range this technique of storage should be acceptable in nearly all floppy disk applications.

If the minimum index offset (0) is used, the storage address range would be 1-128 inclusive. Note that this routine does not permit address 0 to be used for floppy disk write data storage.

An alternate method of fetching write data uses a data stack and the PUL instruction. This method of data fetching is not acceptable in most floppy disk applications because if an error interrupt did occur during the write operation, up to seven bytes of write data storage would be overwritten by the interrupt's stacking of the MPU registers. In the read operation, stacking is an acceptable method of storing data and saves considerable time in the read loop (See the read operation program listing).

When a write operation is either completed or aborted, the PIA's should be restored to the pre-read condition. This serves two purposes. It protects the data on the diskette in that a multiple malfunction would be required to inadvertly turn on write current. In addition, the preparatory steps required to begin a read operation are reduced.

The integration of this write routine with a typical host program is described in section 5-4.6.4-3.

5-4.8　SPECIAL OPERATIONS — UPC LOOKUP

One of the main advantages of direct MC6800 control of the floppy disk system is the "higher level of intelligence" attainable with special applications programs. In this section the special application — UPC Lookup will be discussed.

UPC means Universal Product Code. This is the bar code used on the labels of many grocery store commodities to identify the product for electronic point of sale terminals. In present systems a scanner is used to

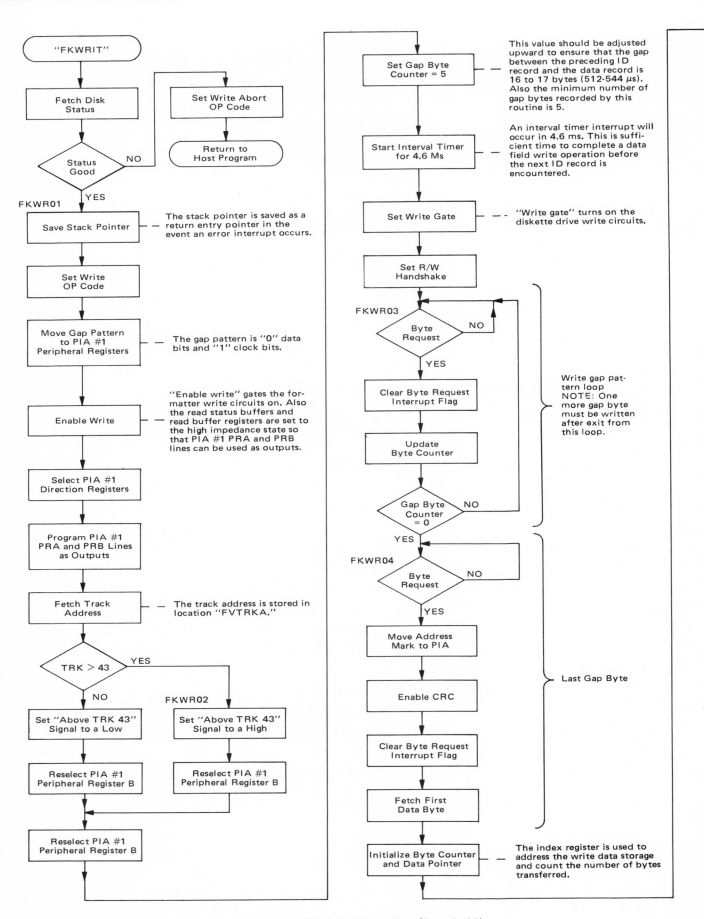

FIGURE 5-4.7.4-2 Write Flow (Sheet 1 of 2)

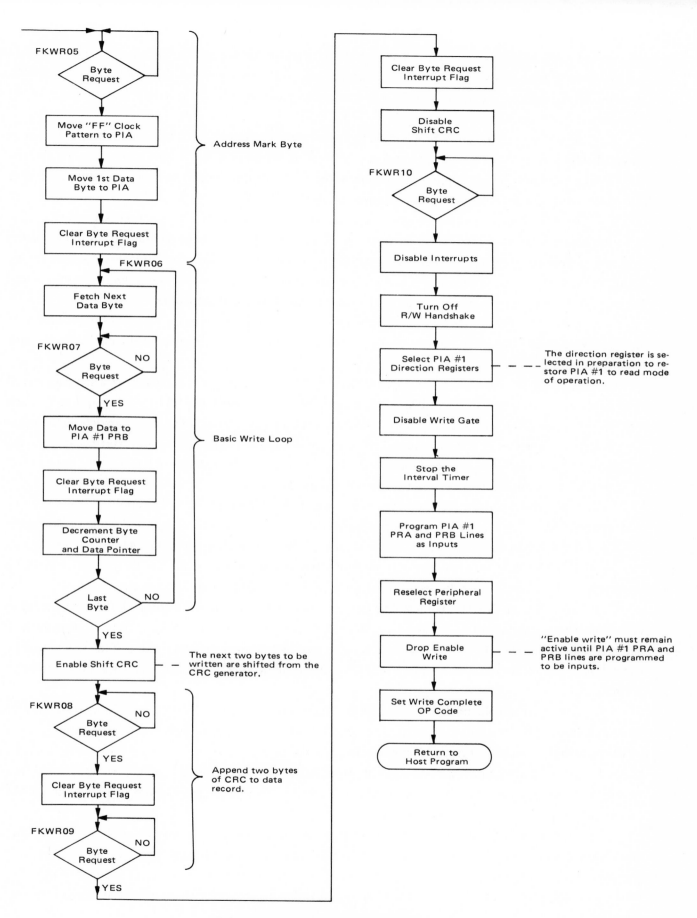

FIGURE 5-4.7.4-2 Write Flow (Sheet 2 Of 2)

read the UPC Code. Then the code is transferred via the terminal communication facilities to a remote computer system. Price and descriptive information is obtained from mass storage and then transmitted back to the POS terminal. From that point the transaction for that commodity is continued as though the information was keyed into the terminal manually.

There are many potential problems in this system, the greatest of which is that if the remote system is down, all of the terminals are down with respect to UPC lookup. Many proposals have been made to localize the UPC lookup storage by using floppy disk systems at the terminal. But the cost has been prohibitive because DMA and large amounts of RAM storage are required.

The UPC lookup may be thought of as a read-only process. That is, it is not necessary that the local terminals have the ability to record data on the floppy disk. The UPC files can be recorded at a central location such as a grocery chain central headquarters or in the "backroom" of the store itself. Because ths diskettes are highly portable they can be delivered with new grocery shipments. By limiting the terminal to a read-only floppy disk system there is an immediate cost saving in the floppy disk hardware.

If DMA is not required to recover the data in a microprocessor based terminal further hardware savings are realized. But these savings are even greater due to the "intelligence level" of the floppy disk control programs.

Assume that the data on the floppy disk is in IBM 3740 format. This means that each data record field is 128 bytes. But the UPC record does not require 128 bytes. Assume that 18 bytes are required for each UPC record. Then seven UPC records could be stored in each data record field. The ideal situation, in this case, is that only 18 bytes of RAM is required for UPC data storage. This can be achieved because of the micro-processor's ability to perform a logical or "key" search. A UPC record can be "keyed" by the UPC code itself. The resulting track format is shown in Figure 5-4.8-1.

Figure 5-4.8-2 is a system level flow chart which shows how a UPC lookup could be integrated in a POS system. Figure 5-4.8-3 is the assembled program listing with commentary for a UPC lookup task. Figure 5-4.8.4 is a flow chart of the read and search portion of the UPC lookup program routines.

The FKSRCH program not only performs the search for UPC data but also gathers diagnostic information which can be used to determine if error recovery attempts should be made.

Note in the FKLKUP that a simple decode of the two low order bytes of the UPC code is used to determine the track address of the desired data. The UPC characters in this example system are single bytes with decimal values 0 through 9. The track address is calculated by finding the decimal value of the two low order characters (0-99) and dividing by 2. Then 8 is added to the result in order to determine a track address 8 through 57 inclusive.

This is a simple track address decode which provides even distribution of the UPC records throughout the 50 UPC tracks if it can be assumed that the UPC codes are consecutively assigned by the grocery product packagers. In actual practice this will seldom be the case and a more complex track decode would be required. The track assignment decode may vary from day to day. Therefore it may be required for the track decode to be recorded on the diskette at a central location. Then the program would be moved into RAM memory during the POS system initialization.

In summary, a task such as UPC lookup can be made feasible at the local level using techniques similar to those documented in this manual. But the UPC task is just one of many applications of a non-DMA approach toward floppy disk. The UPC is just a specific case of the more general logical or keyed search. The main advantage of direct MPU control of the floppy disk is that the programs can be tailored to the specific task requirements.

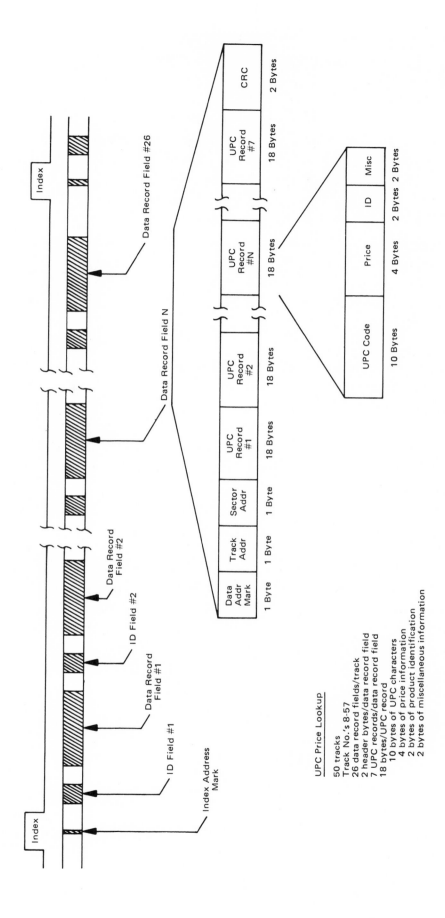

FIGURE 5-4.8-1. UPC Track Format

UPC Price Lookup

50 tracks
Track No.'s 8-57
26 data record fields/track
2 header bytes/data record field
7 UPC records/data record field
18 bytes/UPC record
  10 bytes of UPC characters
  4 bytes of price information
  2 bytes of product identification
  2 bytes of miscellaneous information

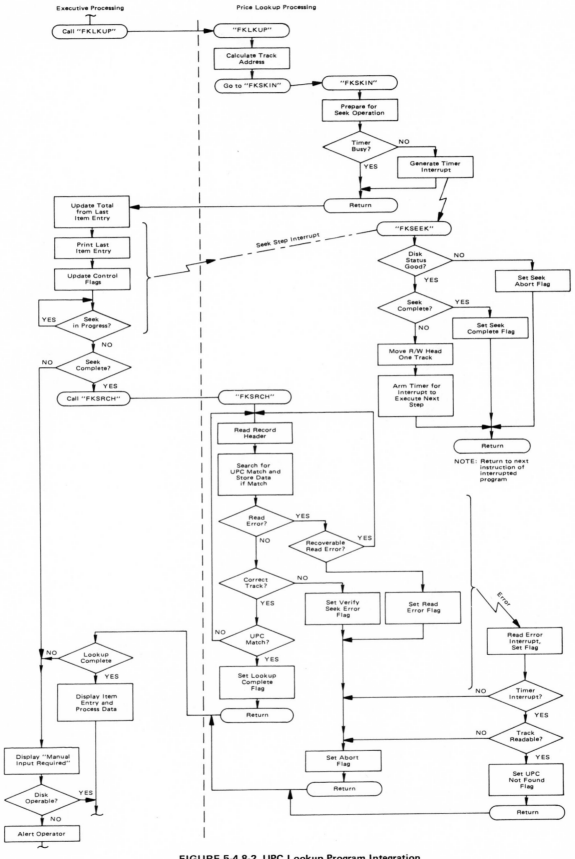

FIGURE 5-4.8-2. UPC Lookup Program Integration

5-186

```
01820                      * UPC LOOKUP PREPARATION ROUTINE


01840                      * THIS ROUTINE CALCULATES ONE OF 50 TRACKS
01850                      * FROM THE LEAST SIGNIFICANT TWO DECIMAL
01860                      * CHARACTERS OF THE UPC CODE. THE RESULTANT
01870                      * TRACK IS THEN STORED IN "FYTRKA" AND THE
01880                      * THE SEEK PREPARATION ROUTINE IS BRANCHED TO.
01890                      * TRACKS 8 THROUGH 57 CONTAIN THE UPC DATA.


01910 5048 D6 17  FKLKUP LDA B  FYUPC+10   GET LSC OF UPC CODE
01920 504A 96 16         LDA A  FYUPC+9    GET 2ND LSC OF UPC CODE
01930 504C 27 05         BEQ    FKLU02     BRANCH IF 2ND CHAR = 0
01940 504E CB 0A  FKLU01 ADD B  #10        CONVERT DECIMAL-BINARY
01950 5050 4A            DEC A
01960 5051 26 F9         BNE    FKLU01     LOOP UNTIL CONVERSION COMPL
01970 5053 54     FKLU02 LSR B             DIVIDE RESULT BY 2
01980 5054 C1 31         CMP B  #49        TEST RESULT MAGNITUDE
01990 5056 23 05         BLS    FKLU03     BRANCH IF TRK ADDR GOOD
02000 5058 86 40         LDA A  #%01000000
02010 505A 97 00         STA A  FYABOR     SET LOOKUP ABORT CODE
02020 505C 39            RTS               RETURN TO EXEC PROGRAM
02030 505D D7 04  FKLU03 STA B  FYTRKA     STORE TRACK ADDRESS
02040 505F 20 0A         BRA    FKSKIN     GO TO SEEK PREP
```

TABLE 5-4.8-3. UPC Search Routine (Sheet 1 of 10)

```
03040                    * UPC SEARCH ROUTINE


03060                    * THIS ROUTINE SEARCHS FOR THE DESIRED UPC DATA
03070                    * AND WHEN FOUND STORES THE DATA.

03090                    * THE DATA ON FLOPPY DISK IS RECORDED IN IBM 3740
03100                    * FIXED FORMAT. THE FOLLOWING IS A BREAKDOWN
03110                    * OF THE UPC RECORD STORAGE.
03120                    *    UPC ASSIGNED TRACKS          = 8-57
03130                    *    NO. OF ASSIGNED TRACKS       = 50
03140                    *    DATA RECORD FIELDS PER TRACK = 26
03150                    *    TOTAL BYTES PER DATA FIELD   = 128
03160                    *    BYTES PER FIELD HEADER       = 2
03170                    *    BYTES PER UPC RECORD         = 18
03180                    *    UPC RECORDS PER DATA FIELD   = 7
03190                    *    UPC RECORDS PER TRACK        = 182
03200                    *    TOTAL AVAILABLE UPC RECORDS  = 9100

03220                    * THE FOLLOWING IS A BREAKDOWN OF THE UPC RECORD:
03230                    *    UPC CODE      = 10 BYTES
03240                    *    PRICE         = 4 BYTES
03250                    *    MESSAGE ADDR  = 2 BYTES
03260                    *    MISCELLANEOUS = 2 BYTES

03280                    * EACH DATA RECORD FIELD CONTAINS 7 UPC RECORDS.
03290                    * THE FIRST TWO BYTES OF THE DATA RECORD FIELD
03300                    * CONTAIN HEADER INFORMATION. THE FIRST BYTE
03310                    * IS THE TRACK ADDRESS AND THE SECOND BYTE IS
03320                    * THE SECTOR ADDRESS.

03340                    * EACH UPC RECORD CONSISTS OF A 10 BYTE UPC CODE
03350                    * WHICH SERVES AS A "KEY" TO 8 BYTES OF PRICE
03360                    * AND DESCRIPTIVE INFORMATION.

03380                    * A UPC SEARCH IS BEGUN BY READING THE FIRST
03390                    * DATA ADDRESS MARK WHICH OCCURS. THEN THE
03400                    * FIRST DATA BYTE IS COMPARED WITH THE TRACK
03410                    * ADDRESS ("FYTRKA"). THE NEXT BYTE IS READ
03420                    * AND STORED IN "FYFLG2." THEN THE FIRST 10 BYTES
03430                    * OF EACH 18 BYTE UPC RECORD IS COMPARED AGAINST
03440                    * THE DESIRED UPC CHARACTERS. IF A MATCH IS FOUND
03450                    * THE NEXT 8 BYTES ARE STACKED IN MEMORY. IF NO
03460                    * MATCH IS FOUND IN ONE OF THE SEVEN UPC RECORDS
03470                    * THE OPERATION REPEATS FOR THE NEXT DATA RECORD
03480                    * FIELD. HOWEVER, ONCE THE FIRST DATA RECORD FIELD
03490                    * IS READ WITHOUT A CRC ERROR THE SECTOR ADDRESS
03500                    * ("FYFLG2") LOCATION IN MEMORY IS NOT CHANGED.
```

TABLE 5-4.8-3. UPC Search Routine (Sheet 2 of 10)

```
03530          * THIS PROCESS CONTINUES FOR 2 REVOLUTIONS OF THE
03540          * DISKETTE GOVERNED BY A 340MS INTERVAL TIMER
03550          * SETTING. IF THE DATA CANNOT BE FOUND IN TWO
03560          * REVOLUTIONS ERROR FLAGS ARE SET AS A RESULT
03570          * OF AN INTERVAL TIMER INTERRUPT AND THE UPC
03580          * SEARCH OPERATION IS ABORTED.

03600          * FLAG BYTES ARE USED TO DIRECT THE PROGRAM FLOW.
03610          * DEFINITIONS OF THE FLAG BYTES ARE AS FOLLOWS:

03630          *   "FVFLG1"
03640          * FLAG 1 IS SET IF THE FIRST HEADER BYTE DOES NOT
03650          * MATCH THE DESIRED TRACK ADDRESS ("FVTRKA").
03660          * THE FLAG IS RESET IF A CRC ERROR OCCURS AFTER
03670          * READING THE DATA RECORD FIELD. IF NO CRC ERROR
03680          * OCCURS AND FLAG 1 IS SET, A SEEK ERROR FLAG
03690          * IS SET AND THE UPC SEARCH IS ABORTED.

03710          *   "FVFLG2"
03720          * FLAG 2 IS SET BY STORING THE 2ND HEADER BYTE
03730          * IN LOCATION "FVFLG2." THE FLAG IS SET ONLY ONCE
03740          * DURING THE 1ST ERROR FREE READ OF A DATA RECORD
03750          * FIELD. IF THE FLAG IS SET IT MEANS THAT A TRACK
03760          * MATCH WAS FOUND.

03780          *   "FVFLG3"
03790          * FLAG 3 MEANS THE UPC SEARCH WAS SUCCESSFUL.
03800          * IF A CRC ERROR OCCURS FLAG 3 IS CLEARED.

03820          *   "FVFLG4"
03830          * FLAG 4 IS A CRC ERROR COUNTER. IF THE FIRST
03840          * 5 DATA FIELDS HAVE CRC ERRORS THE READ ERROR
03850          * IS CONSIDERED TO BE NON-RECOVERABLE. IF ANY
03860          * OF THE FIRST FIVE DATA FIELDS READ HAVE NO
03870          * CRC ERRORS, ANY SUBSEQUENT CRC ERRORS INCREMENT
03880          * FLAG 4. ONCE A DATA RECORD FIELD HAS BEEN READ
03890          * WITHOUT ERROR FURTHER ERRORS ARE CONSIDERED TO
03900          * BE RECOVERABLE UNTIL THE INTERVAL TIMER ABORTS
03910          * THE SEARCH OPERATION.

03930          *   "FVFLG5"
03940          * FLAG 5 IS A COUNTER WHICH INDICATES THE NUMBER
03950          * OF DATA FIELDS PASSED WITHOUT A UPC MATCH AND
03960          * NO UPC ERRORS.
```

TABLE 5-4.8-3. UPC Search Routine (Sheet 3 of 10)

```
03980          * AN OPERATION/ABORT FLAG IS MAINTAINED FOR
03990          * PURPOSES OF COMMUNICATION WITH THE HOST PROGRAM.
04000          * THE OPERATION/ABORT FLAG IS STORED IN RAM
04010          * LOCATION "FVABOR" AS FOLLOWS:

04030          *     10011000   UPC SEARCH IN PROGRESS
04040          *     01011000   UPC SEARCH ABORTED BY PROGRAM
04050          *     01111000   UPC SEARCH ABORTED BY INTERRUPT
04060          *     00111010   UPC RECORD NOT FOUND
04070          *     00011010   UPC SEARCH COMPLETE
04080          *     01111111   SEEK VERIFY ERROR
```

TABLE 5-4.8-3. UPC Search Routine (Sheet 4 of 10)

```
04100 5081 8D F0    FKSRCH BSR     FKERST   CLEAR ERROR LATCHES
04110 5083 4F               CLR A
04120 5084 C6 67            LDA B  #%01100111   SET ERROR STATUS MASK
04130 5086 F4 8041          AND B  FP2PRB   FETCH MASKED STATUS
04140 5089 27 03            BEQ    FKSR01   SKIP IF STATUS GOOD
04150 508B 7E 51DE          JMP    FKSR26   BAD STATUS,EXIT

04170              * THE FOLLOWING ERROR STATUS IS CHECKED:
04180              *    BIT 6 - NOT READY
04190              *    BIT 5 - HEAD NOT LOADED
04200              *    BIT 2 - OVERRUN
04210              *    BIT 1 - DISK SYSTEM INOPERABLE
04220              *    BIT 0 - NOT IN SYNC

04240 508E 86 98    FKSR01 LDA A  #%10011000
04250 50C0 97 00           STA A  FVABOR   STORE OP CODE
04260 50C2 9F 09           STS    FVSVSP   SAVE STACK POINTER
04270 50C4 CE 3F1E         LDX    #$3F1E
04280 50C7 FF 8042         STX    FP2CRA   ENABLE ERROR INTERRUPTS
04290 50CA CE 0122         LDX    #$10MS+34  LOAD 340MS TIMEOUT
04300 50CD FF 8010         STX    FP3PRA   START INTERVAL TIMER
04310 50D0 CE FB7F  FKSR02 LDX    #$FB7F   PRELOAD DATA MARK MATCH
04320 50D3 86 80           LDA A  #256-128
04330 50D5 97 06           STA A  FVBCNT   STORE FIELD BYTE CNTR
04340 50D7 9E 07           LDS    FVDADR   POINT TO DATA STACK
04350 50D9 D6 04           LDA B  FVTRKA   PRELOAD TRACK ADDRESS
04360 50DB 86 24           LDA A  #%00100100
04370 50DD B7 8082         STA A  FP1CRA   ENABLE R/W HANDSHAKE
04380 50E0 86 2B    FKSR03 LDA A  #%00101011   PRELOAD ENABLE CRC
04390 50E2 F5 8080         BIT B  FP1PRA   CLR BYTE READY INTERR FLAG
04400 50E5 B7 8040         STA A  FP2PRA   ENABLE CRC

04420              * THE DISK SYSTEM IS NOW ARMED FOR DATA RECOVERY

04440 50E8 86 01           LDA A  #%00000001   PRELOAD 1ST BIT MASK
04450 50EA B5 8081  FKSR04 BIT A  FP1PRB
04460 50ED 27 FB           BEQ    FKSR04   WAIT FOR 1ST BIT
04470 50EF B1 8082  FKSR05 CMP A  FP1CRA
04480 50F2 2B FB           BMI    FKSR05   WAIT FOR BYTE READY
04490 50F4 BC 8080         CPX    FP1PRA   COMPARE FOR DATA MARK
04500 50F7 27 07           BEQ    FKSR06
04510 50F9 86 2F           LDA A  #%00101111
04520 50FB B7 8040         STA A  FP2PRA   DROP ENABLE CRC
04530 50FE 20 E0           BRA    FKSR03   DO AGAIN,LOOK FOR 1ST BIT

04550              * THE PROGRAM WILL RESTART THE READ OPERATION
04560              * UNTIL A DATA ADDRESS MARK IS FOUND.
```

TABLE 5-4.8-3. UPC Search Routine (Sheet 5 of 10)

```
04590                      * THE DATA ADDRESS MARK HAS BEEN FOUND.
04600                      * BEGIN READING DATA.

04620 5100 86 6B   FKSR06 LDA A   #%01101011
04630 5102 B7 8040         STA A   FP2PRA   RAISE READ ENABLE
04640 5105 B1 8082  FKSR07 CMP A   FP1CRA
04650 5108 25 FB           BCS     FKSR07   WAIT FOR BYTE READY
04660 510A F0 8080         SUB B   FP1PRA   COMPARE TRACK ADDR
04670 510D 27 42           BEQ     FKSR12   BRANCH IF CORRECT TRACK

04690                      * THE 1ST DATA BYTE OF THE DATA RECORD FIELD IS
04700                      * THE TRACK ADDRESS.  IF THE WRONG TRACK ADDRESS
04710                      * HAS BEEN READ IT IS A POSSIBLE SEEK ERROR.
04720                      * BECAUSE IT IS NOT YET KNOWN THAT THE RECOVERED
04730                      * DATA IS VALID FLAG 7 IS SET WHICH WILL BE
04740                      * TESTED IF THERE IS NO CRC ERROR AT THE END OF
04750                      * THE DATA RECORD FIELD.

04770 510F D7 17           STA B   FYFLG1   SAVE TRK ERROR DELTA
04780 5111 C6 81           LDA B   #256-127

04800                      * THE FOLLOWING INSTRUCTION  SEQUENCE SKIPS OVER
04810                      * THE NUMBER OF BYTES INDICATED IN ACCUMULATOR B
04820                      * IN NEGATIVE BINARY FORMAT

04840 5113 F5 8082  FKSR08 BIT B   FP1CRA
04850 5116 2A FB           BPL     FKSR08   WAIT FOR BYTE READY
04860 5118 F5 8080         BIT B   FP1PRA   CLR INTERR FLAG
04870 511B 5C              INC B            DECREMENT BYTE COUNTER
04880 511C 26 F5           BNE     FKSR08   LOOP UNTIL LAST BYTE


04900                      * CRC PROCESSING.

04920 511E F1 8082  FKSR09 CMP B   FP1CRA
04930 5121 2B FB           BMI     FKSR09   WAIT FOR 1ST CRC BYTE
04940 5123 F5 8080         BIT B   FP1PRA   CLR INTERR FLAG
04950 5126 86 2F           LDA A   #%00101111   PRELOAD STOP READ
04960 5128 C6 08           LDA B   #%00001000   PRELOAD TST CRC MASK
04970 512A F1 8082  FKSR10 CMP B   FP1CRA
04980 512D 2B FB           BMI     FKSR10   WAIT FOR 2ND CRC BYTE
04990 512F F4 8081         AND B   FP1PRB   FETCH CRC STATUS
05000 5132 B7 8040         STA A   FP2PRA   STOP READ
05010 5135 86 34           LDA A   #%00110100
05020 5137 B7 8082         STA A   FP1CRA   TURN OFF R/W HANDSHAKE
05030 513A 5D              TST B
05040 513B 27 5E           BEQ     FKSR20   BRANCH IF CRC =00
```

TABLE 5-4.8-3. UPC Search Routine (Sheet 6 of 10)

```
05070                           * CRC ERROR DETECTED

05090                           * CRC ERRORS ARE COUNTED TO DETERMINE IF READ
05100                           * ERRORS ARE RECOVERABLE OR NOT.  THIS
05110                           * INFORMATION IS ALSO USEFUL IN DIAGNOSING
05120                           * DISK SYSTEM MALFUNCTIONS.

05140 513D 7C 001A              INC     FVFLG4    INCREMENT CRC ERR CNTR
05150 5140 7D 001B              TST     FVFLG5
05160 5143 26 83                BNE     FKSR02    IF FLG 5, READ NEXT RECORD
05170 5145 86 05                LDA A   #5
05180 5147 91 1A                CMP A   FVFLG4
05190 5149 23 4A                BLS     FKSR19    BRANCH IF CRC ERRORS <= 5


05210                           * NORMAL EXIT ENTRY POINT

05230 514B 7F 8010 FKSR11 CLR   FP3PRA    STOP INTERVAL TIMER
05240 514E 7E 51D5        JMP   FKSR25    GO TO ENDING PROCESSING
```

TABLE 5-4.8-3. UPC Search Routine (Sheet 7 of 10)

```
05260                            * READ THE 2ND HEADER BYTE.
05270                            * THE 1ST HEADER BYTE HAS BEEN READ AND MATCHES
05280                            * THE TRACK ADDRESS. CONTINUE READING.

05300  5151 D7 19    FKSR12 STA B  FYFLG3    CLEAR FLAG 3
05310  5153 F1 8082  FKSR13 CMP B  FP1CRA
05320  5156 2B FB           BMI    FKSR13    WAIT FOR 2ND HEADER BYTE
05330  5158 B6 8080         LDA A  FP1PRA    FETCH SECTOR ADDR
05340  515B D1 18           CMP B  FYFLG2
05350  515D 26 02           BNE    FKSR14    BRANCH IF NOT 1ST SECTOR
05360  515F 97 18           STA A  FYFLG2    SET FLAG 2

05380                            * IF FLAG 2 IS ALREADY SET DO NOT OVERWRITE.
05390                            * FLAG 2 CONTAINS THE SECTOR ADDRESS OF THE 1ST
05400                            * DATA RECORD FIELD RECOVERED WITHOUT A CRC
05410                            * ERROR.


05430                            * THE FOLLOWING SERIES OF INSTRUCTIONS ATTEMPTS
05440                            * TO MATCH THE 1ST 10 BYTES OF THE UPC RECORD
05450                            * WITH THE DESIRED UPC CODE.

05470  5161 CE 000A  FKSR14 LDX    #10       LOAD MATCH POINTER
05480  5164 A6 FF    FKSR15 LDA A  FKMTCH,X    GET 1ST UPC CHAR
05490  5166 F6 8082  FKSR16 LDA B  FP1CRA
05500  5169 2A FB           BPL    FKSR16    WAIT FOR BYTE READY
05510  516B B1 8080         CMP A  FP1PRA
05520  516E 26 4C           BNE    FKSR23    BRANCH IF NOT UPC MATCH
05530  5170 09              DEX              DECREMENT MATCH POINTER
05540  5171 26 F1           BNE    FKSR15    LOOP FOR 10 BYTE MATCH

05560                            * THE UPC MATCH WAS SUCCESFUL. STACK THE NEXT
05570                            * 8 BYTES OF UPC DATA.

05590  5173 C6 85           LDA B  #127+7    SET BYTE COUNTER TO 7
05600  5175 F5 8082  FKSR17 BIT B  FP1CRA
05610  5178 2A FB           BPL    FKSR17    WAIT FOR BYTE READY
05620  517A B6 8080         LDA A  FP1PRA    FETCH DATA FROM DISK
05630  517D 36              PSH A            STACK DATA
05640  517E 5A              DEC B            DECREMENT DATA BYTE CNTR
05650  517F 2B F4           BMI    FKSR17    LOOP FOR 7 BYTES
05660  5181 D7 19           STA B  FYFLG3    SET FLAG 3

05680                            * FLAG 3 INDICATES THE UPC SEARCH WAS SUCCESSFUL.

05700  5183 D6 05           LDA B  FYBCNT    LOAD FIELD BYTE CNT
05710  5185 F5 8082  FKSR18 BIT B  FP1CRA
05720  5188 2A FB           BPL    FKSR18    WAIT FOR BYTE READY
05730  518A B6 8080         LDA A  FP1PRA    FETCH LAST DATA BYTE
05740  518D 36              PSH A
```

TABLE 5-4.8-3. UPC Search Routine (Sheet 8 of 10)

```
05760                          * UPC MATCH WAS SUCCESSFUL.
05770                          * PREPARE TO SKIP REMAINING BYTES, IF ANY.

05790 518E CB 12                 ADD  B   #18        ADJUST FIELD BYTE CNT
05800 5190 27 8C                 BEQ      FKSR09     IF LAST BYTE, DO CRC CHK
05810 5192 7E 5113               JMP      FKSR08     IF NOT LAST BYTE, SKIP OUT


05830                          * A CRC ERROR HAS BEEN DETECTED BUT IT IS
05840                          * ASSUMED TO BE A RECOVERABLE ERROR.
05850                          * CLEAR FLAG 2 AND READ THE NEXT DATA RECORD
05860                          * FIELD.


05890 5195 4F           FKSR19 CLR A
05900 5196 97 18               STA  A   FVFLG2     CLEAR FLAG 2
05910 5198 7E 50D0               JMP      FKSR02     READ NEXT RECORD


05940                          * CRC = 00, END OF DATA RECORD FIELD.

05960 519B C6 80         FKSR20 LDA  B   #%10000000    PRELOAD SEEK ERROR FLAG
05970 519D 86 27               LDA  A   #%00100111    FORM SEEK ERR OP CODE
05980 519F 7D 0017             TST      FVFLG1
05990 51A2 26 A7               BNE      FKSR11     IF FLAG 1, ABORT

06010                          * FLAG 1 WAS SET IF THE TRACK ADDRESS DESIRED DID
06020                          * DID NOT MATCH WITH THE FIRST HEADER BYTE.

06040 51A4 7D 0019             TST      FVFLG3
06050 51A7 27 05               BEQ      FKSR21     SKIP IF NOT FLAG 3
06060 51A9 86 42               LDA  A   #%01000010    FORM OP CODE MASK
06070 51AB 7E 514B             JMP      FKSR11     EXIT LOOKUP ROUTINE

06090                          * FLAG 3 WAS SET IF THE UPC MATCH WAS SUCCESSFUL.

06110 51AE 7C 001B   FKSR21 INC      FVFLG5     SET FLAG 5
06120 51B1 7E 50D0               JMP      FKSR02     READ NEXT RECORD

06140                          * FLAG 5 IS INCREMENTED EACH TIME A DATA FIELD IS
06150                          * READ WITHOUT ERROR, BUT NO UPC MATCH WAS FOUND.
```

TABLE 5-4.8-3. UPC Search Routine (Sheet 9 of 10)

```
06180                        * THE FOLLOWING SERIES OF INSTRUCTIONS SKIPS OVER
06190                        * THE REMAINING UPC BYTES WHEN A UPC MATCH WAS
06200                        * NOT MADE.

06220  51B4 F6 8082  FKSR22  LDA B   FP1CRA
06230  51B7 2A F9             BPL     FKSR22    WAIT FOR BYTE READY
06240  51B9 F5 8080           BIT B   FP1PRA    CLR INTERR FLAG
06250  51BC 09       FKSR23  DEX               DECREMENT POINTER

06270                        * "FKSR23" IS THE ENTRY INTO THIS LOOP

06290  51BD 26 F5             BNE     FKSR22    LOOP TILL POINTER EXHAUSTED



06310                        * THE FOLLOWING SERIES SKIPS OVER THE 8 BYTES OF
06320                        * UPC DATA. IF THERE ARE SUBSEQUENT UPC RECORDS
06330                        * A UPC MATCH WILL BE ATTEMPTED AGAIN.

06350  51BF D6 05             LDA B   FYBCNT    GET FIELD BYTE CNTR
06360  51C1 86 F8             LDA A   #256-8    LOAD BYTE CNTR
06370  51C3 B5 8082  FKSR24  BIT A   FP1CRA
06380  51C6 2A F9             BPL     FKSR24    WAIT FOR BYTE READY
06390  51C8 B5 8080           BIT A   FP1PRA    CLR INTERR FLAG
06400  51CB 4C                INC A             UPDATE BYTE COUNTER
06410  51CC 26 F5             BNE     FKSR24    LOOP FOR 8 BYTES
06420  51CE CB 12             ADD B   #18       ADJUST FIELD BYTE CNTER
06430  51D0 26 8F             BNE     FKSR14    BRNCH IF NOT END OF FIELD
06440  51D2 7E 511E           JMP     FKSR09    GO TO CRC PROCESS



06460                        * ENDING PROCESSING

06480  51D5 CE 3E16  FKSR25  LDX     #$3E16
06490  51D8 FF 8042           STX     FP2CRA    DISABLE ERROR INTERRUPTS
06500  51DB 30                TSX               PNT TO DATA WITH INDEX REG
06510  51DC 9E 0B             LDS     FYSVSP    RESTORE STACK POINTER

06530                        * EXIT SEQUENCE ENTRY POINT IF STATUS ERROR

06550  51DE D7 01    FKSR26  STA B   FYSTAT    STORE ERROR STATUS
06560  51E0 88 58             EOR A   #%01011000    FORM OP/ABORT CODE
06570  51E2 97 00             STA A   FYABOR    STORE OP/ABORT CODE
06580  51E4 39                RTS               RETURN TO EXEC PROGRAM
```

TABLE 5-4.8-3. UPC Search Routine (Sheet 10 of 10)

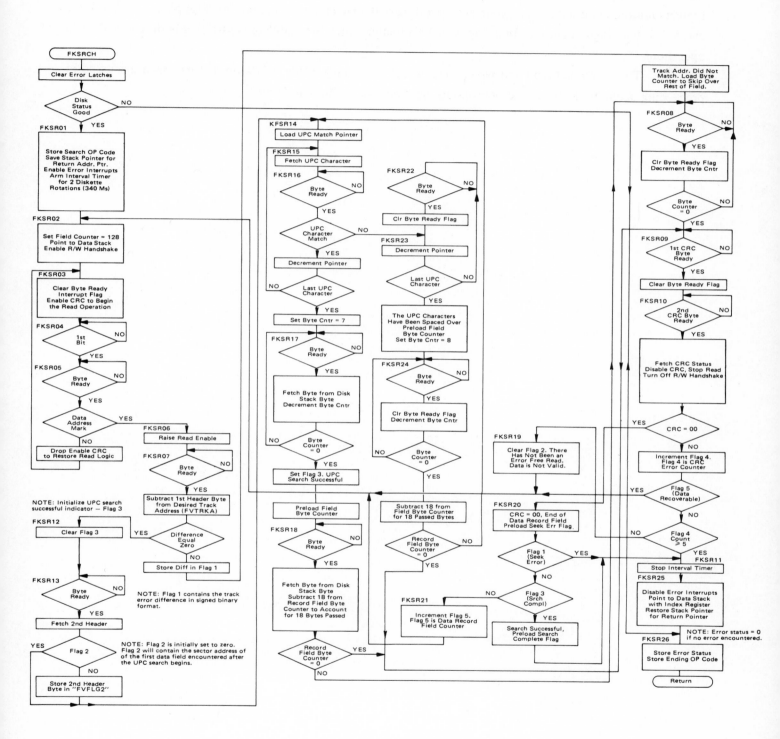

FIGURE 5-4.8-4. UPC Search Program Flow Chart

5-4.9 INTEGRATED READ/WRITE LOGIC

Up to this point the discussion of the read and write logic has been treated separately. In the case of the UPC Lookup, it was shown that there are applications where the write controls are not needed. But the more typical requirement is a design capable of controlling both read and write operations. Figures 5-4.9-1, 5-4.9-2 and 5-4.9-3 are logic diagrams for a floppy disk formatter which is capable of controlling both read and write operations.

The combined read and write logic is just a marriage of the hardware that has been discussed in preceeding sections. Refer to the appropriate Sections for additional detail.

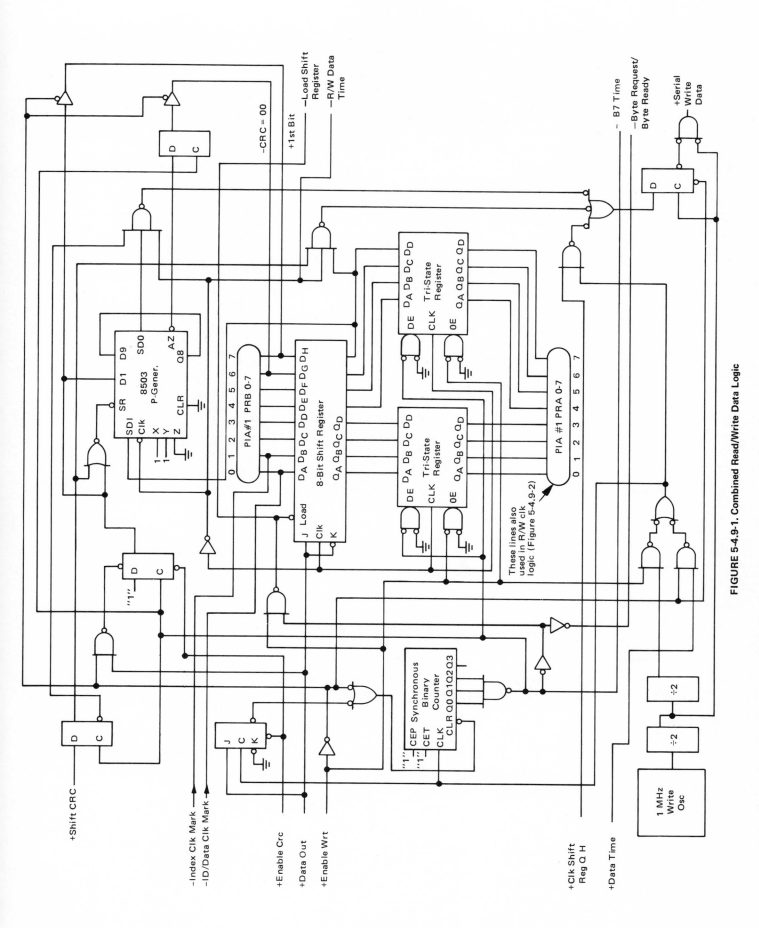

FIGURE 5-4.9-1. Combined Read/Write Data Logic

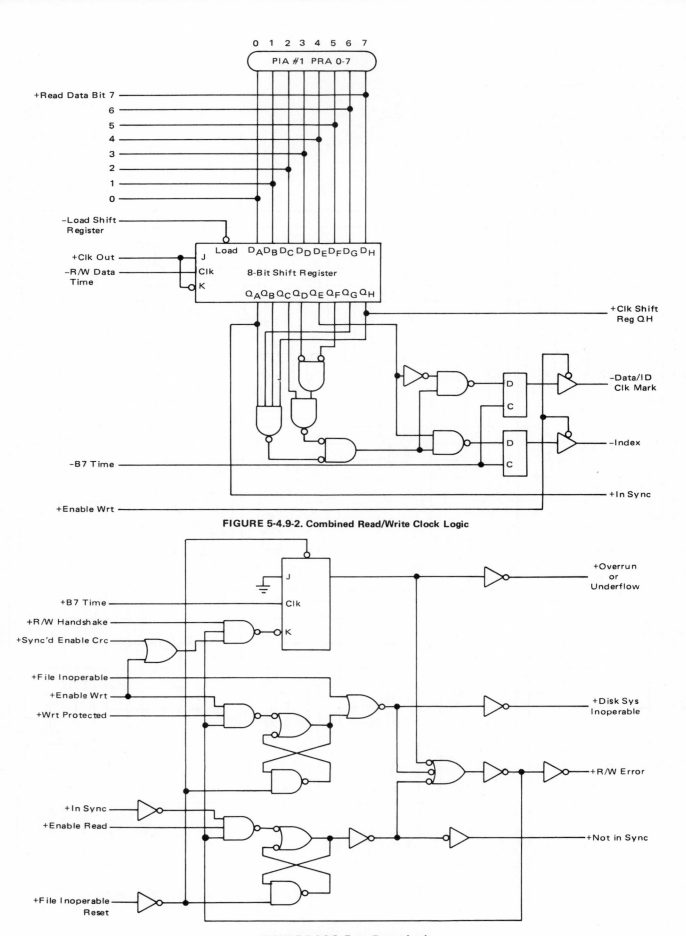

FIGURE 5-4.9-2. Combined Read/Write Clock Logic

FIGURE 5-4.9-3. Error Detect Logic

5-200

APPENDIX 5-4.A
SHUGART ASSOCIATES
SA900/901
Diskette Storage Drive

SPECIFICATION SUMMARY

Performance Specifications

Capacity (Unformatted)	Per Disk	3.1 megabits
	Per Track	41 kilobits
Data Transfer Rate		250 kilobits/second
Access Time	Track to Track	10 MS
	Settling Time	10 MS
Average Access Time		260 MS
Rotational Speed		360 RPM
Average Latency		83 MS
Recording Mode		Frequency Modulation

Media Characteristics

Cartridge Required	SA900	SA100 or IBM "Diskette"
	SA901	SA101
Physical Sectors	SA900	0
	SA901	32
Index		1
Tracks		77
Density	Recording	3200 bpi (approx. inside track)
	Track	48 TPI

Additional Features for SA900/901

50 Hz - 100 VAC, single phase

60 Hz - 208/230 VAC, single phase

50 Hz - 208/230 VAC, single phase

Write Protect (SA901 only)

–12 or –15V option to replace -5V input

Chassis Slide

10½" High Front Plate for use with

Chassis Slide

5.25" x 11" Front Plate

5.25" x 10" Front Plate

READ ERROR RATE

1×10^9 bits read/soft error (nominal)

1×10^{12} bits read/hard error (nominal)

SEEK ERROR RATE

1 seek error in 10^6 seeks

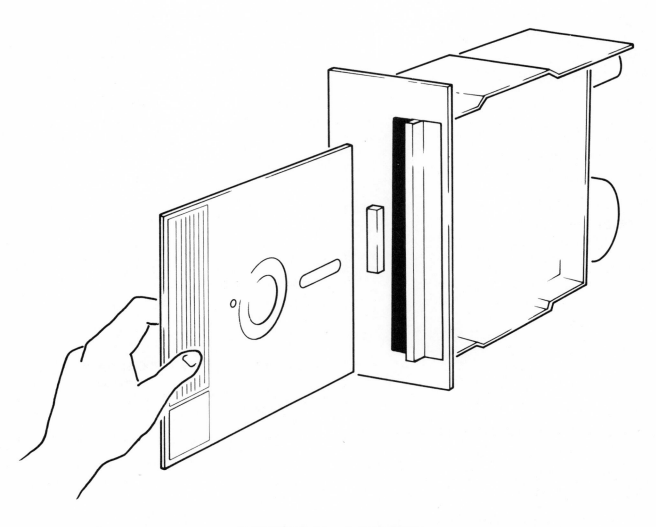

FIGURE 5-4.A-2. Loading SA900/901

SA900/901
DISKETTE STORAGE DRIVE

FUNCTIONAL CHARACTERISTICS

GENERAL OPERATION

The SA900/901 Diskette Drive consists of read/write and control electronics, drive mechanism, read/write head, track positioning mechanism, and the removable Diskette. These components perform the following functions:

- Interpret and generate control signals.

- Move read/write head to the selected track.

- Read and write data.

The relationship and interface signals for the internal functions of the SA900/901 are shown in Figures 5-4.A-3 and 5-4.A-4 respectively.

The Head Positioning Actuator positions the read/write head to the desired track on the Diskette. The Head Load Actuator loads the Diskette against the read/write head and data may then be recorded or read from the Diskette.

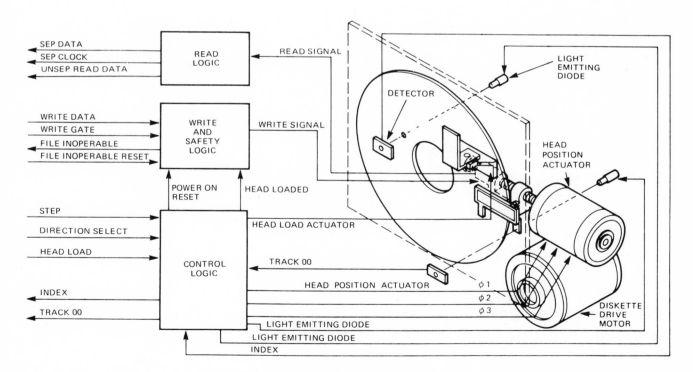

FIGURE 5-4.A-3 SA900 Functional Diagram, One Sector Hole

5-203

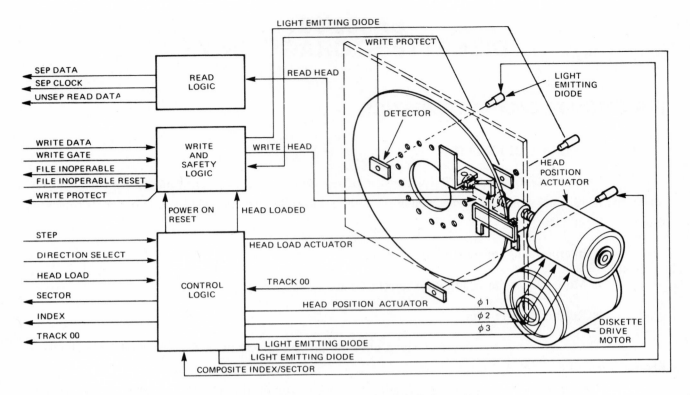

FIGURE 5-4.A-4 SA901 Functional Diagram, 32 Sector Holes

The electronics are packaged on one PCB. The PCB contains:

(1) Index Detector Circuits (Sector/Index for 901).

(2) Head Position Actuator Driver

(3) Head Load Actuator Driver

(4) Read/Write Amplifier and Transition Detector

(5) Data/Clock Separation Circuits

(6) Safety Sensing Circuits

(7) Write Protect (SA901 only)

An electrical stepping motor (Head Position Actuator) and lead screw positions the read/write head. The stepping motor rotates the lead screw clockwise or counterclockwise in 15° increments. A 15° rotation of the lead screw moves the read/write head one track position. The using system increments the stepping motor to the desired track.

The Diskette drive motor rotates the spindle at 360 rpm through a belt-drive system. 50 or 60 Hz power is accommodated by changing the drive pulley. A registration hub, centered on the face of the spindle, positions the Diskette. A clamp that moves in conjunction with the latch handle fixes the Diskette to the registration hub.

The read/write head is in direct contact with the Diskette. The head surface has been designed to obtain maximum signal transfer to and from the magnetic surface of the Diskette with minimum head/Diskette wear.

The SA900/901 head is a single element read/write head with straddle erase elements to provide erased areas between data tracks. Thus normal tolerance between media and drives will not degrade the signal to noise ration and insures Diskette interchangeability.

The read/write head is mounted on a carriage which is located on the Head Position Actuator lead screw. (See Figure 5-4.A-5) The Diskette is held in a plane perpendicular to the read/write head by a platen located on the base casting. This precise registration assures perfect compliance with the read/write head. The Diskette is loaded against the head with a load pad actuated by the head load solenoid.

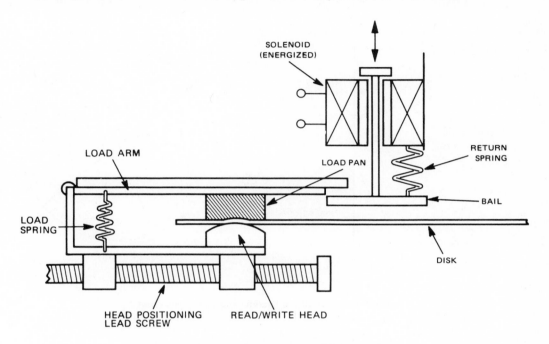

FIGURE 5-4.A-5 Head Load and Carriage Assembly

DISKETTE

The recording media used in the SA900 Diskette Storage Drive is a Mylar* disk enclosed in a plastic envelope. The characteristics of the disk and envelope are:

Disk Diameter	7.875 inches
Envelope Size	8 inches x 8 inches
Rotational Speed	360 RPM
Rotational Period	166.67 ms
Average Latency	83.33 ms
Number of Tracks	77
Bit Density Inside Track	3200 bpi approx.

The SA100 Diskette media is IBM compatible and can be used in the SA900 or the IBM 3740 Data Entry System. (See Figure 5-4.A-6A)

The SA101 Diskette is used with the SA901 and differs from the SA100 in that there are 32 sector holes and a file protect hole. (See Figure 5-4.A-6B)

*Trademark of Dupont Corp.

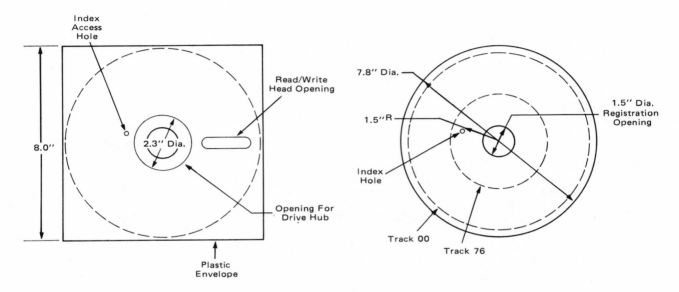

FIGURE 5-4.A-6A SA100 Diskette and Cartridge Layout

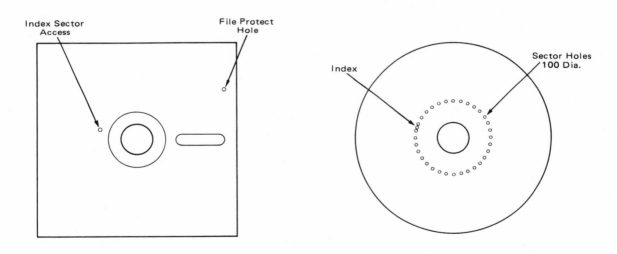

FIGURE 5-4.A-6B SA101 Diskette and Cartridge Layout

SA900/901
DISKETTE STORAGE DRIVE

ELECTRICAL INTERFACE

The interface of the SA900/901 Diskette drive can be divided into two categories: Signal and Power. The following sections provide the electrical definition for each line.

SIGNAL INTERFACE

The signal interface consists of the lines required to control the SA900/901 Diskette Storage drive and transfer data to and from the unit. All lines in the signal interface are digital in nature and either provide signals to the drive (input) or provide signals to the user (output).

Input

There are six (6) input signal lines to the SA900/901 Diskette Storage drive; each line has the following input specifications.

V_{in} 0V − .4V = logical zero = true

V_{in} 2.5V − 5.5V = logical one = false

Input Impedance = 150Ω

DIRECTION SELECT

This interface signal defines the direction of motion of the R/W head when the Step line is pulsed. An open circuit or logical one level defines the direction as out, and if a pulse is applied to the Step line the R/W head will move away from the center of the disk. Conversely, if this input is shorted to ground or a logical zero level is applied the direction of motion is defined as in and if a pulse is applied to the Step line the R/W head will move towards the center of the disk.

STEP

This interface line is a control signal which causes the R/W head to move with the direction of motion defined by the Direction Select line. The access motion is initiated on each logical zero to logical one transition of this signal. The timing restrictions on this signal are shown in Figure 5-4.A-13.

LOAD HEAD

This interface line performs two functions on all machines at or above E.C. level 45. (The EC level can be found in the rear upper corner of the PCB.) One function is to remove the 24 volts from the stepper motor which will allow the motor to run cooler. This means to either step, read or write. The head load line must be a logical 0 level. This function can be crippled by cutting a trace on the PCB. Then 24 volts will be applied to the stepper at all times. This trace has been labeled ''R'' for easy identification.

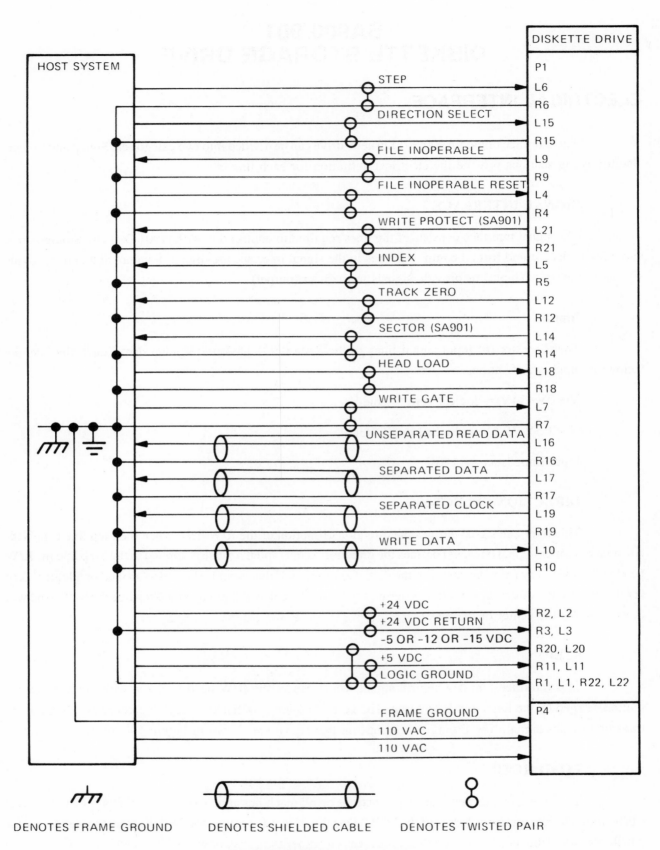

DENOTES FRAME GROUND · DENOTES SHIELDED CABLE · DENOTES TWISTED PAIR

FIGURE 5-4.A-7 Standard Interface Lines

It also is a control signal to an actuator that allows the disk to be moved into contact with the R/W head. An open circuit or logical one deactivates the head load actuator and causes a bail to lift the pressure pad from the disk, which removes the load from the disk and R/W head. A logical zero level on this signal activates the head load actuator and allows the pressure pad to bring the disk into contact with the R/W head with the proper contact pressure.

FILE INOPERABLE RESET

This interface line provides a direct reset on the File Inoperable latch. The inactive level for this signal is a logical one. The File Inoperable condition is reset with a logical zero level applied to this line. **Note:** Under no circumstances should the drive be operated with this signal at a constant logical zero level since all data safety circuitry will be defeated.

WRITE GATE

Write Gate is an interface line which controls the writing of data on the disk. A logical one level on this interface line turns off the current source to the write drivers along with the current sinks for the write current. A logical zero level on this line enables the write current source and current sinks, and disables the stepping circuitry.

WRITE DATA

This interface line provides the data to be written on the disk and each transition from the logical one level to logical zero level causes the current through the R/W head to be reversed. Input impedance for Write Data = 100Ω.

Output

There are six (6) output signal lines from the SA900 Disk Storage drive, and eight (8) from the SA901. Each line has the following output specifications:

$V_{out} = 0V - .4V$ logical zero = true

Each output line appears as an open circuit (transistor in cut-off) for the logical one level. (False)

Maximum sink current = 100 ma.

TRACK 00

The Track 00 interface signal indicates when the R/W head is positioned at track zero (the outer most data track) and the access circuitry is driving current through phase one of the stepping motor. This signal is at a logical one level when the R/W head is not at track zero and is at a logical zero level when the R/W head is at track zero.

FILE INOPERABLE

File Inoperable is the output of the data safety circuitry and is at a logical zero level when a condition which jeopardizes data integrity has occured. Logically the signal is defined as follows:

File Inoperable = (Write Gate . Write I Sense)

+ (Write Gate . Write I Sense)

+ (Write Gate . Head Load)

+ (Write Gate . Write Data)

+ (Write Gate . Door Closed)

INDEX

This interface signal is provided by the disk drive once each revolution (166.67 ms) to indicate the beginning of the track. Normally, this signal is a logical one level and makes the transition to the logical zero level for a period of 1.7 ms (.4 ms SA091) once each revolution. The timing of this signal is shown in Figure 5-4.A-8.

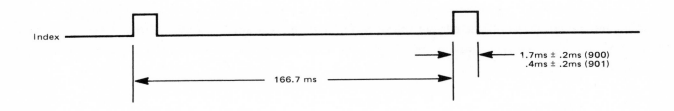

FIGURE 5-4.A-8 Index Timing

SECTOR (SA901 ONLY)

This interface signal is provided by the disk drive 32 times each revolution. Normally, this signal is a logical one level and makes the transition to the logical zero level for a period of .4 ms 32 times each revolution. The timing of this signal is shown in Figure 5-4.A-9.

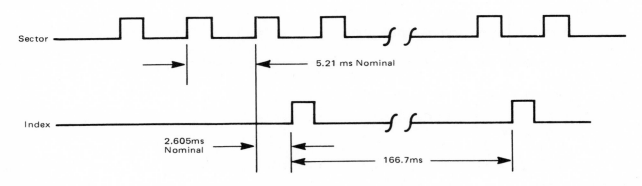

FIGURE 5-4.A-9 Index/Sector Timing

WRITE PROTECT (SA901 ONLY)

This interface signal is provided by the disk drive to allow the user an indication when a write protected diskette is inserted in the SA901. The signal is a logical one level when the diskette is not protected and a logical zero when it is protected.

SEPARATED DATA

Separated Data is the interface line over which read data is sent to the using system. The frequency modulated signal written on the disk is demodulated by the drive electronics and the data pulses are sent to the using system over this interface line. Normally, this signal is a logical one level and each data bit recorded on the disc causes a transition to the logical zero level for 200 ns. The timing for this signal is shown in Figure 5-4.A-15.

SEPARATED CLOCK

The Separated Clock interface line provides the using system the clock bits recorded on the disk in frequency modulation recording. The levels and timing are identical to the Separated Data line except that a separated clock pulse occurs each $4\mu s$.

UNSEPARATED READ DATA

The Unseparated Read Data interface line provides raw data (clock and data bits together) to the using system that requires it. The levels and timing for this signal are shown in Figure 5-4.A-15.

POWER INTERFACE

The SA900/901 Diskette Storage Drive requires both AC and DC power for operation; the AC power is used for the drive motor while the DC power is used for the electronics and stepping motor. The power requirements are defined in the following sections.

AC Power

110 ± 10% VAC @ .75A
50/60 ± .5 Hz single phase

DC Power

+5 ± 0.25 VDC @ 1.5A max. 50 mV ripple
−5 ± 0.25 VCD @ .20A max. 50 mV ripple
+24 ± 1.20 VCD @ 2.0A max.
100 mV ripple
DC POWER OPTIONS (−5 VDC Replacement)
−12 ± .6 VDC @ .20A max. 50 mV ripple
(cut trace "L")
−15 ± .75 VDC @ .20A max. 50 mV ripple
(cut trace "L" and "M")

INTERFACE CIRCUITRY

Shugart Associates provides interface circuitry to connect the SA900/901 with the host system via lines with 150 ohms characteristic impedance. The drivers and receivers are divided into two categories —

those lines carrying data and those lines carrying control information.

The following two sections describe the circuitry recommended for interfacing the SA900/901 with the host system.

Figure 5-4.A-10 shows the interface circuitry for the Read Data, Separated Data, Separated Clock, and Write Data interface lines.

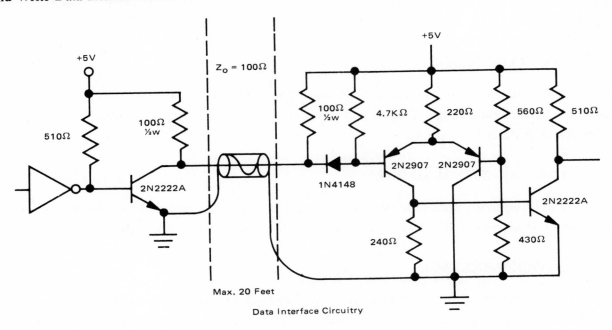

FIGURE 5-4.A-10 Data Line Driver/Receiver Combination

Data Line Driver

The line drivers for these interface signals must be capable of sinking 110 ma in the logical true state with the maximum voltage in this state no greater than .3 volts with respect to logic ground. When the line driver is in the logical false state, the driver transistor is in cutoff and the voltage at the output of the driver should be no less than 3.0v with respect to logic ground.

Control Line Driver

The line driver for these signals consist of an open collector 2N2222A transistor. The driver must be able to sink a maximum of 37 ma. in the logical true state with a maximum voltage of .3 volts with respect to logic ground. When the line driver is in the logical false state the driver transistor is in cutoff and the collector cutoff current should be no greater than 10 nanoamperes.

Data Line Receiver

The line receiver for the four interface lines is basically a Schmitt trigger with the switching threshold at 1.7 volts to enhance the noise immunity on these signal lines. The signal line is terminated in 100Ω ($\pm5\%$) for use with 93 to 100Ω coaxial cable.

Figure 5-4.A-11 shows the interface circuitry for the control lines between the SA900/901 and the host system.

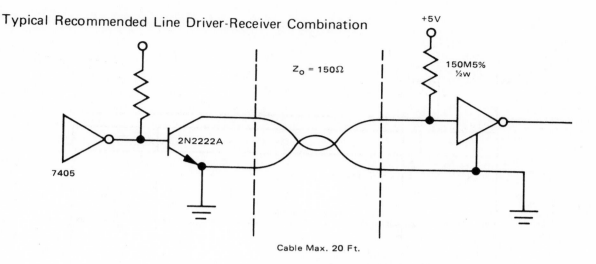

Typical Recommended Line Driver-Receiver Combination

FIGURE 5-4.A-11 Control Signal Driver/Receiver Combination

Control Line Receiver

The line receiver consists of a standard 7400 family TTL gate with a termination resistor of 150Ω ($\pm5\%$) to $+5$ volts. The input characteristics for this receiver are:

Maximum logical state voltage = .8 v.

Minimum logical false state voltage = 2.0 v.

Note: These are measured at the input to the receiver.

For a detailed discussion of IBM 3740 compatibility, the system designer should read Shugart Associates Guide to IBM 3740 Compatibility (Publication number SA 0001-2).

TRACK ACCESSING

Seeking the R/W head from one track to another is accomplished by selecting the desired direction utilizing the Direction Select interface line and then pulsing the Step line. Multiple track accessing is accomplished by repeated pulsing of the Step line until the desired track has been reached. Each pulse on the Step line will cause the R/W head to move on track either in or out depending on the Direction Select line.

The head load line must be active (logical 0 level) in order to activate the stepper. When not Accessing, Reading or Writing it is not necessary to have power to the stepper; therefore, the head load line controls the 24 volts to the stepper motor which allows it to remain cooler. This function can be crippled by cutting a trace which has been provided on the PCB. This trace has been labeled ''R'' for easy identification.

Figure 5-4.A-12 shows an SA901 recording format using sector recording.

Step Out

With the Direction Select line at a plus logic level (2.5V to 5.5V) a pulse on the Step line will cause the R/W head to move one track away from the center of the disk. The pulse(s) applied to the Step line and the Direction Select line must have the timing characteristics shown in Figure 5-4.A-13.

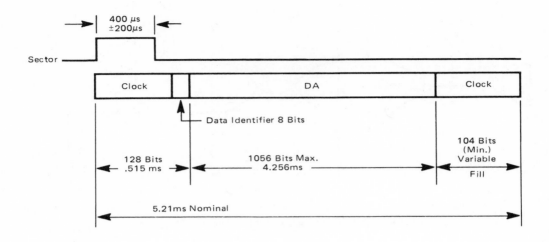

FIGURE 5-4.A-12 Sector Recording Format (SA 901 only)

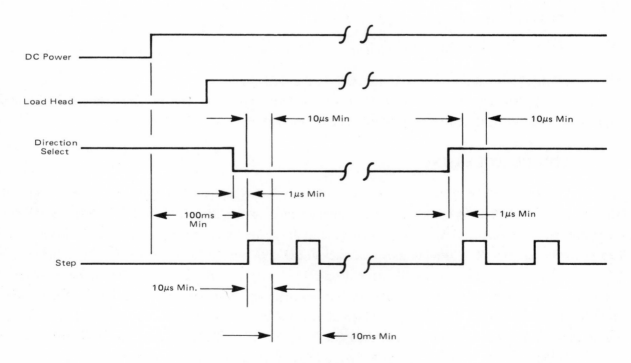

FIGURE 5-4.A-13 Track Access Timing

Step In

With the Direction Select line at a minus logic level (0V to .4V), a pulse on the Step line will cause the R/W head to move one track closer to the center of the disk. The pulse(s) applied to the Step line must have the timing characteristics shown in Figure 5-4.A-13.

These timing specifications are required in order to guarantee that the R/W head position has stabilized prior to reading.

READ OPERATION

Reading data from the SA900/901 Diskette Storage drive is accomplished by activating the interface line, "Load Head" and "Write Gate" is not active. The timing relationships required to initiate a read sequence are shown in Figure 5-4.A-14.

Once reading has commenced, the two interface lines, Separated Data and Separated Clock provide the read data. The timing of the read signals, Separated Data, and Separated Clock are shown in Figure 5-4.A-15.

WRITE OPERATION

In order to write data on the SA900/901 Diskette Storage drive, certain timing relationships must be assured. These timing requirements are required to:

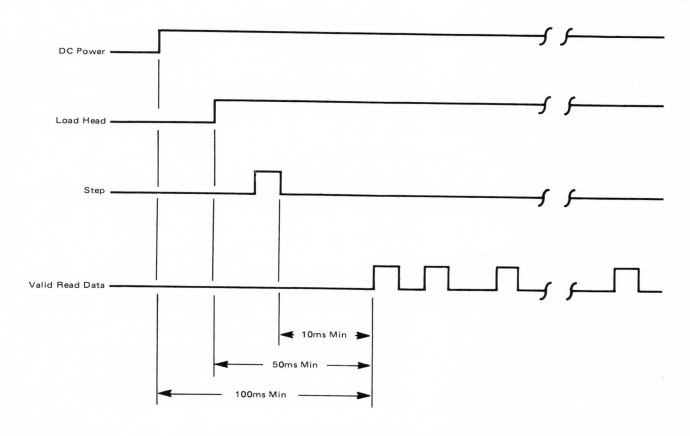

FIGURE 5-4.A-14 Read Initiate Timing

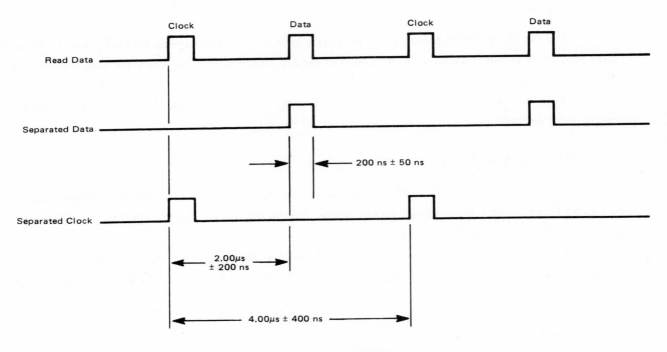

FIGURE 5-4.A-15 Read Signal Timing

(1) Avoid destroying data due to a hardware failure or the position of the R/W head has not stabilized.

These timing requirements are defined in Figure 5-4.A-16.

In order to ensure that a hardware failure or operator interference does not cause the unintentional loss of data, data safety circuitry is provided. If the data safety circuitry detects an undesirable condition within the drive a latch is set, writing is inhibited, and the signal File Inoperable is sent to the user. File Inoperable is defined by:

File Inoperable = (Write Gate . Write I Sense)
+ (Write Gate . Write I Sense)
+ (Write Gate . Head Load)
+ (Write Gate . Write Data)
+ (Write Gate . Door Closed)

POWER SEQUENCING

Applying AC and DC power to the SA900/901 can be done in any sequence, however, once AC power has been applied, a 4 second delay must be introduced before any Read or Write operation is attempted. This delay is for stabilization of the Diskette rotational speed. Also, initial position of the R/W head with respect to data tracks is indeterminant immediately after application of DC power. In order to assure proper positioning of the R/W head prior to any read/write operation, a Step Out operation should be performed until the Track 00 indicator becomes active.

The Load Head signal can be applied any time after DC power has been applied, however, the signal must be true for a minimum of 50 ms prior to a read or write operation.

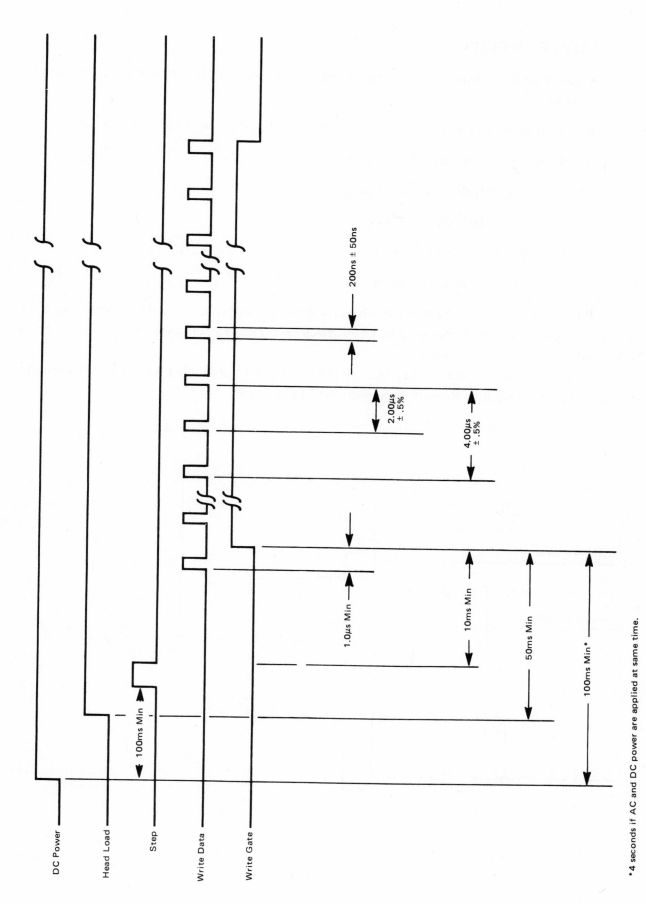

FIGURE 5-4.A-16 Write Initiate Timing

SAFETY CIRCUITS

- Safety Circuits check for component failures, using system operational errors, and operator errors.

The safety circuit, File Inop, in the SA900/901 is designed to check for the following:

(1) Write gate with no write current sense.

(2) No write gate with write current sense.

(3) Write gate without the head loaded.

(4) Write gate with no write data.

(5) Write gate with the door opened.

Figure 5-4.A-17 shows the functional diagram of the File Inop circuit. It is the responsibility of the using system to test the -File Inop interface line. Upon detection of -File Inop, the using system should activate -File Inop Reset and retry the operation.

When -File Inop becomes active, the SA900/901 will inhibit any further write operations until the fault is corrected, and File Inop Reset or Power on reset is presented.

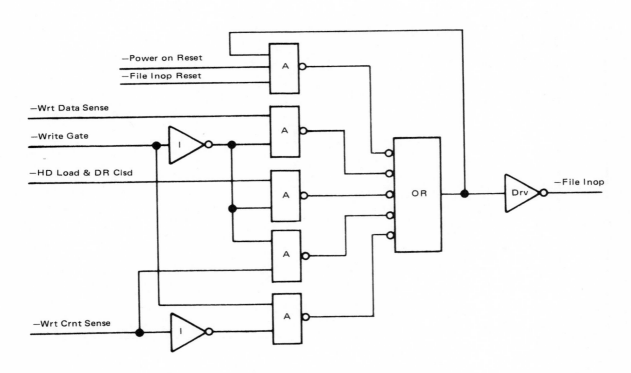

FIGURE 5-4.A-17 File Inop Circuit

APPENDIX 5-4.B
ORBIS MODEL 74 DISKETTE DRIVE
(Courtesy Orbis Systems, Inc.)

ORBIS MODEL 74 DISKETTE DRIVE

5-4.B.1 EQUIPMENT SPECIFICATIONS

The equipment specifications for the Model 74 Diskette Drive are as follows:

5-4.B.1.1 ACCESSING TIME

Average Latency	83 mS
Access Time	6 mS track to track; 14 mS Settle
Head Load Time	16 mS/14mS Settle

5-4.B.1.2 RECORDING

Mode	Double Frequency (Standard)
Density (nominal)	1836 bpi (outer track)
	3268 bpi (inner track)
Data Transfer Rate	250,000 Hz nominal
Sectors (soft)	IBM 3740 or equivalent
Sectors (hard)	Up to 32

5-4.B.1.3 DATA CAPACITY (Unformatted)

Bits/Track	41,664
Bytes/Track	5,208
Bits/Byte	8
Tracks/Disk	77
Bits/Disk	3,208,128

5-4.B.1.4 DISKETTE (IBM Compatible)

Disks/Cartridge	1 (8 x 8 inches including envelope)
Useable Recording Surfaces/ Disk Cartridge	1 or 2
Disk Surface Diameter	7.88 inches
Recording Diameters	Track 76 (inner) 2.0290 inches nominal;
	Track 00 (outer) 3.6123 inches nominal
Disk Surface Coating	Magnetic Oxide
Disk Rotational Speed	360 ± 9 rpm

5-4.B.1.5 READ/WRITE/ERASE HEAD

Head/Unit	1
Track Width	.014 inch
Track Spacing	0.02083 inch (48 tracks per inch)
Erase to Read/Write Gap	.033 ± 0.003 inch

5-4.B.1.6 PHYSICAL (Approx.)

Height	4.53 inches
Width	9.01 inches
Depth	14.12 inches
Weight	15 lbs.

5-4.B.1.7 ELECTRICAL

Power Supply (Supplied by User)

dc
+24 volts (± 5%) @ 1.5A
+5 volts (± 5%) @ 0.75A
−12 volts (± 5%) @ 0.10A (Early Machines Only)

ac
100 Vac ± 10% 50/60 Hz ± 0.5 Hz
115 Vac ± 10% 60 Hz ± 0.5 Hz
208/230 Vac ± 10% 60 Hz ± 0.5 Hz
240 Vac ± 10% 50 Hz ± 0.5 Hz

5.4.B.1.8 DATA INTEGRITY

Soft Error Rate > 1 in 10^{10} Bits
Hard Error Rate < 1 in 10^{12} Bits

THEORY OF OPERATION

5-4.B.2 GENERAL

The Model 74 consists of control and read/write electronics, diskette drive motor, read/write head, track access mechanism, and removable diskette cartridge. The basic functions of the Model 74 are:

Receive and generate control signals

Access the appropriate track

Write or read data on command

The functions of the Model 74 and the required interface signals to and from the using system are shown in Figure 5-4.B-1. The Read, Write, File Unsafe and Control Logic are the interface electronics between the host system and the drive. The stepping motor positions the read/write head to the desired track on the diskette. The head load solenoid loads the disk against the read/write head and data may then be recorded on or read from the diskette. Each of the logic blocks and signal names shown are later discussed under Logic and R/W Functional Descriptions.

The electronic circuitry is packaged on one Printed Wiring Board (PWB).
The PWB contains:

(1) Index Transducer Circuit

(2) Track Position Stepping Motor Circuits

(3) Head Load Circuit

(4) Read/Write Circuits

(5) File Unsafe Sensing Circuits

(6) Drive Selection Circuits

The stepping motor and lead screw positions the read/write head. The stepping motor rotates the lead screw clockwise or counterclockwise in 15° increments. A 15° rotation of the moves the read/write head one track position. The host system steps the stepping motor to the desired track. Track verification is accomplished by checking track and/or sector address.

The diskette drive motor rotates the spindle at 360 rpm through a belt-drive system. 50 or 60 Hz power is accommodated by means of a pulley change. A registration cone, centered on the face of the spindle, positions the diskette. A clamp (that closes with mechanical door linkage) fixes the diskette to the registration cone.

The read/write head is in contact with the diskette when loaded. The head surface has been designed to obtain maximum signal transfer to and from the magnetic surface of the disk with minimum head/diskette wear. The tunnel erase DC erases the inter-track area to improve off track signal-to-noise ratio and permit diskette interchangeability from unit to unit.

The read/write head is mounted on a carriage that is moved by the stepper motor drive shaft. Head load is achieved when the diskette is loaded against the rigidly mounted head by moving a load pad against the diskette with the solenoid actuated bail. Head to diskette compliance is achieved by restraining the diskette between the head and the load pad.

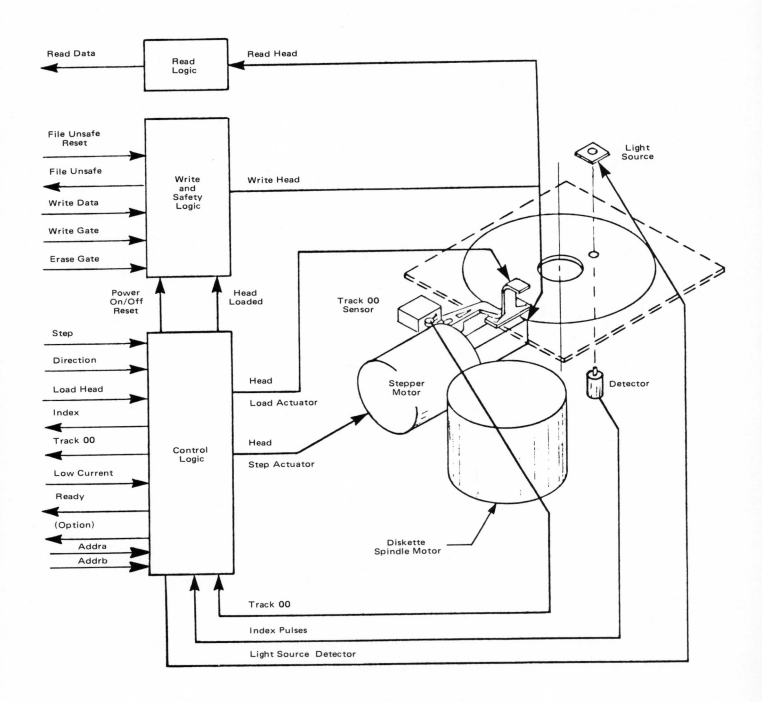

FIGURE 5-4.B-1 Model 74 Functional Block Diagram

FUNCTION	DISKETTE DRIVE CONNECTOR J1	FUNCTION	DISKETTE DRIVE CONNECTOR J1
DRIVE ADDR A	1	RETURN	26
RETURN	2	-LOW CURRENT	27
KEY	3	RETURN	28
KEY	4	-STEP	29
-READ DATA	5	RETURN	30
RETURN	6	-IN (DIRECTION)	31
-READY	7	RETURN	32
RETURN	8	-LOAD HEAD	33
-SECTOR*	9	RETURN	34
RETURN	10	-SEP CLOCK*	35
-INDEX	11	RETURN	36
RETURN	12	-SEP DATA*	37
-WRITE DATA	13	RETURN	38
RETURN	14	DRIVE ADDR B	39
-ERASE GATE (Early Machines Only)	15	RETURN	40
RETURN	16	+5 VOLTS	41
-WRITE GATE	17	+5 VOLTS	42
RETURN	18	−12 VOLTS(Early Machines Only)	43
-FILE UNSAFE	19	0 VOLTS	44
RETURN	20	+24 VOLT RETURN	45
-FILE PROTECT*	21	+24 VOLT RETURN	46
RETURN	22	+24 VOLT RETURN	47
-TRACK 00	23	+24 VOLTS	48
RETURN	24	+24 VOLTS	49
-UNSAFE RESET	25	+24 VOLTS	50

*Option Signals

TABLE 5.4-B-3 Interface Pin Assignments

5-4.B.2 INTERFACE DESCRIPTION

The interface of the 74 is divided into two categories: Signal/Data Interface and Power Interface. The initial Power up and Read/Write Sequence are shown in Figures 5-4.B-3 and 5-4.B-4.

5-4.B.4 SIGNAL AND DATA INTERFACE

5-4.B.4.1 INPUT LINES

There are nine low active TTL input lines to the 74: Direction, Step, Load Head, File Unsafe Reset,

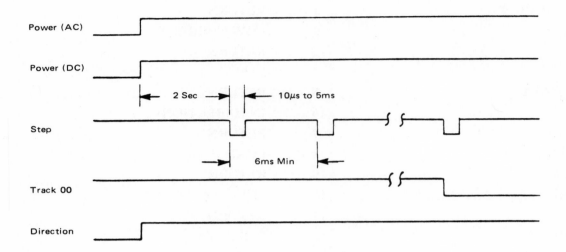

FIGURE 5-4.B-3 Power Up Sequence

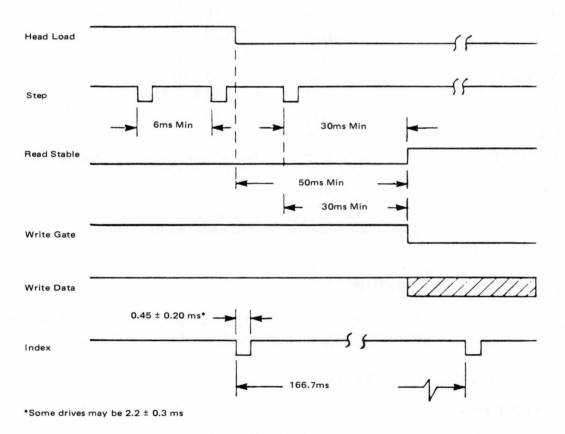

*Some drives may be 2.2 ± 0.3 ms

FIGURE 5-4.B-4 Read/Write Sequence

Write Gate, Write Data, Drive Addr A, Drive Addr B, and Low Current. Each line has the following characteristics (refer to Figure 5-4.B-5):

Logic 1	−Active — 0V to 0.4V
Logic 0	−Inactive — +2.5V to +5.5V
Input Impedance	−220 ohms to +5V and 330 ohms to GND.

(1) Direction (-In)

This interface signal defines the direction of motion of the R/W head when the Step line is pulsed. A low active level on this line causes the Head Position Mechanism to move the read/write head towards the center of the disk when the Step line is pulsed. With the Direction line at an inactive level, a pulse on the Step line causes the Head Position Mechanism to move the read/write head away from the center of the disk. The state of Direction must not change until 200 nS after the leading edge of the Step pulse.

(2) Step

A low active level (10 μS min) on this line will cause the read/write head to be moved one track. The direction of movement is controlled by the Direction line. The state of Direction line is sampled 100 ± 30 nsec after the leading edge of step. Access timing relationships conform to Figure 5-4.B-3.

(3) Load Head

A low active level on this line causes the storage element to be placed in close proximity to the read/write head for data recording or retrieval. Load Head may be activated at any time after power has been applied; however, this line must be activated at least 50 mS prior to a read or write operation. During periods of no data transfer this line should be deactivated to provide for maximum storage element and head life.

(4) File Unsafe Reset

A low active level (200 nS minimum) on this line resets the File Unsafe Latch, providing the capability of a write retry operation without the need for operator intervention.

(5) Write Gate

A low active level on this line enables the write current source, and disables the stepping circuitry (see Section 4.5.2 for further clarification).

(6) Write Data

This interface line provides the data to be written on the disk. Each transition to a low active level on this line causes write current through the write coils to be reversed. A 200nS wide pulse is required for each flux reversal to be written.

(7) Erase Gate

The Erase Gate input controls the DC Current through the erase element to provide tunnel erase while writing on the disk. A low active level on this line turns on constant current to the erase head. (Refer to Figure 5-4.B-6 for timing considerations.)

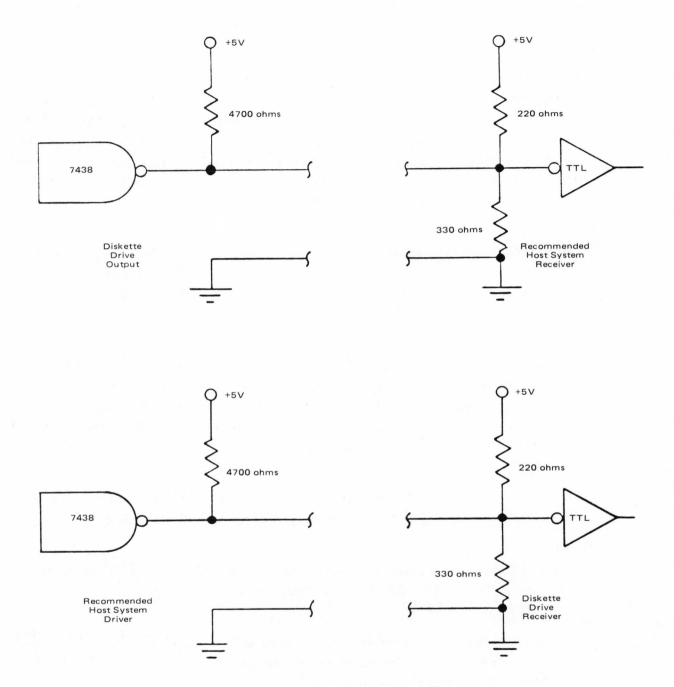

FIGURE 5-4.B-5 Interface Driver and Receiver

(8) Low Current

A low active level on this line is recommended for writing on tracks 44 through 76. This input is used to lower the write current which consequently improves the read output resolution of the inner tracks.

(9) Drive Addr A & B

The interface lines may be used to define one of 4 drives to be selected in the following manner:

Drive	Address	
B	A	
0	0	Drive 0 0 = Inactive
0	1	Drive 1 1 = Active
1	0	Drive 2
1	1	Drive 3

5-4.B.4.2 OUTPUT LINES

There are five output lines from the 74: Index, Track 00, File Unsafe, Read Data, and Ready. Each line has the following characteristics (refer to Figure 5-4.B-5):

Active	0 to 0.4V
Inactive	4700 ohms to +5V
Maximum Sink	47 mA

(1) Index

This interface signal is provided by the disk drive once each revolution (166.7 mS) to indicate the beginning of the track. This signal makes a transition to a low active level for a period of 0.45 ± 0.20 mS* (Refer to Figure 5-4.B-4).

(2) Track 00

A low active level on this line indicates that the read/write head is positioned at track 00. The signal is valid 10 mS after the last Step command.

(3) File Unsafe

A low active level on this line indicates that a condition which may jeopardize data integrity has occurred. File Unsafe may be reset by activating the File Unsafe Reset line. (See WRITE MODE for list of File Unsafe conditions.)

(4) Read Data

Data is output to the host system in the same form as write data from the host system. Each flux reversal sensed on the storage element will result in a transition to a low active level for a 200 nS period on this line.

(5) Ready

A low active level on this line indicates that a diskette is loaded and rotating in the drive and that the front door is closed.

---

*Some drives may be 2.2 ± 0.3 mS.

APPENDIX 5-4.C
CAL COMP 140 DISKETTE DRIVE
(Courtesy Cal Comp Corporation)

Century Data
A DIVISION OF
CALCOMP

5-4.C.1 **DESCRIPTION**

The Century Data Model 140 Floppy Disk Drive is a high speed, random access, disk storage unit which utilizes a flexible disk cartridge as the storage unit which utilizes a flexible disk cartridge as the storage medium. Up to 3.20 million bits of data may be stored on the single recording surface of the flexible disk. When utilizing the IBM 3740 data format, 1.94 million bits of data may be recorded. The Model 140 Floppy Disk Drive features 48 tracks-per-inch and 3200 bits-per-inch technologies to provide media interchangeability with the IBM 3740 series of data recording equipment.

The Model 140 contains features and options whereby a systems designer may incorporate the Model 140 into his data storage system with a minimum of effort. Among these are a positive pressurized media chamber, precise media registration, write protect capability, sector outputs, and a choice of data outputs.

Figure 5-4.C-1 shows the size and composition of the floppy disk cartridge.

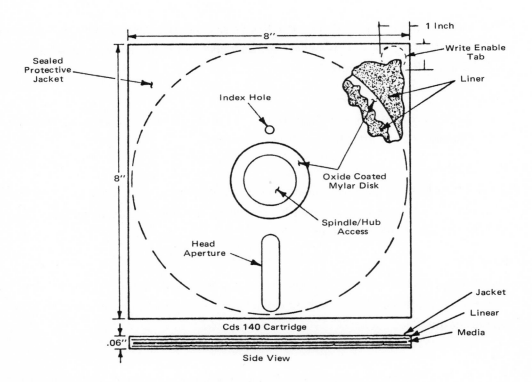

FIGURE 5-4.C-1 Floppy Disk Cartridge

The disk drive comprises a read/write head positioning system, data decoder, and I/O gated control and status circuits. Drive voltage is obtained from the host system, as well as, +24 and +5 vdc voltage requirements.

I/O interface signals are routed between the controller and disk drive(s) in a radial or daisy-chain fashion via standard paddle board connectors.

In multiple disk drive applications, each drive is individually selectable. Availability status of a disk drive for on-line operations bypasses the addressing circuits; thereby, permitting ready status to be monitored on a status interrupt basis.

5-4.C.2 PHYSICAL AND ELECTRICAL CHARACTERISTICS

Tables 5-4.C-2, 5-4.C-3 and 5-4.C-4 provide the physical and electrical characteristics and Table 5-4.C-5 gives the pertinent specifications.

Height	8.40 inches
Width	4.90 inches
Depth	15.75 inches including connector
Weight	18 pounds

TABLE 5-4.C-2 Physical Characteristics

AC Power	50Hz+0.5Hz 100 vac ±10%, single phase
	208 vac ±10%, single phase
	220 vac ±10%, single phase
	240 vac ±10%, single phase
	60Hz+0.5Hz 100 vac ±10%, single phase
	115 vac ±10%, single phase
	208 vac ±10%, single phase
	230 vac ±10%, single phase
DC Power	+5 vdc ±2% at 1.5 amperes
	+24 vdc ±5% at 1.0 amperes

TABLE 5-4.C-3 Power Requirements

Temperature	60°F to 100°F with maximum gradient of 20°F/hour
Relative Humidity	20% to 80%, 78°F maximum wet bulb
Heat Dissipation	540 BTU/hour

TABLE 5-4.C-4 Operating Environment

Storage Capacity	
Unformatted	
Per Disk	3,208,128 Bits
Per Track	41,664 Bits
Formatted (IBM 3740)	1,943,552 Bits
Per Disk	1,943,552 Bits
Per Track	26,624 Bits
Sector	1,024 Bits
Number of Tracks	77
Recommended Coding Technique	Double Frequency (FM)
Bit Transfer Rate	250,000 bits/sec, nominal
Positioning Mechanism	Stepper Motor, electrical detent
Head Stabilization Time	10 milliseconds
Head Load Time	16 milliseconds
Rotational Speed	360 RPM ± 2.5% (167 millisecond/revolution)
Motor Start Time (To Ready)	2 seconds maximum

TABLE 5-4.C-5 Specifications

6-5.C.3 INPUT/OUTPUT SIGNALS

A list of input and output signals, and characteristics, is provided in Tables 5-4.C-5 and 5-4.C-6, respectively.

Signal Name	Definition
SELECT/	A unique signal used to enable communication between a disk drive and its controller. This line must be low (0V) to be active.
WRITE ENABLE/	Enable recording of data on the flexible disk. This line must be low (0V) to be active. When this line is high (+5V), reading from the flexible disk is enabled.
WRITE DATA/	This line carries low active (0V) pulses representing data to be recorded on the flexible disk. Write current reverses direction on the trailing edge of each pulse. Pulses must be 0.2 to 1.5 microseconds wide with a maximum repetition rate of 2.0 microseconds.
ABOVE TRACK 43/	This line is used to control write current amplitude, guaranteeing IBM 3740 media interchangeability. This line must be high (+5V) when recording on tracks 0 through 43, and low (0V) when recording on tracks 44 through 76. ABOVE TRACK 43 must be stabilized 10 microseconds before activating WRITE ENABLE.
STEP/	This line is used in conjunction with DIRECTION and is used to cause the read/write head to be moved from track to track. A low pulse (0V) of 2 microseconds to 4 milliseconds causes the head to move one track in the direction specified by the DIRECTION line. Maximum step rate is 167 steps per second (6 milliseconds per step).
DIRECTION	This line is used in conjunction with STEP to cause the read/write head to be moved from track to track. When this line is high (+5V), direction is IN (higher numbered tracks). When this line is low (0V), direction is OUT (lower numbered tracks). This line must be stable 100 nanoseconds minimum before activating STEP and remain in the appropriate state for the duration of the step period.
HEAD LOAD/	This line is used to move the flexible disk against the read/write head for data recording or retrieval. This line must be low (0V) to be active. A 16 millisecond delay is required after activating this line prior to commencing data transfers to allow for media loading.
PLO SYNC/	A low level (0V) pulse 12 microseconds wide will cause the PLO data separator to sync to preamble 0's for data tracking.

TABLE 5-4.C-6 140 Disk Drive Output Signals

Signal Name	Definition
READ DATA	This line transmits read data to the controller. Exact line definition and timing characteristics depend on the data separator present within the drive. When no data separator is present within the drive, this line has no function.
With Standard One-Shot Separator	This line is a NRZ data line with the one-shot separator. The level of the line represents data. A one bit is represented by a low (0V) level, and a zero bit is represented by a high (+5V) level. The READ CLOCK line is used to clock data into the controller.
Read DATA (Continued) With Optional PLO Data Separator	This line outputs data pulses with the PLO separator. A one bit is represented by an 800 nanosecond low (0V) level pulse. A zero bit is represented by the absence of a pulse. The READ CLOCK line is used to clock data into the controller.
READ CLOCK/	Exact meaning and timing characteristics of this line depend on the data separator used within the drive.
With No Data Separator	When no data separator is used within the drive, this line outputs unseparated data (clocks and data). This output is provided for the systems designer who desires to use his own encoding scheme or provide data separation in the controller. This output may be used to enable detection of IBM 3720-type address marks by the controller. A modified one-shot decoder with a missing pulse detector will allow detection of 3740 address marks. Each flux reversal read from the disk is output as a 300 ± 100 nanosecond wide low (0V) pulse.
With One-Shot Separator	This line will output 300 ± 100 nanosecond wide low (0V) pulses representing separated clocks. The trailing edge of these pulses are used to strobe the READ DATA line into the controller.
With PLO Separator	This line will output 800 nonosecond wide low (0V) pulses representing separated clocks. These pulses occur simultaneously with pulses occurring on the READ DATA line.
INDEX/	The leading edge of a 450 microsecond wide low (0V) pulse on this line represents the beginning of track. This pulse occurs once per revolution of the flexible disk.
TRACK 00/	When this line is low (0V), the read/write head is positioned over track 00. This line is intended as a head position reference. When this line is active, the stepper motor drive circuits are inhibited from further outward movement.
READY	A low level (0V) on this line indicates that the flexible disk is up to speed. This line is not gated by SELECT and is thus a unique line. This line serves as an interrupt to the controller and is particularly useful during flexible disk changes.
SECTOR/	Low level (0V) pulses on this line represent sector marks. Sector pulses are 1 millisecond wide.
WRITE PROTECTED/	A low level (0V) on this line indicates that a write enable tab is not present on the flexible disk in the drive, thus no writing may take place.

TABLE 5-4.C-6 140 Disk Drive Output Signals

5-4.C.4 INTERFACE REQUIREMENTS

Table 5-4.C-7 gives the interface logic levels and the I/O cable specifications.

Specifications	Characteristics
Logic Levels High Low	 +5.5V to +2.2V +0.4V to 0.0V
Signal Cable Length Type Conductor Size Twists per foot	 20 feet maximum Twisted pairs (40 pair) No. 24 or No. 26 AWG 30

TABLE 5-4.C-7

5-4.C.5 FUNCTIONAL DESCRIPTION

The disk drive is a mass memory device featuring a floppy disk and contact recording. The 250 kHz transfer rate provides a high speed interchange of data between the disk drive and a host controller. The disk drive(s) may be connected in a radial or daisy-chained configuration with individual selection and status monitoring.

The disk drive requires operator intervention in loading and unloading the floppy disk, after which the controller remotely operates the unit. Low-voltage, control signals, drive motor power, and write data are supplied by the controller, while the disk drive responds with operating status and read data.

The disk drive (Figure 5-4.C-8) comprises the following functional circuits and mechanisms:

- Drive mechanism
- Head load mechanism
- Positioning mechanism
- Head load mechanism

- Power-on/ready logic
- Read/Write head positioning logic
- Read/write logic

Drive Mechanism

The drive system provides rotational disk movement using a single-phase motor selected to match primary power of the controller system (see Figure 5-4.C-9). Various drive motors are available that accommodate primary power ranging between 100 and 240 vac at 50 or 60 Hz. The disk drive attains ready status within two seconds of primary power application.

The drive motor also provides positive pressurization by an impeller (squirrel cage) fan mechanically connected to one end of the rotor shaft.

Rotation of the disk is provided by a belt and pulley connected to the other side of the motor. The drive pulley and drive belt are selected for either 50 or 60 Hz input power. Floppy disk rotational speed is 360 rpm. The disk is engaged with the drive by the spindle mechanism centering cone.

THE CDS 140

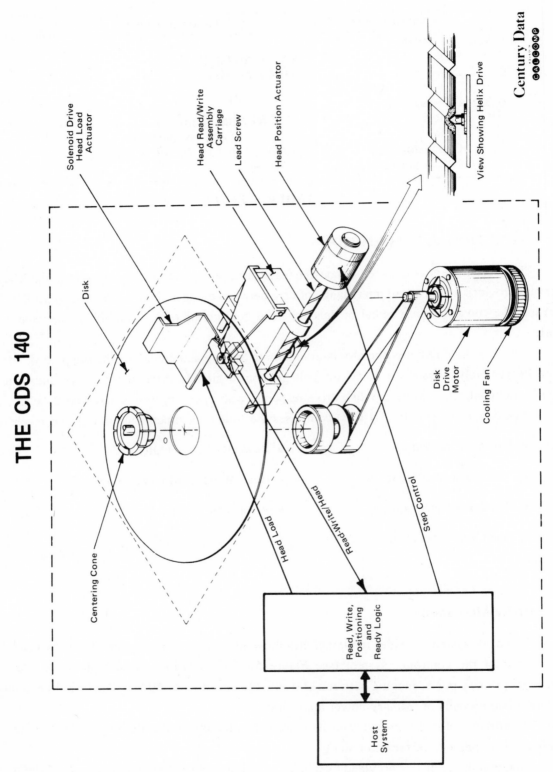

Solenoid Drive Head Load Actuator

Head Read/Write Assembly Carriage

Lead Screw

Head Position Actuator

Disk

Centering Cone

Disk Drive Motor

Cooling Fan

View Showing Helix Drive

Century Data

Head Load

Read/Write/Head

Step Control

Read, Write, Positioning and Ready Logic

Host System

FIGURE 5-4.C-8 The CDS 140

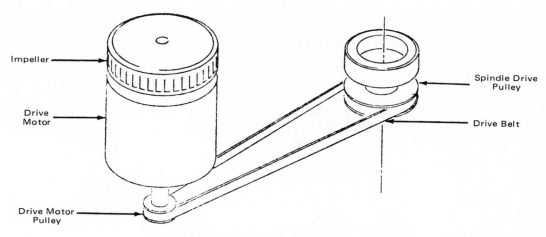

FIGURE 5-4.C-9 Drive Mechanism

5-4.C.5.1 Spindle Mechanism

The spindle mechanism consists of a centering-cone and a load plate. In the unload position, the load plate is pivoted upwards creating an aperture through which the floppy disk is inserted. In this position, the centering-cone disengages the disk from the drive mechanism.

To load a disk, the operator inserts the floppy disk then presses down on the load handle which latches the load plate in the operating mode. The centering-cone is mechanically linked to the load plate and is activated at the same time (see Figure 5-4.C-10).

The centering cone is an open splined device that performs two functions: (1) engages disk media and drive mechanism and (2) positions the disk media in the correct track alignment.

As the load plate is pivoted to the load position, the centering-cone enters the floppy disk center. At approximately 80 mils from full-down position, a centering cone expander is automatically activated. This device then expands the centering-cone which grips the inner diameter of the disk media in the correct track alignment.

Track 00 (home) position serves as the disk drive reference track. This position is sensed by a photo-transducer which generates track 00 status. This status is sent to the controller for initial track positioning. All track addressing is relative. The controller generates step pulses to position the carriage from the current track to a new track.

5-4.C.5.2 Positioning Mechanism

The positioning mechanism comprises a carriage assembly and a bi-directional stepper motor (see Figure 5-4.C-11). The stepper motor rotational movements are converted to linear motion by the rotor helix drive.

The read/write head mount rides in the grooved helix shaft and is held in horizontal alignment by the way. When the stepper motor is pulsed, the helix drive rotates clockwise or counterclockwise moving the mount in or out.

The stepper motor includes four pair of quadrature windings. In detent, current flows in one winding and maintains the rotor in electro-magnetic detent. For positioning one or more step pulses are sequentially applied to quadrature windings, causing an imbalance in the electro-magnetic field. The stepper motor, consequently, revolves through detent positions until the step pulses are halted. The rotor then locks in that

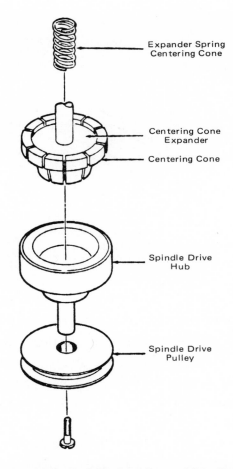

FIGURE 5-4.C-10 Centering Cone and Drive Hub

Expander Spring
Centering Cone

Centering Cone
Expander

Centering Cone

Spindle Drive
Hub

Spindle Drive
Pulley

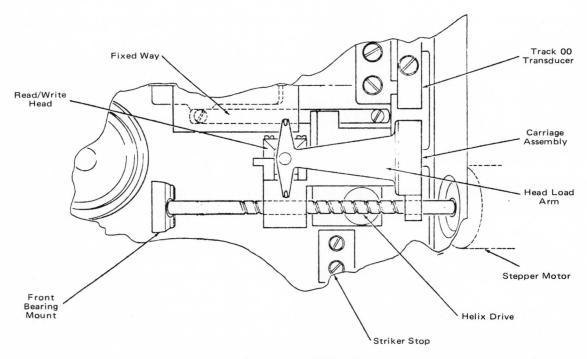

Fixed Way

Read/Write
Head

Track 00
Transducer

Carriage
Assembly

Head Load
Arm

Stepper Motor

Front
Bearing
Mount

Helix Drive

Striker Stop

FIGURE 5-4.C-11 Positioning Mechanism

position. The sequence in which the stepper motor quadrature windings are pulsed dictates rotational direction and, subsequently, higher or lower track addressing from a relative position.

5-4.C.5.3 Head Load Mechanism

The head load mechanism is basically a relay driver and a solenoid. When activated by HEAD LOAD/, the spring-loaded head load pad is released and rests in parallel alignment with the floppy disk surface. Part of the casting provides the lower alignment dimensional surface while the head load solenoid bar provides the upper alignment surface.

In the load position the read/write head tang rides between these two alignment surfaces and maintains the read/write head in contact with the disk surface.

The load pad is located behind the read/write head and holds the floppy disk flat against the lower alignment block.

To minimize disk surface and read/write head wear, the head load signal is gated with SELECT. In the deselect or idle mode, head loading is automatically disabled. The head load command requires a 16 millisecond execution time.

5-4.C.5.4 Power-On/Ready Logic

Initially the controller applies ac drive motor power which, in turn, initializes the ready circuit (see Figure 5-4.C-12). Rotational speed is measured by comparing index repetition rate to a ramp signal. When 60

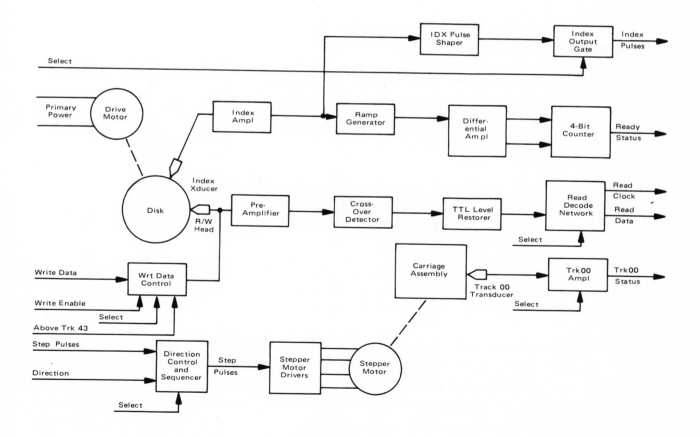

FIGURE 5-4.C-12 Model 140 Functional Block Diagram

5-237

percent rotational speed is attained, the ramp level is less than index pulse timing. This condition is detected by a differential amplifier whose output is applied to the parallel load input of a 4-stage counter.

Prior to attaining speed, the 4-stage counter is held in the cleared state and maintains a not ready status output. Once speed is increased to the operational level, the parallel load signal is inhibited and the counter is incremented by index. At a 12-count, the decoded output inhibits further index counting and switches the ready line to a low or disk drive ready status.

Ready status is not gated SELECT, allowing the controller to monitor this condition through a status interrupt feature. The controller may elect to issue track addressing while waiting ready status. The positioning system operates independently of the disk drive mechanism.

5-4.C.5.5 Read/Write Head Positioning Circuits

The read/write head positioning logic responds to STEP/pulses and the DIRECTION signal from the controller. The number of step pulses designates track position. DIRECTION provides the step pulse sequence; thereby, signifying a clockwise or a counter-clockwise decode.

The rotational decode is applied to Darlington drivers connected to the stepper motor quadrature windings. The 2-bit decode successively enables one winding at a time, causing the read/write head to traverse one track position.

Track 00 is optically detected by a photo-diode transducer. This position is attained by the controller issuing a step-out command followed by approximately 100 stepping pulses. The positioning system responds, by moving the read/write head to track 00, developing track 00 status, and inhibiting any further outward movement.

5-4.C.5.6 Read/Write Logic

The read/write logic incorporates a single read/write head to record and retrieve data. Data is recorded wide by the write circuit, then confined to 0.012-inch track width by the tunnel erase coil (see Figure 5-4.C-13).

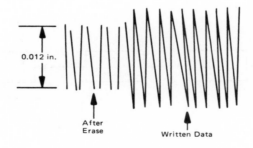

FIGURE 5-4.C-13 Tunnel Erase

Each bit (clock or data) produces a flux change that is concentrated on a small area of the recording surface. Flux pattern polarity is alternated for successive bits through the use of dual write coils, wound anti-phase fashion. This technique assists data recovery during a read operation.

Flux transitions are detected by the read coils as the head passes over data. The analog output of the read coils is applied to a differential amplifier for pre-amplification. Data is recovered from the bipolar signal by a crossover detector whose output is linearly shaped then coupled to a read decode network.

APPENDIX 5-4.D
RECORDING FORMATS
(COURTESY SHUGART ASSOCIATES)

5-4.D   Recording Format

5-4.d.1   The format of the data recorded on the Diskette is totally a function of the host system. Data is recorded on the diskette using frequency modulation as the recording mode, i.e., each data bit recorded on the diskette has an associated clock bit recorded with it. Data written on and read back from the diskette takes the form as shown in Figure 5-4.D-1. The binary data pattern shown represents a 101.

5-4.d.2   Bit Cell

As shown in Figure 5-4.D-2, the clock bits and data bits (if present) are interleaved. By definition, a Bit Cell is the period between the leading edge of one clock bit and the leading edge of the next clock bit.

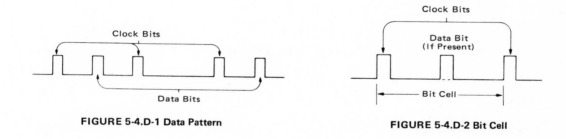

FIGURE 5-4.D-1 Data Pattern   **FIGURE 5-4.D-2 Bit Cell**

5-4.d.3   Byte

A Byte, when referring to serial data (being written onto or read from the disc drive), is defined as eight (8) consecutive bit cells. The most significant bit cell is defined as bit cell 0 and the least significant bit cell is defined as bit cell 7. When reference is made to a specific data bit (i.e., data bit 3), it is with respect to the corresponding bit cell (bit cell 3).

During a write operation, bit cell 0 of each byte is transferred to the disc drive first with bit cell 7 being transferred last. Correspondingly, the most significant byte of data is transferred to the disc first and the least significant byte is transferred last.

When data is being read back from the drive, bit cell 0 of each byte will be transferred first with bit cell 7 last. As with reading, the most significant byte will be transferred first from the drive to the user.

Figure 5-4.D-3 illustrates the relationship of the bits within a byte and Figure 5-4.D-4 illustrates the relationship of the bytes for read and write data.

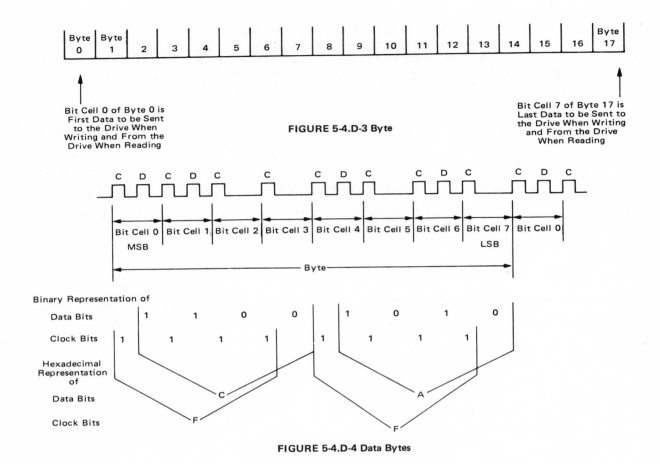

FIGURE 5-4.D-3 Byte

FIGURE 5-4.D-4 Data Bytes

5-4.D.4 Tracks

The SA900/901 is capable of recording up to 77 tracks of data. The tracks are numbered 0-76. Each track is made available to the R/W Head by accessing the head with a stepper motor and carriage assembly. Track accessing will be covered in Section 5.5.

Basic Track Characteristics:

Number of bits/track	41,300 bits
Index Pulse Width	1.7 ± .5 ms
Index/Sector Pulse Width (SA901 only)	.4 ± .2 ms

5-4.D.5 Track Format

Tracks may be formatted in numerous ways and are dependent on the using system. The SA900/901 use index and sector recording formats respectively.

5-4.D.5.1 Index Recording Format

In this Format, the using system may record one long record or several smaller records. Each track is started by a physical index pulse and then each record is preceded by a unique recorded identifier. This type of recording is called soft sectoring. Figure 5-4.D-5 shows a typical Index Recording Format.

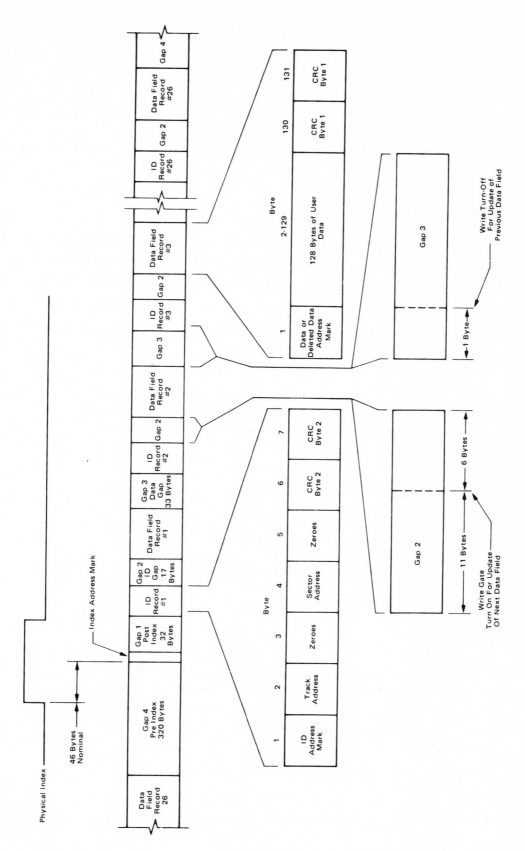

FIGURE 5-4.D-5 Track Format

5-4.D.5.2 Sector Recording Format

In this Format, the using system may record up to 32 sectors (records) per track. Each track is started by a physical index pulse and each sector is started by a physical sector pulse. This type of recording is called hard sectoring. Figure 5-4.D-6 shows a typical Sector Recording Format.

5-4.D.6 Typical Track Index Format

Figure 5-4.D-7 shows a track Format, which is IBM compatible, using Index Recording Format with soft sectoring.

5-4.d.6.1 Gaps (Ref. Figure 5-4.D-7)

Each field on a track is separated from adjacent fields by a number of bytes containing no data bits. These areas are referred to as gaps and are provided to allow the updating of one field without affecting adjacent fields. As can be seen from Figure 5-4.D-7, there are four different types of gaps on each track.

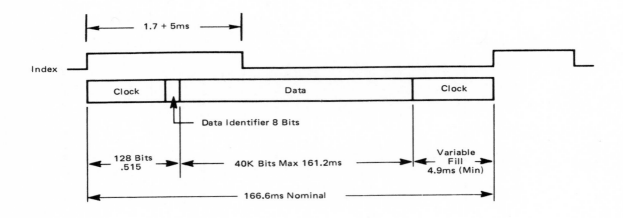

FIGURE 5-4.D-6 Index Recording Format

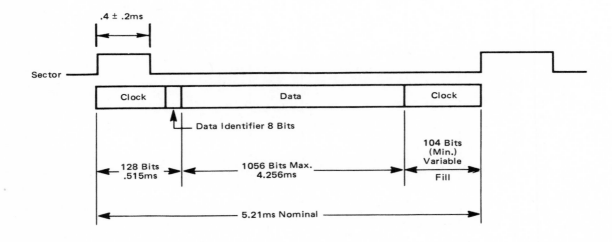

FIGURE 5-4.D-7 Sector Recording Format

5-242

Gap 1 Post-Index Gap

This gap is defined as the 32 bytes between Index Address Mark and the ID Address Mark for Sector one (excluding the address mark bytes.) This gap is always 32 bytes in length and is not affected by any updating process.

Gap 2 ID Gap

The seventeen bytes between the ID Field and the Data Field is defined as Gap 2 (ID Gap). This gap may vary in size slightly after the Data Field has been updated.

Gap 3 Data Gap

The thirty-three bytes between the Data Field and the next ID Field is defined as Gap 3 (Data Gap). As with the ID Gap, the Data Gap may vary slightly in length after the adjacent Data Field has been updated.

Gap 4 Pre-Index Gap

The three hundred and twenty bytes between the last Data Field on a track and the Index Address Mark is defined as Gap 4 (Pre-Index Gap). Initially, this gap is nominally 320 bytes in length; however, due to write frequency tolerances and disc speed tolerances this gap may vary slightly in length. Also, after the data field of record 26 has been updated, this gap may again change slightly in length.

5-4.D.6.2 Address Marks

Address Marks are unique bit patterns one byte in length which are used in this typical recording format to identify the beginning of ID and Data Fields and to synchronize the deserializing circuitry with the first byte of each field. Address Mark bytes are unique from all other data bytes in that certain bit cells do not contain a clock bit (all other data bytes have clock bits in every bit cell). There are four different types of Address Marks used. Each of these used to identify different types of fields.

Index Address Mark

The Index Address Mark is located at the beginning of each track and is a fixed number of bytes in front of the first record. The bit configuration for the Index Address Mark is shown in Figure 5-4.D-8.

ID Address Mark

The ID Address Mark byte is located at the beginning of each ID Field on the diskette. The bit configuration for this Address Mark is shown in Figure 5-4.D-9.

Data Address·Mark

The Data Address Mark is located at the beginning of each nondeleted Data Field on the diskette. The bit configuration for this Address Mark is shown in Figure 5-4.D-10.

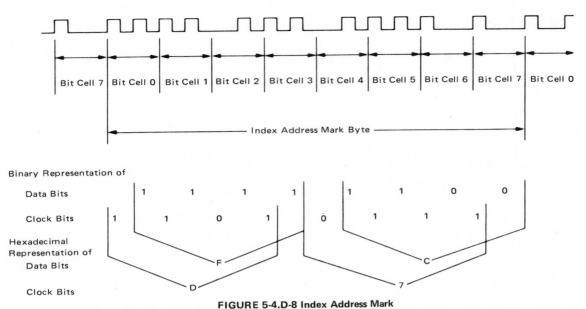

FIGURE 5-4.D-8 Index Address Mark

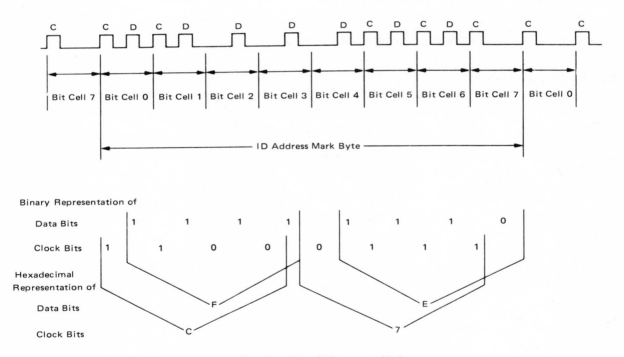

FIGURE 5-4.D-9 ID Address Mark

Deleted Data Address Mark

The Deleted Data Address Mark byte is located at the beginning of each deleted Data Field on the diskette. The bit configuration for this Address Mark is shown in Figure 5-4.D-11.

5-4.D.6.3 CRC

Each field written on the diskette is appended with two Cyclic Redundancy Check (CRC) bytes. These two CRC bytes are generated from a cyclic permutation of the data bits starting with bit zero of the address mark and ending with bit seven of the last byte within a field (excluding the CRC bytes). When a field is read back from a diskette, the data bits (from bit zero of the address mark to bit seven of the second CRC byte) are divided by the same generator polynomial. A non-zero remainder indicates an error within the data read back from the drive while a remainder of zero indicates the data has been read back correctly from the disk.

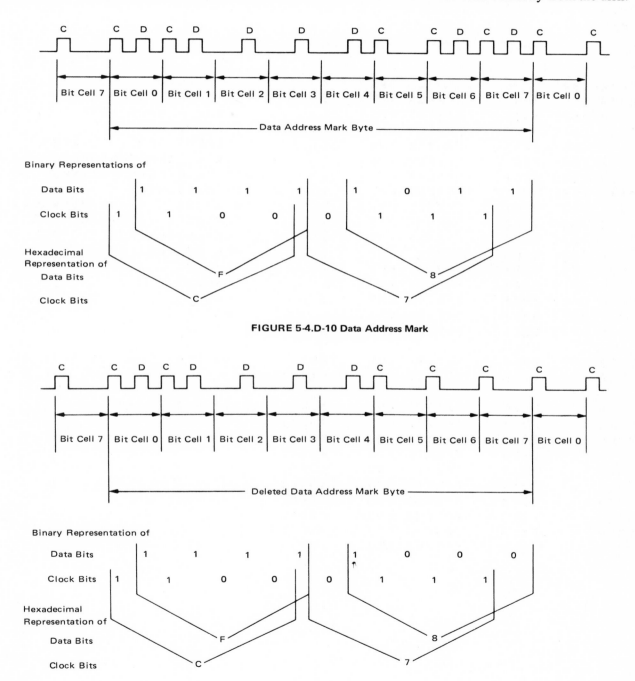

FIGURE 5-4.D-10 Data Address Mark

FIGURE 5-4.D-11 Deleted Data Address Mark

APPENDIX 5-4.E FLOPPY DISK PROGRAM LISTINGS

FLDISK

```
00010
00020
00030

00050

00070 0000                    ORG    0
00080 0000 0001    FVABOR RMB  1        OP/ABORT CODE
00090 0001 0001    FVSTAT RMB  1        ERROR STATUS WORD
00100 0002 0001    FVDELT RMB  1        TRACK DELTA
00110 0003 0001    FVCTRK RMB  1        CURRENT TRACK ADDRESS
00120 0004 0001    FVTRKA RMB  1        TARGET TRACK ADDRESS
00130 0005 0001    FVDMRK RMB  1        ID/DATA MARK PATTERN
00140 0006 0001    FVBCNT RMB  1        BYTE COUNTER
00150 0007 0002    FVDADR RMB  2        READ DATA STACK ADDRESS
00160 0009 0002    FVTIME RMB  2        VARIABLE INTERVAL TIME
00170 000B 0002    FVSYSP RMB  2        TEMP STACK PTR STORAGE
00180 000D 000A    FVUPC  RMB  10       UPC STORAGE AREA
00190 0017 0001    FVFLG1 RMB  1        FLAG 1
00200 0018 0001    FVFLG2 RMB  1        FLAG 2
00210 0019 0001    FVFLG3 RMB  1        FLAG 3
00220 001A 0001    FVFLG4 RMB  1        FLAG 4
00230 001B 0001    FVFLG5 RMB  1        FLAG 5

00250      00FF    FKDATA EQU  255      INDEX OFFSET FOR DATA STORE
00260      00FF    FKMTCH EQU  FKDATA

00280      8080    FP1PRA EQU  $8080    PIA ADDRESSES
00290      8081    FP1PRB EQU  $8081
00300      8082    FP1CRA EQU  $8082
00310      8083    FP1CRB EQU  $8083
00320      8040    FP2PRA EQU  $8040
00330      8041    FP2PRB EQU  $8041
00340      8042    FP2CRA EQU  $8042
00350      8043    FP2CRB EQU  $8043
00360      8010    FP3PRA EQU  $8010
00370      8011    FP3PRB EQU  $8011
```

```
00390                    * INTERVAL TIMER 8-BIT PRESCALE CONSTANTS

00410        0005    C1US    EQU     5          1 MICROSECOND CLOCK
00420        0004    C10US   EQU     4          10 MICROSECOND CLOCK
00430        0003    C100US  EQU     3          100 MICROSECOND CLOCK
00440        0002    C1MS    EQU     2          1 MILLISECOND CLOCK
00450        0001    C10MS   EQU     1          10 MILLISECOND CLOCK

00470                    * INTERVAL TIMER 16-BIT PRESCALE CONSTANTS

00490        0500    S1US    EQU     1280       1 MICROSECOND CLOCK
00500        0400    S10US   EQU     1024       10 MICROSECOND CLOCK
00510        0300    S100US  EQU     768        100 MICROSECOND CLOCK
00520        0200    S1MS    EQU     512        1 MILLISECOND CLOCK
00530        0100    S10MS   EQU     256        10 MILLISECOND CLOCK
00540 5000                   ORG     $5000
```

```
00580                    *INTERRUPT DRIVEN SEEK/RESTORE ROUTINE

00600                    *   THIS ROUTINE EXECUTES A ONE TRACK STEP OF
00610                    * A SEEK OR RESTORE SEQUENCE. THE DISKETTE
00620                    * DRIVE MOVES THE HEAD ONE TRACK POSITION
00630                    * EACH TIME THE STEP SIGNAL IS PULSED.
00640                    * ENTRY INTO THIS ROUTINE IS GOVERNED BY
00650                    * INTERRUPTS FROM THE INTERVAL TIMER. THE
00660                    * TIMER IS PRESET TO 9.9 MILLISECONDS FOR
00670                    * EACH STEP.  THE NUMBER OF TRACKS THE HEAD
00680                    * MUST MOVE FOR A SEEK OPERATION IS STORED
00690                    * IN RAM LOCATION "FVDELT." FOR A RESTORE
00700                    * OPERATION "FVDELT" IS PRESET TO 83 TO INSURE
00710                    * THAT THE MAXIMUM NUMBER OF TRACKS (77) CAN
00720                    * BE STEPPED. WHEN THE SEEK OR RESTORE IS
00730                    * COMPLETED OR ABORTED "FVDELT" IS SET TO
00740                    * ALL ONES. WHILE THE SEEK IS IN PROGRESS
00750                    * BIT 7 OF "FVDELT" IS ZERO.

00770                    * RAM LOCATION "FVCTRK" CONTAINS THE CURRENT
00780                    * TRACK ADDRESS OF THE HEAD. THE VALUE
00790                    * "FVCTRK" IS IN SIGNED BINARY FORMAT.
00800                    * IF THE SEEK DIRECTION IS FORWARD
00810                    * (FROM TRACK 00) "FVCTRK" IS A POSITIVE
00820                    * BINARY NUMBER, I.E. BIT 7 IS ZERO. IF
00830                    * THE SEEK DIRECTION IS REVERSE (TOWARD
00840                    * TRACK 00) "FVCTRK" IS A NEGATIVE BINARY
00850                    * NUMBER, I.E. BIT 7 IS A ONE.

00870                    * DISK STATUS IS CHECKED EACH STEP. IF
00880                    * THE STATUS IS GOOD AND THE SEEK OR
00890                    * RESTORE IS NOT COMPLETE THE INTERVAL TIMER
00900                    * IS RESTARTED TO TIME OUT THE NEXT STEP.
00910                    * AN EXCEPTION TO THE ABOVE IS IF SEEK
00920                    * COMPLETE IS DETECTED ("FVDELT" BIT 7=1)
00930                    * DURING A RESTORE OPERATION THE TIMER IS NOT
00940                    * RESTARTED AND THE RESTORE OPERATION IS
00950                    * ABORTED. IF SEEK COMPLETE, RESTORE COMPLETE
00960                    * OR A STATUS ERROR IS DETECTED THE TIMER
00970                    * IS NOT RESTARTED.
```

```
00990                    * AN OPERATION/ABORT FLAG IS MAINTAINED
01000                    * IN RAM LOCATION "FYABOR" AS FOLLOWS:
01010                    *     0001000X SEEK/RESTORE IN PROGRESS
01020                    *     0101000X SEEK/RESTORE ABORTED
01030                    *     0001001X SEEK/RESTORE COMPLETE
01040                    *        X=0 SEEK OPERATION
01050                    *        X=1 RESTORE OPERATION
```

```
01080 5000 96 00   FKSEEK LDA A   FVABOR   FETCH OP CODE
01090 5002 46             ROR A            IF RESTORE OP, CARRY=1
01100 5003 C6 62          LDA B   #%01100010   SET STATUS MASK
01110 5005 F4 8041        AND B   FP2PRB   FETCH MASKED STATUS
01120 5008 D7 01          STA B   FVSTAT   STORE ERROR STATUS
01130 500A 26 16          BNE     FKSK02   BRANCH IF ERROR

01150              * ERROR STATUS CHECKED:
01160              *    BIT 1 = DISK SYSTEM INOPERABLE
01170              *    BIT 5 = NOT HEAD LOAD
01180              *    BIT 6 = NOT READY

01200 500C 7A 8002        DEC     FVDELT   DECREMENT TRK DELTA
01210 500F 2B 19          BMI     FKSK04   BRANCH IF SEEK COMPLETE
01220 5011 7C 8003        INC     FVCTRK   UPDATE CURRENT TRK
01230 5014 B6 8040        LDA A   FP2PRA   FETCH CONTROL WORD

01250              * READING THE DISK CONTROL WORD FP2PRA
01260              * AUTOMATICALLY GENERATES THE STEP
01270              * PULSE.

01290 5017 24 02          BCC     FKSK01   BRANCH IF NOT RESTORE OP
01300 5019 2B 1D          BMI     FKSK07   BRANCH IF TRK 00

01320              * RESTORE OPERATION IS COMPLETE
01330              * WHEN TRACK 00 IS DETECTED.

01350 501B CE 0363 FKSK01 LDX    #S100US+99
01360 501E FF 8010        STX     FP3PRA   REARM TIMER FOR 9.9MS
01370 5021 39             RTS              RETURN TO INTERRUPT POLL




01390              * ERROR DETECTED IN STATUS

01410 5022 86 50   FKSK02 LDA A   #%01010000   PRELOAD SEEK ABORT FLAG
01420 5024 C6 FF   FKSK03 LDA B   #$FF
01430 5026 D7 02          STA B   FVDELT   RESTORE TRK DELTA
01440 5028 20 02          BRA     FKSK05   GO TO EXIT PREPARATION
```

```
01470                         * SEEK COMPLETE DETECTED

01490 502A 86 12      FKSK04 LDA A  #%00010010   PRELOAD SEEK COMPL FLAG
01500 502C C6 3C      FKSK05 LDA B  #%00111100
01510 502E F7 8042           STA B  FP2CRA   DISABLE STEP PULSE
01520 5031 24 02             BCC    FKSK06   BRANCH IF NOT RESTORE
01530 5033 86 51             LDA A  #%01010001   PRELOAD RESTORE ABORT

01550                         * RESTORE OP IN PROGRESS IS INDICATED WHEN
01560                         * THE CARRY BIT IS SET. BECAUSE THE TRACK
01570                         * DELTA IS SET TO A HIGH VALUE (83) PRIOR
01580                         * TO BEGINNING A RESTORE OPERATION AN ERROR
01590                         * IS IMPLIED IF SEEK COMPLETE IS DETECTED.
01600                         * BEFORE TRACK 00 STATUS IS SENSED.
01610                         * ALSO THIS PATH IS TAKEN IF DISK STATUS IS
01620                         * BAD DURING A RESTORE OPERATION.

01640 5035 97 00      FKSK06 STA A  FYABOR   SET OP/ABORT FLAG WORD
01650 5037 39                RTS             RETURN TO INTERRUPT POLL


01670                         * RESTORE OPERATION COMPLETE

01690 5038 86 10      FKSK07 LDA A  #%00010000
01700 503A B7 8041           STA A  FP2PRB   SET FORWARD DIRECTION
01710 503D B6 8040           LDA A  FP2PRA   GENERATE STEP PULSE

01730                         * THE FORWARD STEP IS USED TO RESTORE THE HEAD
01740                         * STEPPER MOTOR TO TRACK 00 PHASE.

01760 5040 0C                CLC             CLEAR RESTORE OP FLAG
01770 5041 7F 0003           CLR    FYCTRK   SET CURRENT TRK TO 00
01780 5044 86 13             LDA A  #%00010011   RESTORE COMPLETE FLAG
01790 5046 20 DC             BRA    FKSK03   GO TO RESTORE EXIT PREP


01820                         * UPC LOOKUP PREPARATION ROUTINE

01840                         * THIS ROUTINE CALCULATES ONE OF 50 TRACKS
01850                         * FROM THE LEAST SIGNIFICANT TWO DECIMAL
01860                         * CHARACTERS OF THE UPC CODE. THE RESULTANT
01870                         * TRACK IS THEN STORED IN "FYTRKA" AND THE
01880                         * THE SEEK PREPARATION ROUTINE IS BRANCHED TO.
01890                         * TRACKS 8 THROUGH 57 CONTAIN THE UPC DATA.
```

```
01910  5048  D6 17       FKLKUP LDA B   FVUPC+10     GET LSC OF UPC CODE
01920  504A  96 16              LDA A   FVUPC+9      GET 2ND LSC OF UPC CODE
01930  504C  27 05              BEQ     FKLU02       BRANCH IF 2ND CHAR = 0
01940  504E  CB 0A       FKLU01 ADD B   #10          CONVERT DECIMAL-BINARY
01950  5050  4A                 DEC A
01960  5051  26 F9              BNE     FKLU01       LOOP UNTIL CONVERSION COMPL
01970  5053  54          FKLU02 LSR B                DIVIDE RESULT BY 2
01980  5054  C1 31              CMP B   #49          TEST RESULT MAGNITUDE
01990  5056  23 05              BLS     FKLU03       BRANCH IF TRK ADDR GOOD
02000  5058  86 40              LDA A   #%01000000
02010  505A  97 00              STA A   FVABOR       SET LOOKUP ABORT CODE
02020  505C  39                 RTS                  RETURN TO EXEC PROGRAM
02030  505D  D7 04       FKLU03 STA B   FVTRKA       STORE TRACK ADDRESS
02040  505F  20 0A              BRA     FKSKIN       GO TO SEEK PREP


02070                   * SEEK/RESTORE PREPARATION ROUTINE


02090                   *   THIS ROUTINE PREPARES THE DISKETTE DRIVE
02100                   * AND RAM LOCATIONS FOR A SEEK OR RESTORE
02110                   * OPERATION. FOR A RESTORE OPERATION THE CURRENT
02120                   * TRACK ADDRESS ("FVCTRK") IS PRESET TO 83 AND
02130                   * THE TARGET TRACK ADDRESS ("FVTRKA") IS
02140                   * CLEARED TO 00. FOR A SEEK OPERATION THE
02150                   * CURRENT TRACK VALUE IS DETERMINED BY THE LAST
02160                   * SEEK OR RESTORE OPERATION. THE TRACK DELTA
02170                   * ("FVDELT") IS CALCULATED BY SUBTRACTING THE
02180                   * CURRENT TRACK FROM THE TARGET TRACK AND
02190                   * CONVERTING THE SIGNED BINARY RESULT TO A
02200                   * POSITIVE BINARY NUMBER.

02220                   * THE DIRECTION OF THE SEEK IS DETERMINED BY
02230                   * SIGN OF THE TRACK DELTA BEFORE IT IS CONVERTED
02240                   * TO A POSITIVE BINARY NUMBER. IF THE SIGN IS
02250                   * NEGATIVE THE SEEK IS REVERSE (TOWARD TRK 00).

02270                   * TO INITIATE THE INTERRUPT DRIVEN SEEK ROUTINE
02280                   * A DUMMY INTERVAL TIMER INTERRUPT IS GENERATED
02290                   * IF THE TIMER IS NOT BUSY.  IF THE TIMER IS
02300                   * BUSY IT IS ASSUMED THAT THE INTERRUPT WILL
02310                   * OCCUR WHEN THE TIMER RUNS OUT, SO A DUMMY
02320                   * INTERVAL TIMER INTERRUPT IS NOT GENERATED.
02330                   * THUS INTERFERENCE WITH CONCURRENT OPERATIONS
02340                   * USING THE TIMER IS ELIMINATED, I.E. THE SEEK
02350                   * WILL NOT BEGIN UNTIL THE TIMER IS AVAILABLE.
```

```
02380                     * RESTORE OPERATION ENTRY = "FKRSTR"


02400  5061  0F     FKRSTR  SEI              MASK SYSTEM INTERRUPTS
02410  5062  7F 0004         CLR    FYTRKA    TARGET TRACK = 00
02420  5065  C6 53           LDA B  #83       PRELOAD ARTIFICIAL CURR TRK
02430  5067  86 11           LDA A  #%00010001    PRELOAD RESTORE OP CODE
02440  5069  20 05           BRA    FKSP01


02460                     * SEEK OPERATION ENTRY = "FKSKIN"


02480  506B  0F     FKSKIN  SEI              MASK SYSTEM INTERRUPTS
02490  506C  D6 03           LDA B  FYCTRK    FETCH CURRENT TRACK
02500  506E  86 10           LDA A  #%00010000    PRELOAD SEEK OP CODE
02510  5070  97 00    FKSP01 STA A  FYABOR    STORE OP CODE
02520  5072  5D              TST B
02530  5073  2A 01           BPL    FKSP02    BRANCH IF "FYCTRK" POSITIVE
02540  5075  50              NEG B            MAKE "FYCTRK" POSITIVE

02560                     * SINCE "DYCTRK" IS IN SIGNED BINARY FORMAT IT
02570                     * IS NECESSARY TO CONVERT IT TO POSITIVE BEFORE
02580                     * CALCULATING THE TRACK DELTA.

02600  5076  96 04    FKSP02 LDA A  FYTRKA    FETCH TARGET TRACK
02610  5078  10              SBA              CALCULATE TRACK DELTA
02620  5079  2A 07           BPL    FKSP03    BRANCH IF DELTA POSITIVE
02630  507B  40              NEG A            MAKE DELTA POSITIVE
02640  507C  50              NEG B            NEGATE CURRENT TRK ADDR.

02660                     * "FYCTRK" IS A NEGATIVE BINARY NUMBER IF THE
02670                     * SEEK IS REVERSE

02690  507D  97 02           STA A  FYDELT    STORE TRACK DELTA
02700  507F  4F              CLR A            PRELOAD REVERSE DIRECTION
02710  5080  20 04           BRA    FKSP04
02720  5082  97 02    FKSP03 STA A  FYDELT    STORE TRACK DELTA
02730  5084  86 10           LDA A  #%00010000    PRELOAD FORWARD DIRECT.
02740  5086  B7 8041  FKSP04 STA A  FP2PRB    SET DISK DIRECTION
02750  5089  D7 03           STA B  FYCTRK    STORE CURRENT TRK ADDRESS
02760  508B  8D 16           BSR    FKERST    RESET DISK ERROR LATCHES
02770  508D  86 24           LDA A  #%00100100
02780  508F  B7 8042         STA A  FP2CRA    ENABLE STEP PULSE
02790  5092  B6 8010         LDA A  FP3PRA    FETCH TIMER STATUS
02800  5095  85 07           BIT A  #%00000111    MASK NON-TIMER STATUS
02810  5097  26 08           BNE    FKSP05    BRANCH IF TIMER BUSY
02820  5099  8A 05           ORA A  #C1US
02830  509B  B7 8010         STA A  FP3PRA    -START INTERVAL TIMER
02840  509E  7F 8011         CLR    FP3PRB    -FOR IMMEDIATE INTERRUPT
02850  50A1  0E     FKSP05  CLI              CLEAR SYSTEM INTERRUPT MASK
02860  50A2  39              RTS              RETURN TO HOST PROGRAM
```

```
02890                    *   THIS ROUTINE RESETS THE DISKETTE DRIVE
02900                    *   ERROR LATCHES AND SELECTS THE DRIVE.


02920 50A3 86 0F     FKERST LDA A    #%00001111
02930 50A5 B7 8040           STA A    FP2PRA    RESET ERROR LATCHES
02940 50A8 86 2F             LDA A    #%00101111
02950 50AA B7 8040           STA A    FP2PRA    REMOVE RESET & SELECT DRIVE
02960 50AD BC 8040           CPX      FP2PRA    CLEAR ERROR INTERRUPT FLAGS

02980                    *  THE "CPX" INSTRUCTION PERFORMS A DUMMY READ
02990                    *  TO "FP2PRA & FP2PRB" TO CLEAR THE PIA
03000                    *  INTERRUPT FLAGS.

03020 50B0 39                 RTS
```

03040   * UPC SEARCH ROUTINE

03060   * THIS ROUTINE SEARCHS FOR THE DESIRED UPC DATA
03070   * AND WHEN FOUND STORES THE DATA.

03090   * THE DATA ON FLOPPY DISK IS RECORDED IN IBM 3740
03100   * FIXED FORMAT. THE FOLLOWING IS A BREAKDOWN
03110   * OF THE UPC RECORD STORAGE:
03120   *   UPC ASSIGNED TRACKS   = 8-57
03130   *   NO. OF ASSIGNED TRACKS   = 50
03140   *   DATA RECORD FIELDS PER TRACK   = 26
03150   *   TOTAL BYTES PER DATA FIELD   = 128
03160   *   BYTES PER FIELD HEADER   = 2
03170   *   BYTES PER UPC RECORD   = 18
03180   *   UPC RECORDS PER DATA FIELD   = 7
03190   *   UPC RECORDS PER TRACK   = 182
03200   *   TOTAL AVAILABLE UPC RECORDS   = 9100

03220   * THE FOLLOWING IS A BREAKDOWN OF THE UPC RECORD:
03230   *   UPC CODE   = 10 BYTES
03240   *   PRICE   = 4 BYTES
03250   *   MESSAGE ADDR = 2 BYTES
03260   *   MISCELLANEOUS= 2 BYTES

03280   * EACH DATA RECORD FIELD CONTAINS 7 UPC RECORDS.
03290   * THE FIRST TWO BYTES OF THE DATA RECORD FIELD
03300   * CONTAIN HEADER INFORMATION. THE FIRST BYTE
03310   * IS THE TRACK ADDRESS AND THE SECOND BYTE IS
03320   * THE SECTOR ADDRESS.

03340   * EACH UPC RECORD CONSISTS OF A 10 BYTE UPC CODE
03350   * WHICH SERVES AS A "KEY" TO 8 BYTES OF PRICE
03360   * AND DESCRIPTIVE INFORMATION.

03380   * A UPC SEARCH IS BEGUN BY READING THE FIRST
03390   * DATA ADDRESS MARK WHICH OCCURS. THEN THE
03400   * FIRST DATA BYTE IS COMPARED WITH THE TRACK
03410   * ADDRESS ("FVTRKA"). THE NEXT BYTE IS READ
03420   * AND STORED IN "FVFLG2." THEN THE FIRST 10 BYTES
03430   * OF EACH 18 BYTE UPC RECORD IS COMPARED AGAINST
03440   * THE DESIRED UPC CHARACTERS. IF A MATCH IS FOUND
03450   * THE NEXT 8 BYTES ARE STACKED IN MEMORY. IF NO
03460   * MATCH IS FOUND IN ONE OF THE SEVEN UPC RECORDS
03470   * THE OPERATION REPEATS FOR THE NEXT DATA RECORD
03480   * FIELD. HOWEVER, ONCE THE FIRST DATA RECORD FIELD
03490   * IS READ WITHOUT A CRC ERROR THE SECTOR ADDRESS
03500   * ("FVFLG2") LOCATION IN MEMORY IS NOT CHANGED.

```
03530              * THIS PROCESS CONTINUES FOR 2 REVOLUTIONS OF THE
03540              * DISKETTE GOVERNED BY A 340MS INTERVAL TIMER
03550              * SETTING. IF THE DATA CANNOT BE FOUND IN TWO
03560              * REVOLUTIONS ERROR FLAGS ARE SET AS A RESULT
03570              * OF AN INTERVAL TIMER INTERRUPT AND THE UPC
03580              * SEARCH OPERATION IS ABORTED.

03600              * FLAG BYTES ARE USED TO DIRECT THE PROGRAM FLOW.
03610              * DEFINITIONS OF THE FLAG BYTES ARE AS FOLLOWS:

03630              *  "FVFLG1"
03640              * FLAG 1 IS SET IF THE FIRST HEADER BYTE DOES NOT
03650              * MATCH THE DESIRED TRACK ADDRESS ("FVTRKA").
03660              * THE FLAG IS RESET IF A CRC ERROR OCCURS AFTER
03670              * READING THE DATA RECORD FIELD. IF NO CRC ERROR
03680              * OCCURS AND FLAG 1 IS SET, A SEEK ERROR FLAG
03690              * IS SET AND THE UPC SEARCH IS ABORTED.

03710              *  "FVFLG2"
03720              * FLAG 2 IS SET BY STORING THE 2ND HEADER BYTE
03730              * IN LOCATION "FVFLG2." THE FLAG IS SET ONLY ONCE
03740              * DURING THE 1ST ERROR FREE READ OF A DATA RECORD
03750              * FIELD. IF THE FLAG IS SET IT MEANS THAT A TRACK
03760              * MATCH WAS FOUND.

03780              *  "FVFLG3"
03790              * FLAG 3 MEANS THE UPC SEARCH WAS SUCCESSFUL.
03800              * IF A CRC ERROR OCCURS FLAG 3 IS CLEARED.

03820              *  "FVFLG4"
03830              * FLAG 4 IS A CRC ERROR COUNTER. IF THE FIRST
03840              * 5 DATA FIELDS HAVE CRC ERRORS THE READ ERROR
03850              * IS CONSIDERED TO BE NON-RECOVERABLE. IF ANY
03860              * OF THE FIRST FIVE DATA FIELDS READ HAVE NO
03870              * CRC ERRORS, ANY SUBSEQUENT CRC ERRORS INCREMENT
03880              * FLAG 4. ONCE A DATA RECORD FIELD HAS BEEN READ
03890              * WITHOUT ERROR FURTHER ERRORS ARE CONSIDERED TO
03900              * BE RECOVERABLE UNTIL THE INTERVAL TIMER ABORTS
03910              * THE SEARCH OPERATION.

03930              *  "FVFLG5"
03940              * FLAG 5 IS A COUNTER WHICH INDICATES THE NUMBER
03950              * OF DATA FIELDS PASSED WITHOUT A UPC MATCH AND
03960              * NO UPC ERRORS.
```

```
03980              * AN OPERATION/ABORT FLAG IS MAINTAINED FOR
03990              * PURPOSES OF COMMUNICATION WITH THE HOST PROGRAM.
04000              * THE OPERATION/ABORT FLAG IS STORED IN RAM
04010              * LOCATION "FVABOR" AS FOLLOWS:

04030              *     10011000   UPC SEARCH IN PROGRESS
04040              *     01011000   UPC SEARCH ABORTED BY PROGRAM
04050              *     01111000   UPC SEARCH ABORTED BY INTERRUPT
04060              *     00111010   UPC RECORD NOT FOUND
04070              *     00011010   UPC SEARCH COMPLETE
04080              *     01111111   SEEK VERIFY ERROR
```

```
04100 5081 8D F0   FKSRCH BSR    FKERST   CLEAR ERROR LATCHES
04110 5083 4F              CLR A
04120 5084 C6 67           LDA B  #%01100111   SET ERROR STATUS MASK
04130 5086 F4 8041         AND B  FP2PRB   FETCH MASKED STATUS
04140 5089 27 03           BEQ    FKSR01   SKIP IF STATUS GOOD
04150 508B 7E 51DE         JMP    FKSR26   BAD STATUS,EXIT

04170                 * THE FOLLOWING ERROR STATUS IS CHECKED:
04180                 *     BIT 6 - NOT READY
04190                 *     BIT 5 - HEAD NOT LOADED
04200                 *     BIT 2 - OVERRUN
04210                 *     BIT 1 - DISK SYSTEM INOPERABLE
04220                 *     BIT 0 - NOT IN SYNC

04240 508E 86 98   FKSR01 LDA A  #%10011000
04250 50C0 97 00           STA A  FYABOR   STORE OP CODE
04260 50C2 9F 09           STS    FYSYSP   SAVE STACK POINTER
04270 50C4 CE 3F1E         LDX    #$3F1E
04280 50C7 FF 8042         STX    FP2CRA   ENABLE ERROR INTERRUPTS
04290 50CA CE 0122         LDX    #S10MS+34   LOAD 340MS TIMEOUT
04300 50CD FF 8010         STX    FP3PRA   START INTERVAL TIMER
04310 50D0 CE FB7F FKSR02 LDX    #$FB7F   PRELOAD DATA MARK MATCH
04320 50D3 86 80           LDA A  #256-128
04330 50D5 97 06           STA A  FYBCNT   STORE FIELD BYTE CNTR
04340 50D7 9E 07           LDS    FYDADR   POINT TO DATA STACK
04350 50D9 D6 04           LDA B  FYTRKA   PRELOAD TRACK ADDRESS
04360 50DB 86 24           LDA A  #%00100100
04370 50DD B7 8082         STA A  FP1CRA   ENABLE R/W HANDSHAKE
04380 50E0 86 2B   FKSR03 LDA A  #%00101011   PRELOAD ENABLE CRC
04390 50E2 F5 8080         BIT B  FP1PRA   CLR BYTE READY INTERR FLAG
04400 50E5 B7 8040         STA A  FP2PRA   ENABLE CRC

04420                 * THE DISK SYSTEM IS NOW ARMED FOR DATA RECOVERY

04440 50E8 86 01           LDA A  #%00000001   PRELOAD 1ST BIT MASK
04450 50EA B5 8081 FKSR04 BIT A  FP1PRB
04460 50ED 27 FB           BEQ    FKSR04   WAIT FOR 1ST BIT
04470 50EF B1 8082 FKSR05 CMP A  FP1CRA
04480 50F2 2B FB           BMI    FKSR05   WAIT FOR BYTE READY
04490 50F4 BC 8080         CPX    FP1PRA   COMPARE FOR DATA MARK
04500 50F7 27 07           BEQ    FKSR06
04510 50F9 86 2F           LDA A  #%00101111
04520 50FB B7 8040         STA A  FP2PRA   DROP ENABLE CRC
04530 50FE 20 E0           BRA    FKSR03   DO AGAIN,LOOK FOR 1ST BIT

04550                 * THE PROGRAM WILL RESTART THE READ OPERATION
04560                 * UNTIL A DATA ADDRESS MARK IS FOUND.
```

```
04590                       * THE DATA ADDRESS MARK HAS BEEN FOUND.
04600                       * BEGIN READING DATA.

04620 5100 86 69   FKSR06 LDA A    #%01101011
04630 5102 B7 8040         STA A    FP2PRA    RAISE READ ENABLE
04640 5105 B1 8082 FKSR07 CMP A    FP1CRA
04650 5108 25 FB          BCS      FKSR07    WAIT FOR BYTE READY
04660 510A F0 8080         SUB B    FP1PRA    COMPARE TRACK ADDR
04670 510D 27 42          BEQ      FKSR12    BRANCH IF CORRECT TRACK

04690                       * THE 1ST DATA BYTE OF THE DATA RECORD FIELD IS
04700                       * THE TRACK ADDRESS.  IF THE WRONG TRACK ADDRESS
04710                       * HAS BEEN READ IT IS A POSSIBLE SEEK ERROR.
04720                       * BECAUSE IT IS NOT YET KNOWN THAT THE RECOVERED
04730                       * DATA IS VALID FLAG 7 IS SET WHICH WILL BE
04740                       * TESTED IF THERE IS NO CRC ERROR AT THE END OF
04750                       * THE DATA RECORD FIELD.

04770 510F D7 17          STA B    FVFLG1    SAVE TRK ERROR DELTA
04780 5111 C6 81          LDA B    #256-127

04800                       * THE FOLLOWING INSTRUCTION  SEQUENCE SKIPS OVER
04810                       * THE NUMBER OF BYTES INDICATED IN ACCUMULATOR B
04820                       * IN NEGATIVE BINARY FORMAT.

04840 5113 F5 8082 FKSR08 BIT B    FP1CRA
04850 5116 2A FB          BPL      FKSR08    WAIT FOR BYTE READY
04860 5118 F5 8080         BIT B    FP1PRA    CLR INTERR FLAG
04870 511B 5C             INC B              DECREMENT BYTE COUNTER
04880 511C 26 F5          BNE      FKSR08    LOOP UNTIL LAST BYTE


04900                       * CRC PROCESSING.

04920 511E F1 8082 FKSR09 CMP B    FP1CRA
04930 5121 2B FB          BMI      FKSR09    WAIT FOR 1ST CRC BYTE
04940 5123 F5 8080         BIT B    FP1PRA    CLR INTERR FLAG
04950 5126 86 2F          LDA A    #%00101111    PRELOAD STOP READ
04960 5128 C6 08          LDA B    #%00001000    PRELOAD TST CRC MASK
04970 512A F1 8082 FKSR10 CMP B    FP1CRA
04980 512D 2B F9          BMI      FKSR10    WAIT FOR 2ND CRC BYTE
04990 512F F4 8081         AND B    FP1PRB    FETCH CRC STATUS
05000 5132 B7 8040         STA A    FP2PRA    STOP READ
05010 5135 86 34          LDA A    #%00110100
05020 5137 B7 8082         STA A    FP1CRA    TURN OFF R/W HANDSHAKE
05030 513A 5D             TST B
05040 513B 27 5E          BEQ      FKSR20    BRANCH IF CRC =00
```

```
05070                      * CRC ERROR DETECTED

05090                      * CRC ERRORS ARE COUNTED TO DETERMINE IF READ
05100                      * ERRORS ARE RECOVERABLE OR NOT.  THIS
05110                      * INFORMATION IS ALSO USEFUL IN DIAGNOSING
05120                      * DISK SYSTEM MALFUNCTIONS.

05140 513D 7C 001A              INC     FYFLG4      INCREMENT CRC ERR CNTR
05150 5140 7D 001B              TST     FYFLG5
05160 5143 26 89               BNE     FKSR02      IF FLG 5, READ NEXT RECORD
05170 5145 86 05               LDA A   #5
05180 5147 91 1A               CMP A   FYFLG4
05190 5149 23 4A               BLS     FKSR19      BRANCH IF CRC ERRORS <= 5


05210                      * NORMAL EXIT ENTRY POINT

05230 514B 7F 8010 FKSR11   CLR     FP3PRA      STOP INTERVAL TIMER
05240 514E 7E 51D5            JMP     FKSR25      GO TO ENDING PROCESSING
```

```
05260                       * READ THE 2ND HEADER BYTE.
05270                       * THE 1ST HEADER BYTE HAS BEEN READ AND MATCHES
05280                       * THE TRACK ADDRESS. CONTINUE READING.

05300  5151 D7 19   FKSR12 STA B   FYFLG3   CLEAR FLAG 3
05310  5153 F1 8082 FKSR13 CMP B   FP1CRA
05320  5156 2B FB          BMI     FKSR13   WAIT FOR 2ND HEADER BYTE
05330  5158 B6 8080        LDA A   FP1PRA   FETCH SECTOR ADDR
05340  515B D1 18          CMP B   FYFLG2
05350  515D 26 02          BNE     FKSR14   BRANCH IF NOT 1ST SECTOR
05360  515F 97 18          STA A   FYFLG2   SET FLAG 2

05380                       * IF FLAG 2 IS ALREADY SET DO NOT OVERWRITE.
05390                       * FLAG 2 CONTAINS THE SECTOR ADDRESS OF THE 1ST
05400                       * DATA RECORD FIELD RECOVERED WITHOUT A CRC
05410                       * ERROR.


05430                       * THE FOLLOWING SERIES OF INSTRUCTIONS ATTEMPTS
05440                       * TO MATCH THE 1ST 10 BYTES OF THE UPC RECORD
05450                       * WITH THE DESIRED UPC CODE.

05470  5161 CE 000A FKSR14 LDX     #10      LOAD MATCH POINTER
05480  5164 A6 FF   FKSR15 LDA A   FKMTCH,X  GET 1ST UPC CHAR
05490  5166 F6 8082 FKSR16 LDA B   FP1CRA
05500  5169 2A FB          BPL     FKSR16   WAIT FOR BYTE READY
05510  516B B1 8080        CMP A   FP1PRA
05520  516E 26 4C          BNE     FKSR23   BRANCH IF NOT UPC MATCH
05530  5170 09             DEX              DECREMENT MATCH POINTER
05540  5171 26 F1          BNE     FKSR15   LOOP FOR 10 BYTE MATCH

05560                       * THE UPC MATCH WAS SUCCESFUL. STACK THE NEXT
05570                       * 8 BYTES OF UPC DATA.

05590  5173 C6 86          LDA B   #127+7   SET BYTE COUNTER TO 7
05600  5175 F5 8082 FKSR17 BIT B   FP1CRA
05610  5178 2A FB          BPL     FKSR17   WAIT FOR BYTE READY
05620  517A B6 8080        LDA A   FP1PRA   FETCH DATA FROM DISK
05630  517D 36             PSH A            STACK DATA
05640  517E 5A             DEC B            DECREMENT DATA BYTE CNTR
05650  517F 2B F4          BMI     FKSR17   LOOP FOR 7 BYTES
05660  5181 D7 19          STA B   FYFLG3   SET FLAG 3

05680                       * FLAG 3 INDICATES THE UPC SEARCH WAS SUCCESSFUL.

05700  5183 D6 06          LDA B   FYBCNT   LOAD FIELD BYTE CNT
05710  5185 F5 8082 FKSR18 BIT B   FP1CRA
05720  5188 2A FB          BPL     FKSR18   WAIT FOR BYTE READY
05730  518A B6 8080        LDA A   FP1PRA   FETCH LAST DATA BYTE
05740  518D 36             PSH A
```

```
05760                               * UPC MATCH WAS SUCCESSFUL.
05770                               * PREPARE TO SKIP REMAINING BYTES, IF ANY.

05790 518E CB 12            ADD  B    #18        ADJUST FIELD BYTE CNT
05800 5190 27 8C            BEQ       FKSR09     IF LAST BYTE, DO CRC CHK
05810 5192 7E 5113          JMP       FKSR08     IF NOT LAST BYTE, SKIP OUT



05830                               * A CRC ERROR HAS BEEN DETECTED BUT IT IS
05840                               * ASSUMED TO BE A RECOVERABLE ERROR.
05850                               * CLEAR FLAG 2 AND READ THE NEXT DATA RECORD
05860                               * FIELD.


05890 5195 4F        FKSR19 CLR  A
05900 5196 97 18            STA  A    FYFLG2     CLEAR FLAG 2
05910 5198 7E 50D0          JMP       FKSR02     READ NEXT RECORD



05940                               * CRC = 00, END OF DATA RECORD FIELD.

05960 519B C6 80     FKSR20 LDA  B    #%10000000    PRELOAD SEEK ERROR FLAG
05970 519D 86 27            LDA  A    #%00100111    FORM SEEK ERR OP CODE
05980 519F 7D 0017          TST       FYFLG1
05990 51A2 26 A7            BNE       FKSR11    IF FLAG 1, ABORT

06010                               * FLAG 1 WAS SET IF THE TRACK ADDRESS DESIRED DID
06020                               * DID NOT MATCH WITH THE FIRST HEADER BYTE.

06040 51A4 7D 0019          TST       FYFLG3
06050 51A7 27 05            BEQ       FKSR21    SKIP IF NOT FLAG 3
06060 51A9 86 42            LDA  A    #%01000010    FORM OP CODE MASK
06070 51AB 7E 514B          JMP       FKSR11    EXIT LOOKUP ROUTINE

06090                               * FLAG 3 WAS SET IF THE UPC MATCH WAS SUCCESSFUL.

06110 51AE 7C 001B   FKSR21 INC       FYFLG5    SET FLAG 5
06120 51B1 7E 50D0          JMP       FKSR02    READ NEXT RECORD

06140                               * FLAG 5 IS INCREMENTED EACH TIME A DATA FIELD IS
06150                               * READ WITHOUT ERROR, BUT NO UPC MATCH WAS FOUND.
```

```
06180                           * THE FOLLOWING SERIES OF INSTRUCTIONS SKIPS OVER
06190                           * THE REMAINING UPC BYTES WHEN A UPC MATCH WAS
06200                           * NOT MADE.

06220 51B4 F6 8082 FKSR22 LDA B   FP1CRA
06230 51B7 2A F9          BPL     FKSR22      WAIT FOR BYTE READY
06240 51B9 F5 8080        BIT B   FP1PRA      CLR INTERR FLAG
06250 51BC 09      FKSR23 DEX                 DECREMENT POINTER

06270                           * "FKSR23" IS THE ENTRY INTO THIS LOOP

06290 51BD 26 F5          BNE     FKSR22      LOOP TILL POINTER EXHAUSTED




06310                           * THE FOLLOWING SERIES SKIPS OVER THE 8 BYTES OF
06320                           * UPC DATA. IF THERE ARE SUBSEQUENT UPC RECORDS
06330                           * A UPC MATCH WILL BE ATTEMPTED AGAIN.

06350 51BF D6 05          LDA B   FYBCNT      GET FIELD BYTE CNTR
06360 51C1 86 F8          LDA A   #256-8      LOAD BYTE CNTR
06370 51C3 B5 8082 FKSR24 BIT A   FP1CRA
06380 51C6 2A F9          BPL     FKSR24      WAIT FOR BYTE READY
06390 51C8 B5 8080        BIT A   FP1PRA      CLR INTERR FLAG
06400 51CB 4C             INC A               UPDATE BYTE COUNTER
06410 51CC 26 F5          BNE     FKSR24      LOOP FOR 8 BYTES
06420 51CE CB 12          ADD B   #18         ADJUST FIELD BYTE CNTER
06430 51D0 26 8F          BNE     FKSR14      BRNCH IF NOT END OF FIELD
06440 51D2 7E 511E        JMP     FKSR09      GO TO CRC PROCESS




06460                           * ENDING PROCESSING

06480 51D5 CE 3E16 FKSR25 LDX    #$3E16
06490 51D8 FF 8042        STX     FP2CRA      DISABLE ERROR INTERRUPTS
06500 51DB 30             TSX                 PNT TO DATA WITH INDEX REG
06510 51DC 9E 08          LDS     FYSVSP      RESTORE STACK POINTER

06530                           * EXIT SEQUENCE ENTRY POINT IF STATUS ERROR

06550 51DE D7 01   FKSR26 STA B   FYSTAT      STORE ERROR STATUS
06560 51E0 88 58          EOR A   #%01011000   FORM OP/ABORT CODE
06570 51E2 97 00          STA A   FYABOR      STORE OP/ABORT CODE
06580 51E4 39             RTS                 RETURN TO EXEC PROGRAM
```

06600   * FLOPPY DISK READ ROUTINE

06620   * THIS ROUTINE READS AND STORES ONE ID OR ONE
06630   * DATA RECORD.

06650   * THE READ DATA RATE IS GOVERNED PRIMARILY BY
06660   * THE ROTATIONAL SPEED OF THE DISKETTE. THE
06670   * WORST CASE READ DATA RATE IS DETERMINED BY
06680   * ALLOWING FOR THE ACCUMULATION OF THE
06690   * ROTATIONAL SPEED ERROR DURING THE WRITE
06700   * OPERATION PLUS THE SPEED ERROR DURING THE READ
06710   * OPERATION. THE DESIGN CRITERION OF THIS ROUTINE
06720   * IS TO OPERATE AT MAX/MIN DATA RATES OF:
06730   *   29.75 TO 34.25 MICROSECONDS/BYTE

06750   * SYNCHRONIZATION OF PROGRAM TIMING TO THE READ
06760   * DATA RATE IS ACCOMPLISHED BY WAITING UNTIL BYTE
06770   * READY OCCURS. BYTE READY IS RECOGNIZED BY THE
06780   * PROGRAM WHEN THE CA1 INPUT TO PIA #1 MAKES A
06790   * HIGH TO LOW TRANSITION AND SETS BIT 7 OF
06800   * CONTROL REGISTER A (INTERR FLAG #1) TO A ONE.
06810   * THE INTERRUPT FLAG IS POLLED FOR BY THE PROGRAM.
06820   * AFTER BYTE READY IS RECOGNIZED THE DATA IS
06830   * FETCHED FROM THE PIA. MOVING THE DATA FROM
06840   * THE PIA TO THE MPU AUTOMATICALLY CLEARS THE
06850   * INTERRUPT FLAG.

06870   * THE INTERVAL TIMER IS USED TO ABORT THE READ
06880   * OPERATION IF THE READ IS NOT COMPLETED BEFORE
06890   * THE TIME SPECIFIED IN "FVTIME" IS EXHAUSTED.
06900   * OTHER ERROR INTERRUPTS INCLUDE:
06910   *   A.   SYSTEM INOPERABLE
06920   *   B.   OVERRUN
06930   *   C.   NOT READY

06950   * DATA IS STACKED INTO A BUFFER AREA
06960   * SPECIFIED BY THE CONTENTS OF "FVDADR." WHEN
06970   * THE READ OPERATION IS COMPLETE THE ADDRESS OF
06980   * THE LAST DATA BYTE IS TRANSFERRED TO THE INDEX
06990   * REGISTER.

07010   * ACCUMULATOR B IS USED AS THE DATA BYTE COUNTER
07020   * IN THE READ ROUTINE. THE INITIAL BYTE COUNT
07030   * MUST BE STORED IN "FVBCNT." THIS VALUE IS
07040   * REQUIRED TO BE IN NEGATIVE BINARY FORMAT.
07050   * USING THE IBM 3740 FORMAT, THE DATA RECORD IS
07060   * 128 BYTES. THEREFORE THE BYTE COUNTER WILL HAVE
07070   * A "1" IN BIT 7 THROUGHOUT DATA TRANSFER. THE "1"
07080   * IN BIT 7 ENABLES ACCUMULATOR B TO BE USED AS A
07090   * BIT TEST MASK FOR BYTE READY AS WELL AS A BYTE
07100   * COUNTER.

```
07120              *  AN OPERATION/ABORT FLAG IS MAINTAINED IN RAM
07130              *  LOCATION "FYABOR" AS FOLLOWS:
07140              *     10001000   READ OPERATION IN PROGRESS
07150              *     01001000   READ OPERATION ABORTED BY PROGRAM
07160              *     01101000   READ OPERATION ABORTED BY INTERRUPT
07170              *     00001010   READ OPERATION COMPLETE
```

```
07200  51E5  86 88      FKREAD  LDA A   #%10001000    -PRESET READ IN
07210  51E7  97 00              STA A   FVABOR        ----PROGRESS OP CODE
07220  51E9  BD 50A3            JSR     FKERST

07240                   * "FKERST" IS A DISK SYSTEM ERROR LATCH RESET
07250                   * SUBROUTINE. THIS ROUTINE ALSO SELECTS THE
07260                   * DISKETTE DRIVE AND CLEARS PIA #2 ERROR
07270                   * INTERRUPT FLAGS.

07290  51EC  86 E6              LDA A   #%11100110   SET ERROR STATUS MASK
07300  51EE  B4 8041            AND A   FP2PRB       FETCH MASKED STATUS
07310  51F1  26 74              BNE     FKRD09       BRANCH IF ERROR

07330                   * ERROR STATUS CHECKED
07340                   *     BIT 0 = NOT IN SYNC
07350                   *     BIT 1 = DISK SYSTEM INOPERABLE
07360                   *     BIT 2 = OVERRUN
07370                   *     BIT 5 = NOT HEAD LOADED
07380                   *     BIT 6 = NOT READY

07400  51F3  9F 09              STS     FVSVSP       SAVE STACK POINTER
07410  51F5  9E 07              LDS     FVDADR       POINT TO DATA STACK
07420  51F7  CE 3F1E            LDX     #$3F1E
07430  51FA  FF 8042            STX     FP2CRA       ENABLE ERROR INTERRUPTS
07440  51FD  DE 09              LDX     FVTIME       FETCH TIMER VARIABLE
07450  51FF  FF 8010            STX     FP3PRA       START INTERVAL TIMER
07460  5202  CE 3E16            LDX     #3E16        PRELOAD DISABLE INTERRUPTS
07470  5205  D6 05              LDA B   FVBCNT       LOAD BYTE COUNTER
07480  5207  86 24              LDA A   #%00100100
07490  5209  B7 8082            STA A   FP1CRA       ENABLE R/W HANDSHAKE
07500  520C  86 2B      FKRD01  LDA A   #%00101011    PRELOAD ENABLE CRC
07510  520E  F5 8080            BIT B   FP1PRA       CLR BYTE RDY INTERR FLAG
07520  5211  B7 8040            STA A   FP2PRA       ENABLE CRC

07540                   * FOR A READ OPERATION "ENABLE CRC" ARMS THE
07550                   * READ CIRCUITS TO SYNCHRONIZE TO THE FIRST
07560                   * "1" DATA BIT DETECTED.

07580  5214  96 05              LDA A   FVDMRK       PRELOAD DATA MARK
07590  5216  76 8081    FKRD02  ROR     FP1PRB       MOVE 1ST BIT TO CARRY
07600  5219  24 FB              BCC     FKRD02       WAIT UNTIL 1ST BIT
07610  521B  F5 8082    FKRD03  BIT B   FP1CRA
07620  521E  2A FB              BPL     FKRD03       WAIT FOR BYTE READY
07630  5220  B1 8080            CMP A   FP1PRA       COMPARE MARK PATTERN
07640  5223  26 05              BNE     FKRD04       BRANCH IF NOT MARK
07650  5225  F5 8081            BIT B   FP1PRB
07660  5228  2A 07              BPL     FKRD05       BRANCH IF ID/DATA MRK
07670  522A  86 2F      FKRD04  LDA A   #%00101111
07680  522C  B7 8040            STA A   FP2PRA       DROP ENABLE CRC
07690  522F  20 DB              BRA     FKRD01       DO AGAIN,LOOK FOR 1ST BIT
```

```
07710 5231 86 6B    FKRD05 LDA A  #%01101011
07720 5233 B7 8040         STA A  FP2PRA    RAISE READ ENABLE

07740                  * "READ ENABLE" ENABLES THE NOT IN SYNC
07750                  * ERROR DETECTION LOGIC. "NOT IN SYNC" IS A
07760                  * LATCHED ERROR SIGNAL WHICH IS SET WHEN THE
07770                  * CLOCK RECOVERY CIRCUITS DO NOT
07780                  * DETECT A "1" BIT AT CLOCK TIME AND "READ
07790                  * ENABLE" IS SET.


07810                  * THE FOLLOWING SERIES OF INSTRUCTIONS IS THE
07820                  * BASIC READ LOOP

07840 5236 F5 8082 FKRD06 BIT B  FP1CRA
07850 5239 2A FB         BPL    FKRD06   WAIT FOR BYTE READY
07860 523B B6 8080       LDA A  FP1PRA   GET DATA & CLR INTERR FLAG
07870 523E 36            PSH A           STORE DATA
07880 523F 5C            INC B           UPDATE BYTE COUNTER
07890 5240 26 F4         BNE    FKRD06   LOOP UNTIL LAST BYTE


07910 5242 F1 8082 FKRD07 CMP B  FP1CRA
07920 5245 2B FB         BMI    FKRD07   WAIT FOR 1ST CRC BYTE RDY

07940                  * ACCUMULATOR B IS 00 AT THIS TIME. THE "CMPB"
07950                  * AND "BMI" INSTRUCTIONS TEST THE BYTE READY
07960                  * INTERRUPT FLAG (FP1CRA, BIT 7). IF THE FLAG IS
07970                  * A ""0" THE PROGRAM LOOPS BACK TO "FKRD07."

07990 5247 F5 8080       BIT B  FP1PRA   CLEAR INTERRUPT FLAG
08000 524A 86 2F         LDA A  #%00101111   PRELOAD STOP READ
08010 524C C6 08         LDA B  #%00001000   LOAD TST CRC MASK
08020 524E F1 8082 FKRD08 CMP B  FP1CRA
08030 5251 2B FB         BMI    FKRD08   WAIT FOR 2ND CRC BYTE
08040 5253 F4 8081       AND B  FP1PRB   FETCH CRC STATUS
08050 5256 B7 8040       STA A  FP2PRA   STOP READ
08060 5259 FF 8042       STX    FP2CRA   DISABLE INTERRUPTS
08070 525C 7F 8010       CLR    FP3PRA   STOP INTERVAL TIMER
08080 525F 86 34         LDA A  #%00110100
08090 5261 B7 8082       STA A  FP1CRA   TURN OFF R/W HANDSHAKE
08100 5264 30            TSX             XFER DATA POINTER TO INDEX
08110 5265 9E 09         LDS    FYSYSP   RESTORE STACK POINTER
```

```
08130 5267 D7 01    FKRD09 STA B   FYSTAT    STORE ERROR STATUS
08140 5269 27 02           BEQ     FKRD10    SKIP IF NO READ ERROR
08150 526B C6 42           LDA B   #%01000010   SET OP CODE MODIFIER
08160 526D C8 0A    FKRD10 EOR B   #%00001010   GENERATE ENDING OP CODE
08170 526F D7 00           STA B   FYABOR    STORE OP/ABORT CODE

08190               * THE OP/ABORT CODE IS GENERATED FROM THE
08200               * VALUE OF ACCUMULATOR B. IF ANY ERROR
08210               * STATUS IS PRESENT B IS NON ZERO. IN THAT CASE
08220               * THE OP CODE MODIFIER IS SET. IF NO ERROR STATUS
08230               * EXISTS ACCUMULATOR B IS ZERO. THEN:

08250               *                ERROR           NO ERROR
08260               *              --------         --------
08270               *      B =     01000010         00000000
08280               *  EOR B =     00001010         00001010
08290               *              --------         --------
08300               *   CODE =     01001000         00001010

08320 5271 39              RTS               RETURN TO HOST PROGRAM
```

```
08350              * FLOPPY DISK WRITE DATA ROUTINE

08370              * THIS ROUTINE OBTAINS BYTE PARALLEL DATA FROM
08380              * RAM STORAGE AND MOVES THE DATA TO THE DISK
08390              * FORMATTER. DATA IS THEN WRITTEN ON THE DISKETTE
08400              * IN SERIAL.

08420              * A CRYSTAL OSCILLATOR IS USED TO GENERATE THE
08430              * WRITE FREQUENCY. THEREFORE, THE WRITE DATA
08440              * RATE WILL DEVIATE ONLY SLIGHTLY. THIS ROUTINE
08450              * WILL OPERATE WITH AS MUCH AS + OR - 5%
08460              * FREQUENCY DEVIATION.

08480              * DATA IS MOVED FROM MEMORY USING INDEXED MODE
08490              * ADDRESSING. THIS ROUTINE USES THE INDEX REGISTER
08500              * AS BOTH A MEMORY ADDRESS REGISTER AND AS A
08510              * BYTE COUNTER. BECAUSE OF THE TIMING REQUIREMENTS
08520              * OF THE FLOPPY DISK THE INDEX REGISTER IS TESTED
08530              * FOR ZERO TO DETERMINE THE END OF THE DATA
08540              * TRANSFER. TESTING FOR ZERO PLACES ADDRESSING
08550              * CONSTRAINTS ON THE LOCATION OF THE WRITE DATA
08560              * STORAGE AREA. THE HIGHEST ADDRESS OF THIS AREA
08570              * IS DETERMINED BY ADDING THE MAXIMUM OFFSET
08580              * VALUE TO THE DATA LENGTH:
08590              *     MAX ADDRESS = 255 (OFFSET) + 128 (DATA)
08600              *                 = 383

08620              * THE INTERVAL TIMER IS ARMED TO INTERRUPT THE
08630              * SYSTEM AFTER 4.6 MILLISECONDS. THIS INSURES
08640              * THAT IF THERE IS A HARDWARE MALFUNCTION THE
08650              * ONLY RECORD AFFECTED IS THAT ONE WHICH WAS TO
08660              * BE WRITTEN.

08680              * OTHER ERROR INTERRUPTS INCLUDE:
08690              *     A. SYSTEM INOPERABLE
08700              *     B. UNDERFLOW
08710              *     C. INDEX
08720              *     D. NOT READY

08740              * THE "ABOVE TRK 43" SIGNAL IS SET TO A "1" OR
08750              * "0" PRIOR TO BEGINNING THE DATA TRANSFER. THE
08760              * RAM LOCATION "FYTRKA" IS USED TO DETERMINE THE
08770              * PRESENT LOCATION OF THE HEAD.
```

08790	* SYNCHRONIZATION OF THE WRITE DATA RATE TO THE
08800	* PROGRAM IS ACCOMPLISHED BY WAITING UNTIL A BYTE
08810	* REQUEST OCCURS. THIS WAIT LOOP CONSISTS OF
08820	* TESTING BIT 7 OF PIA #1 CONTROL REGISTER A
08830	* AND LOOPING BACK TO TEST THE BIT AGAIN IF IT
08840	* HAD BEEN "0." AFTER A "1" BIT IS DETECTED
08850	* A DATA BYTE IS MOVED TO THE PIA. AFTER
08860	* THE BYTE HAS BEEN MOVED A DUMMY READ CLEARS
08870	* THE INTERRUPT FLAG. FAILURE TO EXECUTE THE
08880	* DUMMY READ BEFORE THE NEXT BYTE REQUEST WILL
08890	* CAUSE AN UNDERFLOW ERROR SIGNAL TO LATCH.
08910	* WHEN THE WRITE ROUTINE IS COMPLETED OR ABORTED
08920	* THE PIA'S ARE RETURNED TO READ MODE
08940	* AN OPERATION/ABORT FLAG IS MAINTAINED IN RAM
08950	* LOCATION "FVABOR" AS FOLLOWS:
08960	* 10000100 WRITE OPERATION IN PROGRESS
08970	* 01000100 WRITE OPERATION ABORTED BY PROGRAM
08980	* 01100100 WRITE OPERATION ABORTED BY INTERRUPT
08990	* 00000110 WRITE OPERATION COMPLETE

```
09020 5272 86 EF     FKWRIT LDA A   #%11101111    SET STATUS MASK
09030 5274 B4 8041           AND A   FP2PRB   FETCH MASKED STATUS
09040 5277 97 01            STA A   FYSTAT   STORE ERROR STATUS
09050 5279 27 05            BEQ     FKWR01   BRANCH IF STATUS GOOD

09070                * ERROR STATUS CHECKED:
09080                *    BIT 0 = NOT IN SYNC
09090                *    BIT 1 = DISK SYSTEM INOPERABLE
09100                *    BIT 2 = UNDERFLOW
09110                *    BIT 3 = WRITE PROTECTED
09120                *    BIT 5 = NOT HEAD LOADED
09130                *    BIT 6 = NOT READY
09140                *    BIT 7 = INDEX

09160 527B 86 44            LDA A   #%01000100
09170 527D 97 00            STA A   FYABOR   STORE ABORT CODE
09180 527F 39               RTS              RETURN TO HOST PROGRAM

09200 5280 9F 08     FKWR01 STS      FYSYSP   SAVE STACK POINTER
09210 5282 86 84            LDA A   #%10000100
09220 5284 97 00            STA A   FYABOR   STORE WRITE OP CODE
09230 5286 CE FF00          LDX      #$FF00
09240 5289 FF 8080          STX      FP1PRA   MOVE GAP PATTERN TO PIA

09260                * "FF" IS MOVED TO FP1PRA AND "00" IS MOVED TO
09270                * FP1PRB. "FF" IS THE GAP CLOCK PATTERN AND
09280                * "00" IS THE GAP DATA PATTERN.

09300 528C 86 AD            LDA A   #%10101101
09310 528E B7 8040          STA A   FP2PRA   ENABLE WRITE

09330                * "ENABLE WRITE" GATES THE FORMATTER WRITE
09340                * CIRCUITS ON. BECAUSE "WRITE GATE" IS OFF THE
09350                * SERIAL DATA IS NOT TRANSFERRED TO THE DRIVE.
09360                * ALSO, THE READ STATUS SIGNALS WHICH ARE ROUTED
09370                * TO PIA #1 ARE SWITCHED TO A HIGH IMPEDANCE
09380                * STATE BY "ENABLE WRITE" IN PREPARATION TO
09390                * CHANGING THE PIA #1 I/O LINES FROM INPUTS TO
09400                * OUTPUTS.

09420 5291 CE 3030          LDX      #$3030
09430 5294 FF 8082          STX      FP1CRA   SELECT DIRECTION REGS
09440 5297 CE FFFF          LDX      #$FFFF
09450 529A FF 8080          STX      FP1PRA   DEFINE PIA #1 LINES OUTPUTS
```

```
09470 529D C6 34            LDA B  #%00110100   PRELOAD FP1CRA CONTROL
09480 529F 86 29            LDA A  #43
09490 52A1 91 04            CMP A  FYTRKA       TEST TRK ADDR > 43
09500 52A3 22 02            BHI    FKWR02       BRANCH IF > 43
09510 52A5 86 23            LDA A  #43-8
09520 52A7 88 13  FKWR02    EOR A  #%00010011   FORM TRK > 43 CONTR WOR
09530 52A9 B7 8083          STA A  FP1CRB       SET ABOVE TRK 43

09550              * THE TRK > 43 CONTROL WORD IS GENERATED FROM THE
09560              * VALUE 43 AS FOLLOWS:

09580              *                  TRK > 43                 TRK =/< 43
09590              *                  --------                 --------
09600              *    43 =         00101011     43-8 =       00100011
09610              *    EOR#         00010111                  00010111
09620              *                 --------                  --------
09630              *    FP1CRB       00111100                  00110100

09650              * IF THE TRACK IS GREATER THAN 43 THE CB2 SIGNAL
09660              * OF PIA #1 IS SET TO A HIGH. ALSO PERIPHERAL
09670              * REGISTER B IS SELECTED BY BIT 2.

09690 52AC F7 8082          STA B  FP1CRA       SELECT PERIPHERAL REG A
09700 52AF C6 F9            LDA B  #256-5       SET BYTE COUNTER = 5
09710 52B1 86 24            LDA A  #%00100100   PRELOAD R/W HANDSHAKE
09720 52B3 CE 032E          LDX    #S100US+46
09730 52B6 FF 8010          STX    FP3PRA       ARM TIMER FOR 4.6 MS
09740 52B9 CE C7FB          LDX    #$C7FB       PRELOAD ADDRESS MARK
09750 52BC 7A 8040          DEC    FP2PRA       SET WRITE GATE

09770              * SERIAL WRITE DATA IS GATED INTO THE DRIVE AT
09780              * THIS TIME.

09800 52BF F5 8080          BIT B  FP1PRA       CLR BYTE REQUEST
09810 52C2 B7 8082          STA A  FP1CRA       SET R/W HANDSHAKE
09820 52C5 86 A8            LDA A  #%10101000   PRELOAD ENABLE CRC
09830 52C7 F5 8082  FKWR03  BIT B  FP1CRA
09840 52CA 2A F9            BPL    FKWR03       WAIT FOR BYTE REQUEST
09850 52CC F5 8080          BIT B  FP1PRA       CLR INTERRUPT FLAG
09860 52CF 5C               INC B               UPDATE BYTE COUNTER
09870 52D0 26 F5            BNE    FKWR03       LOOP UNTIL LAST GAP BYTE
09880 52D2 F1 8082  FKWR04  CMP B  FP1CRA
09890 52D5 2B F9            BMI    FKWR04       WAIT FOR BYTE REQUEST
09900 52D7 FF 8080          STX    FP1PRA       MOVE ADDR MARK TO PIA
09910 52DA B7 8040          STA A  FP2PRA       ENABLE CRC
09920 52DD F5 8080          BIT B  FP1PRA       CLEAR INTERRUPT FLAG
09930 52E0 86 FF            LDA A  #$FF         PRELOAD CLK PATTERN
09940 52E2 F6 017F          LDA B  FKDATA+128   GET 1ST DATA BYTE
09950 52E5 CE 007F          LDX    #127         LOAD BYTE COUNTER
09960 52E8 B5 8082  FKWR05  BIT A  FP1CRA
09970 52EB 2A F9            BPL    FKWR05       WAIT FOR BYTE REQUEST
09980 52ED B7 8080          STA A  FP1PRA       MOVE CLK PATTERN TO PIA
```

```
09990  52F0  F7 8081           STA B   FP1PRB    MOVE 1ST BYTE TO PIA
10000  52F3  F5 8080           BIT B   FP1PRA    CLR INTERRUPT FLAG
10010  52F6  C6 A0             LDA B   #%10100000  PRELOAD SHIFT CRC


10030                          * THE FOLLOWING SERIES OF INSTRUCTIONS IS THE
10040                          * BASIC WRITE LOOP.

10060  52F8  A6 FF      FKWR06 LDA A   FKDATA,X   FETCH NEXT DATA BYTE
10070  52FA  F5 8082    FKWR07 BIT B   FP1CRA
10080  52FD  2A F8             BPL     FKWR07    WAIT FOR BYTE REQUEST
10090  52FF  B7 8081           STA A   FP1PRB    MOVE DATA TO PIA
10100  5302  F5 8080           BIT B   FP1PRA    CLR INTERRUPT FLAG
10110  5305  09                DEX               DECREMENT BYTE COUNTER
10120  5306  26 F0             BNE     FKWR06    LOOP UNTIL LAST BYTE


10140  5308  F7 8040           STA B   FP2PRA    SHIFT CRC
10150  530B  F5 8082    FKWR08 BIT B   FP1CRA
10160  530E  2A F8             BPL     FKWR08    POLL FOR 1ST CRC BYTE
10170  5310  F5 8080           BIT B   FP1PRA    CLR INTERRUPT FLAG
10180  5313  7F 8081           CLR     FP1PRB    MOVE "00" TO DATA PIA
10190  5316  86 AD             LDA A   #%10101101  PRELOAD DROP WRITE GATE
10200  5318  C6 A8             LDA B   #%10101000  PRELOAD STOP SHIFT CRC
10210  531A  F5 8082    FKWR09 BIT B   FP1CRA
10220  531D  2A F8             BPL     FKWR09    POLL FOR 2ND CRC BYTE
10230  531F  F5 8080           BIT B   FP1PRA    CLR INTERRUPT FLAG
10240  5322  F7 8040           STA B   FP2PRA    STOP SHIFT CRC
10250  5325  CE 3E16           LDX     #$3E16    PRELOAD DISABLE INTERRUPTS
10260  5328  C6 AF             LDA B   #%10101111  PRELOAD STOP WRITE
10270  532A  F5 8082    FKWR10 BIT B   FP1CRA
10280  532D  2A F8             BPL     FKWR10    POLL FOR LAST BYTE REQUEST
10290  532F  FF 8042           STX     FP2CRA    DISABLE INTERRUPTS
10300  5332  CE 3030           LDX     #$3030    -GATE R/W HANDSHAKE OFF
10310  5335  FF 8082           STX     FP1CRA    - AND SELECT DIRECT. REG.
10320  5338  B7 8040           STA A   FP2PRA    DROP WRITE GATE

10340                          * "WRITE GATE" IS DROPPED 30 TO 38 MICROSECONDS
10350                          * AFTER THE LAST BYTE REQUEST. THIS ENSURES THAT
10360                          * THE LAST CRC BYTE HAS PASSED THE TRIMMER ERASE
10370                          * COIL IN THE R/W HEAD.

10390  533B  7F 8010           CLR     FP3PRA    STOP INTERVAL TIMER
10400  533E  CE 0000           LDX     #0
10410  5341  FF 8080           STX     FP1PRA    CHANGE PIA #1 TO INPUTS
10420  5344  CE 3434           LDX     #$3434
10430  5347  FF 8082           STX     FP1CRA    RESELECT PERIPHERAL REG.
10440  534A  F7 8040           STA B   FP2PRA    DROP ENABLE WRITE

10460                          * PIA #1 IS NOW IN READ MODE.

10480  534D  86 05             LDA A   #%00000110
```

```
10490 534F 97 00        STA A   FVABOR      SET WRITE COMPLETE FLAG
10500 5351 39           RTS                 RETURN TO HOST PROGRAM
10520                   END
```

SYMBOL TABLE

```
C100US 0003 C10MS  0001 C10US  0004 C1MS   0002 C1US   0005
FKDATA 00FF FKERST 50A3 FKLKUP 5048 FKLU01 504E FKLU02 5053
FKLU03 505D FKMTCH 00FF FKRD01 520C FKRD02 5216 FKRD03 521B
FKRD04 522A FKRD05 5231 FKRD06 5236 FKRD07 5242 FKRD08 524E
FKRD09 5267 FKRD10 525D FKREAD 51E5 FKRSTR 5061 FKSEEK 5000
FKSK01 5013 FKSK02 5022 FKSK03 5024 FKSK04 502A FKSK05 502C
FKSK06 5035 FKSK07 5038 FKSKIN 506B FKSP01 5070 FKSP02 5076
FKSP03 5082 FKSP04 5086 FKSP05 50A1 FKSR01 50BE FKSR02 50D0
FKSR03 50E0 FKSR04 50EA FKSR05 50EF FKSR06 5100 FKSR07 5105
FKSR08 5113 FKSR09 511E FKSR10 512A FKSR11 514B FKSR12 5151
FKSR13 5153 FKSR14 5161 FKSR15 5164 FKSR16 5166 FKSR17 5175
FKSR18 5185 FKSR19 5195 FKSR20 519B FKSR21 51AE FKSR22 51B4
FKSR23 518C FKSR24 51C3 FKSR25 51D5 FKSR26 51DE FKSRCH 50B1
FKWR01 5280 FKWR02 52A7 FKWR03 52C7 FKWR04 52D2 FKWR05 52E8
FKWR06 52F3 FKWR07 52FA FKWR08 530B FKWR09 531A FKWR10 532A
FKWRIT 5272 FP1CRA 8082 FP1CRB 8083 FP1PRA 8080 FP1PRB 8081
FP2CRA 8042 FP2CRB 8043 FP2PRA 8040 FP2PRB 8041 FP3PRA 8010
FP3PRB 8011 FVABOR 0000 FVBCNT 0006 FVCTRK 0003 FVDADR 0007
FVDELT 0002 FVDMRK 0005 FVFLG1 0017 FVFLG2 0018 FVFLG3 0019
FVFLG4 001A FVFLG5 001B FVSTAT 0001 FVSVSP 000B FVTIME 0009
FVTRKA 0004 FVUPC  000D S100US 0300 S10MS  0100 S10US  0400
S1MS   0200 S1US   0500
```

CHAPTER 6

6. SYSTEM DESIGN TECHNIQUES

6-1 INTRODUCTION

Development of a microprocessor based system is similar in most respects to the design of conventional SSI/MSI systems. Both approaches must include the steps shown in Figure 6-1-1: specification, system flow charts, hardware design, and test and debug. However, the MPU based design adds another dimension. As indicated in Figure 6-1-2, the designer also has the option of software to consider and must decide whether each task is best done using the conventional approach or the software approach.

The additional decisions should not be construed as an additional burden; they are in fact the key to developing the most cost effective system. Study of the system specification will often provide indications as to the best approach. In addition to the MPU and its associated memory and interface devices, three additional elements are present in a typical system design: (1) the actual peipheral equipment that is dictated by the system specification; (2) any conventional electronics required to control the peripherals; (3) the "intelligence" that enables the MPU to perform the required control and data processing functions.

In an MPU based design, "intelligence" refers to the control program, a sequence of instructions that will guide the MPU through the various operations it must perform. During development, the designer uses the MC6800's predefined instruction set to prepare a control program that will satisfy the system requirements. The program, usually called "software" at this point, is then stored in read-only memory that can be accessed by the MPU during operation, thus becoming the system's intelligence. Once in memory, the program is often called "firmware," however, it is common to find the terms software and firmware used interchangeably in this context.

When peripherals satisfying the system requirement have been selected, the designer can begin to consider tradeoffs that will result in the most cost effective program. The presence of the MPU and control program in the system provides the designer with tradeoff opportunities not available in conventional designs.

The remainder of this Chapter explores many of the considerations involved by describing the system development for a representative microprocessor system.

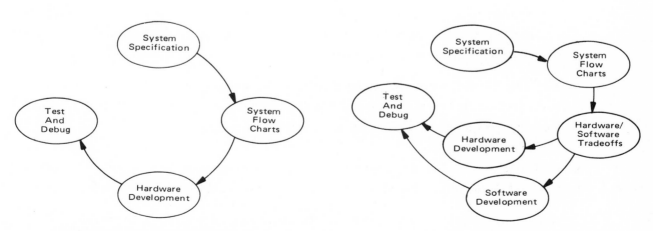

FIGURE 6-1-1: Conventional Design Cycle   FIGURE 6-1-2: MPU-Based Design Cycle

System integration considerations are best demonstrated by applying them to a specific problem. The design of an MPU based Point-of-Sale (POS) Transaction Terminal suitable for use in retail food stores will demonstrate typical system integration procedures.

The minimum requirement for such a Terminal is that it must perform all the functions currently performed by mechanical registers in the cash transaction supermarket checkout environment. The two primary requirements are that it must be simple to operate and capable of reliable stand-alone operation. Beyond this, a number of other highly desirable features are possible using an MPU based system:

(1) Data entry can be either through conventional keyboard or by electronic scanning of labels on the products. The grocery industry has recently adopted a Universal Product Code (UPC) that will eventually be used industry wide. A modern terminal must include the capability to process this code; since the code provides manufacturer and product identification rather than price information, the Terminal should have an on-board price look-up capability. Fortunately, this is within the capability of a relatively inexpensive floppy-disk unit.

(2) The Terminal can control auxiliary devices such as Electronic scales, change making machines, and stamp dispensers. Electronic control and data signals make possible a modular design; if desired for aesthetic and/or operator comfort reasons, remote location can be used for the visual display, scales, keyboard, etc.

(3) Data for use in inventory control and transaction accounting can be accumulated on a machine readable (magnetic tape, for example) medium for later use by the store's management. The MPU can also provide the capability of real time interrogation as to volume of business, cash balances, etc.

(4) The Terminal should automatically calculate such things as the total price after entry of the weight and price per unit weight, total price of multiple items upon entry of a unit price and number of items, and Sales Tax due on a transaction.

(5) Addition of a communications channel, while not necessary to the basic function, provides several advantages. Communication channels between the Terminals and a central control point can be used to update price look-up files, transfer transaction data, and perform on line interrogation from a remote location. The communications channel also permits automated remote authorization for cashing checks.

(6) The MPU can also monitor operator procedures and its own peripheral devices with little increase in system cost. Incorrect procedures or equipment malfunctions can be indicated by means of warning lights or diagnostic messages via the display system.

An MPU oriented block diagram of a POS terminal incorporating many of the features just described is shown in Figure 6-4.1-1. In addition to the MPU electronics, the Terminal includes the following functions:

(1) A scanning wand for optical reading of labels bearing the Universal Product Code.

(2) A 16-character display for visually indicating entry data.

(3) A printer suitable for providing a printed paper record of the transaction details.

(4) A cassette tape system for capturing data in a machine readable format.

(5) A floppy-disk system for use in automatic price look-up.

(6) A communications channel for data interchange between the Terminal and a central controller.

(7) A keyboard for manual entry of data.

A functional description of each of the peripheral devices is included in Chapter 5. However, since the keyboard plays a large role in operating procedures, a partial explanation of its features and operating characteristics is included here. The data entry keyboard is shown schematically in Figure 6-2-2. It includes eleven keys for entering numerical data (digits 0–9 plus decimal point) and fifteen function keys.

The seemingly simple task of totaling the price of individual items and receiving the dollar amount due is complicated by the wide variety of activities included in a typical supermarket transaction. For instance, bulk produce items must be weighed and the price calculated; most items are taxable, however, some may not be. Currently most non-produce items have the price indicated on the package; the future trend is toward incorporating the Universal Product Code supplemented by in-house numerical codes. In addition to cash, the customer may offer checks, stamps, coupons, and refundable items such as bottles in payment. The Terminal design must include methods for handling all these possibilities and yet keep the operating procedures simple.

The numeric and decimal point keys are used to manually enter numerical data for the following categories: price in dollars and cents, weight in pounds, number of identical items (for simplifying multiple item entry), and numerical codes, either UPC or in-house.

The operating procedures selected assume that a numeric entry is the first step in manual data entry. The type of data is then specified by an appropriate function key. An entry representing the number of identical items is identified by closing the Quantity key; closure of the Weight key following a numeric entry indicates that the data is a weight in pounds. Up to eight product categories are identified by following a numeric price entry with the appropriate Category key.

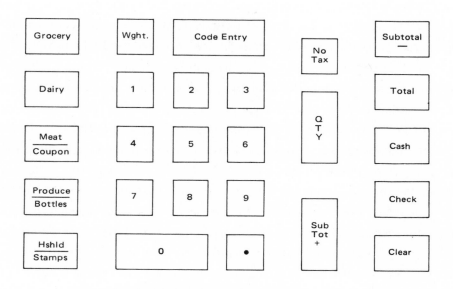

FIGURE 6-2-1: POS Keyboard Configuration

The operator may enter price and weight data in either order; similarly, in multiple item entries either the quantity or the price may be entered first. Data entry procedures are explained further in the following description of the action taken by the Terminal for various combinations of inputs.

The simplest item entry consists of numerical price followed by a product category. Closure of the Subtotal Plus key then indicates the end of the item entry sequence. The Terminal responds by updating the current running total and displaying and printing the item entry data. Note: This is performed automatically when the Terminal is in the code entry mode i.e., no Subtotal Plus is required.

The next entry mode in order of complexity is a price/category accompanied by a quantity entry. The Quantity key permits entry of multiple items with a single price entry and may be used with either price or UPC data entry. A numeric/quantity entry either before or after a price/category entry causes the Terminal to calculate and print/display the total price of multiple entries after the Subtotal Plus completes the entry sequence.

The Terminal interprets a price/category entry accompanied by a numeric/weight entry as price per pound and weight in pounds. The Terminal accepts up to four digits plus the decimal point for weight entries and automatically calculates/displays/prints the total item price.

Closure of the Code Entry Key alerts the Terminal that the next item entry will be UPC numerical data. Entry may then be made either by label scanner or keyboard. The Terminal will respond to each valid data entry by first displaying and printing the price and then sounding an audible "Approval" tone. The Terminal automatically recognizes a valid data entry, hence no closure of Subtotal Plus is required during UPC entry. Multiple item UPC entry is accomplished by means of a numeric/quantity entry prior to the code entry. The UPC entry mode is cancelled by a Code Entry key closure following the last UPC entry. Visual display of the last item price continues until another entry is made.

Five keys are provided for indicating merchandise categories: Grocery, Dairy, Meat, Produce, and Household. Three of the keys serve the dual purpose of indicating one of the three refund categories, Coupons, Bottles, or Stamps. As indicated earlier, the category entry is made immediately after price has been entered. If Subtotal Minus is used to conclude an item entry concerning the three dual purpose keys, the appropriate refundable category is assigned by the Terminal.

Closure of the Subtotal Minus key indicates that the preceeding numeric entry is to be deducted from the current total. The calculate/display/print format is determined by the data entry immediately preceeding closure of the Subtotal Minus key. If the entry was an unqualified numeric, the Terminal subtracts that amount from the current transaction total and displays/prints the amount entered and a minus sign. If the numeric entry is followed by one of the categories, Coupon, Bottles, or Stamps the Terminal subtracts the amount and displays/prints category, price, and minus sign. The unqualified numeric deduction allows operator correction of erroneously entered data. Partially entered data (prior to a subtotal closure) is erased by a Clear key closure.

Closure of the Total key indicates the end of a transaction entry sequence. Used immediately following Subtotal Plus/Minus entry, it causes the current transaction total to be printed and displayed. A second closure of the Total key following display/print causes the terminal to first calculate and print the tax due on the transaction and then display/print the new total including tax. The No Tax key is used just prior to subtotaling an entry upon which no tax is to be included. The Terminal keeps track of such entries and deletes them from the tax calculations.

At this point, several transaction conclusion alternatives are possible :(a) Numeric entry of amount of cash tendered followed by closure of the Cash key causes the Terminal to display/print the amount of cash entered. A Clear key closure will now calculate and display/print the change due, release the cash drawer, and dispense change and/or stamps via dispensing machines, if used. (b) Numeric entry of the amount tendered by check followed by a Check key closure causes the Terminal to display/print amount of the check entered. If the check is to be accepted without authorization, closure of the Clear key now calculates and displays/prints the change due, releases the cash drawer, and dispenses change and/on stamps. If the Terminal is to be used for obtaining check cashing authorization, up to a nine digit I.D. number followed by a Code Entry closure may be used prior to entering the amount tendered. This sequence causes the terminal to obtain authorization or rejection via the communications channel. The result is displayed/printed and audible "Approval" or "Disapproval" is sounded. If, after a rejection, the check is to be accepted anyway (after personal authorization by the store manager, for example) a numeric/Check entry followed by a closure of the Clear key allows the transaction to be concluded as above. If, after rejection, the transaction is to be converted to cash, numeric entry of the cash tendered followed by closure of the Cash key concludes the transaction as in (a) above.

The keys can be used in combination to perform several additional functions. Transactions may be voided at any time. If the current transaction has not yet been totaled, the Total key must be closed momentarily to form a total. Sequential closure of Subtotal Minus, Cash, Total, then voids the transaction. If the total is currently displayed and the tax calculated, the same sequence voids the transaction, i.e., sequential closure of Subtotal Minus, Cash, Total. Tax is not permanently recorded internally until one of the valid transaction completion routines has been carried out. The voiding of a transaction is printed on the register tape.

The contents of the Terminal may be modified by using coded entries. Codes are available for adding or removing cash and for cashing checks. A numerical entry followed by a Code Entry closure causes the Terminal to respond by displaying "Add Cash," "Remove Cash," or "Cash Check," depending on the code selected. The operator may then enter the amount involved and close the total key. The Terminal will automatically make the appropriate adjustments to running balances. Modification of the contents should be done between normal transactions.

The Code Entry key also provides a means of interrogating and instructing the Terminal through the keyboard. A numeric entry followed by a Code Entry closure can be used to (a) Display/print current transaction count number and total dollar sales for the current work shift, (b) Display/print current transaction count number and total check balance, (c) Display/print current transaction number and cash balance in drawer, or (d) Print transaction count number, operator I.D. number, total sales for the work shift, total cash and check balances, and the difference if any, between sales and receipts. During this operation only a difference between sales and receipts are displayed.

The interrogation mode, i.e., numeric/Code Entry is also used for entering new operator I.D. and initializing at the beginning of an operator shift and causing a Terminal controlled cassette tape data dump through the communications channel.

Once the system requirements are defined, the designer must almost immediately begin making decisions to establish whether a hardware or a software approach will be used for each sub-task.

The tradeoff possibilities can be explored by considering some of the overall design goals. For example, if a high volume production run is anticipated, a logical goal is to minimize hardware costs since each dollar of cost is amplified by the unit count. In such cases, every attempt should be made to eliminate external control hardware by "loading up" the MPU since control programs in memory are generally more economical than generating the same function with conventional logic circuits.

At the opposite extreme are relatively complex systems (with attendent high engineering development costs) that will be produced in limited quantity. In this case, minimizing development cost may be the more important criteria. In typical MPU systems, the peripherals can be obtained from OEM suppliers with varying amounts of the control and drive circuitry provided. Using peripherals with conventional control and drive electronics will simplify the tasks that must be performed by the MPU and will result in a shorter, more economical development cycle.

Typical applications fall somewhere between these two extremes. There will usually be three approaches to consider: the older conventional method, the new programmed method, and a judicious blend of both.

The primary goal using an MPU based design should be to replace as much hardware as possible with a control program that causes the MPU to duplicate the hardware process. This capability is the primary motivation for using an MPU in the first place. In many cases, this approach can be carried to the extreme of eliminating everything except the family devices (MPU, Memory, Interface) and the peripherals themselves. However, in most systems, there are tasks that, if done in hardware, can significantly reduce memory requirements and/or improve the data throughput rate. For this reason, selection of the configuration should not be based on simplistic hardware/software tradeoffs.

The first task of the system designer is to become familiar with the MPU's characteristics. Knowledge concerning the MPU's ability to handle various aspects of the problem will heavily influence the methods that are finally adopted. Such factors as operating speed, the number of working registers and how they can be used, available control features, I/O techniques, addressing modes, and the instruction set will all influence each stage of the development.

The remainder of this section illustrates by example some of the steps involved in reducing a system specification to individual software and hardware tasks. The various options are discussed in context with the Transaction Terminal described in the previous section.

6-3.1   **MEMORY REFERENCE I/O VS DMA I/O**

Memory reference or software I/O refers to the technique of transferring data to and from memory via the MPU and a PIA. For example, to load memory from a peripheral device, the data flow would be to (1) the PIA, to (2) the MPU, to (3) the memory. This is typically accomplished in software by a LDAA (PIA to MPU) instruction addressing the proper PIA followed by a STAA (MPU to Memory) instruction addressing the desired memory location.

DMA, or direct memory access, is a technique by which peripheral data transfer to and from memory is accomplished directly utilizing special DMA hardware. This implies that a DMA transfer is transparent to the

MPU, thus costing no software. However, it does affect system operation; the DMA circuitry must disable the MPU and generate the desired data, address and control signals required to transfer data directly to memory. DMA is discussed in detail in Chapter 4, however, it is worth reviewing here the reasons for disabling the MPU prior to a DMA transfer. During non-DMA operation, the MPU is driving the system busses and control lines. When DMA is required, the DMA hardware is responsible for driving the busses and some of the control lines, therefore, to avoid contention the DMA must "disable" the MPU.

Any of the methods described in Chapter 4 may be used; the cycle stealing method of Section 4-2.2.2 is particularly useful when the DMA transfer requires a quick response. The transfer may begin within 500 nsec after setting the required MPU control lines. This technique is limited to an access of 5 μsec duration because of the MPU refresh requirements.

In the POS system, likely candidates for DMA transfer were the floppy disk and cassette peripherals. However, analysis indicated that neither of these peripherals required DMA hardware. (See Section 2-3 for the analysis.) The floppy disk requires a nominal transfer rate of approximately 31.25 kbytes/sec. The 6800 MPU, utilizing the PIA, can accommodate this transfer rate using software techniques. The cassette transfer rate is even slower, approximately 1.5 kbytes/sec. Even though the data block is long (256 bytes), suggesting DMA usage, the byte rate is very slow compared with the MPU's software capability. As a result, DMA hardware was deemed unnecessary for the defined system. The floppy disk data rate approaches the minimum cycle time that software alone can transfer data from peripheral to MPU. Any peripherals requiring transfer cycle time less than 25 μsec/byte will require DMA techniques.

6-3.2 SOFTWARE VS HARDWARE PERIPHERAL SERVICE PRIORITIZING

Either software or hardware techniques can be used to establish the priority by which peripherals will be serviced. In the software approach, the MPU polls the peripheral devices to determine which peripheral needs service. The priority of peripherals with respect to one another is, therefore, determined by the order in which the software performs the poll. Hardware prioritizing uses external hardware to generate the service requests.

The advantages and disadvantages of both methods are discussed in Section 3-3. Several hardware prioritizing methods are described in Section 4-2.1. In general, hardware techniques are faster, but the software approach eliminates the need for external circuitry.

In keeping with the goal of minimizing external hardware wherever possible and because software polling was found to be adequate, no hardware prioritizing was done on the POS design.

An example of software prioritizing methods was used in the case of the floppy disk. The interrupt must be serviced as quickly as possible once it occurs. In such a case, the MPU can ignore all other service requests and go into a programmed waiting loop until the device asks for service. When the disk is transmitting data to the MPU, the MPU repeatedly asks the disk if data is coming and responds immediately to a request for service.

6-3.3 SOFTWARE VS HARDWARE TIMER

In most systems, the MPU must occasionally perform a time out requirement before continuing with the program. Software can be used to generate the delay in a straightforward fashion by loading a register and decrementing it to zero and then allowing the program to continue. The amount of delay is determined by the value loaded into the register. Other software timing techniques are described in Section 2-3.

Hardware time delays may be generated using any of the conventional methods such as one-shots, shift registers, counters, etc. Programmable counters are particularly useful in MPU systems; they can be parallel loaded from the MPU and decremented to zero similarly to the MPU's internal registers. In this case, however, the zero count is used to generate an interrupt that tells the MPU the timeout is complete. The hardware approach is useful in two situations: (1) When another useful task can be performed by the MPU while a timeout is taking place; (2) When two or more simultaneous but independent delays or timeouts are required for proper system operation.

In the case of the POS terminal design, a hardware timer was incorporated for both purposes. It is used as a matter of efficiency by several of the peripheral subroutines and as a matter of necessity by the disk control routine. The timer used is described in detail in Section 4-2.4.

6-3.4　DISPLAY WITH OR WITHOUT EXTERNAL MEMORY

In general, the hardware/software considerations for specific peripherals are covered in their respective Sections of Chapter 5. (See, for example, Section 5-2.1.2 of the Printer description.) The display circuitry, however, has a direct bearing on overall system efficiency. A Burroughs SSD1000-0060 16 Character Selfscan alphanumeric display panel was selected for the POS design. Data entry is by character from right to left with all displayed characters shifted one position to the left for each new entry. A display such as this raises the question as to whether a display with its own external memory storage should be selected.

The Burroughs SSD1000-0060 Selfscan with memory is straightforward to use with the Motorola M6800 family (see Figure 5-2.2-1). To display a character, the MPU need only store the character code into the PIA interfacing with the display. The PIA then transmits the data and controls to the display. Each character displayed is stored in the display hardware thereby "freezing" the display until the MPU loads a new character.

The 16 character Burroughs Selfscan without memory has essentially the same hardware interface but requires software for memory refresh. The program must establish a 16-byte character buffer in the system memory and periodically (approximately every .4 msec) refresh each character. The display program loads the display by storing the character codes into system memory and sequentially transferring each of the 16 memory words into the display at the desired refresh rate.

The decision whether to use the more expensive display with memory versus additional programming requirements is influenced by the refresh time burdens placed on the executive control program. As usual, the objective is to eliminate hardware suggesting that the display without memory be used, however, the display operation should be examined in context with other system timing requirements. The display requires a new data word every 420 μsec; this relatively slow data rate is well within the MPU's data transfer capability. A more restrictive requirement is that once the MPU is requested to display a word it has nominally 120 μsec to load the character into the display. From the standpoint of the MPU alone, the character could be loaded well within the required 120 μsec but a conflict arises when there are other subsystem routines demanding uninterrupted services. The POS terminal design uses two routines that require uninterrupted service; both the disk and wand operations require dedicated service. As a result, there is a high probability that the display will require refresh while the MPU is locking out all interrupts. If the display is momentarily ignored, the result is not catastrophic, but will cause a visual flicker in the display. Prior to actual program development, the designer has only limited knowledge concerning the number and duration of possible contention problems. As the contention increases, the visual quality of the display degenerates. For this reason, the decision was made to use the display with external memory and not risk sacrificing display quality.

As a general rule, hardware/software tradeoff decisions should be made as early as possible during system development. However, situations often arise in which the pros and cons of each method are initially well balanced. In these circumstances, the final selection can be made later when the problem is better defined. A great advantage of the MPU approach is that design changes are easily incorporated. For example, if the anticipated contention problem discussed in connection with the display does not arise during development, it is a simple matter to modify the display program and switch to the unit without external memory.

An exhaustive discussion of hardware/software tradeoffs is potentially unlimited. It has been the intent here to evoke an awareness of the alternatives without trying to categorize all the possibilities that may arise. Each application will present different problems; the important point is that MPU based designs offer the designer a wide variety of options to chose from.

The final hardware design of the Transaction Terminal was influenced by several considerations in addition to satisfying the specified system requirements. The design differs from a normal protytype in two respects: (1) There was no anticipated follow-on production requirements; (2) The Terminal was to be packaged in a portable configuration. The objectives were to verify the system design described in earlier sections of this manual and provide a portable demonstration vehicle for the M6800 Microprocessor family. A block diagram of the hardware configuration is shown in Figure 6-4.1-1.

Due to the once-only nature of the design, generation of mask-programmed MC6830 ROMs for the program was not economically feasible. An available 8K RAM/ROM[1] memory board was selected instead. This technique of placing control programs in battery-backed RAM instead of ROM is also useful during the field test phase of systems whose operational environment cannot be well defined during development. The system can be easily modified during operational tests, then converted to mask programmable ROM prior to volume production.

The demonstration features where enhanced by including a limited diagnostic capability. This was provided by including an MC6830 ROM containing the MIKbugTM diagnostic program[2]. This firmware would also be useful during field evaluation programs since it includes such features as memory change, register display, memory dump, etc. It also provides a convenient method of loading the Transaction Terminal control program into the 8K memory via an RS232 interface to terminals such as the TI Silent 700[3].

The bulk of the hardware was partitioned into three printed circuit boards as shown in Figure 6-4.1-2.* Because of weight restrictions imposed by the portability requirement, it was necessary to place the tape cassette, the floppy disk, and their associated conventional circuitry in a separate package. The cassette and disk interface to the remainder of the system through a cable and two PIAs located on the board designated as "I/O Card" in Figure 6-4.1-2. The I/O Card (see the Schematic Diagram of Figure 6-4.1-3) also contains the MIKbugTM PIA and terminal interface circuitry, the Restart and Powerfail circuitry, and the ACIA/MODEM telephone communications circuitry.

The remainder of the system hardware is located on the "MPU/Control Card." In addition to the MPU, this board contains:

(1) The MIKbugTM ROM.

(2) Four MC6810 128 X 8 RAMs providing 512 bytes of random access memory used for shared scratchpad and temporary storage by the various subroutines.

(3) MPU ϕ1 and ϕ2 clock circuitry and memory refresh and clock circuits.

(4) Three PIAs and the interface circuitry associated with the printer, keyboard, display, interval timer, UPC scanning wand, and miscellaneous controls and indicators.

(5) Various other timing and control signals for enabling the bus extender and family devices.

---

[1]This memory board was developed for use with Motorola's EXORciserTM system development aid. The memory configuration is described in Section 4-2.5.3 of this manual.

[2]MIKbugTM was developed for use in Motorola's MPU Evaluation Module. The principle features of MIKbugTM and the Evaluation Module are described briefly in Section 7-3 and in detail in the MPU Evaluation Module Users Guide.

[3]Registered Trademark of the Texas Instruments Corporation.

*Figure 6-4.1-2 is on page 6-16.

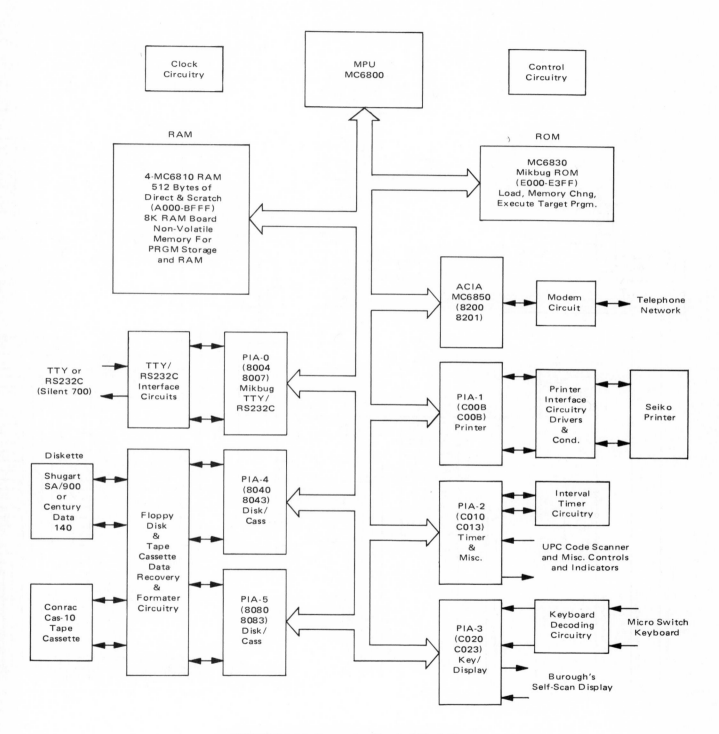

FIGURE 6-4.1-1: Transaction Terminal Block Diagram

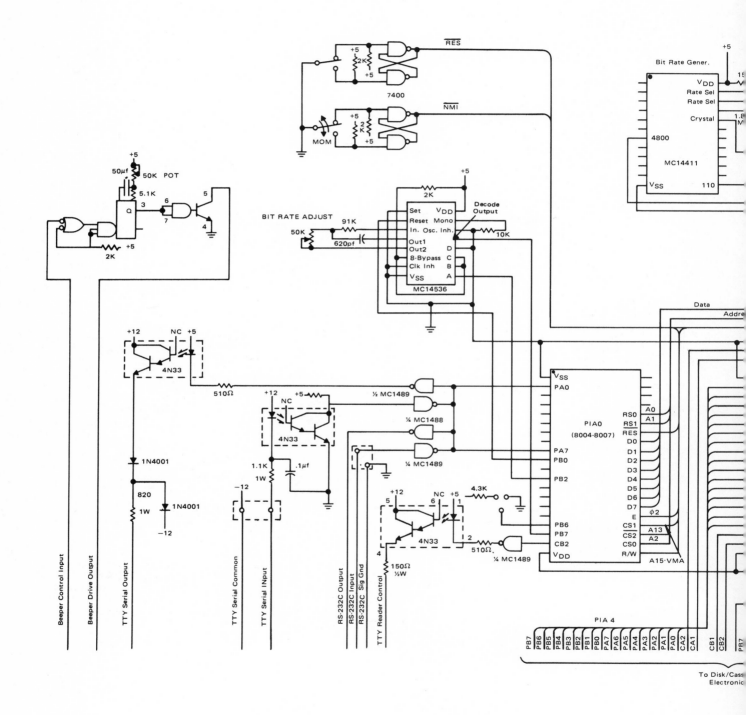

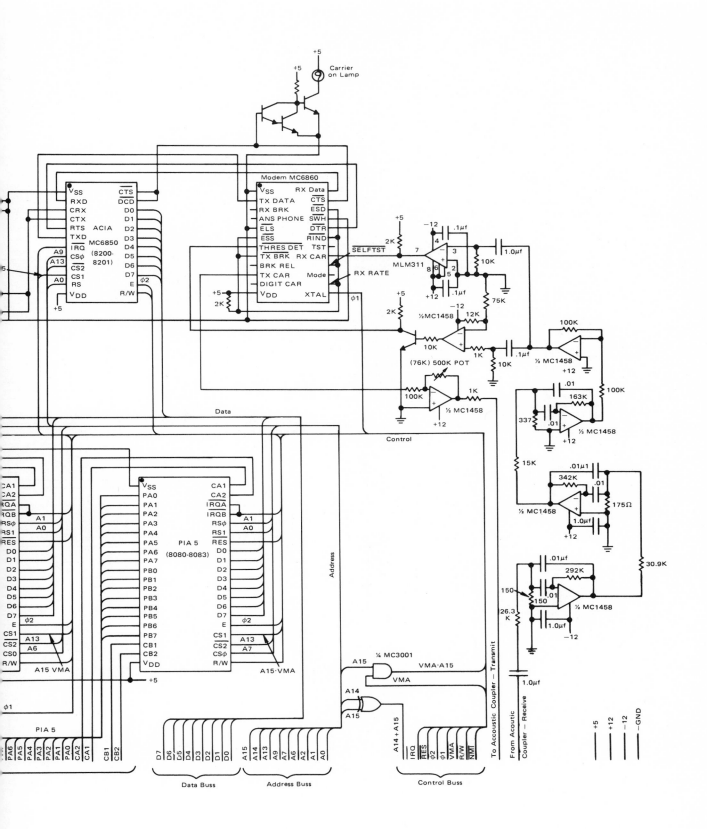

FIGURE 6-4.1-3: I/O Control Card Schematic Diagram

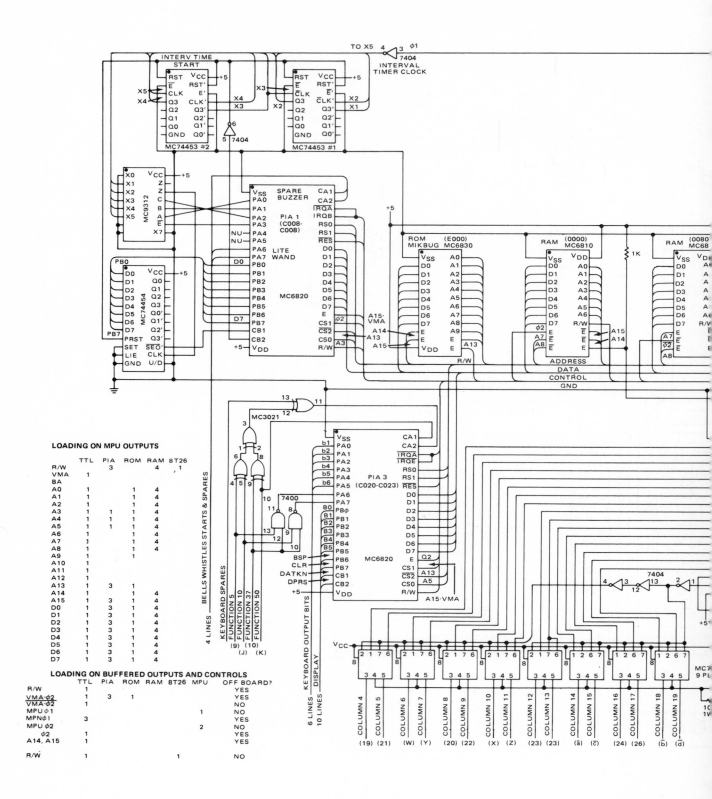

LOADING ON MPU OUTPUTS

	TTL	PIA	ROM	RAM	8T26
R/W		3			1
VMA	1				
BA					
A0	1		1	4	
A1	1		1	4	
A2	1		1	4	
A3	1	1	1	4	
A4	1	1	1	4	
A5	1	1	1	4	
A6	1		1	4	
A7	1		1	4	
A8	1		1	4	
A9	1		1		
A10	1				
A11	1				
A12	1				
A13	1	3	1		
A14	1		1		
A15	1	3	1	4	
D0	1	3	1	4	
D1	1	3	1	4	
D2	1	3	1	4	
D3	1	3	1	4	
D4	1	3	1	4	
D5	1	3	1	4	
D6	1	3	1	4	
D7	1	3	1	4	

LOADING ON BUFFERED OUTPUTS AND CONTROLS

	TTL	PIA	ROM	RAM	8T26	MPU	OFF BOARD?
R/W	1						YES
VMA·φ2	1	3	1				YES
VMA·φ2	1						NO
MPUφ1						1	NO
MPNφ1	3						YES
MPU φ2						2	NO
φ2	1						YES
A14, A15	1						YES
R/W̄	1				1		NO

6-14

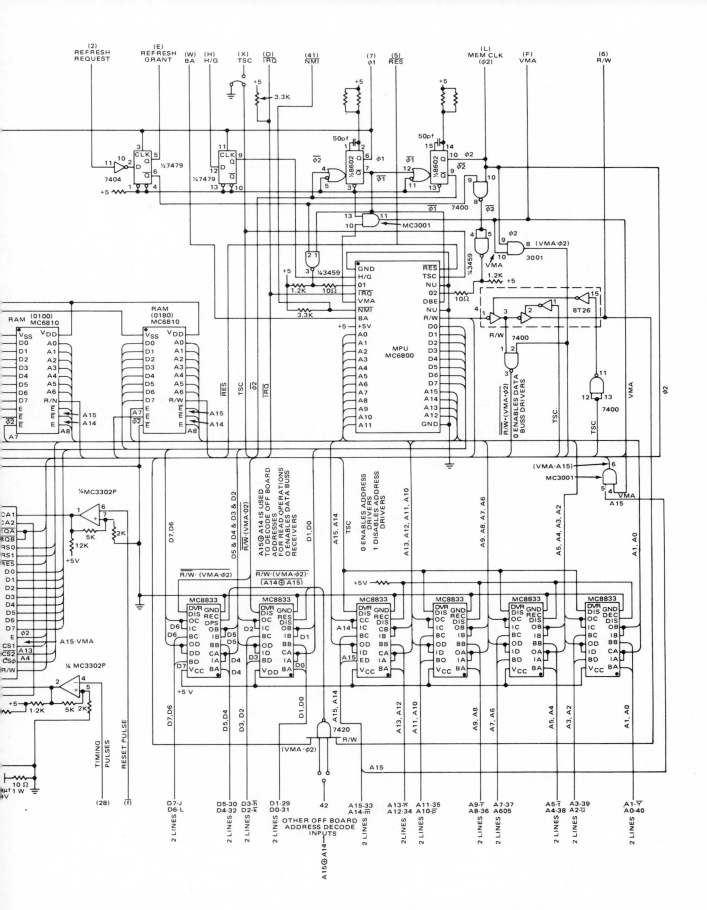

FIGURE 6-4.1-4: MPU Control Card Schematic Diagram

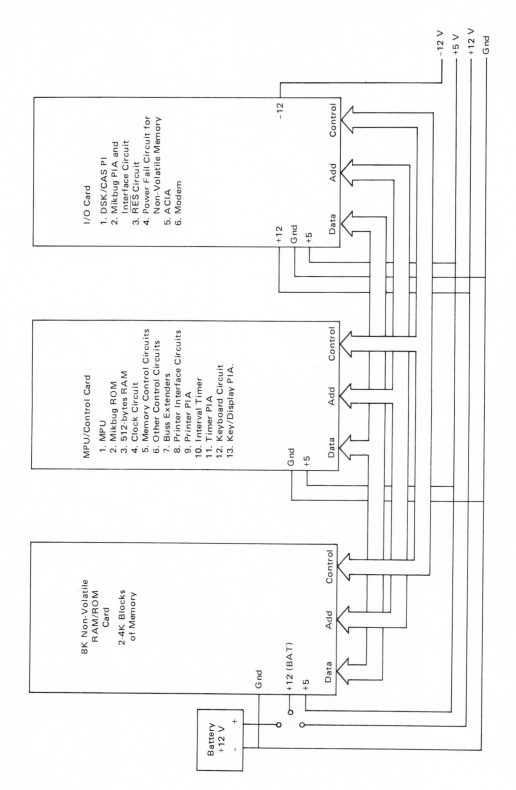

FIGURE 6-4.1-2: Control Circuitry Configuration

The schematic diagram for the MPU/Control Card is shown in Figure 6-4.1-4. The circuitry associated with the individual peripheral devices is described in detail in their respective sections of Chapter 5. This section will describe the remaining circuitry including the MIKbug PIA circuit (a feature of the M6800 Evaluation Module), the clock and control circuits, the BUS EXTENDERS, $\overline{\text{RES}}$ and powerfail circuits, and the ACIA and Modem.

The MIKbug PIA interfaces either teletype (TTY) or RS-232 type devices to the Transaction Terminal (see Figure 6-4.1-5) for purposes of loading programs into RAM or for debugging. The TTY interface is an optically isolated 20 ma current loop. By selecting the appropriate S1 position, either the TTY or the RS232 interface will be enabled, thus allowing the selected interface to function. Paper tape reader control is also provided. The BIT RATE oscillator is used to shift the data in and out of the PIA at the frequency required by the interface selected, i.e., 10 cps for the TTY and 30 cps for the RS232, etc. The oscillator must be adjusted to the frequency required for the desired data transfer rate.

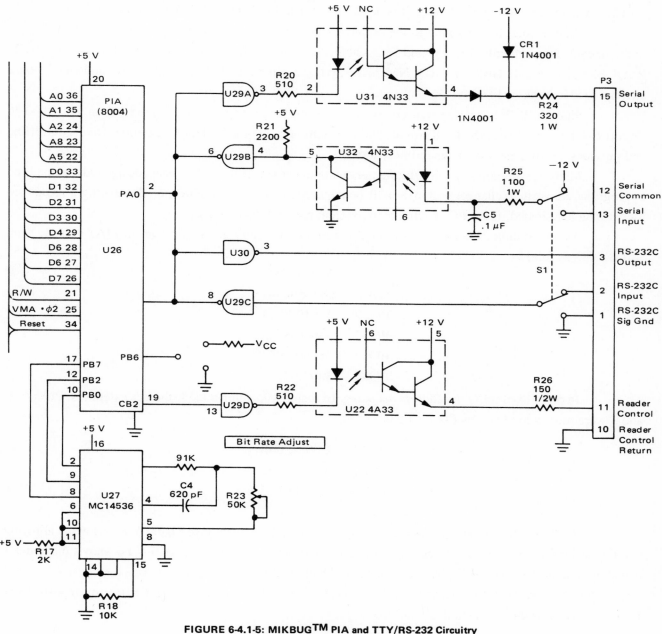

FIGURE 6-4.1-5: MIKBUG™ PIA and TTY/RS-232 Circuitry

Since the 8K memory, 3 PIAs, and the ACIA are located "outside" the bus extenders, some address decoding for the data bus receivers is required in order to prevent contention for control of the data bus. The system memory map is shown in Figure 6-4.1-6. The allocation with respect to address decoding and location with respect to the bus extender is shown in Figure 6-4.1-7.

Note that all "external" memory has A15 and A14 at logic one and zero levels, respectively. By Exclusive ORing A15 and A14 and combining them as shown in Figure 6-4.1-8 with R/W and ($VMA \cdot \phi2$), the data bus receivers are enabled only when devices off the MPU card are addressed, that is, when: $\overline{R/W \cdot (VMA \cdot \phi2) \cdot (A15 + A14)} = 0$. The data bus drivers are enabled whenever $\overline{R/W} (VMA \cdot \phi2) = 0$. The address bus drivers are controlled by the TSC line which is grounded for normal operation and the address bus receivers are disabled at all times. VMA is ANDed with A15 to enable the PIAs via their CS1 inputs. This insures that the address on the bus is valid before the PIA is enabled.

The remaining control circuitry on the MPU card includes the MEMORY refresh control signals and the G/H sync circuit. The memory circuit is described in detail in Section 4-1.5.3 of Chapter 4.

Control lines are provided to the output connector so that future functions such as DMA may be implemented. These include G/H, BA and TSC. Other controls brought out for system operation are $\overline{\text{REFRESH REQUEST}}$, REFRESH GRANT, $\overline{\text{IRQ}}$, $\overline{\text{NMI}}$, $\overline{\text{RES}}$, $\phi1$, $\phi2$ (memory clock), VMA, R/W, and an off board address decode input (A15 $\oplus$ A14).

Since the R/W line is a tri-state output, a tri-state buffer must be used to drive the system. An MC8T26 (Figure 6-4.1-9) was used since it will provide the inversion necessary for the data bus extender driver control line and provides the tri-state output capability required.

Many considerations go into the memory mapping of a system. As the system design is developed and as programs are written, changes will invariably be required in the memory allocation due to programs that are longer than anticipated, more I/O requirements, system partitioning changes, etc.

As an example, the original transaction terminal memory allocation had all PIAs defined from $8008-8083 as follows:

PIA-0	$8004-8007
PIA-1	$8008-800B
PIA-2	$8010-8013
PIA-3	$8020-8023
PIA-4	$8040-8053
PIA-5	$8080-8083

In order to simplify the address decoding for memory location outside the bus extenders, PIAs 1, 2, and 3 were moved to locations C008-C023:

PIA-1	C008-C00B
PIA-2	C010-C013
PIA-3	C020-C023

This allowed the same address decoding scheme at the devices (see Figure 6-4.1-7) while allowing simple "inside"/"outside" decoding for the data bus extender receivers. Figure 6-4.1-7 shows the address decoding scheme used for the Transaction Terminal. Shading of the address line indicates that the line is tied to either a device enable (E or $\overline{\text{E}}$) or a chip select (CSx or $\overline{\text{CSx}}$) line. A 1 indicates the line is tied to a true input (CSx or E) a zero indicates the line is tied to a not true input ($\overline{\text{CSx}}$ or $\overline{\text{E}}$).

FIGURE 6-4.1-6: Transaction Terminal Memory Map

# of Bytes	Address Range	Name	Function
1K Bytes	E3FF – E000	Mikbug ROM	Mikbug Program Firmware
4 Bytes	C023 – C020	PIA-3	Keyboard/Display Interface
4 Bytes	C013 – C010	PIA-2	Interval Timer/Misc. Interface
4 Bytes	C00B – C008	PIA-1	Printer Interface
8K Bytes	BFFF — A000	Block-2 4K RAM/ROM; Block-1 4K RAM/ROM	Program Storage; RAM Storage; RAM Buffers; Mikbug Program RAM
4 Bytes	8083 – 8080	PIA-5	Disk/Cassette Interface
4 Bytes	8043 – 8040	PIA-4	Disk/Cassette Interface
4 Bytes	8007 – 8004	PIA-0	Mikbug TTY/RS232 Interface
5K Bytes	01FF – 0000	RAM	Direct RAM and Shared RAM Scratch Pad Memory

FIGURE 6-4.1-7: Transaction Terminal Address Decoding Chart

FUNCTION/DEVICE	ADDRESS RANGE	COMMENT	A0	A1	A2	A3	A4	A5	A6	A7	A8	A9	A10	A11	A12	A13	A14	A15
Direct & Shared Scratch Memory	0000-007F	Inside Buss Extenders	X	X	X	X	X	X	X	0	0	0	0	0	0	0	0	0
	0080-00FF		X	X	X	X	X	X	X	1	0	0	0	0	0	0	0	0
	0100-017F		X	X	X	X	X	X	X	0	1	0	0	0	0	0	0	0
	0180-01FF		X	X	X	X	X	X	X	1	1	0	0	0	0	0	0	0
Printer PIA 1	C008-C00B		X	X	0	1	0	0	0	0	0	0	0	0	0	0	1	1
Int. Timer/Misc. PIA2	C010-C013		X	X	0	0	1	0	0	0	0	0	0	0	0	0	1	1
Key/Dspl PIA 3	C020-C023	(A15⊕A14)=0	X	X	0	0	0	1	0	0	0	0	0	0	0	0	1	1
MIKBUG ROM	E000-E3FF		X	X	X	X	X	X	X	X	X	X	0	0	0	1	1	1
MIKBUG PIA 0	8004-8007	Outside Buss Extenders	X	X	1	0	0	0	0	0	0	0	0	0	0	0	0	1
DSK/CAS PIA 4	8040-8043		X	X	0	0	0	0	1	0	0	0	0	0	0	0	0	1
DSK/CAS PIA 5	8080-8083	(A15⊕A14)=1	X	X	0	0	0	0	0	1	0	0	0	0	0	0	0	1
ACIA	8200-8201		X	0	0	0	0	0	0	0	0	1	0	0	0	0	0	1
Clock 1 RAM/ROM 4K	A000-AFFF	Full Address Decode	X	X	X	X	X	X	X	X	X	X	X	X	0	1	0	1
Clock 2	B000-BFFF		X	X	X	X	X	X	X	X	X	X	X	X	1	1	0	1

NOTES:
1) Data Buss Extender Receivers Enabled By $\overline{R/W} \cdot (VMA \cdot \phi2) \cdot \overline{(A15 + A14)} = 0$
2) X Indicates Variable Address
3) [shaded] Indicates This Address Line Used For Address Decoding At Chips
   a) 0's are tied to $\overline{CS}$ or $\overline{E}$ Inputs
   b) 1's are tied to CS or E Inputs
4) [box] Used To Indicate That These PIA Are Inside Buss Extenders.

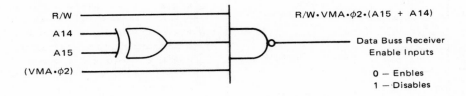

FIGURE 6-4.1-8: Bus Extender Enable/Disable

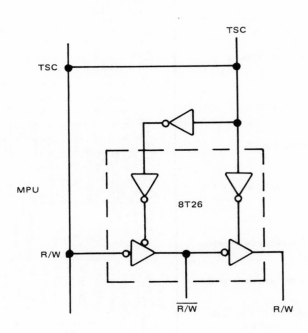

FIGURE 6-4.1-9: MC8T26, Partial Schematic

For this demonstration version of the terminal, the RES and powerfail detect circuit for the non-volatile memory are switches with contact bounce suppression circuitry. The RES (restart or reset) is a push button switch used to initialize and restart the system at power on and if the system malfunctions. The power fail detect function is switched prior to AC power off so that the memory refresh circuitry will operate from the battery during transportation of the demonstration terminal.

6-4.2   TRANSACTION TERMINAL SOFTWARE DEVELOPMENT

6-4.2.1   Software Background Preparation

The first stage of the software development is to define the tasks required of the system software. Section 6-2 describes the POS terminal requirements and provides the specification from which to work. The keyboard data entry procedure becomes a large portion of the main (executive) program and serves as a logical starting point from which to begin generating the system flow charts.

Table 6-4.2.1-1 summarizes the actions that would need to be taken for each keyboard or wand entry. The table categorizes each entry procedure indicating what action will be required of the executive program and peripheral. The left hand column shows how the entry is made; the middle column shows what is occurring in the peripherals; and the right hand column shows what action the program must take. The function of the table is to organize the necessary house-keeping requirements as items are entered and delineate some of the data

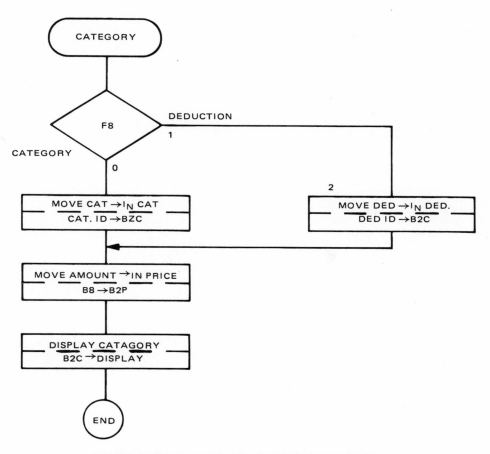

FIGURE 6-4.2.1-1: Flow for Key Entry Data (Sheet 1 of 15)

manipulation that will be required of the program. Such a table also helps the designer visualize the operation for each item entry and becomes a first pass at a set of low level flow charts. No attempt is made yet to weave them together into a common flow.

Notice that item entry is double buffered. As each new item is entered (I_n) it is immediately displayed. The program stores both the present (I_{n-1}) item information (i.e., price, category, quantity, etc.). Upon completion of a current item entry (subtotal plus): (1) pertinent data of I_{n-1} is outputted to the printer, (2) a new partial product is calculated, and (3) I_n is shifted into I_{n-1}. Using this procedure, operator errors may be "cleared" on the current item entry without affecting the printout hard copy.

The next step in program development is an outgrowth of Table 6-4.2.1-1, still focusing on the keyboard operation. The entry procedure of Table 6-4.2.1-1 is translated into a flow diagram for each key on the transaction terminal keyboard. These diagrams, shown in Figure 6-4.2.1-1, merely summarize housekeeping requirements in another format and show the flow of data between defined memory buffers, test of programmable flags, and interaction with peripherals. There is a separate flow diagram for each key or group of keys on the keyboard (see Figure 6-2-2 for a representation of the transaction keyboard). For example, all numeric entries are grouped into a single "number" flow. The only other groupings are the product category keys (i.e., grocery, dairy, meat/coupon, produce/bottles, and household/stamps). These two groups combined with the remaining transaction keys result in the thirteen distinct flow diagrams contained within Figure 6-4.2.1-1 and the buffer and flag assignments of Tables 6-4.2.1-2 and 6-4.2.1-3, respectively.

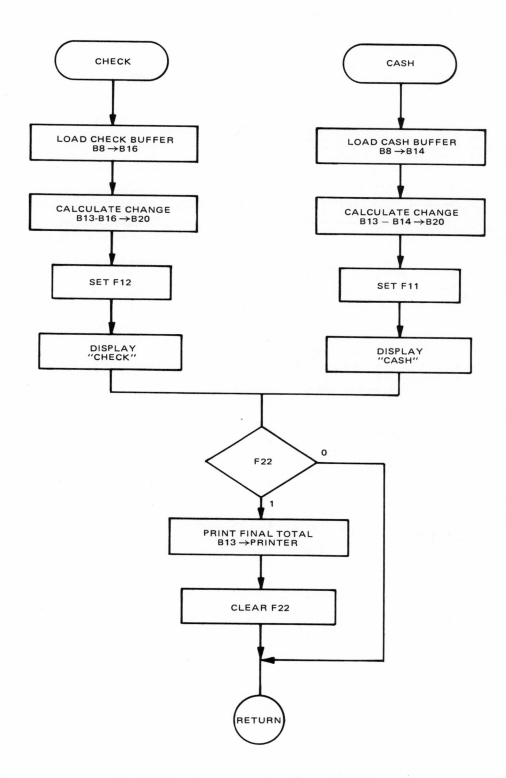

FIGURE 6-4.2.1-1: Flow for Key Entry Data (Sheet 2 of 15)

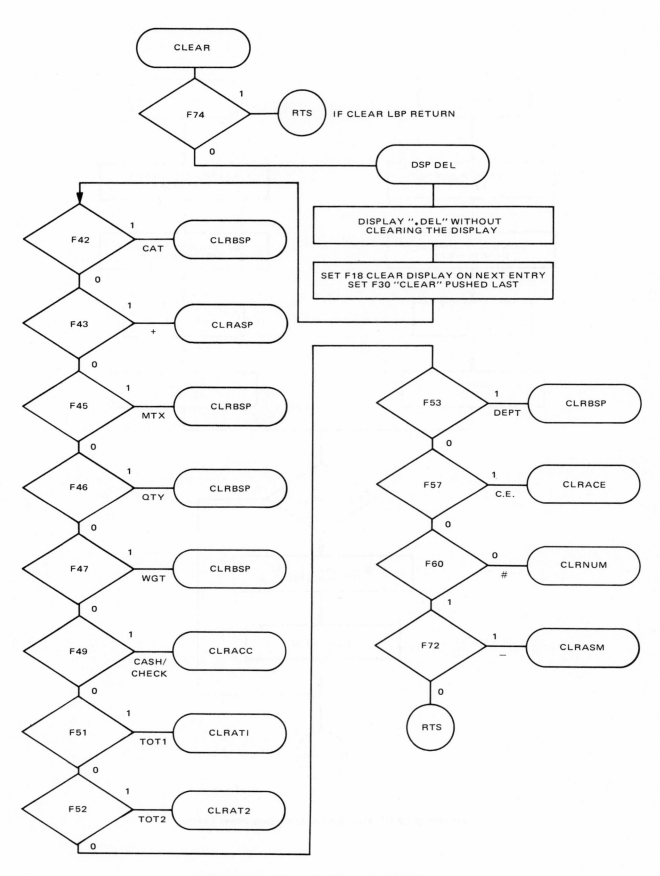

FIGURE 6-4.2.1-1: Flow for Key Entry Data (Sheet 3 of 15)

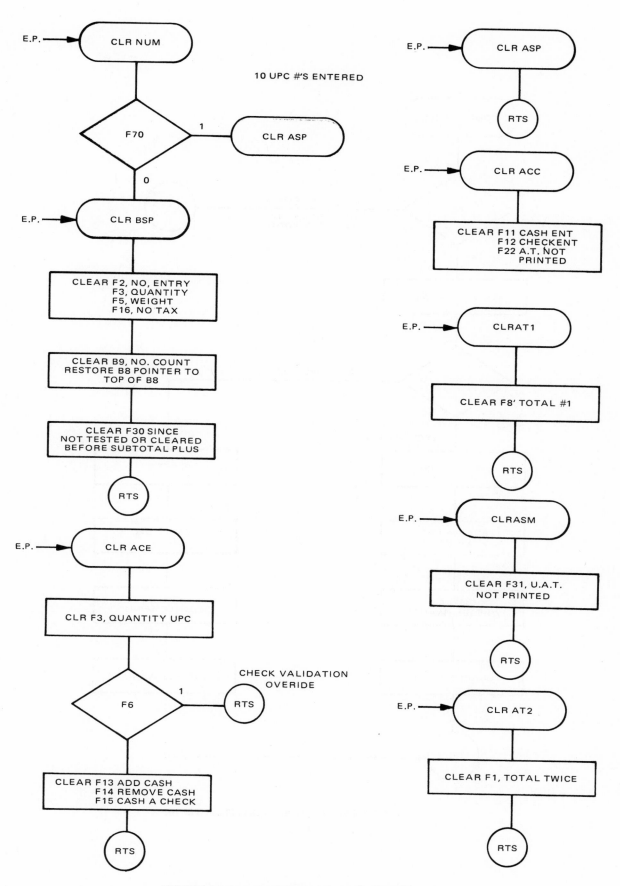

FIGURE 6-4.2.1-1: Flow for Key Entry Data (Sheet 4 of 15)

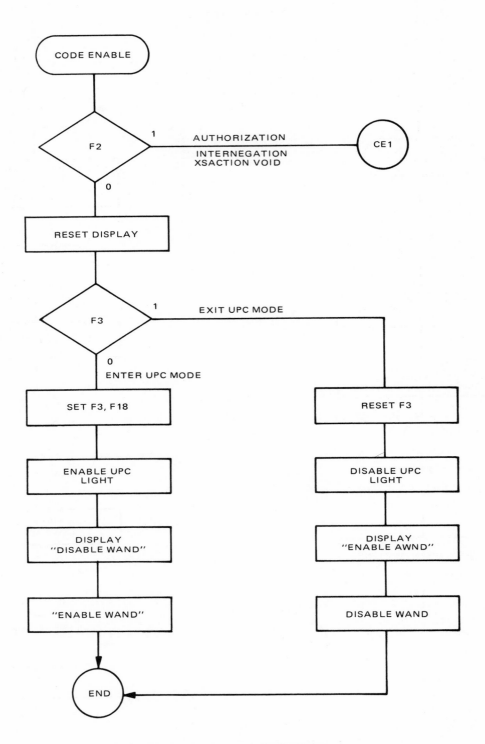

FIGURE 6-4.2.1-1: Flow for Key Entry Data (Sheet 5 of 15)

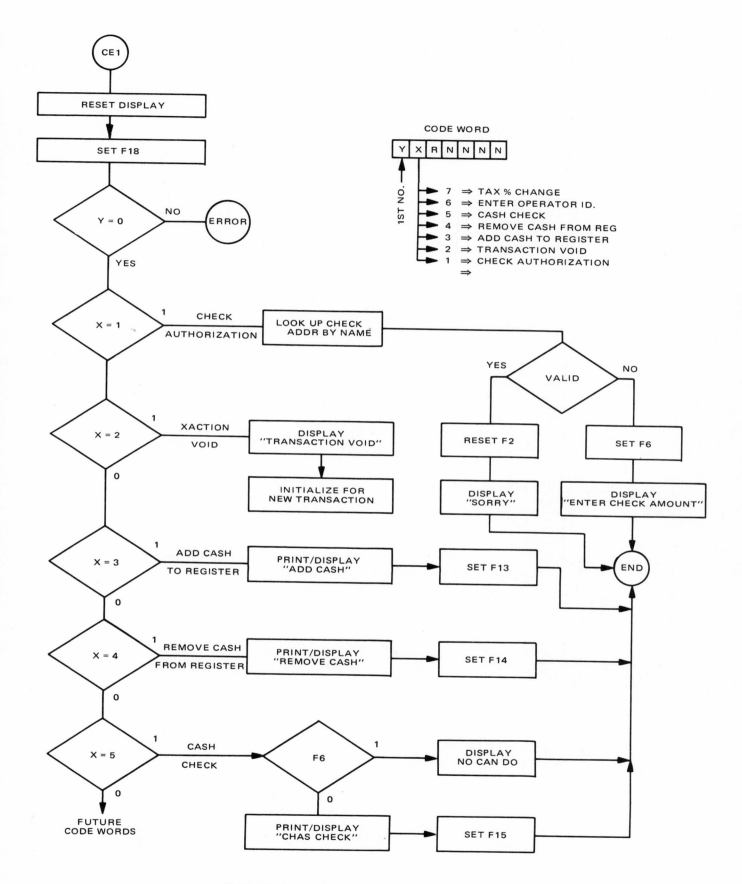

FIGURE 6-4.2.1-1: Flow for Key Entry Data (Sheet 6 of 15)

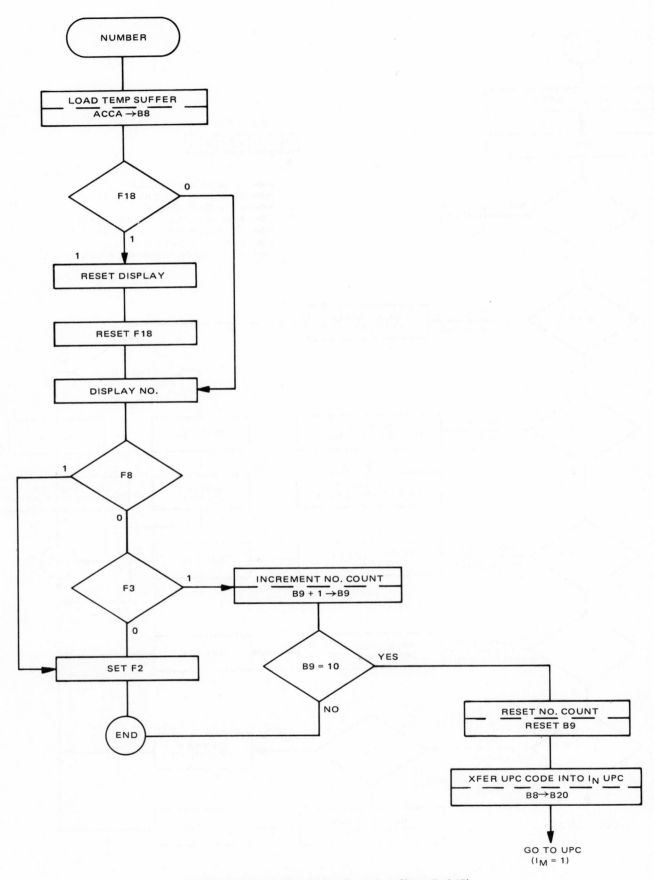

FIGURE 6-4.2.1-1: Flow for Key Entry Data (Sheet 7 of 15)

6-28

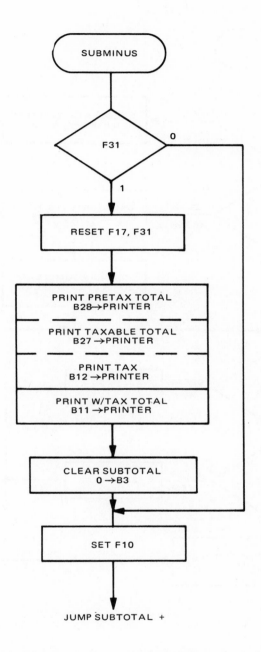

FIGURE 6-4.2.1-1: Flow for Key Entry Data (Sheet 8 of 15)

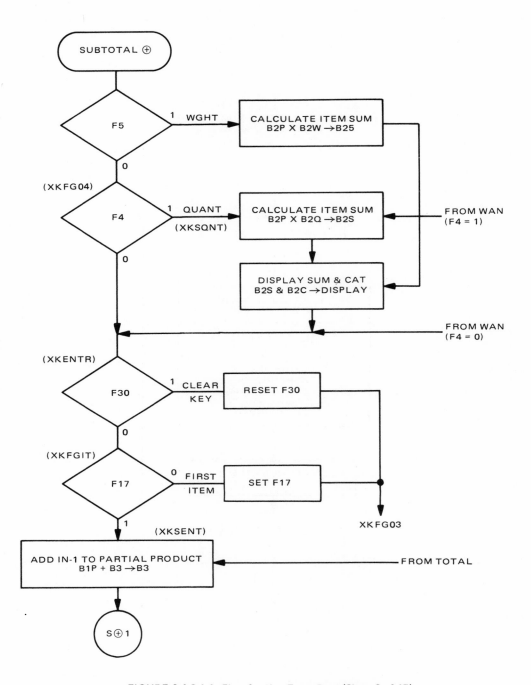

FIGURE 6-4.2.1-1: Flow for Key Entry Data (Sheet 9 of 15)

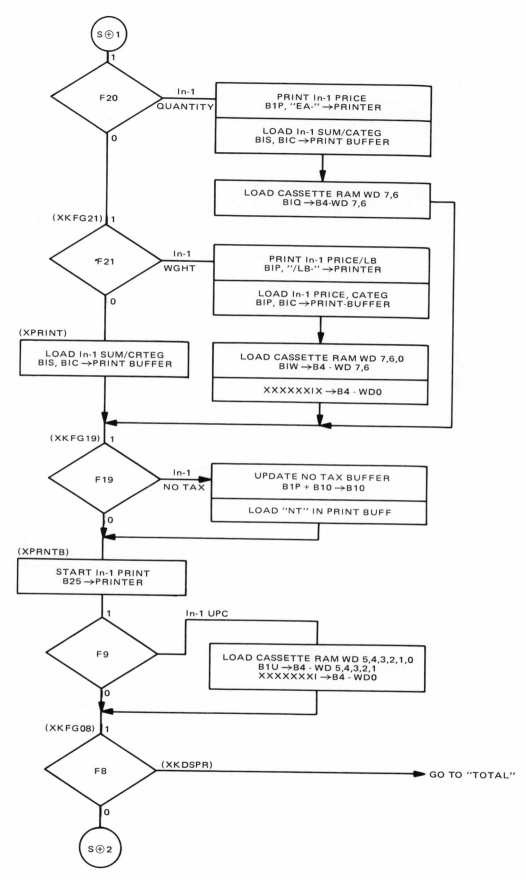

FIGURE 6-4.2.1-1: Flow for Key Entry Data (Sheet 10 of 15)

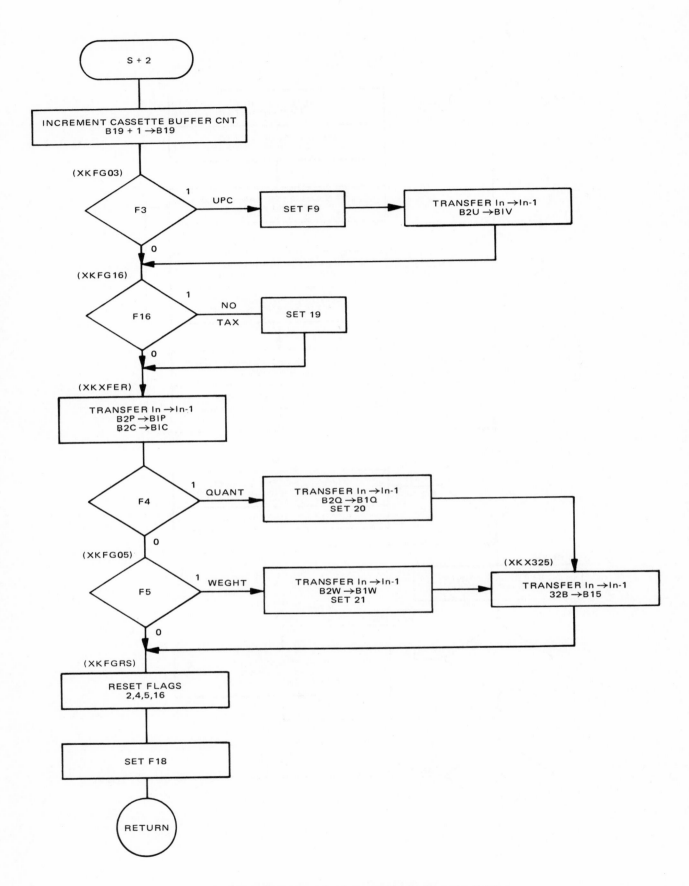

FIGURE 6-4.2.1-1: Flow for Key Entry Data (Sheet 11 of 15)

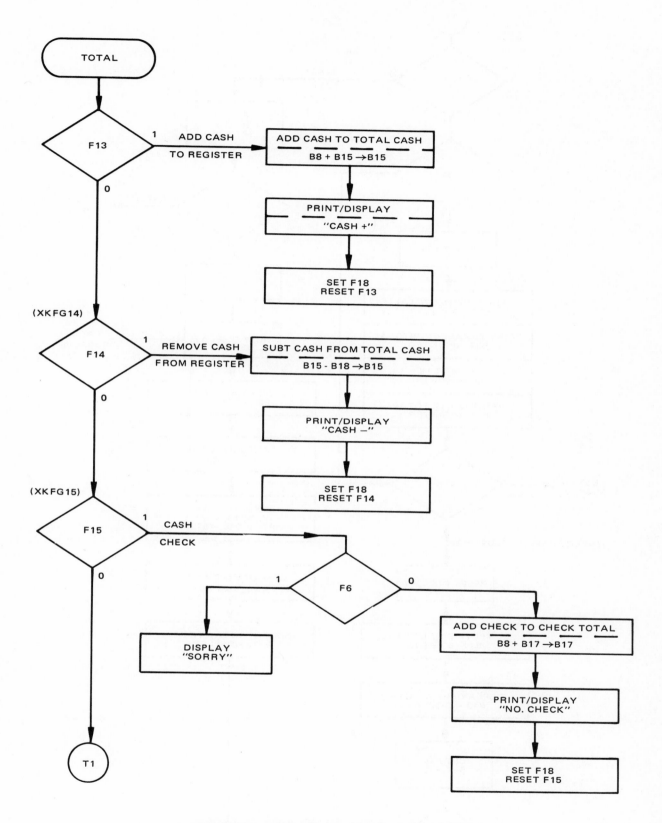

FIGURE 6-4.2.1-1: Flow for Key Entry Data (Sheet 12 of 15)

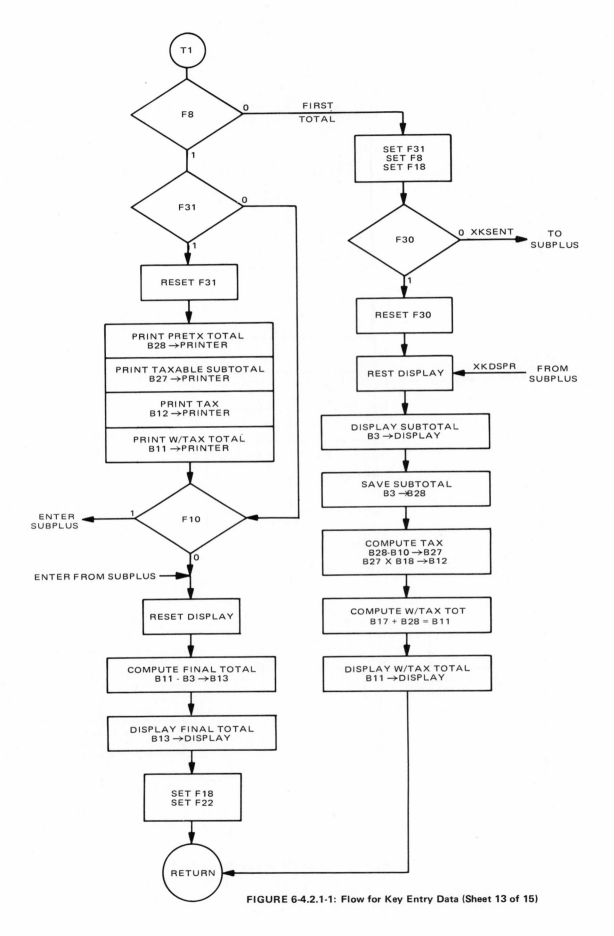

FIGURE 6-4.2.1-1: Flow for Key Entry Data (Sheet 13 of 15)

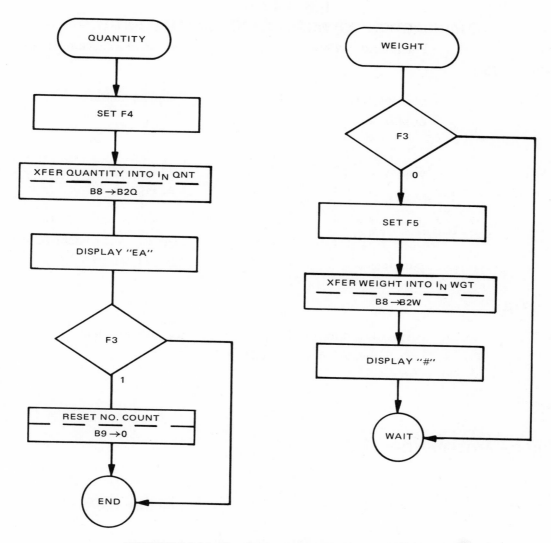

FIGURE 6-4.2.1-1: Flow for Key Entry Data (Sheet 14 of 15)

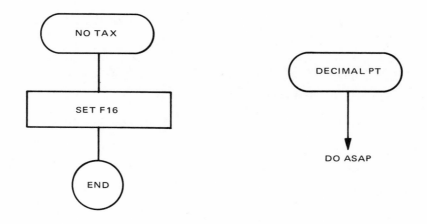

FIGURE 6-4.2.1-1: Flow for Key Entry Data (Sheet 15 of 15)

Keyboard	Peripheral Action	Executive Program Action
STANDARD ENTRY		
#5	reset display display # 5	load temp buffer
CATEGORY	display #*cat* 51 4 1	load In category load In price
SUB +	display #*cat* 51 4 11 print In−1	add In−1 to partial product load In−1 into cassette buffer move In to In−1
NO TAX ENTRY		
NO TAX	depress key prior to SUB + (standard entry) or 10#s (UPC entry)	set ''no tax'' flag
SUB + 10# (UPC)		
STANDARD/QUANTITY ENTRY		
OPTION 1:		
#s	reset display display #	load temp buffer
CATEGORY	display #*cat* 51 4 1	load In category load In price
#	display #*cat*# 51 4 11	load temp buffer
QUANTITY	display #*cat*#ea* 51 4 112 1	load In quantity
SUB +	display #* 51 4 11 print In−1	compute In total add In−1 to partial product load In−1 into cassette buffer move In to In−1
OPTION 2:		
#	reset display display #	load temp buffer

Keyboard	Peripheral Action	Executive Program Action
QUANTITY	display #ea* 12 1	load In quantity
#s	display #ea*# 12 15	load temp buffer
CATEGORY	display #ea*#*cat* 12 151 4 1	load In category load In price
SUB +	display #*cat* 51 4 11 print In−1 approval tone	compute In total add In−1 to partial product load In−1 into cassette buffer move In to In−1

STANDARD/WGT ENTRY

OPTION 1:

Keyboard	Peripheral Action	Executive Program Action
#s	reset display display #	load temp buffer
CATEGORY	display #*cat* 51 4 1	load In category load In price
#s	display #*cat*# 51 4 14	load temp buffer
WEIGHT	display #*cat*## 51	load In weight
SUB +	display #*cat* 51 4 11 print In−1	compute In total add In−1 to partial product load In−1 into cassette buffer move In to In−1

OPTION 2:

Keyboard	Peripheral Action	Executive Program Action
#s	reset display display # 4	load temp buffer
WEIGHT	display ## 41	load In weight

Keyboard	Peripheral Action	Executive Program Action
#s	display ### 415	load temp buffer
CATEGORY	display ###*cat* 4151 4 1	load In category load In price
SUB +	display #*cat* 51 4 11	compute In total
	print In−1	add In−1 to partial product load In−1 into cassette buffer move In to In−1
KYBD UPC ENTRY		
CODE ENTRY	reset display display UPC*ENTRY 3 1 5 turn on UPC light	enable wand
#s	reset display display # 10	load tump buffer
10#s	go to disk routine reset display display #*cat* 51 5 11 print In−1	load In UPC add In−1 to partial product load In−1 into cassette buffer move In to In−1 reset # count
WAND UPC ENTRY		
CODE ENTRY	reset display display UPC*ENTRY 3 1 5 turn on UPC light	enable
WAND INPUT	go to disk routine reset display display #*cat* print In−1	load In UPC add In−1 to partial product load In−1 into cassette buffer move In to In−1

Keyboard	Peripheral Action	Executive Program Action
KYBD UPC/QUANT ENTRY		
#s	reset display display #	load temp buffer increment # count
QUANTITY	display #ea* 12 1	reset # count load In quantity
#s	display #ea*# 12 110	load temp buffer increment # count
10#s	reset display display #*cat* 51 5 11	load In UPC; compute In total add In−1 to partial product reset # count load In−1 into cassette buffer move In to In−1
WAND UPC/QUANT ENTRY (in UPC mode)		
#	reset display display #	load temp buffer increment # count
QUANTITY	display #ea* 12 1	load In quantity reset # count
WAND	reset display display #*cat* 51 5 11	load In UPC; compute In total add In−1 to partial product reset # count load In−1 into cassette buffer move In to In−1

EXIT UPC MODE

(#) operator may not exit the UPC mode subsequent to depressing a # key

| CODE ENTRY | reset display
display UPC DISABLE
disable UPC light
disable wand | |

TRANSACTION TOTAL

| SUB + | display #*cat*
51 4 11
print In−1 | update buffers |

Keyboard	Peripheral Action	Executive Program Action
TOTAL	reset display	add In−1 to partial product
	display #*PRETAX*TOT	load In−1 into cassette buffer
	51 6 1	
	print In−1	
	print # PRETAX TOTAL	
TOTAL	reset display	xxxx tax
	display #*TOTAL	compute post tax total
	51	store tax/total on casette buffer
	print tax/deductions	
	print # TOTAL	
CASH ENTRY		
#	reset display	load temp buffer
	display #	
CASH	display #CA	load cash buffer
	5 2	
DECIMAL POINT	display #CA*#CHG	calculate change
	5 215 3	reset flags and buffers
	print cash	store on cassette tape
	print change	update register cash buffer
	open register drawer	
CHECK ENTRY — no authorization		
#	reset display	load temp buffer
	display #	
CHECK	display #CK	load check buffer
	5 2	
DECIMAL POINT	display #CK*#CHG	update register check buffer
	5 215 3	calculate change
	print check	store on cassette tape
	print change	reset flags and buffers
	open register drawer	
DEDUCTION ENTRY — (between 1st and 2nd total)		
#	reset display	load temp buffer
	display #	

Keyboard	Peripheral Action	Executive Program Action
CATEGORY	display #*DED*	load deduct
	41 4 1	load deduct price
SUB −	display #*DED*	load deduct buffer
	41 4 11	

MULTIPLE DEDUCTION ENTRY

OPTION 1:

#	reset display	load temp buffer
	display #	
QUANTITY	display #ea*	load In quantity
	12 1	
#	display #ea*#	load temp buffer
	12 15	
CATEGORY	display #ea*#*DED*	load deduct
	12 151 4 1	load deduct price
SUB −	reset display	calculate mult price
	display #*DED*	load deduct buffer
	51 4 11	

MULTIPLE DEDUCTION ENTRY

OPTION 2:

#	reset display	load temp buffer
	display #	
CATEGORY	display #*DED*	load deduct
	41 4 1	load deduct price
#	display #*DED*#	load temp
	41 4 11	
QUANTITY	display #*DED*#ea*	load In category
	51 4 112 1	
SUB −	reset display	calculate multiple price
	display #*DED*	load deduct buffer
	51 4 11	

Keyboard	Peripheral Action	Executive Program Action
CHECK ENTRY — with authorization/approval		
# (01nnn)	reset display display #	load temp buffer
CODE ENTRY	display ENTER*CHECK*AMNT 5 1 5 1 4	look up check
#	reset display display #	load temp buffer
CHECK	display #CK	load check buffer
DECIMAL POINT	display #CK*#CHG 52 15 3 print check print change open register drawer	update register check buffer calculate change load cassette reset flags and buffers
CHECK ENTRY — with authorization (override disapproval)		
# (01nnn)	reset display display #	load temp buffer
CODE ENTRY	display #*SORRY 1 5	look up check
#	reset display display #	load temp buffer
CHECK	display #CK 5 2	load check buffer
DECIMAL POINT	display #CK*#CHG 5 215 3 print check print change open register drawer	update register check buffer calculate change load cassette reset flags and buffers
CASH ENTRY — subsequent to check disapproval		
#(01nnn)	reset display display #	load temp buffer
CODE ENTRY	display #*SORRY 1 5	look up check

Keyboard	Peripheral Action	Executive Program Action
#	reset display	load temp buffer
	display #	
CASH	display #CA	load cash buffer
	5 2	
DECIMAL POINT	display #CA*#CHG	update cash buffer
	5 215 3	calculate change due
	print cash	load cassette
	print change	reset flags and buffers
	open register	

TRANSACTION VOID

# (02)	reset display	load temp buffer
	display #	
CODE ENTRY	display "TRANSACTION VOID"	reset transaction buffer and flags

DELETE PRESENT ENTRY

#,CAT,WT,QTY,NO TAX	Same as a "standard" entry	
CLEAR	reset display	reset In buffers and flags

DELETE PREVIOUS ENTRY

delete previous item:

SUB +	Same as a "standard" entry	
CLEAR	display DEL#*cat* *DEL	
	6 51 4 111 3	

DELETE PREVIOUS DEDUCTION

SUB −	Same as "deduction" entry	
CLEAR	display #*DED* *DEL	update deduct total
	41 4 111 3	

DELETE CASH ENTRY

CASH	Same as "cash" entry	
CLEAR	display #CA*DEL	reset cash buffer
	52 1 3	

Table 6-4.2.1-1

Keyboard	Peripheral Action	Executive Program Action
DELETE CHECK ENTRY		
CHECK	Same as "check" entry	
CLEAR	display #CK*DEL 52 1 3	reset check buffer
ADD CASH — (between transactions)		
#s (03nn)	display #	load temp buffer
CODE ENTRY	reset display print/display "add cash"	
#s	reset display display #	load temp buffer
TOTAL	print/display #*CASH+	update register cash buffer
REMOVE CASH — (between transactions)		
#s (04nn)	display #	load temp buffer
CODE ENTRY	reset display print/display "remove cash"	
#s	reset display display #	load temp buffer
TOTAL	print/display #*CASH−	update register cash buffer
CASH CHECK — (between transactions)		
#s	reset display display #	load temp buffer
CODE ENTRY	reset display print/display "cash check"	
#s	reset display display #	load temp buffer
TOTAL	print/display #*CHECK	

extra heads & titles

Table 6-4.2.1-2
TRANSACTION TERMINAL KEYBOARD BUFFERS

Buffer Number	Description
B1C	In−1 CATEGORY POINTER
B1P	In−1 PRICE
B1Q	In−1 QUANTITY
B1W	In−1 WEIGHT
B1S	In−1 SUM (IF QUANTITY/WEIGHT ENTRY)
B1U	In−1 UPC CODE
B2P	In PRICE
B2Q	In QUANTITY
B2W	In WEIGHT
B2S	In SUM (IF QUANTITY/WEIGHT ENTRY)
B2C	In CATEGORY POINTER
B2U	In UPC CODE
B3	TRANSACTION/DEDUCTION PARTIAL PRODUCT
B4	CASSETTE RAM BUFFER
B5	TRANSACTION NUMBER
B8	TEMPORARY BUFFER (UNPACKED BCD)
B9	UPC KEYBOARD NUMBER COUNT
B10	TRANSACTION NONTAX SUMMATION (PRICE SUMMATION)
B11	POST TAX TOTAL
B12	TRANSACTION TAX
B13	DEDUCTION TOTAL
B14	SINGLE TRANSACTION CASH
B15	TOTAL CASH IN REGISTER
B16	SINGLE TRANSACTION CHECK
B17	TOTAL CHECKS IN REGISTER
B18	TAX PERCENT
B19	CASSETTE BUFFER COUNT
B20	TRANSACTION CHANGE
B22	TOTAL DOLLAR SALES
B23	OPERATOR IDENTIFICATION NUMBER
B24	LOOKUP KEY SUBROUTINE MSP ADDRESSES (line 1140)
B25	PRINTER BUFFER
B26	DISPLAY BUFFER
B27	TAXABLE TOTAL
B28	PRETAX TOTAL

Table 6-4.2.1-3
TRANSACTION TERMINAL KEYBOARD FLAGS

Flag No.	Description	Set	Reset	Test
F1	"TOTAL" KEY DEPRESSED TWICE	TOTAL	INITIALIZE (SU,BT)	SUBTOTAL −
F2	NUMBER ENTRY	NUMBER	INITIALIZE (SU,BT,BI) CLEAR CODE ENTRY SUBTOTAL +	CLEAR CODE ENTRY
F3	UPC ENTRY MODE	CODE ENTRY QUANTITY WEIGHT	INITIALIZE (SU) CODE ENTRY	CODE ENTRY NUMBER SUBTOTAL +
F4	In MULTIPLE ITEM ENTRY	QUANTITY	INITIALIZE (SU,BT,BI) CLEAR SUBTOTAL +	SUBTOTAL + SUBTOTAL −
F5	In WEIGHT ENTRY	WEIGHT	INITIALIZE (SU,BT,BI) CLEAR SUBTOTAL +	SUBTOTAL +
F6	INVALID CHECK	CODE ENTRY	INITIALIZE (SU) CLEAR	CHECK CLEAR CODE ENTRY TOTAL
F7	ITEM DELETION	SUBTOTAL −	INITIALIZE (SU,BT) SUBTOTAL +	SUBTOTAL + TOTAL
F8	"TOTAL" KEY DEPRESSED ONCE	TOTAL	INITIALIZE (SU) TOTAL	CATEGORY NUMBER SUBTOTAL + SUBTOTAL − TOTAL
F9	In−1 UPC ENTRY	SUBTOTAL +	INITIALIZE (SU)	SUBTOTAL +
F10	DEDUCTION ENTRY	SUBTOTAL −	INITIALIZE (SU) CATEGORY	SUBTOTAL − TOTAL
F11	CASH ENTRY	CASH	INITIALIZE (SU) SUBTOTAL −	CLEAR
F12	CHECK ENTRY	CHECK	INITIALIZE (SU,BT) SUBTOTAL −	CLEAR SUBTOTAL −

Table 6-4.2.1-3
TRANSACTION TERMINAL KEYBOARD FLAGS
(Sheet 2 of 2)

Flag No.	Description	Set	Reset	Test
F13	ADD CASH TO REGISTER	CODE ENTRY	INITIALIZE (SU) TOTAL	TOTAL
F14	REMOVE CASH FROM REGISTER	CODE ENTRY	INITIALIZE (SU) TOTAL	TOTAL
F15	CASH A CHECK	CODE ENTRY	INITIALIZE (SU) TOTAL	TOTAL
F16	In NO TAX FLAG	NO TAX	INITIALIZE (SU,BT,BI) CLEAR SUBTOTAL +	SUBTOTAL +
F17	In−1 HAS BEEN LOADED	SUBTOTAL +	INITIALIZE (SU,BT)	SUBTOTAL +
F18	DISPLAY IS FULL	INITIALIZE (BT,BI) CLEAR CODE ENTRY SUBTOTAL + SUBTOTAL − TOTAL	INITIALIZE (SU)	NUMBER
F19	In−1 NO TAX FLAG	SUBTOTAL +	INITIALIZE (SU,BT)	SUBTOTAL +
F20	In−1 MULTIPLE ITEM ENTRY	SUBTOTAL +	INITIALIZE (SU,BT)	SUBTOTAL +
F21	In−1 WEIGHT ENTRY	SUBTOTAL +	INITIALIZE (SU,BT)	SUBTOTAL +
F22	FINAL TOTAL MUST POINT	TOTAL BE PRINTED	CASH/CHECK	DECIMAL
F29	PRINTER FINISHED	PRINT ROUTINE	PRINT ROUTINE	SUBTOTAL + TOTAL
F30	CLEAR LAST PUSHED	CLEAR		
F31	PRETAX TOTAL MUST PRINTED	TOTAL	TOTAL SUBTOTAL −	

6-4.2.2 Development of Macro Flow Diagram

The groundwork has been laid. The transaction terminal specification has been translated into a detailed set of flow charts that describe the action required when a given key is depressed. At this point, the development consists of 13 independent flow diagrams. A high level program may now be defined to interweave all programs into an operating system.

The macro flow of the executive program is shown in Figure 6-4.2.2-1. The flow diagram has two basic elements: initialization and item entry. The initialization is further broken down into three elements. The first, system startup, initializes the entire system from a power on condition. The other two initialization routines are entered between items and transactions.

The item entry procedure indicated in Figure 6-4.2.2-1 becomes the basis for the entire terminal operation. The terminal has two methods of data entry: the keyboard or an electronic scan of encoded labels on the products (wand). The executive program is organized so that both the keyboard and wand are serviced on a polling basis. Immediately after initialization, the MPU begins a software poll of the keyboard and wand, looping until service is requested.

If the keyboard requests service, the MPU begins to decode the input data to determine which key has been depressed (keyboard decode). This data is then checked to determine if the key is allowed and the data is processed. This check is accomplished by a Failsafe Interlock routine that protects the executive program from processing data as a result of an operator error.

Data from the keyboard may be either standard price/category or ten numbers to represent the universal product code (see Section 5-1.2 for a description of the UPC). If the entry is standard, the executive will process the data as required. If the data is the result of a UPC entry, the executive will first access the floppy disk to obtain price/category information. Upon data retrieval from the disk, the executive will then process data.

If the wand requests service, the executive jumps to the wand interpreter routine. Here the stream of 0's and 1's read optically from a label is converted into ten UPC numbers. The UPC numbers are then used by the disk program to access the associated price/category information (similar to a disk lookup as a result of 10 UPC numbers entered from the keyboard). Once the information is retrieved from the disk, the executive program begins normal processing of data.

As seen in Figure 6-4.2.2-1, the executive program returns to the polling loop until all necessary data to enter an item is entered from the keyboard. If the item is a standard keyboard entry, the "subtotal +" key terminates the item. If the item is a keyboard UPC entry (10 numbers), the tenth key depressed initiates disk lookup and item processing. The item entry is automatically considered complete at the tenth number entry and the "subtotal +" terminator is not required. All wand entries are also considered complete item entries. Once the item entry is completed, the MPU then reinitializes for either a new item or transaction. If the transaction is complete, the MPU also accesses the cassette and saves the transaction data on tape.

The preceding discussion of Figure 6-4.2.2-1 is intended to review the high level flow of the transaction terminal executive program without regard to detail. The following sections will examine the macro flow in greater detail to demonstrate the developmental process and, in some instances, show the final objective — the source code itself.

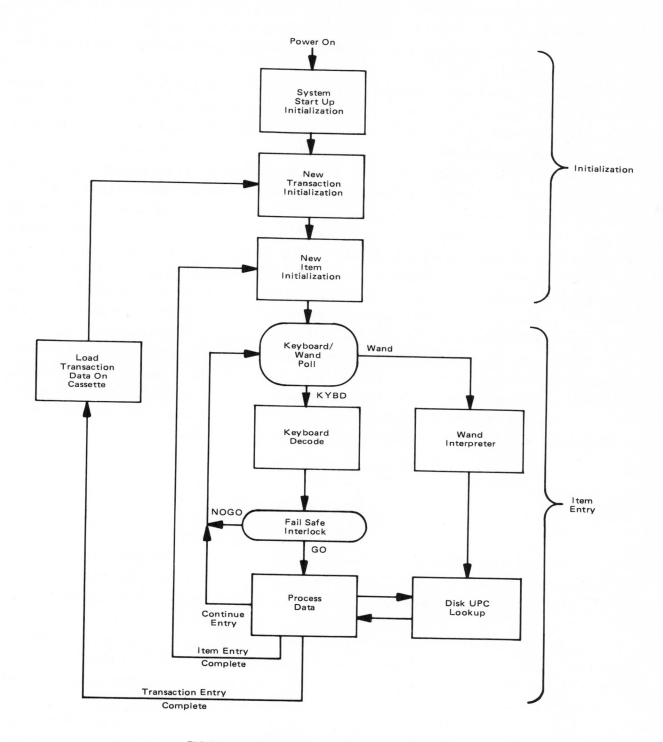

FIGURE 6-4.2.2-1: Transaction Terminal Flow Diagram

6-4.2.3 Technique of Executive Program Organization

Development of the executive program requires organized bookkeeping from the beginning. In the flow diagrams of Figure 6-4.2.1-1, the tabulation of buffers and flags are just a first pass at the requirements of the executive program. Recognizing that growth is inevitable, program management techniques must be developed to organize the program formation.

A desirable management technique is to partition the potentially extensive program into shorter controllable units. The program "blocks" of Figure 6-4.2.2-1 are, for example, identified as separate subroutines. As the program grows, the content of and number of subroutines often continually changes. Then with this procedure, only related subroutines need to be updated and reassembled as alterations are made.

Individual subroutines must often reference labels used in other subroutines and/or the executive program. Housekeeping is simplified by organizing the labels used to identify subroutine entry points, PIA registers, RAM buffer/scratchpad, and fixed constants in ROM into an index or cross reference file. The label file for this sytem, XLABEL, is shown as Figure 6-4.2.3-1. It defines a list of constant memory locations or addresses that the various subroutines may reference during assembly. This eliminates the need for maintaining individual label files with each routine as it is developed. It also insures that duplicate label naming will not later complicate debugging since the Assembler will flag such errors during program development. Note that the listing provides visibility as to the actual memory addresses represented by the lables. This is useful when looking for a place to "insert" additional buffer locations and/or I/O devices if the system should be expanded.

The specific location of RAM, ROM, and I/O addresses is determined by the actual hardware configuration (see Section 6-4.1 for a description of the hardware system). The locations shown in the label file are assigned in accordance with the hardware. For example, the printer PIA is located in memory starting at C008 (HEX). The statement ORG C008 defines the memory address which the subsequent labels will begin filling. Therefore, the labels on lines 110 – 130 will be assigned the following values:

$$
\begin{array}{rcl}
\text{XP1DRA} & = & \text{C008} \\
\text{XP1CRA} & = & \text{C009} \\
\text{XP1DRB} & = & \text{C00A} \\
\text{XP1CRB} & = & \text{C00B}
\end{array}
$$

In this fashion, the four address labels used in the routines to communicate with the printer have been identified in the software to match the hardware wiring. Should the hardware design require moving the PIA to a different memory area, the software can be modified accordingly by simply changing the ORG statement in Table 6-4.2.3-1, line 90.

RAM memory is the second category of lables defined in Figure 6-4.2.3-1. Similarly to the PIA address labels, the RAM labels are prefaced by an ORG statement to define where the memory block begins. Subsequent labels are then assigned a portion of memory as defined by the associated RMB (Reserve Memory Byte) assembler directive.

General purpose constants used by executive subroutines are also categorized in the ROM memory section of the listing of Figure 6-4.2.3-1. Examples seen in Figure 6-4.2.3-1 define such items as the ASCII code for the alpha-numeric characters, canned display messages, and program masks.

```
00010                              NAM    XLABEL
00020                              OPT    NG
00025                              OPT    NS
00030                        *  NAME:  XLABEL
00060                        ***********************************************
00070                        *****       PIA ADDRESSES      *****************
00080                        ***********************************************
00090 C008                           ORG    $C008      PRINTER
00100 C008 0001             XP1DRA RMB    1
00110 C009 0001             XP1CRA RMB    1
00120 C00A 0001             XP1DRB RMB    1
00130 C00B 0001             XP1CRB RMB    1
00140 C010                           ORG    $C010      INTERVAL TIMER
00150 C010 0001             XP2DRA RMB    1          PA-7  WAND INPUT
00160 C011 0001             XP2DRB RMB    1          PA-6  LIGHT OUTPUT   1=ACTIV
00170 C012 0001             XP2CRA RMB    1          CA-2  BUZZER CONTROL
00180 C013 0001             XP2CRB RMB    1          CA1 SPARE
00200 C020                           ORG    $C020      KEYBOARD/DISPLAY
00210 C020 0001             XP3DRA RMB    1
00220 C021 0001             XP3CRA RMB    1
00230 C022 0001             XP3DRB RMB    1
00240 C023 0001             XP3CRB RMB    1
00250 8040                           ORG    $8040      DISK/CASSETTE
00260 8040 0001             XP4DRA RMB    1
00270 8041 0001             XP4DRB RMB    1
00280 8042 0001             XP4CRA RMB    1
00290 8043 0001             XP4CRB RMB    1
00300 8080                           ORG    $8080      DISK/CASSETTE
00310 8080 0001             XP5DRA RMB    1
00320 8081 0001             XP5DRB RMB    1
00330 8082 0001             XP5CRA RMB    1
00340 8083 0001             XP5CRB RMB    1
00350                        ***********************************************
00360                        ******  RAM MEMORY BUFFERS   ******************
00370                        ***********************************************
00380           0000        START0 EQU    $0000
00390 0000                           ORG    START0
00400           0000        XKMIBA EQU    START0     BOTTOM OF MEMORY
00410           0200        XKMITA EQU    START0+512    TOP OF MEMORY
00420 0000 000A             XVMB2U RMB    10         I/N UPC UNPACKED NUMBER
00430 000A 0001             DVABOR RMB    1          DISK OPERATIONS FLAG
00440 000B 0001             DVDELT RMB    1          DISK SEEK STATUS FLAG
00450           0080        START1 EQU    $0080
00460 0080                           ORG    START1
00470           0000        XKFWAM EQU    START1/256    FLAG WORD BUFFER-10 WOR
00480           0000        TEMP1  EQU    XKFWAM*256
00490           0080        XKFWAL EQU    START1-TEMP1
00500 0080 000A                      RMB    10
00510 008A 0003             XTMPLR RMB    3          MULTIPLIER
00520           008A        XVSAV1 EQU    XTMPLR     XKLDDR BUFFER
00530           008C        XVSAV2 EQU    XTMPLR+2    XKLDDR BUFFER
00540 008D 0005             XTMPLC RMB    5          MULTIPLICAD
```

FIGURE 6-4.2.3-1: XLABEL Assembly Listing (Sheet 1 of 6)

```
00550 0092 0008   XTPROD RMB    8          RESULT
00560 009A 0002   XVMPLR RMB    2          MULTIPLIER POINTER (M)
00570      009A   XVADDP EQU    XVMPLR     POINTER FOR XKADD ADD RROUT
00580 009C 0002   XVPROD RMB    2          RESULT POINTER (P)
00590      008C   XKMPLC EQU    XTMPLC-1    CALCULATE POINTER OFFSETS
00600      0089   XKMPLR EQU    XTMPLR-1
00610      0091   XKRSLT EQU    XTPROD-1
00620 009E 0001   XKDVSR RMB    1          DIVISOR   UNSIGNED HEX NUMBE
00630 009F 0002   XKDVND RMB    2          DIVIDEND      "     "     "
00640 00A1 0002   XKQUOT RMB    2          QUOTIENT
00650 00A3 0001   XKDSPL RMB    1          LEFT DISPLACEMENT OF REMAIN
00660 00A4 0001   XVFLG1 RMB    1          DEFINE GENERAL PURPOSE
00670 00A5 0001   XVFLG2 RMB    1          BUFFERS.
00680 00A6 0001   XVFLG3 RMB    1
00690 00A7 0001   XVFLG4 RMB    1
00691 00A8 0004          RMB    4          AVAILABLE FOR USE
00700      00A7   XVKBTP EQU    XVFLG4
00710 00AC 0005   XVMB2P RMB    5          I/N PRICE
00720 00B1 0005   XVMB1P RMB    5          I/N-1 PRICE
00730 00B6 0005   XVMB2S RMB    5          I/N SUM
00740 00BB 0003   XVMB2W RMB    3          I/N WEIGHT
00750 00BE 0005   XVMB27 RMB    5          TAXABLE TOTAL
00760 00C3 0005   XVMB3  RMB    5          PART PROD;100,10,1,.1,.01
00770 00C8 0004   XVMB7  RMB    4          I/N DEDUCTION AMOUNT
00780 00CC 0011   XVMB26 RMB    17         DISPLAY BUFFER
00790 00DD 0010   XVMB25 RMB    16         PRINTER BUFFER
00791 00ED 0005   XVMB1S RMB    5          I/(N-1) SUM
00792 00F2 0003   XVMB1W RMB    3          I/(N-1) WEIGHT
00800                     ◆◆   EXTENDED RAM   ◆◆   ADDRESSES 256 OR ABOVE   ◆◆
00810 0100               ORG    256
00820 0100 0009          RMB    9          STACK KEYBOARD BUFFER-10 WO
00830 0109 0001   XVTPB8 RMB    1          TOP OF KYBD STACK
00840 010A 0002   XVMB1C RMB    2          I/N-1 CATEGORY POINTER
00850 010C 0001   XVMKNC RMB    1          KEYBOARD NUMBER COUNT
00860 010D 0002   XVMSGP RMB    2          DISPLAY MESSAGE POINTER
00870 010F 0002   XVMB8P RMB    2          BUFFER 8 POINTER
00880 0111 0002   XVMB2C RMB    2          I/N CATEGORY POINTER
00890 0113 0002   XVTEMP RMB    2          2-BYTE TEMP STORAGE
00900 0115 0004   XVMB6  RMB    4          I/N DEDUCT DESCRIPTION
00910 0119 0001   XVMB2Q RMB    1          QUANTITY
00920 011A 0002   XVMSTK RMB    2          TEMP STACK POINTER BUFFER
00930 011C 0002   IVSERV RMB    2          SERVICE ROUTINE STARTING AD
00940 011E 0001   PRCNTR RMB    1          PAPER RIBBON FEED TIME
00950                     ◆                COUNTER
00960 011F 0002   PVTXBF RMB    2          PRINTER BUFFER POINTER
00970 0121 0002   PVXBFR RMB    2          CHARACTER FILE ADDRESS
00980 0123 0001   PVCFBF RMB    1          CHARACTER FILE BUFFER
00990 0124 0001   BF1DRB RMB    1          PRINTER DATA REGISTER
01000 0125 0002   WCBFAD RMB    2          CHARACTER BUFFER ADDRESS
01010      0125   WDUMBF EQU    WCBFAD     DUMMY BUFFER
01020 0127 0001   WFLAG  RMB    1          BAR/SPACE FLAG
01030      0127   WF712  EQU    WFLAG      7-12 FLAG
```

FIGURE 6-4.2.3-1: XLABEL Assembly Listing (Sheet 2 of 6)

```
01040  0128  0001    WSPCNT  RMB    1          SPACE COUNT
01050  0129  0001    WBRCNT  RMB    1          BAR COUNT
01060        0129    WCHRCT  EQU    WBRCNT     CHARACTER COUNT
01070  012A  0001    W34MOD  RMB    1          3/4 MODULE COUNT TIME
01080  012B  0002    WBEND1  RMB    2          WBEND # BUFFERS
01090  012D  0002    WBEND2  RMB    2
01100  012F  0002    WBEND3  RMB    2
01110  0131  0002    WBEND4  RMB    2
01120  0133  0002    WMODTM  RMB    2          MODULE TIME
01130  0135  0002    WTSAMP  RMB    2          SAMPLE TIME
01140  0137  0002    WSBFAD  RMB    2          STORAGE BUFFER ADDRESS
01150  0139  000C    WSTGBF  RMB    12         WAND STORAGE BUFFER
01160  0145  0005    XVMB10  RMB    5          NO TAX BUFFER
01161  014A  0001    XVMB1Q  RMB    1          I/(N-1) QUANTITY
01162  014B  0005    XVMB28  RMB    5          PRETAX TOTAL
01163  0150  0005    XVMB12  RMB    5          TAX
01164  0155  0005    XVMB11  RMB    5          AFTER TAX TOTAL
01165  015A  0005    XVMB13  RMB    5          FINAL TOTAL
01170                ++++++++++++++++++++++++++++++++++++++++++++++++++++++
01180                +++++      LINKING SUBROUTINES      +++++++++++++++++++
01190                ++++++++++++++++++++++++++++++++++++++++++++++++++++++
01200  A043                   ORG    $A043
01210                + XKINIT - 3 ROUTINES
01220  A043  0003    XKBGIN  RMB    3          JMP SFTP
01230  A046  017D    XKTEND  RMB    381        PUL,PUL,JMP XKBGIN
01240                + XKYBRD - INCLUDES POLL AND KEYBOARD DECODE
01250  A1C3  0100    XKSFTP  RMB    256        JMP SFTP
01260                +XKFLAG - 3 SUBROUTINES - RTS
01270  A2C3  0003    XKTSTF  RMB    3
01280  A2C6  0003    XKSETF  RMB    3
01290  A2C9  0070    XKRSTF  RMB    112
01300                +XKPRIC - 2 ROUTINES
01310  A339  0003    XKDECP  RMB    3          JMP XKNUMB
01320  A33C  01FD    XKNUMB  RMB    509        RTS
01330                +XKCATY - 5 SUBROUTINES -RTS
01340  A539  0003    XKGROC  RMB    3
01350  A53C  0003    XKDAIR  RMB    3
01360  A53F  0003    XKMTCP  RMB    3
01370  A542  0003    XKPRBO  RMB    3
01380  A545  0100    XKHSST  RMB    256
01390                +  SUBPLUS - 5 ROUTINES
01400  A645  0003    XKSUBP  RMB    3          RTS   SUBTOTAL+ KEY ROUTINE
01410  A648  0003    XKSENT  RMB    3          JMP XKDSPR  FROM/TO TOTAL
01420  A64B  0003    XKSQNT  RMB    3          JMP XKENTR  ENTRY FROM WAND
01430  A64E  0003    XKENTR  RMB    3          RTS   ENTRY FROM WAND ROUTIN
01450  A651  01E5    XKADD   RMB    485        RTS   UNPACKED ADD ROUTINE
01460  A836  000F    XKNTAX  RMB    15
01470  A845  39      XKSUBM  RTS
01480  A846  00FF            RMB    255
01490  A945  39      XKCODE  RTS
01500  A946  023F            RMB    575
01510  AB85  0040    XKQNTY  RMB    64
```

FIGURE 6-4.2.3-1: XLABEL Assembly Listing (Sheet 3 of 6)

```
01520 ABC5 39        XKWGHT RTS
01530 ABC6 007F             RMB     127
01540                * TOTAL - 2 SUBROUTINES
01550 AC45 0003      XKTOTL RMB     3
01560 AC48 01FD      XKDSPR RMB     509
01570 AE45 39        XKCHCK RTS
01580 AE46 003F             RMB     63
01590 AE85 39        XKCASH RTS
01600 AE86 003F             RMB     63
01610 AEC5 39        XKCLER RTS
01620 AEC6 00FF             RMB     255
01630                *XKSAFE - 15 SUBROUTINES-RTS
01640 AFC5 0003      PUSHCL RMB     3
01650 AFC8 0003      PUSHNU RMB     3
01660 AFCB 0003      PUSHDP RMB     3
01670 AFCE 0003      PUSHCA RMB     3
01680 AFD1 0003      PUSHSP RMB     3
01690 AFD4 0003      PUSHSM RMB     3
01700 AFD7 0003      PUSHCE RMB     3
01710 AFDA 0003      PUSHNX RMB     3
01720 AFDD 0003      PUSHQT RMB     3
01730 AFE0 0003      PUSHWT RMB     3
01740 AFE3 0003      PUSHTO RMB     3
01750 AFE6 0003      PUSHCC RMB     3
01760 AFE9 0003      GETSET RMB     3
01770 AFEC 0620      FAKESP RMB     1568
01780                *XKWAND - 2 SUBROUTINES-RTS
01790 B60C 39        XKWAND RTS
01800 B60D 0002             RMB     2
01810 B60F 39        XKIWND RTS
01820 B610 02AF             RMB     687
01830                *DKDSPL - 3 SUBROUTINES-RTS
01840 B8BF 0003      DKINIT RMB     3
01850 B8C2 0003      DKSDSP RMB     3
01860 B8C5 0054      DKINTR RMB     84          RTI
01870                *PKPRNT - 4 SUBROUTINES
01880 B919 0003      PKIPRT RMB     3           RTS
01890 B91C 0003      PKNTRL RMB     3           RTS
01900 B91F 0003      PRNTIR RMB     3           RTI
01910 B922 0003      PRNTIT RMB     3           RTI
01920 B925 0003      PPRRBN RMB     3           RTS
01930 B928 0003      PKLNFD RMB     3           RTS
01940 B92B 0003      PKLFMD RMB     3           RTS
01950 B92E 0003      PKPHDR RMB     3           RTS
01960 B931 0122             RMB     290
01970 BA53 0055      XKDIVD RMB     85          RTS
01980 BAA8 0080      XKRUPT RMB     128         RTI
01990 BB28 0064      XKMULT RMB     100         RTS
01992                *INTIME - 1 SUBROUTINE
01995 BB8C 0032      IKINIT RMB     50          RTS
01995                * FORMAT - 10 ROUTINES
01995 BBBE 0003      XKPRCD RMB     3           RTS
```

FIGURE 6-4.2.3-1: XLABEL Assembly Listing (Sheet 4 of 6)

```
01995 BBC1 0003      XKPRCP RMB      3
01995 BBC4 0003      XKMSGD RMB      3
01995 BBC7 0003      XKMSGP RMB      3
01996 BBCA 0003      XKASC  RMB      3
01996 BBCD 0003      XKINTP RMB      3
01996 BBD0 0003      XKINTD RMB      3
01996 BBD3 0003      XPRTW  RMB      3
01996 BBD6 0003      XKBLKP RMB      3
01996 BBD9 00C8      XKBLKD RMB      200
02000                ++++++++++++++++++++++++++++++++++++++++++++++++++
02010                ++++++      ROM MEMORY CONSTANTS      ++++++++++++++++
02020                ++++++++++++++++++++++++++++++++++++++++++++++++++
02030 BE00                  ORG      $BE00
02040 BE00 01      BEGIN  FCB      $01,$02,$04,$08,$10,$20,$40,$80
02050                ++   LOAD FLAG SERVICE MASK TABLE CONSTANTS
02060      00BE      XKFMAM EQU      BEGIN/256
02070      BE00      TEMP2  EQU      XKFMAM*256
02080      0000      XKFMAL EQU      BEGIN-TEMP2
02090                ++   PRINTER CHARACTER FILE   ++
02100 BE08 30      PKCF00 FCC      /0123456789ABCDEFGHIJKLMNOP/
02110 BE22 51             FCC      AQRSTUVWXYZ+$,-./A
02120                ++   HEADER MESSAGE   ++
02130 BE32 20      XKHEAD FCC      16,   WELCOME TO
02140 BE42 20             FCC      16,   THE MOTOROLA
02150 BE52 20             FCC      16, GROCERY   STORE
02160 BE62 20             FCC      16, DATE  12/10/74
02170                ++   MULTIPLY LOOKUP TABLE ++
02180                ++   INTERLACED WITH DISPLAY CONSTANTS ++
02190 BE72 01      XKTTAB FCB      1,2,3,4,5,6,7,8,9    TABLE ++
02200      BE61      XKMTAB EQU      XKTTAB-17    TABLE ADD OFFSET ++
02210 BE7B 20      XKDARY FCC      / DARY ^/
02220 BE82 5E      XKMSGL FCB      $5E
02230 BE83 04             FCB      4,6,8,$10,$12,$14,$16,$18    TABLE ++
02240 BE8B 20      XKGRCY FCC      / GRCY ^/
02250 BE92 0002             RMB      2         ++   TWO SPARE CONSTANT BYTE
02260 BE94 09             FCB      9,$12,$15,$18,$21,$24,$27    TABLE ++
02270 BE9B 20      XKMEAT FCC      / MEAT ^/
02280 BEA2 0003             RMB      3         ++   THREE SPARE CONSTANT BY
02290 BEA5 16             FCB      $16,$20,$24,$28,$32,$36    TABLE ++
02300 BEAB 20      XKPROD FCC      / PROD ^/
02310 BEB2 45      XKEA   FCC      /EA-^/
02320 BEB6 25             FCB      $25,$30,$35,$40,$45    TABLE ++
02330 BEBB 20      XKHSHD FCC      / HSHD ^/
02340 BEC2 54      XKTOAL FCC      /TOTAL/
02350 BEC7 36             FCB      $36,$42,$48,$54
02360 BECB 20      XKEACH FCC      / EA ^/
02361 BED0 2F      XKLB   FCC      A/LB-^A
02370 BED5 0003             RMB      3         ++   THREE SPARE CONSTANT BY
02380 BED8 49             FCB      $49,$56,$63    TABLE ++
02390 BEDB 20      XKBOTT FCC      / BOTT ^/
02400 BEE2 20      XKSTMP FCC      / STMP ^/
02410 BEE9 64             FCB      $64,$72    TABLE ++
```

FIGURE 6-4.2.3-1: XLABEL Assembly Listing (Sheet 5 of 6)

```
02420 BEEB 20    XKREDY FCC    / READY ^/
02430 BEF3 20    XKCOUP FCC    / COUP ^/
02440 BEFA 81           FCB    $81         TABLE **
02445 BEFB 2A    XKDEL  FCC    /* DEL^/
02450      00BE  XKLIST EQU    XKMTAB/$100  CALCULATE MULTILPY TAB
02460      BE00  XKLSTT EQU    XKLIST*$100  ADDRESSES
02470      0061  XKLSTL EQU    XKMTAB-XKLSTT
02480      2700  S256US EQU    $2700
02490            *
02500            * FOLLOWING IS A FLOW OF EXEC PROGRAM MOVEMENT:
02510            *
02520            * SFT TO KYBD TO IDIOT TO KYBD TO BUTTON TO SFT
02530            *    (JSR)   (JSR)    (RTS)    (JMP)      (RTS)
02540            *
02550            * SFT TO WAND TO DISK TO EXEC TO SUBP TO SFT
02560            *    (JSR)   (JMP)    (JMP)    (JMP)   (RTS)
02580            *  16 - BIT TIMER PRESCALE CONSTANTS
02600                   END
```

FIGURE 6-4.2.3-1: XLABEL Assembly Listing (Sheet 6 of 6)

"Linking Subroutines" is the final section of the XLABEL program and is used to identify starting addresses of subroutines. Each subroutine has a six character label as a "header" in the first instruction, Interprogram jumps are then referenced by the header label. If, for example, the program desires to jump from the XKSUBP program to the XKMULT program, the XLABEL will provide a link between the two by providing an address for the assembler. Also note that the exit for each program is identified as an aid to program management. PUSHSM is, for example, exited by a return from subroutine (RTS) instruction, implying that the program may be called by either a branch to subroutine (BSR) or jump to subroutine (JSR) instruction.

In summary, management of labels of all subroutines are concentrated in the XLABEL program. When all the subroutines are ultimately combined into a single executive program, the XLABEL program will no longer be useful. However, XLABEL or some similar procedure is a useful method of linking undefined labels during program development.

6-4.2.4 Description of Macro Flow Diagram Initialization

Initialization

The first task of the software is initialization. As shown in Figure 6-4.2.2-1, the initialization is organized into three different elements; start-up, new transaction, and new item. The system start-up initialization is entered from the MPU's power on sequence. The MPU obtains the starting address of the Initialization sequence as described in Section 3-2.3. For this system, the program counter is loaded with a value A043 to begin the start-up initialization. The portion of the start-up sequence for initializing memory, PIAs and peripherals, is shown in Figure 6-4.2.4-1.

Memory initialization first clears all scratch pad locations from 0000 to 01FF. This area of memory will contain temporary flags and buffers for the executive program as items are entered into the terminal. The remainder of the memory initialization presets flag 18 (lines 240 – 250) and establishes the top address of buffer 8 (lines 270 – 280).

Initialization of the PIAs is the next step in the start up routine. This segment of the program loads the control and data direction registers of the PIAs to define the characteristics of the interface. As an example, lines 490 – 500 load 06 into the keyboard control register. This defines the CA1 control line of the PIA to be an input which is active on a low-to-high transition but does not cause an interrupt to the MPU. As a result, a subsequent rising edge from the keyboard strobe (CA1) will set an interrupt flag in the PIA.

A thorough understanding of the initialization routines requires a working knowledge of the PIA and each peripheral device. The PIA operation and details of coding are described in Section 3-4.1. The detailed description of PIA operation with their associated peripherals are in Chapter 5.

Table 6-4.2.4-1 shows initialization code for PIAs interfacing with the keyboard, display, interval timer, and miscellaneous controls. Additional initialization of the PIAs is performed within the peripheral subroutines referenced in lines 630 – 772. These subroutines set up both the PIAs and their peripheral for entry of data into the terminal.

The remainder of the initialization routines shown in Figure 6-4.2.2-1 perform housekeeping functions when entering new items or new transactions. When entering item information from the keyboard, i.e., price, category, quantity, etc., the entry is closed with a "subtotal +." The MPU will then process the item and return to "new item initialization" to prepare for the next entry. When initializing for a new entry, the MPU resets appropriate flags and buffers and begins to poll for the next entry.

After finishing a transaction, the MPU returns to the initialization routine to prepare for the next transaction. At this point, a major portion of memory must be cleared before the MPU returns to the waiting loop

```
00010                           NAM     XKINITO
00010                           OPT     LIST
00010                      ◆   NAME:  XKINIT
00020                      ◆   REV:    2.0  01-31-75

00040 A043                      ORG     $A043
00050 A043 7E A049 XKBGIN JMP     YKBGIN
00060 A046 7E A0A7 XKTEND JMP     YKTEND
00070           ◆◆◆◆◆◆◆◆◆◆◆◆◆◆◆◆◆◆◆◆◆◆◆◆◆◆◆◆◆◆◆◆◆◆◆◆◆◆◆◆◆◆
00080           ◆◆◆◆                SYSTEM INITIALIZATION       ◆◆◆◆◆◆◆◆
00090           ◆◆◆◆◆◆◆◆◆◆◆◆◆◆◆◆◆◆◆◆◆◆◆◆◆◆◆◆◆◆◆◆◆◆◆◆◆◆◆◆◆◆
00100 A049 01       YKBGIN NOP
00110 A04A 0F              SEI
00120 A04B 8E 01FF          LDS     #$01FF
00120 A04E CE BAA8          LDX     #XKRUPT
00121 A051 FF FFF8          STX     $FFF8
00130           ◆
00140           ◆          INITIALIZE MEMORY BUFFERS ◆◆◆◆◆◆◆◆◆◆◆◆◆◆◆◆
00150           ◆
00160           ◆          INITIALIZE FLAGS AND BUFFERS ◆◆◆◆◆◆◆◆◆◆◆◆◆
00170 A054 CE 0200          LDX     #XKMITA   CLEAR MEMORY TOP ADDRESS
00180 A057 6F 00   XK0190 CLR     X
00190 A059 09              DEX               GET NEXT LOWER ADDRESS
00200 A05A 8C FFFF          CPX     #XKMIBA-1  SEE IF BOTTOM ADDRESS CL
00210 A05D 26 F8            BNE     XK0190    LOOP UNTILL RANGE CLEARED
00240 A05F 86 18            LDA A   #$18      SET FLAG 18
00250 A061 BD A2C6          JSR     XKSETF
00260           ◆◆INITIALIZE        B8 ADDRESS POINTER
00270 A064 CE 0109          LDX     #XVTPB8
00280 A067 FF 010F          STX     XVMB8P
00410           ◆
00420           ◆ INITIALIZE PIAS ◆◆◆◆◆◆◆◆◆◆◆◆◆◆◆◆◆◆◆◆◆◆◆◆◆◆◆◆◆◆◆◆
00430           ◆          INITIALIZE KEYBOARD PIA
00440           ◆
00450 A06A 7F C021          CLR     XP3CRA    SET CRA=0
00460 A06D 7F C020          CLR     XP3DRA    SET DATA DIRECTION
00470 A070 4F               CLR A
00480 A071 43               COM A
00490 A072 C6 06            LDA B   #$06
00500 A074 F7 C021          STA B   XP3CRA   SET CONTROL REG A=06
00510 A077 C6 2C            LDA B   #$2C
00520           ◆◆          INITIALIZE DISPLAY PIA
00530 A079 BD B8BF          JSR     DKINIT
00540           ◆                            REGISTER B = 00
00550           ◆◆ INTERVAL TIMER / MISC PIA
00560           ◆ PA0-PA5    SCALE FACTOR
00570           ◆ PB0-PB7    BINARY COUNT
00580           ◆ PA7        WAND INPUT
00590           ◆ PA6        LIGHT OUTPUT
00600           ◆ CA2        BUZZER CONTROL
00610           ◆ CA1        SPARE
00620           ◆ PA4,PA5    NOT USEABLE/CARD PIN LIMITED
```

FIGURE 6-4.2.4-1: System Initialization Assembly Listing (Sheet 1 of 2)

```
00630 A07C BD BB8C        JSR      IKINIT
00740                  ♦♦INITIALIZE PRINTER PIA
00750 A07F BD B919        JSR      PKIPRT
00760                  ♦           INITIALIZE DISK AND CASETTE ♦♦♦♦♦♦♦♦♦♦♦♦♦♦
00770 A082 01             NOP
00771 A083 01             NOP
00772 A084 01             NOP
00780                  ♦           INITIALIZE WAND ♦♦♦♦♦♦♦♦♦♦♦♦♦♦♦♦♦♦♦♦♦♦♦♦♦
00790 A085 BD B60F        JSR      XKIWND
00800                  ♦INITIALIZE FOR FAILSAFE ROUTINE ♦♦♦♦♦♦♦♦♦♦♦♦♦♦♦♦♦♦♦
00810 A088 BD AFE9        JSR      GETSET
00811 A08B 01             NOP
00812 A08C 0E             CLI                 ENABLE INTERRUPTS
00820 A08D CE BEEB        LDX      #XKREDY     DISPLAY RDY MESSG.
00830 A090 BD B8C2        JSR      DKSDSP
00831 A093 C6 03          LDA B    #3          LOAD LINE FEED COUNT
00832 A095 BD B928        JSR      PKLNFD      GO LINE FEED
00832 A098 CE BE32        LDX      #XKHEAD
00832 A09B C6 04          LDA B    #4          GET HEADER PARAMETERS
00833 A09D BD B92E        JSR      PKPHDR      GO PRINT HEADER
00834 A0A0 C6 02          LDA B    #2
00835 A0A2 BD B928        JSR      PKLNFD      2 LINE FEEDS
00840 A0A5 20 16          BRA      XKSFT
00850                  ♦♦♦♦♦♦♦♦♦♦♦♦♦♦♦♦♦♦♦♦♦♦♦♦♦♦♦♦♦♦♦♦♦♦♦♦♦♦♦♦♦♦♦♦♦♦♦♦♦♦♦
00860                  ♦♦♦♦♦♦♦♦ NEW TRANSACTION INITIALIZATION ♦♦♦♦♦♦♦♦♦♦♦
00870                  ♦♦♦♦♦♦♦♦♦♦♦♦♦♦♦♦♦♦♦♦♦♦♦♦♦♦♦♦♦♦♦♦♦♦♦♦♦♦♦♦♦♦♦♦♦♦♦♦♦♦♦
00880                  ♦
00880                  ♦       ♦♦♦♦♦BEEPER♦♦♦♦♦
00880                  ♦
00880 A0A7 B6 C012 YKTEND LDA A   XP2CRA      GET BEEPER CONTROL REGISTEE
00880 A0AA 16             TAB                 SAVE BEEPER OFF CNTRL BYTE
00880 A0AB 84 C7          AND A    #%11000111  CLR CNTRL BITS
00880 A0AD 8A 28          ORA A    #%00101000   SET CNTRL BITS TO TURN
00880                  ♦                        ON BEEPER
00880 A0AF B7 C012        STA A    XP2CRA      STORE CNTRL BYTE IN PIA
00880 A0B2 B6 C010        LDA A    XP2DRA      READ DATA REG TO FIRE BEEPE
00881 A0B5 F7 C012        STA B    XP2CRA      STORE BEEPER OFF CNTRL BYTE
00890 A0B8 32             PUL A               CLR RTS FROM STACK
00900 A0B9 32             PUL A
00910 A0BA 7E A043        JMP      XKBGIN      LOOP BACK FOR NEXT CUSTOMER
00920 A0BD 7E A1C3 XKSFT  JMP      XKSFTP
00930                     END
```

FIGURE 6-4.2.4-1: System Initialization Assembly Listing (Sheet 2 of 2)

to await the next transaction. The only data saved during the transaction initialization are buffers containing cumulative transaction information such as total sales, cash in register, and checks cashed.

Software Poll

The software poll for keyboard or wand service shown in Figure 6-4.2.2-1 is the central feature of the executive program. When initialization is complete, the polling routine is entered to await new data from either the wand or keyboard. At this point, the MPU goes into a software loop that inspects the keyboard and wand PIAs.

Figure 6-4.2.4-2 is an assembly listing of the software poll. The instructions on lines 80 –100 turn on a "ready" light to indicate to the operator that the MPU is prepared to accept new data entry. The next instruction, CLI, clears the interrupt mask in the MPU, thus enabling peripheral interrupts that may occur while polling. As a result, peripherals such as the display or printer may continue to be serviced while in the polling routine. It should be noted that the keyboard or wand is not allowed to interrupt the system. The "keyboard strobe" sets an interrupt flag in the PIA control register but is programmed at initialization to disable an interrupt to the MPU. The wand input is tied to a PIA data line and, therefore, is not able to generate interrupts to the MPU since only PIA control inputs may generate inputs. While the keyboard and wand are primary input devices, they are under the control of an operator who can re-enter the data if the MPU is temporarily busy with another task.

The MPU begins the actual polling by reading the keyboard PIA control register (line 130). Referring to Figure 6-4.2.4-3 and 6-4.2.4-4, the keyboard interface may set either of two interrupt flags in the control register. An important feature to point out is that the "clear" key signal is not encoded in the same manner as the other keys — it has a separate control input to the PIA. For this reason, when a keyboard request does occur, the MPU first checks the status of the "clear" signal (line 160). If clear is active, a "clear" key code is loaded into the accumulator for subsequent use by the keyboard decode routine. In this manner, the "clear" key shares the same software path with all other keys. The MPU then turns off the "ready" light (lines 220 –240) and jumps to the keyboard decode.

If a request for keyboard service does not exist, the MPU will inspect the status of the wand by inspecting the wand data bit for a logic "0" or "1." If the data signal is at a logic "0," the wand is assumed to be reading a white band. The UPC level is surrounded by a white border, therefore, when the wand first sees white, the MPU prepares for entry into the wand service routine. The MPU will turn off the "ready" light and exit the software poll in preparation for accepting wand data. If the wand is not in use, the MPU will return to the beginning of the software poll to repeat the cycle. The system remains in the software polling loop until either the keyboard or wand make a request for service.

Keyboard Decode

Data from the keyboard is presented to the PIA interface in the format shown in Figure 6-4.2.4-4. Each of the keys is encoded as an 8-bit word which the MPU decodes to determine which key has been depressed. The 8-bit word is brought in the MPU during the software poll and is saved in accumulator A. The "keyboard decode" routine, Figure 6-4.24-5, then uses the data in accumulator A to determine the key in question. The decode technique successively tests each of the eight bits working from the most significant bit (bit 7).

If bit 7 is 1, the MPU need only check bit 6 to determine whether this is a subtotal + or subtotal − . If bit 7 is 0, the MPU continues to decode by inspecting bit 6 for the "code enable" key. The process continues in this manner until the key is identified.

The primary purpose of the decode routine is to determine which data processing routine to enter; but the decode includes one other function — it is to provide entry into the "failsafe interlock" routine. Once the decode routine determines the key to be serviced, it will first jump to the failsafe subroutine to determine if the key

```
00010                           NAM     XKYBRD
00010                           OPT     LIST
00010                    *   NAME:   XKYBRD
00020                    *   REV:    2.0   02-01-75
00030 A1C3                      ORG     $A1C3
00059                    ***********************************************************
00060                    *****          SOFTWARE POLL FOR SERVICE        ***********
00061                    ***********************************************************
00072 A1C3 01         XKSFTP NOP
00074 A1C4 OF                   SEI
00076 A1C5 01                   NOP
00078 A1C6 01                   NOP
00080 A1C7 F6 C010               LDA B  XP2DRA          TURN ON READY LIGHT
00090 A1CA CA FO                 ORA B  #$F0            SET PA-6
00100 A1CC F7 C010               STA B  XP2DRA
00110 A1CF 0E                    CLI                    ENABLE INTERRUPTS
00120                    *   KEYBOARD REQUEST ?
00130 A1D0 B6 C021               LDA A  XP3CRA          READ KEYBOARD PIA CONTROL
00140 A1D3 85 C0                 BIT A  #$C0            CHECK CRA7,CRA6
00150 A1D5 27 19                 BEQ    XK1065          IF NO REQUEST, CHECK WAND
00160 A1D7 85 40                 BIT A  #$40            CHECK FOR CLEAR KEY
00170 A1D9 27 07                 BEQ    XK1040          IF NO, CONTINUE KYBD SERVIC
00180 A1DB 86 18                 LDA A  #$18            IF YES, LOAD CLEAR CODE
00190 A1DD F6 C020               LDA B  XP3DRA          CLEAR INTERRUPT
00200 A1E0 20 03                 BRA    XK1045
00210 A1E2 B6 C020 XK1040 LDA A  XP3DRA          LOAD KYBD DATA/CLEAR INTERR
00220 A1E5 F6 C010 XK1045 LDA B  XP2DRA          TURN OFF READY LIGHT
00230 A1E8 C4 BF                 AND B  #$BF            CLR PA-6
00240 A1EA F7 C010               STA B  XP2DRA
00250 A1ED BD A203               JSR    XKKYIN          GO TO KYBD ROUTINE,ACCA=DAT
00260                    *
00270                    *  WAND SERVICE REQUEST?
00280                    *
00290 A1F0 B6 C010 XK1065 LDA A  XP2DRA          IS WAND ON SPACE, B7=0?
00310 A1F3 2B CE                 BMI    XKSFTP          IF NOT LOOP BACK
00320 A1F5 F6 C010               LDA B  XP2DRA          TURN OFF READY LIGHT
00330 A1F8 C4 BF                 AND B  #$BF            CLR PA-6
00340 A1FA F7 C010               STA B  XP2DRA
00350 A1FD BD B60C               JSR    XKWAND          OTHERWISE, GO TO WAND ROUTI
00360 A200 7E A1C3               JMP    XKSFTP
```

FIGURE 6-4.2.4-2: Software Poll for Service Assembly Listing

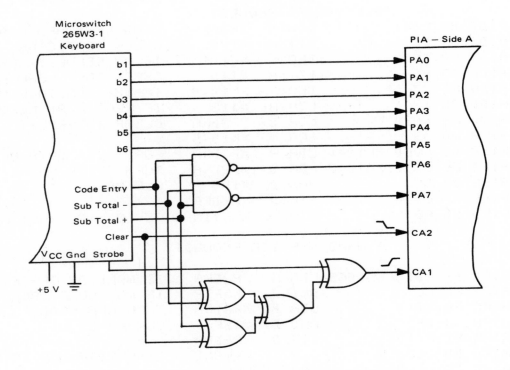

FIGURE 6-4.2.4-3 Keyboard/PIA Hardware Interface

Key Function	Key Number	Code to PIA							
		b7	b6	b5	b4	b3	b2	b1	b0
0	43	0	0	0	0	0	0	0	0
1	13	0	0	0	0	0	0	0	1
2	14	0	0	0	0	0	0	1	0
3	15	0	0	0	0	0	0	1	1
4	23	0	0	0	0	0	1	0	0
5	24	0	0	0	0	0	1	0	1
6	25	0	0	0	0	0	1	1	0
7	33	0	0	0	0	0	1	1	1
8	34	0	0	0	0	1	0	0	0
9	35	0	0	0	0	1	0	0	1
. (Demical pt.)	45	0	0	0	0	1	0	1	0
Grocery	1	0	0	0	0	0	0	0	1
Dairy	11	0	0	0	0	0	0	1	0
Meat/Coupon	21	0	0	0	0	0	0	1	1
Produce/Bottles	31	0	0	0	0	0	1	0	0
Hshld/Stamps	41	0	0	0	0	0	1	0	1
Weight	3	0	0	1	0	0	0	0	0
No Tax	7	0	0	1	0	0	0	1	1
Quantity	17	0	0	1	0	0	1	1	1
Total	20	0	0	1	0	1	0	1	0
Cash	30	0	0	1	0	1	1	1	1
Check	40	0	0	1	1	0	0	1	1
Code Entry	5	0	1	Will be holding					
Subtotal (—)	10	1	0	data from					
Subtotal (+)	37	1	1	previous entry					
Clear	50			[C2 interrupt]					
		0	0	0	1	1	0	0	0
Strobe	—			[C1 interrupt]					

1. Strobe will be high while any key is closed

FIGURE 6-4.2.4-4 Keyboard Coding/PIA Interface

in question is allowed at this point in a transaction. Referring back to Figure 6-4.2.4-5, there is a prescribed entry procedure that the keyboard operator must follow. If the operator depresses a key that is disallowed at that point of entry, the failsafe routine will ignore the key and return to the software poll to wait for another entry. This does not mean that the operator must follow a rigid entry procedure. The intent is to prevent the executive routine from operating on incomplete data. If, for example, the operator depresses three numbers after a decimal point, the failsafe routine will ignore the third number, thereby preventing the executive routine from operating on this last entry.

The failsafe routine categorizes all keys into 11 classes. When a key is depressed, the failsafe routine then determines, on the basis of the state of the entry, which class of keys is allowed. The failsafe routine, therefore, has 11 subroutines, each of which is entered from the keyboard decode routine shown in Figure 6-4.2.4-5. Notice the comments in Figure 6-4.2.4-5 which asks the question "allowed?" There are 11 such comments throughout the listing, each of which identifies an entry into the failsafe routine. When the keyboard routine determines which key has been depressed, it then jumps to the corresponding failsafe subroutine (1 of 11). The failsafe routine will determine whether or not the entry is to be permitted. If allowed, the failsafe routine will issue a return from subroutine thereby re-entering the decode routine. The decode return will continue execution by jumping into the appropriate "data process" routine. If the key is not allowed, the failsafe routine will read from the stack twice (to restore the stack pointer as a result of the JSR to the failsafe subroutine) and then jump to the software poll.

6-4.2.4 Keyboard Interlock Program

As programs were developed for the keybaord and display, including rudimentary transaction calculations, it became obvious that some sort of keyboard interlock was needed to prevent unwanted key input sequences from hanging up program flow. A program, XKSAFE, was developed which allows only the desired input sequences (defined in Table 6-4.2.1-1). A positive feedback audible approval tone or "beep" is generated when an allowed key is depressed.

Keys depressed out of sequence are ignored by the system and no "beep" is generated. The operator may then enter a proper key without any corrections. If an erroneous allowed key is depressed, i.e., a wrong number, etc., the CLEAR key will return the transaction to the start of the erroneous entry.

The program is a sequence of flag checking routines which determines from the states of the tested flags where the current operation is in an allowed transaction flow and then determines the set of keys allowable for the next key entry. The flow is divided into four parts as shown in Figure 6-4.2.4-6:

(1) Initialization (Figure 6-4.2.4-7)

(2) Entry Routines (Figure 6.4.2.4-8)

(3) Main Processing (Figure 6-4.2.4-9)

(4) Defining Sections (Figure 6-4.2.4-10)

The Initialization subroutine is used at power on and before each new transaction. It simply sets and clears the flags required for the start of a transaction (see Figure 6-4.2.4-7).

The entry routines are entered from the keyboard interrogation routine. Each section sets and clears flags according to the key that has been depressed (see Figure 6-4.2.4-8).

The main body of the program follows the entry routines and determines the point where the

```
00370                   ++++++++++++++++++++++++++++++++++++++++++++++++++
00380                   +++++     KEYBOARD  INTERROGATION     +++++++++++++
00390                   ++++++++++++++++++++++++++++++++++++++++++++++++++
00400                   ++ SUBTOTAL + OR SUBTOTAL - ?
00410 A203 16      XKKYIN TAB
00420 A204 2A 0F             BPL     XK3045      IF NO, CONTINUE INTERROGATI
00430 A206 58               ASL B
00440 A207 2B 06             BMI     XK3035
00450 A209 BD AFD4           JSR     PUSHSM      ALLOWED?
00460 A20C 7E A845           JMP     XKSUBM      GO TO "SUB -" ROUTINE ‹
00470 A20F BD AFD1 XK3035    JSR     PUSHSP      ALLOWED?
00480 A212 7E A645           JMP     XKSUBP      GO TO "SUB+" ROUTINE
00490                   +
00500                   ++ CODE ENTRY KEY ?
00510                   +
00520 A215 58      XK3045 ASL B
00530 A216 2A 06             BPL     XK3065      IF NO,CONTINUE INTERROGATIO
00540 A218 BD AFD7           JSR     PUSHCE      ALLOWED?
00550 A21B 7E A945           JMP     XKCODE      GO TO "CODE" ROUTINE
00560                   +
00570                   +
00580                   ++ GROUP A ?
00590                   +
00600 A21E 58      XK3065 ASL B
00610 A21F 2A 33             BPL     XK3165      IF NO,CONTINUE INTERROGATIO
00620 A221 58               ASL B
00630 A222 2A 06             BPL     XK3090
00640 A224 BD AFE6           JSR     PUSHCC      ALLOWED?
00650 A227 7E AE85           JMP     XKCASH      GO TO "CASH" ROUTINE
00660 A22A 58      XK3090 ASL B
00670 A22B 2A 0F             BPL     XK3120
00680 A22D 58               ASL B
00690 A22E 2A 06             BPL     XK3115
00700 A230 BD AFE6           JSR     PUSHCC      ALLOWED?
00710 A233 7E AE45           JMP     XKCHCK      GO TO "CHECK" ROUTINE
00720 A236 BD AFE3 XK3115    JSR     PUSHTO      ALLOWED?
00730 A239 7E AC45           JMP     XKTOTL      GO TO "TOTAL" ROUTINE
00740 A23C 58      XK3120 ASL B
00750 A23D 2A 06             BPL     XK3135
00760 A23F BD AFDD           JSR     PUSHQT      ALLOWED?
00770 A242 7E AB85           JMP     XKQNTY      GO TO "QUANTITY" ROUTINE
00780 A245 58      XK3135 ASL B
00790 A246 2A 06             BPL     XK3155
00800 A248 BD AFDA           JSR     PUSHNX      ALLOWED?
00810 A24B 7E A836           JMP     XKNTAX      GO TO "NO TAX" ROUTINE
00820 A24E BD AFE0 XK3155    JSR     PUSHWT      ALLOWED?
00830 A251 7E ABC5           JMP     XKWGHT      GO TO "WEIGHT" ROUTINE
```

FIGURE 6-4.2.4-5: Keyboard Decode Assembly Listing (Sheet 1 of 2)

```
00840                         ◆
00850                         ◆◆ GROUP B
00860                         ◆
00870 A254 58       XK3165 ASL  B
00880 A255 2A 2C           BPL     XK3270      IF NO, CONTINUE INTERROGATI
00890 A257 58              ASL  B
00900 A258 2A 06           BPL     XK3190
00910 A25A BD AFC5         JSR     PUSHCL      ALLOWED?
00920 A25D 7E AEC5         JMP     XKCLER      GO TO "CLEAR" ROUTE
00930 A260 D7 A7    XK3190 STA  B  XVKBTP      SAVE NUMBER
00940 A262 BD AFCE         JSR     PUSHCA      ALLOWED?
00950 A265 D6 A7           LDA  B  XVKBTP      RESTORE NUMBER
00960 A267 58              ASL  B
00970 A268 2A 0A           BPL     XK3225
00980 A26A 58              ASL  B
00990 A26B 58              ASL  B
01000 A26C 2A 03           BPL     XK3220
01010 A26E 7E A545         JMP     XKHSST      GO TO "HOUSEHLD/STAMPS" ROU
01020 A271 7E A542 XK3220 JMP     XKPRBO      GO TO "PRODUCE/BOTTLES" ROU
01030 A274 58       XK3225 ASL  B
01040 A275 2A 09           BPL     XK3260
01050 A277 58              ASL  B
01060 A278 2A 03           BPL     XK3255
01070 A27A 7E A53F         JMP     XKMTCP      GO TO "MEAT/COUPON" ROUTINE
01080 A27D 7E A53C XK3255 JMP     XKDAIR      GO TO "DAIRY" ROUTINE
01090 A280 7E A539 XK3260 JMP     XKGROC      GO TO "GROCERY" ROUTINE
01100                         ◆
01110                         ◆◆ DECIMAL POINT ?
01120                         ◆
01130 A283 81 0A    XK3270 CMP  A  #$0A
01140 A285 26 10           BNE     XK3300
01150 A287 86 49           LDA  A  #$49        WAS LBP CASH OR CHECK?
01160 A289 BD A2C3         JSR     XKTSTF
01170 A28C 27 03           BEQ     NOEND1      IF NOT, CONTINUE
01180 A28E 7E A046         JMP     XKTEND      IF SO, INITIATE X-ACTION END
01190 A291 BD AFCB NOEND1 JSR     PUSHDP      ALLOWED?
01200 A294 7E A339         JMP     XKDECP      GO TO "DECIMAL POINT" ROUTI
01210                         ◆
01220                         ◆◆ NUMBER ?
01230                         ◆
01240 A297 97 A7    XK3300 STA  A  XVKBTP      SAVE KEYBOARD DATA
01250 A299 81 00           CMP  A  #00         IS ⌗ = 0
01260 A29B 27 07           BEQ     XK3308
01270 A29D 86 73           LDA  A  #$73        IF NOT, RESET FLAG 73
01280 A29F BD A2C9         JSR     XKRSTF
01290 A2A2 20 05           BRA     XK3311
01300 A2A4 86 73    XK3308 LDA  A  #$73        IF EQUAL, SET 73
01310 A2A6 BD A2C6         JSR     XKSETF
01320 A2A9 BD AFC8 XK3311 JSR     PUSHNU      ALLOWED?
01330 A2AC 96 A7           LDA  A  XVKBTP      RESTORE KEYBOARD DATA
01340 A2AE 7E A33C         JMP     XKNUMB      GO TO "NUMBER" ROUTINE
01350                         END
```

FIGURE 6-4.2.4-5: Keyboard Decode Assembly Listing (Sheet 2 of 2)

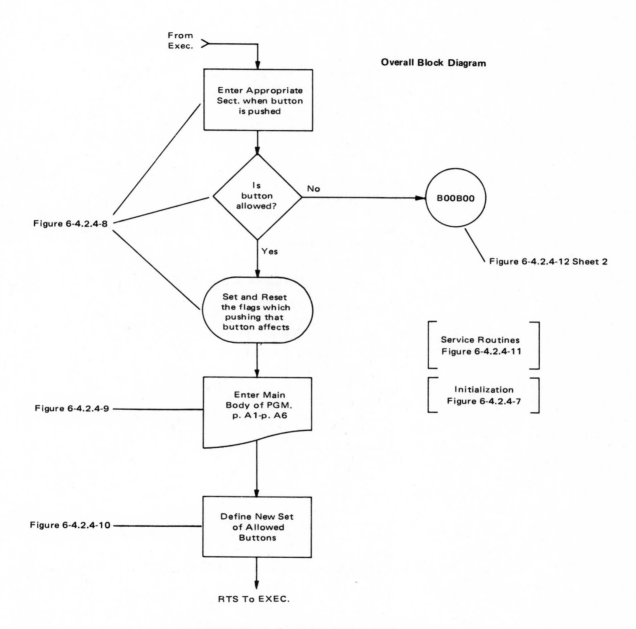

FIGURE 6-4.2.4-6: XK Safe General Flow Diagram

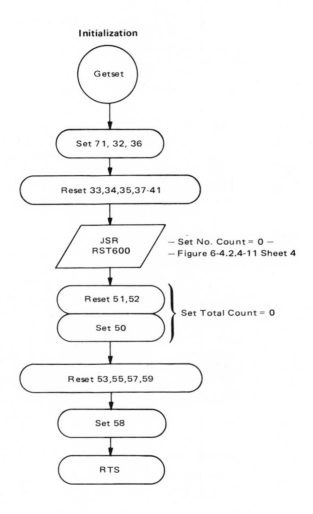

FIGURE 6-4.2.4-7: XKSafe Initialization Section Flow Chart

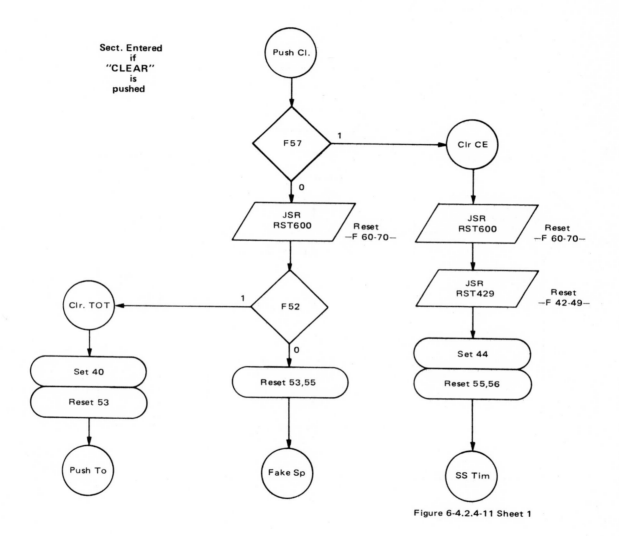

Sect. Entered
if
"CLEAR"
is
pushed

Figure 6-4.2.4-11 Sheet 1

FIGURE 6-4.2.4-8: XKSafe Entry Point Flow Charts (Sheet 1 of 7)

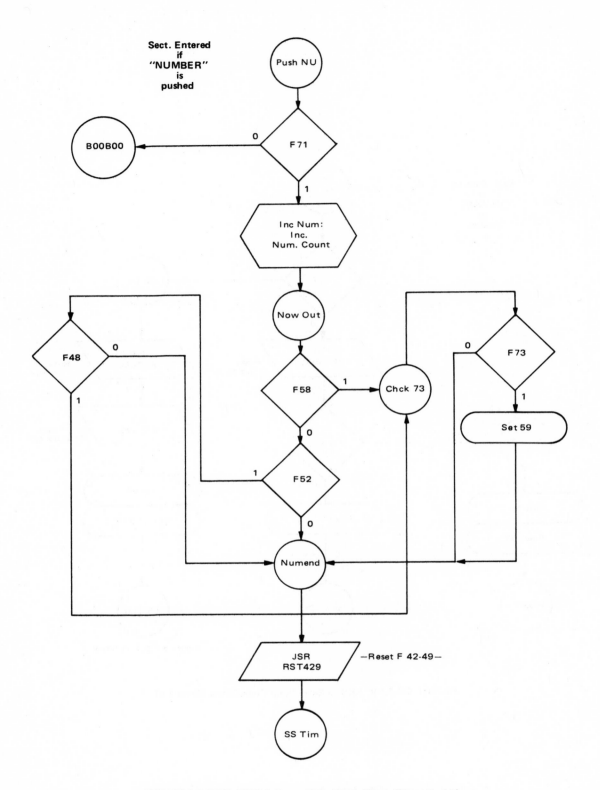

FIGURE 6-4.2.4-8: XKSafe Entry Point Flow Charts (Sheet 2 of 7)

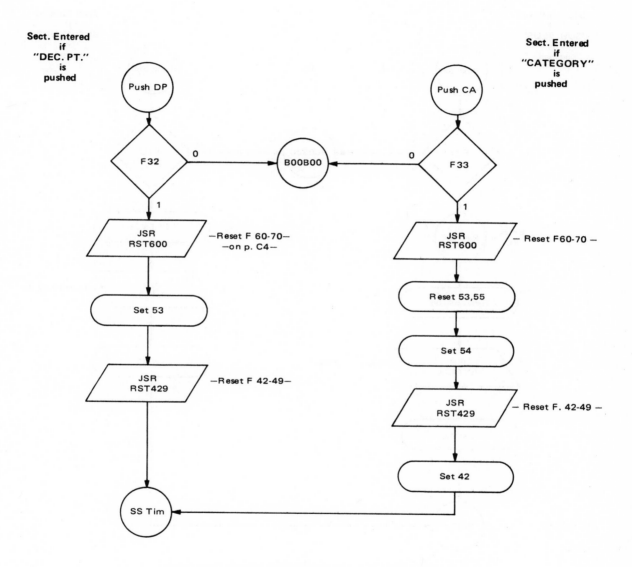

FIGURE 6-4.2.4-8: XKSafe Entry Point Flow Charts (Sheet 3 of 7)

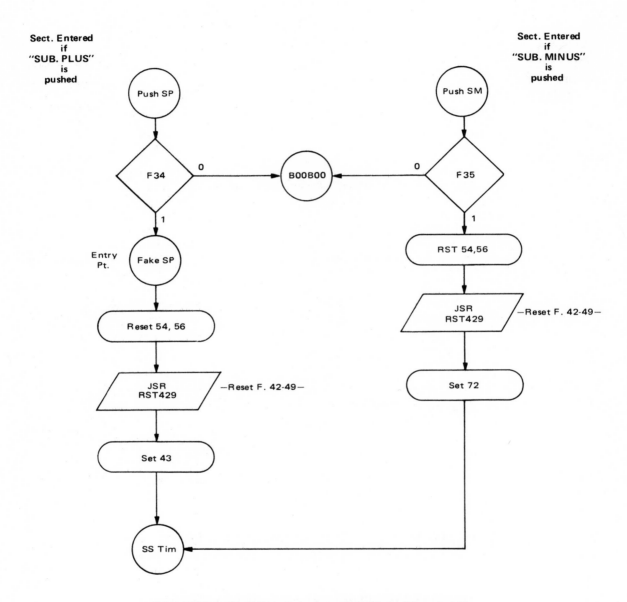

FIGURE 6-4.2.4-8: XKSafe Entry Point Flow Charts (Sheet 4 of 7)

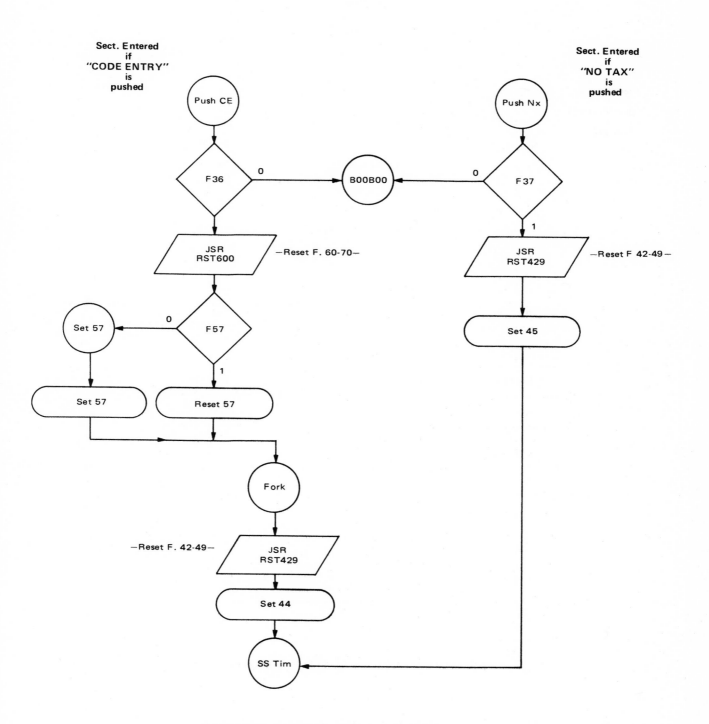

FIGURE 6-4.2.4-8: XKSafe Entry Point Flow Charts (Sheet 5 of 7)

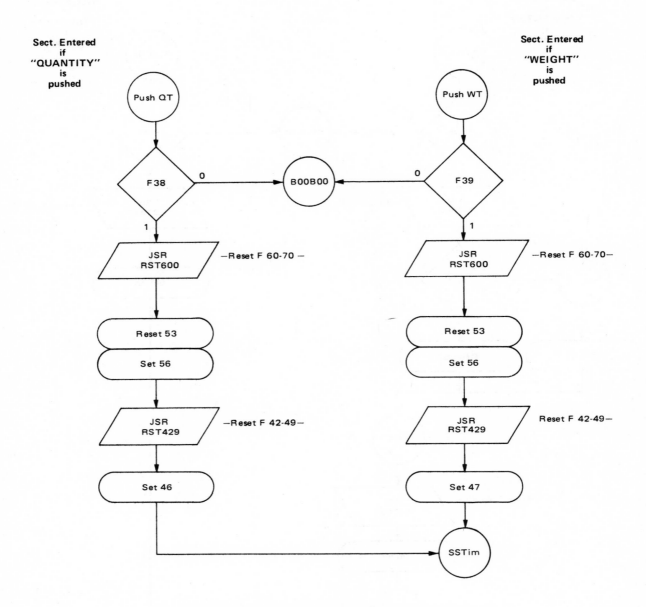

FIGURE 6-4.2.4-8: XKSafe Entry Point Flow Charts (Sheet 6 of 7)

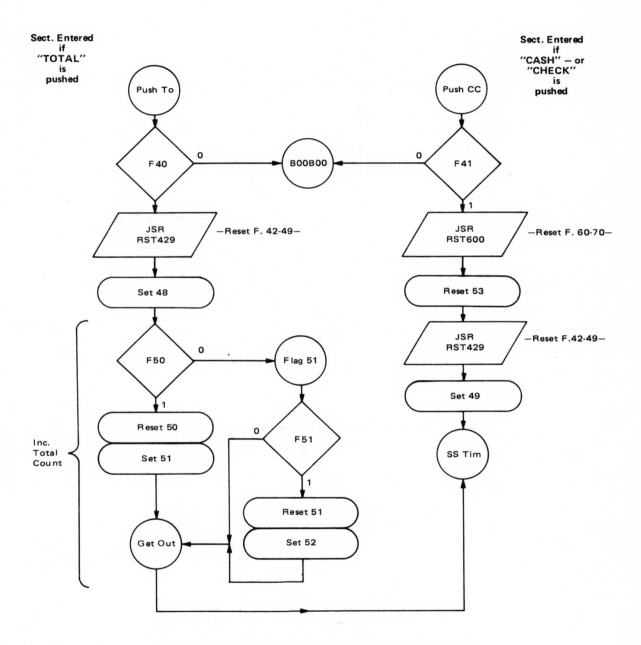

FIGURE 6-4.2.4-8: XKSafe Entry Point Flow Charts (Sheet 7 of 7)

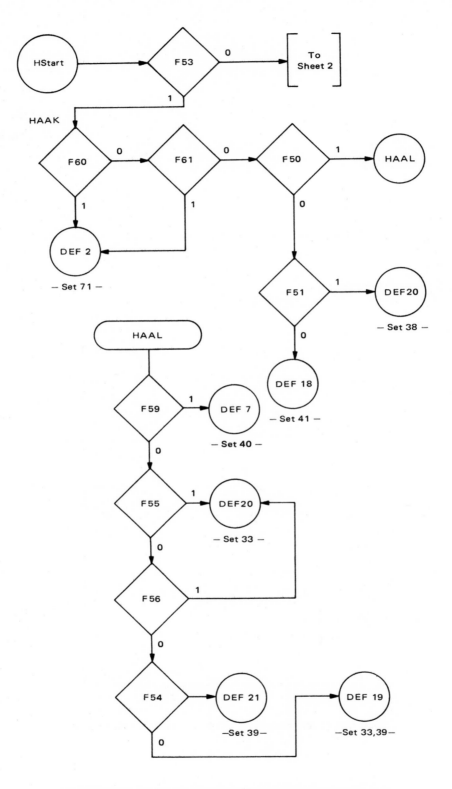

FIGURE 6-4.2.4-9: XKSafe Main Processing Flow Chart (Sheet 1 of 5)

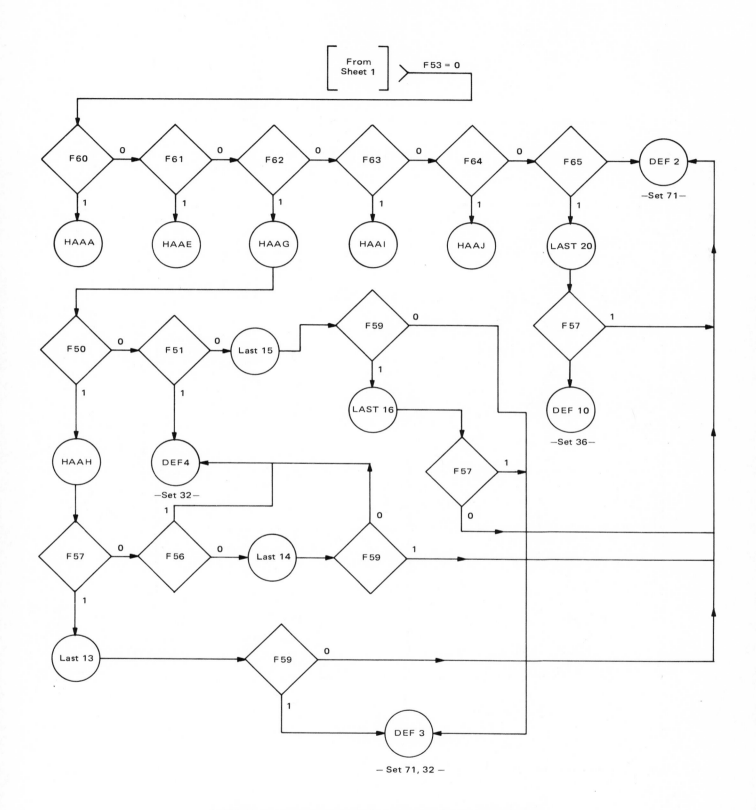

FIGURE 6-4.2.4-9: XKSafe Main Processing Flow Chart (Sheet 2 of 5)

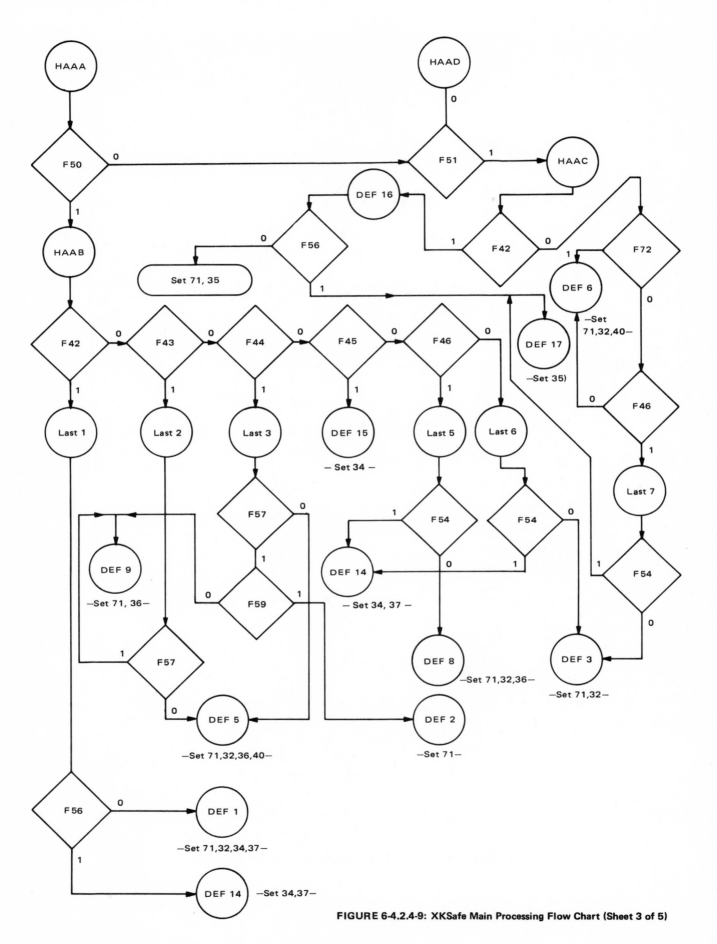

FIGURE 6-4.2.4-9: XKSafe Main Processing Flow Chart (Sheet 3 of 5)

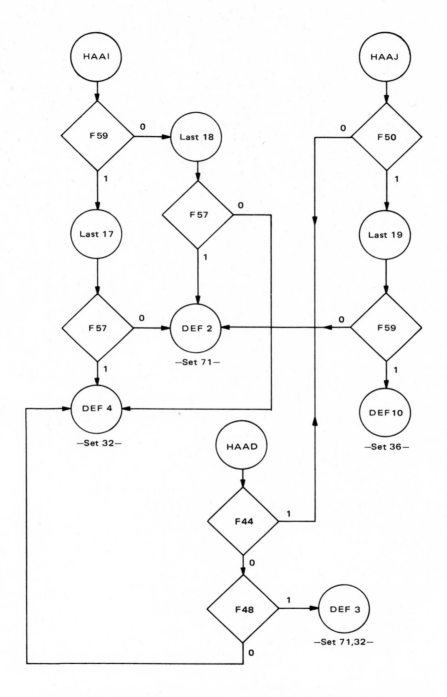

FIGURE 6-4.2.4-9: XKSafe Main Processing Flow Chart (Sheet 4 of 5)

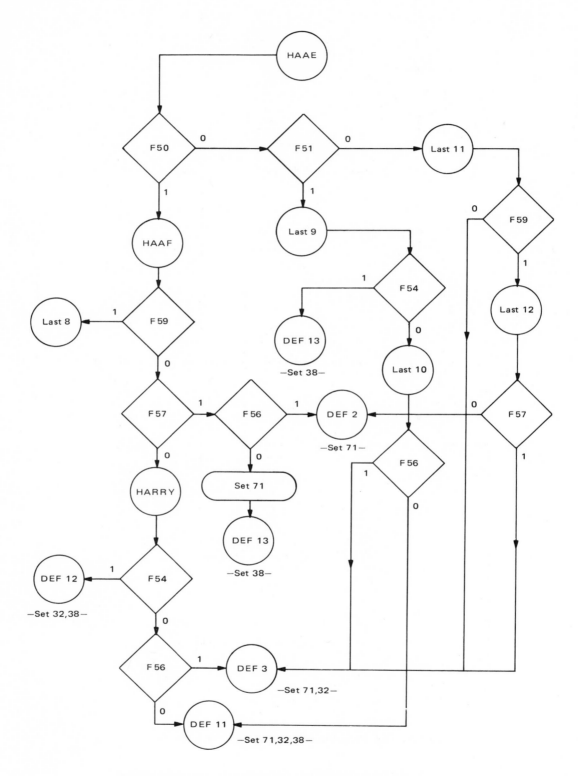

FIGURE 6-4.2.4-9: XKSafe Main Processing Flow Chart (Sheet 5 of 5)

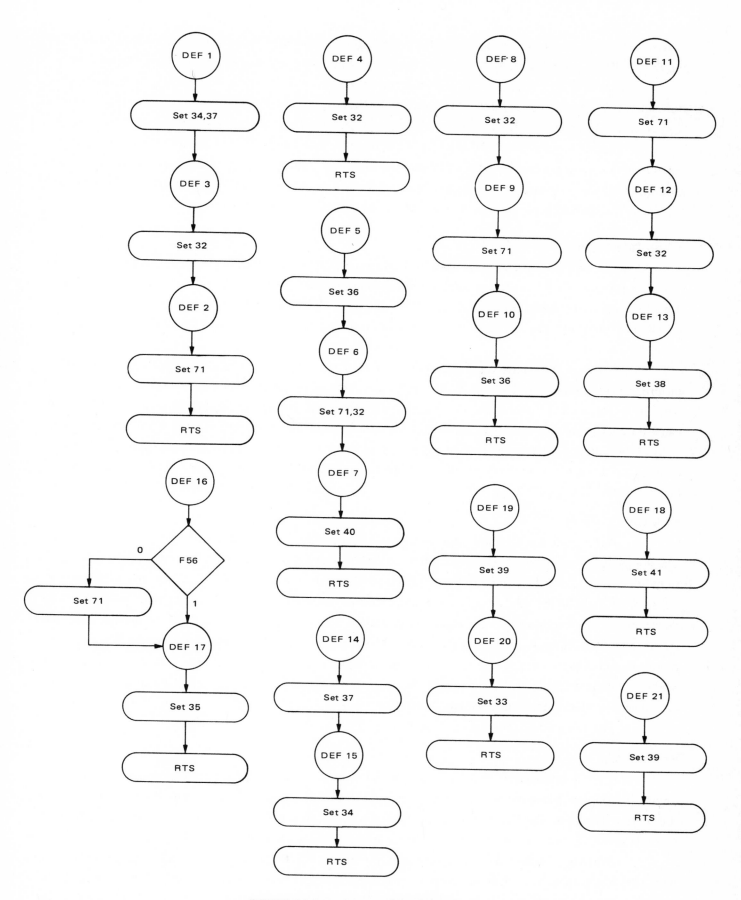

FIGURE 6-4.2.4-10: XKSafe Defining Section

transaction flow is for the present entry by checking the appropriate flag. Once this is accomplished, it clears all the BUTTON ALLOWED FLAGS before going to the appropriate defining section (see Figure 6-4.2.4-9).

The BUTTON ALLOWED FLAGS are then set by the defining sections as determined by how far the transaction has progressed as defined in the main body of the program (see Figure 6-4.2A-10). The service routine flow is shown in Figure 6-4.2.4-11. Flags referred to in the flow charts are summarized in Figure 6-4.2.4-12.

From the flow charts and flag tables, the complexity and length of the program becomes obvious. The assembled code occupies about 1.5K of memory, a significant portion of the system's program. A detailed description of the program is not included since each terminal design would require a specialized interlock program. The XKSAFE program is included as an example of microprocessor flexibility.

Wand Interpreter

The wand interpreter program translates the recovered UPC code into a binary word. The scanner "sees" white and black bands on the UPC label and translates them into logic levels; a white band represents a logic "0" and a black band represents a logic "1." These logic signals are then brought into the MPU via a PIA data line. At this point, the Wand software takes over to convert the stream of 1's and 0's into 10 BCD characters stored into RAM.

Entry into the wand routine is always from the software poll. A green ready light will be turned on when the program enters the software poll. At this time, the operator may scan the UPC labels to enter data. The wand data line will be at a logic level 1 until the scanner first sees the white border surrounding the actual label. This will cause the data line to go to "0" indicating to the MPU that a wand input has been initiated. At this time, the MPU will exit the polling routine and enter the wand interpreter routine. The actual operation of the interpreter routine is detailed in Section 5-1.1. When the routine is completed and the UPC code is in memory, the wand routine jumps directly to the "Disk UPC Lookup" to convert the UPC numbers into price/category information.

Disk UPC Lookup

A floppy disk is included in the system to act as a lookup file for Universal Product Code information The floppy disk is called upon for information when the keyboard enters UPC data or the wand scans a UPC label. In either case, the disk UPC lookup program is entered to convert the 10 UPC numbers into price/category information. Briefly, the UPC input becomes an address to the floppy disk. The data addressed by the UPC code then contains the necessary price/category information. The lookup routine transfers the desired data into memory while concurrently storing a status word, and then returns control to the executive routine. The executive routine then checks the status word to determine if the floppy disk completed a valid read. If the read is invalid, the MPU displays an error message and returns to the software poll. If the UPC lookup is valid, the program continues execution by entering the "process data" routine.

The floppy disk routines are described in detail in Section 5-4.

Process Data

The "Process Data" routine is the workhorse of the executive program. Depending upon the entry mode, this routine must maintain control of the majority of flags and buffers in the system. Program execution in this routine is best described with reference to Figure 6-4.2.1-1. Here the keyboard entries are categorized into 13 separate flow diagrams. These flow charts then become the nucleus of the processing program.

When data is entered from the keyboard, the MPU jumps to the keyboard decode routine to determine which key has been depressed. If the entry passes the interlock test, the decode routine will then enter one of 13 subroutines to process the data. The word "processing" does not have a singular description in this context. If, for example, the "no tax" key is depressed, the processing consists only of setting flag 16 (refer to Figure 6-4.2.1-1). At the other extreme, use of the "subtotal +" key causes the MPU to do extensive housekeeping since this key completes an item entry. Therefore, the processing routine must calculate sums, issue data to the printer and display, and update numerous flags and buffers. The flow for the "processing" for each class of keyboard entry is shown in Figure 6-4.2.2-1. After the data is processed, the executive will return to the polling routine and wait for the next input.

When operating on UPC inputs, the disk UPC lookup routine is entered to translate the data into price/category information. The lookup routine will store the resultant data into the same memory buffers as if the entry was from the keyboard. The lookup routine them jumps to the processing routine at the subtotal + entry point. The UPC entry continues execution in the subtotal + flow to complete the item entry processing.

When processing is completed, the routine exits to one of three areas of the executive program each of which ultimately returns to the polling sequence to receive new data. An incomplete entry returns directly from the processing routine to the poll. If, for example, the operator has entered only the price of an item the program still requires a category key and subtotal +. The process routine continues to return directly to the software poll until a "subtotal +" key is depressed. At this time, all item information is entered, and upon completion of processing, the MPU will jump to the "new item initialization" to prepare the program for the next item entry. It should be noted that each wand scan is considered to be a complete item entry. The disk lookup enters the subtotal + subroutine to process data and, therefore, exits to the new item initialization before returning to the poll. The final exit from the processing routine is at completion of a transaction. When the decimal point key is depressed subsequent to a cash or check entry, the transaction is over. At this time, the processing routine will store all transaction data into a magnetic tape cassette. The cassette routine transfers price/category information stored in memory to provide a daily summation stored on the cassette. At completion of the cassette transfer, the "new transaction initialization" is entered to preset the executive program for a new entry. The cassette operation is described in more detail in Section 5-3.

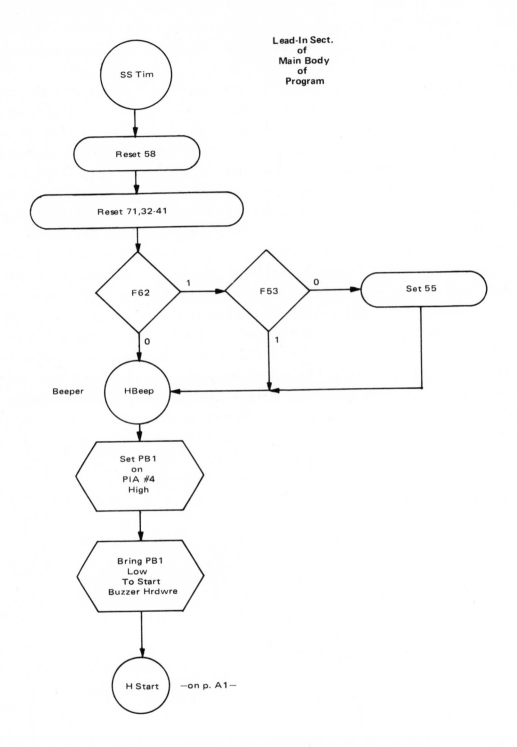

FIGURE 6-4.2.4-11: XKSafe Service Routine Flow Charts (Sheet 1 of 5)

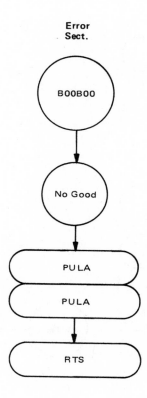

FIGURE 6-4.2.4-11: XKSafe Service Routine Flow Charts (Sheet 2 of 5)

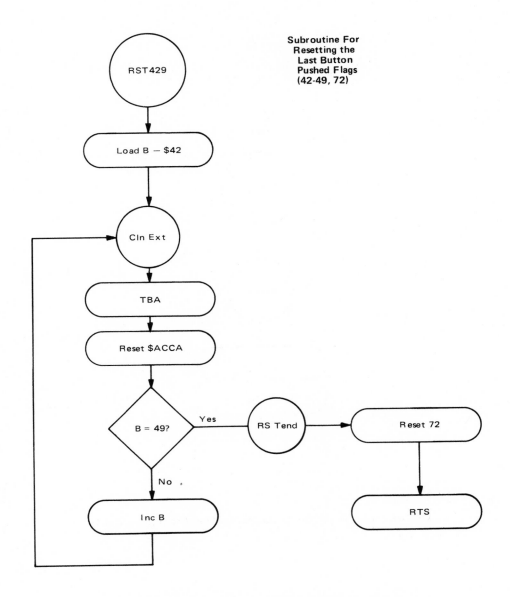

Subroutine For
Resetting the
Last Button
Pushed Flags
(42-49, 72)

FIGURE 6-4.2.4-11: XKSafe Service Routine Flow Charts (Sheet 3 of 5)

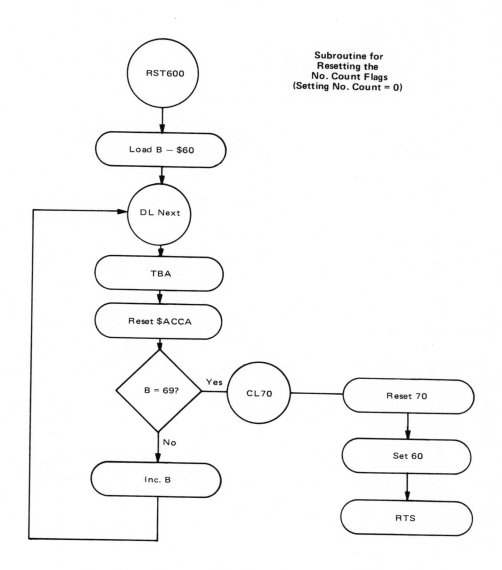

FIGURE 6-4.2.4-11: XKSafe Service Routine Flow Charts (Sheet 4 of 5)

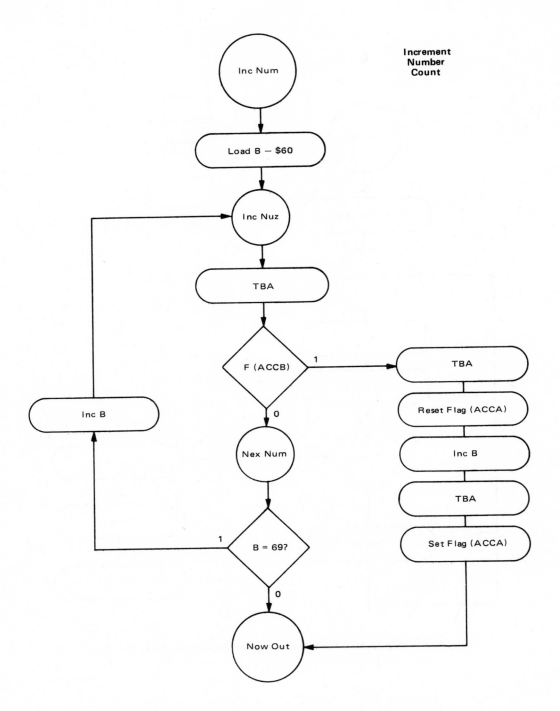

Increment
Number
Count

FIGURE 6-4.2.4-11: XKSafe Service Routine Flow Charts (Sheet 5 of 5)

Button Allowed Flags

Flag No.	Button
71	#
32	DP
33	CAT
34	⊕
35	⊖
36	CE
37	NTX
38	Q+Y
39	WGHT
40	TOT
41	{ Cash { Check

Last Button Pushed Flags

Flag No.	Button
42	CAT
43	⊕
44	CE
45	NTX
46	Qty
47	Wght
48	TOT
49	{ Cash { Check
72	⊖

Special Flags

73 — Is # = 0?

Total Counter Flags

Flag No.	Total Count
50	0
51	1
52	2

No. Counter Flags

Flag No.	No. Count
60	0
61	1
62	2
63	3
64	4
65	5
66	6
67	7
68	8
69	9
70	10

Other Flags

Flag No.	Func.
53	DP
54	CAT
55	Qty-Wght A
56	Qty-Wght B
57	CE
58	Last Entry END
59	Zero

FIGURE 6-4.2.4-12: Flag Reference Summary

6-4.3 INTERRUPT CONTROL

There is another program flow, transparent to the flow of Figure 6-4.2.2-1, associated with the transaction terminal. It is the program flow (See Figure 6-4.3-1) required for servicing interrupts generated by the system peripherals. The $\overline{IRQA}$ and $\overline{IRQB}$ lines of all the peripheral PIA's are tied together and connected to the $\overline{IRQ}$ input of the MPU. When a peripheral needs service, it issues an interrupt request for service through a PIA. When the MPU recognizes that an interrupt request is present, it jumps to the interrupt polling program XKRUPT. An assembly listing of the polling program is shown in Figure 6-4.3-2.

The addresses decoded for the $\overline{IRQ}$ vector in the Transaction Terminal are E3F8 and E3F9 in the MIKBUG ROM. The MIKBUG $\overline{IRQ}$ service routine jumps to the address stored in RAM locations A000 and A001. These memory locations were set to the interrupt polling routine's starting address when the Transaction Terminal program was loaded.

The interrupt polling routine, XKRUPT, checks the appropriate PIA control registers for interrupt flag bits and, in some cases, the interrupt request enable/disable bits as well. The $\overline{IRQ}$ enable/disable bits must be checked on those peripherals which generate continuous interrupt requests that set the IRQA(B) flag bits but are not allowed to generate an IRQ when the peripheral is not in use. The printer, for example, is continuously generating timing signals and the IRQB1 (CRB−b7) flag is periodically set to 1, however, the $\overline{IRQB}$ line is not brought low except during a print cycle when the enable bit (CRB−b0) is set to 1. By first checking the flag bit (CRB−b7) and, if it is set, checking the enable bit (CRB−b0) it can be determined if the printer has requested service via the CB1 line. See Section 5-2.1.4 for additional details.

Two subroutines are provided, one to check the IRQA(B)1 flag and enable bit (IRQ1FM), the other to check the IRQA(B)2 flag and its associated control bits (IRQ2FM). (See the code in Figure 6-4.3-1.)

IRQ1FM shifts the IRQ1 flag into the carry. If the carry is clear, indicating no interrupt, a return is initiated. If the carry is set, indicating an interrupt request, the enable is tested by a BITA instruction. If the enable is clear, a return is executed; if the enable is set, a JMP X is executed. The index register (X) is set to the value of the service routine starting address and ACCA loaded with the appropriate PIA control register prior to jumping to the subroutine.

IRQ2FM shifts the IRQA(B)2 bit to the MSB (sign bit) position. If the byte is positive (b7 = 0, IRQA(B)2 shifted = 0) a return is executed. If negative (b7 = 1) the byte is shifted left one more bit so that the CA2 (CB2) output control bit (CRA(B)−b5) is now in the MSB position. The routine executes a return if the bit is 1 indicating that CA2(CB2) is an output. If the bit = 0, the enable bit, CRA(B)−b3, (now ACCA−b5 after 2 shifts) is tested. If the enable is clear, a return is executed; if the enable is set, a JMP X is executed where X is the service routine address.

The interrupt polling sequence determines the peripheral priority structure. Assume, for example, that an interval timer interrupt and a printer timing interrupt occur at the same time. The poll would jump to PRNTIT which clears the $\overline{IRQA(B)}$ flag, removing its influence on the $\overline{IRQ}$ line to the MPU. The RTI following completion of PRNTIT then clears the interrupt mask and allows the interval time interrupt to be recognized.

The first test in the poll checks for disk read/write operation. Since an interrupt generated when this flag is set could be an overwrite error, the disk must stop writing as soon as possible. This flag will only be set when the system is under control of the disk program so all other interrupts are masked and will be ignored. The cassette and printer interrupts follow in the poll and use the subroutines described above. The display interrupt is never masked, therefore, the poll only checks the control register flag bit.

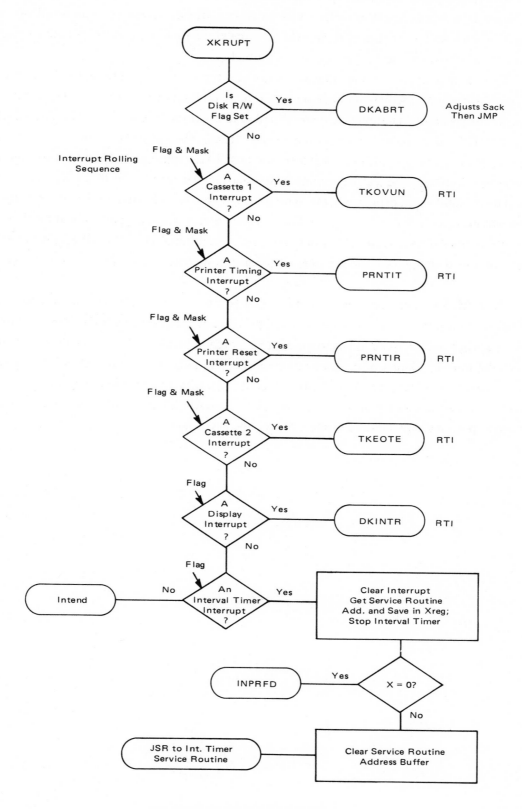

FIGURE 6-4.3-1: Interrupt Control Flow Chart

Only the interval timer interrupt remains to be checked. Like the display, it is never masked and the flag bit is tested. If the flag is clear, the interrupt was not generated by the system and is assumed to be noise and the poll returns. If the $\overline{\text{IRQ}}$ line continues to be held low, the system will loop in the polling routine until some corrective action is taken or the $\overline{\text{IRQ}}$ is allowed to go high.

If the interval timer flag is set, the routine stops the timer, clears the interrupt and flag, and then checks the service address and jumps there if one is present. If there is no service routine address, the poll checks for a printer line feed in progress. (The timer service routine also returns to this point.) If there is a line feed, the line feed counter (PRCNTR) is decremented and checked for zero. If zero, the line feed is terminated, otherwise, the disk status is checked for a seek as would be done if there was no line feed in progress. If a seek is in progress, a jump to seek subroutine is initiated. The seek subroutine returns and another check of the disk status is made for a seek in progress. If there is still a seek in progress, the routine ends. If not, a check is made for a line feed still in progress. (If no seek was previously in progress, the routine branched here.) If not, the poll ends. If the line feed requires more time, the interval timer is set for 10 ms and started before returning. This allows the printer line feed and disk seek operation to simultaneously use the interval timer thus increasing the effectiveness (throughput) of the system.

The $\overline{\text{NMI}}$ interrupt is used by the system to start the transaction terminal program. The line is tied to a push button switch which, when depressed, will pull the line low generating an $\overline{\text{NMI}}$ interrupt at the MPU. The $\overline{\text{NMI}}$ service routine in MIKBUG jumps to the address stored in locations A006 and A007. The locations are loaded with the starting address of the transaction terminal initialization routine XKBGIN, A04A. Once the program has been loaded into RAM, an $\overline{\text{NMI}}$ will start the transaction terminal program without the use of MIKBUG "G" (execute user's program) function. Since the RAM is non-volatile and is battery backed up, the system may be powered down and restarted by using the $\overline{\text{NMI}}$ interrupt.

```
00010                            NAM    XKRUPT
00010                            OPT    LIST
01000                      ◆     NAM    XKRUPT
01020                      ◆     REV    1.2
01110 BAA8                       ORG    $BAA8
01480                      ◆  THE INTERRUPT POLL CHECKS THE PIA CONTROL
01490                      ◆  REGISTERS TO SEE WHICH PIA CAUSED THE
01500                      ◆  INTERRUPT.  IF MORE THAN ONE IS POSSIBLE
01510                      ◆  THE PRIOROTY IS DETERMINED BY THE
01520                      ◆  SEQUENCE OF THE POLL.
01570 BAA8 B6 C00B XKRUPT LDA A  XP1CRB    IF IRQB1 FLG IS SET AND
01580 BAAB CE B922        LDX    #PRNTIT    THE IRQB INTRPT IS ENABLED
01590 BAAE BD BAE1        JSR    IRQ1FM    JMP TO PRNTIT (PRINTER)
01600 BAB1 B6 C009        LDA A  XP1CRA    IF IRQA1 FLG IS SET AND
01610 BAB4 CE B91F        LDX    #PRNTIR    THE IRQA INTRPT IS ENABLED
01620 BAB7 BD BAE1        JSR    IRQ1FM    JMP TO PRNTIR (PRINTER)
01660 BABA B6 C023 INDSPL LDA A  XP3CRB    TEST IF DISPLAY FLAG SET
01670 BABD 2A 03          BPL    INTIME    NO,CHECK NEXT
01680 BABF 7E B8C5        JMP    DKINTR    YES JUMP TO DISPLAY ROUTINE
01690 BAC2 B6 C013 INTIME LDA A  XP2CRB    IS TIMER FLAG SET?
01700 BAC5 2A 19          BPL    INTEND    NO:END
01700 BAC7 B6 C010        LDA A  XP2DRA    STOP INTERVAL TIMER
01700 BACA 84 40          AND A  #%01000000   BY CLEARING SCALE FACTO
01700 BACC B7 C010        STA A  XP2DRA
01710 BACF B6 C011        LDA A  XP2DRB    DUMMY READ TO CLEAR INTRPT
01730 BAD2 FE 011C        LDX    IVSERV    GET SERVICE ROUTINE ADDRESS
01740 BAD5 27 FE          BEQ    ◆         BRANCH ON SELF
01760 BAD7 4F             CLR A            IF ADD PRESENT
01770 BAD8 B7 011C        STA A  IVSERV    CLEAR SERVICE ADDRESS
01780 BADB B7 011D        STA A  IVSERV+1
01790 BADE AD 00          JSR    X         JUMP TO SERVICE SUBROUTINE
01800                      ◆  INT. TIMER SERV. SUBROU. MUST END IN RTS
01980 BAE0 3B      INTEND RTI              RETURN
01990                      ◆  SUBROUTINE TO TEST FOR CA1 (CB1)
01990                      ◆  INTERRUPTS BY CHECKING BOTH THE
01990                      ◆  IRQ1 FLAG AND ITS IRQ ENABLE BIT.
01990                      ◆     LDAA   WITH THE PIA CNTRL REG ADDRESS
01990                      ◆     LDX    WITH THE INTERRUPT SERV. ADD.
01990                      ◆     JSR  IRQ1FM
01990 BAE1 84 81   IRQ1FM AND A  #$81      MASK UNWANTED BITS
01990 BAE3 81 81          CMP A  #$81      TEST IF ENABLED WITH
01990                      ◆                         FLAG SET
01991 BAE5 26 04          BNE    IRQEND    NO  END
01991 BAE7 32             PUL A            IF SET ADJUST STACK
01991 BAE8 32             PUL A            AND JUMP TO THE INTRPT
01991 BAE9 6E 00          JMP    X         SERVICE ROUTINE
01991 BAEB 39      IRQEND RTS              RETURN TO POLL
01991                      ◆  SUBROUTINE TO TEST FOR CA2 (CB2)
01991                      ◆  INTERRUPTS BY CHECKING BOTH THE
01991                      ◆  IRQ2 FLAG AND ITS ASSOCIATED
01991                      ◆  CONTROL BITS
```

FIGURE 6-4.3-2: Interrupt Poll Assembly Listings (Sheet 1 of 2)

```
01992              ◆      LDAA   WITH THE PIA CNTRL REG ADD
01992              ◆      LDX    WITH THE INTERRUPT SERV. ADD
01992              ◆      JSR  IRQ2FM
01992 BAEC 84 68  IRQ2FM  AND A  #$68       MASK UNWANTED BITS
01992 BAEE 81 48           CMP A  #$48       TEST IF INPUT, ENABLED, AND
01992              ◆                              INTRPT FLAG SET
01992 BAF0 26 F9          BNE    IRQEND      NO  END
01992 BAF2 32             PUL A              YES  ADJUST STACK AND
01992 BAF3 32             PUL A              JUMP TO THE INTRPT
01993 BAF4 6E 00          JMP    X           SERVICE ROUTINE
```

FIGURE 6-4.3-2: Interrupt Poll Assembly Listings (Sheet 2 of 2)

CHAPTER 7

7. SYSTEM DEVELOPMENT TASKS

The development of any system is, in a sense, like Figure 7-1 where the desired end product is shown as being analogous to the visible above-water portion of an iceberg. It is only this portion that contributes to the ultimate success (or failure) of a project. Beneath the surface are the many necessary steps that must be performed if the project is to be successful. Such tasks as design, prototyping, evaluation, documentation, etc., must be performed regardless of whether or not the design incorporates an MPU.

In one respect, using a microprocessor simplifies the effort. Major reasons for using an MPU are, after all, to reduce the design cycle time and replace many conventional logic packages with a few LSI devices. However, in order to benefit fully from the attendant reductions in evaluation time and manufacturing cost, the additional tasks introduced by the use of the MPU must be handled efficiently.

The main additional task in an MPU-based system is generation of the control program that will eventually serve as the system's "intelligence". This program, while generally referred to as "software" throughout the development stage, will ultimately be stored in the system memory in most designs. This

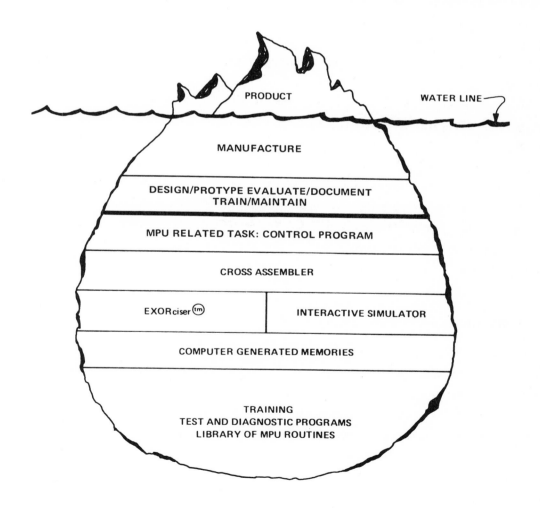

FIGURE 7-1: System Development: Like an Iceberg

Chapter briefly describes the design aids and products that Motorola provides for assistance in efficiently performing this task. The principle items, as shown in the lower portion of the iceberg, are the Cross Assembler, an Interactive Simulator, and an EXORciser.

The recommended procedure for developing and verifying a design using these aids is indicated in the Flowchart of Figure 7-2. Briefly, the control program is written, assembled, simulated, and exercised. The output of the process is system documentation and a tape suitable for generating appropriate memories. Each of these steps are discussed in subsequent sections of this Chapter, however, greater detail can be obtained by referring to the M6800 Programming Manual and the several manuals associated with the EXORciser.

7-1 ASSEMBLY OF THE CONTROL PROGRAM

While programs can be written in the MPU's language, that is, binary numbers, there is no easy way for the programmer to remember the particular binary number that corresponds to a given operation. For this reason, the MPU's instructions are assigned a three letter mnemonic symbol that suggests the definition of the instruction. Normally, the program is written as a series of source statements using this symbolic language and then translated into machine language. The translation can be done manually using an alphabetic listing of the symbolic instruction set such as that shown in Table 7-1-1. More often, the translation is accomplished by means of a special computer program. When the target program is assembled by the same microprocessor (or computer) that it will run on, the program that performs the assembly is referred to simply as an Assembler. If, as is often the case, the target program is assembled by some other computer, the process is referred to as cross-assembly.

Motorola provides such a program, the M6800 Cross-Assembler, on several[1] nationwide timesharing services. This permits subscribers to the services to efficiently assemble their control programs as indicated in Figure 7-2. The source program is entered via their in-house terminal and assembled. If necessary, the host system's Edit package is available for incorporating corrections and changes. In addition to the assembled output file, the Cross-Assembler provides other useful outputs. If the user is satisfied that the code as assembled is correct, a punched paper tape that is compatible with Motorola's EXORciser and ROM programming computer can be generated. The Cross-Assembler also provides a hard-copy output of the Assembly Listing. For properly commented and formatted programs, this Listing is an important part of the system documentation.

7-1.1 M6800 CROSS-ASSEMBLER SYNTAX

The syntax or language requirements for using the Motorola Assembler (and other support software) falls into one of two categories: (a) Requirements for conversing with the host computers operating system; (2) Requirements for conversing with the Motorola programs.

The first category varies from service to service. The documentation of the specific service being used should be obtained and referred to when using the support software. Where references are made to the host computers syntax in this Chapter, the General Electric procedures are shown. The emphasis in this Chapter is

---

[1]G.E. plus others to be announced later. The M6800 Cross-Assembler and the other special programs (Simulator, Build Virtual Machine, Help) described in this Chapter are maintained by Motorola and are dynamic programs that are constantly being improved. The descriptions in this Chapter reflect the status as of the time this Manual was printed. All changes are indicated in the Help program and can be obtained at the actual time the programs are to be used.

PROCEDURE FOR DESIGNING AND VERIFYING A SYSTEM USING THE MOTOROLA M6800 MICROCOMPUTER

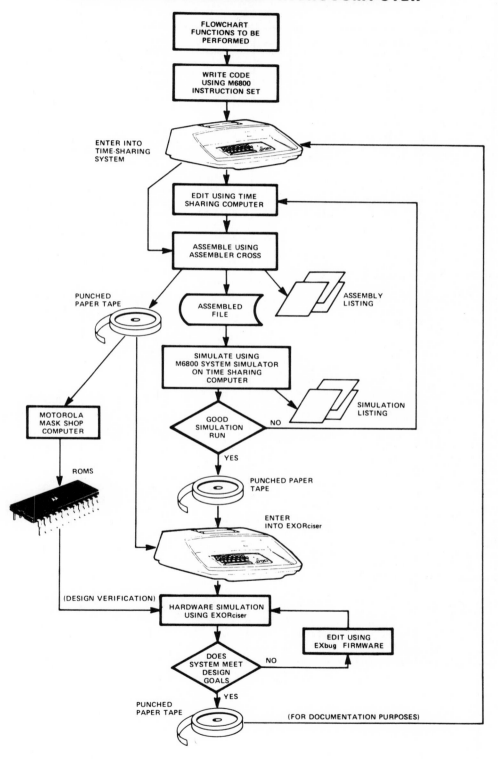

FIGURE 7-2:

TABLE 7-1-1: Alphabetic Listing of Instruction Mnemonics

Mnemonic Code	Addr. Mode	Hex Code
ADA	Inherent	1B
ADC(A)	Immediate	89
ADC(A)	Direct	99
ADC(A)	Indexed	A9
ADC(A)	Extended	B9
ADC(B)	Immediate	C9
ADC(B)	Direct	D9
ADC(B)	Indexed	E9
ADC(B)	Extended	F9
ADD(A)	Immediate	8B
ADD(A)	Direct	9B
ADD(A)	Indexed	AB
ADD(A)	Extended	BB
ADD(B)	Immediate	CB
ADD(B)	Direct	DB
ADD(B)	Indexed	EB
ADD(B)	Extended	FB
AND(A)	Immediate	84
AND(A)	Direct	94
AND(A)	Indexed	A4
AND(A)	Extended	B4
AND(B)	Immediate	C4
AND(B)	Direct	D4
AND(B)	Indexed	E4
AND(B)	Extended	F4
ASL(A)		48
ASL(B)		58
ASL	Indexed	68
ASL	Extended	78
ASR(A)		47
ASR(B)		57
ASR	Indexed	67
ASR	Extended	77
BCC	Relative	24
BCS	Relative	25
BEQ	Relative	27
BGE	Relative	2C
BGT	Relative	2E
BHI	Relative	22
BIT(A)	Immediate	85
BIT(A)	Direct	95
BIT(A)	Indexed	A5
BIT(A)	Extended	B5
BIT(B)	Immediate	C5
BIT(B)	Direct	D5
BIT(B)	Indexed	E5
BIT(B)	Extended	F5
BLE	Relative	2F
BLS	Relative	23
BLT	Relative	2D

Mnemonic Code	Addr. Mode	Hex Code
BMI	Relative	2B
BNE	Relative	26
BPL	Relative	2A
BRA	Relative	20
BSR	Relative	8D
BVC	Relative	28
BVS	Relative	29
CBA	Inherent	11
CLC	Inherent	0C
CLI	Inherent	0E
CLR(A)		4F
CLR(B)		5F
CLR	Indexed	6F
CLR	Extended	7F
CLV	Inherent	0A
CMP(A)	Immediate	81
CMP(A)	Direct	91
CMP(A)	Indexed	A1
CMP(A)	Extended	B1
CMP(B)	Immediate	C1
CMP(B)	Direct	D1
CMP(B)	Indexed	E1
CMP(B)	Extended	F1
COM(A)		43
COM(B)		53
COM	Indexed	63
COM	Extended	73
CPX	Immediate	8C
CPX	Direct	9C
CPX	Indexed	AC
CPX	Extended	BC
DAA	Inherent	19
DEC(A)		4A
DEC(B)		5A
DEC	Indexed	6A
DEC	Extended	7A
DES	Inherent	34
DEX	Inherent	09
EOR(A)	Immediate	88
EOR(A)	Direct	98
EOR(A)	Indexed	A8
EOR(A)	Extended	B8
EOR(B)	Immediate	C8
EOR(B)	Direct	D8
EOR(B)	Indexed	E8
EOR(B)	Extended	F9
INC(A)		4C
INC(B)		5C
INC	Indexed	6C
INC	Extended	7C

Mnemonic Code	Addr. Mode	Hex Code
INS	Inherent	31
INX	Inherent	08
JMP	Indexed	6E
JMP	Extended	7E
JSR	Indexed	AD
JSR	Extended	BD
LDA(A)	Immediate	86
LDA(A)	Direct	96
LDA(A)	Indexed	A6
LDA(A)	Extended	BE
LDA(B)	Immediate	CE
LDA(B)	Direct	DE
LDA(B)	Indexed	EE
LDA(B)	Extended	FE
LDS	Immediate	8E
LDS	Direct	9E
LDS	Indexed	AE
LDS	Extended	BE
LDX	Immediate	CE
LDX	Direct	DE
LDX	Indexed	EE
LDX	Extended	FE
LSR(A)		44
LSR(B)		54
LSR	Indexed	64
LSR	Extended	74
NEG(A)		40
NEG(B)		50
NEG	Indexed	60
NEG	Extended	70
NOP	Inherent	02
ORA(A)	Immediate	8A
ORA(A)	Direct	9A
ORA(A)	Indexed	AA
ORA(A)	Extended	BA
ORA(B)	Immediate	CA
ORA(B)	Direct	DA
ORA(B)	Indexed	EA
ORA(B)	Extended	FA
PSH(A)		36
PSH(B)		37
PUL(A)		32
PUL(B)		33
ROL(A)		49
ROL(B)		59
ROL	Indexed	69
ROL	Extended	79
ROR(A)		46
ROR(B)		56
ROR	Indexed	66

Mnemonic Code	Addr. Mode	Hex Code
ROR	Extended	76
RTI	Inherent	3B
RTS	Inherent	39
SBA	Inherent	10
SBC(A)	Immediate	82
SBC(A)	Direct	92
SBC(A)	Indexed	A2
SBC(A)	Extended	B2
SBC(B)	Immediate	C2
SBC(B)	Direct	D2
SBC(B)	Indexed	E2
SBC(B)	Extended	F2
SEC	Inherent	0D
SEI	Inherent	0F
SEV	Inherent	0B
STA(A)	Direct	97
STA(A)	Indexed	A7
STA(A)	Extended	B7
STA(B)	Direct	D7
STA(B)	Indexed	E7
STA(B)	Extended	F7
STS	Direct	9F
STS	Indexed	AF
STS	Extended	BF
STX	Direct	DF
STX	Indexed	EF
STX	Extended	FF
SUB(A)	Immediate	80
SUB(A)	Direct	90
SUB(A)	Indexed	A0
SUB(A)	Extended	B0
SUB(B)	Immediate	C0
SUB(B)	Direct	D0
SUB(B)	Indexed	E0
SUB(B)	Extended	F0
SWI	Inherent	3F
TAB	Inherent	16
TAP	Inherent	06
TBA	Inherent	17
TPA	Inherent	07
TST(A)		4D
TST(B)		5D
TST	Indexed	6D
TST	Extended	7D
TSX	Inherent	30
TXS	Inherent	35
WAI	Inherent	3E

on the language requirements of the Motorola programs. These requirements are constant and, except for minor variations in format, do not vary from system to system.

The source program is nothing more than a list of instructions that the MPU is to execute during system operation. All that is required is that the mnemonic instructions used by the programmer to write the program be translated into binary machine language acceptable to the MPU. However, if the Cross-Assembler is to be used to perform the translation, the language and format described in the following paragraphs should be used.

The source program is written in an assembler language consisting of the 72 executive instructions and the assembly directives shown in Table 7-1.1-1. The assembly directives are useful in generating, controlling, and documenting the source program. With the exceptions of FCB, FCC, and FDB, they do not generate code. The characters recognized by the Assembler include A through Z of the alphabet, the integers ϕ through 9, and the four arithmetic operators $+$, $-$, $*$, and $/$. In addition, the following special prefixes and separating characters may be used:

   # (pounds sign) specifies the immediate mode of addressing.
   $ (dollar sign) specifies a hexadecimal number.
   @ (commercial at) specifies an octal number.
   % percent) specifies a binary number.
   ' apostrophe) specifies an ASCII literal character.
SPACE
Horizontal TAB
CR (carriage return)
 , (comma)

The character set is a subset of ASCII (American Standard Code for Information Interchange, 1968) and includes the ASCII characters, 20 (SP) through 5F ($\leftarrow$). The ASCII code is shown in Table 7-1.1-2.

END — End of Program

The assembler directive "END", if used, marks the end of a source program, and can be followed only by a statement containing the assembler directive "MON". The operator in the last statement of a source program must be either "END" or "MON". If the program ends with a "MON" directive, the use of "END" is optional. The "END" directive must not be written with a label, and it does not have an operand.

EQU — Equate Symbol

The "EQU" directive is used to assign a value to a symbol. The "EQU" statement must contain a label which is identical with the symbol being defined. The operand field may contain the numerical value of the symbol (decimal, hexadecimal, octal, or binary). Alternatively, the operand field may be another symbol or an expression which can be evaluated by the Assembler. The special symbol "*" which represents the program counter must not be used.

Examples of valid "EQU" statements:

Data	Label	Operator	Operand
0A01	SUN	EQU	$A01
0003	AB	EQU	3
0A01	AA	EQU	SUN
0A04	AC	EQU	AB+AA
0FC1	ABC	EQU	$FC1

If a symbol or an expression is used in the operand field, only one level of forward referencing will assemble correctly. This reflects a two-pass characteristic of the assembly process. An illegal example of two levels of forward referencing would be:

E	EQU	Y
Y	EQU	C
C	EQU	5

This will not assemble correctly because E will not be assigned a numerical value at the end of pass 2. E and Y are both undefined throughout pass 1 and will be listed as such at the end of pass 1. E is undefined throughout pass 2 and will cause an error message.

FCB — Form Constant Byte

The "FCB" directive may have one or more operands, separated by commas. An 8-bit unsigned binary number, corresponding to the value of each operand is stored in a byte of the object program. If there is more than one operand, they are stored in successive bytes. The operand field may contain the actual value (decimal, hexadecimal, octal or binary) or be a symbol or an expression which can be assigned a numerical value by the Assembler. An "FCB" directive followed by one or more void operands separated by commas will store zeros for the void operands. An "FCB" directive may be written with a label.

TABLE 7-1.1-1 Assembler Directives (Sheet 1 of 6)

Examples of valid "FCB" directives:

Location	Data	Label	Operator	Operand
0000	FF	TOP	FCB	$9FF
0001	00	TAB	TCB	,$F,23,
0002	0F			
0003	17			
0004	00			
0005	E5		FCB	*+$E0

FCC — Form Constant Characters

The "FCC" directive translates strings of characters into their 7-bit ASCII codes. Any of the characters which correspond to ASCII hexadecimal codes 20 (SP) thru 5F (←) can be processed by this directive. Either of the following formats may be used:

1. Count, comma, text. Where the count specifies how many ASCII characters to generate and the text begins following the first comma of the operand. Should the count be longer than the text, spaces will be inserted to fill the count. Maximum count is 255.

2. Text enclosed between identical delimiters, each being any single character. (If the delimiters are numbers, the text must not begin with a comma.)

If the string in the operand consists of more than one character, the ASCII codes corresponding to the successive characters are entered into successive bytes of memory.

An "FCC" directive may be written with a label.

Examples of valid "FCC" directives:

Location	Data	Label	Operator	Operand
0A00	54	MSG1	FCC	TEXT
0A01	45			
0A02	58			
0A03	54			
0A04	54	MSG1	FCC	9,TEXT
0A05	45			
0A06	58			
0A07	54			
0A08	20			
0A09	20			
0A0A	20			
0A0B	20			
0A0C	20			

TABLE 7-1.1-1 Assembler Directives (Sheet 2 of 6)

FDB — Form Double Constant Byte

The "FDB" directive may have one or more operands separated by commas. The 1-bit unsigned binary number, corresponding to the value of each operand is stored in two bytes of the object program. If there is more than one operand, they are stored in successive bytes. The operand field may contain the actual value (decimal, hexadecimal, octal or binary) or be a symbol or an expression which can be assigned a numerical value by the assembler. An "FDB" directive followed by one or more void operands separated by commas will store zeros for the void operands.

An "FDB" directive may be written with a label.

Examples of valid "FDB" directives:

Location	Data	Label	Operator	Operand
0010	0002	TWO	FDB	2
0012	0000	MASK	FDB	,$F,$EF,,$AFF
0014	000F			
0016	00EF			
0018	0000			
001A	0AFF			

MON — Return to Console

The assembler directive "MON", if used, must be in the last statement of a source program. (See assembler directive "END" above.) The "MON" directive instructs the assembler that the source program just completed is the last to be assembled, and will return control to the user at the keyboard of the terminal by printing the input request "READY".

The last statement of a source program must contain either "END" or "MON". If the last statement of the program has "END" as its operator, the Assembler will request another file upon completion of assembly, by printing:

```
SI FILENAME
?
```

If the user does not wish to assemble another file he may type ".EOF" (i.e. type a period followed by an "END OF FILE" character). The assembler directive "MON" must not be written with a label, and no operand is used.

NAM — Name

The "NAM" (or NAME) directive names the program, or provides the top of page heading text meaningful to users of the assembly. The "NAM" directive must not be written with a label. The "NAM" directive cannot distinguish the operand field from the comment field. Both the operand field and the comment field are treated as continuous text.

TABLE 7-1.1-1 Assembler Directives (Sheet 3 of 6)

OPT — Option

The "OPT" directive is used to give the programmer optional control of the format of assembler output. The "OPT" directive is not translated into machine code. No label may be used with the "OPT" directive. The options are written in the operand field following the directive, and are separated by commas.

The available options are:

Long Form	Short Form	
LIST	L	Selects listing of the assembly in long format (selected by default).
SLIST	SLIS	Selects listing of the assembly in an abbreviated form.
NOLIST	NOL NL	Suppresses the printing of the assembly listing.
SYMBOL	SYMB S	Causes the symbol table to be printed (selected by default).
NOSYMBOL	NOSYMB NOS NS	Suppresses the printing of the symbol table.
GENERATE	GENE G	Causes full printing of all code generated by FCC directive (selected by default).
NOGENERATE	NOGENE NGENE NOG NG	Causes only one line of listing to be generated by FCC directive.
ERROR	E	Selects printing of error messages in long format (selected by default).
SERROR	SER	Selects printing of error messages in an abbreviated form.
NOERROR	NERROR NOE NE	Suppresses the printing of error messages.
PAGE		Causes the listing to be page formatted and to have a heading on each page (selected by default).
NOPAGE	NPAGE	Causes the listing to be continuous without page formatting.
TAB	T	Causes horizontal formatting of the listing (selected by default).
NOTAB	NOT NT	Suppresses horizontal formatting of the listing.

TABLE 7-1.1-1 Assembler Directives (Sheet 4 of 6)

DB8		Octal display base.
DB10		Decimal display base
DB16		Hexadecimal display base (selected by default).
MEM	M	Instructs the assembler to save the object program in a permanent file.
NOMEM	NOM NM	Assembler does not save the object program (selected by default).

ORG — Origin

The assembler directive "ORG" defines the numerical address of the first byte of machine code which results from the assembly of the immediately subsequent section of a source program. There may be any number of "ORG" statements in a program. The "ORG" directive sets the program counter to the value expressed in the operand field.

The operand field may contain the actual value (decimal, hexadecimal, octal or binary) to which the program counter is to be set or may contain a symbol or an expression which can be assigned a numerical value by the assembler. The special symbol "*", which represents the program counter must not be used.

The location counter is initialized before each assembly. If no "ORG" statement appears at the beginning of the program, the location counter will begin as if an "ORG" zero had been entered.

Examples of valid "ORG" statements:

	Location	Data	Label	Operator	Operand
(1)	0064		(blank)	ORG	100
(2)	AF23		(blank)	ORG	$AF23
(3)			BEGIN	EQU	$1100
	1100		(BLANK)	ORG	BEGIN

PAGE —Advance Paper to Top of Next Page

The "PAGE" directive causes the Assembler to advance the paper to the top of the next page. The PAGE directive does not appear on the program listing. No label or operand is used, and no machine code results.

RMB —Reserve Memory Bytes

The "RMB" directive causes the location counter to be increased by the value of the operand field. This reserves a block of memory whose length is equal to the value of the operand field. The operand field may contain the actual number (decimal, hexadecimal, octal or binary) equal to the number of

TABLE 7-1.1-1 Assembler Directives (Sheet 5 of 6)

bytes to be reserved or may be a symbol or an expression which can be assigned a numerical value by the assembler.

The block of memory which is reserved by the "RMB" directive is unchanged by that directive.

The "RMB" directive may be written with a lable.

Examples of valid "RMB" directives follow:

Location	Data	Label	Operator	Operand
0100	00		RMB	4
0104	00	TABLE 1	RMB	20
0118	00	TABLE 2	RMB	20

SPC — Space Lines

The "SPC" directive provides vertical spaces for formatting the program listing. It does not itself appear in the listing. The number of lines to be left blank is stated by an operand in the operand field.

The operand would normally contain the actual number (decimal, hexadecimal, octal or binary) equal to the number of lines to be left blank. A symbol or an expression is also allowed but must be assigned a numerical value during assembly by means of an EQU statement.

TABLE 7-1.1-1 Assembler Directives (Sheet 6 of 6)

ASCII CHARACTER SET (7-BIT CODE)								
M.S. CHAR L.S. CHAR	0 000	1 001	2 010	3 011	4 100	5 101	6 110	7 111
0 0000	NUL	DLE	SP	0	@	P	'	p
1 0001	SOH	DC1	1	1	A	Q	a	g
2 0010	STX	DC2	"	2	B	R	b	r
3 0011	ETX	DC3	#	3	C	S	c	s
4 0100	EOT	DC4	$	4	D	T	d	t
5 0101	ENQ	NAK	%	5	E	U	e	u
6 0110	ACK	SYN	&	6	F	V	f	v
7 0111	BEL	ETB	'	7	G	W	g	w
8 1000	BS	CAN	(	8	H	X	h	x
9 1001	HT	EM	)	9	I	Y	i	y
A 1010	LF	SUB	*	:	J	Z	j	z
B 1011	VT	ESC	+	;	K	[	k	{
C 1100	FF	FS	,	<	L	\	l	:
D 1101	CR	GS	−	=	M	]	m	}
E 1110	SO	RS	●	>	N	↑	n	~
F 1111	SI	VS	/	?	O	↓	o	DEL

TABLE 7-1.1-2 ASCII Code

7-1.1.1 Line Numbers

When preparing a source program for entry via a timesharing terminal, each source statement is normally assigned a line number. The line number is followed by a SPACE and the character position immediately following that SPACE is then the first character position of the source statement. The line numbers are usually assigned in multiples of a base so that additional statements can be inserted later, if necessary. For example, numbering as 1, 5, 10, 15, 20, etc., leaves room for 4 statements to be added between each of the original statements.

7-1.1.2 Field of the Source Statement

Each statement in the source program may have from one to four fields: a label, a mnemonic operator (instruction), an operand, and a comment. Each statement must have at least the mnemonic operator field. An operand may or may not be required, depending on the nature of the instruction. The comment field is optional at the programmer's convenience for describing and documenting the program.

The successive fields in a statement are normally separated by one or more spaces. An exception to this rule occurs for instructions that use dual addressing in the operand field and for instructions that must distinguish between the two accumulators. In these cases, A and B are "operands" but the space between them and the operator may be omitted. This is commonly done, resulting in apparent four character mnemonics for those instructions.

If the statement includes a label, it must begin in the first character position of the statement field. A SPACE in the first position will indicate that no label is included with the statement. Note that if line numbers are being used, there must be two or more spaces between the number and the operator when labels are not used.

7-1.1.3 Labels

Labels may be up to six characters long and use any alphanumeric combination of the character set with the restriction that the first character be alphabetic. Three single character labels, A, B, and X, are reserved for referring to accumulator A, accumulator B, and the Index Register, respectively. In general, labels may correspond to either numerical values or memory locations. The use of symbolic references to memory permits initial programming to be done without using specific absolute memory locations.

Labels are required for source statements that are the destination of jump and branch instructions. (Such an instruction would have the same label as its operand.) Labels may be used with any executable instruction at the option of the programmer.

A label is normally used with the assembly directives FCB, FCC, FDB, and RMB. A label must be used with the directive EQU and will be equated to the symbol which the EQU statement is defining. Labels must not be used with the other assembler directives. See Table 7-1.1-1 for examples.

7-1.1.4 Operands

The operand field can contain numerical values, labels, or algebraic expressions that can be evaluated by the Assembler. Such expressions can include the arithmetic operators + (addition), − (subtraction), * (multiplication), or / (division).

The assembler evaluates expressions algebraically from left to right without parenthetical grouping, with no heirarchy of precedence among the arithmetic operators. A fractional result, or intermediate result, if obtained during the evaluation of an expression, will be truncated to an integer value. The use of expressions in the source language does not imply any capability of the microprocessor to evaluate those expressions, since the expressions are evaluated during assembly and not during execution of the machine language program.

7-1.1.5 Comments

Comments for improving understanding of the program can be included in source statements by inserting a SPACE and then the comment after the operand. If the instruction does not require an operand, everything following the insertion of one or more SPACEs after the operator will be treated as a comment.

Additional documentation information will appear on the assembler generated program listing if an asterisk is used in the first character position of a statement. Everything following the asterisk is then converted into a comment and does not affect the machine language generated by the assembler.

7-1.2 ACCESSING A TIMESHARE SERVICE

As indicated earlier, the details of accessing vary from service to service, however, the following example based on the G.E. system serves to illustrate the procedure. It is assumed that a series of source statements have been prepared and are to be entered into the host computer in preparation for assembly.

(1) Dial the telephone number assigned for computer access.

(2) When the network responds, enter HHHH on the keyboard so that the terminal's speed can be determined.

(3) In each case, conclude entries with a carriage return. The computer acknowledges entries by providing a line feed.

(4) Enter user number and password.

(5) If the computer requests additional identification, a code may be entered for additional protection of the program. If this is unnecessary, enter a carriage return to bypass.

(6) Identify the system language that will be used by the Assembler. The Motorola Cross-Assembler language is identified by entering: FIV.

(7) When the computer acknowledges a command, rather than merely the entry of information, it responds with the word ''READY'' in addition to the usual line feed.

(8) After identifying the system, the user must specify whether an old or new file is to be used. Therefore, the user must enter: OLD:xxxxxx where xxxxxx represents the name of the old file that is to be changed, or NEW:xxxxxx where xxxxxx is the name of the new program.

(9) After the computer has responded ''READY'', the source statements may be entered, line by line.

(10) The computer must be told to make a permanent record of the entires. This is done by giving

the command: SAVE. If this is not done, the computer will not recognize the name of the old file if called for later; the program will have to be entered again.

(11) When the source program is ready to be assembled, the Assembler is called by entering: RUN MPCASM

(12) If an assembled program is to be simulated, the Simulator may be called by entering: RUN MPSSIM

(13) If the user wants to change the memory file form, address range, or name of the assembled program or to link it to another memory file, the Build Virtual Machine program may be called by entering: RUN MPBVM

(14) Build Virtual Machine can also be used to punch out a tape of the assembled program for entering the EXORciser or to order ROM from Motorola.

7-1.3   **ENTERING A SOURCE PROGRAM**

Entry of a typical source program is illustrated in Figure 7-1.3-1. It is recommended that the input be "saved" in the host computers permanent files following every few lines of code. This protects against loss due to a system failure. This is shown in the example by the SAVE command entered following the source statement numbered 200. Note that the command REP (replace) is used to "save" subsequent statements. This is a characteristic of the G.E. system.

Figure 7-1.3-2 shows the results of listing a previously entered program. It is assumed that the system is accessed at a later time after AAA was entered. Note that the file OLD AAA is called, i.e., AAA is now an "old" file.

```
NEW AAA

READY
SYS FIV

READY
100   NAM ITEM2
110   OPT MEM
120   * ADDITION OF TWO MULTIPLE-PRECISION
130   * BINARY-CODED-DECIMAL NUMBERS.
140   *
150 NB EQU 8      SPECIFIES 8-BYTE OPERANDS.
160   *
170   * BEGIN SUBROUTINE.
180   ORG $1000
190 BCD LDA B #NB
200   LDX ADDR   LOADS DATA ADDRESS.
SAVE
READY
210   CLC
220 NEXT LDA A NB-1,X   START LOOP
230   ADC A 2*NB-1,X
240   DAA
250   STA A 2*NB-1,X
260   DEX
270   DEC B
280   BNE NEXT   END OF LOOP
290   RTS        END OF BCD SUBROUTINE.
300   *
REP

READY
310   *
320   * BEGIN MAIN PROGRAM......
330   * TEST OF SUBROUTINE BCD.
340   ORG $1100
350   LDS #$13F   INITIALIZE STCK PNTR.
360   LDX #P      LOADS ADDRESS OF P.
370   STX ADDR
380   JSR BCD
390   NOP
400   BRA *-1     END OF MAIN PROGRAM.
REP

READY
410   *
420   *
430   * ALLOCATE A DATA AREA IN
440   * READ-WRITE MEMORY.
450   ORG $0100
460   * (1) FOR THE SUBROUTINE.
470 ADDR RMB 2
480   * (2) FOR THE MAIN PROGRAM.
490 P RMB NB
500 Q RMB NB
510 RES RMB NB
520   END
530   MON
REP

READY       NOTE: System Commands Entered by User are Underlined.
```

FIGURE 7-1.3-1: Entering the Source Program "AAA"

READY
LIST

AAA   18:10EST   01/24/75

```
100  NAM ITEM2
110  OPT MEM
120  * ADDITION OF TWO MULTIPLE-PRECISION
130  * BINARY-CODED-DECIMAL NUMBERS.
140  *
150 NB EQU 8       SPECIFIES 8-BYTE OPERANDS.
160  *
170  * BEGIN SUBROUTINE.
180  ORG $1000
190 BCD LDA B #NB
200  LDX ADDR    LOADS DATA ADDRESS.
210  CLC
220 NEXT LDA A NB-1,X   START LOOP
230  ADC A 2*NB-1,X
240  DAA
250  STA A 3*NB-1,X
260  DEX
270  DEC B
280  BNE NEXT  END OF LOOP
290  RTS         END OF BCD SUBROUTINE.
300  *
310  *
320  * BEGIN MAIN PROGRAM......
330  * TEST OF SUBROUTINE BCD.
340  ORG $1100
350  LDS #$13F    INITIALIZE STCK PNTR.
360  LDX #P       LOADS ADDRESS OF P.
370  STX ADDR
380  JSR BCD
390  NOP
400  BRA *-1     END OF MAIN PROGRAM.
410  *
420  *
430  * ALLOCATE A DATA AREA IN
440  * READ-WRITE MEMORY.
450  ORG $0100
460  * (1) FOR THE SUBROUTINE.
470 ADDR RMB 2
480  * (2) FOR THE MAIN PROGRAM.
490 P RMB NB
500 Q RMB NB
510 RES RMB NB
520  END
530  MON
```

NOTE: System Commands Entered by User are Underlined.

FIGURE 7-1.3-2: Listing of the Source Program "AAA"

7-1.4 ASSEMBLING A SOURCE PROGRAM

Prior to assembly, a source program must have been placed in memory accessible to the Assembler (see previous section). When the Assembler is called, it will request that a source input file (SI) be specified. This source input file will be the source program that was previously saved.

If a MEM option was included in the source program, the Assembler will also request that a memory file (MF) be named. At this time, the user must specify a name for the file that is different from the source input file name. The machine language code resulting from the assembly will be stored in that file.

After the assembly is completed, the Assembler prints out a listing of the code that was generated. The OPT (Option) assembly directive may be included in the source program and allows the user to vary the format of the Assembly Listing. If other options are not specified, the Assembler will automatically select the fullest format (see the OPT directive in Table 7-1.1-1 for a list of the options). The long format for a representative line from an Assembly Listing is shown in Figure 7-1.4-1.

A sample Assembly Listing for the program AAA is shown in Figure 7-1.4-2. A number of the characteristics of source statements and the assembly process are illustrated:

(1) Instruction labels: BCD, NEXT.

(2) Assembler directives: NAM, OPT, EQU, ORG, RMB, END.

(3) Assembler directive labels: NB, ADDR, P, Q, RES.

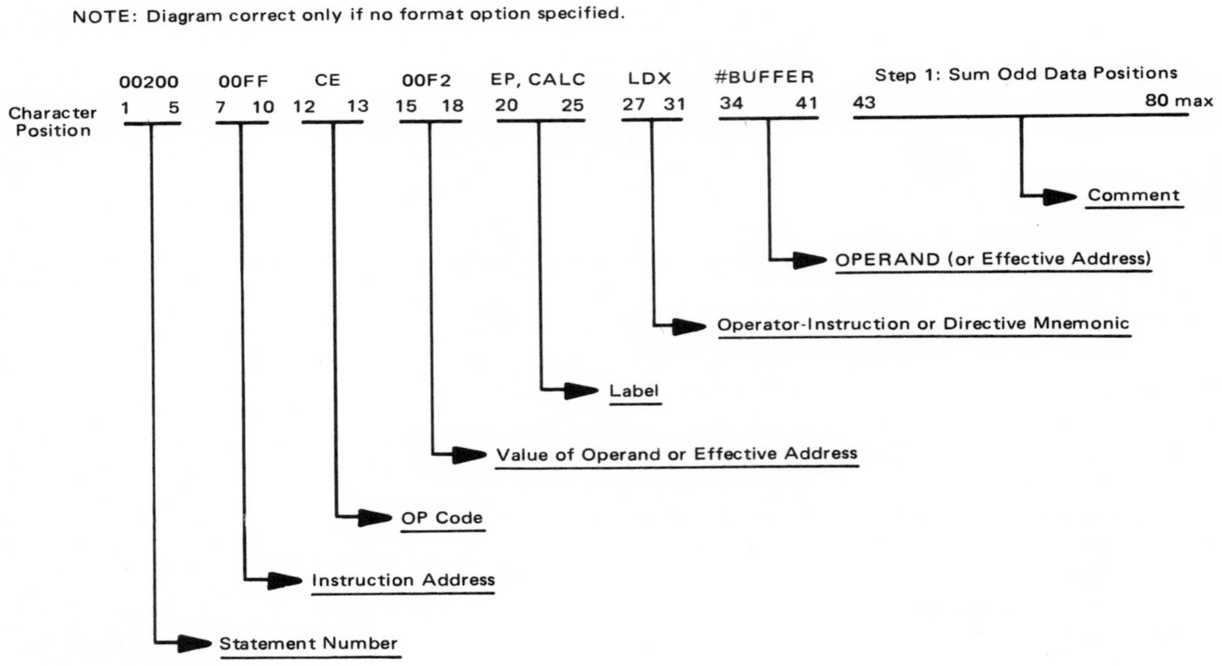

NOTE: Diagram correct only if no format option specified.

FIGURE 7-1.4-1: Fields of Assembly Listing

MPCASM   15:19EST   01/24/75

MOTOROLA SPD, INC. OWNS AND IS RESPONSIBLE FOR MPCASM
        COPYRIGHT 1973 & 1974 BY MOTOROLA INC

      MOTOROLA MPU CROSS ASSEMBLER, RELEASE 1.2

    ENTER SI FILENAME
?AAA

    ENTER MF FILENAME
?DEF456

DEFAULT MACHINE FILE 06/20/74.

    PAGE 1 ITEM2 01/24/75 15:19.00


```
00100                        NAM     ITEM2
00110                        OPT     MEM
00120               ◆ ADDITION OF TWO MULTIPLE-PRECISION
00130               ◆ BINARY-CODED-DECIMAL NUMBERS.
00140               ◆
00150       0008    NB     EQU     8            SPECIFIES 8-BYTE OPERANDS.
00160               ◆
00170               ◆ BEGIN SUBROUTINE.
00180 1000                   ORG     $1000
00190 1000 C6 08    BCD     LDA B   #NB
00200 1002 FE 0100          LDX     ADDR        LOADS DATA ADDRESS.
00210 1005 0C              CLC
00220 1006 A6 07    NEXT    LDA A   NB-1,X      START LOOP
00230 1008 A9 0F            ADC A   2◆NB-1,X
00240 100A 19              DAA
00250 100B A7 17            STA A   3◆NB-1,X
00260 100D 09              DEX
00270 100E 5A              DEC B
00280 100F 26 F5            BNE     NEXT        END OF LOOP
00290 1011 39              RTS                 END OF BCD SUBROUTINE.
```

NOTE: System Commands Entered by User are Underlined.

FIGURE 7-1.4-2: Assembly Listing for Sample Program "AAA" (Sheet 1 of 2)

```
00300            ◆
00310            ◆
00320            ◆  BEGIN MAIN PROGRAM......
00330            ◆  TEST OF SUBROUTINE BCD.
00340 1100              ORG    $1100
00350 1100 8E 013F      LDS    #$13F       INITIALIZE STCK PNTR.
00360 1103 CE 0102      LDX    #P          LOADS ADDRESS OF P.
00370 1106 FF 0100      STX    ADDR
00380 1109 BD 1000      JSR    BCD
00390 110C 02           NOP
00400 110D 20 FD        BRA    ◆-1         END OF MAIN PROGRAM.
00410            ◆
00420            ◆
00430            ◆  ALLOCATE A DATA AREA IN
00440            ◆  READ-WRITE MEMORY.
00450 0100              ORG    $0100
00460            ◆  (1) FOR THE SUBROUTINE.
00470 0100 0002  ADDR   RMB    2
00480            ◆  (2) FOR THE MAIN PROGRAM.
00490 0102 0008  P      RMB    NB
00500 010A 0008  Q      RMB    NB
00510 0112 0008  RES    RMB    NB
00520                   END
```

SYMBOL TABLE

```
NB    0008  BCD   1000  NEXT  1006  ADDR   0100  P      0102
Q     010A  RES   0112
```

PROGRAM STOP AT 0

USED   20.72 UNITS

FIGURE 7-1.4-2: Assembly Listing for Sample Program "AAA" (Sheet 2 of 2)

(4) Comments in comment field and also on lines where an asterisk appeared in the first character position of the source program.

(5) Instructions without labels, on lines in the source program where two spaces separated the line number and operation mnemonic.

(6) Operands consisting of an expression to be evaluated by the Assembler: NB-1, 2* NB-1, 3* NB-1, *-1.

(7) Operands indicating immediate addressing: #NB, #$13F, #P, so that NB, which is equal to 8, is loaded into accumulator B (line 190), $13F, a hexadecimal number, is loaded into the stack pointer register (line 350), and the address labeled P, rather than its contents, is loaded into the Index (X) register (line 360).

During the assembly of the source file, the Assembler may detect inconsistencies or deletions in the usage of some symbols, labels, operation codes or directives that prevent it from continuing. Errors of this type are printed out on the terminal, and it is up to the user to correct the referenced source statement before attempting to reassemble. Other errors may be detected by the Assembler, such as undefined or doubly defined symbols, out-of-range relative addressing or syntax that do not prevent the Assembler from continuing but cause an incorrect assembly. These errors are identified at the end of the incorrect assembly. A list of typical error messages that might be printed out are shown in Table 7-1.4-1. If an error message not included in the list should be encountered, the user can obtain additional information from the HELP program (see Section 7-1.6).

There are many additional errors that the Assembler cannot recognize, and the Assembly Listing must be checked carefully to see that the addresses, operations and data that have been assembled are accessible or executable and that the program can run to completion. For instance, note that in the sample program AAA (Figure 7-1.4-2), the operand of the instruction on Line 400 is: *-1. This is one of the three uses of the asterisk, and, in this case, refers to the present value of the program counter. BRA *-1 is an instruction to branch to one less than the present value of the program counter which causes the program to continue execution at the preceding instruction located at 110C. Note that this instruction is a NOP and has no effect other than advancing the program to the next instruction. During an examination of the Assembly Listing or during Simulation, it would be seen that this is not a very useful pair of instructions; the program would hang up, continuously repeating these two instructions.

It should be noted that an error-free assembly does not mean the program will perform the desired function. A good assembly means only that the language of the M6800 system has been used properly. Significant programs will usually still require some additional debugging.

7-1.5   SIMULATION

The M6800 Simulator is a special program that simulates the logical operation of the MC6800 Microprocessor. It is designed to execute object programs generated by the M6800 Cross-Assembler and is useful for checking and debugging assembled programs prior to committing them to ROM "firmware".

7-1.5.1   Simulator Commands

The Simulator is normally controlled[1] by means of an interactive conversation with the operator via

---

[1]It is also possible to simulate programs in a batch-processing mode. Refer to the M6800 Programming Manual for details.

0201

    201   NAM DIRECTIVE ERROR
           MESSAGE: ****ERROR 201
           MEANING: THE SOURCE PROGRAM DOES NOT START WITH A NAM DIR-
                    ECTIVE STATEMENT OR THE NAM DIRECTIVE IS MISSING.

0202

    202   LABEL OR OPCODE ERROR
           MESSAGE: ****ERROR 202
           MEANING: THE LABEL OR OPCODE SYMBOL DOES NOT BEGIN WITH AN
                    ALPHABETIC CHARACTER.

0203

    203   STATEMENT ERROR
           MESSAGE: ****ERROR 203
           MEANING: THE STATEMENT IS BLANK OR ONLY CONTAINS A LABEL.

0204

    204   SYNTAX ERROR
           MESSAGE: ****ERROR 204
           MEANING: THE STATEMENT IS SYNTACTICALLY INCORRECT.

0205

    205   LABEL ERROR
           MESSAGE: ****ERROR 205
           MEANING: THE STATEMENT LABEL DOES NOT END WITH A SPACE.

0206

    206   REDEFINED SYMBOL
           MESSAGE: ****ERROR 206
           MEANING: THE SYMBOL HAS PREVIOUSLY BEEN DEFINED.

0207

    207   UNDEFINED OPCODE
           MESSAGE: ****ERROR 207
           MEANING: THE SYMBOL IN THE OPCODE FIELD IS NOT A VALID
                    OPCODE MNEMONIC OR DIRECTIVE.

0208

    208   BRANCH ERROR
           MESSAGE: ****ERROR 208
           MEANING: THE BRANCH COUNT IS BEYOND THE RELATIVE BYTE'S
                    RANGE. THE ALLOWABLE RANGE IS:

$$(*+2) - 128 < D < (*+2) + 128$$

                      WHERE: * = ADDRESS OF THE FIRST BYTE OF THE
                                BRANCH INSTRUCTION
                          D = ADDRESS OF THE DESTINATION OF THE
                                  BRANCH INSTRUCTION.

TABLE 7-1.4-1. Assembler Error Messages (Sheet 1 of 3)

0209

209   ILLEGAL ADDRESS MODE
      MESSAGE: ****ERROR 209
      MEANING: THE MODE OF ADDRESSING IS NOT ALLOWED WITH THE OP-
               CODE TYPE.

0210

210   BYTE OVERFLOW
      MESSAGE: ****ERROR 210
      MEANING: A CONSTANT CONVERTED TO A VALUE GREATER THAN 255
               (DECIMAL).

0211

211   UNDEFINED SYMBOL
      MESSAGE: ****ERROR 211
      MEANING: THE SYMBOL DOES NOT APPEAR IN A LABEL FIELD.

0212

212   DIRECTIVE OPERAND ERROR
      MESSAGE: ****ERROR 212
      MEANING: SYNTAX ERROR IN THE OPERAND FIELD OF A DIRECTIVE.

0213

213   EQU DIRECTIVE SYNTAX ERROR
      MESSAGE: ****ERROR 213
      MEANING: THE STRUCTURE OF THE EQU DIRECTIVE IS SYNTACTI-
               CALLY INCORRECT OR IT HAS NO LABEL.

0214

214   FCB DIRECTIVE SYNTAX ERROR
      MESSAGE: ****ERROR 214
      MEANING: THE STRUCTURE OF THE FCB DIRECTIVE IS SYNTACTI-
               CALLY INCORRECT.

0215

215   FDB DIRECTIVE SYNTAX ERROR
      MESSAGE: ****ERROR 215
      MEANING: THE STRUCTURE OF THE FDB DIRECTIVE IS SYNTACTI-
               CALLY INCORRECT.

0216

216   DIRECTIVE OPERAND ERROR
      MESSAGE: ****ERROR 216
      MEANING: THE DIRECTIVE'S OPERAND FIELD IS IN ERROR.

0217

217   OPT DIRECTIVE ERROR
      MESSAGE: ****ERROR 217
      MEANING: THE STRUCTURE OF THE OPT DIRECTIVE IS SYNTACTIC-
               ALLY INCORRECT OR THE OPTION IS UNDEFINED.

TABLE 7-1.4-1. Assembler Error Messages (Sheet 2 of 3)

0218

    218   ADDRESSING ERROR
         MESSAGE: ****ERROR 218
         MEANING: AN ADDRESS WAS GENERATED WHICH LIES OUTSIDE THE
                    LEGAL MEMORY BOUNDS OF THE VIRTUAL MACHINE FILE.
                    TO EXTEND THE LAST ADDRESS (LWA) OF THE MACHINE
                    (MF FILE); RUN THE MPBVM PROGRAM. ENTER "LW LWA"
                    WHERE LWA IS THE NEW LAST WORD ADDRESS. THE
                    SYSTEM WILL PROMPT THE USER FOR THE NAME OF THE
                    MF FILE.

0220

    220   PHASING ERROR
         MESSAGE: ****ERROR 220
         MEANING: THE VALUE OF THE P COUNTER DURING PASS 1 AND
                    PASS 2 FOR THE SAME INSTRUCTION IS DIFFERENT.

0221

    221 - SYMBOL TABLE OVERFLOW
         MESSAGE: ****ERROR 221
         MEANING: THE SYMBOL TABLE HAS OVERFLOWED. THE NEW SYMBOL
                    WAS NOT STORED AND ALL REFERENCES TO IT WILL BE
                    FLAGGED AS AN ERROR.

0222

    222 - SYNTAX ERROR IN THE SYMBOL
         MESSAGE: ****ERROR 222
         MEANING: THE SYMBOL WHICH USED AN OPERAND WAS REDEFINED OR
                    HAS AN ERROR IN IT'S DEFINITION. THIS ERROR IS ONLY
                    USED TO SHOW WHERE THE SYMBOL WAS USED.

0223

    223 - THE DIRECTIVE CANNOT HAVE A LABEL
         MESSAGE: ****ERROR 223
          MEANING: THE DIRECTIVE CANNOT BE LABELED. REMOVE THE LABEL.

0224

    224 - ERROR IN USING THE OPTION DIRECTIVES OTAPE OR MEMORY
         MESSAGE: ****ERROR 224 XXXXX
         MEANING: THE OTAPE=FILENAME OR MEMORY=FILENAME IS NOT THE
                    FILENAME USED ON THE 1ST OCCURRENCE OF THE OPTION.
                    OR THE OPTION WAS TURN OFF (NOMEMORY) AND A FILE-
                    NAME WAS SPECIFIED.

TABLE 7-1.4-1. Assembler Error Messages (Sheet 3 of 3)

a timesharing terminal. Simulator requests for input may be responded to using any of the following typical commands:

1. Format Control for Commands and Print-Out

IB2   Set input number base to BINARY

IB8   Set input number base to OCTAL

IB10   Set input number base to DECIMAL

IB16   Set input number base to HEXADECIMAL

These commands are used to set the format control of the Simulator to the number base of the user. Thereafter, the user enters commands with this base. There is a choice of binary (IB2), octal (IB8), decimal (IB10), or hexadecimal (IB16).

DB8   Set display number base to OCTAL.

DB10   Set display number base to DECIMAL.

DB16   Set display number base to HEXADECIMAL.

Notes: (i) The format of the above commands is invariable, and does not depend on the current input number display base.

(ii) The display base command does not apply to the display of the number of cycles of execution time, which is always shown as a 7-digit decimal number.

These commands select the number base that the simulator will use when it prints out information for the user. There is a choice of octal (DB8), decimal (DB10), or hexadecimal (DB16). The one exception is the print out of execution time cycles, which is always displayed in decimal.

SD   IOEPXABCST

This command selects the registers that will be displayed by the D command. It does not cause them to be displayed. The user may select any or all of the following ten:

IA — instruction address
OC — Operation mnemonic code
EA — effective address
P — program counter
X — index register
A — accumulator A
B — accumulator B
C — condition codes
S — stack pointer
T — time

IA can also be addressed as I, OC as O, and EA as E as in the command format line above. The contents of all these registers are printed out by the Simulator as initial status when the name of the memory file is entered. In addition, the first item of the initial status display is a two letter code which informs the user of the input and display base being used. This code consists of the letters, H (hexadecimal), D (decimal), O (octal), and B (binary). Binary can be used as an input base, but not as a display base. The first letter is the input base and the second is the display base.

Initial status display:

HH	IA	OC	EA	P	X	A	B	C	S	T
0000	***	0000*	0000	0000	00	00	000000	0000	0000000

In the above example, HH means that both the input and display base are hexadecimal.

HRn

This command causes the Simulator Register Header to be displayed, at intervals of n lines of print. The header has the same appearance as in the initial status display.

LM

List each command before it is executed. Useful as a check and reminder after a string of commands has been entered.

NOLM

To not list command before execution. Normally used sometime after an LM command has been entered when the echo listing is no longer desired.

2. Set Values

SM s,n_0,n_1,n_2, ...,n_m

Set memory location s to n_0, s + 1 to n_1, s + 2 to n_2, ..., s + m to n_m.

This command is used to load specified data into selected memory addresses. By altering the machine code stored in particular addresses, the program instructions can be changed or modified to improve the program. The contents of the selected memory addresses can be checked with the Display Memory (DM) command. SM requires only the lowest memory address in a continuous sequence. Each data value specified is automatically placed in the next higher address. These data values are separated by commas.

SR Pn_1,Xn_2,An_3,Bn_4,Cn_5,Sn_6

Set registers to the respective values represented by n_1, n_2, . . ., n_6. Register codes may be in any order and only the registers to be changed need be entered.

This command is used to load specified data into selected registers. It can also be used to move the Simulator around in the program by resetting the program counter to a different instruction and then doing a Trace or Run. After using the Set Register (SR) command, the contents of those registers can be checked by using the Display D, command.

3. Display Values

DM s,n

> Display memory starting at the memory location s and displaying n locations. Numerical values will be displayed in the display number base selected by the DB command. The numerical values are followed by ASCII literal interpretations of the 7-bit codes from hexadecimal value 20 through 5F.

> The DM command displays up to sixteen memory locations per line of print. This is shown by the following example, for which the input and display bases had been set previously to hexadecimal (by simulator commands IB16 and DB16):

?SM 18F0,00,11,22,33,44,55,66,77,88,99,0AA,0BB,0CC,0DD,0EE,0FF

?DM 18F0, 10

18F0 00 11 22 33 44 55 66 77 88 99 AA BB CC DD EE FF . . ''3DU. . . . .

> Each line of memory display shows the numerical address of the first memory location being displayed. This is followed by the numerical coding of the specified number of successive memory locations. The numerical codes are followed by their corresponding ASCII literal interpretations. For the ASCII literals, only bit positions 0 through 6 are considered, bit No. 7 being ignored. Literals corresponding to seven bit codes 20 through 5F are printed, all others are indicated by a period (.). As an example, note that the contents of the first two locations, 00 and 11, are less than 20 and, hence, cause periods to be printed instead of ASCII literals. The last 10 locations contain values greater than 5F and also display as periods.

D

> Display the registers selected with the SD command. Numerical values will be displayed in the display number base selected by the DB command.

DL

> Display the last instruction previously executed.

4. Program Execution

Tn

> Trace n instructions, printing the selected registers after each instruction is executed.

Rn

> Run n instructions without printing, and then print the selected registers.

> The trace command traces the execution of successive instructions of the program. The format of the trace is identical with that of the second line of the display of initial status, as described above. The run command (Rn) also results in a printed line in the same format, but this is printed after execution of the specified number of instructions.

The trace may also include register header lines, in the form described earlier. The frequency of appearance of the register header line in the trace depends on the value set in by the Display Register Header command (HRn).

The user may command either Trace mode or Run mode. The trace mode (T) is selected for a number (n) of instructions specified by the user. The n instructions are then executed, and the simulator displays the contents of selected registers after the execution of each instruction. The trace is capable of showing the current status of all of the registers of the programming model, the address and coding of the current instruction, the source language mnemonic operator corresponding to the instruction, and the total time of execution in cycles.

The user has complete control of the content of the trace and by using a simulator command (SD) is able to set the display so as to eliminate unwanted elements.

The Run mode (R), like the Trace, is selected for a number (n) of instructions specified by the user. The successive instructions are executed without display by the simulator until n instructions have been executed. The nth instruction is then displayed in the same format as for the trace.

5. Repetition

RCn

Execute the next command n times. If the command RCn is the last command in a line, the command which will be repeated is the first command in the next command line.

A typical application could be for increment or decrement instructions which are part of a counter subroutine. Repeating the instruction advances the counter.

RLn

Execute the remaining portion of the command line (to the right of the RLn command) n times. If the command RLn is the last command in a line, it will have no effect. The RLn command must not be included in the definition of a MACRO command.

6. Memory File Status

SS

Save the simulator status in the memory file. All register settings and selected options are saved. The MACRO library and current MPU memory pages are not saved. Useful for terminating an incomplete simulation that will be resumed later.

RS

Restores status saved by SS command. The saved status is transferred from the memory file back into the Simulator registers.

EX

Exit from the simulator after saving the status as for the SS command, and also saving the MACRO library, and all of memory including the current memory pages. Informs host computer that present usage of Simulator is complete.

Numerical Substitution in the Commands

Where applicable, n, n0, n1, n2, ... , nm, and s are replaced by numbers when entering a simulator command. The number so substituted will be interpreted as octal, decimal, or hexadecimal, according to the input base set previously by a command IB2, IB8, IB10, or IB16.

Hexadecimal Input

When entering a hexadecimal number in a simulator command, the hexadecimal number must begin with a digit from 0 to 9. If the hexadecimal number would otherwise begin with A, B, C, D, E or F, a leading zero must be used.

7-1.5.2 Operating the Simulator

After the host computer has been accessed as described in Section 7-1.2 (for the G.E. system), the Simulator is called by the command RUN MPSSIM followed by a carriage return. Once accessed, the Simulator will request a source input file. The user responds with the name of the desired memory file as assigned during assembly of the original source program. The Simulator extracts control information, the source language, and the machine code from the memory file. It then prints out the initial status of the microprocessor registers and then requests a command by typing a question mark on the next line. Thereafter, each time the Simulator prints a question mark, the user may respond by entering a Simulator command, a Macro command, or a string of commands and/or Macros. A Macro (see Section 7-1.5.3) is itself a string of Simulator commands which are performed in the order entered each time the Macro name is entered. Any portion of a program may be simulated by setting the P (program) register to the address of the first instruction and using the Trace or RUN commands to cause the Simulator to advance through the program.

If a single command is being entered, it is followed by typing a carriage return to put the command into effect. More than one simulator command may be entered in reply to a simulator request. The multiple commands are entered on a single line with a period (.) typed between the commands as a separator. The string of commands is followed by a carriage return which puts the commands into effect in serial order from left to right. The string of commands entered in a single line must not exceed 70 characters. The simulator will accept minor variations of format in the entering of commands such as extra spaces inserted in a string of commands in some instances.

The use of some of the Simulator commands is illustrated in the following examples:

Example I:

Assume that the user wishes to have the simulator perform as follows:

1. Save the simulator status in the memory file.

2. Set the display registers so as to display the program counter, and the accumulators A and B.

3, Display the registers as selected at (2).

4. Trace five instructions.

The commands to carry out this sequence may be entered on a single line, in response to a simulator command request, as follows:

? SS.SD PAB.D.T5

Example II:

Assume that a one line command is to be entered to do the following:

1. Set the program counter to hexadecimal 1000, and register A to hexadecimal value A0.
2. Set four memory locations, beginning at hexadecimal address 5000, to the hexadecimal values 12, 34, CD, and EF.
3. Display the four memory locations set by the instruction (2).
4. Display the registers as previously selected.
5. Trace sixteen instructions.

Assuming that the input base (IB) has been set to hexadecimal, the commands required for the above sequence may be entered on a single line as follows:

? SR P1000, A0A0.SM5000, 12,34,0CD,0EF.DM5000,4.D.T10

In this example, there are some formatting details that should be noted:

(1) After the SR command, there is a space preceding the first designated register.

(2) There is no space between the register designation and the data value to be entered.

(3) The designated register and its data value is separated by a comma from the next one.

(4) When the data value is a hexadecimal digit greater than 9, a zero must precede it. (Data value 0A0 into the A register, Data value 0EF into memory address 5003)

(5) SM requires only the lowest memory address in a continuous sequence. Each data value specified is automatically placed in the next highest address. These data values are separated by commas.

(6) DM requires the number of memory addresses to be specified.

(D refers to the registers previously designated on the same line (P and A).

7-1.5.3   Macro Commands

Macros are special user defined commands that cause the Simulator to carry out a string of normal commands. By carefully defining a few macros that include all the repetitious commands, the time and effort of reentering those commands each time they are required is saved. Instead, only the Macro is entered. The Macros, once defined, can be saved in a Macro Library in memory for recall during later similar simulations.

Naming a MACRO Command

A Macro command may be named and defined in reply to any of the simulator command requests (after the initial status display). The format for naming and defining a MACRO is as follows:

? Name [Definition]

The name may consist of from 1 to 4 alphabetic characters. The definition of the Macro command is enclosed in brackets, following the name.

(Any combination of 1 to 4 letters may be used for the name even if it is identical with one of the simulator commands. However, in such a case, the Macro takes precedence, so that the simulator command which it displaces cannot then be used except within the definition of a Macro.)

The simplest type of Macro command consists of a series of constant simulator commands, which are to be put into effect in the order written. The definition in this case consists of the corresponding string of simulator commands, with a period (.) as a separator.

Calling a Constant Macro Command

A Macro command is put into effect exactly the same as any of the simulator commands. The name of the Macro is typed as if it were a simulator command. The names of one or more Macros may be included in a string of commands entered on a single line, in response to a simulator command request. The Macro names are separated by periods (.) the same as for basic simulator commands. The Macro, or a string of commands including one or more Macros, is put into effect by the carriage return. Examples:

Example I:

Assume that the one-line string of commands shown below is frequently required.
?SS.SD PAB.D.R5

To avoid repetitive typing, the Macro "AB" may be defined by typing the following in replay to a simulator command request:

?AB[SS.SD PAB.D.R5]

The string of commands will be put into effect by calling the Macro AB followed by a carriage return:

? AB

Example II:

To replace the sequence of simulator commands which could be typed:

? SR P1000,A0A0.SM5000,12,34,0CD,0EF

A Macro command, which may be named "CD", could be defined by entering as follows:

? CD[SR P1000,A0A0.SM5000,12,34,0CD,0EF]

Both of these Macros, AB and CD, having once been defined are retained by the Simulator for further usage.

In some cases, the same Macro could be useful if only the memory addresses, registers, data content or trace and run cycles requested by it were different. That is, the Macro command remains constant but the relevant parameters are variable.

There are two ways to do this, called Parameter Substitution, and Text Substitution.

Parameter Substitution

Example 1:

Consider the sequence of simulator commands entered as follows:

? SM5000,0A2.R15.D.DM5000,1

A constant Macro, say "EF", could be defined. This might be entered by:

? EF [SM5000,0A2.R15.D.DM5000,1]

However, this can be replaced by a Macro in which the address and the numerical data can be substituted at the time that the MACRO is called. To do this, the numbers are replaced by symbols, consisting of the pound sign (#) followed by a serial number.

In place of the above constant Macro substitute a Macro with two numerical parameters denoted by #1 and #2. The Macro would be defined by:

? EF[SM#1,#2.R15.D.DM#1,1]

The foregoing Macro with not more than two numerical parameters, may be called, in response to a simulator command request, as follows:

? EF,5000,0A2

The actual values 5000 and A2 are substituted for the parameters represented by #1 and #2. (This format assumes that the input base (IB) has been set to hexadecimal.)

The Macro could also be called in a string of commands, as for example by:

? R20.T5.EF,5000,0A2.T5

Example 2:

Another set of Simulator commands might be:

? SM5000,12,34, 0CD,0EF.R50.D.DM5000,0C

To provide for substitution of all of the numerical content, this could be replaced by a Macro defined by:

? GH[SM#1,#2.R#3.D.DM#1,#4]

It should be noted that there are four substitutable parameters here. In this case, the Text Substitution mode must be used to call the Macro since there are more than two parameters.

Text Substitution Validity

In text substitution, the parameters in the Macro represented by #1, #2, etc., are replaced by specified text when the Macro is called. The text corresponding to each parameter is delineated by the colon (:) and the semi-colon (;) in the calling command.

More generally, the text corresponding to any parameters may be any string comprising alphanumeric symbols, spaces, and commas, subject to the following rule: when every text has been substituted for the corresponding parameter, the result must be identical with a valid constant Macro command, consisting of a sequence of simulator commands separated by periods.

Accordingly, the text substitution mode allows for substituting commands, as well as numerical data, whenever a Macro command containing parameters is called.

For the example Macros, GH and EF defined previously, the Text Substitution call is as follows:

? GH:5000:12,34, 0CD,0EF:50:0C
? EF:5000:0A2

The Macro could also be called in a string of commands, as for example by:

? R20.T5.GH:5000:12,34,0CD,0EF:50:0C;T5

and

? R20.T5.EF:5000:0A2;T5

Text Substitution of Simulator Commands

The general nature of the Text Substitution method requires only that a valid Macro result from the substitution. For this reason, it is also feasible to replace an undefined symbol in the Macro with one or more Simulator commands.

Example:

Consider again the Macro command GH and suppose that the user anticipates that he may need to run or trace variable numbers of instructions between the SM and D commands. A Macro command could be defined by:

? IJ[SM#1,#2.#3.D.DM#1,#4]

The Macro command might be called by entering:

? IJ:5000:12,34,0CD,0EF:R10.T10.R30:0C;T5

The four substitutable parameters are replaced by text, as follows:

#1 — 5000
#2 — 12,34,0CD,0EF
#3 — R10.T10.R30
#4 — 0C

The semi-colon (;) denotes the close of the Macro command.

Restrictions in Defining a Macro Command

The line of typing including the name, brackets, and definition, must not exceed 70 characters.

When substitution of parameters or text takes place, a virtual Macro command is formed. The virtual Macro command must not exceed 70 characters.

A Macro command must not be used within the definition of another Macro command.

The simulator command ''RLn'' must not be included in the definition of a Macro command.

To Delete a Macro Command

To delete one or more previously defined Macro commands named "Nam 1", "Nam 2", respond to any simulator command request in the following format:

? MD,Nam 1,Nam2, . . .,Nam N

For example, to delete previously defined Macro commands named AB,EFG, JKLM, respond as follows:

? MD,AB,EFG,JKLM

Macro Library Commands

MS   Save the current Macro library in the memory file.

MR   Read in the Macro library from the memory file. (Destroys the current library).

ML   List the current Macro library and the number of characters remaining in the library for more Macro storage.

MD,Nam1,Nam2,. . . .,NamN

    Delete the Macro commands named "Nam1", "Nam2". . . . . ."NamN", from the Macro library.

7-1.5.4   Sample Simulated Program

Figure 7-1.5.4-1 illustrates the print out by the Simulator of a sample program (see Section 7-1.4, Figure 7-1.4-2 for an Assembly Listing) which adds together two 8 byte binary coded decimal (bcd) numbers. This program is saved in memory file "DEF456."

Explanation of Sample Simulation

Initital Status

The first two lines of printed output, shown after MF filename DEF456, are the display of the initial register status of the memory file. The case shown in the tables represents the first simulated execution of the program "AAA" (see Section 7-1.5.4), following the assembly of the program. The initial status of the memory file is such that the input and display bases are both hexadecimal, all possible registers will be displayed, and all registers, including time, are set to zero.

If execution of the program contained in the specified memory file had been simulated previously, the initial status might differ from that represented, both in format and in content.

Simulator Command Requests

Following the initial status display, the simulator prints the first simulator command request, indicated by a question mark (?). In response to successive simulator command requests, the typed commands and definitions described below have been entered.

Repetition of Commands and Input Base Definition

In the example shown, the operator has replied to the first simulator command request with a string

```
RUN MPSSIM


MPSSIM          11:42EST     01/28/75



MOTOROLA SPD, INC. OWNS AND IS RESPONSIBLE FOR MPSSIM
       COPYRIGHT 1973 & 1974 BY MOTOROLA INC

      MOTOROLA MPU SIMULATOR, RELEASE 1.1

   ENTER MF FILENAME
?DEF456

DEFAULT MACHINE FILE 06/20/74.
  HH IA  OC    EA   P    X    A   B    C     S    T
  0000 ◆◆◆   0000 0000 0000 00  00 000000 0000 0000000
?LM.IB16

LM.
IB 16.
?SETP[LM.SD IOEPXABCST.IB16.DB16.HR5.SR P1100,T0]

SETP[LM.SD IOEPXABCST.IB16.DB16.HR5.SR P1100,T0]
?SX[SM 0102,#1]

SX[SM 0102,#1]
?SY[SM 010A,#1]

SY[SM 010A,#1]
?ZSUM[SM 0112,0,0,0,0,0,0,0,0]

ZSUM[SM 0112,0,0,0,0,0,0,0,0]
?DMEM[NOLM.DM 0102,8.DM 010A,8.DM 0112,8.LM]

DMEM[NOLM.DM 0102,8.DM 010A,8.DM 0112,8.LM]
?ML

ML.
   MACRO LIBRARY LISTING


  SETP  [LM.SD IOEPXABCST.IB16.DB16.HR5.SR P1100,T0]
  SX    [SM 0102,#1]
  SY    [SM 010A,#1]
  ZSUM  [SM 0112,0,0,0,0,0,0,0,0]
  DMEM  [NOLM.DM 0102,8.DM 010A,8.DM 0112,8.LM]


1056 REMAINING CHARACTERS
```

NOTE: User Input Underlined.

FIGURE 7-1.5-4-1: Simulation of "AAA" (Sheet 1 of 3)

```
?SETP

SETP; LM.
SETP; SD IOEPXABCST.
SETP; IB 16.
SETP; DB 16.
SETP; HR 5.
SETP; SR P1100,T0.
?SX:13,57,90,24,68,09,75,31

SX:13,57,90,24,68,09,75,31; SM 0102,13,57,90,24,68,09,75,31.
?SY:92,58,14,70,36,74,18,52

SY:92,58,14,70,36,74,18,52; SM 010A,92,58,14,70,36,74,18,52.
?ZSUM

ZSUM; SM 0112,0,0,0,0,0,0,0,0.
?DMEM.D

DMEM; NOLM.
 0102 13 57 90 24 68 09 75 31 .W.$...1
 010A 92 58 14 70 36 74 18 52 .X..6..R
 0112 00 00 00 00 00 00 00 00 ........
D.
 HH IA    OC    EA   P    X    A  B    C      S     T
  0000 ◆◆◆    0000◆1100 0000 00 00 000000 0000 0000000
?TOE

T OE.
 ◆1100 LDS   ◆1102◆1103 0000 00 00 000000◆013F 0000003
 ◆1103 LDX   ◆1105◆1106◆0102 00 00 000000 013F 0000006
 ◆1106 STX   ◆0101◆1109 0102 00 00 000000 013F 0000011
 ◆1109 JSR   ◆013E◆1000 0102 00 00 000000◆013D 0000020
 HH IA    OC    EA   P    X    A  B    C      S     T
 ◆1000 LDA B◆1001◆1002 0102 00◆08 000000 013D 0000022
 ◆1002 LDX   ◆0101◆1005 0102 00 08 000000 013D 0000027
 ◆1005 CLC   ◆1005◆1006 0102 00 08 000000 013D 0000029
 ◆1006 LDA A◆0109◆1008 0102◆31 08 000000 013D 0000034
 ◆1008 ADC A◆0111◆100A 0102◆83 08 00N0V0 013D 0000039
 HH IA    OC    EA   P    X    A  B    C      S     T
 ◆100A DAA   ◆100A◆100B 0102 83 08 00N000 013D 0000041
 ◆100B STA A◆0119◆100D 0102 83 08 00N000 013D 0000044
 ◆100D DEX   ◆100D◆100E◆0101 83 08 000000 013D 0000048
 ◆100E DEC B◆100E◆100F 0101 83◆07 000000 013D 0000050
 ◆100F BNE   ◆1010◆1006 0101 83 07 000000 013D 0000054
```

FIGURE 7-1.5.4-1: Simulation of "AAA" (Sheet 2 of 3)

```
HR 100.
NOLM.
  HH IA    OC      EA    P     X     A  B    C      S       T
  100F  BNE     1010  1006◆0100◆93◆06  000000  013D  0000079
  100F  BNE     1010  1006◆00FF◆83◆05  000000  013D  0000104
  100F  BNE     1010  1006◆00FE◆04◆04  00000C  013D  0000129
  100F  BNE     1010  1006◆00FD◆95◆03  000000  013D  0000154
  100F  BNE     1010  1006◆00FC◆04◆02  00000C  013D  0000179
  100F  BNE     1010  1006◆00FB◆16◆01  H0000C  013D  0000204
  100F  BNE     1010◆1011◆00FA◆06◆00  000Z0C  013D  0000229
?T5.DMEM

  ◆1011 RTS   ◆013F◆110C  00FA  06  00  000Z0C◆013F  0000234
  ◆110C NOP   ◆110C◆110D  00FA  06  00  000Z0C  013F  0000236
  ◆110D BRA   ◆110E◆110C  00FA  06  00  000Z0C  013F  0000240
  ◆110C NOP   ◆110C◆110D  00FA  06  00  000Z0C  013F  0000242
  ◆110D BRA   ◆110E◆110C  00FA  06  00  000Z0C  013F  0000246
   0102 13 57  90 24 68 09 75 31  .W.$...1
   010A 92 58  14 70 36 74 18 52  .X..6..R
   0112 06 16  04 95 04 83 93 83  ........
?RS.EX

RS.
EX.

PROGRAM STOP AT 0

USED    22.11 UNITS
```

FIGURE 7-1.5.4-1: Simulation of "AAA" (Sheet 3 of 3)

of two simulator commands. These commands instruct the simulator to repeat all commands (LM), and to set the input base to hexadecimal (IB16).

Entering the command IB16 is actually redundant in this example, since as is shown by the initial status display, the input base was already hexadecimal.

The simulator repeats the IB16 command, because of the preceding entry of the LM command. All subsequent commands will be repeated by the simulator until the LM command is cancelled by "NOLM".

Definition of Macro Commands

The user has next defined five Macro commands, to facilitate running the program. The purposes of the Macro commands are as follows:

SETP —to set the program counter to the beginning of the program, at hexadecimal address 1100; to ensure format control for repeating commands, displaying all possible registers in the trace, and printing a header line every five lines of the trace; to ensure that input and display bases are both hexadecimal: to set initial cycle time to zero.

SX —to facilitate entry of the first of the two 8-byte bcd numbers which are to be added together; this number will be placed in memory at consecutive addresses beginning at hexadecimal 0102.

SY —to facilitate entry of the second of the two 8-byte bcd numbers which are to be added together; this number will be placed in memory at consecutive addresses beginning at hexadecimal 010A.

ZSUM —to enter zeros in the memory locations where the result of the bcd addition will be stored, beginning at hexadecimal address 0112.

DMEM—to display the locations in memory where the two bcd numbers which are to be added together are stored, and where the bcd sum is stored; NOLM and LM are used to eliminate the repetition of commands during execution of this Macro.

Macro Library Listing

The operator then entered a command (ML) to obtain a listing of the Macro library. The simulator displays the Macros SETP, SX, SY, ZSUM and DMEM, in a standard format. This is followed by an indication of the space which remains for MACRO definitions, expressed as the number of remaining characters.

Program and Data Initialization

The operator next initialized the program by calling successively the Macros SETP, SX, SY and ZSUM. Text substitution is used with the Macros SX and SY to enter the values of the two 8-byte binary-coded-decimal numbers which are to be added together.

In the example shown, numbers have been entered for carrying out the addition represented by:

$$1357902468097531$$
$$+9258147036741852$$

Display of Program and Data Initialization

The operator then called the Macro "DMEM", and entered the display command (D). The Macro

"DMEM" display the operands of the arithmetic program which have been entered into the memory, and also displays the memory locations where the result will be stored, and which have been set to zero. The display command (D), at this point, enables the user to check that the program counter has been set to the start of the program at hexadecimal address 1100.

Execution of the bcd Addition

The operator then entered a command to trace 14 instructions (T0E). After repeating this command the simulator has executed and traced 14 instructions in the program, reaching the end of the first pass through the loop in the subroutine.

The operator then decided to eliminate the header line and the repetition of commands and run the program to the end of the last pass through the loop in the subroutine, then obtain a display of the registers at the end of the loop on each pass. This was achieved by the string of commands:

?HR100.NOLM.RC7.R7

The command HR100 has set the header interval to a sufficiently high value to eliminate the header in the remainder of the execution.

To verify that execution of the addition is complete, the user entered a command to trace five instructions, (T5), and on the same line has called the MACRO command DMEM for displaying the results of the computations. The trace shows that execution has returned to the main program (RTS) and has entered the perpetual loop of two instructions (NOP and BRA). The purpose of the perpetual loop is to provide an easily recognized indication of the completion of the computations but should be removed when the program is satisfactorily debugged.

The display of memory obtained by calling the Macro "DMEM" shows the results of the 8-byte binary-coded-decimal addition as follows:

$$1357902468097531$$
$$+9258147036741852$$
$$\overline{0616049504839383}$$

which is the correct result.

Exit from the Simulator

The user entered a string of two commands to restore the status (RS) and to exit from the simulator (EX). The RS command has restored the registers to the status after program initialization and before execution of the program. Following the EX command the computer system has printed information regarding system status and usage.

7-1.5.5 Simulation Results

The comparison of an instruction sequence as shown in the Assembly Listing of Figure 7-1.4-2, and as traced by the Simulator, provides some insight into the internal operations of the microprocessor. The content of the accumulators, index register and stack pointer can be checked before and after each instruction. The instruction address begins with the starting point specified in the ORG directive and advances by the number of bytes required for each instruction. The program counter indicates where the next instruction is located. Of particular significance is the condition code register which shows the effect of accumulator operations, register data transfers and the base status for conditional branching. The T display keeps the count of expended microprocessor cycles. By subtraction of the beginning from the end count, the duration of instruction sequences, loops and subroutines can be calculated. The stack pointer and index register should be checked to make sure they are not overlapping memory reserved for other program instructions or parameters.

Furthermore, when an instruction which manipulates the stack pointer is executed, it should be observed that the pointer moves accordingly. For example, a JSR instruction causes the stack pointer to be decremented two addresses. At the end of the subroutine, the RTS instruction increments it by two, thus restoring it to its former setting. In the same way, the Push Data instruction decrements the pointer by one, while the Pull Data instruction restores it.

Memory addresses for temporary storage of data may be examined at crucial points in the program to make sure the expected value has been stored. The PIA control and data registers may be checked the same way, since they appear to the microprocessor and the Simulator as memory addresses too.

Errors

Errors detected by the Simulator are printed out in the same format as Assembly errors. Typical Simulator errors are listed in Table 7-1.5.5-1.

7-1.6   HELP

HELP is a special program designed to provide on-line assistance to the users of the Motorola support software. It can be called to obtain additional information on error messages printed out during operation of the Assembler, Simulator, or Build Virtual Machine programs. In addition, it includes a Help Message File that provides up-to-date information on improvements and new developments in the M6800 System. The Message File is organized into groups. Following are the groups, the related message number range, and the HELP command which places the HELP program in the group mode.

```
CMD           SYSTEM              MESSAGE NUMBER RANGE
---   ---------------------      --------------------
 E            ERRORS              0000  TO  0999
 B      BUILD VIRTUAL MACHINE     1000  TO  1999
 A           ASSEMBLER            2000  TO  2999
 S           SIMMULATOR           3000  TO  3999
 H             HELP               4000  TO  4999
             RESERVED             5000  TO  9999
```

To obtain additional information while running the other software programs, HELP is called by entering: RUN HELP. Then enter the HELP error command, E, followed by the number of the error message in question. A current listing of the error messages is shown in Table 7-1.6-1. For a listing of all the error messages, enter E followed by 1 to 999. At the completion of the listing, the user must enter the exit command, EX, in order to return to other programs.

HELP can be invoked from within[1] the Simulator and Build Virtual Machine programs by entering a Help command in response to any command request. An up-to-date list of all the Simulator and Build Virtual

---

[1]Because the Assembler operates in the batch mode, to obtain HELP during assembly, the user must exit from the Assembler and enter the Help program by RUN HELP.

```
0301
    301   UNDEFINED SIMULATOR COMMAND
          MESSAGE:   ****ERROR 301 MMMMM
          MEANING:   AN UNDEFINED SIMULATOR COMMAND WAS ENTERED.
0302
    302   SYNTAX ERROR
          MESSAGE:   ****ERROR 302 MMMMM
          MEANING:   THE STRUCTURE OF THE SIMUALTOR COMMAND IS SYNTAC-
                     TICALLY INCORRECT.
0303
    303   MACRO DEFINITION ERROR
          MESSAGE:   ****ERROR 303 MMMMM
          MEANING:   THE MD SIMULATOR COMMAND CANNOT BE USED IN A MACRO
                     DEFINITION.
0304
    304   MACRO NOT IN LIBRARY
          MESSAGE:   ****ERROR 304 MMMMM
          MEANING:   THE MACRO TO BE DELETED USING THE MD COMMAND IS
                     NOT IN THE MACRO LIBRARY.
0305
    305   MACRO DEFINITION ERROR
          MESSAGE:   ****ERROR 305 MMMMM
          MEANING:   THE RL SIMULATOR COMMAND CANNOT BE USED IN A MACRO
                     DEFINITION.
0306
    306   REGISTER OVERFLOW
          MESSAGE:   ****ERROR 306 MMMMM
          MEANING:   AN OPERAND IN THE SR COMMAND IS TOO LARGE FOR
                     THE ASSOCIATED REGISTER.
0307
    307   MACRO LIBRARY OVERFLOW
          MESSAGE:   ****ERROR 307 MMMMM
          MEANING:   THERE IS INSUFFICIENT STORAGE IN THE MACRO LI-
                     BRARY FOR THE NEW MACRO.  THE MACRO IS NOT STORED.
0308
    308   MACRO DEFINITION ERROR
          MESSAGE:   ****ERROR 308 MMMMM
          MEANING:   THE MACRO VARIABLE PARAMETER (#N) IS GREATER THAN
                     30.
0309
    309   COMMAND BUFFER OVERFLOW
          MESSAGE:   ****ERROR 309 MMMMM
          MEANING:   MORE THAN 72 CHARACTERS WERE ENTERED AS A COMMAND
                     LINE.  THE TOTAL NUMBER OF CHARACTERS IN A COMMAND
                     LINE INCLUDES THOSE CHARACTERS IN A MACRO DEFIN-
                     ITION IF THE COMMAND LINE CONTAINS A MACRO CALL.
0310
    310   HELP REQUEST
          MESSAGE:   ****ERROR 310 MMMMM
          MEANING:   ENTER "HP ALL B" FOR A COMPLETE LIST OF ALL SIM-
                     ULATOR COMMANDS.
```

TABLE 7-1.5.5-1. Typical Simulator Errors (Sheet 1 of 2)

0311
```
    311  SYNTAX ERROR
         MESSAGE:  ****ERROR 311 MMMMM
         MEANING:  SYNTAX ERROR IN THE SIMULATOR'S HELP COMMAND.
```
0312
```
    312  ILLEGAL HELP MESSAGE NUMBER
         MESSAGE:  ****ERROR 312 MMMMM
         MEANING:  THE HELP MESSAGE NUMBER WAS NOT FOUND IN THE HELP
                   MESSAGE FILE.
```
0313
```
    313  ADDRESSING ERROR
         MESSAGE:  ****ERROR 313 MMMMM
         MEANING:  AN ATTEMPT TO STORE BEYOND THE DEFINED MEMORY
                   BOUNDS OF THE VIRTUAL MACHINE FILE WAS MADE.
```
0314
```
    314  SYNTAX ERROR IN A SET OR CLEAR BREAK POINT
         MESSAGE:  ****ERROR 314 MMMMM
         MEANING:  THERE IS A SYNTAX IN THE SIMULATOR'S
                   BP, BS, OR BC COMMAND.
```
0315
```
    315  ILLEGAL MEMORY ADDRESS
         MESSAGE:  ****ERROR 315 MMMMM
         MEANING:  A BREAK POINT REQUEST TO CLEAR OR SET A BREAK
                   POINT AT AN ILLEGAL MEMORY ADDRESS FOR THE "MF"
                   FILE. USE "BD" TO DISPLAY BREAK POINTS SET OR
                   CLEARED.
```
0316
```
    316  NO BREAK POINT SET AT MEMORY ADDRESS
         MESSAGE:  ****ERROR 316 MMMMM
         MEANING:  NO BREAK POINT FLAG WAS SET AT THE MEMORY LOCA-
                   TION ON THE REQUEST TO CLEAR IT'S FLAG. USE "BD"
                   TO DISPLAY BREAK POINTS STILL SET.
```
0317
```
    317  COMMAND NOT TERMINATED WITH A PERIOD
         MESSAGE:  ****ERROR 317 MMMMM
         MEANING:  THE COMMAND WAS NOT TERMINATED WITH A PERIOD OR
                   OR THE COMMAND HAS UNSED PARAMETERS.
```
0318
```
    318  SYNTAX ERROR IN "ON" OR "OF" COMMAND
         MESSAGE:  ****ERROR 318 MMMMM
         MEANING:  SYNTAX ERROR IN THE "ON" OR "OF" COMMAND.
                   A) UNDEFINED CODE, NOT X, A, B, S, T, BP, MF OR F.
                   B) OPERATION NOT =, < OR >.
                   C) DEFINING A MACRO FOR THE COMMAND SECTION OF A
                      "ON" IS ILLEGAL.
                   D) NO COMMAND FOLLOWS THE CONDITIONS.
```
0319
```
    319  "ON" COMMAND NOT FOUND IN THE "ON" LIBRARY
         MESSAGE:  ****ERROR 319 MMMMM
         MEANING:  THE "ON" COMMAND WAS NOT FOUND IN THE "ON" CON-
                   DITION LIBRARY.
```
0320
```
    320  ILLEGAL INTERRUPT TYPE OR TIME BASE IS ZERO
         MESSAGE:  ****ERROR 320 MMMMM
         MEANING:  WHEN A "IR" COMMAND IS USED, THE INTERRUPT TYPE
                   IS UNDEFINED OR THE DELTA TIME BASE FOR THE FIRST
                   INTERRUPT IS ZERO.
```

TABLE 7-1.5.5-1. Typical Simulator Errors (Sheet 2 of 2)

0001

001   FILE IS NOT A "MF" FILE
       MESSAGE: ****ERROR 001 LU FILENAME:PASSWORD:USER-ID
       MEANING: THE FILE WHOSE FILENAME WAS ENTERED IN RESPONSE TO
                  THE "ENTER MF FILENAME" REQUEST IS NOT A VIRTUAL
                  MACHINE FILE.   THE LOGICAL UNIT IDENTIFIER (LU),
                  THE FILENAME, THE PASSWORD, AND THE USER-ID OF THE
                  FILE CAUSING THE ERROR IS LISTED IN THE ERROR MES-
                  SAGE.   THE SYSTEM WILL REPEAT THE REQUEST.
0002

002   MF VERSION NUMBER ERROR
       MESSAGE: ****ERROR 002 MF FILENAME:PASSWORD:USER-ID
       MEANING: THE "MF" OPENED IN RESPONSE TO THE "ENTER MF FILE-
                  NAME" REQUEST IS NOT A CURRENT VIRTUAL MACHINE
                  FILE.   THE FILE CAN BE CONVERTED TO THE CURRENT
                  VERSION BY RUNNING THE BUILD VIRTUAL MACHINE PRO-
                  GRAM (MPBVM).
0003

003   TERMINATION DUE TO OLD MF VERSION
       MESSAGE: ****SYSTEM ABORT 003
       MEANING: THE PROGRAM WAS ABORTED BECAUSE OF AN "OLD" VIRTUAL
                  USING THE BUILD VIRTUAL MACHINE PROGRAM (MPBVM).
0004

004   TERMINATION DUE TO OPEN FILE ERRORS
       MESSAGE: ****SYSTEM ABORT 004
       MEANING: FIVE CONSECUTIVE, UNSUCCESSFUL ATTEMPTS WERE
                  MADE TO OPEN A FILE.   THE PROGRAM IS ABORTED.
0005

005   ERROR IN THE '.X' JOB CONTROL COMMAND
       MESSAGE: ****ERROR 05 IIIIII
       MEANING: THE JOB CONTROL COMMAND ENTERED IN RESPONSE
                  TO A REQUEST FOR A FILENAME IS IN ERROR.
                  IIIIII IS THE CHARACTER LOCATION WHERE
                  COMMAND PROCESSOR STOPPED SCANNING THE COMMAND.
0011

011   FILE IS BUSY
       MESSAGE: ****ERROR 011 LU FILENAME:PASSWORD:USER-ID
       MEANING: THE FILE WHOSE FILENAME WAS ENTERED IN RESPONSE TO
                  A SYSTEM REQUEST TO OPEN A FILE IS CURRENTLY OPEN
                  AND IS BEING USED BY THIS OR ANOTHER USER.   THE
                  FILE IS NOT AVAILABLE TO THE CURRENT USER.   THE
                  LOGICAL UNIT IDENTIFIER (LU), THE FILENAME, THE
                  PASSWORD, AND THE USER-ID OF THE FILE APPEAR IN
                  THE ERROR MESSAGE.

TABLE 7-1.6-1. HELP Error Messages (Sheet 1 of 7)

0012

    012   FILE DOES NOT EXIST
           MESSAGE: ****ERROR 012 LU FILENAME:PASSWORD:USER-ID
           MEANING: THE FILE WHOSE FILENAME WAS ENTERED IN RESPONSE TO
                   A SYSTEM REQUEST TO OPEN A FILE DOES NOT EXIST.
                   THE PASSWORD, AND THE USER-ID APPEAR IN THE ERROR
                   MESSAGE.

0013

    013   INCORRECT ACCESS PRIVELEGES
           MESSAGE: ****ERROR 013 LU FILENAME:PASSWORD:USER-ID
           MEANING: THERE WAS NO READ PERMISSION ASSIGNED TO A FILE
                   WHOSE FILENAME WAS ENTERED IN RESPONSE TO A SYS-
                   TEM REQUEST TO OPEN A FILE. THIS ERROR OCCURS
                   ONLY WHEN THE USER ATTEMPTS TO ACCESS A FILE IN
                   ANOTHER USER'S CATALOG. THE LOGICAL UNIT IDENTI-
                   FIER (LU), THE FILENAME, THE PASSWORD, AND THE
                   USER-ID OF THE FILE APPEAR IN THE ERROR MESSAGE.

0014

    014   INCORRECT PASSWORD
           MESSAGE: ****ERROR 014 LU FILENAME:PASSWORD:USER-ID
           MEANING: AN INCORRECT PASSWORD WAS SUPPLIED WITH THE FILE-
                   NAME IN RESPONSE TO A SYSTEM REQUEST TO OPEN A
                   FILE. THE LOGICAL UNIT IDENTIFIER (LU), THE FILE-
                   NAME, THE PASSWORD, AND THE USER-ID APPEAR IN THE
                   ERROR MESSAGE.

0015

    015   UNSPECIFIED OPEN ERROR
           MESSAGE: ****ERROR 015 LU FILENAME:PASSWORD:USER-ID
           MEANING: AN OPEN ERROR OTHER THAN 011-014 OCCURRED WHEN
                   AN ATTEMPT TO OPEN THE FILE WAS MADE. THE LOGICAL
                   UNIT IDENTIFIER (LU), THE FILENAME, THE PASSWORD,
                   AND THE USER-ID APPEAR IN THE ERROR MESSAGE.

0016

    016   FILE IS NOT A "MF" FILE
           MESSAGE: ****ERROR 016 LU FILENAME:PASSWORD:USER-ID
           MEANING: THE FILE WHOSE FILENAME WAS ENTERED IN RESPONSE TO
                   THE "ENTER MF FILENAME" REQUEST IS NOT A VIRTUAL
                   MACHINE FILE. THE LOGICAL UNIT IDENTIFIER (LU),
                   THE FILENAME, THE PASSWORD, AND THE USER-ID OF THE
                   FILE CAUSING THE ERROR IS LISTED IN THE ERROR MES-
                   SAGE. THE SYSTEM WILL REPEAT THE REQUEST.

0017

    017   NO MF OPENED
           MESSAGE: ****ERROR 017
           MEANING: DUE TO A PRIOR OPEN ERROR, A VIRTUAL MACHINE FILE
                   HAS NOT BEEN OPENED.

TABLE 7-1.6-1. HELP Error Messages (Sheet 2 of 7)

0018

018   FILE TYPE DOES NOT AGREE WITH REQUEST TYPE
      MESSAGE: **** ERROR 018 LU FILENAME:PASSWORD:USER-ID
      MEANING: THE FILE TYPES DO NOT AGREE FOR THE FILENAME
                 AND THE SYSTEM'S REQUEST. ONE MAY BE BINARY AND
                 THE OTHER MAY BE ASCII OR SOME OTHER COMBINATION
                 LIKE THAT. THE LOGICAL UNIT IDENTIFIER (LU), THE
                 FILENAME, THE PASSWORD, AND THE USER-ID OF THE
                 FILE CAUSING THE ERROR ARE LISTED IN THE ERROR
                 MESSAGE.

0024

024   FILE WAS NOT UNSAVED
      MESSAGE: ****ERROR 024 LU FILENAME:PASSWORD:USER-ID
      MEANING: THE FILE, FILENAME ON LOGICAL UNIT LU WAS NOT UN-
                 SAVED BECAUSE 1) THE FILE WAS BUSY, 2) THE FILE
                 DID NOT EXIST, 3) OR PASSWORD OR USER-ID IN ERROR.

0025

025   COMPUTER SYSTEM DEPENDENT ERROR CODE
      MESSAGE: ****ERROR 025 IIIII
      MEANING: AN ERROR CODE WAS FOUND WHICH WAS NOT EXPECTED
                 BY THE SYSTEM. THIS ERROR MESSAGE SHOULD BE
                 PASSED ON TO MOTORALA'S MPU PROGRAMMING STAFF.
                 IIIIII IS THE ERROR CODE WHICH IS COMPUTER
                 DEPENDENT.

0050

050   DEFAULT MF USED.
      MESSAGE: ****WARNING 050
      MEANING: THE REQUESTED MF FILE DID NOT EXIST. THE BUILD
                 VIRTUAL MACHINE PROGRAM SUPPLIED A DEFAULT VIRTUAL
                 MACHINE FILE. THE DEFAULT MF IS IDENTIFIED BY
                 THE FILENAME AND PASSWORD WHICH WAS ENTERED IN
                 RESPONSE TO A SYSTEM REQUEST TO OPEN A FILE.

0051

051   FILE IS BUSY
      MESSAGE: ****WARNING 051 LU FILENAME:PASSWORD:USER-ID
      MEANING: THE FILE WHOSE FILENAME WAS ENTERED IN RESPONSE TO
                 A SYSTEM REQUEST TO OPEN A FILE IS BUSY. THE FILE
                 IS PROBABLY BEING USED BY ANOTHER USER OR BY THE
                 CURRENT USER. THE LOGICAL UNIT IDENTIFIER (LU),
                 THE FILENAME, THE PASSWORD, AND THE USER-ID AP-
                 PEAR IN THE ERROR MESSAGE. THE OPEN REQUEST
                 CAN BE REPEATED AT A LATER TIME.

0052

052   OLD VERSION NUMBER FOR MF FILE
      MESSAGE: ****WARNING 052
      MEANING: THE MF FILE WHICH WAS OPENED IN RESPONSE TO A
                 SYSTEM REQUEST TO OPEN A FILE HAS AN OLD VERSION
                 NUMBER. THE FILE CAN BE UPGRADED TO CURRENT
                 STANDARDS BY EXECUTING THE BUILD VIRTUAL UM COM-
                 MAND.

TABLE 7-1.6-1. HELP Error Messages (Sheet 3 of 7)

0078

078   NO MORE DISK SPACE
      MESSAGE: ****SYSTEM ABORT 078 IIIIII
      MEANING: A) MARK III - THE SYSTEM'S PSU STORAGE IS
                   USED UP. IT CANNOT CREATE A FILE IIIIII
                   PSU LONG. CALL YOUR G.E. SALEMAN, SYSTEM
                   ERROR MORE DISK DRIVERS NEEDED.
                B) SIGMA 9 - YOUR ACCOUNT CANNOT CREATE A
                   FILE IIIIII GRANULES LONG. PACK YOUR ACCOUNT
                   BY LOGGING OFF AND LOGGING ON AGAIN OR
                   REQUESTING YOUR ACCOUNT BE AUTHORIZED FOR
                   MORE DISK SPACE.

0079

079   THE FILE ORGANIZATION DOES NOT AGREE WITH REQESTED FILE
      MESSAGE: ****SYSTEM ABORT 079
      MEANING: THE REQUESTED FILE'S ORGANIZATION IS DIFFERENT
                THAN THE FILE BEING OPENED. ONE FILE IS BINARY
                THE OTHER IS AN ASCII FILE; ETC.

0080

080   FILE IS BUSY
      MESSAGE: ****SYSTEM ABORT 080
      MEANING: THE REQUESTED FILE IS BUSY. THE SYSTEM ABORTS
                AFTER MAKING 5 TRIES TO OPEN THE FILE AFTER
                A DELAY OF SEVERAL SECONDS.

0081

081   DEFAULT MF FILE NOT AVAILABLE
      MESSAGE: ****SYSTEM ABORT 081
      MEANING: THE REQUESTED MF FILE DID NOT EXIST AND THE SYS-
                WAS UNABLE TO SUPPLY THE DEFAULT MACHINE FILE.
                THIS IS NOT A USER ERROR. NOTIFY THE SYSTEM PRO-
                GRAMMER.

0082

082   UNABLE TO OPEN A SYSTEM SCRATCH FILE
      MESSAGE: ****SYSTEM ABORT 082
      MEANING: THE SYSTEM WAS UNABLE TO OPEN A SCRATCH FILE.
                THIS IS NOT A USER ERROR. NOTIFY THE SYSTEM PRO-
                GRAMMER. NOTE: SCRATCH FILES ARE CREATED AND
                UNSAVED BY THE SYSTEM FOR USE AS INTERMEDIATE WORK
                AREAS. IT IS POSSIBLE THAT THESE FILES MAY NOT
                BE UNSAVED DURING A "SYSTEM CRASH" THE USER
                SHOULD DELETE ANY SCRATCH FILES WHICH MAY BE IN
                HIS CATALOG. SCRATCH FILE NAMES APPEAR AS SCRNNN
                WHERE NNN IS A THREE DIGIT NUMBER FROM 000 TO 099

0083

083   UNDEFINED MF VERSION NUMBER
      MESSAGE: ****SYSTEM ABORT NNNNNN
      MEANING: THE VIRTUAL MACHINE FILE WHICH WAS OPENED CONTAINS
                AN UNDEFINED VERSION NUMBER. THE PROGRAM CANNOT
                PROCEED AND IS TERMINATED. THE FILE IS PROBABLY
                NOT A VIRTUAL MACHINE FILE. NNNNNN IS THE UNDE-
                FINED VERSION NUMBER.

TABLE 7-1.6-1. HELP Error Messages (Sheet 4 of 7)

0091

```
091    FILE IS BUSY
       MESSAGE:  ****ATTN: 091
       MEANING:  THE FILE WHOSE FILENAME WAS ENTERED IN RESPONSE TO
                 A SYSTEM REQUEST TO OPEN A FILE IS BUSY.  ANOTHER
                 ATTEMPT TO OPEN THE FILE IS BEING MADE.
```

0092

```
092    DEFAULT MF USED
       MESSAGE:  ****ATTN: 092
       MEANING:  THE REQUESTED MF FILE DID NOT EXIST.  THE BUILD
                 VIRTUAL MACHINE PROGRAM SUPPLIED A DEFAULT VIRTUAL
                 MACHINE FILE.  THE DEFAULT MF IS IDENTIFIED BY
                 THE FILENAME AND PASSWORD WHICH WAS ENTERED IN
                 RESPONSE TO A SYSTEM REQUEST TO OPEN A FILE.
```

0099

```
099    BUILDING DEFAULT MF
       MESSAGE:  ****ATTN: 099
       MEANING:  THE BUILD VIRTUAL MACHINE PROGRAM IS GENERATING
                 THE DEFAULT VIRTUAL MACHINE FILE.  THIS FUNCTION
                 CAN ONLY BE PERFORMED BY THE ADMINISTRATIVE USER.
```

0101

```
101    ILLEGAL BUILD VIRTUAL COMMAND
       MESSAGE:  ****ERROR 101 AAAAAA
       MEANING:  AN ILLEGAL BUILD VIRTUAL MACHINE COMMAND WAS
                 ENTERED.  AAAAAA IS THE AREA OF THE COMMAND LINE
                 CONTAINING THE ILLEGAL COMMAND.
```

0102

```
102    SYNTAX ERROR
       MESSAGE:  ****ERROR 102 AAAAAA
       MEANING:  THE STRUCTURE OF THE COMMAND IS LOGICALLY INCOR-
                 RECT.  AAAAAA IS THE AREA OF THE COMMAND CONTAIN-
                 ING THE ERROR.
```

0103

```
103    INVALID LAST WORD ADDRESS
       MESSAGE:  ****ERROR 103 IIIII
       MEANING:  AN ILLEGAL VALUE WAS USED FOR THE SIZE OF MEMORY
                 IN THE LW COMMAND.  IIIII IS THE DECIMAL EQUIVA-
                 LENT OF THAT VALUE.  LEGAL VALUES MUST BE A MUL-
                 TIPLE OF 256-1 (N*256-1) AND IN THE RANGE 255 -
                 65535
```

0104

```
104    MACRO IS NOT IN THE "CF" MACRO LIBRARY
       MESSAGE:  ****ERROR 104 MMMM
       MEANING:  THE ERROR OCCURRED WHILE TRYING TO COPY MACROS
                 FROM THE "CF" FILE TO THE "MF" FILE.  ONE OF THE
                 THE REQUESTED MACROS, MACRO MMMM, WAS NOT FOUND.
```

TABLE 7-1.6-1. HELP Error Messages (Sheet 5 of 7)

0105

    105   DUPLICATE MACRONAME IN "MF" MACRO LIBRARY
           MESSAGE: ****ERROR 105 MMMM
           MEANING: THE ERROR OCCURRED WHILE TRYING TO COPY MACROS
                    FROM THE "CF" FILE TO THE "MF" FILE. A MACRO
                    OF THE SAME NAME AS THE ONE TO BE TRANSFERRED
                    ALREADY EXISTS IN THE "MF" FILE. MMMM IS THE NAME
                    OF THE MACRO. NO TRANSFER OCCURRED.

0106

    106   INSUFFICIENT MACRO LIBRARY SPACE AVAILABLE
           MESSAGE: ****ERROR 106 MMMM
           MEANING: THE ERROR OCCURRED WHILE TRYING TO COPY MACROS
                    FROM THE "CF" FILE TO THE "MF" FILE. MMMM IS THE
                    MACRO FOR WHICH THERE IS INSUFFICIENT SPACE.

0107

    107   ILLEGAL MACRONAME
           MESSAGE: ****ERROR 107 MMMM
                    MMMM ARE THE FIRST 4 CHARACTERS OF THE NAME.

0108

    108   NULL FIELD
           MESSAGE: ****ERROR 108
           MEANING: MORE INFORMATION IS NEEDED FOLLOWING THE COMMAND
                    FIELD. THE FIELD FOLLOWING THE COMMAND IS BLANK.

0109

    109   FILENAME ALREADY USED
           MESSAGE: ****ERROR 109 LU FILENAME:PASSWORD:USER-ID
                    THE NAME OF AN EXISTING FILE WAS GIVEN IN RESPONSE
                    TO AN OPERATION REQUIRING A "NEW" FILE. INCLUDED
                    IN THE ERROR MESSAGE ARE THE OLD FILE'S FILENAME,
                    PASSWORD, USER-ID, AND A TWO-CHARACTER LOGICAL UNIT
                    IDENTIFIER.

0110

    110   ILLEGAL ADDRESS
           MESSAGE: ****ERROR 110 NNNNNN
           MEANING: AN ILLEGAL ADDRESS WAS ENCOUNTERED. THE AD-
                    DRESS MAY BE GREATER THAN THE LWA (LAST WORD
                    ADDRESS) FOR THE VIRTUAL MACHINE. THE CURRENT
                    LWA VALUE CAN BE DISPLAYED BY ENTERING THE MO
                    COMMAND. NNNNNN IS THE ILLEGAL ADDRESS.

0111

    111   EXECUTION CHECK
           MESSAGE: ****ERROR 111
           MEANING: EXECUTION OF A BUILD VIRTUAL COMMAND WAS HALTED
                    BECAUSE AN OLD VERSION "MF" FILE WAS LOADED WITH
                    THE MF COMMAND THE MF FILE MUST BE UPDATED WITH
                    THE UM COMMAND BEFORE THE CURRENT COMMAND CAN BE
                    EXECUTED.

TABLE 7-1.6-1. HELP Error Messages (Sheet 6 of 7)

0112

    112   CHECKSUM ERROR
           MESSAGE: ****ERROR 112 NNNNNN
           MEANING: A CHECKSUM ERROR OCCURRED WHILE LOADING MEMORY
                       FROM A "ROM" FILE (IM COMMAND). NNNNNN IS THE
                       RECORD NUMBER CONTAINING THE CHECKSUM ERROR.
0113

    113   ROM RECORD ERROR
           MESSAGE: ****ERROR 114 NNNNNN
           MEANING: AN ILLEGAL, OUT OF ORDER, OR MISSING ROM RECORD
                       OCCURRED AT RECORD NUMBER NNNNNN.
0190

    190   MACRO WAS SUCCESSFULLY TRANSFERRED
           MESSAGE: ATTN: 190 MMMM
           MEANING: MACRO MMMM WAS SUCCESSFULLY TRANSFERRED FROM THE
                       "CF" FILE TO THE "MF" FILE.
0401

    401   HELP MESSAGE NUMBER NOT FOUND
           MESSAGE: ****ERROR 401
           MEANING: THE HELP MESSAGE NUMBER COULD NOT BE FOUND IN THE
                       HELP MESSAGE FILE.
0402

    402   ILLEGAL HELP MESSAGE NUMBER
           MESSAGE: ****ERROR 402
           MEANING: THE HELP MESSAGE NUMBER IS OUTSIDE THE RANGE OF
                       VALID HELP MESSAGE NUMBERS.
0403

    403   UNDEFINED HELP COMMAND
           MESSAGE: ****ERROR 403
           MEANING: AN UNDEFINED HELP COMMAND WAS ENTERED.
0404

    404   SYNTAX ERROR
           MESSAGE: ****ERROR 404
           MEANING: THE STRUCTURE OF THE HELP COMMAND IS SYNTACTICALLY
                       INCORRECT.

TABLE 7-1.6-1. HELP Error Messages (Sheet 7 of 7)

Machine commands can be obtained by entering the Simulator Help command: HP ALL B. A current listing of the commands is shown in Table 7-1.6-2. Note that this is a more complete list than the typical commands shown in Section 7-1.5.5 where the Simulator is explained.

When using HELP from within the Simulator, varying amounts of information can be obtained, depending on the format used to enter the request. The response will be as follows for the various command formats:

Command Format	Response
HP nnnn	Print index information relating to the HELP message identified by the 1 to 4 digit number "nnnn".
HP nnnnT	Print text relating to the HELP message identified by the 1 to 4 digit number "nnnn".
HP nnnnB	Print index and text relating to the HELP message identified by the 1 to 4 digit number "nnnn".
HP CMD	Print index information relating to the simulator command specified by "CMD".
HP CMD T	Print text relating to the simulator command specified by "CMD".
HP CMD B	Print index and text relating to the simulator command specified by "CMD".
HP ALL	Print an index of all simulator commands.
HP ALL T	Print text for all simulator commands.
HP ALL B	Print index and text for all simulator commands.

Additional general information concerning the HELP program can be obtained by calling out the HELP messages. A partial listing of current HELP messages is listed in Table 7-1.6-3. It should be noted that HELP is a dynamic program that is constantly being updated to reflect the latest status of the M6800 System Support Software. It is advisable to occasionally access the HELP message file since it includes information concerning revisions and improvements as well as error and command data.

7-1.7 BUILD VIRTUAL MACHINE

The Build Virtual Machine (BVM) program provides a way of managing files generated during the development of software for the M6800 system. It is used to: (1) Structure a virtual Machine File (MF) that duplicates the configuration desired for the actual system; (2) Merge and/or load Object Files into the Machine File; (3) Create a formatted tape of the Machine File for generating the required ROM patterns.

A full description of BVM is beyond the scope of this Manual[1], however, study of the BVM commands listed in Table 7-1.6-2 of the preceding Section will give an indication of the program's capability. It is of interest here to consider the steps required to generate a tape for ordering the ROMs in which the MC6800 control program will reside.

---

[1]See the M6800 Programming Manual for a detailed description of BVM.

1001

CC - COPY COMMAND FROM MACRO LIBRARY
FORMAT: CC MACRONAME-1[,MACRONAME-2,...]
FUNCTION: THE MACRO COMMANDS SPECIFIED BY THE MACRONAME
            LIST ARE COPIED FROM THE MACRO LIBRARY OF THE
            SOURCE FILE INTO THE MACRO LIBRARY OF THE DES-
            TINATION FILE. THE SOURCE FILE IS IDENTIFIED
            BY THE CF COMMAND AND THE DESTINATION FILE IS
            IDENTIFIED BY THE MF COMMAND.

EXAMPLES: CC MACA
            MACRO MACA IS COPIED FROM THE CF FILE TO THE MF
            FILE.

            CC A,B,C
            THREE MACROS, A, B, AND C ARE COPIED.

1002

CF - COPY FILE
FORMAT: CF FILENAME-1
FUNCTION: THE "CF" COMMAND LOADS THE FILE "FILENAME-1" INTO
            A WORK AREA. THE COPY FILE IS THE SOURCE FILE
            FOR ALL COPY FUNCTIONS.

EXAMPLES: CF MEMFIL
            THE MACHINE FILE "MEMFIL" IS IDENTIFIED AS THE
            SOURCE FILE FOR ALL COPY FUNCTIONS.

1003

CM - COPY MEMORY
FORMAT: CM FWA-1,LWA-1[,FWA-2]
FUNCTION: MEMORY IS COPIED FROM THE "CF" FILE INTO THE "MF"
            FILE. FWA-1 IS THE FIRST WORD ADDRESS OF THE
            TRANSFER, LWA-1 IS THE LAST WORD ADDRESS, AND
            FWA-2 IS THE FIRST WORD ADDRESS OF THE "MF" FILE
            WHERE THE DATA IS RECEIVED. FWA-2 IS OPTIONAL
            AND IS ASSUMED TO BE EQUAL TO FWA-1 IF OMITTED.

EXAMPLES: CM 0,0FF
            MEMORY IS COPIED FROM LOCATIONS 0 THROUGH FF
            FROM THE CF FILE INTO LOCATIONS 0 THROUGH FF
            OF THE MF FILE.

            CM 0100,2FF,1000
            MEMORY IS COPIED FROM LOCATIONS 100 THROUGH 2FF
            OF THE CF FILE AND RELOCATED TO LOCATIONS 1000
            TO 11FF OF THE MF FILE.

1004

DB - SET DISPLAY BASE
FORMAT: DB BASE-1   (WHERE BASE-1 = 8, 10 OR 16)
FUNCTION: THE DISPLAY BASE IS SET TO OCTAL, DECIMAL,
            OR HEXADECIMAL WHEN BASE-1 IS 8, 10, OR 16,
            RESPECTIVELY.

EXAMPLES: DB 8
            NUMERIC OUTPUT FROM THE DM COMMAND WILL BE DIS-
            PLAYED IN OCTAL.

TABLE 7-1.6-2. HELP Listing of Simulator and BVM Commands (Sheet 1 of 13)

1005

DF - SET DISPLAY FLAG
FORMAT: DF FLAG-1   (WHERE FLAG-1 = 1, 2, OR 3)
FUNCTION: MEMORY DUMPS WILL APPEAR IN NUMERIC, CHARACTER,
             OR BOTH WHEN FLAG-1 IS 1, 2, OR 3, RESPECTIVELY.
             THE DEFAULT SETTING IS 3.

EXAMPLES: DF 2
             OUTPUT FROM THE DM COMMAND WILL BE DISPLAYE IN
             CHARACTER FORMAT ONLY.

1006

DM - DISPLAY MEMORY
FORMAT: DM FWA-1,WCT-1
FUNCTION: WCT-1 WORDS OF MEMORY BEGINNING AT LOCATION FWA-1
             ARE DISPLAYED. THE FORMAT OF THE DISPLAY IS
             DETERMINED BY THE DF SWITCH. MEMORY IS DUMPED
             FROM THE "MF" FILE.

EXAMPLES: DM 100,20
             DISPLAY 20 (HEXADECIMAL) WORDS OF MEMORY STARTING
             FROM LOCATION 100.

1007

EX - NORMAL EXIT FROM MPBVM SYSTEM
FORMAT: EX
FUNCTION: ANY UPDATED INFORMATION IS SAVED. THE "MF" AND
             "CF" FILES ARE CLOSED.

EXAMPLES: EX
             THE BUILD VIRTUAL SESSION IS TERMINATED.

1008

HP - HELP
FORMAT: HP MESSAGECODE-1[SWITCH-1]
FUNCTION: INFORMATION ABOUT MESSAGECODE-1 IS PRINTED.
             MESSAGECODE-1 HAS ONE OF THE FOLLOWING FORMS:
             NNNN   WHERE NNNN IS A NUMBER FROM 1 TO 9999
                     CORRESPONDING TO ANY HELP MESSAGE
             CMD   WHERE CMD IS A BUILD VIRTUAL COMMAND
             ALL   WHERE THE WORD "ALL" REQUESTS THAT
                     INFORMATION FOR ALL BUILD VIRTUAL COM-
                     MANDS BE PRINTED.
             SWITCH-1 CONTROLS THE AMOUNT OF DETAIL TO BE
             PRINTED AND HAS ONE OF THE FOLLOWING FORMS:
             I   PRINT INDEX OF MESSAGE ONLY
             T   PRINT TEXT OF MESSAGE ONLY
             B   PRINT BOTH THE INDEX AND TEXT
             IF SWITCH-1 IS OMITTED, THEN OPTION I IS USED.

             ENTER 'HP 4012 B' FOR INFORMATION ON THE SYN-
             TAX USED IN THE HELP MESSAGES.

             ENTER 'HP ALL I' FOR A LIST OF ALL BUILD VIRTUAL
             COMMANDS.

TABLE 7-1.6-2. HELP Listing of Simulator and BVM Commands (Sheet 2 of 13)

1009

    IB - SET INPUT BASE
        FORMAT   IB BASE-1   (WHERE BASE-1 IS 2, 8, 10, OR 16)
        FUNCTION: THE INPUT BASE IS SET TO BINARY, OCTAL, DECIMAL,
                   OR HEXADECIMAL WHEN BASE-1 IS 2, 8, 10, OR 16,
                   RESPECTIVELY.

        EXAMPLES: IB 8
                   THE INPUT BASE IS SET TO OCTAL. ALL NUMBERS
                   IN THE COMMANDS WILL BE INTERPRETED AS OCTAL
                   UNLESS THERE IS DIFFERENT BASE IMPLIED AS PART
                   OF THE BASE (IE., DM 0,$10 WILL DUMP 10 HEX-
                   ADECIMAL LOCATIONS).

1010

    IM - INPUT MEMORY (FROM ROM FILE)

        FORMAT: IM FILENAME-1[,MAB-1]
        FUNCTION: MEMORY IS READ FROM A ROM FILE (CREATED BY THE
                   OM COMMAND) AND STORED IN THE "MF" FILE.
                   MAB-1 IS A MEMORY ADDRESS BIAS AND IS OPTIONAL.
                   WHEN INCLUDED, IT IS ADDED TO THE ADDRESS OF
                   EACH MEMORY LOCATION BEFORE THE DATA IS STORED.

        EXAMPLES: IM BACKUP
                   MEMORY IS LOADED FROM THE ROM FILE "BACKUP" AND
                   IS STORED IN THE MF FILE.

                   IM BACKUP,1000
                   MEMORY IS LOADED FROM THE ROM FILE "BACKUP" AND
                   IS STORED IN THE MF FILE AFTER RELOCATING EACH
                   WORD OF MEMORY 1000 LOCATIONS FORWARD.

                   IM BACKUP,0FFFE
                   BECAUSE OF THE WRAP-AROUND CHARACTERISTIC OF
                   MEMORY, EACH WORD OF MEMORY FROM THE ROM FILE
                   IS RELOCATED BACKWARD 2 LOCATIONS.

1011

    LW - SET LAST WORD ADDRESS OF MEMORY
        FORMAT: LW LWA-1
        FUNCTION: THE LAST WORD OF MEMORY IS DEFINED TO BE LWA-1.
                   LWA-1 MUST BE A MULTIPLE OF 256-1 (N*256-1) AND
                   IN THE RANGE 255-65535. ANY ADDITIONAL MEMORY
                   ADDED TO THE "MF" FILE IS PRESET TO ZERO.

        EXAMPLES: LW 3FF
                   THE LAST WORD ADDRESS OF MEMORY IS DEFINED TO
                   BE HEXADECIMAL 3FF.

1012

    MF - MACHINE FILE
        FORMAT: MF FILENAME-1
        FUNCTION: THE MF COMMAND LOADS FILE FILENAME-1 INTO A WORK
                   AREA. THE CC, CF, DM, IM, LW, ML, MO, OM, RF,
                   SM, TI, AND UM COMMANDS ALL REQUIRE A MF FILE
                   TO BE LOADED PR   SOURCE
        EXAMPLES: MF MEMORY
                   THE MACHINE FILE "MEMORY" IS IDENTIFIED AS THE
                   MF FILE.

TABLE 7-1.6-2. HELP Listing of Simulator and BVM Commands (Sheet 3 of 13)

1013
```
    ML - MACRO LISTING
        FORMAT:     ML
        FUNCTION:   A DIRECTORY OF THE MACRO LIBRARY IN THE
                    MF FILE IS PRINTED.

        EXAMPLES:   ML
```
1014
```
    MO - MACHINE ORGANIZATION
        FORMAT:     MO
        FUNCTION:   THE CONFIGURATION OF THE "MF" FILE IS PRINTED.

        EXAMPLES:   MO
```
1015
```
    OM - OUTPUT MEMORY
        FORMAT:     OM FILENAME-1(FWA-1,LWA-1[,RFWA-1])
                            [(FWA-2,LWA-2[,RFWA-2])...]
        FUNCTION:   OUTPUTS THE SPECIFIED REGIONS OF MEMORY FROM THE
                    "MF" FILE INTO FILE FILENAME-1.  FWA-1 IS THE
                    FIRST WORD ADDRESS AND LWA-1 IS THE LAST WORD
                    ADDRESS OF THE FIRST REGION.  RFWA-1 IS THE ROM
                    MEMORY FIRST WORD ADDRESS.  IF PRESENT, MEMORY
                    IS RELOCATED TO THIS STARTING ADDRESS IN THE ROM
                    OUTPUT FILE.
                        ROM PAPER TAPE FORMAT
                    BYTE 1 - RECORD TYPE
                        S0 - HEADER RECORD
                        S1 - DATA RECORD
                        S9 - END OF FILE RECORD
                    BYTE 2 - RECORD LENGTH IN BYTES (DOES NOT
                        INCLUDE BYTE 1)
                    BYTE 3 - UPPER BYTE OF MEMORY ADDRESS
                    BYTE 4 - LOWER BYTE OF MEMORY ADDRESS
                    LAST
                    BYTE   - CHECKSUM OF BYTES.  THE CHECKSUM +
                        THE SUM OF BYTES = 255 (MODULO 256).
                        ALL BYTES BETWEEN BYTE 4 AND THE
                        CHECKSUM BYTE ARE DATA BYTES.  THE
                        MEMORY ADDRESS OF THE FIRST DATA
                        BYTE IS IN BYTES 3 AND 4.  SUCCESSIVE
                        DATA BYTES HAVE SUCCESSIVE MEMORY
                        ADDRESSES.

        EXAMPLES:   OM TOM(0,0FF)
                    MEMORY IS OUTPUT IN ROM PAPER TAPE FORMAT INTO
                    FILE "TOM".  THE REGION OF MEMORY OUTPUT IS
                    LOCATIONS 0 THROUGH FF.

                    OM DICK(100,1FF,2000)
                    THE ADDRESSES FOR THE REGION OF MEMORY FROM
                    TIONS 100 THROUGH 1FF ARE REASSIGNED TO LOCATIONS
                    2000 THROUGH 20FF BEFORE BEING OUTPUT INTO ROM
                    FILE "DICK".

                    OM,HARRY(0,2FF)(300,4FF,600)
                    TWO REGIONS OF MEMORY ARE OUPUT TO ROM FILE
                    "HARRY"  ADDRESSES FOR THE SECOND REGION ARE
                    REASSIGNED TO LOCATIONS 600 THROUGH 7FF.
```

TABLE 7-1.6-2. HELP Listing of Simulator and BVM Commands (Sheet 4 of 13)

1016

    RF - RENAME FILE
        FORMAT: RF FILENAME-1
        FUNCTION: A DUPLICATE COPY OF THE "MF" FILE IS MADE AND IS
                    RENAMED FILENAME-1. THE OLD "MF" FILE AND ITS
                    FILENAME ARE SAVED.

        EXAMPLES: RF NEWNAM
                    A COPY OF THE MF FILE WAS MADE AND RENAMED "NEWNAM

1017

    SM - SET MEMORY
        FORMAT: SM FWA-1,VALUE-1[,VALUE-2,...]
        FUNCTION: LOCATION FWA-1 IS SET TO VALUE-1, THE NEXT LOCA-
                    TION IS SET TO VALUE-2, ETC.

        EXAMPLES: SM 10,1
                    THE CONTENTS OF LOCATION 10 IS SET TO 1.

                    SM 20,1,2,3,4,5,6,7,8
                    THE CONTENTS OF LOCATIONS 20 THROUGH 27 ARE SET
                    TO 1 THROUGH 8.

1018

    TI - ENTER "MF" TITLE
        FORMAT: TI.
        FUNCTION: BUILD VIRTUAL WILL REQUEST A LINE OF TEXT BY
                    PRINTING: " ENTER TITLE TEXT".
                    ENTER ONE LINE OF TEXT AND A CARRIAGE RETURN.
                    BUILD VIRTUAL WILL CONTINUE TO REQUEST TEXT UNTIL
                    A BLANK LINE IS ENTERED OR THE LABEL BUFFER IS
                    FILLED. THE TITLE OR MACHINE FILE'S LABEL WILL BE
                    PRINTED EACH TIME THE FILE IS OPENED OR WHEN THE
                    "MO" COMMAND IS USED.

        EXAMPLES: TI.MO.
                    ENTER TITLE TEXT
                     THIS IS THE 1ST LINE OF THE TITLE
                    ENTER TITLE TEXT
                     THIS IS LINE 2 OF THE TITLE
                    ENTER TITLE TEXT

                    THE TITLE WILL BE ENTER AND THAN THE MEMORY
                    ORGANIZATION WILL BE PRINT.

1019

    UF - UNSAVE FILE
        FORMAT: UF FILENAME-1[,FILENAME-2,...]
        FUNCTION: THE FILES WHOSE NAMES APPEAR IN THE FILENAME LIST
                    ARE DELETED FROM THE USER'S LIBRARY.

        EXAMPLES: UF PETE
                    MACHINE FILE "PETE" ID DELETED FROM USER
                    CATALOG.

                    UF FILE1,FILE2,FILE3
                    THE THREE FILES, FILE1, FILE2, AND FILE3 ARE
                    DELETED.

TABLE 7-1.6-2. HELP Listing of Simulator and BVM Commands (Sheet 5 of 13)

1020

UM - UPDATE MACHINE FILE
      FORMAT: UM
      FUNCTION: THE "MF" FILE IS UPDATED TO THE LATEST MPU STAND-
                  ARDS. AN "OLD VERSION" ERROR MESSAGE WILL INFORM
                  THE USER WHEN TO UPDATE THE "MF" FILE.

      EXAMPLES: UM

1985

MP9VM - BUILD VIRTUAL RELEASE 1.4
      1) THE "UF" COMMAND WILL UNSAVE BOTH BINARY AND ASCII FILES.
      2) THE "OM" COMMAND NO LONGER HANGS UP IF THE FILENAME IS
         IS NOT INCLUDED IN THE COMMAND.
      3) MULTIPLE LINES OF TEXT MAY BE ENTERED ON A "TI" COMMAND.
      4) THE "IM" (INPUT MEMORY FROM ROM FILE) COMMAND ADDED.

1990

      *** THIS IS A NEW RELEASE OF THE BUILD VIRTUAL. ***
FOR MORE INFORMATION LIST MESSAGE TEXT FOR 1990 IN "HELP"
      EX: RUN HELP, TYPE-IN "T 1990" CARRIAGE RETURN

TO LIST THE CHANGES TO THE NEW BUILD VIRTUAL TYPE-IN THE FOLLOWING

      1) LIST THE INDEX TO THE CHANGES.
         TURN OFF THE "T" (TEXT) TOGGLE AND TURN ON THE "I" (INDEX)
         TOGGLE. THE TOGGLE'S STATUS WILL BE PRINTED EACH TIME IT
         IS TYPED IN. EX: TYPE-IN "T T CR" (CR => CARRIAGE RETURN)
         NOW SET THE TOGGLES AND TYPE-IN "1980 TO 1989 CR"
         THIS WILL LIST THE INDEXES OF THE RELEASES.

      2) LIST THE INDEX AND TEXT OF THE CHANGES.
         TURN ON THE "I" AND "T" TOGGLES AND AND TYPE-IN
         "1980 TO 1989 CR".

      3) LIST ALL HELP MESSAGES WHICH HAVE CHANGED.
         TURN ON THE "I" TOGGLE AND TURN OFF THE "T" TOGGLE THAN
         TYPE-IN "06/11/74 TO 11/10/74 CR" THIS WILL LIST THE
         INDEX OF ALL THE MESSAGES IN HELP WHICH HAVE BEEN CHANGED
         OR ADDED TO THE MESSAGE FILE.

      4) TO EXIT HELP, TYPE-IN "EX CR".

3001

BC - BREAK POINT CLEAR

      FORMAT: BC
      FUNCTION: CLEARS ALL BREAK POINTS AND SETS THE BREAK
                  POINT FLAG TO RESET.

      FORMAT: BC ADR-1[,ADR-2,...]
      FUNCTION: CLEARS ONLY THE BREAK POINTS SET AT MEMORY
                  ADDRESSES ADR-1,ADR-2,...

TABLE 7-1.6-2. HELP Listing of Simulator and BVM Commands (Sheet 6 of 13)

3002

BD - DISPLAY BREAK POINTS
    FORMAT: BD
    FUNCTION: DISPLAY THE BREAK POINT FLAG (RESET, ALL OR
                  STORE) AND ALL MEMORY ADDRESSES WHERE A BREAK
                  P INT IS SET.

3003

BP - SET BREAK POINTS FOR READ AND STORE ALL.
    FORMAT: BP ADR-1[,ADR-2,...]
    FUNCTION: SET BREAK POINTS AT MEMORY ADDRESSES ADR-1,
                  ADR-2,... THE SIMULATOR WILL STOP AND
                  PRINT THE SELECTED REGISTERS WHENEVER A BREAK
                  POINT LOCATION IS READ OR STORED INTO. BREAK
                  POINTS MAY BE SET ON ANY BYTE OF MEMORY. THERE
                  IS NO LIMIT ON THE NUMBER OF BREAK POINTS.

    FORMAT: BP
    FUNCTION: SET THE BREAK POINT FLAG TO ALL MODES.

    FORMAT: NOBP OR NBP
    FUNCTION: SET THE BREAK POINT FLAG TO RESET. (BREAK
                  POINTS SET IN MEMORY ARE NOT CHANGED.)

3004

BS - SET BREAK POINTS FOR STORE ONLY
    FORMAT: BS ADR-1[,ADR-2,...]
    FUNCTION: SET BREAK POINTS AT MEMORY ADDRESSES ADR-1,
                  ADR-2,... THE SIMULATOR WILL STOP AND PRINT
                  THE SELECTED REGISTERS WHENEVER A BREAK POINT
                  LOCATION IS STORED INTO.

    FORMAT: BS
    FUNCTION: SET THE BREAK POINT FLAG TO STORE MODE.

    FORMAT: NOBS OR NBS
    FUNCTION: SET THE BREAK POINT FLAG TO RESET. (BREAK
                  POINTS SET ON MEMORY ARE NOT CHANGED.)

3005

D - DISPLAY REGISTERS
    FORMAT: D
    FUNCTION: THE CONTENTS OF THE REGISTERS SELECTED WITH THE
                  SD COMMAND ARE DISPLAYED. NUMERICAL VALUES ARE
                  DISPLAYED IN THE DISPLAY BASE SELECTED BY THE DB
                  COMMAND.

3005

DB - SET DISPLAY BASE
    FORMAT: DB BASE-1   (WHERE BASE-1 = 8, 10 OR 16)
    FUNCTION: THE DISPLAY BASE IS SET TO OCTAL, DECIMAL,
                  OR HEXADECIMAL WHEN BASE-1 IS 8, 10, OR 16,
                  RESPECTIVELY

    EXAMPLES: DB 8
                  NUMERIC OUTPUT FROM THE DM COMMAND WILL BE DIS-
                  PLAYED IN OCTAL.

TABLE 7-1.6-2. HELP Listing of Simulator and BVM Commands (Sheet 7 of 13)

3007

DF - SET DISPLAY FLAG
FORMAT: DF FLAG-1   (WHERE FLAG-1 = 1, 2, OR 3)
FUNCTION: MEMORY DUMPS WILL APPEAR IN NUMERIC, CHARACTER,
            OR BOTH WHEN FLAG-1 IS 1, 2, OR 3, RESPECTIVELY.
            THE DEFAULT SETTING IS 3.

EXAMPLES: DF 2
            OUTPUT FROM THE DM COMMAND WILL BE DISPLAYE IN
            CHARACTER FORMAT ONLY.

3008

DL - DISPLAY LAST INSTRUCTION
FORMAT: DL
FUNCTION: DISPLAY THE LAST INSTRUCTION PREVIOUSLY EXECUTED.

3009

DM - DISPLAY MEMORY
FORMAT: DM FWA-1,WCT-1
FUNCTION: WCT-1 WORDS OF MEMORY BEGINNING AT LOCATION FWA-1
            ARE DISPLAYED. THE FORMAT OF THE DISPLAY IS
            DETERMINED BY THE DF SWITCH. MEMORY IS DUMPED
            FROM THE "MF" FILE.

EXAMPLES: DM 100,20
            DISPLAY 20 (HEXADECIMAL) WORDS OF MEMORY STARTING
            FROM LOCATION 100.

3010

EX - EXIT
FORMAT: EX
FUNCTION: EXIT FROM THE SIMULATOR AFTER SAVING THE STATUS
            AS FOR THE SS COMMAND, AND ALSO SAVING THE MACRO
            LIBRARY, AND ALL OF MEMORY INCLUDING THE CURRENT
            MEMORY PAGES.

3011

HR - SET HEADER COUNT
FORMAT: HR COUNT-1
FUNCTION: PRINT THE REGISTER HEADER LINE EVERY COUNT-1
            LINES OF PRINT.

TABLE 7-1.6-2. HELP Listing of Simulator and BVM Commands (Sheet 8 of 13)

3012

HP - HELP
       FORMAT: HP MESSAGECODE-1[SWITCH-1]
       FUNCTION: INFORMATION ABOUT MESSAGECODE-1 IS PRINTED.
                      MESSAGECODE-1 HAS ONE OF THE FOLLOWING FORMS:
                         NNNN   WHERE NNNN IS A NUMBER FROM 1 TO 9999
                                 CORRESPONDING TO ANY HELP MESSAGE
                         CMD   WHERE CMD IS A SIMULATOR COMMAND
                         ALL   WHERE THE WORD "ALL" REQUESTS THAT
                                 INFORMATION FOR ALL SIMULATOR COMMANDS
                                 BE PRINTED.
                      SWITCH-1 CONTROLS THE AMOUNT OF DETAIL TO BE
                      PRINTED AND HAS ONE OF THE FOLLOWING FORMS:
                         I   PRINT INDEX OF MESSAGE ONLY
                         T   PRINT TEXT OF MESSAGE ONLY
                         B   PRINT BOTH THE INDEX AND TEXT
                      IF SWITCH-1 IS OMITTED, THEN OPTION I IS USED.

                      ENTER 'HP 4012 B' FOR INFORMATION ON THE SYN-
                      TAX USED IN THE HELP MESSAGES.

                      ENTER 'HP ALL I' FOR A LIST OF ALL SIMULATOR
                      COMMANDS.
3013

IB - SET INPUT BASE
       FORMAT   IB BASE-1 (WHERE BASE-1 IS 2, 8, 10, OR 16)
       FUNCTION: THE INPUT BASE IS SET TO BINARY, OCTAL, DECIMAL,
                      OR HEXADECIMAL WHEN BASE-1 IS 2, 8, 10, OR 16,
                      RESPECTIVELY.

       EXAMPLES: IB 8
                      THE INPUT BASE IS SET TO OCTAL. ALL NUMBERS
                      IN THE COMMANDS WILL BE INTERPRETED AS OCTAL
                      UNLESS THERE IS DIFFERENT BASE IMPLIED AS PART
                      OF THE BASE (IE., DM 0,$10 WILL DUMP 10 HEX-
                      ADECIMAL LOCATIONS).
3014

IR - SET INTERRUPT REQUEST
       FORMAT: IR FWA-1[,LWA-1]
       FUNCTION: NO DOCUMENT AVAILABLE.
3015

LM - LIST MACRO SWITCH
       FORMAT: LM
       FUNCTION: LIST EACH COMMAND BEFORE IT IS EXECUTED. ENTER
                      THE NOLM COMMAND TO INHIBIT THE PRINTING OF EACH
                      COMMAND.
3016

MD - MACRO DELETE
       FORMAT: MD MACRO-1[,MACRO-2,...]
       FUNCTION: DELELTE MACROS MACRO-1, MACRO-2, ... FROM THE
                      MACRO LIBRARY.

TABLE 7-1.6-2. HELP Listing of Simulator and BVM Commands (Sheet 9 of 13)

3017

```
ML - MACRO LISTING
    FORMAT:     ML
    FUNCTION:   A LISTING OF THE MACRO LIBRARY AND THE AVAILABLE
                STORAGE REMAINING FOR NEW MACROS IS PRINTED.
```

3018

```
MR - MACRO RESTORE
    FORMAT:     MR
    FUNCTION:   RESTORE THE MACRO LIBRARY WHICH WAS SAVED BY THE
                LAST MS OR EX COMMAND.
```

3019

```
MS - SAVE MACRO LIBRARY
    FORMAT:     MS
    FUNCTION:   THE CURRENT MACRO LIBRARY (AS IT APPEARS WHEN
                DISPLAYED WITH THE ML COMMAND) IS SAVED IN THE
                MACHINE FILE.
```

3020

```
OF - DELETE 'ON' COMMANDS
    FORMAT:     OF [CONDITION-1]
    FUNCTION:   'ON' COMMANDS ARE REMOVED FROM THE 'ON' CONDITION
                LIBRARY. IF THE CONDITION-1 IS SPECIFIED, THEN
                ONLY THAT 'ON' COMMAND IS REMOVED. IF NO CONDI-
                TION IS SPECIFIED THEN ALL 'ON' CONDITIONS ARE
                REMOVED. SEE THE 'ON' COMMAND FOR CONDITION-1'S
                FORMAT.

    EXAMPLES:   OF
                REMOVES ALL 'ON' COMMANDS FROM THE LIBRARY.

                OF,A=0FF.
                REMOVE ONLY THE 'ON' COMMAND WITH THE CONDITION
                A=0FF.
                WILL BE DELETED.
```

3021

```
OL - LIST THE 'ON' CONDITION LIBRARY
    FORMAT:     OL
    FUNCTION:   A LISTING OF THE 'ON' CONDITION LIBRARY AND THE
                AVAILABLE STORAGE REMAINING FOR NEW 'ON' COMMANDS
                WILL BE PRINTED.
```

TABLE 7-1.6-2. HELP Listing of Simulator and BVM Commands (Sheet 10 of 13)

3022

ON - SET AND STORE A 'ON' CONDITION COMMAND INTO THE LIBRARY
     FORMAT: ON,CONDITION-1,COMMAND-1.
     FUNCTION: WHEN CONDITION-1 IS TRUE, THE CURRENT COMMAND
                  LINE IS TERMINATED. THE COMMAND COMMAND-1 IS THEN
                  EXECUTED. THE 'LM' COMMAND SHOULD BE ON SO THE
                  COMMANDS ARE LISTED BEFORE THEY ARE EXECUTED.

                  CONDITION FORMAT: CODE-1 [OPERATION-1 VAULE-1]
                  WHERE CODE-1 IS ANY OF THE FOLLOWING REGISTER
                  CODES:
                   X - INDEX REGISTER
                   A - ACCUMULATOR A
                   B - ACCUMULATOR B
                   S - STACK POINTER
                   T - TIME
                  OR FAULT CODES:
                   BP - BREAK POINT FAULT
                   MF - MEMORY FAULT
                   F - ALL OTHER FAULTS
                  OPERATION-1 IS OPTIONAL AND MAY BE ANY OF THE
                  FOLLOWING LOGICAL OPERTIONS:
                   = IF THE CODE EQUALS THE VAULE THE CONDITON IS
                     TRUE AND THE COMMAND IS EXECUTED.
                   < IF THE CODE IS LESS THAN THE VAULE THE CONDI-
                     TION IS TRUE AND THE COMMAND IS EXECUTED.
                   > IF THE CODE IS GREATER THAN THE VAULE THE CON-
                     DITION IS TRUE AND THE COMMAND IS EXECUTED.
                  VALUE-1 IS THE PARAMETER WHICH IS COMPARED TO
                  CODE-1 AND IS INCLUDED IN THE CONDITION IF AND
                  ONLY IF OPERATION-1 IS INCLUDED.

                  COMMAND-1 IS ANY COMMAND OR MARCO WITH OR WITHOUT
                  PARAMETERS. ONLY ONE COMMAND CAN BE ENTERED. THE
                  FIRST PERIOD TERMINATES THE COMMAND LINE.

                  ONLY ONE REGISTER 'ON' COMMAND MAY BE ENTERED AT
                  A TIME, BUT MULTIPLE FAULTS MAY BE TESTED.

     EXAMPLES: ON,A>0F2,SAM,1,2.
                  ON THE A ACCUMULATOR GREATER THAN $F2 (HEX) THE
                  MACRO COMMAND 'SAM' AN IT'S PARAMETERS WILL BE
                  EXECUTED. (THE TRACE OR RUN WILL BE STOPPED)

                  ON,BP=100,DM,100,5.
                  WHEN A BREAK POINT OCCURS AT LOCATION 100, THE
                  TENTS OF MEMORY LOCATIONS 100 THRU 104 WILL BE
                  DISPLAYED. THE TRACE OR RUN WILL BE STOPPED.

                  ON,BP,DM,100,5
                  WHEN ANY BREAK POINT OCCURS, THE CONTENTS OF MEM-
                  ORY LOCATIONS 100 THRU 104 WILL BE DISPLAYED. THE
                  SIMULATOR WILL REQUEST A COMMAND.
3023

PF - SIMULATE POWER FAIL
     FORMAT: PF
     FUNCTION: SIMULATES POWER FAIL BY PUSHING THE REGISTERS
                  ONTO THE STACK AND LOADING THE POWER FAIL VECTOR
                  (LAST WORD ADDRESS-3) INTO THE P REGISTER.

TABLE 7-1.6-2. HELP Listing of Simulator and BVM Commands (Sheet 11 of 13)

3024

PI - PRINT INTERRUPT REQUESTS WHEN THEY OCCUR
    FORMAT: PI [,L]
    FUNCTION: NO DOCUMENT AVAILABLE.

3025

PO - SIMULATE POWER ON
    FORMAT: PO
    FUNCTION: SIMULATES THE POWER ON BY LOADING THE POWER ON
                VECTOR (LAST WORD ADDRESS-1) INTO THE P REGISTER
                AND LOADING RANDOM INFORMATION INTO THE OTHER
                REGISTERS.

3026

R - RUN
    FORMAT: R COUNT-1
    FUNCTION: RUN COUNT-1 INSTRUCTIONS WITHOUT PRINTING, AND
                THEN PRINT THE REGISTERS SELECTED BY THE SR COM-
                MAND. THE INPUT BASE OF COUNT-1 IS SET BY THE
                IB COMMAND.

3027

RC - REPEAT COMMAND
    FORMAT: RC COUNT-1
    FUNCTION: THE NEXT COMMAND IS EXECUTED COUNT-1 TIMES. IF
                THE RC COMMAND IS THE LAST COMMAND IN A LINE,
                THEN THE FIRST COMMAND IN THE NEXT LINE WILL BE
                REPEATED COUNT-1 TIMES.

3028

RL - REPEAT LINE
    FORMAT: RL COUNT-1
    FUNCTION: THE REMAINING PORTION OF THE COMMAND LINE (TO
                THE RIGHT OF THE RL COMMAND) IS EXECUTED COUNT-1
                TIMES. THE RL COMMAND WILL HAVE NO EFFECT IF IT
                IS THE LAST COMMAND IN THE LINE.

3029

RS - RESTORE SIMULATOR STATUS
    FORMAT: RS
    FUNCTION: RESTORE THE SIMULATOR STATUS SAVED WITH THE SS
                COMMAND.

3030

SD - SELECT DISPLAY REGISTERS
    FORMAT: SD REGISTER-1[REGISTER-2...]
    FUNCTION: REGISTERS REGISTER-1, REGISTER-2, ... ARE SELECT-
                ED TO BE DISPLAYED WHEN THE D, DL, R, AND T COM-
                MANDS ARE EXECUTED. REGISTER-1, REGISTER-2, ...
                CAN BE ANY OF THE FOLLOWING ONE CHARACTER CODES:
                    I - INSTRUCTION ADDRESS
                    O - OPERATOR MNEMONIC CODE
                    E - EFFECTIVE ADDRESS
                    P - PROGRAM COUNTER
                    X - INDEX REGISTER
                    A - ACCUMULATOR A
                    B - ACCUMULATOR B
                    C - CONDITION CODES
                    S - STACK POINTER
                    T - TIME

TABLE 7-1.6-2. HELP Listing of Simulator and BVM Commands (Sheet 12 of 13)

3031

    SM - SET MEMORY
        FORMAT: SM FWA-1,VALUE-1[,VALUE-2,...]
        FUNCTION: LOCATION FWA-1 IS SET TO VALUE-1, THE NEXT LOCA-
                     TION IS SET TO VALUE-2, ETC.

        EXAMPLES: SM 10,1
                     THE CONTENTS OF LOCATION 10 IS SET TO 1.

                     SM 20,1,2,3,4,5,6,7,8
                     THE CONTENTS OF LOCATIONS 20 THROUGH 27 ARE SET
                     TO 1 THROUGH 8.
3032

    SR - SET REGISTER
        FORMAT: SR REGISTER-1 VALUE-1[,REGISTER-2 VALUE-2,...]
        FUNCTION: THE REGISTERS IN THE LIST ARE SET TO THEIR RE-
                     SPECTIVE VALUES. REGISTER-1, REGISTER-2, ... CAN
                     BE ANY OF THE FOLLOWING ONE CHARACTER CODES:
                         P - PROGRAM COUNTER
                         X - INDEX REGISTER
                         A - ACCUMULATOR A
                         B - ACCUMULATOR B
                         C - CONDITION CODES
                         S - STACK POINTER
                         T - TIME
3033

    SS - SAVE SIMULATOR STATUS
        FORMAT: SS
        FUNCTION: SAVE THE SIMULATOR STATUS IN THE MEMORY FILE.
                     ALL REGISTER SETTINGS AND SELECTED OPTIONS ARE
                     SAVED. THE MACRO LIBRARY AND CURRENT MPU MEM-
                     ORY PAGES ARE NOT SAVED.
3034

    TB - TRACE BRANCHES
        FORMAT: TB [COUNT-1]
        FUNCATION: RUN COUNT-1 INSTRUCTIONS AND PRINT THE SELECTED
                     REGISTERS AFTER EVERY BRANCH, JMP, JSR, BSR, RTI,
                     RTS, OR SWI INSTRUCTION IS EXECUTED. IF COUNT-1
                     IS OMITTED ONLY ONE INSTRUCTON IS EXECUTED. SEE
                     COMMANDS SD AND DB FOR SELECTING THE REGISTERS
                     DISPLAYED AND THE DISPLAY BASE

        EXAMPLES: TB 7
                     RUN 7 INSTRUCTIONS AND TRACE ANY BRANCHES FOUND
                     (PRINT THE SELECTED REGISTERS).
3035

    T - TRACE INSTRUCTION EXECUTION
        FORMAT: T COUNT-1
        FUNCTION: COUNT-1 INSTRUCTIONS ARE TRACED. THE REGISTERS
                     THE EXECUTION OF EACH INSTRUCTION.

TABLE 7-1.6-2. HELP Listing of Simulator and BVM Commands (Sheet 13 of 13)

4000

HELP DIRECTORY

FOR MORE INFORMATION CONCERNING A GIVEN SUBJECT ENTER THE
SUBJECT'S INDEX FOLLOWED BY A CARRIAGE RETURN.

    INDEX   SUBJECT
    4011   HELP COMMANDS
    4012   SYNTAX NOTATION CONVENTION
    4013   MESSAGE FILE

4011

HELP COMMANDS

GENERAL: THE HELP SYSTEM OPERATES ON A MESSAGE FILE. THE MESSAGE
         FILE CONSISTS OF ENGLISH TYPE STATEMENTS DESIGNED TO ASSIST
         THE USER WITH MOTOROLA'S MPU SOFTWARE. THERE IS AN INDEX
         AND A TEXT PART TO EACH MESSAGE. MESSAGE CREATION DATES AND
         MESSAGE NUMBERS ARE ASSIGNED TO THE MESSAGES. THE MESSAGES
         ARE FURTHER ORGANIZED INTO SYSTEM GROUPS. THERE ARE INDI-
         VIDUAL MESSAGE GROUPS FOR ERRORS, FOR THE ASSEMBLER,
         BUILD VIRTUAL MACHINE, SIMULATOR, AND HELP SYSTEMS. A USER
         MAY ACCESS THE MESSAGES BY SPECIFYING A MESSAGE NUMBER, A
         RANGE OF MESSAGE NUMBERS, A RANGE OF CREATION DATES, OR THE
         ENTIRE MESSAGE FILE. A MODE CAN BE ENTERED WHERE THE RANGE-
         OF-DATES AND PRINT-ALL-MESSAGES COMMANDS APPLY ONLY TO THE
         SELECTED GROUP (ERRORS, ASSEMBLER, BUILD VITUAL, SIMULATOR,
         OR HELP GROUPS). THREE TOGGLE COMMANDS SELECT/DESELECT THE
         PRINTING OF THE MESSAGE NUMBER-CREATION DATE, INDEX, AND
         TEXT PORTIONS OF EACH MESSAGE.

PRINT MESSAGE COMMANDS

    COMMAND: NUMBER-1
    FUNCTION: PRINT MESSAGE NUMBER-1

    COMMAND: NUMBER-1,NUMBER-2,NUMBER-3,...
    FUNCTION: PRINT MESSAGES NUMBER-1, NUMBER-2, NUMBER-3 ...

    COMMAND: NUMBER-1 TO NUMBER-2
    FUNCTION: PRINT ALL MESSAGES FROM MESSAGE NUMBER NUMBER-1
               TO MESSAGE NUMBER NUMBER-2.

    COMMAND: DATE-1
    FUNCTION: PRINT ALL MESSAGES WHICH WERE ENTERED (CREATED)
               FROM DATE-1 UNTIL TODAY'S DATE. DATES ARE
               ENTERED IN THE FORMAT: MM/DD/YY WHERE MM IS THE
               MONTH, DD IS THE DAY, AND YY IS THE YEAR.

    FORMAT: DATE-1 TO DATE-2
    FUNCTION: PRINT ALL MESSAGES WHICH WERE ENTERED (CREATED)
               FROM DATE-1 TO DATE-2.

    COMMAND: ALL
    FUNCTION: PRINT EVERY MESSAGE IN THE MESSAGE FILE OR EVERY
               COMMAND WAS PREVIOUSLY EXECUTED.

TABLE 7-1.6-3. HELP Messages (Sheet 1 of 3)

SELECT GROUP COMMANDS

COMMAND: C
FUNCTION: SELECT THE ASSEMBLER'S MESSAGE GROUP.

COMMAND: B
FUNCTION: SELECT THE BUILD VIRTUAL MESSAGE'S GROUP.

COMMAND: E
FUNCTION: SELECT THE ERROR'S MESSAGE GROUP.

COMMAND: H
FUNCTION: SELECT THE HELP SYSTEM'S MESSAGE GROUP.

COMMAND: S
FUNCTION: SELECT THE SIMULATOR'S MESSAGE GROUP.

TOGGLE COMMANDS

COMMAND: I
FUNCTION: TOGGLE THE PRINT INDEX SWITCH (ON/OFF)

COMMAND: N
FUNCTION: TOGGLE THE PRINT MESSAGE NUMBER SWITCH (ON/OFF)

COMMAND: T
FUNCTION: TOGGLE THE PRINT TEXT SWITCH (ON/OFF)

COMMAND: P
FUNCTION: TOGGLE THE PAGING SWITCH (ON/OFF)
            THE HELP MESSAGE WILL BE PRINTED ON 65 LINES PER
            PAGE. (53 LINES OF TEXT).

EXIT COMMAND

COMMAND: EX
FUNCTION: EXIT THE HELP SYSTEM.

NOTES: 1. MULTIPLE COMMANDS CAN BE ENTERED ON A SINGLE LINE BY
            SEPERATING THE COMMANDS WITH A SPACE.

        2. A SIMILAR HELP STRUCTURE IS CURRENTLY AVAILABLE IN
            THE BUILD VIRTUAL MACHINE AND SIMMULATOR SYSTEMS.
            USER INSTRUCTIONS FOR THESE HELP SYSTEMS ARE PROVIDED
            IN THE RESPECTIVE SYSTEM.

TABLE 7-1.6-3. HELP Messages (Sheet 2 of 3)

SYNTAX NOTATION CONVENTION

GENERAL   - BUILD VIRTUAL AND SIMULATOR COMMANDS CONSIST
             OF A COMMAND CODE FOLLOWED, USUALLY BY ONE OR
             MORE OPERANDS.   OPERANDS PROVIDE THE SPECIFIC
             INFORMATION FOR THE COMMAND TO PERFORM THE
             REQUESTED OPERATION.   THE FOLLOWING SET OF SYM-
             BOLS IS USED TO DEFINE THE FORMAT OF EACH COM-
             MAND, BUT THEY SHOULD NEVER BE ENTERED AS PART
             OF THE COMMAND.
               -   HYPHEN
               [ ] BRACKETS
               ... ELLIPSIS

COMMANDS - BUILD VIRTUAL AND SIMULATOR COMMANDS ARE TWO
             LETTER MNEMONIC CODES.   MACRO COMMANDS (USER
             DEFINED COMMANDS) CONSIST OF ONE TO FOUR LETTER
             CODES.   A COMPLETE LIST OF THE SYSTEM COMMANDS
             IS PRINTED WHEN THE 'HP AL I' COMMAND IS ENTERED
             DURING A BUILD VIRTUAL OR SIMULATOR SESSION   A
             LIST OF ALL MACRO COMMANDS IS PRINTED WHEN THE 'ML
             COMMAND IS ENTERED.

OPERANDS - OPERANDS ARE IDENTIFIED BY THE HYPHEN.   AN
             OPERAND WILL CONSIST OF A SYMBOLIC NAME FOLLOWED
             BY THE HYPHEN WHICH IS FOLLOWED BY A NUMBER.   A
             USER SUPPLIED VALUE IS SUBSTITUTED FOR THE OPERAND
             IN THE COMMAND LINE.   THE HYPHEN AND THE NUMBER
             APPENDED TO EACH SYMBOLIC NAME IS USED TO DIFFER-
             ENTIATE AMONG THE POSSIBLE MULTIPLE OCCURRENCES OF
             A GIVEN OPERAND IN A COMMAND DEFINITION.

HYPHENS   - HYPHENS IDENTIFY AN OPERAND IN THE STATEMENT DEF-
             INITION.   THEY ARE NOT ENTERED IN THE ACTUAL COM-
             MAND.

BRACKETS - BRACKETS IMPLY OPTIONAL INPUT.   EVERTHING WITHIN
             A MATCHED PAIR OF BRACKETS IS OPTIONAL AND MAY BE
             OMITTED.   THE BRACKETS ARE NOT INCLUDED IN THE

             COMMAND LINE.
             NOTE: THE USE OF THE BRACKETS IN THE DEFINITION OF
                   COMMAND SYNTAX AND FORMAT IS NOT TO BE CON-
                   FUSED WITH THEIR USE IN MA CRO DEFINITIONS.

ELLIPSIS - AN ELLIPSIS INDICATES THAT THE PRECEDING ITEM OR
             GROUPS OF ITEMS MAY BE REPEATED MORE THAN ONCE
             IN SUCCESSION.

TABLE 7-1.6-3. HELP Messages (Sheet 3 of 3)

As the result of assembly, the original source program was converted into numerical machine language acceptable to the microprocessor. If the Assembler option "Memory" was chosen, the entire assembled program was saved by the timeshare computer and may now be used to create an output tape. This tape will not contain any of the source language, comments or Assembler directives provided by the Assembler listing. It will, however, contain all of the machine language instructions, addresses and data specified by the source program.

To create the output tape, the first step is to select and reformat the appropriate memory files. This is accomplished by using the Build Virtual Machine program on the timeshare service. The resulting reconfigured file is given a new name and saved. The next, and final step, is performed by requesting the timeshare computer to list the new file on a terminal that has the ability to punch or record a tape. The required BVM commands for generating the tape are repeated as Table 7-1.7-1 for review.

As an example of their use, the sequence for generating a tape using the Texas Instruments "Silent 700" terminal will be described.

(1) Access the host computer as described in Section 7-1.2.

(2) In response to the query "Type Old or New", type "OLD".

(3) In response to the query "File Name", type the name of the present memory file.

(4) Call the Build Virtual Machine program by typing "RUN MPBVM."

(5) MPBVM answers with a message and then a question mark.

(6) Enter "MF XYZ", where "XYZ" is the name of the memory file.

(7) In response to the next question mark, type "OM NEW (FA,LA)" where "NEW" is the name selected for a new memory file to be configured by BVM. "FA" means the first address in memory of the user's program, and "LA" means the last address. These addresses are entered in hexadecimal notation.

(8) When BVM again responds with a question mark, it means the new reconfigured file has been created.

(9) Next type "EX". This command causes the new file to be saved and then exits the BVM program.

(10) At this time, the terminal should be prepared for either printing or recording a tape of the new file.

(11) For the "SILENT 700", a tape cassette is inserted, rewound and loaded. The Record control is placed on-line, tape format control set to line, and keyboard and printer turned on if a printed-out check listing of the tape is desired.

(12) The user types "OLD NEW" where "NEW" is the name of the file that was created in Step 8.

(13) When the terminal prints "ready", type "LIST N H". This command will cause the file to be listed without a header when a carriage return is typed.

MF - MACHINE FILE
        FORMAT: MF FILENAME-1
        FUNCTION: THE MF COMMAND LOADS FILE FILENAME-1 INTO A WORK
                     AREA. THE CC, CF, DM, IM, LW, ML, MO, OM, RF,
                     SM, TI, AND UM COMMANDS ALL REQUIRE A MF FILE
                     TO BE LOADED PR   SOURCE

        EXAMPLES: MF MEMORY
                     THE MACHINE FILE "MEMORY" IS IDENTIFIED AS THE
                     MF FILE.

OM - OUTPUT MEMORY
        FORMAT: OM FILENAME-1(FWA-1,LWA-1[,RFWA-1])
                        [(FWA-2,LWA-2[,RFWA-2])...]
        FUNCTION: OUTPUTS THE SPECIFIED REGIONS OF MEMORY FROM THE
                     "MF" FILE INTO FILE FILENAME-1. FWA-1 IS THE
                     FIRST WORD ADDRESS AND LWA-1 IS THE LAST WORD
                     ADDRESS OF THE FIRST REGION. RFWA-1 IS THE ROM
                     MEMORY FIRST WORD ADDRESS. IF PRESENT, MEMORY
                     IS RELOCATED TO THIS STARTING ADDRESS IN THE ROM
                     OUTPUT FILE.
                             ROM PAPER TAPE FORMAT
                     BYTE 1 - RECORD TYPE
                         S0 - HEADER RECORD
                         S1 - DATA RECORD
                         S9 - END OF FILE RECORD
                     BYTE 2 - RECORD LENGTH IN BYTES (DOES NOT
                              INCLUDE BYTE 1)
                     BYTE 3 - UPPER BYTE OF MEMORY ADDRESS
                     BYTE 4 - LOWER BYTE OF MEMORY ADDRESS
                     LAST
                     BYTE   - CHECKSUM OF BYTES. THE CHECKSUM +
                              THE SUM OF BYTES = 255 (MODULO 256).
                              ALL BYTES BETWEEN BYTE 4 AND THE
                              CHECKSUM BYTE ARE DATA BYTES. THE
                              MEMORY ADDRESS OF THE FIRST DATA
                              BYTE IS IN BYTES 3 AND 4. SUCCESSIVE
                              DATA BYTES HAVE SUCCESSIVE MEMORY
                              ADDRESSES.

        EXAMPLES: OM TOM(0,0FF)
                     MEMORY IS OUTPUT IN ROM PAPER TAPE FORMAT INTO
                     FILE "TOM". THE REGION OF MEMORY OUTPUT IS
                     LOCATIONS 0 THROUGH FF.

                     OM DICK(100,1FF,2000)
                     THE ADDRESSES FOR THE REGION OF MEMORY FROM
                     TIONS 100 THROUGH 1FF ARE REASSIGNED TO LOCATIONS
                     2000 THROUGH 20FF BEFORE BEING OUTPUT INTO ROM
                     FILE "DICK".

                     OM HARRY(0,2FF)(300,4FF,600)
                     TWO REGIONS OF MEMORY ARE OUPUT TO ROM FILE
                     "HARRY". ADDRESSES FOR THE SECOND REGION ARE
                     REASSIGNED TO LOCATIONS 600 THROUGH 7FF.

TABLE 7-1.7-1: BVM "Machine File" and "Output Memory" Commands

(14) The terminal Record button is pressed and a carriage return is typed on the Keyboard.

(15) The program machine code will now be recorded on the tape. Simultaneously, if the printer is turned on, it is listed line by line on the terminal.

The resulting tape is suitably formatted either for ordering ROMs or for entry into an EXORciser for further debug and checkout with the system peripherals.

7-2   THE EXORCISER

The EXORciser (Figure 7-2-1) is a flexible test instrument based on actual M6800 hardware devices. Because of this it can be used as an extension of the system prototype for evaluating and improving hardware/software compatibility. It includes built-in diagnostic and utility programs that can be used to debug the prototype system.

In contrast to the Simulator, which is a software program, the EXORciser is primarily hardware. Programs under development can be run with the actual system peripheral hardware under real time conditions. This allows both the software and hardware to be modified as required to improve system operation.

A typical EXORciser configuration is shown in block diagram form in Figure 7-2-2.

FIGURE 7-2-1: The EXORciser

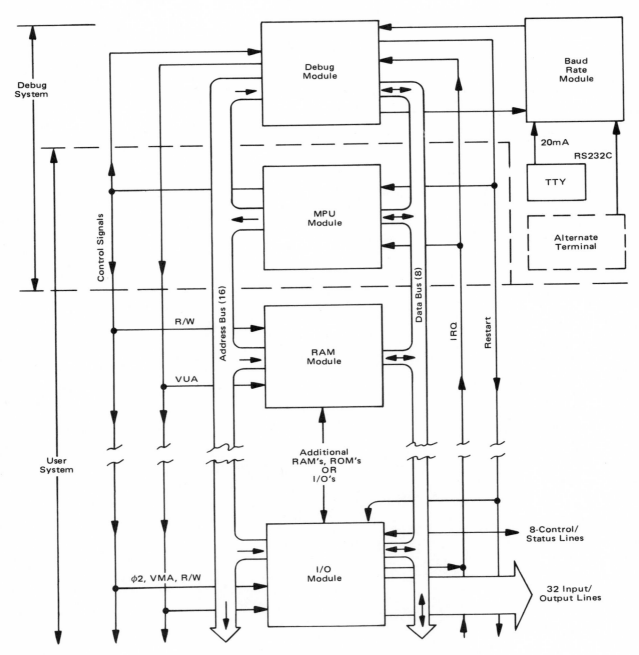

FIGURE 7-2-2: Typical EXORciser^{tm} System Block Diagram

7-2.1 HARDWARE COMPONENTS

The EXORciser chassis fits conveniently on a table top or in a rack. Communication with the user is through a separate data terminal keyboard and printer. The EXORciser controls are on its front panel. The microprocessor, memory, input/output interface, and other additional system elements are contained on plug-in boards which connect to the system busses on the backplane when the boards are inserted.

The basic EXORciser contains three functional modules. Two of these are mounted on separate plug-in boards. They are:

(1) Microprocessor Module

(2) Debug Module

The third, contained in the housing, is the Baud Rate Module which interfaces to the communication terminal.

In addition to the housing, control panel, card cage, and the two modules mentioned above, the EXORciser also has a power supply with reserve for up to 14 plug-in boards. This means there are 12 slots available for additional boards to implement the system configuration, since the EXORciser control nucleus only occupies two.

7-2.1.1 Hardware Specifications

The basic M6800SDT EXORciser Assembly consists of:

1. Equipment Housing: (Includes Chassis, Power Supply, Card Cage for 14 cards, and Band Rate Module.)

Chassis

Size: Tabletop:	7″ × 17½″ × 19¼″
Rackmount:	7″ × 17″ × 19″
Weight:	45 lbs. maximum

Module Compartment	Accommodates fourteen 5¾" × 9¾" modules
Front Panel Controls:	ON/OFF switch
	ABORT pushbutton switch
	RESTART pushbutton switch
Rear Control	Baud Rate Switch
	(110-9600 Baud) 8 pos.

Power Supply

AC Power Requirements:	60 Hz, 120 ± 10% VAC, 300 Watts
DC Power Supplies:	+5 VDC @ 15A
	+12 VDC @ 2.5A
	−12 VDC @ 1A
Operating Environment:	0°C to 55°C
Indicators (Front Panel):	RUN, ON/OFF, and Battery

Baud Rate Module

- Communications Clock Circuit
- Twelve switch selectable baud rates from 110 to 9600
- TTY (20 milliamp) and/or RS232C.

2. Microprocessor Module

- Complete microprocessor (MC6800)
- System crystal clock (1 MHz or external osc.)
- 8-Bit data word
- Bi-directional data bus
- 16-bit address bus
- 72 Instructions — variable length
- Seven addressing modes
- Variable length stack
- Real time interrupt capability
- Restart capability
- Non-Maskable interrupt
- Six internal registers — two accumulators, index register, program counter, stack pointer, condition code register
- 2μsec instruction cycle (1 MHz clock)
- Memory ready circuit for slow memories

This Card includes the MPU, and the necessary peripheral circuitry to provide the clock, powerfail/Restart and DMA functions. The clock circuit generates two phase signals for use by the MPU and the rest of the system. All Address, data, and control lines are equipped with bus drivers and brought out to the connector.

The DMA circuitry is utilized to transfer data to or from other devices at high speed and allows the use of memory units that operate at any speed up to the 1 MHz maximum.

3. DEBUG Module

Hardware Features

- Stop-on-address comparison circuit
- Provision for executing one instruction at a time
- ABORT and RESTART pushbutton switches
- Address selectable scope trigger

Programmed Features (EXbug)

- Load (reads tape into RAM)
- Verify (compare tape with memory)
- Punch (outputs memory contents on tape)
- Print (prints memory contents on terminal)
- Search (searches tape for desired object program)
- Examine and/or change memory
- Set/reset breakpoints
- Set breakpoint loop count
- Display/change registers
- Trace n instructions
- Trace to address
- Search memory for bit pattern
- Calculate offset for branch instructions
- Hex-octal-decimal conversions

4. Table Top Cover Kit or Rack Mounting Kit

The table top version is designated as M6800SDT-T(0) and the Rack mounted version is designated as M6800SDT-R(0)

Optional Items Include:

1. I/O Module (PIA's sold separately)   (Spec. 1810-103)
2. Static RAM Module (2K × 8)   (Spec. 1810-102)
3. Universal Wirewrap Module   (Spec. 1810-105)
4. Extender Module   (Spec. 1810-104)
5. Rack Mounting Kit   (Spec. 1810-106)
6. Table Top Cover Kit   (Spec. 1810-108)

Input/Output Module (optional)

- Four 8-bit peripheral data busses (TTL compatible)
- Each buss programmable for any input/output combination
- Wirewrap sockets for special interface circuits
- Eight individually controlled interrupt input lines — four usable as peripheral control lines
- Handshake control logic for input/output peripheral operation
- High impedance three-state and direct Darlington transistor drive peripheral lines
- Program controlled interrupt and interrupt mask capability
- Address select logic switchable to any memory location.

Static RAM Module (optional)

- 2K $\times$ 8 random access memory using 1K $\times$ 1 RAMs
- Address select logic for each 1K block assignment
- Expandable to 65K
- RAM/ROM control per 1K $\times$ 8 block of memory
- +5 VDC (only) operation
- No clocks required
- Compatible with Microprocessor Module
- 1μsec cycle time
- Interfaced via bus driver/receiver

Universal Wirewrap Module

- Plug-in board to accommodate integrated circuit sockets
- Wirewrap pins for simple breadboarding of prototype designs

Extender Module

- Plug-in board to extend another board for easy access to components.

7-2.2   SOFTWARE COMPONENTS

7-2.2.1   EXORciser Control

The EXORciser is controlled by EXbug, a diagnostic program which resides in 3072 bytes of ROM on the Debug board. This board also includes 256 bytes of RAM which the EXbug program uses to store interrupt addresses and variable parameters.

EXbug never has to be loaded into the EXORciser since it is permanently stored in ROM. The user's target program, however, must be loaded into the EXORciser's memory. EXbug performs this function along with several related ones.

After the tape holding the user's program (generated by the BVM program on the time share terminal), has been placed in position, EXbug is commanded to Search. When it locates the beginning of the program, it prints out an identification header. EXbug is then commanded to Load. This operation transfers the target program from tape into EXORciser memory. At this time, it is advisable to verify that the machine code of the tape has been corrected stored in memory. To do this, the tape is rewound to the beginning of the program, and EXbug is given the command, VERF. Each byte of memory is then compared with the corresponding byte on tape. Checksum errors are detected and printed out on the terminal. MAID, the debugging function of EXbug, may then be used to examine and alter memory or to trace, modify, or run the program.

After the program has been debugged or for an interim inspection, it may be desirable to print it or put it back on tape again. When given the command, PRNT, and the appropriate memory addresses, EXbug will output each stored byte to the terminal. To copy the program onto tape, the user first positions the tape and turns the recorder on. The EXbug command PNCH with the beginning and end memory addresses of the program, will then cause it to copied, byte by byte, from memory onto the tape.

7-2.2.2   MAID

The MAID (Motorola Active Interface Debug) routine of the EXORciser EXbug control program enables the user to perform the following operations in debugging a program:

- Examine and change data in a memory location.
- Examine and change the data in the MPU program registers and counters.
- Calculate the offset in the relative addressing mode.
- Insert, display, and remove breakpoints in the program.
- Freerun or trace the target program under MAID control.
- Perform decimal-octal-hexadecimal conversions.
- Search memory for a bit pattern.

These operations are carried out when one or more of the MAID control commands are entered on the data terminal keyboard. With the exception of the decimal-octal-hexadecimal base conversions, numerical values or addresses associated with the commands must be entered in hexadecimal notation.

After executing a command, MAID prints out an asterisk to indicate it is ready for another one. If MAID can not perform the command, it indicates this by ringing the bell on the terminal. In either case, the asterisk signifies that EXbug is still running the MAID routine and another command may be entered. The MAID commands are summarized in Table 7-2.2.2-1.

7-2.3 MEMORY UTILIZATION

As shown on the memory map of Figure 7-2.3-1 the EXORciser has an addressing range of 65,536 bytes. Therefore, the highest address is 65,535 or hexadecimal FFFF. This address, and the one below it are reserved for the Restart subroutine of EXbug. The entire EXbug program is assigned the highest 4096 bytes of the addressing range. The three ROMs which contain permanent EXbug instructions have hexadecimal addresses F000 to FC00. Addresses FF00 to FFFF are used for interrupt subroutines, to stack register contents, and to keep track of variable program parameters. The remaining EXbug addresses, FC00 to FF00, are assigned to devices within the system, such as the PIA's and ACIA's for input/output.

The target program is assigned to memory addresses between 0000 and F000. This is a range of 61,440 bytes of storage. Few systems require this large memory capacity, therefore, it can be allocated to minimize the number of address bits for unambiguous access, or to simplify microprocessor operations. As an example, suppose that the target program is to be stored in two 1024 byte ROMs. Each one has an addressing range of 400 hexadecimal. One ROM can be assigned addresses 4000 to 43FF, and the other 4400 to 47FF. Address lines left unconnected cause the respective bit to appear as a 0. Therefore the first ROM address can be specified:

bit	15	14	13	12	11	10	9	8	7	6	5	4	3	2	1
value	0	1	0	0	0	0	X	X	X	X	X	X	X	X	X	X

NOTE: X represents either a 1 or a 0

Address lines 10, 11, 12, 13, and 15 are left unconnected. For this address range Line 14 is always 1, therefore it can be connected to a ROM chip select line. The remainder of the address is determined by bits 0 to 9. Only address lines 0-9 and 14 have to be tied to the microprocessor address buss in this case.

The second ROM would be connected the same way, except for line 10, which should also be tied to a chip select line. A similar procedure can be used for the PIA'S, ACIA's, or other system components.

MAID Command	Description
n	Print the contents of memory location n and enable the EXORciser to change the contents of this memory location.
LF	Print the contents of the next sequential memory location and enable the EXORciser to change the contents of this memory location. (LF — Line Feed Character)
↑	Print the contents of the previous sequential memory location and enable the EXORciser to change the contents of this memory location. (↑ — up arrow character or SHIFT and N characters)
n;V	Set a breakpoint at memory location n.
$V	Display the breakpoint memory locations.
n;P	Continue executing from the encounter breakpoint until this breakpoint is encountered n times.
n;U	Remove the breakpoint at memory location n.
;U	Remove all the breakpoints.
n;W	Search for the n bit pattern.
$M	Display the search mask.
;G	Executes the user program starting at the auto restart memory location.
n;G	Execute user program starting at memory location n.
$R	Display/change the user program registers.
;P	Continue executing from the current program counter setting.
CR	(Carriage Return) Close open address and accept next command.
;S	Disable stop-on-address interrupt, leaving stop address at location previously set.
;T	Discontinue trace mode.
#n	Convert the decimal number n to its hexadecimal equivalent.
#n $ n	Convert the hexadecimal number n to its decimal equivalent.
# @ n	Convert the octal number n to its hexadecimal equivalent.
n;O	Calculate the address offset (for relative addressing mode instructions).
$T	Set the trace mode.
;N	Trace one instruction.
N	Trace one instruction.
n;N	Trace n instructions.
$S	Display/set the stop-on-address compare.

TABLE 7-2.2.2-1 MAID Control Commands

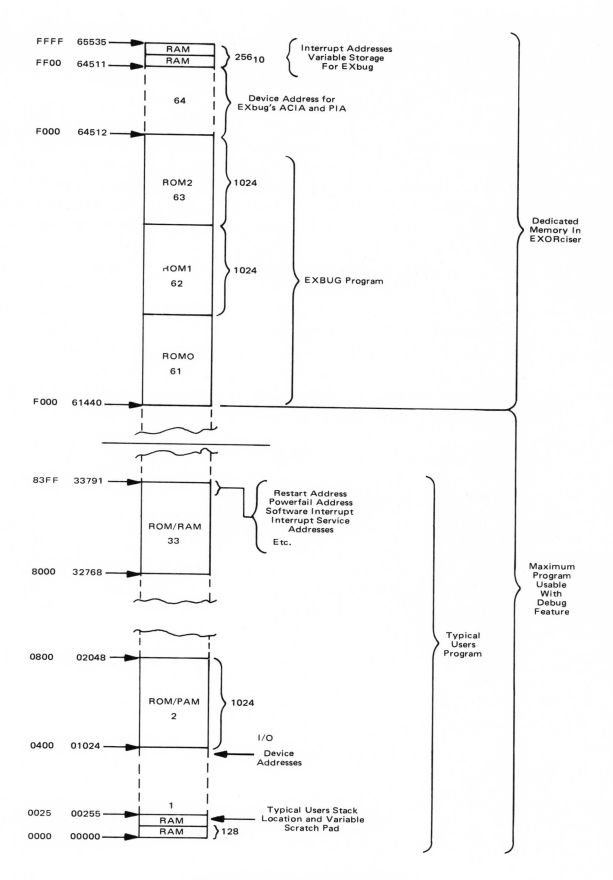

FIGURE 7-2.3-1: Memory Map and Addressing

Microprocessor operations are more efficient if a fewer number of bytes, and processor cycles, are needed to access memory. Those locations which are the object of frequent Load and Store instructions, within the user's program, should be assigned an address in the range 00 to FF. They can then be defined by a single byte of machine code, rather than two. This permits the Assembler to use direct addressing instead of extended for the relevant memory access instructions. This can result in a saving in memory size and cycle time of up to 33%.

EXbug assumes that the average target program may be contained within half of the maximum range of the EXORciser memory. For this reason EXbug expects address 83FF to be the top of the target memory range, and looks for the user specified interrupt subroutine pointers in bytes 83F8 to 83FF when initialized. These pointers are then transferred to locations FFF8 to FFFF in EXbug's memory. If the user prefers a different top of memory location for the interrupt pointers, however, the alternate preferred top of memory location may be entered into EXbug address FF00, using the memory change command of MAID. After the interrupt pointers have been placed in the preferred locations, they are transferred to EXbug's memory when the user presses the ABORT button.

In order to allow for program expansion within memory, it is recommended that the program initially be placed in the approximate middle of the addressing range. This would be address 8000 to 83FF if less than 1024 bytes, 7C00 to 83FF for a 2048 byte program, 7400 to 83FF for 4096 bytes, 7C00 to 83FF for a 2048 byte program, 7400 to 83FF for 4096 bytes, etc. In this manner, the program instructions are expanded downward in memory. At the same time, the scratch pad and stack area, in the bottom 256 bytes may be expanded upward.

7-2.4 HARDWARE OPERATIONS AND CONTROLS

7-2.4.1 Combined Hardware/Software

Many of the EXORciser features are entirely implemented by software routines, but a number of them also utilize hardware to achieve the desired results. One of the special hardware circuits included on the DEBUG card generates a "Psuedo Powerfail" interrupt. The $\overline{\text{NMI}}$ and $\overline{\text{RES}}$ (Restart) inputs to the Microprocessor are switched OFF and then ON again after a short delay. The Microprocessor then performs the "power down" and "Restart" functions even though the system power has remained on at all times. Other hardware/software features are:

(a) Trace (or Run) one instruction

(b) Multiple loop breakpoint

(c) Stop-on-address

Run-One-Instruction

When the command to "trace" ($T) or "run" one (or more) instructions is entered (n;N), the hardware cycle counter is enabled and an RTI instruction is executed. This utilizes 12 clock cycles to move the contents of pseudo registers established on the stack into the internal registers of the MPU Unit. The instruction addressed by the P counter (just loaded) is started but since the hardware cycle counter was preset to 13, a pseudo powerfail interrupt is initiated after the 1st cycle. The MPU completes the instruction in progress, whether it is one, two, or three bytes and then enters a normal "Restart" routine by fetching the Restart routine's address from the top two bytes of memory. These bytes are always reserved for this purpose. (When the EXORciser was first turned ON, the EXbug program preset its own entry address into those top locations.) As a result, when a pseudo powerfail occurs, the program stops running after completing the current instruction, and returns to EXbug. EXbug's "Restart" routine stores the contents of all internal registers in memory and prints them out on the terminal. The system then waits for the next command.

Multiple Loop Breakpoint

The Breakpoint routine utilizes the "Run-one-instruction" routines; therefore, whenever the second breakpoint is tested (by entering n;P) it will also depend on the hardware counter to interrupt the system.

Stop-On-Address

This is another of the combination Hardware/Software features. It is called by typing the command $S, which then transmits the desired address to the comparators in the DEbug card. Whenever the selected address appears on the address bus, a Psuedo Powerfail interrupt is started. On completion of the instruction at that address, the program enters the EXbug routine to save the internal registers on the stack and display them (on the printer). The program counter is displayed, and this identifies the program location which activated the Stop-On-Address compare. The system then waits for another command.

7-2.4.2 ABORT Button Circuit

One of the unique features of the EXORciser is the ABORT circuit. It operates similarly to the other Pseudo Powerfail functions except it is manually activated. When a typical program is being tested, and it "runs away", or locks-up in a loop, (which occasionally happens with an untried program), the ABORT button should be pressed. This causes a printout on the TTY which identifies the location (P counter) and all other internal register contents (so the diagnosis of the cause can be determined). The system then waits for the next command. The recovery occurs in this case without reinitialization so that prior work is not destroyed.

7-2.4.3 RESTART Button Circuit

Occasionally, when a program "runs away" (due to improper instructions), it destroys some of the preset data in various places throughout memory. If this included EXbug stack contents, the ABORT button could not restore operation in EXbug. If this occurs, the "RESTART" button must be used to reinitialize the system in the same way as initial Turn-On or a true power failure. It is not the same, however, because any program already in RAM will not be lost by use of the RESTART button.

7-2.4.4 VMA Inhibit Decoder

A requirement of the technique of utilizing EXbug routines, at addresses above the users program in memory, is that the users program must be inhibited whenever interrupts are serviced or EXbug routines are entered. Since a user's program might not be fully decoded (and need not be) it could respond along with EXbug. To prevent this, a decoder circuit is included in the Debug card which inhibits VMA to the users program whenever an address in EXbug is encountered.

7-2.4.5 Asynchronous Communications Interface

The EXORciser utilizes an ASR33 Teletype[1] (or equivalent) for the user to communicate with the system. It provides the means to enter commands, load data via the tape reader, punch (or record) data from memory, or to display the status or data for examination.

An interface is provided which uses duplex serial data in ASCII format. Either 20 milliamperes neutral circuitry or RS232C is accommodated. Also a switchable baud rate is available (from 110 to 9600 baud) to work with a variety of terminals. This circuitry is implemented on a separate card located in the rear of the EXORciser chassis. The RS232C interface and the variable baud rates make it possible to use a number of teletype substitutes but the TI 733 ASR/KSR[2] is particularly recommended. The EXbug program accommodates 30 baud printers and 1200 baud transfer rates for recording and playback of cassettes. The 12 times improvement in program loading or recording speed plus the much reduced noise level, makes a dramatic difference in efficiency of EXORciser operations.

7-2.4.6 Scope SYNC

A connector is installed on the DEBUG card and 4 thumbwheel switches are provided on the DEBUG card to implement a Scope SYNC feature. The switches can be adjusted to correspond to any address in the range 0 to 65K. When peripheral interface circuitry is being debugged, it is frequently very helpful to examine the signals on the control leads for that peripheral while triggering the scope at a particular time in the input or output cycle. By setting the thumbwheels to correspond to a specific address in the peripheral service routine, and by causing the program to loop through that routine if necessary, a careful study of the signals can be made.

7-2.5 INTERRUPTS

The MPU reserves two bytes at the top of memory for each of four interrupt vectors. Each two byte vector contains the starting address of the subroutine to be used when the corresponding interrupt occurs. The MPU always completes its current instruction before recognizing an interrupt. Then, automatically, without programmed instructions, it transfers the contents of its registers, program location and status to the memory stack and carries out the subroutine. At the conclusion of the subroutine, a RTI instruction restores the stacked information to the MPU.

Three of the four interrupts are used by the EXORciser for internal control, but can be exploited for additional system functions providing that these do not conflict with EXbug. They are: (1) $\overline{\text{NMI}}$, (2) $\overline{\text{Reset}}$, (3) SWI. The fourth one, the Hardware interrupt, is intended for use with the prototype interface. These interrupts are described below.

7-2.5.1 $\overline{\text{NMI}}$

The Non-Maskable-Interrupt is best used to signal when urgent control operations are to be performed independently of the program. For this reason, it is often used to detect imminent power failure conditions. The EXORciser also reacts to certain user commands by means of this interrupt:

---

[1]Teletype is a trademark of the Teletype Corp.
[2]Texas Instruments Co.

(1) MAID commands to run through a breakpoint or trace the target program, as follows:

      n;G (commence program execution at address n)

      ;G (commence program execution at Restart address)

      ;N (run one instruction)

      N (run one instruction)

      n;N (run n instructions)

      $T (run instructions until select address reached)

      ;P (proceed from current instruction)

      n;P (proceed from current instruction through breakpoint n times)

(2) STOP-ON-ADDRESS COMPARE ($S) also uses the $\overline{\text{NMI}}$ interrupt, although it does not involve breakpoints or tracing. It is obtained by means of a hardware comparator on the EXORciser DEbug Module.

(3) ABORT sets the $\overline{\text{NMI}}$ interrupt when the front panel button is pressed. Program control is returned to EXbug.

$\overline{\text{NMI}}$ always causes the MPU registers to be printed. The memory addresses for the $\overline{\text{NMI}}$ vector are bytes FFFC and FFFD.

7-2.5.2 $\overline{\text{RESET}}$

This interrupt occurs when the EXORciser is first turned on, or if the front panel RESTART button is pressed. EXbug is reinitialized and the EXORciser's internal I/O interfaces are set with starting parameters. These control the baud rate of the attached data terminal and Debug Module hardware. The Reset subroutine is also performed if the $\overline{\text{NMI}}$ interrupt is set by a power failure. The interrupt vector for the Reset subroutine is at memory addresses FFFE and FFFF.

If program control is lost and the ABORT button does not return it to EXbug, the RESTART button should be pressed to reinitialize the EXORciser. MAID may then be called to check that the user's program has not been altered.

7-2.5.3 SWI

The software interrupt is generated by a program instruction, and as such, is not maskable. As in the case of all other interrupts, however, the MPU is automatically masked while the interrupt subroutine is being performed. If desired, the user may deliberately defeat this mechanism by putting a Clear Interrupt Mask instruction (CLI) in the interrupt subroutine. The SWI vector is at locations FFFA and FFFB. The EXORciser uses this interrupt in MAID to execute breakpoints that have been set in the program. The breakpoint target instruction is temporarily replaced by an SWI instruction. This switches control to EXbug when the breakpoint is encountered, and the MPU registers are printed out. Other uses of SWI are to simulate interrupt-driven synchronous I/O operations, or to insert entire display, data retrieval or test subroutines into a predefined program without having to change more than a single instruction byte.

7-2.5.4 Hardware Interrupt

Unless the MPU actively scans the status of I/O devices attached to the system, it depends on this interrupt to signal peripheral conditions. Like user designed equipment that must perform peripheral functions most efficiently, the EXORciser interfaces to the MPU with PIA and ACIA chips. These programmable devices can be set to provide essential control signals, while buffering data and interrupts to the MPU. In order to expand EXORciser control to the prototype peripherals, the user connects additional PIA's or ACIA's into the system to act as the interface. The chip and register select lines of the PIA's or ACIA's are tied to appropriate bits of the address buss, corresponding to the addresses to be used in the prototype equipment. The MPU data buss is directly connected to the PIA's or ACIA's. If the prototype hardware was constructed on an EXORciser type plug-in board, all of these connections are made simultaneously when the board is inserted into the EXORciser, since the EXORciser backplane ties all board sockets into the MPU busses and control lines. Under ordinary circumstances, the PIA or ACIA interrupt lines are wire-ored to the MPU. The interrupt signal is not ambiguous, however, since any or all of the interrupts can be selectively inhibited by the MPU.

For "instant" interfacing and least prototype development time, it is recommended that the EXORciser I/O Module be used. This optional printed circuit plug-in board can be ordered with the EXORciser. It allows the user to quickly set the PIA register addresses and, by means of screwdriver adjustable switches, connect two peripheral data busses to each one of its two PIA's. Additional circuitry in the form of integrated circuits in 14, 16 or 24 pin wire-wrap sockets may also be added.

Interrupts from the user's equipment to the PIA or ACIA are latched and held until the MPU dismisses them. Depending on their urgency, the target program may react immediately, or when it has reached a particular instruction. This is possible because the MPU can mask all interrupts or enable only particular PIA sections. In any case, when the interrupt is recognized the MPU automatically stacks its registers and status. It next fetches the subroutine pointer from locations FFF8 and FFF9. The interrupt subroutine is then performed, and an RTS instruction returns the MPU to its central program. If this was the MAID routine of EXbug, control commands previously entered by the user will be carried out during and after the interrupt subroutine.

Care must be taken to avoid using the MAID Trace command when an interrupt is anticipated. If this occurs, EXbug may lose control of the EXORciser. This effect is due to the MPU receiving the $\overline{\text{NMI}}$ and hardware interrupts simultaneously, each of which have a separate subroutine pointer address. The RESTART button must then be pressed to reinitialize the EXORciser. One method to avoid tracing through an interrupt is to set breakpoints around it and then use the program run (;P) to go from the first breakpoint to the second. The first breakpoint is set into the program just before the interrupt mask is cleared or when a PIA input is expected. The second is placed in the top of the interrupt subroutine. The program run command will then carry the system through the interrupt into the subroutine without tracing intermediate instructions. After the second breakpoint is encountered, tracing may be resumed through an RTI instruction at the end of the subroutine.

A frequently used technique for dealing with multiple wire-ored hardware interrupts is for the interrupt subroutine to scan each of the interrupt generating PIA's or ACIA's. They may be assigned relative priorities by the program, and if their interrupt flags are set, appropriate instructions executed according to the priority sequence.

7-2.6   TEST SIGNALS

System address, data and control signals are readily available for observation since the EXORciser backplane (see Figure 7-2.6-1) distributes them to all the board connectors. An extender board may be plugged into an empty connector, or used to lift an operating board above the chassis. To observe a signal, oscilloscope probes can then be placed on the appropriate board connector pin or to a wirewrap pin on the board. The following signals are common to all EXORciser boards:

Component Side Pin Number	Function	Circuit Side	Function	Component Side Pin Number	Function	Circuit Side	Function
A	+5VDC	1	+5VDC	$\overline{A}$		23	
B	+5VDC	2	+5VDC	$\overline{B}$		24	
C	+5VDC	3	+5VDC	$\overline{C}$		25	
D	$\overline{IRQ}$	4	Go/HALT	$\overline{D}$		26	
E	$\overline{NMI}$	5	$\overline{RESET}$	$\overline{E}$		27	
F	VMA	6	R/W	$\overline{F}$		28	
H	GND	7	01	$\overline{H}$	$\overline{D3}$	29	$\overline{D1}$
J	02	8	GND	$\overline{J}$	$\overline{D7}$	30	$\overline{D5}$
K	GND	9	GND	$\overline{K}$	$\overline{D2}$	31	$\overline{D0}$
L	Memory Clock	10	VUA	$\overline{L}$	$\overline{D6}$	32	$\overline{D4}$
M	−12VDC	11	−12VDC	$\overline{M}$	A14	33	A15
N	TSC	12	Ref. Req.	$\overline{N}$	A13	34	A12
P	B.A.	13	Ref. Gnt.	$\overline{P}$	A10	35	A11
R	Memory Ready	14		$\overline{R}$	A9	36	A8
S	Refresh Clock	15		$\overline{S}$	A6	37	A7
T	+12VDC	16	+12VDC	$\overline{T}$	A5	38	A4
U		17		$\overline{U}$	A2	39	A3
V		18		$\overline{V}$	A1	40	A0
W		19		$\overline{W}$	GND	41	GND
X		20		$\overline{X}$	GND	42	GND
Y		21		$\overline{Y}$	GND	43	GND
Z		22					

FIGURE 7-2.6-1 Exorciser Backplane Connections for all Boards

BI-DIRECTIONAL DATA LINES ($\overline{D0}$-$\overline{D7}$) — The bi-directional data lines D0 through D7 permit the transfer of data between the EXORciser MPU and other modules. The data bus output drivers are three-state devices that remain in the high impedance (off) state except when the MPU performs a memory write operation.

ADDRESS BUS (A0-A15) — The sixteen address bus lines are inputs to the bus receiver and select the memory location to be accessed (write into or read from) by the EXORciser MPU.

NON-MASKABLE INTERRUPT ($\overline{NMI}$) — This TTL output requests that the EXORciser MPU performs a non-maskable interrupt sequence. As with the Interrupt Request Signal, the processor will complete the current instruction that is being executed before it recognizes the $\overline{NMI}$ signal. The interrupt mask bit in the Condition Code Register has no effect on $\overline{NMI}$.

The Index Register, Program Counter, Accumulators, and Condition Code Register are stored away on the stack. At the end of the cycle, a 16-bit address will be loaded that points to a vectoring address which is located in memory locations FFFC and FFFD. An address loaded at these locations causes the MPU to branch to a non-maskable interrupt routine in memory.

VALID USERS ADDRESS (VUA) — This output when true indicates to the other Modules that there is a valid address on the bus and the EXORciser is not addressing an EXbug routine. It is capable of sinking 20 ma. and the voltage levels are TTL compatible.

PHASE 1 CLOCK (ϕ1) — The ϕ1 clock is the first phase of the non-overlapping clock signals.

PHASE 2 CLOCK (ϕ2) — The ϕ2 clock is the second phase of the non-overlapping clock signals.

READ/WRITE SIGNAL (R/W) — This is generated by the EXORciser MPU and determines whether the MPU is to read (high) data from or write (low) data into other modules or devices. The normal standby state of this signal is read (high). Three-State Control going high will cause Read/Write to go into the off (high impedance) state. Also, when the MPU is halted, R/W will be in the off state.

VALID MEMORY ADDRESS (VMA) — This input when true indicates to the DEBUG Module that there is a valid address on the address bus. This signal is not used by other modules in the EXORciser. See VUA.

$\overline{RESET}$ (also called MASTER RESET) — The $\overline{RESET}$ TTL compatible output, when low, resets the PIA circuits on the I/O Modules and when high restarts the MPU. This line goes low each time the EXORciser RESTART switch is actuated or when power is first applied to the EXORciser.

GO/HALT (G/H) — The GO/HALT line is pulled up to 5 volts by the circuitry on the DEBUG card. This TTL "1" is the Go condition for the MPU Module. The user can control this line through the bus if desired. When this input is in the high state, the machine will fetch the instruction addressed by the program counter and start execution. When it is low, all activity in the MPU will be halted. This input is level sensitive. In the halt mode, the MPU will stop at the end of an instruction, Bus Available will be at a one level, Valid Memory Address will be at a zero, and all other three-state lines will be in the three-state mode.

The halt line must go low with the leading edge of phase one to insure single instruction operation. If the halt line does not go low with the leading edge of phase one, one or two instruction operations may result, depending on when the halt line goes low relative to the phasing of the clock.

THREE-STATE CONTROL (TSC) — This input causes all of the address lines and the Read/Write line to go into the off or high impedance state. The Valid Memory address and Bus Available signals will be forced low. The data bus is not affected by TSC and has its own enable, (Data Bus Enable). In DMA applications, the Three-State Control line should be brought high on the leading edge of the Phase One Clock. The $\phi 1$ clock must be held in the high state for this function to operate properly. The address bus will then be available for other devices to directly address memory. Since the MPU is a dynamic device, it must be refreshed periodically or destruction of data will occur in the MPU.

INTERRUPT REQUEST ($\overline{\text{IRQ}}$) — This input requests that an interrupt sequence be generated within the MPU. The processor will wait until it completes the current instruction that is being executed before it recognizes the request. At that time, if the interrupt mask bit in the Condition Code Register is not set (interrupt masked), the MPU will begin an interrupt sequence. The Index Register, Program Counter, Accumulators, and Condition Code Register are stored away on the stack. Next the MPU will respond to the interrupt request by setting the interrupt mask bit high so that no further interrupts may occur. At the end of the cycle, a 16-bit address will be loaded that points to a vectoring address which is located in memory locations FFF8 and FFF9. An address loaded at these locations causes the MPU to branch to an interrupt routine in memory.

The Go/Halt line must be in the Go (high) state for interrupts to be recognized. If it is in the Halt (low) state, the MPU will be halted and interrupts will have no effect.

BUS AVAILABLE (BA) — The Bus Available signal will normally be in the low state; when activated, it will go to the high state indicating that the microprocessor has stopped and that the address bus is available. This will occur if the Go/Halt line is in the Halt (low) state or the processor is in the WAIT state as a result of the execution of a WAIT instruction. At such time, all three-state output drivers will go to their off state and other outputs to their normally inactive level. The processor is removed from the WAIT state by the occurrence of a maskable or non-maskable interrupt.

MEMORY CLOCK — This clock signal provides basic timing for the optional 8K memory boards, DMA if used, and memory refresh cycles. It is synchronized with $\phi 2$ of the MPU clock.

REFRESH CLOCK — This clock determines the frequency of MPU and dynamic memory refresh cycles.

$\overline{\text{REFRESH REQUEST}}$ — This signal indicates when the MPU and dynamic memory should be refreshed.

REFRESH GRANT — This signal acknowledges the Refresh Request, when an MPU clock cycle has been stolen to refresh the MPU and/or dynamic memory.

MEMORY READY — This signal is used when interfacing slow memories ($T_{ACC} > 575$ nanosec.). If this signal is brought low, it will stretch the high portion of $\phi 2$ of all clocks.

+5 VOLTS — This voltage is available to all EXORciser boards. Total load should not exceed 15 amps

+15 VOLTS — This voltage is available to all EXORciser boards. Total load should not exceed 2.5 amps.

−12 VOLTS — This voltage is available to all EXORciser boards. Total load should not exceed 1.0 amp.

GROUND — Common electrical reference point for all EXORciser voltages, signals and chassis. When grounding an oscilloscope, or connecting external circuitry, care must be taken to avoid noise pickup at the ground point. There are ten separate grounds on the EXORciser backplane, tied together at a single point, that can be selected for minimum noise on a particular signal line.

All the card slots in the EXORciser housing are wired in parallel so any card could be inserted in any slot. However, the I/O and Universal Wirewrap cards require 1¼ inches between slots while the MPU RAM and Debug Modules (which are standard PC construction) require only ⅝''. The slots are arranged so that the 6 in the center are ⅝'' apart while the 4 on each side are spaced 1¼''.

The M6800 Microprocessor Family utilizes an Address and Data Bus structure to interconnect all units and uses the technique of treating all peripherals as memory. Address decoding is thus provided for each I/O channel. Output from or input to a peripheral via the Microprocessor Bus is achieved by "Storing to" or "Loading from" a specific address which has been assigned to the PIA's or ACIA's.

In the EXORciser, each Module has MC8T26 Bus Driver/Receivers incorporated so that an almost unlimited number of memory or I/O Modules can be used. Also each memory or I/O Module is equipped with address decoding which utilizes hexadecimally marked, screwdriver adjustable switches to provide instant address assignment for rapid system assembly.

Special Signals

The following signals are not bussed to all boards, but provide essential timing for an individual module or device:

MPU Module Only:

> DATA BUS ENABLE (DBE) — This input is the three-state control signal for the MPU data bus and will enable the bus drivers when in the high state. This input is TTL compatible; however in normal operation, it should be driven by the phase two clock. During an MPU read cycle, the data bus drivers will be disabled internally. When it is desired that another device control the data bus such as in Direct Memory Access (DMA) applications, DBE should be held low.

FRONT PANEL

> RUN — The RUN signal is present whenever the MPU is executing in user memory (0 to 60K).
>
> ABORT (Two Lines) — These two inputs are connected to a cross-coupled TTL anti-bounce circuit so that one line is normally low and the other high. The EXORciser ABORT switch is SPDT and connected so that the grounded side is transferred to the other line when the button is pressed. The output of this circuit is used to activate $\overline{NMI}$.
>
> RESTART (Two Lines) — These two inputs are connected to a cross-coupled TTL anti-bounce circuit so that one line is normally low and one high. The EXORciser RESTART switch is SPDT and connected so that the grounded side is transferred to the other line when the button is pressed. The output of this circuit is the $\overline{RESET}$ signal.

Baud Rate Module:

> READER ON — This signal is the output of a TTL F/F in series with 510 ohms and is applied to the Baud Rate Module and used to control the reader of a modified teletypewriter. This line provides approximately 5 ma. to drive the diode in the optical coupler.
>
> TTY $\overline{SERIAL\ OUT}$ — This signal is the output of a TTL inverter with a series 510 ohm resistor. It is intended to drive the diode of an optical coupler on the Baud Rate Module. The signal switches the 20 milliampre line to the teletype in response to the data from the UART.
>
> RS232 INPUT — The RS232 OUT line transfers serial data through the level conversion in the Baud Rate Module to the terminal device. This output is TTL compatible at this point.
>
> RS232 INPUT — The RS232 INPUT line is a TTL compatible input through which data is received in a serial format from the level converters on the Baud Rate Module.
>
> TTY SERIAL INPUT — The $\overline{TTY\ SERIAL\ INPUT}$ line is a TTL compatible input through which data is received in a serial format from the TTY inputs on the Baud Rate Module.

RS232 DTR — This input is TTL compatible. The signal is generated on the Baud Rate card.

CLOCK (CLK) — The CLK input from the Baud Rate Module determines the baud rate at which the EXORciser will exchange data with its terminal device. This input is TTL compatible and represents two standard loads. (3.2 ma. at 0.4V)

STOP BIT SELECT — This input is TTL compatible. When high, two stop bits are selected by the UART. When low, one stop bit is selected. The signal is generated by the Baud Rate Module in the EXORciser.

Reader and Punch Control

The 1.1 version of the EXbug program is designed to work with several models of teletypes as well as with a Texas Instruments ASR733 Cassette/printer terminal with 1200 baud and Remote Device Control options.

The EXbug program utilizes the usual ASCII control codes to control teletypes equipped with Automatic Readers and punches. The codes are: (Shown in hexadecimal notation)

DC1 Reader ON — (11)
DC2 Punch ON — (12)
DC3 Reader OFF — (13)
DC4 Punch OFF — (14)

The program also includes routines to control teletypes which have been modified by the addition of a reader control relay. A Flip/Flop on the DEbug card and an optical coupler (U4) on the Baud Rate Card implement this function. The "D" type Flip/Flop is set by outputting to address FCF4, a data word in which bit 5 is a "1". This turns the reader relay ON. Since both these methods of control are included, either type of teletype will work.

TI ASR733 Operation

The Texas Instruments ASR733 terminal recommended for use with this version of EXbug utilizes an Remote Device Control (RDC) card to provide the extra control functions needed for control of the printer and Cassettes when using the 1200 baud option. For 10 and 30 character per second (CPS) rates, the tape is started and stopped (in playback) by the usual ASCII Reader Control codes DC1 and DC3 but for 120 CPS operation the "Block Forward" command of the RDC card (DLE,7) is used to control the Cassette. The printer is commanded ON and OFF by the (DLE,9) and (DLE,0) codes to avoid garbled printing. In initialization, the Auto Device "ON" code (DLE,:) is used to make sure the RDC card will respond.

Baud Rate Control

Another feature of "EXBUG 1.1" is its ability to be adjusted for operation at various baud rates. Programs written for a TTY require at least two character times (200 milliseconds) for the carriage to return. For this reason, the CR is issued followed by a (LF) Line Feed so that the next character will print at the beginning of the next line. When the TI terminal is used at 30 characters per second, the carriage return time is similar so it is necessary to insert 4 additional character delays by outputting null characters (0). The command S30. is typed to accomplish this.

In the case where the Verify routine is used, it is very desirable to run the tape at 1200 baud but also necessary to print the differences found (between the tape and memory). Since the Printer mechanism will only print at 30 characters per second and the data transfer rate is at 120 CPS, three null characters are inserted between each character to be printed and 22 nulls are output after each carriage return. Typing ''S120'' after the baud rate has been set for 1200 baud, switches this version (1.1) of EXbug to provide this format.

Formatted Binary Object Program Tapes (i.e. LOAD, VERF, SRCH and PNCH)

The first four routines in EXbug involve the handling of ''Formatted Binary Object Program Tapes.'' These tapes are generated by the MPU Build Virtual Machine Program on timeshare, or by the PNCH routine in EXbug. The tape can be the conventional paper tape (if the system terminal is a Teletype) or may be a Cassette tape such as that produced by the Texas Instruments ASR33 terminal. The procedure for using the Build Virtual Machine time-share program to generate a suitably formatted tape is described in Section 7-1.7.

This Section is included in order to summarize the principle features of the EXORciser. For additional information, the several Manuals provided with the EXORciser should be referred to.

7-3   EVALUATION MODULE

The M6800 Evaluation Module is a pre-engineered assembly that provides an efficient means of becoming familiar with the M6800 Microcomputer family of parts. The Module (see Figure 7-3-1) is designed to demonstrate the M6800 Family operating with their specified loading at clock frequencies up to 1.0 MHz. In addition to its use for evaluating the family devices, it can be used to enter and de-bug simple programs including the operation/control of peripheral devices. The circuit configuration is shown in block diagram form in Figure 7-3-2. A brief summary of the specifications is shown in Table 7-3-1.

FIGURE 7-3-1: The Evaluation Module

An interface is provided for either a 20 ma current loop TTY or an RS-232C compatible terminal. The terminal can be used to communicate with the Module's diagnostic control program, MIKBUG. The MIKBUG program is stored in read only memory, and in conjunction with the terminal can be used to perform the following functions:

- Load data into the Evaluation Modules random access memory.

- Display and, if desired, change the data in the Modules random access memory.

- Print out or generate a tape of the data stored in the modules memory.

- Display and, if desired, change the contents of the MPU's registers.

- Run User Programs

- Evaluate Interrupts

- Set Breakpoints

The use of each of these features plus a complete description of the Module is provided in the M6800 Evaluation Module User's Guide; it may be referred to for additional details.

Characteristics	Specifications
Power Requirements:	+5 VDC @ 2A +12 VDC @ 250 mA −12 VDC @ 250 mA
Clock Frequency:	100 KHz to 1 MHz (adjustable)
Signal Characteristics: Connector (P1) Address bus Data bus	Three-state TTL voltage compatible
Input	TTL voltage compatible
Output	Three-state TTL voltage compatible
Input and output commands	TTL voltage compatible
MC6820 Peripheral Interface Adapter (P2) Data signals PA0–PA7 input/output lines	TTL voltage compatible
PA0–PB7 input/output lines	Three-state TTL voltage compatible
Control Signals CA1, CA2, and CB1	TTL voltage compatible
CB2	Three-state TTL voltage compatible
Terminal Interface Specifications (P3) Data transfer rate	110 or 300 Baud
Signal characterisitcs	TTY or RS-232C Compatible
Reader control signal	Control signal for modified TTY devices
Data Format	ASCII

TABLE 7-3-1 Evaluation Module Specifications

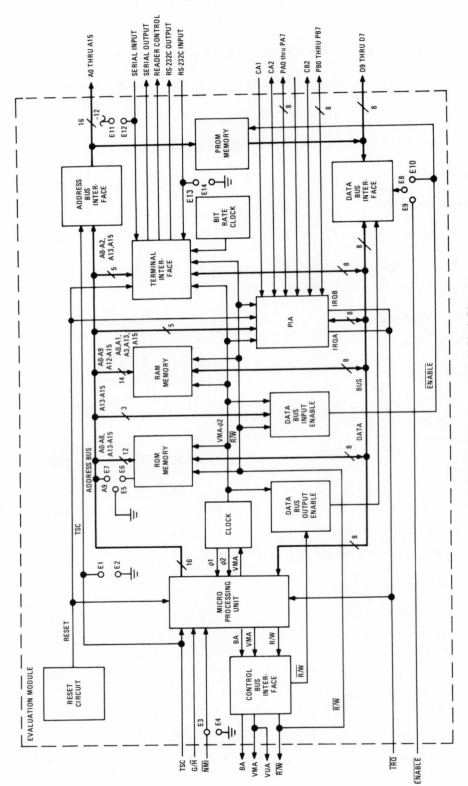

FIGURE 7-3-2: Evaluation Module Block Diagram

The Module includes two PIAs. One is used for the terminal interface, however, the other is available for general use. It can be used in exactly the same manner as in an EXORciser or a prototype hardware design for interfacing to peripherals. This PIA has, for instance, been used to control a TTY type keyboard and a self-scan visual display used in conjunction with a portable demonstration kit for the Evaluation Module.

A memory map of the Evaluation Module is shown in Figure 7-3-3. The Module provides up to 640 bytes (hex addresses 0000 to 027F) for storage of evaluation programs. The 128 bytes of random access memory at base memory address A000 is used as scratch-pad memory for the MIKBUG firmware. MIKBUG is located at base memory address E000. An interface is provided for adding additional blocks of memory. The additional memory could be located anywhere from 0000 through DFFF except for addresses 8004 through 800B and A000 through A07F.

In addition to the Evaluation Module printed circuit assemble itself, the following items are provided:

- An 86-pin connector compatible with the P1 connector of the Module

- TTY/RS-232C 16-pin Flatribbon Cable W1 for connection between the Module and a terminal.

- PIA Connector/Flatribbon Cable W2 for connecting the Module to external peripheral devices.

- M6800 Evaluation Module Users Guide which contains a complete description of the Module and includes detailed operating instructions.

This package provides a simple but useful method for evaluating the M6800 Family's characteristics in a realistic environment.

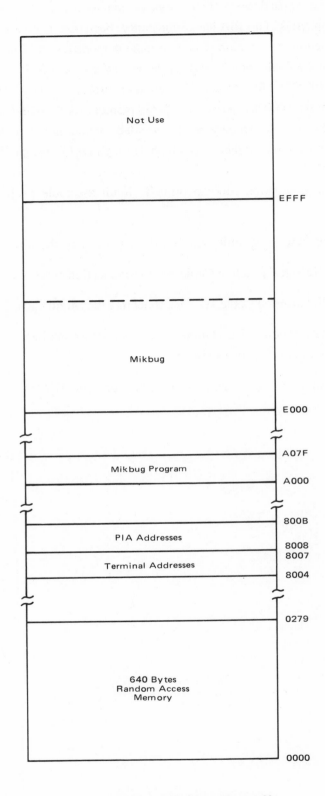

FIGURE 7-3-3: Evaluation Module Memory Map

APPENDIX A
(Questions and Answers)

1   M6800 SYSTEMS OPERATION

Q 1.   **Is it possible to read a PIA address unintentionally?**

A 1.   Yes. If the PIA is assigned an address in memory such that the address location immediately preceding it contains a single byte (inherent address mode) instruction, then the execution of that instruction will cause the PIA to be read. The MPU always fetches the byte following the operator byte. If the PIA address that is read happens to be a Data Register, then the interrupt flags may be inadvertently cleared. This may be avoided by separating PIA addresses from the main program by at least a single byte gap.

Q 2.   **What is the MPU's drive capability?**

A 2.   The MPU can drive 130 pf of capacitance and one standard TTL load while operating at 1 MHz. Since the PIA, RAM, and ROM have Data Bus load capacitances of 10 pf, 15 pf, and 15 pf, respectively, the MPU can drive from 7 to 10 family devices at 1 MHz.

Q 3.   **What is the state of the PIA's I/O lines at initialization?**

A 3.   The $\overline{\text{RES}}$ signal to the PIA will reset all six of the internal registers (Control, Data Direction, and Output Data) to zero. Since all the Data Direction Register bit positions are zero, the I/O Data lines PA0-PB7 and PB0-PB7 will be established as inputs. Since b5 of both Control Registers is zero, the CA2 and CB2 control lines are also established as inputs. This has the following effect on lines that will later be established as outputs (that is, they may be hardwired to the inputs of external logic elements): Since the B side of the PIA has three-state outputs and the lines are initially established as inputs, they represent a high impedance "off" device and will not affect the inputs of gates that may be connected. The A side lines have an internal pullup resistor and will "look" like logic ones to gate inputs. External circuitry tied to the A side should require active low signals if they are not to be affected by $\overline{\text{RES}}$.

On the B side lines that are to be established as outputs and used to drive active high Darlington inputs, a resistor to ground can be used to avoid initial turn on:

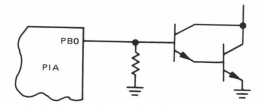

If the output lines are to drive TTL and must be active high, the peripheral logic should be disabled with a hardware control during the initialization sequence. Note that, as far as system operation is concerned, the initial state of some lines may not matter. For example, in a tape cassette system if the motion control circuitry is disabled during initialization, the other lines such as direction and speed are "don't cares."

Recommended procedure for initializing the PIAs is as follows:

1. Set b2 = 1 in the Control Register in order to select the Data Register.

2. Write the desired initial logic states into the Data Register.

3. Then establish the required outputs by selecting the Data Direction Register by setting b2 = 0 in the Control Register and writing the appropriate pattern into the Direction Register.

Q 4.   **What causes the PIA to miss interrupts when the MPU is halted or in the WAIT mode?**

A 4.   While there are nominally no restrictions on the format of interrupt signals into CA1, CA2, CB1, and CB2 of the PIA, there are certain combinations of system situations that require special consideration. Assume that the interrupt signal format follows one of the cases shown in Figure A1 and that the PIA has been conditioned by the MPU to recognize the transition polarity represented by the "trailing edge" of the interrupt pulse.

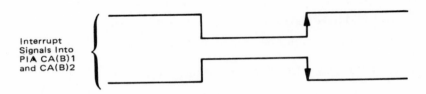

Interrupt
Signals Into
PIA CA(B)1
and CA(B)2

FIGURE A1. Interrupt Signal Format

The design of the PIA is such that at least one E pulse must occur between the inactive and active edges of the input signal if the interrupt is to be recognized. Relative timing requirements are shown in Figure A2. Note that an internal enable signal that is initiated by the first positive transition of E following the inactive edge of the input signals is included.

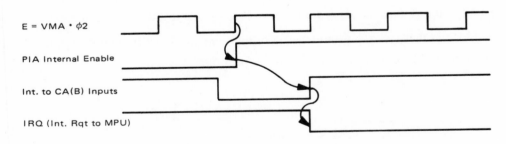

E = VMA · φ2

PIA Internal Enable

Int. to CA(B) Inputs

IRQ (Int. Rqt to MPU)

FIGURE A2. Interrupt Enabling

When the MPU has been halted either by hardware control or execution of the Wait For Interrupt (WAI) instruction, its VMA output goes low. Since VMA is normally used to generate the Enable signal (E = VMA· φ2) either of these two conditions temporarily eliminates the E signal. The effect of this on the trailing edge interrupt format is shown in Figure A3 where it is assumed that VMA went low and eliminated the Enable pulses before the PIA's interrupt circuitry was properly conditioned to recognize the active transition. It should be noted that this condition occurs only when an active transition is preceded by an inactive transition and there are no intervening E pulses.

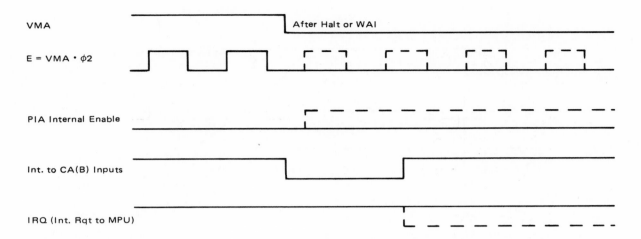

FIGURE A3. Interrupt Not Properly Enabled

If this combination occurs during system operation, valid interrupts will be ignored. Either of two simple precautions can be adopted. If the format of the interrupt signals is up to the designer, the potential problem can be avoided simply by not using the pulse-with-trailing-edge-interrupt format.

If this format is compulsory, it is recommended that $\phi2$ be used as the Enable signal with VMA ANDed with an address line and applied to one of the PIA's chip select inputs as shown in Figure A4.

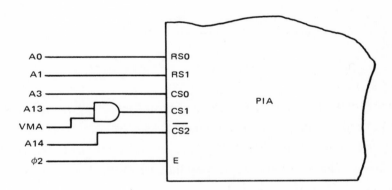

FIGURE A4. Alternate E Generation

Q 5. Is there any change in the CA2 (CB2) line if it is set to a logic "0" (Control Register bits 5, 4, 3, are 110 respectively — defining CA2 (CB2) as an output) and then the control register is put in the handshake mode (CR bits 5, 4, 3, are changed to 10X, respectively)?

A 5. When the control register bits are changed to put the PIA in the handshake mode, the CA2 (CB2) lines remain low.

Q 6. What are the threshold points for the M6800 family from which the delays are measured?

A 6. The M6800 input thresholds are specified as Logic 1 = 2.0v, Logic 0 = 0.8v; the delays are measured from these points. TTL and M6800 family devices provide output signals having logic 1 = 2.4v and logic 0 = 0.4v, providing 400 mv of noise margin. The delays are measured as shown:

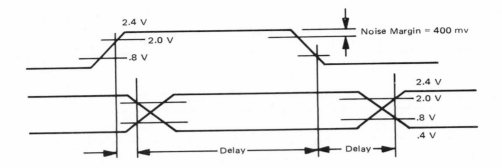

Q 7. **What happens in the ACIA when a control word is loaded after an ACIA reset condition? (How is the ACIA initialized in the system?)**

A 7. When power is turned on in the system, the ACIA interrupts may be enabled and generate a system interrupt. This can happen if there is a glitch in the power supply as the power came on:

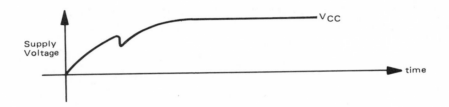

The procedure for initializing the ACIA is to do a master-reset by writing into the control register (CR1=1; CR0=1), while the interrupts are masked in the system. The master reset clears the interrupt, transmit data register empty, and receive data register full flags, and clears both the receive and transmit data registers. The ACIA interrupts may then be enabled as required.

NOTE: Since a master reset clears the Transmitter buffer, an interrupt will be generated from the ACIA provided the Transmitter Interrupt Enable (TIE) is activated when loading the control register subsequent to the master reset.

Q 8. **How large a load is the MC8T26 bus driver?**

A 8. The MC8T26 has a PNP input and loads the MPU as shown:

$$200 \ \mu a \text{ max at ``0''}$$
$$25 \ \mu a \text{ max at ``1''}$$
$$\approx 10 \text{ pf input capacitance}$$

Q 9. **Why is 100 KHz specified as the minimum operating frequency?**

A 9. The MPU is a dynamic device and (like dynamic memories) requires refreshing via the clock. The maximum time between refresh transitions on the clock line is 5 μs corresponding to an MPU cycle time of 10 μs; or a frequency of 100 KHz.

2 M6800 CONTROL

Q 1.   **Can DBE be tied to a DC level?**

A 1.   No, the DBE signal is used to refresh the output buffers which are dynamic. DBE cannot be held in one state for more than 4.5 μs without degrading the data held in the output buffers.

Q 2.   **What does DBE control?**

A 2.   DBE controls the three-state enable on the data output buffers. When DBE is low, the data output buffers are in the high impedance state. When DBE is high, the data output buffers drive the data bus. The data output buffers are also in the high impedance state during the execution of a read cycle (R/W = 1).

Q 3.   **What should be used as a DBE control signal?**

A 3.   Most applications will use $\phi 2$ as the DBE control signal. A longer data hold time requirement during a write cycle may be met by holding DBE high past the trailing edge of $\phi 2$. The MPU data setup time (T$_{ADS}$) can be shortened from the 200 ns specified by bringing DBE high before the leading edge of $\phi 2$. The exact timing relationships are currently being characterized.

Q 4.   **What is the relationship od DBE and TSC?**

A 4.   DBE is the three-state strobe for the data buffers while TSC is the three-state strobe for the address bus and the R/W line. TSC also forces VMA low. In many applications, it will be desired that the MPU always drive the bus, thus, TSC will be tied low. In other applications, TSC will be used to implement a Direct Memory Access, (DMA), or to force VMA low during system power-up rather than using $\overline{\text{RESET}}$ to disable the devices on the bus. DBE and TSC cannot be tied together because DBE must change states every 5 μs whereas, in many systems, TSC will be tied low.

Q 5.   **Will interrupts ($\overline{\text{IRQ}}$ or $\overline{\text{NMI}}$) and $\overline{\text{RESET}}$ be recognized while the MPU is halted?**

A 5.   Interrupts will not be acted on while the MPU is halted. These control signals are latched on the MPU and will be serviced as soon as the MPU is taken out of the halted state. $\overline{\text{RESET}}$ going low while the MPU is halted causes the following: VMA-low, BA-low, Data Bus-high impedance, R/W-Read State, and the Address Bus will contain the restart address FFFE.

Q 6.   **What happens if the MPU is halted and the +5 volt power fails?**

A 6.   The MPU stops program execution and all internal register contents will be lost.

Q 7.   **How can one tell whether the MPU has halted?**

A 7.   When the MPU is halted the BA signal will be high. The MPU completes execution of an instruction before halting. Once the execution is completed, BA will go high within 470 nsec after the leading edge of the next $\phi 2$ signal. Whenever BA goes high the MPU is inactive (halted) and the address bus, R/W line and data bus are available for use by another device for as long as necessary. One caution to be observed is that TSC going high will force BA low whether or not the MPU is halted. When the MPU is halted all MPU outputs are in the high impedance state, therefore, there is no reason for TSC to be high, however if it is brought high BA will go low and the indication that the MPU is halted will be lost.

Q 8.   **What is the timing relationship between $\overline{\text{HALT}}$ and BA?**

A 8.   If $\overline{\text{HALT}}$ is low during the first 100ns of $\phi1$ in the last cycle of an instruction the MPU will halt at the end of that instruction. If $\overline{\text{HALT}}$ is not low during the first 100ns of $\phi1$ in the last cycle of an instruction the MPU will halt at the end of the next instruction. The fastest instructions such as LDAA (Immediate) execute in $2\mu s$ while the longest instructions such as SWI require $12\mu s$ to execute, (assuming a 1 MHz clock rate). Depending on the instruction being executed when $\overline{\text{HALT}}$ goes low, BA will go high no sooner than $2\mu s$ and no longer than $14\mu s$ after the negative transition of $\overline{\text{HALT}}$.

Q 9.   **How is single instruction execution accomplished with the MC6800?**

A 9.   Single instruction execution is accomplished by holding the $\overline{\text{HALT}}$ line active low and pulsing the $\overline{\text{HALT}}$ line high for one clock cycle when an instruction is to be executed. The transitions of this pulse must occur within 100ns of the leading edge of $\phi1$. The machine will come out of the halted mode and execute the next instruction which will require from 2 to 12 machine cycles to complete. After completion of the current instruction the MPU will return to the halted mode. In order to avoid incorrect operation of the MPU when "stepping" through a program at a very high rate, the $\overline{\text{HALT}}$ line must not be pulsed high until the MPU has completed executing the instruction commanded by the previous $\overline{\text{HALT}}$ pulse. The BA signal going high will indicate that the MPU has halted and is available for another single cycle pulse on the $\overline{\text{HALT}}$ line.

Q 10.   **What effect on the other MPU signals does a low logic level on the $\overline{\text{RESET}}$ pin have?**

A 10. $\overline{\text{RESET}}$ is intended to be used to initiate the power up sequence. $\overline{\text{RESET}}$ should be held low while power is coming up and for at least 8 clock cycles after the power supply voltage goes above 4.75 volts to properly initialize the MPU. During this time the address bus, R/W line, VMA line and data bus will be in an indeterminate state. If any devices on the data bus could accept a write pulse during this time (a battery backed RAM for example) they should be disabled until $\overline{\text{RESET}}$ goes high to avoid system problems. After 8 clock cycles VMA will go low and $\overline{\text{RESET}}$ may be brought high causing the MPU to vector to the restart addresses FFFE and FFFF.

Q 11.   **With the MPU power up and the system running can $\overline{\text{RESET}}$ be pulsed low to re-initialize the system?**

A 11.   Yes. Assuming that the processor has been running for at least 8 clock cycles, the processor can be restarted by pulsing the $\overline{\text{RESET}}$ line low. This pulse must remain low for at least three $\phi2$ cycles.

         While the $\overline{\text{RESET}}$ line is low the MPU output signal will go to the following states: VMA-low, BA-low, Data Outputs-high impedance, R/W (Read State), and the Address Bus will contain the restart address FFFE. This will occur within 300 ns of the $\phi1$ cycle following the $\phi1$ cycle in which $\overline{\text{RESET}}$ went low.

Q 12.   **How can a DMA channel be implemented with the MC6800 MPU?**

A 12.   Two methods of controlling the MPU to allow DMA involve the use of the $\overline{\text{HALT}}$ and TSC lines.

     (a) When the $\overline{\text{HALT}}$ line is pulled low the MPU will finish the current instruction and then go into the halt mode as indicated by BA being high. All address lines, data lines, and R/W lines will be in the high impedance state, allowing the DMA channel to assume these functions. VMA will be forced low. Once the MPU enters the halt state (which can take up to 14 nsec to finish the current instruction), DMA transfers can begin and control the bus as long as necessary. The speed of DMA is limited only by the constraints imposed by the memory system speed and DMA controller design.

(b) TSC used in combination with stretching of the clock signals can provide a DMA channel which allows DMA transfers without stopping MPU program execution. In order to transfer DMA information using this technique TSC is brought high on the leading edge of $\phi1$ when a DMA transfer is requested. While TSC is held high the $\phi1$ clock is held in the high state and the $\phi2$ clock is held in the low state in order to stop program execution by cycle stealing. Assuming that DBE is driven by $\phi2$ the result of pulling TSC high will be to place the address bus, R/W line, and the data bus in the high impedance state. VMA and BA will be forced low. Due to the use of dynamic registers within the MPU the clock signals cannot be held in any given state for more than $4.5\mu s$ producing a lower limit on clock frequency of 100KHz. This factor limits DMA transfers on the bus to this $4.5\mu s$ interval when $\phi1$ is held high. After the $4.5\mu s$ interval when $\phi1$ is being held high the MPU must be clocked in order to refresh the dynamic registers. This technique of DMA has the advantage of fast response to a request for a DMA transfer (TSC = 1) but has a limitation on how much data can be transferred in one block. Halting the machine as described in (a) has a longer response time before DMA transfers can start but there is no limitation to the block size of the DMA data.

Q 13. **What control signals could be used to select ROMS, RAMS, and PIA/ACIA?**

A 13. VMA, R/W and $\phi2$ are all available to enable RAMS, ROMS and PIA/ACIA's. In some cases it may be desirable to eliminate one of these enabling signals so that enable input may be freed for address decoding. The following discussion indicates which control signals could be deleted for a given device and the effects on the system operation.

ROM — R/W and $\phi2$ can be used to enable the ROMS without using the VMA signal. Not using the VMA signal means that the ROM may be enabled during a non-memory reference read cycle (VMA would be low but since it is not used the ROM may be enabled). A false read of the ROM will have no effect on the system and if the non-memory reference cycle had been a write then the R/W signal would have disabled the ROM.

RAM — VMA can be left off as an enable to a RAM if the MPU will not be halted, WAI Instruction executed or if the TSC will not be used. Either of these conditions cause the Address lines and the R/W lines to float which could produce a false write into RAM if not protected by VMA. During normal operation of the MPU only one instruction, TST, causes a false write to memory (i.e. the write line going low without VMA also going low). This instruction does not pose a problem because it first reads the memory and then rewrites the data read. If VMA was used to enable the RAM this false write would not occur, however, since the memory is rewritten with the same data no problem occurs by not using VMA as an enable.

PIA/ACIA — All three signals must be used to enable or select a PIA or ACIA. Both of these devices automatically clear the Interrupt Flags when the MPU reads the PIA or ACIA data registers so that a false read of a PIA or ACIA may cause an interrupt on CA1, CB1, CA2, or CB2 to be missed. In addition it is suggested that VMA•ϕ2 not be used as an Enable signal for a PIA because if the machine is halted, ($\overline{\text{HALT}}$ active or WAI instruction) VMA is forced low removing the clock from the PIA. Without the Enable input to the PIA an external interrupt may not be recognized. ϕ2 should be used for the PIA Enable signal so that the PIA Enable clock always occurs whether or not the MPU is halted. VMA may then be taken directly to chip select inputs or be gated with address signals to the chip select inputs.

3 M6800 INTERRUPT OPERATION

Q 1. **What happens if the interrupt mark is set (I=1) and (a) a SWI occurs; (b) a WAI occurs?**

A 1. (a) The interrupt service routine indicated by the SWI vector will be processed. The Interrupt Mask status (I=1) will be saved on the stack with the other Condition Code Register bits. The RTI at the end of the service routine then restores the I=1 status when the stacked condition code register is returned to the MPU.

(b) If a WAI is executed while the Interrupt Mask is set, the MPU will cycle in a wait loop unless a non-maskable interrupt (NMI) occurs.

Q 2. **Is the interrupt mask always cleared after an RTI?**

A 2. An RTI returns the I to the status that existed before the interrupt occurred. If the interrupt mask is set then only the NMI or SWI can cause interrupts. The interrupt mask will be set following execution of RTI if it was set prior to the above interrupts.

Q 3. **If power goes down how does the programmer know where the MPU contents are stacked?**

A 3. If the system uses NMI as a power fail detect input and there is non-volatile memory in the system the MPU status will be saved on the stack. As part of the NMI service routine the STS instruction can be used to store the stack pointer into a predetermined non-volatile memory location. If the MPU status is also to be saved the stack must be in non-volatile memory.

Q 4. **How can the NMI input be used as an operator interrupt?**

A 4. If NMI is not used for starting a power down sequence, it may be used directly as an operator interrupt by having an operator interrupt service routine specified at the NMI vector location.

If NMI is used for power down and operator interrupt, some external circuitry may be added so that a test in the NMI service routine can determine whether a power fail or an operator interrupt has occurred. In the diagram shown below, the test may be accomplished by reading the PIA data bit, PAO. If NMI occurs, a test of the appropriate PIA data register will determine whether a power down or an operator interrupt occurred.

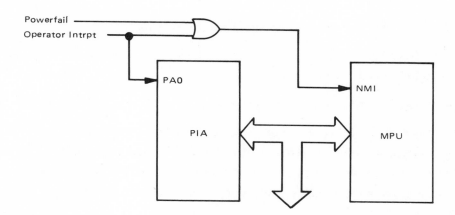

Q 5.   **What instructions set the interrupt mask?**

A 5.   TAP, SEI, SWI, WAI (after interrupt occurs).

The interrupt mask will also be set by $\overline{\text{NMI}}$, $\overline{\text{RES}}$, and $\overline{\text{IRQ}}$ interrupt inputs to the MPU.

Q 6.   **If $\overline{\text{NMI}}$ occurs while the MPU is halted will the MPU respond to the NMI when it is returned to the "go" state?**

A 6.   Yes, there are flip-flops in the MPU to save $\overline{\text{NMI}}$ and $\overline{\text{IRQ}}$. When the halt condition is removed, the MPU will execute one instruction and then operate on $\overline{\text{NMI}}$.

Q 7.   **How will the MPU react to the following conditions?**

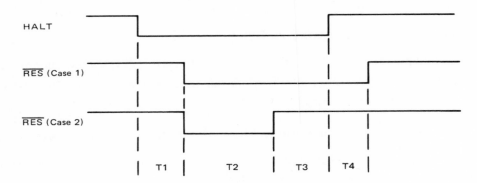

A 7.   In both cases the MPU will eventually recognize the $\overline{\text{RES}}$. The $\overline{\text{RES}}$ sequence will be initiated when $\overline{\text{RES}}$ goes high in Case 1 and when $\overline{\text{HALT}}$ goes high in Case 2. During T1, the MPU is halted and its outputs are in the three-state high impedance mode. When the $\overline{\text{RES}}$ line goes low at the beginning of T2, a halt latch is reset, the MPU goes out of three-state, and (after 3 machine cycles) the Address bus is outputting FFFE, the most significant half of $\overline{\text{RES}}$ vector address

In Case 1, the $\overline{\text{HALT}}$ line goes high and the MPU waits in its current state until $\overline{\text{RES}}$ high at the end of T4; the MPU then fetches the starting address of the RES service routine from FFFE and FFFF and processes the $\overline{\text{RES}}$ interrupt.

In Case 2, the $\overline{\text{RES}}$ line goes high at the end of T2 and the MPU loads the Program Counter with the data (starting address of $\overline{\text{RES}}$ routine) from locations FFFE and FFFF and enters the halt mode again. The $\overline{\text{RES}}$ service routine begins executing when $\overline{\text{HALT}}$ goes high at the end of T3.

Q 8.   **Can the Interrupt Mask be changed by the TAP instruction?**

A 8.   Yes. The contents of accumulator A is stored in the Condition Code Register, including the Interrupt Mask. Note that bits 6 and 7 will not be stored.

Q 9.   **What happens when an $\overline{\text{NMI}}$ interrupt occurs during a SWI?**

A 9.   It is a characteristic of the MPU that if an $\overline{\text{NMI}}$ occurs while a Software Interrupt (SWI) is being executed, the interrupt vector will be retrieved from the IRQ location rather than either the SWI or $\overline{\text{NMI}}$ locations. If there is a possibility of this situation developing during system operation, precautions should be taken to avoid an ambiguous result. In most applications, the $\overline{\text{NMI}}$ must be recognized and serviced whenever it occurs.

A simple procedure is to always set a flag immediately prior to each use of SWI:

```
NOP
SEI
INC NMIFLG        Set possible NMI Flag.
SWI               Execute Software Interrupt
DEC NMIFLG        Clear flag if SWI was normal
CLI
    .

    .
```

Testing this flag can then be made the first step of the normal IRQ service routine. As an example, assume that the IRQ vector has been fetched and directs program control to IRQ service routine START:

```
START      TST      NMIFLG       Was this NMI via SWI?
           BEQ      IRQSVC       No, branch to normal IRQ
           JMP      NMIAUX       Yes, go to NMI Service routine


IRQSVC     xxx      xxxxxx
             .

             .

             .
```

For a normal $\overline{\text{IRQ}}$, the flag will be zero and the routine will branch to the normal service routine, IRQSVC. If the IRQ was entered via a Simultaneous SWI-NMI, the flag is non-zero and control is transferred to an auxiliary NMI routine, NMIAUX:

```
               .

               .

               .

NMIAUX     TSX                   Get SP into X reg
           TST      6,X          Lobyte of PC on Stack = ϕϕ?
           BNE      HIBYTE       Yes, go decrement Hibyte
           DEC      5,X          No, decrement lobyte
HIBYTE     DEC      6,X          Decrement Hibyte
NMISVC     xxx      xxxxx        Begin normal NMI service
             .

             .

             .
```

A normal $\overline{\text{NMI}}$ would be vectored to NMISVC. If NMISVC is entered via a simultaneous SWI/$\overline{\text{NMI}}$ and it is required that the program resume normal operation following service of the non-maskable interrupt, NMIAUX will insure an orderly return to the main program. The NMIAUX sequence causes the value of the Program Counter that was stacked by the SWI instruction to be decremented by one so that the stacked program counter is pointing to the SWI instruction's location. This will cause the SWI instruction to re-execute following an RTI from the NIMSVC service routine. Program flow will then proceed as if the $\overline{\text{NMI}}$ had not occurred. If there is no system requirement to return to the SWI sequence, the auxiliary instructions can be deleted and exit from START becomes JMP NMISVC. Note that the system initialization procedure should include provisions for clearing the NMIFLG flag. Note also that $\overline{\text{IRQ}}$ is masked while the NMI flag (NMIFLG) is set to prevent an improper branch at IRQ START.

Q 10. **When will the MPU recognize an $\overline{\text{IRQ}}$ pulse?**

A 10. The $\overline{\text{IRQ}}$ input is latched internal to the MPU providing the pulse duration is at least two MPU cycles. Therefore, the MPU will recognize pulses active for two cycles. Three exceptions are to be noted as follows:

1. If $I_M = 1$ while a pulse occurs, the MPU will miss the interrupt.

2. If $\overline{\text{IRQ}}$ and $\overline{\text{NMI}}$ are active concurrently, the MPU will recognize $\overline{\text{NMI}}$. In so doing, the interrupt latches are reset and the IRQ pulse will be lost.

3. If $\overline{\text{IRQ}}$ occurs during an SWI instruction, the pulse will be lost because SWI clears the interrupt latches.

Q 11. **What happens if an $\overline{\text{NMI}}$ occurs after an $\overline{\text{IRQ}}$ but before the MPU enters the $\overline{\text{IRQ}}$ service routine?**

A 11. The instruction being executed when the $\overline{\text{IRQ}}$ occurred will be completed. The $\overline{\text{IRQ}}$ interrupt sequence will be initiated and continue (for 9 cycles) until the MPU status has been stacked. Assuming that $\overline{\text{NMI}}$ occurs during this interval, the MPU will select $\overline{\text{NMI}}$ since it has higher priority. (Note that if $\overline{\text{IRQ}}$ was a pulse, it is permanently lost unless it lasts until the Interrupt Mask is cleared by software.) The MPU fetches the starting address of the $\overline{\text{NMI}}$ service routine from locations FFFC and FFFD and begins servicing the non-maskable interrupt. If the $\overline{\text{IRQ}}$ line is still low when the Interrupt Mask is cleared by either a CLI during the NMI service routine or the RTI at the end of it, a normal $\overline{\text{IRQ}}$ will then be initiated.

Q 12. **Assume $I_m = 1$, $\overline{\text{IRQ}}$ is active (low), and I_m on the stack $= 0$; then an RTI is encountered. Will one instruction after the RTI be executed?**

A 12. No. the $\overline{\text{IRQ}}$ will be serviced prior to the instruction.

Q 13. **Assume $I_m = 1$, $\overline{\text{IRQ}}$ is active, and I_m on the stack $= 1$; then an RTI is encountered. Will the interrupt be recognized after the RTI has executed?**

A 13. No. The next program instruction will be executed. $\overline{\text{IRQ}}$ will not be serviced until I_m is reset by software.

Q 14. **Will the MPU recognize an interrupt occurring during the last cycle of an instruction during that instruction?**

A 14. Yes. The interrupt must occur during the second to the last cycle of an instruction if it is to be recognized during that instruction. The interrupt inputs are sampled during $\phi 2$ and clocked during the next $\phi 1$ so the interrupt must be present $\simeq 200$ ns prior to the end of the $\phi 2$ in the last cycle of an instruction if it is to be recognized during that instruction. The first cycle of any given instruction is considered to be the OP CODE fetch from memory.

Q 15. **If the Interrupt Mask is set and an interrupt is pending, how fast does the MPU recognize the interrupt after the mask is cleared by a CLI instruction?**

A 15. The interrupt will be serviced not more than one instruction after execution of the CLI. If the opcode of the instruction immediately preceding the CLI instruction has a zero in its least significant bit position, a pending interrupt will be recognized as soon as execution of CLI is complete. If there was a one in the least significant bit position of the previous instruction's opcode, the instruction following the CLI will be executed before the pending interrupt is recognized.

The Wait for Interrupt instruction (WAI) is often used to expedite the handling of interrupts by causing the MPU to stack its contests and enter a waiting mode. It is normally used in anticipation of an interrupt that requires the quickest possible handling. It is possible for the MPU to hang-up in the wait mode if the WAI instruction is used following a Clear Interrupt Mask instruction (CLI) if the anticipated interrupt is already pending when CLI executes and the interrupt is serviced as soon as the mask clears. Completion of the interrupt service routine will return the program to the WAI instruction and cause the MPU to begin waiting for an interrupt that has already been serviced. If the opcode of the instruction immediately preceding the CLI instruction had a one in its least significant bit position, clearing of the Interrupt Mask by CLI is sufficiently delayed such that execution of the WAI instruction begins before the interrupt can be recognized and the desired result is obtained. That is, WAI executes and then the interrupt is serviced rather than vice versa. It is recommended that whenever WAI is preceded by CLI, the CLI should be preceded by a NOP:

.
.
.

NOP
CLI
WAI

.
.
.

Use of the NOP insures that the least significant bit of the instruction preceding CLI will contain a one.

Q 16. **How is $\overline{\text{NMI}}$ masked once it is activated?**

A 16. The $\overline{\text{NMI}}$ is not masked. The $\overline{\text{NMI}}$ input is reactivated 3 cycles prior to executing the first instruction of the service routine. Another $\overline{\text{NMI}}$ input will be recognized if a falling edge occurs after this time.

Q 17. **When are the $\overline{\text{IRQ}}$ and $\overline{\text{NMI}}$ reactivated during the interrupt service routine?**

A 17. Both are reactivated after the 9th cycle of the interrupt sequence, i.e., after they have been tested to see which interrupt input caused the sequence to start.

Q 18. **How fast can the MPU service an interrupt?**

A 18. The MPU can vector to the first instruction of the interrupt service routine in $13 \rightarrow 23$ clock periods depending on what instruction is being executed and how far that execution has progressed at the time of the interrupt.

Q 19. Why is the interrupt mask placed in front of the $\overline{\text{IRQ}}$ flip-flop?

A 19. The interrupt mask is placed prior to the $\overline{\text{IRQ}}$ flip-flop to prevent the flip-flop from being set again by the present interrupt. The interrupt sequence sets the interrupt mask bit just prior to resetting the interrupt flops.

Q 20. How fast can an interrupt be serviced using the WAI instruction?

A 20. Four MPU cycles are required to start the interrupt sequence after a WAI instruction

Q 21. When is a pull up resistor required for the $\overline{\text{IRQ}}$ and $\overline{\text{NMI}}$ MPU inputs?

A 21. When multiple signals are wired to the interrupt inputs, a $3.3\text{K}\Omega$ pull up resistor is recommended.

Q 22. Will the MPU recognize $\overline{\text{IRQ}}$ and $\overline{\text{NMI}}$ when in a single instruction mode of execution, i.e., G/H high for one $\phi1$ high clock cycle?

A 22. The $\overline{\text{IRQ}}$ and $\overline{\text{NMI}}$ interrupts will not be recognized in this mode of operation.

Q 23. When does the MPU recognize an $\overline{\text{IRQ}}$ or an $\overline{\text{NMI}}$ when the $\overline{\text{HALT}}$ line goes high and the interrupt is present?

A 23. The MPU will execute one instruction after the Go/Halt line goes high before the $\overline{\text{IRQ}}$ or $\overline{\text{NMI}}$ is recognized.

Q 24. What happens if an $\overline{\text{NMI}}$ occurs immediately after the $\overline{\text{RES}}$ line goes high?

A 24. Since the stack is undefined at this time the MPU status will be stored at some unknown location in memory, overwriting any RAM programs if the stack pointer happened to be pointing at them. Similarly if an $\overline{\text{IRQ}}$ occurs after the interrupt mask is cleared and before the stack pointer is initialized the MPU status will be stored starting at an unknown location.

It is therefore recommended that the stack pointer be defined (using the LDS instruction) very early in the program.

4 M6800 PROGRAMMING

Q 1.   **What is meant by dual operand addressing?**

A 1.   In computer terminology, "dual operand instructions" refers to instructions which reference two values. The values may be specified as data (immediate operand), contents of a register, or contents of a memory location.

In the MC6800, dual operand instructions reference an accumulator (register) and either data (immediate operand) or a memory address:

IMMEDIATE DUAL
OPERAND INSTRUCTION

Add A #17
Operand #1 = Contents of A
Operand #2 = 17 (decimal)

MEMORY REFERENCE
DUAL OPERAND INSTRUCTION

EOR B $8130
Operand #1 = Contents of B
Operand #2 = Contents of memory location 8130 (hex)

Q 2.   **When is there an arithmetic carry?**

A 2.   *Add Instructions*

Carry occurs when the sum of the binary operand values is greater than 255. When DAA follows an add instruction carry occurs when the sum of the binary coded decimal values is greater than 99. Add instructions include: ADD, ABA, and ADC.

Subtract Instructions

In subtract operations the condition code register carry (C) bit is used as a borrow bit. When the binary subtrahend is greater than the minuend the C bit is set. Otherwise it is cleared. Subtract instructions include: CMP, CBA, NEG SUB, SBA and SBC.

Q 3.   **How is the H bit (bit 5) in the condition code register used?**

A 3.   The "H" stands for Half-carry.

In the MC6800 two BCD digits can be obtained in one eight bit byte. Decimal addition is accomplished by two instructions — an add instruction followed by a DAA (Decimal Adjust Accumulator) instruction.

The MC6800 add instructions are binary adds. The H bit is set during the add when the binary sum of the low order decimal digit (bits 0-3) exceeds 15. When the binary sum is less than or equal to 15 the H bit is cleared. The DAA instruction then uses the H bit to determine how the result of the add must be adjusted to convert the binary sum to decimal. The H bit is affected by the following add instructions: ADDA, ADDB, ABA, ADCA, and ADCB. The H bit is not tested by any branch instructions. If it is desirable to test the H bit a program routine can be written.

Q 4.   **How is decimal subtraction accomplished?**

A 4.   There is no Decimal Adjust Subtract instruction for the MC6800. Decimal subtraction is accomplished by using 9's complement arithmetic. The 9's complement of the subtrahend is found and then added to the minuend plus 1. The 9's complement of a decimal number is found by subtracting each digit from nine. The following subroutine is a decimal subtract routine of 16 digit numbers.

```
◆ DECIMAL SUBTRACT SUBROUTINE FOR 16 DECIMAL DIGIT

◆ THIS ROUTINE SUBTRACTS THE SUBTRAHEND ("SUBTRH")
◆ FROM THE MINUEND ("MINUEN") AND PLACES THE
◆ DIFFERENCE IN "RSLT."

DSUB    LDX     #8          SET BYTE COUNTER
DSUB1   LDA A   #$99
        SUB A   SUBTRH,X    FIND 9'S COMPLEMENT
        STA A   RSLT,X      USE "RSLT" AS TEMP STORE
        DEX                 DECREMENT BYTE COUNTER
        BNE     DSUB1       LOOP UNTIL LAST BYTE
        LDX     #8          RESTORE BYTE COUNTER
        SEC                 SET CARRY TO ADD 1 TO COMPL
DSUB2   LDA A   MINUEN,X    LOAD MINUEND
        ADC A   RSLT,X      ADD COMPLEMENT SUBTRAHEND
        DAA                 DECIMAL ADJUST
        STA A   RSLT,X      STORE DIFFERENCE
        DEX                 DECREMENT BYTE COUNTER
        BNE     DSUB2       LOOP UNTIL LAST BYTE
        RTS                 RETURN TO HOST PROGRAM

◆ THE EXECUTION TIME OF THIS SUBROUTINE IS
◆ 384 MPU CYCLES EXCLUDING THE RTS.
```

Note that if the subtrahend is less than or equal to the minuend a positive 16 digit difference results. This is known as unsigned 16 decimal digit precision subtraction. The preceding subroutine can also be used for signed (algebraic) subtraction. In this case the precision is 15 decimal digits. The high order digit position is used to indicate the sign of the number. A zero in the high order digit means positive and the remaining 15 decimal digits are in true binary coded decimal format. A 9 in the high order digit means minus and the remaining 15 decimal digits are in 9's complement binary coded decimal format.

Q 5.   **What is the difference between the:**

  BGT and BHI instructions?

  BLE and BLS instructions?

A 5.   BGT — Branch if Greater Than

  BHI — Branch if Higher

  BLE — Branch if Less Than or Equal To

  BLS — Branch if Less Than or Same

The BGT and BLE instructions are used to test the result of a signed binary operation. The BHI and BLS instruction is used to test the result of an unsigned binary operation.

When using signed binary notation the high order bit of a byte represents the sign of the value. A "0" in bit seven means positive and a "1" means negative.

In unsigned binary notation, bit 7 of the number implies a weight of 128.

The correlation between signed and unsigned branch tests subsequent to a subtract or compare instruction is as follows:

ACC = Accumulator value of tested instruction.
OPRND = Operand value of tested instruction.

	SIGNED TEST	UNSIGNED TEST
ACC < OPRND	BLT	BCS
ACC < OPRND	BLE	BLS
ACC $\geq$ OPRND	BGE	BCC
ACC $\geq$ OPRND	BGT	BHI

Q 6. **When using the TSX instruction why is the value in the stack pointer register increased by 1?**

A 6. When stacking data in memory the MC6800 first addresses the memory location referenced by the stack pointer register and stores the data. Then the value in the stack pointer register is decremented by one to point to the next stack address.

The TSX instruction adds one to the stack pointer register value as it is transferred to the index register so that the index register is pointing at the last address of the stack that has stacked data. The TXS instruction subtracts one from the index register value as it is transferred to the stack pointer register to reverse the operation.

The value stored in the stack pointer register is not changed due to the execution of the TSX instruction. Likewise, the value stored in the index register is not changed due to the TXS instruction

Q 7. **How fast can data be transferred via a PIA?**

A 7. There are two types of data transfer-synchronous and asynchronous. In synchronous data transfer the source of the data transfer clock is derived from the M6800 system timing. In asynchronous data transfer the data transfer clock is derived separately from the M6800 system timing.

In the following examples it is assumed that the number of words transferred is known prior to entry into the data transfer routine.

EXAMPLE 1: 8-bit Word Synchronous Read Transfer
   NOTE: Accumulator B is the word counter.

```
LOOP      LDAA     PIAPRA        FETCH DATA
          PSHA                   STORE DATA
          DECB                   DECREMENT WORD COUNTER
          BNE      LOOP          LOOP UNTIL DONE
```

Executive time @ 1 μs/cycle = 14 μs
Max data rate = 71.4K words/sec.

EXAMPLE 2: 8-bit Word Asynchronous Read Transfer

   NOTE: a) Accumulator B is the word counter.

   b) PIA Control Register A, bit 7 = 1 signifies a word is ready for transfer.

```
LOOP      LDAA    PIACRA      FETCH CONTROL WORD
          BPL     LOOP        WAIT FOR WORD READY
          LDAA    PIAPRA      FETCH DATA
          PSHA                STORE DATA
          DECB                DECREMENT WORD COUNTER
          BNE     LOOP        LOOP UNTIL DONE
```

Execution time @ 1μs/cycle = 22 μs.

Max data rate = 45.4K words/sec.

EXAMPLE 3: 8-bit Word Asynchronous Write Transfer

   NOTE: a) Index register is the word counter.

   b) PIA Control Register B bit 7=1 signifies a word transfer is requested by the peripheral.

```
LOOP 1    LDAA    DATA, X     FETCH DATA FROM MEMORY
LOOP 2    LDAB    PIACRB      FETCH CONTROL WORD
          BPL     LOOP 2      WAIT FOR WORD REQUEST
          STAA    PIAPRB      MOVE WORD TO PIA
          LDAB    PIAPRB      CLR CRB, BIT 7
          DEX                 DECREMENT WORD COUNTER
          BNE     LOOP 1      LOOP UNTIL DONE
```

Execution time @ 1 μs/cycle = μs.

Max data rate = 33.3K words/sec.

EXAMPLE 4: 16-bit Asynchronous Word Read Transfer

   NOTE: a) Accumulator B is the word counter.

   b) PIA Control Register A, bit 7 =1 signifies a word is ready for transfer.

```
LOOP      LDAA    PIACRA      FETCH CONTROL WORD
          BPL     LOOP        WAIT FOR WORD READY
          LDAA    PIAPRB      FETCH HIGH ORDER BYTE
          PSHA                STORE HIGH ORDER BYTE
          LDAA    PIAPRA      FETCH LOW ORDER BYTE
          PSHA                STORE LOW ORDER BYTE
          DECB                DECREMENT WORD COUNTER
          BNE     LOOP        LOOP UNTIL DONE
```

Execution time @ 1μs/cycle = 3 μs.

Max data rate = 33.3K words/sec or 66.7K bytes/sec.

The maximum data rates shown in the preceding examples represent simple transfer tasks using software polling rather than interrupt service requests. It should be noted that if any other tasks that must be performed while transferring data would reduce the maximum data rate.

INDEX